Health Psychology

A Cultural Approach

Regan A. R. Gurung

University of Wisconsin, Green Bay

THOMSON
™
WADSWORTH

Australia • Brazil • Canada • Mexico • Singapore
Spain • United Kingdom • United States

THOMSON
™
WADSWORTH

Health Psychology: A Cultural Approach
Regan A. R. Gurung

Executive Editor: Michele Sordi
Assistant Editor: Jennifer Keever
Senior Editorial Assistant: Jessica Kim
Technology Project Manager: Erik Fortier
Marketing Manager: Chris Caldeira
Marketing Assistant: Nicole Morinon
Senior Marketing Communications Manager: Tami Strang
Project Manager, Editorial Production: Jennifer Klos
Creative Director: Rob Hugel
Art Director: Vernon Boes

Print Buyer: Lisa Claudeanos
Permissions Editor: Sarah Harkrader
Production Service and Compositor: Graphic World, Inc.
Photo Researcher: Terri Wright
Copy Editor: Graphic World Publishing Services
Illustrator: Graphic World Illustration Studio
Cover Designer: Roger Knox
Cover Image: Jose Ortega/Images.com
Printer: Webcom

Library of Congress Control Number: 2005925200
ISBN 0-534-62640-8

Thomson Higher Education
10 Davis Drive
Belmont, CA 94002-3098
USA

For more information about our products, contact us at:
Thomson Learning Academic Resource Center
1-800-423-0563

For permission to use material from this text or product, submit a request online at **http://www.thomsonrights.com**. Any additional questions about permissions can be submitted by e-mail to **thomsonrights@thomson.com**.

To my parents, Maria Peidade Lucia Gurung and Douglas Narendra Raj Gurung, and my nana, Carmelina Fernandes: I respect all your sacrifices and am grateful for your infinite support. You ensured I wanted for nothing and showed me the value of being true to my cultural beliefs. Dwane and Martha: You know what you mean to me.

Brief Contents

Contents

Health Psychology: Setting the Stage   1

CHAPTER **4**

Stress across Cultures   96

CHAPTER **5**

Coping and Social Support 139

CHAPTER **8**

Factors Surrounding Illness   235

CHAPTER **9**

Pain 257

CHAPTER **10**

Chronic Illness and Death   284

CHAPTER **11**

Psychoneuroimmunology and HIV   315

CHAPTER **12**

Culture and Cancer   347

CHAPTER **13**

Culture and Cardiovascular Disease 382

CHAPTER **14**

The Future of Health Psychology 411

Preface

Is culture really that important? We often seem inclined to discount its importance, partly because we rarely acknowledge its many dimensions. For example, what do your mother, your best friends, and God have in common? They each constitute the major socialization forces of culture. Take parents for example. Whether we do something because they told us to (e.g., "Eat your greens!") or exactly because they told us *not to* (e.g., "Don't smoke!"), parents have a strong influence on us. If our friends exercise, we are more likely to exercise also. As another example, consider religions, which have different prescriptions for what individuals should or should not do. Muslims cannot eat pork or drink alcohol. Hindus cannot eat beef. Unfortunately, textbooks often limit discussions of culture to just race or ethnicity, when a broader discussion is required to fully understand the precedents of health and health behaviors. Culture is not just race or ethnicity; it also includes religion, age, gender, family values, the region of the country in which one was raised, and many other features. Understanding the dynamic interplay of the cultural forces acting on us can greatly enhance how we face the world and how we optimize our way of life.

The key goals of this book are to examine how the areas of health, illness, and medicine can be studied from a psychological and cultural perspective and to introduce the main topics and issues in the area of health psychology together with providing training to judge the scientific quality of research on psychology and medicine. I first describe what health psychology is all about, giving you a good feel for what culture is, together with highlighting key research methods. I build on these basics with an eye-opening chapter on cultural variations in health beliefs and behaviors (how do shamans, acupuncture, yoga, and sweat lodges fit into health?). Together with culture, developmental processes are also critical but understudied contributors to health. Chapter 3 fills the void and is devoted to reviewing basic developmental theories and their associations with health. Then the part many of you are waiting for: unraveling the mysteries of stress and ways to cope. In chapters 4 and 5, I thoroughly discuss the theories explaining stress and the many practical ways to alleviate it. Armed with tools to make everyday life stress-free, I turn to another common aspect of everyday life, health behaviors that many of us do (or try to do more often) and those we try not to do. Chapter 6 describes the main theories predicting health behaviors, and chapter 7 describes some of the main behaviors in detail. The second half of the book turns to topics relating to sickness, such as factors that surround illness (e.g., adherence and patient-practitioner interactions; chapter 8), pain (chapter 9), and chronic illnesses and death (chapter 10), before examining some of the major health concerns/illnesses plaguing society today—HIV, cancer, and cardiovascular disease (chapters 11 to 13). Finally, I end by identifying the major challenges faced by those in the field of health psychology (and by providing some avenues for future exploration and training in this area).

Each chapter gives you a heads-up outline of the key topics I will cover as well as a clear preamble to the main topics to be discussed. Each chapter ends with a concise summary to help you review the major points and a list of the key terms, people, and concepts. To help you better digest the material and elaborate the information for better retention and understanding, I have also written questions designed to help you synthesize, evaluate, and apply the contents of the chapter. Finally, I have provided a short list of *absolutely must-reads*—a selection of essential readings comprising classic articles in the field or *hot-off-the-presses* research studies that are often some of the works most cited by health psychologists. These are essentially the articles that are most likely to be used in any writing on the topic, and I think you will enjoy being in the thick of the action by reading them.

If you think I have missed something, if you have a suggestion for how this book can be improved, if you want to share a way that your culture has influenced your health, or even if you want to share that you really enjoyed learning about health psychology using this book (that's my goal), get in touch. Email me at gurungr@uwgb.edu.

Acknowledgments

It all began with the scholarship and camaraderie of Andy Fiala, Aeron Haynie, Kim Nielsen, and Jennifer Ham, members of the faculty research group who catalyzed me to consider embarking on writing this book. Mary Majewski helped me make the right connections. Neil Lutsky, Jerry Eberhart, Larry Wichlinski, and the Carleton College faculty introduced me to psychology (and Neil fostered my passion to teach it). Barbara and Irwin Sarason and the faculty in the University of Washington psychology program provided my grounding in social and personality psychology, and Shelley Taylor, Christine Dunkel-Schetter, and Margaret Kemeny at UCLA shared their knowledge of health psychology and their valuable friendship. The Psychology and Human Development faculty at the University of Wisconsin, Green Bay, have encouraged me to appreciate human development and are some of the best colleagues one could wish for in academia. I am also grateful to the wonderful students I have had the pleasure to teach and those I look forward to encountering—their responsiveness and eagerness to learn kept my batteries charged and running.

A number of dedicated reviewers read draft chapters and suggested insightful improvements. In particular the following people provided invaluable comments: Lisa Armistead, Georgia State University; Lisa K. Comer, University of Northern Colorado; Sussie Eshun, East Stroudsburg University; Ephrem Fernandez, Southern Methodist University; Deborah Jones, Barry University; Scott F. Madey, Shippensburg University; Charlotte Markey, Rutgers University; Deborah Fish Ragin, Montclair State University; Christy Scott, Tennessee State University; Elizabeth E. Seebach, University of Wisconsin–La Crosse; Aurora Sherman, Brandeis University; Holly Tatum, Colby-Sawyer College; Debra VanderVoort, University of Hawaii at Hilo; John M. Velasquez, University of the Incarnate Word; Susan Walch, University of West Florida; and Michael Wohl, Carleton University.

Michele Sordi, my editor at Wadsworth, has been one of the most important supporters of this book; she is the prototype of the ideal editor and has been a tremendous source of support. I have really enjoyed working with her. I would also like to thank Jessica Kim, Chris Caldeira, and all the Wadsworth staff who worked behind the scenes in bringing this book to life. A final note — Dwane you are a great brother. Martha, you're the best.

About the Author

Regan A. R. Gurung is chair of the Psychology Department and associate professor of Human Development and Psychology at the University of Wisconsin, Green Bay.

Born and raised in Bombay, India, Dr. Gurung received a B.A. in psychology at Carleton College (MN) and Masters and Ph.D. degrees in social and personality psychology at the University of Washington (WA). He then spent three years at UCLA as a National Institute of Mental Health (NIMH) Research fellow.

His early work focused on social support and close relationships, in which he studied how perceptions of support from close others influence relationship satisfaction. His later work investigated cultural differences in coping with stressors such as HIV infection, pregnancy, and smoking cessation. Building on and continuing with his previous interests, he is currently working on increasing physical activity and good nutrition in local schools, decreasing smoking in colleges, and investigating sex differences in self-perceptions of body image, health, and fitness.

He has received numerous local, state, and national grants for his research in health psychology and social psychology regarding cultural differences in stress, social support, smoking cessation, body image, and impression formation. He has published articles in a variety of scholarly journals, including *Psychological Review* and *Personality and Social Psychology Bulletin,* and is a frequent presenter at national and international conferences.

Dr. Gurung is also a dedicated teacher and has strong interests in enhancing faculty development and student understanding. He is co-director of the University of Wisconsin System Teaching Scholars Program, has been a UWGB Teaching Fellow and a UW System Teaching Scholar, and is winner of the Founder's Award for Excellence in Teaching, as well as UW Teaching-at-its-Best, Creative Teaching, and Featured Faculty Awards. He has organized statewide and national teaching conferences and is an active member of the Society for the Teaching of Psychology (APA-Division 2).

When not helping people stay calm, reading, or writing, Dr. Gurung enjoys culinary explorations, travel, and avoiding political discussions of any kind.

Health Psychology: Setting the Stage

Are you healthy? Sounds like a pretty easy question to answer, right? Take a second and try to answer for yourself. What is your answer? If you are like most people, you probably think that you are quite healthy. Even if you do not think you are like most people, you may be more like most people than you know (most people do not think that they are like most other people). How exactly did you arrive at your answer? Did you quickly drop down on the floor and see how many push-ups or sit-ups you could do and how out of breath that made you? Did you put the book down and time how long it took you to sprint to the corner and back? Maybe you put a finger on your wrist and took your pulse. More likely than not, if you do not presently have a cold or another illness, if you have not just fallen down stairs or twisted an ankle, or if you do not have any other sort of physical ailment, you probably immediately answered my opening question with a statement like, "Yes, pretty healthy, I guess."

For most people living in the United States of America, basic indicators of good health include the absence of disease, injury, or illness, a slow pulse, the ability to do many physical exercises, or the ability to run fast. You may be surprised to learn that these all represent only one general way of being healthy, the one sup-

© Bob Llewellyn/ImageState/PictureQuest

Different Pictures of Health These individuals may seem healthy to the naked eye. It is important to also look beyond just physiological health and the lack of disease and consider mental, spiritual, and emotional health.

ported by Western medicine and as seen on television in shows such as *ER (Emergency Room).* The definition of what is healthy varies from person to person and is strongly influenced by his or her way of thinking and his or her upbringing. For some individuals, being happy signifies good health. For others, being spiritually satisfied signifies good health. Are some people right and others wrong? What are the best ways to measure health and what are the different factors that influence how healthy we will be?

The United States is a diverse nation. Many of the 281 million Americans (Census Bureau, 2005) will have different answers to questions about health. Ask the next young child you see what being healthy is, and I can almost guarantee that his or her answer will be different from that of an older person you ask. Someone living in poverty and earning less than $13,000 a year will probably have an answer different from that of someone making $100,000 a year. A Catholic will probably have an answer different from that of a Buddhist. Essentially, a person's cultural background makes a big difference in how he or she answers. Furthermore, many different things that we do influence our health—things that often vary by culture as well. The amount of carbonated beverages that you drink can make a big difference; younger people tend to drink more of these than older people. What you eat, including the amount of fast food you eat, makes a difference too. Again, some cultural groups as a whole tend to eat more fast food than others.

In fact, the answer to the simple question, "Are you healthy?" can vary with where you live, how old you are, what your parents and friends think constitutes health, what your religious or ethnic background is, and what a variety of other factors indicate about you. If you live in mostly-sunny California, your health habits are probably different than if you live in often-chilly Wisconsin (Nelson et al., 2002). Whereas both states are leading producers of dairy products in the United States, the inhabitants of one of these states tend to be significantly heavier than the inhabitants of the other. (Is it the cheese? Is it the lack of sun?) Each factor, such as where you live, your age, or your ethnicity, interacts with others to influence what you do and how healthy you will be. The one word that nicely captures all these different elements that influence health is *culture,* and this book focuses heavily on how our cultural backgrounds influence our health, shape healthy behaviors, prevent illness, and enhance our health and well-being.

The schematic diagram in Figure 1.1 provides a road map for the terrain we will travel in this book. Notice how many different pathways can determine health. I will start by discussing the dissimilar ways that health and culture are defined and measured. Next I will introduce you to the field of health psychology and provide an overview of what health psychology covers. Finally, I will end this chapter with a profile of a multicultural American, a look at how each of us is "multicultural," especially focusing on differences in family structure, and how sociodemographic variables such as gender and income level are critical aspects of culture.

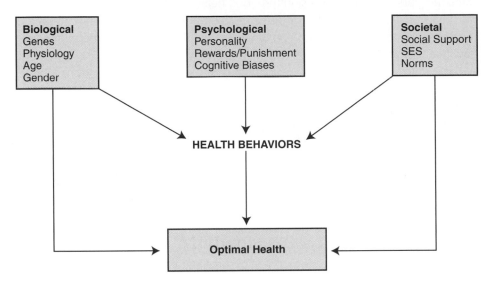

FIGURE 1.1
Health and Its Correlates
Our cultural backgrounds, our biology, and our health behaviors all influence whether we will be healthy or not.

What Is Health?

So let's get back to the issue of health. Newspaper headlines scream the latest health findings almost every day. French fries are bad for you (Gorman, 2002); a glass of wine a day is good for you (Agarwal & Seitz, 2001; Corrao, Rubbiati, Bagnardi, Zambon, & Poikolainen, 2000). Not only is a lot of research reported every day, but often contradictory information is also presented. We tend to pay more attention to the research findings that support our lifestyles and ignore the ones that do not. Much of the media blitz capitalizes on the fact that people in general seem to be paying an increasing amount of attention to attaining healthier lifestyles. Supermarket shelves overflow with supplements to enhance the quality of life, and bookstores overflow with recommendations on how to live better. The answer to the question "What is health?" really depends on who you ask. Let's start with the **WHO** (World Health Organization). This organization defines **health** as a state of complete physical, mental, and social well-being (WHO, 1979, 2003).

As you can see, this is a very general definition and encompasses almost every aspect of life. One aspect that could perhaps be added is "spiritual." Definitions such as this one are relatively common when we look at books or magazines that

Key Health Behaviors Getting 6 to 8 hours of sleep, being physically active, eating a nutritional meal, and not smoking are all important health behaviors that can prolong life.

deal with health in a nonspecific way. One way to see health is as a continuum with optimal health (broadly defined) at one end and poor health at the other, sitting on two ends of a great big teeter-totter (Figure 1.2). The number of healthy things we do in life determines our relative position (closer to optimal health or closer to death) at a particular moment in time. The healthy things we do (e.g., eat and sleep well, exercise, and take time to relax) make the optimal health side

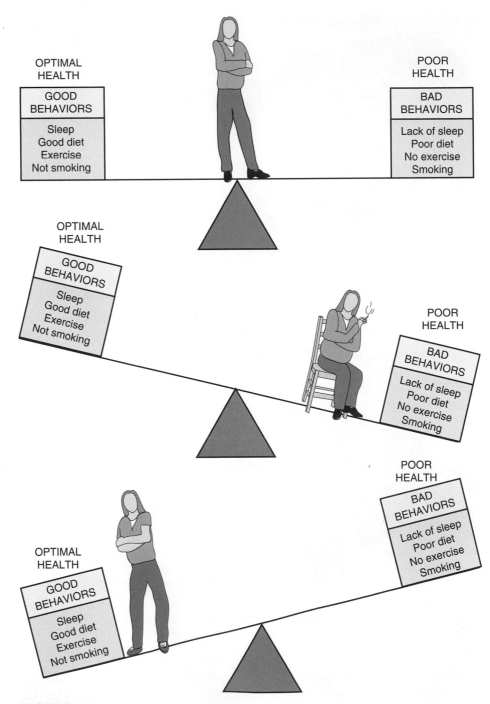

FIGURE 1.2
Health is a Continuum
The sum of the different health behaviors we perform influence where we stand on the balance of health. This is a dynamic process, and although good health behaviors can compensate for some bad ones, you can optimize your health by loading the balance in your favor by practicing as many healthy behaviors as possible.

TABLE 1.1

Examples of Hot and Cold Foods

Hot Yang Foods	Cold Yin Foods
Bamboo	Bean curd and sprouts
Beef	All bland or boiled foods
Broiled, fatty meats	Cabbage family
Catfish	Carrots
Chicken	Celery
Eggplant	Cucumber
Fried foods	Duck
Garlic	Some fish
Ginger	Some fruits (melons, pears)
Rice	Most greens
Green peppers	Honey
Spicy foods	Pork
Leeks and onions	Milk
Liquor	Potatoes
Red foods (beans, peppers, tomatoes, etc.)	Winter squash
Sesame oil	Most white foods
Shellfish	
Sour foods	
Vinegar and wine	

of the teeter-totter heavier. The unhealthy things we do (e.g., get stressed, smoke, and drink excessively) make us tilt toward the poor health side of the balance. This imagery also captures how we sometimes rationalize some unhealthy behaviors by practicing some healthy behaviors to make sure the teeter-totter is leaning in the right direction and we are moving toward the optimal end of the spectrum. Of course, this analogy can only go so far: If you have smoked for 20 or 30 years it will be pretty hard to load the other end of the balance to compensate. Furthermore, it is difficult to compare the extent to which different behaviors translate into longevity. Just because you do not smoke does not mean that you can drink excessively. Just because you may exercise a lot does not mean you can afford to not eat a nutritional diet. Keeping your life tilted toward optimal health is a daily challenge and a dynamic process.

Cross-Cultural Definitions of Health

In Western medical circles, health is commonly defined as the state in which disease is absent (Galanti, 2004). Of course, this definition focuses primarily on the physical or biological aspect of life and correspondingly, this approach taken by Western medicine is often referred to as the **biomedical approach** to health.

TABLE 1.2

Some Cross-Cultural Definitions of Health

Culture	Definition
Western	Absence of disease
Chinese	Balance of yin and yang
	Balance of hot and cold
Indian	Balance of mind, body, and spirit
Mexican	Balance of body types and energies
American Indian	Spiritual, mental, and physical harmony
	Harmony with nature
Hmong	Preventing soul loss
Ethiopian	Preventing spirit possession

I refer to this as the Western approach because many other societies have a different understanding of health. For example, in **Traditional Chinese Medicine** (TCM), health is the balance of the yin and yang, the two complementary forces in the universe (Kaptchuk, 2000). The yin and yang are often translated into hot and cold (two clear opposites), referring to qualities and not temperatures. To be healthy, what you eat and drink and the way you live your life should have equal amounts of hot qualities and cold ones. Balancing hot and cold is a critical element of many different cultures (e.g., Chinese, Indian, and even Mexican) although the foods that constitute each may vary across cultures. Table 1.1 shows examples of hot and cold foods. I provide a complete description of diverse approaches to health in chapter 2.

Other cultures also believe that health is the balance of different qualities (Table 1.2) (Galanti, 2004). Similarly, ancient Indian scholars and doctors defined health as the state in which "the three main biological units, enzymes, tissues and excretory functions are in harmonious condition and when the mind and senses are cheerful." Referred to as **Ayurveda,** or "Knowledge of Life," this ancient system of medicine focuses on the body, the sense organs, the mind, and the soul (Dash, Junius, & Dash, 1997). Another way of looking at health is the approach of Mexican Americans, one of the largest ethnic groups in the United States. Mexican Americans believe that there are both natural biological causes for illness (similar to Western biomedicine) and spiritual causes (Trotter & Chavira, 1997). Whereas Mexican American patients may go to a Western doctor to cure a biological problem, only *curanderos* or healers can be trusted to cure spiritual problems.

American Indians do not even draw distinctions between physical, spiritual, and social entities or between religion and medicine. Instead, most tribes (there are more that 500 different American Indian tribes in America) and especially the Navajo (the largest tribe) strive to achieve a balance between human beings and the spiritual world (Alvord & Van Pelt, 2000). The trees, the animals, the earth, the sky, and the winds are all players in the same game of life. Most of the world's cultures use a more global and widespread approach to assessing health instead of just looking at whether or not disease is absent to determine health (as the biomedical model and most Western approaches do). We will discuss each of these different approaches to health in more detail in the next chapter.

Common Rubrics for Health

Regardless of which one we look at, each definition of health is broad and ambiguous. How can we measure mental, spiritual, and social health? Does just the absence of physical problems or disease equate to health? Can anyone even measure a balanced yin and yang? The answer is not really or at least not by any measure that we know of or use in the United States or in the scientific community and not in a way that we can all agree on. To understand what keeps us healthy, it is important to start with a good measurement of health. As you learn about the field of health psychology you will see that although most researchers will use a common understanding and relatively broad definition of health to guide their general thinking (e.g., a general state of well-being), every researcher uses a different specific measure of health to help understand what makes us healthy. Take a quick look at the major research journals that report on health psychological research, and you will see that different studies use slightly different measures. The main categories of measures vary with the journal. For example, *Health Psychology,* the leading journal in the field and one that publishes the results of studies on the topic of health psychology, will feature many studies in which health is defined in terms of the extent to which health-increasing behaviors are practiced (e.g., how much did the participants in the study exercise in a week?) or in terms of psychological well-being (e.g., what were the participants' scores on the Profile of Mood States, a common measure of mood?). You will also see many studies that assess the extent to which health-decreasing behaviors are practiced. For example, how much does a person smoke? What predicts the amount of alcohol consumed? Other journals, such as *The Annals of the Society for Behavioral Medicine* and *Psychosomatic Medicine,* measure many specific physiological outcomes. For example, what are the levels of immune cells in the blood? Table 1.3 shows sample contents from the three major journals. The bottom line is that from a practical standpoint, health is really measured in a variety of specific ways, ranging from how much healthy behaviors are practiced and basic physiological levels of the body's various systems (e.g., blood pressure, heart rate, or cholesterol level) to the psychological well-being (e.g., levels of depression or optimism) and the practice of "healthy" psychological ways (e.g., good coping skills).

Why Is Culture Important?

One easy answer is "to explain why there are significant differences in the health of European Americans and non-European Americans" (National Center on Minority Health and Health Disparities, 2005). But that's not all.

TABLE 1.3

Sample Contents from the Major Health Psychology Journals

Health Psychology	Annals of the Society for Behavioral Medicine	Psychosomatic Medicine
• Benefit Finding in Multiple Sclerosis and Associations with Positive and Negative Outcomes	Invited Paper: • Toward an Improved Behavioral Medicine	• Effect of Behavioral Interventions on Insulin Sensitivity and Atherosclerosis in the Watanabe Heritable Hyperlipidemic Rabbit
• Condom Use Among High-Risk Adolescents: Testing the Influence of Alcohol Use on the Relationship of Cognitive Correlates of Behavior	Empirical Research: • Beyond Good and Bad Coping: A Multidimensional Examination of Coping with Pain in Persons with Rheumatoid Arthritis	• Inflammatory markers and sleep disturbance in major depression • Depression-Related Hyperglycemia in Type 1 Diabetes: A Mediational Approach
• Ovarian Cancer Patients' Psychological Distress: The Role of Physical Impairment, Perceived Unsupportive Family and Friend Behaviors, Perceived Control, and Self-Esteem	• Coping Strategies and Laboratory Pain in Children with Sickle Cell Disease	• Developmental Heterogeneity in Adolescent Depressive Symptoms: Associations with Smoking Behavior • Depressive Symptoms are Associated with Blunted Cortisol Stress Responses in Very Low-Income Women
• Adherence Across Behavioral Domains in Treatment Promoting Smoking Cessation Plus Weight Control	• Health Beliefs, Personality, and Adherence in Hemodialysis Patients: An Interactional Perspective	• Effects of Treating Exhaustion in Angioplasty Patients on New Coronary Events: Results of the Randomized Exhaustion Intervention Trial (Exit)
• Metacognition, Risk Behavior, and Risk Outcomes: The Role of Perceived Intelligence and Perceived Knowledge	• Correlates of HIV Risk Appraisal in Women	• Potentially Modifiable Factors Associated with Disability Among People with Diabetes • Lifetime Prevalences of Physical Diseases and Mental Disorders in Young Suicide Victims
• Dispositional Optimism, Trait Anxiety, and Coping: Unique or Shared Effects on Biological Response to Fertility Treatment?	• Cigarette Smoking Predicts Development of Depressive Symptoms Among U.S. Adolescents	• Waist-to-Hip Ratio is Positively Associated with Bioavailable Testosterone but Negatively Associated with Sexual Desire in Healthy Premenopausal Women

What do your mother, your best friend, and your religion have in common? They each constitute a way that you learn about acceptable behaviors. Take parents, for example. Whether we do something because they told us to (e.g., "Eat your greens!") or exactly because they told us not to (e.g., "Don't smoke!"), they have a strong influence on us. If our friends exercise, we will be more likely to exercise too. Similarly, religions have different prescriptions for what individuals

TABLE 1.3

Sample Contents from the Major Health Psychology Journals, continued

Health Psychology	Annals of the Society for Behavioral Medicine	Psychosomatic Medicine
• Tailored Interventions for Motivating Smoking Cessation: Using Placebo Tailoring to Examine the Influence of Expectancies and Personalization	• Perceptions of Control, Physical Exercise, and Psychological Adjustment to Breast Cancer in South African Women	• A Multiple-Indicator Multiple-Cause Model for Posttraumatic Stress Reactions: Personality, Coping, and Maladjustment
• Does the Theory of Planned Behavior Mediate the Effects of an Oncologist's Recommendations to Exercise in Newly Diagnosed Breast Cancer Survivors? Results from a Randomized Controlled Trial	• Anger Suppression, Reactivity, and Hypertension Risk: Gender Makes a Difference	• Socioeconomic Status Differences in Coping with a Stressful Medical Procedure
• Experimental Components Analysis of Brief Theory-Based HIV/AIDS Risk-Reduction Counseling for Sexually Transmitted Infection Patients		• Changes in Financial Strain over Three Years, Ambulatory Blood Pressure, and Cortisol Responses to Awakening
• A Longitudinal Study of the Relationship Between Depressive Symptoms and Cigarette Use Among African American Adolescents		• Basal and Stimulated Hypothalamic-Pituitary-Adrenal Axis Activity in Patients with Functional Gastrointestinal Disorders and Healthy Controls
• Interest in Smoking Cessation Among Emergency Department Patients		• Relative-Assessed Psychological Factors Predict Sedation Requirement in Critically Ill Patients.
• Volunteer Support, Marital Status, and the Survival Times of Terminally Ill Patients		• The Antitussive Effect of Placebo Treatment on Cough Associated with Acute Upper Respiratory Infection
		• Symptom Profile of Multiple Chemical Sensitivity in Actual Life
		• Written Emotional Expression Produces Health Benefits in Fibromyalgia Patients
		• Latent Inhibition of Rotation Chair-Induced Nausea in Healthy Male and Female Volunteers

should and should not do. Muslims should not eat pork or drink alcohol. Hindus are prohibited from eating beef. Even where we live can determine our habits. As described before, Californians, on average, are healthier than people in the Midwest (Nelson et al., 2002). Parents, peers, religion, and geography are a few of the key determinants of our behaviors and are examples of what makes up our culture.

Dimensions of Culture

If you think there are many ways to describe health, then get ready for the challenge of defining culture. At first it does not seem too difficult, but both trained psychologists and laypeople often mean different things when they discuss culture. Many use the words culture, ethnicity, and race, as if they mean the same thing. Beyond these specific examples, people also think culture represents a set of ideals or beliefs or sometimes a set of behaviors. Behaviors and beliefs are other accurate components of what culture is. Take the wildly popular *Austin Powers* movies. The actor Mike Myers plays a spy from the late 1960s and early 1970s. The movies rely on the fact that Austin's time period had a recognizable set of behaviors that were thought to be part of a certain carefree type of culture. Sometimes referred to as the "culture of free love," the late 1960s and early 1970s had some clear stereotypes. For example, people during this cultural period had specific ways of dressing (e.g., flared pants and shirts with wide collars), grooming (e.g., the Beatles-like mop-top haircuts), and behaving (e.g., sexual activity was seen in a different light than it is today). Identifying as a member of a certain culture also entails sharing the beliefs and values of others in that culture.

Although we rarely acknowledge it, culture has many dimensions. Many of us limit discussions of culture to race or ethnicity. Look at what happens if you ask someone what she thinks the dominant culture around her is. In most cases, she will identify an ethnic category. Someone in Miami may respond with Cuban. Someone in Minnesota may respond with Scandinavian. When I ask that question in Green Bay, Wisconsin, people often respond Hispanic or Hmong (people from Laos near Vietnam). They sometimes say American Indian because they think that I am asking for which ethnic group is most visible in town. In reality, culture can be a variety of things. The dominant culture in Green Bay is Catholic, but people rarely realize that religion constitutes a form of culture as well. Is there an "American" culture? The Focus section at the end of this chapter will address that question.

Defining Culture

A broader discussion and definition of culture is important for a full understanding of the precedents of health behaviors and health. Culture includes ethnicity, race, religion, age, sex, family values, the region of the country, and many other features. Adolescents belong to a different culture than college students. Even in college, there are different cultures. Some students live in dorms, and some live in apartments off-campus. Also, on campus, there are athletes and musicians, and each group provides different prescriptions for what is correct behavior. It is normal for the athletes to exercise a lot. Aspects of the specific culture we belong to correspondingly influence each of our health behaviors. Understanding the dynamic interplay of cultural forces acting on us can greatly enhance how we face the world and how we optimize our way of life. This book will describe how such cultural backgrounds influence the different behaviors we follow that can influence our health.

There are probably as many different definitions for culture as there are for health. A good way to comprehend the breadth of culture is to see if you know what your own is. For the next 30 seconds, think of all the ways that you would answer the question, "Who am I?" Write down or just think of every response that comes to mind. You will notice that you use many labels for yourself. Social psychologists call this the "Who am I?" test (not a very inventive name, I know) and use it to measure how people describe themselves. You probably generated a number of different descriptors for yourself, and your responses provide a number of different clues about yourself and your culture. Your answers may have included your religious background (e.g., I am Lutheran), your sex (e.g., I am male), or your major roles (e.g., I am a student, daughter, or friend). You may have even mentioned your nationality (e.g., I am American) or your ethnicity (e.g., I am a Latino). So if you really took the 30 seconds I suggested, you should be staggering under the realization that you actually have a lot more culture than you previously expected. Before doing this listing exercise, many European Americans have said things like, "I do not have any culture, I'm just White." Part of the exciting thing about life is that every one of us has different experiences and backgrounds, and we will keep these backgrounds at center stage as we discuss health behaviors and health.

Context and Level of Analysis

The order in which the different descriptors came to your mind gives you a good idea of the aspects of yourself that are most important to you right now. It also alerts us to two critical factors for measuring culture. First, the order in which we use words to describe ourselves often depends on the **context** or the environment that we are in. If you are male and are answering the "Who am I" question sitting in a room full of women, the answer "I am a man" is likely to be near the top of your list. Even if you did not answer with "I am American," I bet that your nationality would be one of the first descriptors that would come to mind if you were on a holiday abroad, say checking out the Tower of London, surrounded by a bunch of local British citizens.

Even though the context can influence our ordering, it does not mean it changes the content of our self-views. This is where the **level of analysis** is important. This means that views of ourselves reside at different levels of conscious awareness. Although you may think of yourself as a "runner," this description may be way down on the list you generated and correspondingly we would have to go to a deeper level of analysis to get at it. If we really want to get a good sense of a person and his or her culture, we have to remember that many different levels could be important and that the context in which we make our assessment can make a world of difference. Take a look at the example shown in Figure 1.3 and notice how the order of ways Manish describes himself varies depending on the context that he is in.

Having culture can offer a person many things. Think about what you may get from being part of a certain culture. Like someone in the army or someone on an athletic team (both cultures of their own), the culture you live in influences ideas

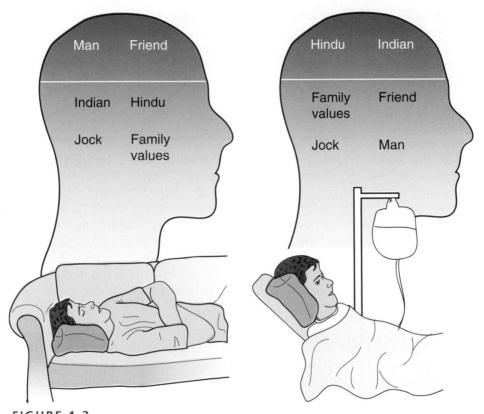

FIGURE 1.3

Levels of Analysis and Context

The context we are in can influence the things that first come to mind when we are asked to describe ourselves. If Manish were awakened from a nap and asked to describe himself, the order of things that would come up would be very different from those if he had an accident and were taken to the hospital. The context (the hospital) would bring different things to the level of consciousness. Being Hindu in a Western hospital may make those aspects of his self-concept more salient.

about what to do, what to wear, how to behave, and even how to feel. These prescriptions of how to be form the basis of the way culture has been defined in the scientific literature. There are many definitions of culture (Soudijn, Hutschemaekers, & Van de Vijver, 1990, analyzed 128 definitions). Next I provide a comprehensive definition of culture that shows you how culture can influence our health behaviors and our health in general.

Culture can be broadly defined as a dynamic, yet stable, set of goals, beliefs, and attitudes shared by a group of people (Matsumoto, 2001). Culture can also include similar physical characteristics (e.g., skin color), psychological characteristics (e.g., levels of hostility), and common superficial features (e.g., hair style and clothing). Culture is dynamic because some of the beliefs held by members in a

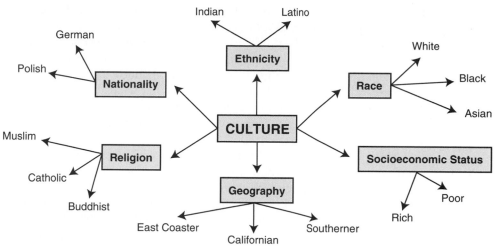

FIGURE 1.4
The Variety of Cultures and Associated Behaviors
There are many different aspects to the definition of culture. The term culture can imply many different things.

culture can change with time. However, the general level of culture stays mostly stable because the individuals change together. The beliefs and attitudes can be implicit, learned by observation, and passed on by word of mouth, or they can be explicit, written down as laws or rules for the group to follow. The most commonly described objective cultural groups consist of grouping by ethnicity, race, sex, and age. Look at Figure 1.4 for a summary of the different types of culture and characteristics. There are also many aspects of culture that are more subjective and cannot be seen or linked easily to physical characteristics. For example, nationality, sex/gender, religion, and geography also constitute different cultural groups, each with its own set of prescriptions for behavior.

Two Major "Cultures"

Two of the most important aspects that define cultural groups are **socioeconomic status (SES)** and sex. Both will be featured frequently throughout this book. SES is becoming one of the most important and widely studied constructs in health psychology (Adler & Ostrove, 1999; Taylor, Repetti, & Seeman, 1997). Almost any study done on this topic shows that poverty and illness tend to go together, often linked by factors such as access to health care and insurance. The poor make up a large percentage of Americans without health insurance. SES is related to a higher occurrence of most chronic and infectious disorders and to higher rates of nearly all major causes of mortality and morbidity (Adler, Boyce, Chesney, Folkman, & Syme, 1993; Macintyre, 1997; Williams & Collins, 1995). Even the neighborhood you live in can be important. Neighborhood SES has been associated with poorer health practices (Petridou et al., 1997) and a variety of other health conditions such as coronary heart disease (Diez-Roux et al., 2001; Robert, 1999). The relationship between SES and health is also fairly direct: the more money you have, the better your health. This relationship is seen for children and for older adults alike. Several ways of measuring SES have been proposed but most include some quantification of family income, parental education, and occupational status. Research shows that SES is associated with a wide array of health, cognitive, and socioemotional outcomes with effects beginning before birth and continuing into adulthood (Bradley & Corwyn, 2002; Gottfried, Gottfried, Bathurst, Guerin, & Parramore, 2003).

Many differences in health are due to sex, an innate, biological characteristic. Men and women react differently to hospitalization (Volicer, Isenberg, & Burns, 1977) and illness in general (Westbrook & Viney, 1983). Although women live longer than men, they report symptoms of illness more frequently and utilize health services to a greater extent (Nathanson, 1977; Waldron, 1991). There are both pros and cons to being female. The female sex hormone estrogen has a protective effect against cardiovascular illness in women younger than age 50 (Orth-Gomer, Chesney, & Wegner, 1998). On the other hand, women are more likely to be victims of violence and sexual assault (Risberg, 1994) and have body image and diet problems (Chesney & Ozer, 1995). Sometimes these differences are due to gender, behaviors determined by socialization, and learning of social roles. For example, sociological factors related to gender include the extra demands of balancing different roles (e.g., being the primary caregiver for children and going to work, Repetti, 1998). Most studies acknowledge these differences by statistically controlling for sex and implicitly (and sometimes explicitly) treating biological sex as a proxy for gender. Remember that sex and gender are not identical constructs although the two are often treated interchangeably (Pryzgoda & Chrisler, 2000).

Our culture has a major impact on behaviors that influence our health. Culture influences some explicit health behaviors. For example: How much do we exercise? Do we drink or smoke? Do we eat well? Culture also influences a whole range of behaviors that indirectly influence our health. For example: How do we form relationships? How many close friends do we have and do we call on them when we are stressed or in need?

Some Important Warnings

Whenever we talk about culture, we often tend to emphasize cultural differences. To some extent, this is a natural human phenomenon. Even if people who are relatively identical in age, ethnicity, and intelligence are randomly separated into two groups and forced to compete with each other, members of each group will tend to believe they are better than those of the other group (e.g., the minimal subgroup paradigm, an important social psychological effect I shall consider in later chapters). Even if we are not competing for resources we still like to emphasize how we are different from other people. There are two major problems here. First, this emphasis on differences often leads us to treat some groups better than others, favoring them for a range of activities and services (I will discuss factors such as prejudice later in this book). For example, we may be more likely to help people who look like us. We may be less likely to give information to someone who is not from a social group we belong to. Second, whenever we deal with an individual from a culture that we are not familiar with, we are likely to use the key ways that he or she is different and generalize from that one person to the entire culture (I will discuss the dangers of stereotyping later as well). By focusing on major group differences, we often forget that differences exist within a group as often as between groups. Let me give you an example.

Take a look at the two bell-shaped curves in Figure 1.5. The horizontal x-axis represents the number of push-ups a person can do, and the vertical y-axis represents the number of people who can do each number of push-ups. Now suppose we walk around town for a few days, and we ask every man and woman we see to get down on the pavement and do as many push-ups as he or she can in 1 minute. We continue this odd little request until we speak to 100 men and 100 women. Each curve you see represents one of the two sexes. So the point of the curve for women above the number 10 basically means that of all the women we talked to (and who agreed to our strange request), 15 could do 10 push-ups. Now you will probably notice that the two curves are slightly set apart from each other. If we were to ask one of the most commonly asked questions in much of psychology, "Are there significant sex differences?" it is easy to see that the answer is yes. The average number of push-ups men can do is significantly higher than the average number of push-ups women can do. You can also see that there are more men who can do 30 or more push-ups than women, and more women than men who can only do 10 or fewer push-ups in 1 minute.

There are two critical things to notice about those two overlapping curves. First, even though there are men who can do more push-ups than women and women who can do fewer push-ups than any man, notice how many men and women can do the same number of push-ups. The entire center portions of each curve overlap (the shaded part). At the heart of it all we are all much more similar than we are dissimilar. Excluding unfortunate and unpredictable circumstances, we all have two eyes, two legs, a nose, and two ears. We all look pretty much the same. We all need to eat, drink, and sleep to live. So why then do we often look at either end of the curves or focus on group differences only? We do so because differences are more noticeable and provide a way to distinguish groups.

Even though we all need to eat, drink, and sleep to live, we vary in how we accomplish each, and how much food, drink, or sleep we need. These variations often make the difference between illness and health. I will draw your attention to these variations in this book. All humans have about 32,000 genes (compare that number with the fruit fly at 18,000 or the worm at 12,000), but a variety of environmental and cultural factors can influence the kind of organisms those genes transcribe onto. Humans share 99.8% of their genes, but that 0.02% of a difference is very important. In short, even though we should always remember that there are more similarities than differences, sometimes we can learn a lot from the differences.

There is something else to notice in Figure 1.5. Take a look at each curve by itself. Notice that there is a lot of diversity in push-up ability *even within each sex*. The average number of push-ups women can do provides a sense of general

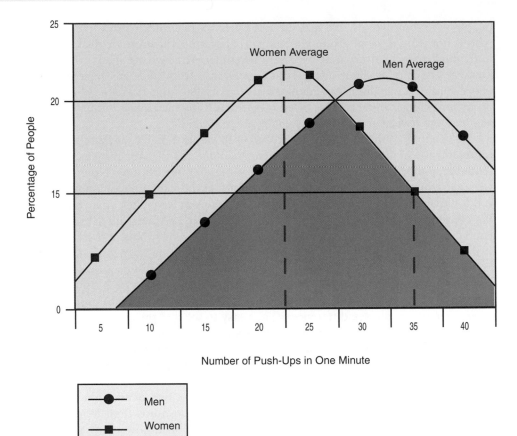

FIGURE 1.5
People within Cultures Vary Too
Although men may be able to do more push-ups than women on average, many women can do more push-ups than a number of men. Notice the number of men and women (shaded) that can do the same number.

ability, but notice the number of women at different stages of ability level. A lot of diversity is seen among women. This is a critical observation to hold on to as we discuss the many different topics in this book. No matter how many significant group differences we see, we must also remember that there are a lot of differences within each culture as well. This basic understanding of the differences *within* versus between cultures applies to every culture we discuss. We can be talking about men and women as in the lighter push-up example above, or we can be comparing young and old, rich and poor, or Mexican American and African American. To make it easier to understand the different aspects of health psychology, I will highlight how groups differ. Every time I do, keep these two overlapping curves at the back of your mind and always remember than these are average group differences only.

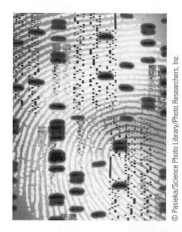

The Biopsychosocial Determinants of Health
Our genes, our psychological states, and our friends and social environments are some of the many factors that influence our health and health behaviors.

Health Psychology's Biopsychosocial Approach

An understanding of the different definitions of culture becomes a useful aid to study health and examine why we do or do not do things that are good for us. Most behaviors that influence health—whether healthy ones such as physical activity and eating nutritionally balanced diets or unhealthy ones such as smoking or drinking excessively—depend heavily on the culture that we grew up in. If both your parents exercised, there is a high probability that you will exercise as well. The fact that behavior is influenced by many different factors outside of the individual is a critical aspect that health psychologists focus on. I will discuss the exact ways that culture influences our development and health behaviors in more detail in chapter 3.

How does the culture that we come from and surround ourselves with influence our health and behaviors? Answering this question with a concerted look at sources of influence outside a person (i.e., not just his or her biology or psychology) is a distinctive feature of the approach taken by health psychologists in studying health. In contrast to the biomedical approach of Western medicine described before, health psychologists use a **biopsychosocial approach.** Most terms used in psychology reflect common sense, and this one is no exception. This type of approach focuses on the biology or physiology underlying health, the psychology or thoughts, feelings, and behaviors influencing health, and the ways that society and culture influence health. This approach goes beyond defining health as the absence of disease and instead forces us to focus on the broader range of the critical determinants of health (Suls & Rothman, 2004).

The Evolution of Health Psychology

The first two components of the biopsychosocial approach—focusing on biology and psychology—represent a current resolution to an ancient debate. For centuries researchers, thinkers, and philosophers have questioned if and how the mind (and psychology) and the body (and our biology) are related and whether this relationship influences health. Is the mind connected to the body? Does it reside in the body? Where is the soul? These are some questions that philosophers and scientists have debated for eons.

The earliest evidence, such as oral traditions and pictorial evidence from early civilizations, suggests that the mind and body were originally considered to be one (Ellenberger, 1970). Spirits invading the body were thought to cause illness, and gruesome solutions such as trephination, the poking of holes in the skull to release spirits, were practiced to make people healthy. Needless to say, this was not a highly successful method (nor was it likely to have been extremely popular with people developing illnesses).

Many of the world's early philosophies seemed to share the view that the mind and the body were intimately connected, and close to 5,000 years ago, both the ancient Chinese Taoist sages and the ancient Indian practitioners of Ayurveda wrote about various ways the mind could calm the body and vice versa (Dash & Junius, 1983; Kaptchuk, 2000; Svoboda, 1992). It is also certain that the rich traditions of medical practice in Egypt and the Middle East around 2000 B.C. (e.g., Mesopotamia, common day Iraq) also focused on this connection (Udwadia, 2000). Greek philosophers around 300 to 400 B.C. challenged this notion and proposed that the mind and the body were separate. Reason and rational thought, basic components of the Greek approach to life, were valued more than the biology of the body, but basic bodily substances were hypothesized to cause different diseases. For example, the Greek philosopher Hippocrates's rational explanation of why people get sick concerned the balance of four major bodily fluids (something that he borrowed from Alcmaeon of Crete). He argued that people got sick or showed different symptoms if the amount of one fluid exceeded that of the others. If you had a lot of blood you would be cheerful; if you had a lot of black bile you would be sad or melancholic. Hippocrates made many other contributions to the biological study of illness and is considered the father of Western biomedicine. In fact, all doctors take the Hippocratic Oath before they practice medicine (Table 1.4).

TABLE 1.4

The Hippocratic Oath

I swear by Apollo Physician and Asclepius and Hygieia and Panaceia and all the gods and goddesses, making them my witnesses, that I will fulfil according to my ability and judgment this oath and this covenant: To hold him who has taught me this art as equal to my parents and to live my life in partnership with him, and if he is in need of money to give him a share of mine, and to regard his offspring as equal to my brothers in male lineage and to teach them this art—if they desire to learn it—without fee and covenant; to give a share of precepts and oral instruction and all the other learning to my sons and to the sons of him who has instructed me and to pupils who have signed the covenant and have taken an oath according to the medical law, but no one else. I will apply dietetic measures for the benefit of the sick according to my ability and judgment; I will keep them from harm and injustice. I will neither give a deadly drug to anybody who asked for it, nor will I make a suggestion to this effect. Similarly I will not give to a woman an abortive remedy. In purity and holiness I will guard my life and my art. I will not use the knife, not even on sufferers from stone, but will withdraw in favor of such men as are engaged in this work.

Whatever houses I may visit, I will come for the benefit of the sick, remaining free of all intentional injustice, of all mischief and in particular of sexual relations with both female and male persons, be they free or slaves. What I may see or hear in the course of the treatment or even outside of the treatment in regard to the life of men, which on no account one must spread abroad, I will keep to myself, holding such things shameful to be spoken about. If I fulfil this oath and do not violate it, may it be granted to me to enjoy life and art, being honored with fame among all men for all time to come; if I transgress it and swear falsely, may the opposite of all this be my lot.

SOURCE: Translation from the Greek by Ludwig Edelstein. From Edelstein, L. (1943). *The Hippocratic Oath: Text, translation, and interpretation.* Baltimore: Johns Hopkins Press.

The French philosopher Rene Descartes (famous for his exclamation, "I think therefore I am"—*Ergo summa cogito*) strengthened many centuries later the Greek idea about the separation of the mind from the body. The hundreds of years that people believed that the mind was separate from the body helped medical science develop as scientists dissected dead bodies and increased our knowledge of human anatomy. The Greek Galen first pioneered the examination of the dead to find the cause of disease although he worked primarily on animals. Centuries later, the study of human anatomy was fine tuned by Andreas Vesalius (1514–1564) and the Italian artist (and the prototypical Renaissance man) Leonardo Da Vinci. Both drew detailed diagrams of the construction of the human body. Human dissections were rarely conducted but were explicitly banned by the Roman Catholic Church, which deemed dissections unholy. Finally, Descartes brokered a deal with the church resulting from a complex set of sociopolitical factors. Active antagonism had existed between the church and science, but the declining power of the church and the draining of church resources due to the Inquisition, made it easier for Descartes to convince the Holy Father that dissections should be allowed. Descartes essentially argued

© ImageState Royalty Free/Alamy

© Image Source/Alamy

© Aflo Foto Agency/Alamy

© IJeff Greenberg/PhotoEdit

Cultural Influences on Behavior To a large extent, our own health behaviors are dependent on the health behaviors of other individuals who share our cultural group.

that because the mind and body were separate, the mind and soul of a person left the body when the person died. Hence, only the biological body was left behind, and it was unimportant. The church accepted this explanation, and human dissections began in earnest.

In the early twentieth century psychology started to play a part in the examination of health. Part of the reason this involvement came so late is that psychology was not a field of study in its own right until around then. Flashing back to your introductory psychology class, you probably remember that the German William Wundt founded the first psychology laboratory in 1879. The first book in psychology, *Principles of Psychology* by Harvard University psychologist William James, was published in 1897. In a precursor of sorts to the biopsychosocial model, James also wrote *Varieties of Religious Experience* (1902) that referred to spirituality, health, and psychology. Also in the late 1890s, Sigmund Freud first generated his ideas about the structure of the human mind. When one mentions Freud's name, people quickly think of couches, bearded psychologists, and other stereotypical Freudian artifacts. Yes, Freud did have clients lie on his couch while he sat behind them and listened to them speak. Yes, we often see pictures of him in a beard and most movie psychoanalysts are similarly bearded (e.g., Billy Crystal in *Analyze This,* Doctor Frasier Crane during his years on the hit TV show *Cheers,* and Robin Williams in *Good Will Hunting* to name a few). These tidbits aside, Freud was one of the earliest health psychologists, though few would call him such.

How did Freud revolutionize the way we look at illness? Freud was the first to draw attention to the possibility that illness could have psychological causes. Trained as a neuroscientist, Freud had a strong biological background. He was perplexed by clients who reported strong symptoms of illness but who lacked physical evidence of illness. He also noticed the work of Pierre Janet and Franz Anton Mesmer, who cured cases of hysteria with hypnosis. In talking to his clients, Freud discovered that many of their physical illnesses were due to psychological issues and that once these issues were resolved, the physical symptoms disappeared. This focus on the workings of the mind in disease was continued later in the twentieth century by the psychoanalysts Franz Alexander and Helen Flanders Dunbar (e.g., Alexander, 1950). Together they established the first formal gathering of individuals interested in studying the influences of the mind on health. This movement within the mainstream medical establishment was coined **psychosomatic medicine.**

The new field of psychosomatic medicine had many supporters, which led to the formation of the first society specifically dedicated to the study of mind and body connections. The American Psychosomatic Society (APS) was formed to "promote and advance the scientific understanding of the interrelationships among biological, psychological, social, and behavioral factors in human health and disease, and the integration of the fields of science that separately examine each, and to foster the application of this understanding in education and improved health care" (APS, 2001). In 1936, the New York Academy of Medicine's joint committee on Religion and Medicine headed by Dunbar assembled a collection of the psychosomatic medical literature, together with publications examining the relationship of religion to health. Dunbar's early collection of articles led her to organize the publishing in 1939 of the first journal for this field, *Psychosomatic Medicine,* which still publishes research today. Although the early movement faltered and received mixed attention because it was based heavily on Freudian ideas and relied heavily on case study methods of research, the APS has survived to this day and is still active with annual meetings and active members.

Another movement within the field of medicine called **behavioral medicine** looks at nonbiological influences on health. Doctors and health care specialists within the medical community were probably always aware that changes in behavior and lifestyle improve health, prevent illness, and reduce symptoms of illness although they did not focus on this fact. The Society of Behavioral Medicine (SBM), a multidisciplinary, nonprofit organization founded in 1978, is dedicated to studying the influences of behavior on health and well-being. This organization brings together different disciplines—nursing, psychology, medicine, and public health—to form an interdisciplinary team. The society's explicit mission is to

Galen

Descartes

Freud

Dunbar

Key Figures in the History of Health Psychology

"foster the development and application of knowledge concerning the interrelationships of health, illness, and behavior" (Society of Behavioral Medicine, 2001). Like *Psychosomatic Medicine* for the APS, the SBM also has its own journal, *The Annals of Behavioral Medicine*.

Other groups of individuals also began to draw attention to the fact that health issues needed to be addressed by a broader approach than the point of

Courtesy of the National Library of Medicine

Early Cures for Illness Many bizarre remedies for illness were experimented with before the discovery of modern medicine, such as bloodletting and leeches.

view taken by the medical establishment. Medical anthropologists are individuals who are committed to improving public health in societies in economically poor nations. Based on the biological and sociocultural roots of anthropology, medical anthropologists have long considered health and medical care within the context of cultural systems although not necessarily using the tools or theoretical approaches of psychologists. In a related fashion, medical sociologists are individuals working within the framework of the medical model, focusing on the role of culture and a person's environment in health and illness. There are many fascinating studies of health and behavior conducted within these different fields that we will draw from and make reference to in this book. These fields and health psychology share common interests and terms. For example, health psychology and medical sociology have been influenced by the field of **epidemiology,** the study of the frequency, distribution, and causes of different diseases with an emphasis on the role of the physical and social environment. We will also be paying close attention to clear-cut outcome measures used by epidemiologists. For example, we shall look at how different biopsychosocial factors relate to the number of cases of a disease that exist at a given point in time, or **morbidity,** and to the number of deaths related to a specific cause, or **mortality.**

Even within mainstream psychology, researchers in social psychology, personality psychology, cognitive psychology, and clinical psychology realize that the basic theories that they derived to describe and predict behavior easily could be used in the study of health and well-being. Beyond just explaining what many laypeople (especially senators in Congress during the late 1960s who begrudged the use of government money to fund psychological studies) considered common-sensical and mundane issues, psychological theorizing can actually save lives! As we will soon see, social psychological theories form one of the core foundations of health psychological research, and many social phenomena can explain why we do what we do. Are children likely to start smoking? What makes a person more or less likely to exercise or eat well? The answers to each of these questions come from theories derived from basic social psychological research.

What Is Health Psychology?

Health psychology is an interdisciplinary subspecialty of psychology dedicated to promoting and maintaining health and preventing and treating illness (Matarazzo, 1982). Health psychologists pay close attention to the way that thoughts, feelings, behavior, and biological processes all interact with each other to influence health and illness. In many ways health psychology is greater than a subfield within the discipline of psychology, as it is built on theoretical ideas and research findings from many other areas in psychology. For example, many of the ways used to understand why we get stressed and how we cope come from social and personality psychology. As previously discussed in the evolution of psychology, even clinical psychologists such as Freud, Alexander, and Dunbar contributed to the development of the field. The biological bases of health have been studied by physiological psychologists. When we discuss the ways that health psychologists try to change behaviors in later chapters, the influence of behaviorists such as Skinner and Watson is apparent. Helping someone to stop smoking or making yourself eat better or exercise more can be accomplished by using basic behaviorist theories (e.g., classical and operant conditioning).

Whenever we refer to Health Psychology (with the capital letters) we refer to the subdivision of the American Psychological Association (**APA Division 38**) that is dedicated to

1. Advancing the contributions of psychology to the understanding of health and illness through basic and clinical research
2. Encouraging the integration of biomedical information about health and illness with current psychological knowledge
3. Promoting education and services in the psychology of health and illness
4. Informing the psychological and biomedical community and the general public about the results of current research and service activities in this area (APA, 2001)

Unlike the Society of Behavioral Medicine or the American Psychosomatic Society, whose members are overwhelmingly physicians, APA's Division of Health Psychology is a group specifically for psychologists. That fact aside, it is also open to (and is driven to foster collaborations with) members of the other health care professions who are interested in the psychological aspects of physical and mental health. The Division's main goals are to (1) understand the etiology and promotion and maintenance of health, (2) prevent, diagnose, treat, and rehabilitate physical and mental illness, (3) study psychological, social, emotional, and behavioral factors in physical and mental illness, and (4) improve the health care system and formulation of health policy.

Main Areas in Health Psychology

The field of health psychology and the contents of this book can be carved into three broad natural segments: (1) stress and coping, (2) health behaviors, and (3) issues in health care. Perhaps closest to the psychological roots of this area, the first part of this book will examine the biopsychosocial determinants of stress and then look at how these same factors can influence how we cope. The next part of the book will first describe the main health psychological theories relating to why we act in various healthy ways using different health behaviors as examples. We will look at the good (e.g., physical activity), the bad (e.g., eating too much fast food), and the ugly (e.g., seeing what smoking can do to a person's teeth and lungs). The last part of the book will focus on different factors relating to health care. These include the complexities of dealing with chronic and terminal illnesses and the different psychological factors influencing the quality of interactions between doctors and patients. I will first set the stage by discussing how different theories of human development and cultural variations can help us understand our health-related behaviors and our health. I will also demonstrate how cultural differences in development (e.g., parenting styles) can influence health behaviors and health. As you move through the book you will also learn about some of the fascinating ways that different cultures approach health and illness.

A Research Primer

Health psychology relies firmly on the scientific method. The key elements of a science are that it is empirical (relying on sense observations and data) and theory driven. The data or empirical evidence is collected in ethical, rigorously controlled, and standardized ways whether you are identifying causes of stress or testing the psychological effects of an intervention to reduce smoking. The research enterprise is a fascinating one and to get a good feel for the results of research (discussed throughout this book), you should have a good idea of the main research designs and data collection methods. Most of you should have encountered research methods in your introductory psychology course so I will briefly discuss the basic issues and then move on to more complex material when I describe some distinctive terms in health psychology research.

The most basic form of research describes relationships between variables. Are heavier people more at risk for cardiovascular disease? Do poorer people smoke more? A **correlation coefficient** is the statistical measure of the association. Correlations range from -1.00 to $+1.00$ with values closer to 1 (regardless of sign) signifying stronger associations. Positive correlations indicate variables that change in the same direction (e.g., higher weight correlates with higher risk of cardiovascular disease). Negative correlations indicate variables that change in opposite directions (e.g., lower socioeconomic status correlates with higher smoking rates).

Correlational studies do not allow us to draw causal conclusions. This does not stop the casual reader or the uninformed and can sometimes lead to mild panic where none is warranted. For example, a study found that oral sex was correlated with incidences of mouth cancer (Alberg et al., 2004). Does this mean that practicing oral sex causes mouth cancer? If the study was correlational, it does not. In fact, the study also showed that oral sex was highly correlated with smoking and drinking, two behaviors more likely to cause mouth cancer. **Experimental designs** help us determine causality. In experiments, the researcher manipulates the variable that is believed to be important—the **independent variable**—and measures how changes in this variable influence another variable—the **dependent variable.** Experiments have two or more groups, each of which experience different levels of the independent variable. If the participants are randomly sampled (everyone in the population has an equal chance of being in the study) and extraneous variables (other variables that may influence the outcome of interest such as socioeconomic status or other health behaviors) are controlled for, then one can be fairly certain that changes in the dependent variable are due to changes in the independent variable. Cause can be determined.

To test whether exercise is good for concentration you can have one group of people exercise (the independent variable) three times a week and the other not exercise. You can then see if the two groups vary in concentration (the dependent variable). In health psychological research it is often impractical and unethical to manipulate key variables of interest (e.g., making people smoke or have oral sex) so groups that naturally vary in the variable of interest are used instead (e.g., compare groups of people who vary in how much they smoke or have oral sex). Because using naturally occurring groups is not a perfect experiment, such designs are referred to as **quasi-experimental designs,** and the independent variables are called subject variables. Examples of common subject variables are age, sex, ethnicity, personality type, occupation, socioeconomic status, and disease state (level or presence of).

Research can also be cross-sectional, conducted at one point in time, or longitudinal, conducted over a period of time and often involving many measures of the key variables. It can be **prospective,** following disease free participants over a period of time to determine whether certain variables (e.g., eating too much fast food) predict disease, or **retrospective,** studying participants with a disease and tracing their histories of health behaviors to determine what caused the disease. You will also hear about **randomized, controlled,** or **clinical trials,** in which one group gets an experimental drug or intervention treatment and a second group unknowingly gets a **placebo** (an inactive substance that appears similar to the experimental drug) or nothing (the control group).

Epidemiological studies often report **prevalence rates,** the proportion of the population that has a particular disease at a particular time (commonly reported as cases per 1,000 or 100,000 people), and **incidence rates,** the frequency of new cases of the disease during a year. Other important terms to watch for in the reporting of health psychological research are **relative risk,** the ratio of incidence or prevalence of a disease in an exposed group to the incidence or prevalence of the disease in an unexposed group, and **absolute risk,** a person's chance of developing a disease independent of any risk that other people may have.

FOCUS on Current Issues

Profile of a Multicultural America

What does it mean to be American? The tragic events surrounding September 11, 2001, brought this question to the foreground. On one hand, we saw most men, women, and children wearing red, white, and blue, waving flags, saluting one united nation, and celebrating the fact that all Americans are the same regardless of ethnicity and religion. Paradoxically, Balbir Singh Sodhi, an Indian American man was shot to death in Arizona because he wore a turban (a head covering consisting of a long cloth that is used to wrap hair that has never been cut since birth). The shooter thought the turban meant that the man was Arab. But, in fact, the turban is the headdress of Sikhs, a religious group originating in India, and more closely associated with Hinduism. Even though Mr. Sodhi was an American, he was shot because he "looked" like an Arab and the terrorists were Arab in origin. So what does it mean to be American? Does it mean being White? Of course, it doesn't. American citizens have many different skin colors, religions, and ways of dressing and that is only the beginning of our country's diversity. America consists of a variety of cultural groups, and it is critical to remind ourselves that not only is the country multicultural but we ourselves are also all multicultural.

The most recent census lists the population the United States as 281 million. That number can be broken down along different cultural lines. An example of a "cultural group" that most people tend to think of first is ethnicity. Of that 281 million population, approximately 13% are African American or Black, approximately 4% are Asian American (including Americans of different Asian backgrounds such as Chinese, Japanese, Korean, and Indian), and approximately 1% are American Indians or Native Americans. The remaining 82% of the population are considered European American or White and include people of Latin American and Spanish ancestry. Commonly referred to as Latinos, the preferred term, or Hispanic (a term applied to this ethnic group by the U.S. government in the 1980 Census), the truth is that people in this same group have their own names for their groups depending on which part of the United States they live in and their specific country of origin. For example, *Hispanic* is preferred in the Southeast and much of Texas, New Yorkers use both *Hispanic* and *Latino*, and in Chicago, *Latino* is preferred (Shorris, 1992). Ethnicity is just one way to carve up the pie.

A second type of "culture" is religion. Of the 281 million Americans, the absolute majority are Christians, accounting for 84% (57% Protestant and 27% Catholic). You may be surprised by the next largest percentage: 8% of Americans do not have any religious affiliation. It is difficult to say whether they are nonbelievers or just practice some personal form of religion. Of the rest, 2% are Jewish. Of note is the fact that some religious groups that we hear a lot about are not really present in very large numbers. Testifying to the fact that we as human beings tend to overestimate the actual occurrence of something just based on the extent to which we hear about it (referred to as the availability heuristic), Muslims only constitute a minute part of the population (between 3.5 and 6 million). Because of political events (e.g., trouble in the Middle East and the War on Terrorism in Afghanistan and Iraq, areas whose populations are predominantly

Muslim), many Americans believe that there are many Muslims in United States (and unfortunately have prejudices against them) when in fact they are a very small minority.

We can also think about culture in terms of ethnicity, different age groups, SES, or different geographical regions. Your biological sex and gender contribute in large part to your sense of self. Different age groups—children, adolescents, teenagers, young adults, or older adults—may experience different stressors. When you break the United States down along these different lines, you realize that there are many such groups that each have their own specific health issues. The numbers in each of these groups change over time too. For example, in 2001 there were 35 million people in the United States older than age 65. In 1990, there were only 31 million. This difference in the age profile can have implications for health care. People living in different parts of the country may have different health behaviors. The southeastern states such as Kentucky and Virginia show some of the highest levels of smoking. A person's SES can have many implications for his or her health. If you have money you can afford healthy food and higher quality health services. In 2001 the median or normative household income level was $42,228 (Census Bureau), but 30% of American households were making less than $25,000 a year. That is not a lot of money to support a family. As you can see, America is multicultural indeed, and we will soon see how these different aspects of culture interact to influence behaviors and health.

Chapter Summary

- There are many different definitions of health, each varying in its culture of origin. Western medicine sees health more as the absence of disease whereas other cultures see health more as a balance of opposing forces or spiritual harmony. The most common definition is that used by the World Health Organization.
- Culture is very broadly defined and includes ethnicity, sex, religion, gender, and nationality. Various dimensions of culture shape our health behaviors and our general health. Individualism and collectivism are examples of basic cultural dimensions. Socioeconomic status and sex are two of the most important cultural variables, each leading to a variety of health differences.
- Health psychology uses a biopsychosocial approach. This approach focuses on the biological, psychological, and sociocultural factors that influence health and health behaviors.
- Theorizing about the extent to which the mind and the body are connected has varied over time and across cultures. The ancient Chinese and Indians saw the two as connected, but the Greeks and other Europeans saw the mind and body as separate. Today we recognize that the two are clearly interconnected, and this connection is critical to understanding health and illness.
- Freud was the first psychologist to link the mind and body together and hypothesize psychological bases for physiological problems. His early views led to the formation of the first organization of behavioral medicine in the late 1930s followed by further growth in the late 1960s.

- Health psychology as a unique area of psychology came to the forefront in the 1970s and has blossomed since then. Its main goals are the prevention of illness, the promotion of health, the understanding of the biopsychosocial aspects of physical and mental illness, and the improvement of the health care system. The main areas of health psychology are stress and coping, health behaviors, and issues in health care.
- Three major organizations cater to those using the biopsychosocial model.
- There are many different types of research design and data collection methods. Research is primarily correlational or experimental in nature. Correlations are the assessment of association between variables. In experiments, researchers manipulate key variables (independent variables) to see the effects on others (dependent variables).

Synthesize, Evaluate, Apply

- How has our view of the mind-body connection changed over time?
- How is health best viewed? What do you feel is the best definition?
- How do different cultures vary in their definition of health?
- What are the components of a good definition of culture?
- What aspects of life are influenced by culture? How is culture transferred?
- What are the different areas of knowledge/psychology that play a role in health psychology?
- What factors can influence responses to the "Who am I?" test?
- A 9-year study (Berkman & Syme, 1979) showed that people who practiced more healthy behaviors lived longer, but examined men and women over the age of 45 only. What aspect of this finding is a challenge for health psychologists (as we try to change the behaviors of younger adults)?
- How are the three main organizations for health psychology different from each other?
- How have the patterns of illness changed over time? How have causes of death changed in the last 300 years?
- Why is the field of health psychology especially needed today?
- Contrast the two approaches used by medicine and health psychology. What are components of each?
- Why are cultural differences important in the context of health?
- How can context and level of analysis play a role in describing culture?
- What areas of society can you see a health psychologist working in?

KEY TERMS, CONCEPTS, AND PEOPLE

absolute risk, 28
Alexander, Franz, 23
APA Division 38, 26
Ayurveda, 8
behavioral medicine, 23
biomedical approach, 7
biopsychosocial approach, 20
context, 13
correlation coefficient, 27
culture, 14
Descartes, René, 21
Dunbar, Helen Flanders, 23
epidemiology, 25
experimental designs, 28

Freud, Sigmund, 22
Galen, 21
health, 4
Health psychology, 26
Hippocrates, 20
independent and dependent
	variable, 28
James, William, 22
level of analysis, 13
morbidity, 25
mortality, 25
placebo, 28
prevalence and incidence
	rates, 28

prospective and retrospective
	studies, 28
psychosomatic medicine, 23
quasi-experimental designs, 28
randomized, controlled, and
	clinical trials, 28
relative risk, 28
socioeconomic status
	(SES), 15
Traditional Chinese
	Medicine, 8
WHO, 4

ESSENTIAL READINGS

Baum, A., & Posluszny, D. M. (1999). Health psychology: Mapping biobehavioral contributions to health and illness. *Annual Review of Psychology, 50,* 137–163.

Matarazzo, J. D. (1980). Behavioral health and behavioral medicine: Frontiers for a new health psychology. *American Psychologist, 35*(9), 807–817.

Suls, J., & Rothman, A. (2004). Evolution of the biopsychosocial model: Prospects and challenges for health psychology. *Health Psychology, 23*(2), 119–126.

Taylor, S. E. (1990). Health psychology: The science and the field. *American Psychologist, 45*(1), 40–50.

WEB RESOURCES

Visit the companion website at **http://psychology.wadsworth.com/gurung1e/,** where you will find online resources for this book, including chapter-by-chapter quizzes, weblinks, and more! You can also visit Wadsworth Psychology Resource Center at **http://psychology.wadsworth.com** to access additional resources.

Health Psychology
http://www.health-psych.org

World Health Organization
http://www.who.int/en

American Psychosomatic Society
http://www.psychosomatic.org

Society for Behavioral Medicine
http://www.sbm.org

Cultural Approaches to Health

Y ou are probably not aware of the number of things that you take for granted. There are many facts that you probably accept easily: The earth is round. It revolves around the sun. These you know. You also may believe you know why some things happen the way they do. If you stay outside in the cold rain without a raincoat, you believe you will catch a cold (at least that is what your mom always told you). If you eat too much fatty food, you know you will put on weight. Every culture has its own beliefs. Many Southeast Asian mothers place a black spot on their babies' heads to ward away the "evil eye" that could cause their babies harm. Kabala-following celebrities such as Madonna and Britney Spears wear red bracelets for the same reason. Some religious groups, such as the Christian Scientists, believe that the use of excessive medication is against God's will. All of us grow up with understandings of how various illnesses are caused. These understandings come from the cultural groups that we are a part of. However, we are not always aware that our understandings of the causes of our good health and of the treatment of sicknesses are culturally dependent. If we believe a virus or bacteria caused an infection, we will be willing to use antibiotic medications to treat it. What if you believed that an infection was caused by the looks of a jealous neighbor or because you had angered the spirits of the wind?

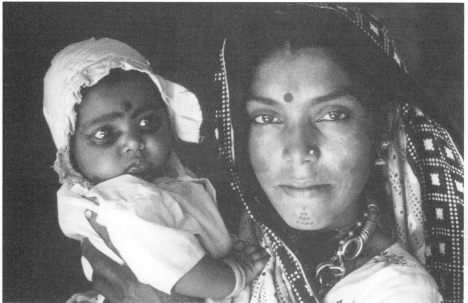

© Lindsay Hebberd/CORBIS

The Evil Eye In cultures around the world, the evil eye is the name for a sickness transmitted— usually without intention—by someone who is envious, jealous, or covetous. Latino and Asian Indian mothers try to make sure their children do not get the "evil eye" by placing large black dots on their children's foreheads.

Different cultures have varied health beliefs and health behaviors. Women in New Mexico and men in Chicago may have the same physical problem, but their doctors must take into account the existing differences in their patients' social systems (differences in culture, beliefs, family structure, and economic class) and their patients' expectations of health care and health care workers to cure them. This chapter describes the major philosophical approaches followed by Americans of different cultural backgrounds. These different approaches can explain some differences in health behaviors. Remember that an effective health psychologist has to be ready to deal with the diversity of people and their beliefs. To help a person stay healthy and recover when sick, you must understand what his or her specific understanding of health and sickness is. Once you understand, you can use variations on the basic tools and theories to intervene and help. I will describe some of America's diverse ethnic and religious beliefs as they relate to health, focusing on contemporary views of the Chinese Taoist and East Indian Ayurvedic approaches to health, Latino folk medicine (curanderismo), and American Indian spiritualism. Be aware that the majority of the beliefs and practices we will discuss have not passed the critical eye of Western scientific inquiry (e.g., spirits cause illness). However, as all good psychologists know, if someone believes something strongly enough, then those beliefs can influence that person's behavior and reactions. It is important to know what different people believe. Even if you do not believe it yourself, shared understanding facilitates communication and successful health and healing.

Varieties of World Medicine

Different cultures have different definitions of health. Each culture evolves with a unique understanding of the creation of human beings and our purpose in life. According to archaeological evidence, our ancestors probably believed that our bodies worked because of magic. Potions, rings, charms, and bracelets were devised to rid the body of the harmful demons and spirits that brought illness and suffering. Some of these ancient beliefs often find their way into popular literature and underlie our enchantment with heady fare such as the *Lord of the Rings* trilogy and even the light and fanciful *Harry Potter* series. A person's eyes in particular were believed to be the sites of power and magic, whereas animal eyes routinely were used in a range of treatments (Monte, 1993). Although still changing, our understanding of the body crystallized about 5,000 years ago when the Chinese, Indians, Greeks, and Egyptians began to study the body extensively. Table 2.1 gives you a sense of when different medical systems evolved and where. The medical traditions and different approaches to health held by most Americans today derive from these early systems.

TABLE 2.1

Key Medical Events In World History

Western Medicine	Chinese Traditional Medicine	American Indian	Mexican/ Mexican American Curanderismo	Other World Cultures and Medicine
Greeks— Hippocrates (400 B.C.) Galen (100 B.C.) Da Vinci (A.D. 1500s) Vesalius (1600s) Harvey (1600s) Pasteur (1800s) Roentgen (1800s) Fleming (Penicillin) (1928)	*The Yellow Emperor's Classic of Internal Medicine* (approximately 100 B.C.)	Europeans first witness native rituals and traditions (approximately A.D. 1500) Folk medicine passed on orally for centuries	Dates unknown Folk medicine passed on orally for centuries	Mesopotamia (4000 B.C.) Indian Ayurveda (4000 B.C.) Egypt (3000 B.C.) Iti (2500 B.C.) Imhotep (2700 B.C.) Unani (A.D. 900)

Western Biomedicine

The most common approach to medicine, **Western biomedicine,** is derived from the work of Greek physicians such as Hippocrates and Galen. This is the medicine that an absolute majority of Americans believe in. American medical schools, hospitals, and emergency rooms all use this Western approach. In our own egocentric way, most Americans refer to any other approach to health and wellness as **complementary** or **alternative medicine.** Chinese acupuncture is perhaps the most commonly known "alternative" medicine, but millions of Americans also practice other means to improve their health (e.g., the use of herbal supplements). Other traditional beliefs and practices will be discussed.

Let us start with perhaps the most common reference point, Western biomedicine. Also referred to as modern medicine, conventional medicine, or **allopathy,** Western biomedicine is one of the most dominant forms of health care in the world today. Hallmarks of this approach are an increasing reliance on technology and the use of complex scientific procedures for the diagnosis and treatment of illness. Treatments using this approach are designed to cause the opposite effect as that created by the disease. If you have a fever, you are prescribed medication to reduce the temperature. Western biomedicine views the body as a biochemical machine with distinct parts. Often called **reductionist,** Western biomedicine searches for the single smallest unit responsible for the illness. Doctors in the West try to localize the cause of an illness to the parts directly surrounding the original point of the problem.

Greek Roots

Western biomedicine often claims the fourth century B.C. Greek, Hippocrates, as its "father," primarily because he was the first to separate medicine from religion and myth and to bring scientific and analytical reasoning to health care. There were physicians before Hippocrates. In the third millennium B.C., physicians in ancient Mesopotamia (modern Iraq) developed an official medical system based on a diagnostic framework that derived from sources as varied as omens and divination techniques and the inspection of livers of sacrificed animals (Porter, 2002). Treatments were coordinated by a head physician and combined religious rites and empirical treatments such as the use of drugs and practicing of surgery. Similarly, the Egypt of the Pharaohs also had a line of physicians. There was Iri, Keeper of the Royal Rectum (the Pharaoh's enema expert), and the most famous, Imhotep, chief physician to the Pharaoh Zozer, both of whom also used large amounts of religious rituals to aid their curing (Udwadia, 2000). Essentially secular medicine only appeared in the Greek-speaking world as practiced by the fifth century B.C. Hippocratic doctors.

Personality psychologists often recount Hippocrates's humoral theory of what made people different. He argued that our personalities were a function of the level of certain bodily fluids or humors. If you had a lot of black bile you would be sad or melancholic. If you had a lot of blood you would be cheerful or sanguine. Because there were very few explicit cures back then, the etiology of disease had not yet been sufficiently mapped out; one of the main roles of the physician was as support provider. Beyond this supportive element of the medical practitioner, none of Hippocrates's healing methods, the use of diet, herbs, and natural remedies, are used by biomedical doctors today. A few centuries later, Galen, the "emperor" of medicine under the Roman empire, and much later the Italian artist Leonardo Da Vinci (in the fifteenth to sixteenth centuries) and the Flemish physician Andreas Vesalius (sixteenth century) greatly advanced Western biomedicine with their studies of human anatomy. William Harvey, an Englishman, first described the circulation of blood and the functioning of the heart in 1628. Biomedicine had its first major boost with the discovery of the high-power microscope. The Dutch naturalist Antonius van Leeuwenhoek ground lenses to magnify objects 300 times. Compare this magnification to that of the electron microscope, invented in 1932, which magnifies specimens to a power of 5 million. Here is a *Trivial Pursuit* curiosity: What was one of the first specimens observed under the lens? (Answer: Human sperm.)

Technological Innovations

Western biomedicine always has been tied heavily to technology. Once the microscope became widely used, blood, saliva, and other bodily fluids were closely examined, leading to a better understanding of the structures and functions of a wide variety of cells. Louis Pasteur really took the next big leap for medicine. As one of the most significant events in the nineteenth century, Pasteur proved that viruses and bacteria could cause disease. In 1878, Pasteur presented his germ theory to the French Academy of Medicine (Udwadia, 2000). Just a few

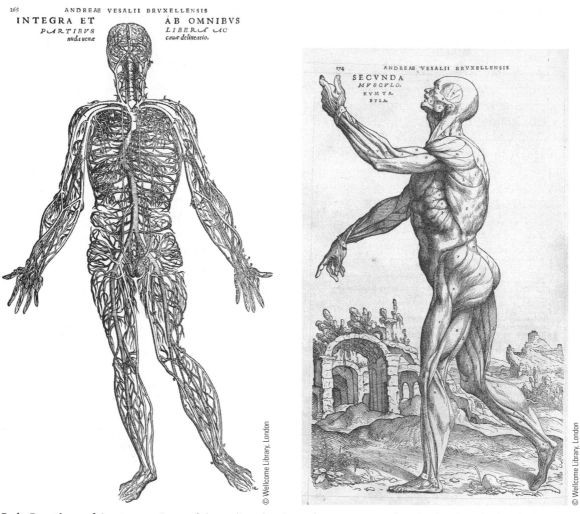

Early Drawings of Anatomy Some of the earliest drawings of anatomy were done by the Flemish physician Andreas Vesalius.

years later in 1885, the German scientist Wilhelm Roentgen discovered x-rays. Roentgen discovered that passing highly charged waves of energy through the body and then onto a sensitive photographic plate created accurate images of the body's interior. This technological advance enabled doctors to look into the body to see what was causing illnesses or problems and together with the microscope took the diagnosis of illness to new heights. More advances in the twentieth century, such as magnetic resonance imaging (MRI) and computerized axial tomography (CAT) scans, led to closer examinations of the body and bodily functions, especially the brain. Technology fueled the drive of Western medicine to find the answers to what causes illness and death by studying the cellular level. Similar to the behavioral psychologist, Western medicinal practitioners primarily focus on what can be observed. The presence of observable factors (e.g., cancerous cells or bacteria) thereby explains any move away from positive health.

Cures and treatment, especially modern pharmacology, developed to attack what was wrong in the body. Medicines, as the biomedical model defines them, are essentially concentrated purified chemical substances that target a particular aspect of the disease process. The chemical composition of some drugs (e.g., **opioids**) mirrors that of naturally occurring substances (e.g., **opiates**). For example, morphine, an opioid that was first extracted in 1805, is identical to chemicals produced by opiates in our body, as there are receptors that accept morphine in our brains. Other milestones in the development of drugs include the discovery of antibacterial sulfonamides in 1935 and the production of antibiotics such as penicillin in the 1940s (although it was first discovered in 1928). Many thousands of different drugs are available today for nearly every ache, pain, or irritation you may have.

The other main element of Western biomedicine is surgery. First practiced by early Egyptians and Peruvians 6,000 years ago, surgery has evolved into an art. If an x-ray reveals a problem or a miniscule camera detects a problem in a vein, artery, or one of the many ducts and tubes that we have (e.g., gastric tract or pulmonary tract), skilled surgeons open up the body and attempt to make things right. Although major surgical milestones have been relatively recent with the first coronary bypass being performed in 1951 and the first heart transplant in 1967, currently there seem to be few operations that cannot be undertaken.

The reliance on technology and the evolution of pharmacology and surgery signal the main approach of Western biomedicine to healing. If you visit a medical doctor with a problem, the routine is straightforward. Your answers to the doctor's questions guide what tests, x-ray studies, or scans you will need. Subsequent test results help the doctor identify the disease-causing agents and medicines or surgical method needed to cure the problem. Health, according to this model, is the absence of disease. The Western doctor starts with a symptom, searches for the underlying mechanisms or causes, and attempts to fight the disease with drugs or surgery. Most Americans believe that germs cause disease and expect to take some sort of pill to treat disease. This main belief of Western medicine is very different from the beliefs and approaches of other cultural groups.

Traditional Chinese Medicine

Traditional Chinese Medicine (TCM) is probably used to treat more people than any other form of medicine (yes, in large part because China is the most populated country in the world). However, even in North America, there are a large number of TCM schools and practitioners. In fact, acupuncture, one form of

TCM, is covered by most health insurance policies (acupuncture will be discussed in the Focus section later on at the end of this chapter). No, feng shui is not a part of TCM, but if you have heard of this Chinese art of arranging your living space to "optimize energy flow," you will have some feel for this very different approach to life. In fact, you will see that you may have been exposed to many aspects of the beliefs underlying TCM.

In TCM, the body is treated as a whole. Every single part of the body is considered to be intrinsically connected to other parts of the body and to what is happening around the person. Critical elements of a healthy life include a person's food choices, relationships, and emotional life. In TCM everyone is a part of a larger creation and lives and flourishes in unison with it. In stark contrast to reductionist Western biomedicine that focuses on a cellular microscopic level of diagnosis, TCM is macroscopic. In TCM humankind is viewed in relation to nature and the physical laws that govern it. Some interesting paradoxes are seen when we compare Western medicine and TCM. Although TCM does not have the concept of a nervous system nor does it recognize the endocrine system, TCM still treats problems the West calls endocrine and neurological disorders. TCM also uses terminology that may appear bizarre to a Westerner. For example, diseases are thought to be caused by imbalances in yin and yang or by too much "heat" or "wind."

Sources of Illness

Two main systems categorize the forces identified in TCM that influence health and well-being: yin and yang (Figure 2.1) and the five phases. According to one Chinese philosophy, all life and the entire universe originated from a single unified source called **Tao** (pronounced "dow" like the stock market index, Dow Jones). The main ideas about the Tao are encompassed in a 5,000-word poem called the *Tao Te Ching* written about 2,500 years ago that describes a way of life from the reign of the "Yellow Emperor" Huang Ti (Reid, 1989). In fact, Chinese medicine is based on *The Yellow Emperor's Classic of Internal Medicine* (approximately 100 B.C.). The Tao is an integrated and undifferentiated whole with two opposing forces—the *yin* and *yang*—that combine to create everything in the universe.

Yin and yang are mutually interdependent, constantly interactive, and potentially interchangeable forces. As you can see in Figure 2.1, each yin and yang contains the seed of the other (the little dot in the center of each comma-shaped component). The circle represents the supreme source or Tao. Yin translates to "shady side of a hill" whereas yang translates to "sunny side of the hill." Yin is traditionally thought of as darkness, the moon, cold, and female, whereas yang is thought of as light, the sun, hot, and male. In TCM, 10 vital organs are divided into five pairs, each consisting of one "solid" yin organ and one "hollow" yang organ. TCM practitioners believe that the yin organs—the heart, liver, pancreas, kidney, and lungs—are more vital than the yang organs, and dysfunctions of yin organs cause the greatest health problems. The paired yang organs are the gallbladder, small intestine, large intestine, and bladder. A healthy individual has a

FIGURE 2.1
The Chinese Symbol for Yin and Yang
The two halves represent the complementary nature of all energy in the universe.

balanced amount of yin and yang. If a person is sick, his or her forces are out of balance. Specific symptoms relate to an excess of either yin or yang. For example, if you are flushed, have a high temperature, are constipated, and have high blood pressure, you have too much yang.

The five phases or elemental activities refer to specific active forces and illustrate the intricate associations that the ancient Chinese saw between human beings and nature (Figure 2.2). Energy or **qi** (pronounced "chee"), another critical aspect of TCM, moves within the body in the same pattern as it does in nature with each season and with different foods helping to optimize energy flow within the body. The five elements of wood, fire, earth, metal, and water each link to a season of the year, a specific organ, and a specific food (Table 2.2). Each element has specific characteristics, is generated by one of the other forces, and is suppressed by another. For example, wood generates fire that turns things to earth that forms metals. The heart is ruled by fire, the liver by wood, and the kidneys by water. Fire provides qi to the heart and then passes qi onto the earth element and correspondingly the stomach, the spleen, and pancreas. Figure 2.3 illustrates how the different elements, seasons, organs, and foods interact.

Figure 2.3 also illustrates how one system depends on another. TCM doctors utilize such diagrams to treat patients. Let's say that a person eats too much salt, which causes kidney disorders. The kidney and bladder (the water element) control the heart and small intestine (fire). Consequently, kidney disorders cause heart disorders and high blood pressure. To treat the condition,

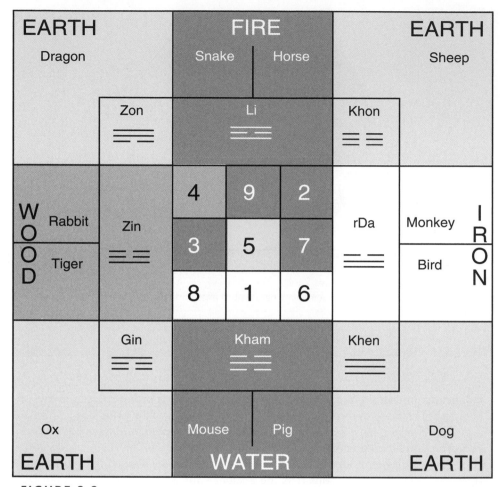

FIGURE 2.2
The Five Elements with Related Numerals and Animals
The five elements are in effect the five energies that, according to Taoist cosmology, comprise the energy matrix of the universe. In Traditional Chinese Medicine theory, these five dynamic bodies (Fire, Water, Wood, Earth, and Metal) balance the internal organs of the human body.

the TCM doctor treats the controlling element, water, by reducing the intake of salt, oils, and fats (which influences body water levels) and increasing mild aerobic exercise (fire).

Treatment

In TCM optimal health consists of balancing yin and yang and optimizing the smooth flow of qi through the body by the coordination of the five elements. Qi flows through the body in 12 precise, orderly patterns called meridians. Merid-

TABLE 2.2

The Chinese Elements and Associations

Elements	Wood	Fire	Earth	Metal	Water
Colors	Blue/green	Red	Yellow	White	Black
Symbols	Dragon	Phoenix	Caldron	Tiger	Tortoise
Seasons	Spring	Summer	Between	Autumn	Winter
Months	1–2	4–5	3, 6, 9, 12	7–8	10–11
Conditions	Rain	Heat	Wind	Clear	Cold
Directions	East	South	Center	West	North
Planets	Jupiter	Mars	Saturn	Venus	Mercury
Days	Thursday	Tuesday	Saturday	Friday	Wednesday
Animals	Scaled	Winged	Naked	Furred	Shelled
Actions	Countenance	Sight	Thought	Speech	Listening
Senses	Sight	Taste	Touch	Smell	Hearing
Sounds	Calling	Laughing	Singing	Lamenting	Moaning
Tastes	Sour	Bitter	Sweet	Acrid/spicy	Salty
Smells	Goatish	Burning	Fragrant	Rank	Rotten
Organs	Liver	Heart	Spleen	Lungs	Kidneys

SOURCE: Kaptchuk (2000).

ians translate from the Chinese term *jing-luo* to mean "to go through something that connects or attaches." In Chinese meridian theory, meridian channels are unseen but embody a form of informational network (Kaptchuk, 2000). The 12 meridians are associated with organs in the body. Two additional meridians unify different systems (Figure 2.4). Blocked meridians can cause illness by bringing about hyperactivity of certain organs and underactivity of others. Without the right amount of qi the organs, tissues, and cells no longer eliminate waste and with the accumulation of such toxins harbor more disease. Thus, many symptoms of diseases are interpreted as the body's efforts to cure itself. The runny nose and sweating of a cold and fever are the body's ways of eliminating the underlying conditions that cause the disease. The meridians can be cleared and qi recharged with acupuncture and specific diets.

The trained TCM physician focuses on both the physiology and the psychology of the individual. Yes, this is similar to the way health psychologists function but with different tools and underlying assumptions. All relevant information, including the symptoms and patients' general life characteristics, such as whether they are happy with their jobs and what they are eating, are all woven together into a "pattern of disharmony." Instead of asking what is *causing* what, the doctor asks what is *related to* what. The aim of treatment is to settle the imbalance. The TCM practitioner prescribes massage, acupuncture or acupressure, herbs, dietary changes, and exercises such as *qi gong* as primary treatments. Qi gong combines movement, meditation, and the regulation of breathing to enhance the flow of qi in the body to improve blood circulation and to promote immune function.

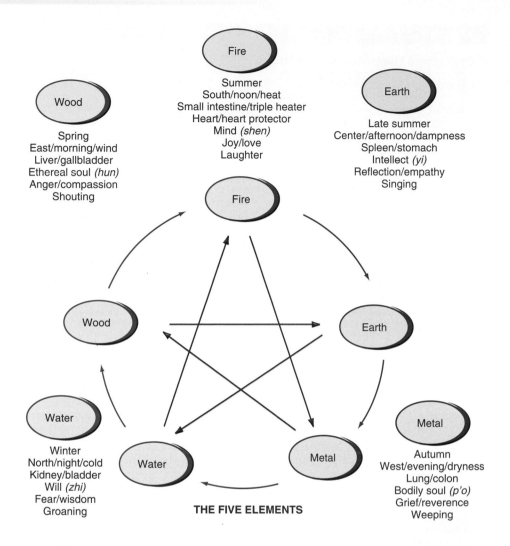

FIGURE 2.3
Balance between Seasons and Organs
The Five-Element theory provides us with an understanding of how our bodies are linked to the seasons, elements, and emotions.

For some North Americans the preceding sections may read like Greek (or Chinese). Meridians? Qi? Yin? Yang? Does any of this work? TCM has been the subject of considerable study for more than 50 years (Kaptchuk, 2000). The Chinese have performed many experimental analyses of traditional medicine, and the results were positive enough to give TCM and Western biomedicine an equal place in modern Chinese hospitals. Not only do many doctors in China provide patients with a prescription for pharmacological drugs as they would

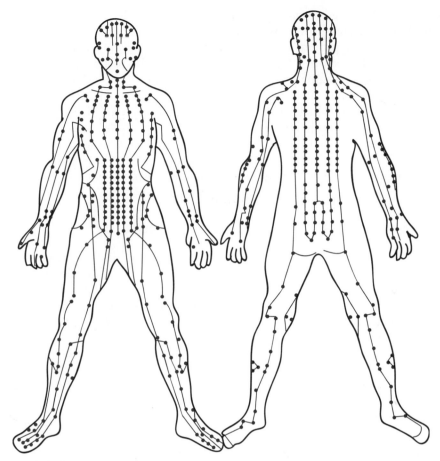

FIGURE 2.4
Meridians
Meridians are the passageways of qi and blood flow through the body. Meridians consist of channels and branches reaching every part of the body. Meridians act as the important route for circulating qi.

receive here in America, but they also provide a prescription for TCM cures (e.g., herbs or ointments). In many Chinese hospitals the two dispensaries sit side by side. Most patients in China as well as in America have the choice of which method to use. Western medicine is used more often for acute problems (by Chinese and Chinese Americans), and TCM is used more often for chronic problems.

Unfortunately, much of the research validating TCM was done without the use of robust Western scientific methodology. Western doctors and scientists do not accept the majority of the Chinese findings (findings for acupuncture are the exception). The Chinese are beginning to use better research methodologies, and research results have begun to satisfy Western doctors. For example, a Western medical examination showed patients to have peptic ulcers, and a Chinese examination of the same patients yielded a diagnosis based on the five elements previously described. Doctors treated these patients with herbs based on TCM, and the patients showed significant recovery 2 months later (Zhou, Hu, & Pi, 1991). Treatment of patients with heart disease provides similar success stories (Zhang, Liang, & Ye, 1995). Much of the research conducted on TCM in America analyzes the constituents of herbs used in treatment, and many such studies show that the active ingredients of the herbs facilitate cures (Chang, Chang, Kuo, & Chang, 1997; Klayman, 1985; Way & Chen, 1999). The growing evidence notwithstanding, it will be some time before TCM is accepted widely, but its time may be sooner than we think.

Ayurveda: Traditional Indian Medicine

You may be more familiar with **Ayurveda,** or traditional Indian medicine, than you realize. No, this is not American Indian medicine (that will be discussed later) but the approach to health that came from the Indian subcontinent. Yoga is a part of Ayurvedic practices. Many herbal supplements in use today came into prominence because of ancient Ayurvedic writings, and various health care products on the market that tout natural bases (e.g., Aveda products) have roots in Ayurveda. Although you do not see as much explicit evidence of this form of medicine in North America (i.e., you see no Ayurveda shops in Little India parts of cities corresponding to Chinese herb shops in Chinatowns), many Americans practice forms of Ayurveda.

Ayurveda originated more than 6,000 years ago and was considered a medicine of the masses. In fact, the basic ideology underlying Ayurveda still influences how health is viewed by many of the billion inhabitants of India today. Many Indian Americans even use the prescriptions of Ayurveda in daily life (e.g., swallowing raw garlic is good for you and chewing on cloves helps toothaches), and many European Americans are using Ayurvedic practices such as yoga and natural supplements. The first two major Ayurvedic texts, the *Charaka Samhita* and the *Sushruta Samhita,* have been dated to 1000 B.C., although Ayurvedic practices are also referred to in the Vedas (3000 to 2000 B.C.), ancient Indian texts containing the wisdom of sages and sacrificial rituals. The *Charaka Samhita* has 120 chapters covering diverse areas such as the general principles of Ayurveda, the causes and symptoms of disease, physiology and medical ethics, prognosis, therapy, and pharmacy (Svoboda, 1992).

Ancient Indian court physicians further developed Ayurvedic practices and were given vast resources because the health of the king was considered equivalent to the health of the state (Svoboda, 1992). Ayurvedic medicine was well developed by the time of the Buddha (500 B.C.) and the rise of Buddhism. Jivaka, the royal physician to the Buddha, was so well known that people actually became Buddhists so he could treat them. When Alexander the Great invaded India in 326 B.C., he even took Ayurvedic physicians back to Greece with him—one of the first times people of the two cultures were exposed to each other. The use of

Ayurveda flourished until A.D. 900 when Muslim invaders came into India and created a new form of medicine called Unani, a combination of Greek and Ayurvedic medicine with Arabic medicine (Udwadia, 2000). Ayurveda continued in different forms even after European forces invaded India around A.D. 1500, bringing Western medicine with them.

The basic core of Ayurvedic medicine parallels the way members of most Asian American cultures view life. A healthy system is made up of healthy units working together in a symbiotic relationship with the well-being of one being indivisible from the well-being of the community, the land, the supernatural world, or the universe. This collectivistic orientation automatically influences perceptions of social support and how people react when they are sick or stressed as I shall discuss in more detail in later chapters.

Sources of Illness

TCM and Ayurveda share many basic similarities. Ayurvedic science also uses the notion of basic elements: five great elements form the basis of the universe. Earth represents the solid state, water the liquid state, air the gaseous state, fire the power to change the state of any substance, and ether, simultaneously the source of all matter and the space in which it exists (Svoboda, 1992). Each of these elements can either nourish the body, balance the body serving to heal, or imbalance the body serving as a poison. Achieving the right balance of these elements in the body is critical to maintaining a healthy state. These elements also combine to form three major forces that influence physiological functions critical to healthy living. Ether and air combine to form the *Vata dosha,* fire and water combine to form the *Pitta dosha,* and water and earth elements that combine to form the *Kapha dosha.* Vata directs nerve impulses, circulation, respiration, and elimination. Pitta is responsible for metabolism in the organ and tissue systems as well as cellular metabolism. Kapha is responsible for growth and protection. We are all made up of unique proportions of Vata, Pitta, and Kapha that cause disease when they go out of balance. These three doshas are also referred to as humors or bodily fluids and correspond to the Greek humors of phlegm (Kapha) and choler (Pitta). There is no equivalent to the Greek humor blood, nor is Vata or "wind" represented in the Greek system (Udwadia, 2000). Similar to the meridians in TCM, the existence of these forces is demonstrated more by inference and results of their hypothesized effects than by physical observation. Vata, Pitta, and Kapha are also associated with specific body type characteristics as shown in Table 2.3.

In addition to diseases caused by the imbalances of the doshas, Ayurveda identifies diseases as having six other key causes. Some diseases are recognized as being due to natural changes in the body, genetic predispositions, trauma, gods or demons, due to the season, or due to deformities present at birth. Again, similar to the Chinese, Ayurvedic sages also evoke the importance of balancing hot and cold. Heat, even the fever of desire for certain foods, is also thought to be an important source of illness.

In general, Ayurvedic practitioners believe that health is a natural state and one maintained by keeping the body clear of toxins and the mind relaxed and

TABLE 2.3

The Major Constitutions of the Body in Ayurvedic Medicine

Characteristic	Vata	Pitta	Kapha
Body frame	Thin, irregular	Medium	Heavy
Weight	Easy to lose Hard to gain	Easy to lose Easy to gain	Hard to lose Easy to gain
Skin	Dark, tans deeply	Light, burns easily	Medium
Sweat	Scanty	Profuse	Moderate
Hair	Dry, coarse, curly Often dark	Fine, straight Light	Oily, thick Brown
Appetite	Variable	Intense	Regular
Climate	Prefers warm	Prefers cool	Prefers change of season
Stamina	Poor	Medium	Good
Speech	Talkative	Purposeful	Cautious
Sex drive	Variable	Intense	Steady
Emotion	Fearful	Angry	Avoids confrontation
Memory	Learns quickly Forgets quickly	Learns quickly Forgets slowly	Learns slowly Forgets slowly

SOURCE: Svoboda (1992).

stress free. The accumulation of toxins can occur when we get stressed and when waste is not effectively eliminated from the body. Consequently, some of the major Ayurvedic treatments involve detoxification and effective waste removal.

Treatment

The Ayurvedic physician uses different methods to diagnose a disease. First, there is a complete inspection of the patient. This involves looking for abnormalities in the body (e.g., discoloration of the skin), listening for abnormal sounds (e.g., irregular breathing), and even smelling the patient because imbalances in diet and the body are thought to result in characteristic odors (especially in the urine). The physician also uses palpitation of the body to feel for problems and often thoroughly interrogates the patient to assess for any changes in lifestyle or routine. After a diagnosis is made, a number of treatments are prescribed.

There are many forms of treatment in the Ayurvedic system of medicine, and many of them have made inroads into the Western consciousness. Some of these treatments exist on the fringe of Western biomedicine as complementary therapies (these are discussed in more detail later in this chapter). Others, such as yoga, are now common in even the smaller cities and towns of this continent (yoga is addressed in Chapter 11). "New age" spiritualists, who probably encountered treatments having origins in Ayurveda on travels through Southeast Asia, also practice many of them. Because imbalance is a source of illness, Ayurvedic medicine employs a number of techniques to reestablish balance. These include purification, surgery, drugs, diet, herbs, minerals, massage, color and gem therapy, homeopathy, acupressure, music, yoga, aromatherapy, and meditation. These treatments can be divided into therapies involving dietary changes and changes of activities at the level of the physical body and in tune with the seasons and climate, therapies aimed to clear the mind, and therapies involving spiritual rituals. Although not labeled "Ayurvedic" you will encounter many of these (especially the last few) in whole health clinics in North America today.

Perhaps one of the most commonly seen forms of Ayurvedic treatments in North America (in alternative medicine circles, spas, and clinics nationwide and especially in California, New Mexico, and New York) is the *Panchakarma* or "five actions." Similar to ancient Egyptian methods to purify the body, Ayurvedic medicine recommends five ways that the body should be purged of toxins: vomiting, laxatives, enemas, nasal medication, and bloodletting. Some of these may sound primitive and you should definitely not try any of them at home, but each is considered critical in a return to health. Other distinctive treatments involve the ingestion of oily and fatty foods as a form of internal purification and making the patient sweat, the latter being a therapy also common to American Indian medicine, as I shall discuss shortly.

The use of plants and herbal remedies plays a major part in Ayurvedic medicine. About 600 different medicinal plants are mentioned in the core Ayurvedic texts. A note of caution: just knowing the name of the plant is not enough. The texts even prescribe how the plant should be grown (e.g., type of soil and water) and where. The use of plants to cure is perhaps one of the key areas in which you will see Ayurveda used in North America. Western drug companies have used a number of plants originally used in India to cure diseases. For example, psyllium seed is used for bowel problems, and other plants are used to reduce blood pressure, control diarrhea, and lessen the risk of liver or heart problems. A substance called forskolin, isolated from the *Coleus forskohlii* plant, has been used in Ayurveda for treating heart disease, and its use has now been empirically validated by Western biomedicine (Ding & Staudinger, 2005).

Curanderismo and Spiritualism

The year 2003 signaled a major change in the cultural face of the United States of America. For the first time in the history of the United States, Americans of Latino descent became the largest minority group, narrowly edging out African Americans (Census Bureau, 2003). Latinos are present in every state in the United States, with large concentrations in California, Texas, and Arizona. Latinos are a very diverse group of people. There are Latinos from Mexico, Puerto Rico, Cuba, the Dominican Republic, and, of course, from Spain (as suggested by the term *Hispanic*). The health beliefs of this large part of the North American population correspondingly become important to consider. We will focus on the beliefs of the largest subgroup of Latinos, Mexican Americans.

Curanderismo is the Mexican American folk-healing system that often coexists side by side with Western biomedicine. Coming from the Spanish verb *curar*

© AP/Wide World Photos

Curandera Maria de Lourdez Gonzales Avila of Mexico City performing an incense cleansing ritual on her students during a workshop in Albuquerque, New Mexico.

meaning "to heal," curanderos are full-time healers. The curandero's office is in the community, often in the healer's own home. There are no appointments, forms, or fees, and you pay whatever you believe the healer deserves. This form of healing relies heavily on the patient's faith and belief systems and uses everyday herbs, fruits, eggs, and oils. In studies beginning as early as 1959, researchers (e.g., Clark, 1959; Torrey, 1969) first focused on "Mexican American cultural illnesses," such as *mal de ojo* (sickness from admiring a baby too much). More recent work (e.g., Trotter & Chavira, 1997) focuses on the healers themselves, their beliefs, training processes, and processes for treatment.

Sources of Illness

The Mexican American cultural framework acknowledges the existence of two sources of illness, one natural and one supernatural. When the natural and supernatural worlds exist in harmony, optimal health is achieved. Disharmony between these realms breeds illness (Madsen, 1968). Beyond this supernatural balance component, the curandero's concept of the cause of illness parallels that of Western biomedicine. Like biomedical practitioners, curanderos believe that germs and other natural factors can cause illness. However, curanderos also believe that there are supernatural causes to illness in addition to natural factors. If an evil spirit, a witch, or a sorcerer causes an illness, then only a supernatural solution will be sufficient for a cure. Illness can also be caused if a person's energy field is weakened or disrupted. Whether diabetes, alcoholism, or cancer, if a spirit caused it, supernatural intervention is the only thing that can cure it. Although curanderos seem to give the devil his due, they are often realistic in their searches for a cause. Trotter and Chavira (1997) conducted extensive interviews with curanderos and report that some identify more supernatural causes than others. For example, a student once asked the authors to take him to a curandero. The student, let's call him Hector, felt hexed by a former girlfriend (he admitted he had treated her badly). Now Hector was feeling sick and exhausted and was performing badly in school. The curandero examined Hector with his magical training and then asked him a series of questions concerning his health behaviors and habits. He determined that instead of a hex, Hector's symptoms developed from too much partying, too much drinking, and not enough studying!

Unlike Western biomedicine and TCM, the practices of curanderismo are based on Judeo-Christian beliefs and customs. The Bible has influenced curanderismo through references made to the specific healing properties of natural substances such as plants (see Luke 10:34). Curanderos's healing and cures are influenced by the Bible's proclamation that belief in God can and does heal directly and that people with a gift from God can heal in his name. The concept of the soul, central to Christianity, also provides support for the existence of saints (good souls) and devils (bad souls). The bad souls can cause illness and the good souls, harnessed by the shamanism and sorcery of the curanderismo, can cure.

Treatment

Curanderos use three levels of treatment depending on the source of the illness: material, spiritual, and mental. Working on the material level, curanderos use things found in any house (eggs, lemons, garlic, and ribbons) and religious symbols (a crucifix, water, oils, and incense). These material things often are designed to either emit or absorb vibrating energy that repairs the energy field around a person. Ceremonies include prayers, ritual sweepings, or cleansings. The spiritual level of treatment often includes the curandero entering a trance, leaving his or her body, and playing the role of a medium. This spiritual treatment allows a spirit to commandeer the curandero's body, facilitating a cure in the patient. On some occasions, the spirit will prescribe simple herbal remedies (via the curandero). On other occasions, the spirit will perform further rituals. The mental level of treatment relies on the power held by the individual curandero, rather than on spirits or materials. Some illnesses (e.g., physical) often are treated by herbs alone, and psychological problems may be treated by a combination of all these types of treatments.

In a manner akin to that of health psychologists, curanderos explicitly focus on social, psychological, and biological problems. The difference is that they add a focus on spiritual problems as well. From a social perspective, the community where the curanderos work recognizes and accepts what the curandero is trying to achieve. The social world is important to the curanderos who evaluate the patient's direct and extended support system. The patient's moods and feelings are weighed together with any physical symptoms. Finally, there is always a ritual petition to God and other spiritual beings to help with the healing process.

Curanderos each have their own set of specializations. For example, midwives (*parteras*) help with births, *sobaderos* treat muscle sprains, and herbalists (*yerberos*) prescribe different plants. For most Mexican Americans, the choice between curanderismo and Western biomedicine is an either/or proposition. Some individuals use both systems, and some stay completely away from Western hospitals as much as they can or because they do not have enough money to use them. Acculturated and higher social class Mexican Americans tend to rely exclusively on Western biomedicine. The existence of this strong cultural and historical folk medicine and the large numbers of its adherents make this approach to illness an important alternative style for us to consider in our study of the psychology of health.

American Indian Medicine

Many elements of the American Indian belief system and the approach to health are somewhat consistent with elements of curanderismo and TCM and provide a strong contrast to Western biomedicine. American Indians comprise about 1% of the population of the United States today. Although approximately 500 nations of American Indians live in the United States, their main beliefs are relatively consistent across the groups. Four practices are common to most: the use of herbal remedies, the employment of ritual purification or purging, the use of symbolic rituals and ceremonies, and the involvement of healers, also referred to as medicine men, medicine women, or **shamans.** Native Americans have utilized and benefited from these practices for at least 10,000 years and possibly much longer.

Sources of Illness

Similar to the ancient Chinese, American Indians believed that human beings and the natural world are closely intertwined. The fate of humankind and the fate of the trees, the mountains, the sky, and the oceans are all linked. The Navajos call this "walking in beauty," a worldview in which everything in life is connected and influences everything else. In this system, sickness is a result of things falling out of balance and of losing one's way in the path of beauty (Alvord & Van Pelt, 2000). Animals are sacred, the winds are sacred, and trees and plants, bugs, and rocks are sacred. Every human and every object corresponds to a presence in the spirit world, and these spirits promote health or cause illness. Spiritual rejuvenation and the achievement of a general sense of physical, emotional, and communal harmony are at the heart of Native American medicine. Shamans coordinate American Indian medicine and inherit the ability to communicate with spirits in much the same way that Mexican American curanderos do. Shamans spend much of their day listening to their patients, asking about their family and their

An American Indian Shaman in a Trance

behaviors and beliefs and making connections between the patient's life and their illness. Shamans do not treat spirits as metaphors or prayers as a way to trick a body into healing. Shamans treat spirits as real entities, respecting them as they would any other intelligent being or living person.

Treatment

Ritual and ceremony play a major role in American Indian medicine. One of the most potent and frequent ceremonies is the sweat lodge (Mehl-Medrona, 1998). Shamans hold lodges or "sweats" for different reasons. Sometimes a sweat purifies the people present; at other times a sweat is dedicated to someone with cancer or another terminal illness. Before each sweat, attendees tie prayer strings and pouches, little bags of red, black, yellow, or white cloth. Each color represents a direction and type of spirit, and the choice of color depends on the ceremony to be performed. Each pouch contains sacred tobacco, the burning of which is believed to please the spirits. The sweat leader, often a shaman, decides on the number of prayer bags depending on why the sweat is needed. The ceremony takes place in a sweat lodge, which looks like a half dome of rocks and sticks covered with blankets and furs to keep the air locked in and the light out. The lodge symbol-

© Joseph Sohm/Alamy

An American Indian Sweat Lodge A fire pit outside the door is where the "elders" or rocks are heated.

izes the world and the womb of Mother Earth. Even though the structure is only a half dome, participants believe that the rest of the sphere continues down inside the earth below it. Heated rocks are placed in a pit in the middle of the half dome. A short distance away from the lodge, a "firekeeper" heats rocks in a wood fire, often for hours before the event. The rocks are called *elders* because the rocks of the earth are seen as ancient observers. The number of rocks used also depends on the type of ceremony and is decided on by the lodge leader. The firekeeper builds a fire, prays over it and with it, and then places the stones in the fire, building the wood up around the rocks. He then keeps the rocks covered until it is time for them to be brought into the lodge (carried in with a pitchfork or shovel). Participants in the sweat sing sacred songs in separate rounds during the ceremony. After each round, the firekeeper brings in another set of hot rocks, and more songs are sung or prayers said. The sequence of prayers, chants, and singing following the addition of hot rocks continues until all the rocks are brought in. The hot stones raise the temperature inside the lodge, leading to profuse perspiration, which is thought to detoxify the body. Because of the darkness and the heat, participants often experience hallucinations that connect to spirit guides or provide insight into personal conditions.

Other ceremonies are also used. For example, the Lakota and Navajo use the medicine wheel, the sacred hoop, and the *sing,* which is a community healing ceremony lasting from 2 to 9 days and guided by a highly skilled specialist called a *singer.* Many healers also employ dancing, sand painting, chanting, drumming (which places a person's spirit into alignment with the heartbeat of Mother Earth), and feathers and rattles to remove blockages and stagnations of energy that may be contributing to ill health. Sometimes sacred stones are rubbed over the part of the person's body suspected to be diseased. Although many American Indians prefer to consult a conventional medical doctor for conditions that require antibiotics or surgery, herbal remedies continue to play a substantial role in treatment of various physical, emotional, and spiritual ailments. The herbs prescribed vary from tribe to tribe, depending upon the ailment and what herbs are available in a particular area. Some shamans suggest that the herbs be eaten directly. Others suggest taking them mixed with water (like an herbal tea) or even with food. Healers burn herbs such as sage, sweet grass, or cedar (called a *smudge*) in almost every ceremony, and let the restorative smoke drift over the patient.

Today most American Indians use a blend of Western biomedicine and American Indian spiritualism. Most reservations usually have both spiritual healers and Western doctors, but frequently traditional American Indians are wary of the doctors and first seek out shamans.

African American Beliefs

In addition to these four basic approaches to health, there are also a wealth of other belief systems that you should be aware of. A full description of all of the different folk medicines existing in the world today is beyond the scope of this book but remember that there are additional belief systems both in Northern America and around the globe that remain for your further explorations. For example, one group I have not discussed explicitly is African Americans. For many members of this cultural group, health beliefs reflect cultural roots that include elements of African healing, medicine of the Civil War South, European medical and anatomical folklore, West Indies voodoo religion, fundamentalist Christianity, and other belief systems. African American communities have become very diverse, especially with the recent arrival of people from Haiti and other Caribbean countries and Africa. Similar to the American Indians, many people of African descent also hold a strong connection to nature and rely on *inyangas* (traditional herbalists). Even today in Africa, hospitals and modern medicines are invariably the last resort in illness. The traditional African seeks relief in the herbal lore of the ancestors and consults the *inyanga,* who is in charge of the physical health of the people (Bradford, 2005). When bewitchment is suspected, which happens frequently among the traditional people of Africa, or there is a personal family crisis or love or financial problem, the patient is taken to a *sangoma* (spiritual diviner or spiritual/traditional healer), who is believed to have spiritual powers and is able to work with the ancestral spirits or spirit guides (Bradford, 2005). The sangoma uses various methods such as "throwing the bones" (*amathambo,* also known by other names depending on the cultural group) or going into a spiritual trance to consult the ancestral spirits or spirit guides to find the diagnosis or cure for the problem, be it bewitchment, love, or other problem. Depending on the response from the higher source, a decision will be made on what herbs and mixes (*intelezis*) should be used and in what manner (e.g., orally, burning). If more powerful medicine is needed, numerous "magical rites" can or will be performed according to rituals handed down from sangoma to sangoma (Bradford, 2005). In South Africa, there are more than 70,000 sangomas or spiritual healers who dispense herbal medicines and even issue medical certificates to employees for purposes of sick leave.

Even though you may have had some awareness of the Greek roots of Western medicine (e.g., the Hippocratic oath taken by doctors) or Chinese medicine (e.g., acupuncture) or even Indian traditional medicine (e.g., the Ayurvedic practice of yoga), other cultural ways of healing such as the sangoma are not as well known and, worse, are often ridiculed by the mass media. For example, many visitors to the city of New Orleans take voodoo tours around the city and joke about sticking pins in dolls made up to look like their bosses or enemies. The story is that a pin in the arm of the doll should cause pain in the arm of the person it is meant to represent. There is a rich history and tradition to voodoo that goes well beyond such parodied anecdotes. Many African Americans believe in a form of folk medicine that incorporates and mirrors aspects of voodoo (really spelled 'vodou'), which is a type of religion derived from some of the world's oldest known religions that have been present in Africa since the beginning of human civilization (Heaven & Booth, 2003). When Africans were brought to the Americas, religious persecution forced them to practice voodoo in secret. To allow voodoo to survive, its followers adopted many elements of Christianity. Today, voodoo is a legitimate religion in a number of areas of the world, including Brazil, where it is called *Candomblé*, and the English-speaking Caribbean, where it is called *Obeah*. In most of the United States, however, White slavers were successful in stripping slaves of their voodoo traditions and beliefs (Heaven & Booth, 2003). A number of other cultures, such as the American Indians described earlier and Hmong Americans, still believe that shamans and medicine men can influence health. Although shamanistic rituals and voodoo rites may seem to be ineffectual ways to cure according to Western science, the rituals have meaning to those who believe in them and should not be ignored or ridiculed.

Are Complementary and Alternative Approaches Valid?

Most of the non-Western approaches to medicine described in this chapter are commonly referred to as complementary or alternative approaches to medicine (CAMs). Voodoo and shamanistic rites do not fall under the CAM umbrella although the term Complementary and Alternative Medicine generally describes any healing philosophies and therapies that mainstream Western (conventional) medicine does not commonly use. Table 2.4 describes the main CAMs.

Earlier, I described how Western medicine started. Spurred on by technological innovations and inquiring minds, Western biomedicine became what we know today. How did different non-Western people discover their methods?

TABLE 2.4

Major Complementary and Alternative Medicines

Acupuncture is a method of healing developed in China at least 2,000 years ago. Procedures involving stimulation of anatomical points on the body by a variety of techniques.

Aromatherapy involves the use of essential oils (extracts or essences) from flowers, herbs, and trees to promote health and well-being.

Ayurveda is a CAM alternative medical system that has been practiced primarily in the Indian subcontinent for 5,000 years. Ayurveda includes diet and herbal remedies and emphasizes the use of body, mind, and spirit in disease prevention and treatment.

Chiropractic focuses on the relationship between bodily structure (primarily that of the spine) and function and how that relationship affects the preservation and restoration of health. Chiropractors use manipulative therapy as an integral treatment tool.

Dietary supplements are products (other than tobacco) taken by mouth that contain a "dietary ingredient" intended to supplement the diet. Dietary ingredients may include vitamins, minerals, herbs or other botanicals, amino acids, and substances such as enzymes, organ tissues, and metabolites.

Electromagnetic fields (EMFs, also called electric and magnetic fields) are invisible lines of force that surround all electrical devices. The Earth also produces EMFs; electric fields are produced when there is thunderstorm activity, and magnetic fields are believed to be produced by electric currents flowing at the Earth's core.

Homeopathic medicine is an alternative medical system. In homeopathic medicine, there is a belief that "like cures like," meaning that small, highly diluted quantities of medicinal substances are given to cure symptoms, when the same substances given at higher or more concentrated doses would actually cause those symptoms.

Massage therapists manipulate muscle and connective tissue to enhance the function of those tissues and promote relaxation and well-being.

Naturopathic medicine proposes that there is a healing power in the body that establishes, maintains, and restores health. Practitioners work with the patient with a goal of supporting this power, through treatments such as nutrition and lifestyle counseling, dietary supplements, medicinal plants, exercise, homeopathy, and treatments from traditional Chinese medicine.

Qi gong is a component of Traditional Chinese Medicine that combines movement, meditation, and regulation of breathing to enhance the flow of *qi* in the body, improve blood circulation, and enhance immune function.

Reiki is a Japanese word representing universal life energy. Reiki is based on the belief that when spiritual energy is channeled through a Reiki practitioner, the patient's spirit is healed, which in turn heals the physical body.

Therapeutic touch is derived from an ancient technique called laying-on of hands. It is based on the premise that the healing force of the therapist affects the patient's recovery; healing is promoted when the body's energies are in balance; and, by passing their hands over the patient, healers can identify energy imbalances.

Source: National Center for Complementary and Alternative Medicine (2005).

The most plausible answer and one supported by contemporary adherents of non-Western treatments is by trial and error. When a person was sick he or she ate the bark or leaves of a number of different herbs. Most of the herbs may not have had any effect, and the person either suffered or died. Some herbs may have produced an immediate cure. Automatically then, that herb would be known to help with that certain ailment. Of course, many practitioners of traditional medicine do not offer the trial and error explanation. The ancient

Chinese text, *The Yellow Emperor's Classic of Internal Medicine,* which is the basis for Traditional Chinese Medicine suggests that communications with the Heavens account for traditional medical practices. Similarly, American Indian shamans and Latino curanderos derive their healing powers from communications with spirits (Trotter & Chavira, 1997). The different origins of traditional beliefs notwithstanding, the fact is that many different cultures (ethnic, racial, religious, and others) have different beliefs about health and illness. Are these valid beliefs? Do the different methods work? This is a question that modern science is beginning to tackle. Given the growing diversity in the composition of North America, a major way to increase the utilization of health services is to learn more about the different cultural approaches to health.

If you are not already surprised by the different aspects of Chinese medicine, curanderismo, and American Indian spiritualism, you may be when you look at what some other peoples in North America actually do to cure themselves. You have heard of special diets (e.g., Atkins, Ornish, and Weil), but there is also a category of treatments called orthomolecular therapies in which patients eat substances such as magnesium, melatonin, and mega-doses of vitamins. Some biological therapies use laetrile (iron and aluminum oxide), shark cartilage, and bee pollen to treat autoimmune and inflammatory diseases. In other CAMs, the body is manipulated. For example, chiropractors and osteopathic manipulators work with the musculoskeletal system. There are separate categories of "energy therapies" such as Reiki. Practitioners channel energy from their spirit to heal the patient's body. Other energy treatments use magnetic and electrical fields to alleviate pain and cure sickness.

In 2004, 36% of people in North America had used some form of complementary medicine according to the National Center for Complementary and Alternative Medicine (Arias, 2004). The *Journal of the American Medical Association* reported that the most popular therapies were herbal medicines, massage, megavitamins, self-help groups, folk remedies, energy healing, and homeopathy (Astin, Marie, Pelletier, Hansen, & Haskell, 1998).

Given the growing exposure of the Western world to non-Western medicines, it is important to ask whether the different approaches meet the rigorous tests of the scientific method before adopting alternate styles of behavior or different cures. The U.S. government recognizes the importance of different approaches to health. In 1998 Congress established the National Center for Complementary and Alternative Medicine (NCCAM) to stimulate, develop, and support research on CAMs for public benefit. In addition to the techniques used by the main approaches described earlier, the NCCAM also studies the effectiveness of other CAMs such as aromatherapy, meditation, acupuncture/acupressure, hypnosis, dance, music and art therapy, and even prayer. Empirical reports of effectiveness trials of CAMs should be ready in the near future.

The critical point to realize about these varying beliefs is that health psychologists must be aware of a person's beliefs to best treat the person. Followers of Western medicine arrive at their beliefs about the values of Western medicine in the same way that the believers of other cultures come to their beliefs about their medical practices. People learn their beliefs from their parents or other people

A Chinese Herbalist Store with Different Jars and Drawers for the Different Herbs

around them. Your mother telling you that your cold is due to a virus establishes a belief system just as someone else's mother telling him or her that his or her cold is due to the evil looks of a neighbor also creates a belief system. In both cases the listening child may believe the story. What people believe influences what they do to remedy the situation. Giving antibiotics to someone who believes his or her cold is due to evil eyes may not yield the same effects as giving antibiotics to someone who believes his or her cold is due to a germ. Belief is a strong tool in the arsenal of the healer and an important element for the health psychologist to consider when attempting to maintain health and prevent illness. Often people educated in the West will express contempt for non-Western ways of looking at health. What do you mean spirits and evil eyes can cause illness? How can the weather and winds make a difference? Why do you have to keep the spirits happy to be healthy? Ideas such as these make some snicker and others roll their eyes in disbelief. Although many non-Western beliefs have not been tested by the scientific method, for many of their practitioners, there is no need to have this proof. A long tradition of believing in a medical practice and having centuries of your ancestors with a certain set of beliefs is enough for many who hold non-Western beliefs. To some extent this is comparable to Christians who have faith in the words of the Bible or Hindus who believe in the Upanishads or the Bhagwad Gita (ancient Hindu scriptures). Scientific evidence is not needed when you have faith. To successfully treat and influence people with different beliefs we have to first know what they believe.

FOCUS on Applications

Acupuncture

"Needles, needles, big long needles, poking into me. A human pin cushion." This is commonly the response I get when I ask people what the word acupuncture brings to mind. Yes, needles are involved. Yes, they are poked into the patient. Yes, the patient often look likes a pincushion. That said, you should also know that the needles are minute, thin, flexible wires, barely a few millimeters thick. The procedure is so painless that if you close your eyes when the needles are being placed, you won't even feel them (believe me, I have tried it many times).

Acupuncture is one of the most scientifically validated forms of alternate medicine and is gaining popularity in hospitals nationwide. In 1993, the Food and Drug Administration estimated that Americans made nearly 12 million visits per year to acupuncture practitioners, spending more than half a billion dollars. The practice of acupuncture in North America only began in the 1970s (as stated earlier, acupuncture has been a part of Chinese traditional medicine for thousands of years). When President Nixon first opened the door to the Far East, journalists who accompanied him on his tour of China witnessed surgeries performed on animals and humans for which no anesthesia was used. Instead, Chinese surgeons used acupuncture with slender needles piercing into predetermined points of the body.

Practitioners of Traditional Chinese Medicine determined that there are as many as 2,000 acupuncture points on the human body connected by 20 pathways (12 main and 8 secondary) called meridians. These meridians conduct energy, or qi, between the surface of the body and its internal organs. Each acupuncture point has a different effect on the qi that passes through it. Acupuncture keeps the balance between yin and yang, thus allowing for the normal flow of qi throughout the body and restoring health to the mind and body.

Several theories have been presented to explain exactly how acupuncture works. One theory suggests that pain impulses are blocked from reaching the spinal cord or brain at various "gates" to these areas. Because a majority of acupuncture points are either connected to (or are located near) neural structures, it is possible that acupuncture stimulates the nervous system. Another theory hypothesizes that acupuncture stimulates the body to produce endorphins, which reduce pain. Other studies have found that opioids (also pain relievers) may be released into the body during acupuncture treatment.

In the late 1970s, the World Health Organization recognized the ability of acupuncture and Traditional Chinese Medicine to treat nearly four dozen common ailments, including neuromusculoskeletal conditions (such as arthritis, neuralgia, insomnia, dizziness, and neck/shoulder pain); emotional and psychological disorders (such as depression and anxiety); circulatory disorders (such as hypertension, angina pectoris, arteriosclerosis, and anemia); addictions to alcohol, nicotine, and other drugs; respiratory disorders (such as emphysema, sinusitis, allergies, and bronchitis); and gastrointestinal conditions (such as food allergies, ulcers, chronic diarrhea, constipation, indigestion, intestinal weakness, anorexia, and gastritis). In 1997, a summary statement released by the National Institutes of Health declared that acupuncture could be useful by itself or in combination with other therapies to treat addiction, headaches, menstrual cramps, tennis elbow, fibromyalgia, myofascial pain, osteoarthritis, lower back pain, carpal tunnel syndrome, and asthma. Other studies have demonstrated that acupuncture may help in the rehabilitation of stroke patients and can relieve nausea in patients recovering from surgery.

Many Western medicine practitioners in North America are actively incorporating acupuncture into mainstream medicine. Some doctors belong to the American Academy of Medical Acupuncture, an organization founded in 1987 by a group of physicians who graduated from an acupuncture training program at the UCLA School of Medicine. Schools for acupuncture training also have been established all across America. Several councils provide structure for the various training schools (e.g., the Council of Colleges of Acupuncture and Oriental Medicine), and accreditation boards (e.g., the Accreditation Commission for Acupuncture and Oriental Medicine [ACAOM]) have brought more acceptance and oversight to the practice of acupuncture in the United States.

Chapter Summary

- Different cultures have varied ideas about what constitutes being healthy and what behaviors are healthy. Such beliefs vary by sex, religion, ethnicity, and nationality, to name a few. Writings about health and illness go as far back as the year 3000 B.C. to the times of the Mesopotamians and Egyptians.
- Western medicine has its roots in the writings of the Greek physicians Hippocrates and Galen. Also called allopathy, this approach focuses on causing the opposite effect from that created by the disease and is driven to rid the body of illness. Clear ideas of anatomy and circulation were some of the early contributions of Greek research to health.
- Western medicine advanced with improvements in technology, specifically the discovery of the microscope and the x-ray and innovations in surgery. Pasteur's work on germ theory showing that germs and bacteria caused illness greatly solidified the focus of Western medicine on physical sources of illness.
- Curanderismo is the Mexican American folk healing system that often coexists with Western medicine. This healing system uses herbs, fruits, eggs, and oils and places a heavy emphasis on spiritual causes of illness. An imbalance between the spiritual and natural world is seen to be the cause of illness.
- Curanderos treat patients on material, spiritual, and mental levels, depending on where the illness is thought to have begun. Spiritual treatments may involve the healer going into a trance and playing the role of a medium. Material treatments involve household items and religious symbols, and mental treatments rely on the power held by the healer.
- Traditional Chinese Medicine (TCM) treats the body as a whole in which every single part is intrinsically linked to other parts and to what is happening around the person. According to TCM, food, relationships, and spiritual harmony are all conducive to health. Diseases are thought to be caused by imbalances in yin and yang.
- Yin and yang are mutually interdependent, interchangeable forces that make up all of the universe. The Tao, or energy force, of the universe is influenced by

the balance of yin and yang and needs to be fostered for optimal health. Main treatments include acupuncture and herbal therapy.

- American Indian medicine also focuses on spiritual balance and living in harmony with nature. The most common practices involve the use of herbal remedies, ritual purification or purging, symbolic rituals and ceremonies, and the involvement of shamans.

Synthesize, Evaluate, Apply

- What are your main beliefs about the cause and cures of illness?
- Where do your beliefs come from? What evidence do you need to support your beliefs?
- What do the different approaches to health have in common?
- Using an empirical scientific approach, evaluate each different approach to health.
- What are the psychological processes by which a health belief can influence recovery?
- Compare and contrast the different philosophical approaches to health.
- Identify the two most significant events in medical history. Rationalize your choice.
- What are the main causes of illness in Traditional Chinese Medicine? To American Indians? In curanderismo?
- Compare and contrast the different treatments used in the different approaches.
- What evidence would you need to see before you tried a new treatment?
- What sociopolitical pressures prevent allowing each American citizen to be reimbursed for whichever treatment he or she desires?
- How should the field of health psychology best use information about diverse approaches to health?
- Identify the critical biopsychosocial factors underlying each diverse approach to health.

KEY TERMS, CONCEPTS, AND PEOPLE

allopathy, 36
Ayurveda, 46
complementary and
    alternative medicine, 36
curanderismo, 49
Da Vinci, Leonardo, 37
Galen, 36

Harvey, William, 37
Hippocrates, 36
opiates and opioids, 39
Pasteur, Louis, 37
qi, 41
reductionist, 36
shamans, 52

Tao, 40
Traditional Chinese Medicine, 39
van Leeuwenhoek, Antonius, 37
Vesalius, Andreas, 37
Western biomedicine, 36

ESSENTIAL READINGS

Kaptchuk, T. J. (2000). *The web that has no weaver: Understanding Chinese medicine.* Chicago: Contemporary Books.

Landrine, H., & Klonoff, E. A. (1992). Culture and health-related schemas: A review and proposal for interdisciplinary integration. *Health Psychology, 11*(4), 267–276.

Landrine, H., & Klonoff, E. A. (2001). Cultural diversity and health psychology. In A. Baum, T. A. Revenson, & J. E. Singer (Eds.), *Handbook of health psychology.* Mahwah, NJ: Erlbaum.

O'Connor, B. B. (1995). *Healing traditions: Alternative medicine and the health professions.* Philadephia: University of Pennsylvania Press.

Trotter, R. T., & Chavira, J. A. (1997). *Curanderismo: Mexican American folk healing.* Athens, GA: University of Georgia Press.

WEB RESOURCES

Visit the companion website at **http://psychology.wadsworth.com/gurung1e/,** where you will find online resources for this book, including chapter-by-chapter quizzes, weblinks, and more! You can also visit Wadsworth Psychology Resource Center at **http://psychology.wadsworth.com** to access additional resources.

Various Cultural Histories of Medicine
http://www.mic.ki.se/History.html

National Center for Complementary and Alternative Medicine
http://nccam.nih.gov

Health and Human Development

Think of those times when you find yourself simultaneously doing a number of things that you know are all not good for you. For example, you walk through your living room and as you pass the television you decide to turn it on for just a moment. You skim through some channels and run into a movie that looks familiar. You have seen it many times before, but decide to watch it just until that part that you love so much or maybe until the next commercial. Then you figure that you may as well take this opportunity to have a snack and a drink. Before you know it, you have watched the entire movie lying mostly motionless on the couch. You have eaten an entire bag of potato chips and have consumed a few cans of your favorite soda (and maybe some of your favorite ice cream). There is nothing wrong with consuming ice cream or snacks or watching television in moderation, but if repeated often, unhealthy eating and low levels of physical activity can have disastrous consequences for your health. Where do these behaviors originate? Were you born with a desire to watch television for long periods of time, to eat fatty, salty food, and to drink high-calorie drinks?

The Interaction between Culture, Development, and Health

Even though we have a natural affinity for some tastes (Bartoshuk, 1988) and our genetic predispositions may make it more or less likely for us to become addicted to some unhealthy behaviors (e.g., drinking), most of our health behaviors are learned during childhood and as we grow. Even taste preferences are largely learned (Rozin, 1990). Our family, our religious group, our ethnicity, the area where we grew up, our gender and sexual orientation, and the socioeconomic level of our family are all cultural factors that shape our behaviors. We spend most of our lives learning the rules and behaviors of the culture we live in. These cultural groups expose us to different experiences, influence how we are treated, and even influence our health. For example, the treatment a doctor prescribes is biased by his or her assumptions about a patient's culture. Male patients receive different treatment from doctors than female patients (Hovelius, 1998); patients from different ethnicities are treated differently: because some ethnicities are seen as being more troublesome, these patients do not get as much attention as others (Galanti, 2004). It is important to understand how culture can influence development and follow through to how it influences our health. For example, socioeconomic status (SES) at different points of a child's lifetime can have different effects on health (Chen, 2004). A focus on human development and how we grow over the lifespan also reveals that health psychologists have to consider different variables for different age groups. The causes of mortality and morbidity vary with age, and as we shall see, the top killers of infants are not the same as those for adolescents or adults (Figure 3.1).

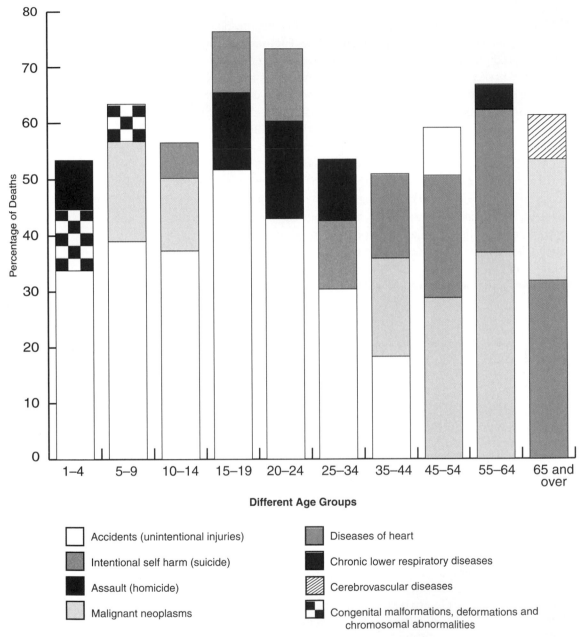

Different Age Groups

Accidents (unintentional injuries)

Intentional self harm (suicide)

Assault (homicide)

Malignant neoplasms

Diseases of heart

Chronic lower respiratory diseases

Cerebrovascular diseases

Congenital malformations, deformations and chromosomal abnormalities

FIGURE 3.1
Differences In Causes of Death Across The Life Span
The major causes of death vary for different age groups supporting the need to keep developmental differences in mind when studying health and health behaviors.
Source: Deaths: Leading causes for 2002. National vital statistics report, 53(17) by R. N., Anderson and B. L. Smith, 2005. Hyattsville, MD: National Center for Health Statistics

What Is Development?

The subfield of **developmental psychology** concentrates on the physiological and psychological changes that occur from conception to death. **Development** is the orderly and sequential changes that occur with the passage of time as an organism grows. For centuries, scientists and philosophers have theorized about how we grow and change. The **biopsychosocial** model, used by health psychologists, provides an easy way to separate how development influences health, especially as it varies across cultures. First I will describe critical milestones in our biological development. Next, I will examine the main theories of human psychological development. Finally, I will describe how societal processes (e.g., the style our parents used to raise us) influence our development. In each of these three areas, I will draw particular attention to the special role of developmental processes in shaping health behaviors and consequently health in general. In addition to understanding the effects of development, it is also important to understand how cultural differences can play a role in development and health, and how health problems, mortality, and morbidity vary across the lifespan.

Biological Development

At the very core, our biology is essentially what determines how long and how comfortably we live. Our biological systems—our brain, heart, lungs, nervous system, circulatory system, and so on—keep us alive and get damaged or compromised when we are sick and when we practice unhealthy behaviors. A key theme of health psychology is that our minds (e.g., how we think), our personalities, and our behaviors influence our bodies and our biology, so our first challenge is to understand how our bodies develop. This will set the stage for us to discuss how our psychology and society can influence this development and consequently our health (and the field of health psychology).

The Prenatal Period

The young infant is born with many predispositions and a genetic inheritance that sets the stage for many future developments. For the baby to have a chance to grow and develop, it has to be born first. Although that may sound like an odd thing to say (or at least extremely obvious), not all pregnancies end with a successful labor and delivery (Dunkel-Schetter, Gurung, Lobel, & Wadhwa, 2001; Wadhwa, Dunkel-Schetter, Chicz-DeMet, Porto, & Sandman, 1996). Furthermore, many things can happen in the time *before* a baby is born (the **prenatal period**), and the less time that the baby has in the womb, or in utero, the less time it will have to grow and develop normally. In fact, the length of **gestation** (time in womb) is one of the most important health psychological outcome variables used to study pregnancy. **Preterm births** (delivery before 37 weeks of gestation) are the most direct causes of **low birth weight** (LBW) babies who have a risk for developmental and mental complications (Newnham, 1998). Extreme preterm and LBW babies have a substantially high risk for infant mortality (McCormick,

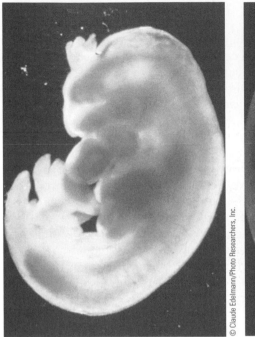
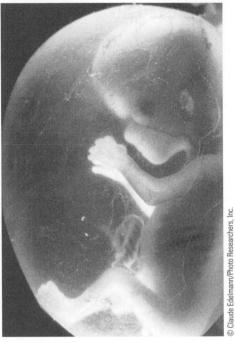

5 week old embryo   14 week old fetus

The Developing Human Being: Different Stages of Prenatal Growth

1985). Something that may surprise you is the fact that the United States has an extremely high rate of LBW babies relative to other industrialized nations, and the rate has been climbing over the past 10 years (David & Collins, 1997). The percentage of LBW infants in the United States is estimated to be 8% compared with 4% for Sweden (UNICEF and WHO, 2004).

As another good example of the usefulness of the biopsychosocial model, the biological development of the fetus can be seriously impacted by the psychological state of the mother—her moods, her feelings, and her thoughts (the *psycho* part)—as well as the networks she has and the social situation she is living in (the *social* part). In fact, the quality of the social environment the mother lives in may prove to be one of the main factors in the influence psychosocial aspects have on healthy biological functioning (Taylor, Repetti, & Seeman, 1997). The biopsychosocial model also provides comprehensive predictions of complications in pregnancy (Smilkstein, Helsper-Lucas, Ashworth, Montano, & Pagel, 1984).

During the nine months before delivery, many clear-cut physiological changes take place. A woman may not even know that she is pregnant until approximately two weeks after conception, when she is unlikely to menstruate (although some women do). However, there are clues. Her breasts may swell and become tender, and some women may become nauseous. Once the sperm and ova fuse to form a

TABLE 3.1

Critical Milestones in Prenatal Development

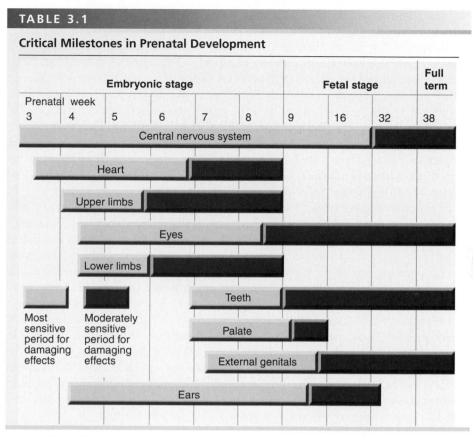

Adapted from Weiten (2005).

fertilized egg (the zygote), the zygote implants itself in the uterine wall and begins to grow, and cells differentiate into various internal structures. By the end of the second week, the organism is called an embryo. At the ninth week of gestation, the embryo is called a fetus, and the time until delivery is called the fetal period (Table 3.1). Of all the senses, only hearing is developed before birth and the fetus shows a preference for the mother's voice. Some mothers believe that playing classical music will improve fetal development. Similarly, you may have heard of the Mozart effect (Rauscher, Shaw, & Ky, 1993), the finding that the cadences and tempo of the classical composer's music can improve performance in certain areas (spatial-temporal tasks such as jigsaw puzzles and some forms of reasoning). However, here is some bad news for classical music fans—the validity of the Mozart effect is questionable (Fudin & Lembessis, 2004).

The developing embryo and fetus are particularly sensitive to teratogens, environmental toxins and drugs capable of causing developmental abnormalities. A key focus for the health psychologist is to ensure that expectant mothers refrain from the use of alcohol, caffeine, nicotine, and other drugs or medications (Calhoun & Alforque, 1996; Zimmer & Zimmer, 1998). Behaviors such as smoking, bad diet, and insufficient medical treatments all negatively affect fetal growth and infant health (McCormick et al., 1990). Some bad habits such as alcohol consumption (by the mother, of course) can even influence the infant when it grows to adolescence (Carmichael et al., 1997). Any alcohol misuse can harm the development of the baby's organs. Fetal exposure to teratogens is higher for ethnic minority populations (Dunkel-Schetter et al., 2001). Stress is particularly dangerous to the prenatal infant and the more stress a mother experiences, the more she risks delivery of a preterm or LBW baby (Wadhwa, Sandman, Porto, Dunkel-Schetter, & Garite, 1993). But let's not forget about the baby's father. Secondhand smoke from the baby's father, for example, as well as stress in the form of emotional or physical harassment, can also interfere with the baby's and mother's health (Dunkel-Schetter et al., 2001).

Two other aspects of pregnancy have strong psychological components: miscarriage and labor/delivery. A miscarriage (medically referred to as a spontaneous abortion) occurs when the zygote, embryo, or fetus is released from the uterus before it is ready to survive on its own. Although not usually publicly discussed, miscarriages happen often. Close to 20% of pregnancies end in miscarriage, and 33% of women have a miscarriage at some point during their reproductive years (DeFrain, Millspaugh, & Xiaolin. 1996). This can be a very traumatic experience, and expecting couples need all the help they can get to cope with this event. Some personality styles can deal with such trauma better than others (more on this in chapters 4 and 5), but the amount of social support provided to the couple, and the way they process their feelings and cope with this event can have major implications for their mental and physical health (Swanson, 2000). Often discussing the problem versus ignoring it eases the emotional pain. Having friends and family express their love and care for the couple at this point is also especially helpful.

Another period when social support can play a major role in pregnancy is during labor and delivery. Childbirth is a stressful event, especially because it involves a threat to both the mother and the infant. Complications arising during this time are the fifth highest cause of infant mortality in the United States (National Center for Health Statistics, 2003). Psychosocial factors (e.g., social support, the mother's personality, or the presence of a companion) all play a major role at this point and also show great differences between cultural groups (Dunkel-Schetter, Sagrestano, Feldman, & Killingsworth, 1996; Keinan, 1997). For example, the family is the most important source of support for African American mothers (Miller, 1992), who report the most support from family followed by Mexican Americans and European Americans (Sagrestano, Feldman, Rini, Woo, & Dunkel-Schetter, 1999).

Infancy and Early Childhood

The growth and development of the newborn infant is dramatic during the first two years of life. Driven by the secretions of the pituitary gland and coordinated by the hypothalamus, hormones pulse through the body, stimulating growth. Based on the work of investigators such as Gesell (1928) and Meredith (1973), we now have a good picture of what normal development for a child should be. As can be seen on the charts in doctors' offices or the charts some parents place against a wall in the house (or the marks they make on walls or door backs) babies grow in an irregular fashion with long intervals between growth spikes and not in a continuous pattern with the same growth every week (Vander Zanden, 2002). The nervous system develops the most rapidly in the early months. How parents interact with their babies is a key factor in infant development. Greater physical contact between the caregiver and child has always been associated with more successful social and physical development (Stern, 1995; Winnicott, 1965), although there is mixed support for this hypothesis. For example, Field (1998) demonstrated that the more a baby is touched and stroked, the faster it develops, but a review of the research suggested that although massage for preterm infants influences clinical outcome measures, such as medical complications or length of stay and caregiver or parental satisfaction, the evidence of benefits for developmental outcomes is weak (Vickers, Ohlsson, Lacy, & Horsley, 2002). Touch does seem to have other important consequences such as playing a role in stress and coping, as we shall discuss in the next chapter (Taylor, Klein, Lewis, Gruenwald, Gurung, & Updegraff, 2000).

During early childhood (ages 2 to 6) the child tends to become more active. Food plays a critical role in muscle growth and the height of the child. This is an important time for parents to watch how much a child eats and when he or she eats. Strength, coordination, and range of motion all continue to increase. Some interesting cultural differences are seen in these early years of development. African American children tend to mature more quickly (as measured by bone growth, percent fat, and number of baby teeth) than European American children (Vander Zanden, 2002). Asian American children show some of the slowest rates of physical change (Keats, 2000).

After early childhood, physical growth slows down in general and children become more skilled in controlling their bodies. Middle childhood (age 7 to adolescence) is the stage during which children tend to be the healthiest and experience significant changes in cognitive development.

Adolescence

Adolescence (ages 12 to 17) can be perhaps one of the most turbulent periods in an individual's life. A flurry of biological activity morphs the child into a young adult and sometimes the grown-up exterior surges ahead of the still underdeveloped interior or cognitive development. This mismatch between biological and psychological factors often has dire health consequences. Adolescence is another critical juncture during which health psychology's biopsychosocial approach nicely reminds us of the different factors we need to focus on.

The key biological milestone in adolescence is **puberty.** At puberty, a genetic timing mechanism activates the pituitary gland and an increasing level of growth hormone is produced in the body. The activation of the pituitary stimulates the manufacture of estrogen and progesterone in girls and testosterone in boys. The increase in sex hormones triggers the growth of secondary sex characteristics, leading to the development of breasts and the beginning of menstruation in women and the deepening of the voice and the growth of facial hair in men. Of direct importance to our study of how different health behaviors may develop, research shows that boys with lower levels of testosterone are more likely to show behavioral problems such as rebelliousness that can catalyze initiating smoking and experimentation with illicit substances (Schaal, Tremblay, Soussignan, & Susman, 1996). In the brain, white matter increases with the growth of fibers that establish connections between brain regions, and the prefrontal cortex, corpus callosum, and temporal lobes increase in size (Paus, 1999).

The age at which puberty hits has been shifting forward in time, demonstrating the possible interaction between our biology and our psychology and society. For example, at the beginning of the twentieth century, the average age for the onset of menstruation was 15 or 16. Less than 100 years later, the average age was just older than 12 (Brumberg, 1997). Why is this the case? The best guesses are increases in stress and higher levels of environmental toxins in contemporary society, but there is no answer yet. Environmental factors combine to make this physiological milestone a great equalizer of ethnic differences. When girls of Jewish, African, Italian, and Japanese descent are raised under the same living conditions, they all begin to menstruate at the same early age (Huffman, 1981). Furthermore, after years of immigration, regardless of ethnicity, girls menstruate earlier in North America than in their countries of origin (Brumberg, 1997). Both boys and girls experience a growth spurt although this tends to happen to girls almost two years before it happens for boys. This spurt continues until around the age of 18. Young adults add on between 7 and 8 inches in height.

Adulthood and Aging

The college years, 18 to 21, are often referred to as the young adult years with adulthood stretching up to at least 65 years of age after which point adults are often referred to as older adults (though there are many 67-year-olds who would take offense to this label). Limited changes in physical development occur after the adolescent years. The body does not appear to have any other specific timed changes occurring for at least another 10 to 30 years after puberty and the adolescent growth spurt. Yet, during this period, our health behaviors are perhaps most important in determining how pain free we live our lives and how long our later years will be. Some changes do happen. The hair tends to thin and turn gray, and many men experience receding hairlines. The storage of body fat also increases and the distribution of fat changes. For example, our bodies store more fat on our waists, causing an increased waist-to-hip ratio (WHR). Higher WHRs are warning signs for coronary heart disease and a signal of excessive wear and tear on the body (Seeman, Singer, Horwitz, & McEwen, 1997). Overall, our bodies tend to put on weight until our mid-50s. Constant physical activity is a must to compensate during these years. We then start to lose weight and slowly our height decreases (after approximately age 60) and our bones shrink (from our body using up the calcium stored in them). Some other clear physiological markers of aging are also present. Hearing and vision degrade first, which can have a severe impact on the quality of day-to-day life by interfering with activities such as driving and walking. Other age-related changes include hormonal functioning are seen, most notably in women.

Menopause, or the ending of the menstrual period, typically occurs in the early 50s. Simultaneously, secretion of a number of female sex hormones decreases, and these changes may be associated with a variety of mood problems and even risks for various diseases (Matthews et al., 1997). Psychology can play a role in this as well. Reactions to menopause vary greatly, depending on the expectations that women have (Matthews, 1992), and many women experience few emotional problems (Dennerstein, 1996). Expecting to experience mood swings and depression can make mood swings and depression more likely to be experienced. The bigger issue on the table is whether women should start taking hormone pills to replace the natural cycle. Hormone replacement therapy was a common practice for many years until 2002 when the intervention arm of the Women's Health Initiative study testing the effects of hormone replacement was halted because women receiving the drug were found to have a higher risk for certain cancers (Rossouw et al., 2002). Some evidence suggests that some forms of hormone replacement may be safe (Bond, Hirota, Fortin, & Col, 2002), but researchers have not reached a consensus as yet.

Although we often stereotype older adults as being weak and forgetful, clearly the natural breakdown of muscles and the loss of memory does not start until much later in life. In a longitudinal study begun in 1956, Schaie (1993) demonstrated that the majority of participants showed no significant decline in most mental abilities until the age of 81. The common saying, "Use it or lose it," is very pertinent (Sandborn, 2000). Maintaining a constant routine of physical activity can prolong good health and activity and ensure that an aging adult can continue to comfortably perform the activities of daily living into their 70s and 80s. Marinelli and Plummer (1999) had members of different community groups

Being Mentally and Physically Active Has Few Age Limits Although there are some natural physiological changes as we age, the greater cause of loss of muscle tone is not using them enough.

participate in regular physical activity. This activity led to an increase in the participants' physical, social, emotional, and intellectual health. Similarly, older adults who have new experiences to occupy their minds, experience less memory loss over time (Ball et al., 2002).

Major Theories of Human Development

Theories about human psychological development over the last 100 or so years have come from and mirrored the different areas of psychology. Developmental theories originated from the psychoanalytical (Sigmund Freud), behavioral (John Watson and B. F. Skinner), cognitive (Piaget), ecological (Bronfenbrenner), and sociological (Vygotsky) schools of thought. Each of these theories provides us with insight into why we do good or bad things for our health. What about an eighth grader's thinking is likely to make him start smoking? Why will a high school student turn rebellious and engage in risky sex? Why will a middle-aged man drive friends away and avoid a close relationship or the social support that could buffer him through times of stress? Developmental theories suggest the answer to these and many other questions pertinent to health psychology.

We all progress through some major, easily identifiable, stages, from infancy, childhood, and adolescence to adulthood and old age. Each stage has its own problems, rituals, and associated expectations that vary by culture. Each stage often starts at different times in different cultural groups. Members of different cultures also may progress through the stages in slightly varying orders and spend different amounts of time within each stage. Developmental theories can be separated into two main categories: social development theories and cognitive development theories. Each constitutes the psychosocial aspects of the biopsychosocial model. All three types of development (physical, social, and cognitive) go hand in hand. The physical changes that take place in the young infant and then the growing adult automatically influence social and cognitive development. The physiological milestones we just discussed correlate with what is going on in the mental realm that is shaped by our interactions with the world. Our first interactions with the world are limited by our physical abilities. The baby cannot walk and depends on the primary caregiver for all needs. As we grow, we venture outside the home and form relationships with friends and romantic partners. The nature of all these relationships can determine how we develop our social skills and is the topic we shall turn to next.

Social Development

Freud Although most often discussed in reference to personality and clinical psychology in introductory psychology books, Sigmund Freud was one of the first psychologists to postulate specific ideas of human development. Freud (1940/1964) believed that the mother-child relationship was critical to social development. He described this relationship with one's mother as, "unique, without parallel, established unalterably for a whole lifetime as the first and strongest love-object and as the prototype of all later love-relationships" (p. 188). Freud called the different levels we progress through psychosocial stages and assumed that we are driven to seek pleasure at each stage (Table 3.2). The specific pleasure sought at each stage is focused around a different part of our body or **erogenous**

TABLE 3.2

Freud's Stages of Psychosocial Development

Stage	Approximate Ages	Erotic Focus	Key Tasks and Experiences
Oral	0–1	Mouth (sucking, biting)	Weaning (from breast or bottle)
Anal	1–3	Anus (expelling or retaining feces)	Toilet training
Phallic	3–6	Genitals (sexuality explored)	Identifying with adult role models; coping with Oedipal crisis
Latency	6–12	None (sexuality refined)	Expanding social contacts
Genital	Puberty onward	Genitals (being sexually intimate)	Establishing intimate relationships; contributing to society through working

Adapted from Weiten (2005).

zone. In the **oral stage,** infants gain pleasure from sucking, chewing, biting, and putting things in their mouth. By the end of the first year, the baby enters the **anal stage,** when pleasure focuses on their anus and the control of their excretions. In the **phallic stage** (approximately ages 3 to 5), the child now derives pleasure from his or her genitals. During this stage a child is thought to develop feelings of desire for the opposite sex parent (the Oedipal complex for boys, and the Electra complex for girls). Girls are thought also to develop penis envy. After a period of latency when the child is thought not to focus on pleasure or sex but to concentrate on cognitive and general social growth, the young adult moves into the final stage of development, the **genital stage.** In this stage, Freud assumed that we now return to the genitals for pleasure again.

You (and probably 96% of other readers) probably wonder how any of this can be pertinent to health psychology. Apart from Freud's role in entwining psychology with the study of health, many theorists have used his description of psychosocial stages to account for a variety of unhealthy behaviors. For example, it is possible that individuals who become addicted to cigarettes or who cannot stop eating are people who did not pass successfully through the oral stage of their development. This failure caused an oral **fixation** for individuals who then continue to derive pleasure from placing things in their mouths (cigarettes or food) even in adulthood. Freud's ideas, no matter how outlandish they may seem to be, were thought to be feasible enough for many tobacco companies to invest vast sums of money to weave sexual themes into their advertisements. Based on Freud's notion that one of the most basic human drives is the drive for pleasure or Eros and that most of our behaviors are fueled by sexual energy or libido, advertisers used (and still use) sex to sell products. We will talk more about this when we discuss smoking in chapter 7. Although Freud's ideas have been criticized, they influenced both John Bowlby's attachment theory and Erik Erikson's stages of development, which I shall discuss next.

Attachment Styles Unlike many animals, we humans are not born ready for action. Our vision is incompletely developed at birth, and we cannot walk for

Courtesy Linda Schmidt

Mother Bonding with Her Newborn Infant Attachment theorists consider the bond between the infant and his or her caregiver to be critical to social development.

nearly a year after birth. The human infant's relationship with its primary caregiver (in most cases his or her mother) is correspondingly critical to survival. The ethnologist Konrad Lorenz (1935) demonstrated **imprinting,** a form of social bonding between the parent and offspring where newborn animals show strong inborn tendencies to bond with their parents. Lorenz's work was modified by John Bowlby (1958), who proposed that the human infant has several instinctual responses such as sucking, crying, following, and smiling. These responses mature during the first year of life and become organized into attachment behavior focused on a specific mother figure. This attachment behavior ensures that the child will have his or her needs met and can be defined as the close emotional bonds that develop between infants and their caregivers. Mary Ainsworth (1978), one of Bowlby's collaborators, expanded this idea further to identify three main attachment styles. A **secure attachment** develops in an infant when the primary caregiver is seen to be attentive, responsive, and approving. The infant feels secure, loved, and confident. If the primary caregiver is not attentive and approving, the infant could develop an **avoidant attachment** style and feel insecure and defensive. Alternatively, a child could develop an **anxious-ambivalent attachment** style and feel fearful and anxious. Each attachment style relates to different psychological and physical behaviors in infants and influences behavior across the life cycle (Parkes, Stevenson-Hinde, & Marris, 1991). Although practical concerns constrain direct tests of the continuity of infant attachment styles into adulthood, it would require a long time to follow an infant from the time of birth to adulthood. Waters, Treboux, Crowell, Merrick, and Albersheim (1995) did just that. Their work and a large number of other studies showed that the three main infant attachment styles represent a useful way to conceptualize adult relationships (Hazan & Shaver, 1987; see Cassidy & Shaver, 1999, for a review).

Despite the appearance that attachment style development is purely biological, substantial cultural differences exist in attachment styles. In the United States, approximately 70% of American infants have a secure style, 20% have an anxious-ambivalent style, and 10% have an avoidant style (Ainsworth, Blehar, & Waters, 1978). In contrast, a study of German infants found that only approximately 35% of infants had a secure style, 15% have an anxious-ambivalent style, and 50% have an avoidant style (Grossman, Grossman, Spangler, Suess, & Unzner, 1985). Similarly, a study of Japanese infants found that the number of secure attachments was similar to that in North America (approximately 70%), but 30% of Japanese infants had an anxious-ambivalent style, and none had an avoidant style (Takahashi, 1986). These discrepancies could have different health implications; for example, symptom reporting is stronger by those with anxious-ambivalent attachment styles (Feeney & Ryan, 1994).

Attachment style is directly relevant to health psychology for two major reasons. First, research shows a direct link between an adult's attachment style and his or her health behaviors (Goodwin, 2003; Myers & Vetere, 2002). Ciechanowski, Walker, Katon, and Russo (2002) showed that attachment style is an important factor in assessing symptom perception and health care utilization. In a study of 701 women, attachment style was significantly associated with the number of symptoms reported. Women with anxious and ambivalent attachment styles had a significantly greater number of physical symptoms compared with secure women. Attachment was also significantly associated with primary care visits and costs. Women who did not have secure attachment styles had the highest primary care costs and utilization. The second connection between attachment and health is indirect. Attachment style is strongly related to the amount of social support a person perceives and receives (DeFronzo, Panzarella, & Butler, 2001; Sarason, Sarason, & Gurung, 2001). Social support, that is, the extent to which we feel loved, esteemed, and cared for, not only helps us cope with stress and chronic illness, but also is a major determinant of whether or not we practice healthy behaviors. If we develop a secure attachment style at a young age, we are more likely to make healthy choices for ourselves and in what we do. We will learn more about social support in the chapter on coping.

Erikson's Eight Stages of Development   Erik Erikson was Freud's academic grandson. Erikson was trained by Freud's daughter Anna Freud and suggested that human beings progress through a series of psychological stages, each with their own **psychosocial crisis**. He argued that how we face each crisis or challenge can determine how well adjusted we are, how happy we are, and how well we function on a day-to-day basis. People's daily behavior will vary as a function of how they resolve the crisis provided by a given stage of development. Look at Table 3.3 for a summary of Erikson's stages and to get a feel for how they relate to health. This relationship between psychosocial development and actions is of direct interest to the health psychologist because it gives us a window into understanding the psychology of why, for example, one eighth grader, Josh, is more likely than another eighth grader, John, to succumb to peer pressure and start to smoke (Trudeau, Lillehoj, Spoth, & Redmond, 2003) or why one young adult may be afraid of committing to a relationship and correspondingly engage in risky sexual behavior.

The first stage corresponds closely to the previous discussion of attachment. The main challenge for an infant is to develop a basic sense of **trust** in the world. An infant's trust develops through interactions with caregivers. You can guess that infants with a secure attachment style are more likely to see the world as a safe place and trust others. In stage 2 and mapping nicely onto physical development, the ability to walk and stand up is now associated with developing a sense of **autonomy.** The child (again with the help of suitable adult interactions) attempts to gain control over his or her own body and make things happen. In stage 3, as cognitive and physical development proceeds, the child has to become comfortable with taking **initiative** and starting interactions and behaviors on his or her own. Stage 4 occurs approximately between the ages of 6 years and puberty as the child develops **competencies.** This age group must become comfortable with interactions at school, including those with their teachers, peers, and playmates.

An important period for health psychologists to study is the adolescent years. Together with the growth spurt and hormonal fluxes associated with "coming of age," the boy or girl now has to decide what he or she believes in and make some sense of different competing ideas all around. Their parents and society and religious and ethnic groups all tell them what is right or wrong. Erikson believed that the major crisis of this period, stage 5, is the discovery of what an individual believes himself or herself to be, a person's **identity.** "Who am I?" and "What do

TABLE 3.3

Erikson's Stages of Social Development

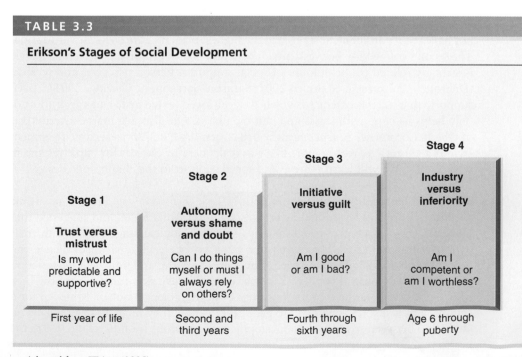

Stage 1	Stage 2	Stage 3	Stage 4
Trust versus mistrust	**Autonomy versus shame and doubt**	**Initiative versus guilt**	**Industry versus inferiority**
Is my world predictable and supportive?	Can I do things myself or must I always rely on others?	Am I good or am I bad?	Am I competent or am I worthless?
First year of life	Second and third years	Fourth through sixth years	Age 6 through puberty

Adapted from Weiten (2005).

I believe is right or wrong?" are perhaps the focal questions of this time period. Uncertainty about the answers to these questions and an unclear sense of self can translate into a slew of negative health behaviors. Teenage rebellion can be viewed as a quest for a unique identity or as a response to a world that is perceived to make you like everyone else. If you ever dyed your hair a wild pink color, wore clothes that shocked your parents, or listened to music that everyone else thought was horrible, you were probably at this phase of identity development. Unfortunately, this is also the time that individuals may experiment with unhealthy behaviors such as smoking, drinking, and risky sexual interactions. For some teens their behaviors are an effort to gain the admiration of peers, and for others these behaviors are statements of uniqueness, but both result from low self-esteem.

In early adulthood, an individual's focus moves out from the immediate self to the relationship between the self and a close other. Erikson believed that the next major step was the development of comfort with **intimacy** (stage 6) and the ability to make full emotional, moral, and sexual commitments to others. An inability to resolve this crisis leads to a sense of isolation and the inability to connect to others. This stage also has great implications for the study of health psychology. Connecting to others and relying on them for support is an important way to cope with stress and illness. Furthermore, good social support networks can ensure that we practice more healthy behaviors and less unhealthy behaviors. Isolated young adults may be more likely to get depressed when they are stressed and may experiment with alcohol and drugs to feel better.

Erikson's last two stages of development view the individual as looking beyond the self and immediate close relationships to his or her place in society

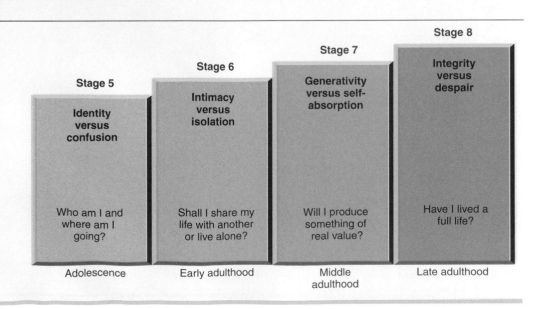

and relationships at work and in other settings. The ability to focus on others—family, friends, society, and even future generations—is referred to as **generativity** (stage 7). You are probably familiar with individuals who do not succeed at this particular challenge. Often called a midlife crisis, during this psychosocial crisis people who cannot look beyond themselves indulge in self-pleasing activities. Not overcoming the crisis at this stage also has significant health consequences for these individuals. They are more likely to have a higher potential to overindulge in alcohol and other drugs and even give up control of healthy regimens because of feelings of meaninglessness. This term has widespread appeal and is often considered more of a colloquial term than a psychological construct. Nevertheless, more than 90% of Americans could provide a definition of the midlife crisis, and these definitions roughly coincide with the definitions used in psychological and psychoanalytic theories of the midlife crisis (Wethington, 2000).

The physical changes of later adulthood often signal that life is ending. Erikson believed that the awareness of our mortality and a tendency to look back over one's life represents the final stage of development. Individuals in this period of later adulthood assess whether their lives have been well spent. Being satisfied with what we have accomplished leads to a sense of **ego-integrity** (stage 8). Feeling disappointed with life, thinking that we are failures, or believing that no one would care if we were to die tomorrow often leads to despair. This psy-

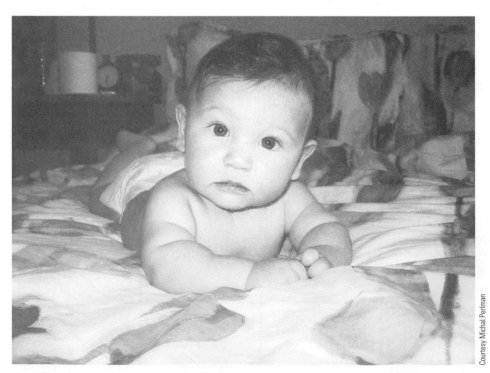

A 5-Month-Old Infant Young Ben is in the sensorimotor stage of cognitive development, interacting with his world by means of his senses and by reaching out to touch.

chological state is not optimal to deal with chronic or terminal illnesses, and this pessimistic mindset can speed our demise. Let's not forget about the bright side of the picture. If we have good interactions with our friends and families (i.e., good social support) and have the needed resources to successfully negotiate each of the different psychological challenges of life, Erikson believed we would live happy, successful lives. From our standpoint as health psychologists, we can extend this to hypothesize that successfully moving through Erikson's eight stages will make us healthier in mind, body, and spirit as well.

Cognitive Development

If we were to identify the dynamic duo of human development, we would probably settle on Erikson and Piaget. Jean Piaget, one of the early followers of the biopsychosocial approach, was trained in biology, psychology, and philosophy. Although both his theories and those of Erikson have been found to have problems (e.g., Lutz & Sternberg, 1999), Piaget's cognitive development theory has profoundly influenced how researchers view the development of children.

Piaget organized cognitive development into periods of a child's life (Table 3.4). The **sensorimotor period** begins in early infancy from birth to about 2 years; the **preoperational period** continues from ages 2 to 7 years. Then follow the **concrete operational** (7 to 11 years) and **formal operational periods** (11 to 15 years). Specific patterns of thinking identify the level of cognitive development. For example, the major development during the sensorimotor stage is the gradual appearance of symbolic thought with the child appearing to use mental images to represent objects such as toys or food. You can tell when a child moves beyond this first stage when he or she grasps the concept of **object permanence,** the knowledge that an object continues to exist even when it is no longer visible.

TABLE 3.4

Piaget's Stages of Cognitive Development

Stage	Description	Age Range
Sensorimotor	An infant progresses from reflexive, instinctual action at birth to the beginning of symbolic thought. The infant constructs an understanding of the world by coordinating experiences with physical actions.	Birth–2 years
Preoperational	The child begins to represent the world with words and images; these words and images reflect increased symbolic thinking and go beyond the connection of sensory information and physical action.	2–7 years
Concrete operational	The child can now reason logically about concrete events and classify objects into different sets.	7–11 years
Formal operational	The adolescent reasons in more abstract and logical ways. Thought is more idealistic.	11–15 years

Adapted from Weiten (2005).

© Regan Gurung

Piaget's Conservation Task A can of soda is poured into each of the glasses above. Maya identified them as being equal. The contents of one glass was then poured into the longer, short glass container. Maya now thinks this longer container has more fluid.

Imagine yourself sitting at a coffee shop and watching people pass by. An attractive person catches your attention and is walking from right to left in front of you when he or she walks behind a large pillar. Do you figure that because you cannot see the person he or she is no longer there? You do not. You wait until the person appears on the other side (or you may even crane your neck to look around the pillar). Infants in the sensorimotor stage do not have this same understanding of the world. If something is hidden from view (even a favorite toy covered by a cloth in front of them), they look around believing it to have disappeared without trying to lift the cloth up and eventually lose interest.

Piaget identified many different such concepts that characterize each of his stages. In the preoperational stage, children do not understand the concept of conservation, the awareness that physical quantities remain constant despite changes in their shape or appearance. Children in this stage are unable to share another person's viewpoint (egocentric), believe that all things are living (animism), and are unable to picture reversing an action (**irreversibility**). Once children master these cognitive abilities they progress into the concrete operational period in which they develop the ability to think about and manipulate ideas, but only if these are tangible and actual (hence concrete). In the last stage of cognitive development, children can perform the different operations to abstract concepts as well. Adolescents can contemplate hypothetical possibilities and think in systematic, logical, and reflective ways.

Although the different developmental theories were originally designed to encompass all human beings, most theorists did not fully factor in cultural differences. Each theory was heavily grounded in the culture of its creator and this limits the extent to which the theory applies to other cultures (Thomas, 2005). Freud developed his ideas in Victorian Vienna. Piaget's Swiss background influenced his ideas. Each theory varies across cultures. For example, in Freud's psychoanalytical theory, cultures vary in how they foster or frustrate healthy progress through psychosexual stages, how suitable political and cultural conditions are for the adoption of the theory, and how well they adapt to the Viennese therapeutic techniques.

When studying development across cultures using Erikson's ideas, it is clear that different cultures vary in the number and sizes of the stages that individuals go through. Piaget's stages are problematic in some cultures when some modes of thinking that are normal in one culture (e.g., syllogisms) are not so in others. In a study comparing children on the island of Tahiti and in Nepal, Levy (1996) found that the Tahitian beliefs about cognitive development and correspondingly how the Tahitians parented their children and fostered their cognitive growth, were far closer to Piaget's position than the Nepalese beliefs. That said, having an understanding of how we develop as we age is critical to predicting why we do the things that we do. You will find that explaining why certain people put their health at risk by eating badly or drinking too much gets a lot easier when you know their stage of development or the social and cognitive development-related challenges they may be experiencing (Figure 3.2).

Major Social Forces Influencing Development

Let's build on our knowledge of the main theories of development and look at the different factors that can help or hinder how we develop. Think back to your childhood. How do you think you learned what was right or wrong? How did you know what was healthy or not healthy? Some of you may respond, "I watched a lot of television and picked things up from Saturday morning cartoons." This is probably an answer your parents would not like to hear. The influence of the media aside, most of us learn healthy behaviors (and sadly, unhealthy ones too) from our parents. Each family is its own culture (nestled in the larger culture of community and nationality), and our parents and family environment can have a great impact on how we process through the different stages of development and the types of behaviors we perform.

The Family

The composition of a family can vary. The **nuclear family** consists of a mother (female), a father (male), and unmarried children. Nuclear families account for approximately 25% of the different types of families in North America. The **blended family** consists of two parents, either or both of whom may have been previously married, with their children. The **extended family** consists of a blended or nuclear family plus grandparents or grandchildren, aunts, uncles, and other relatives. Some ethnic groups are more likely to have extended families living together than others. For example, 31% of African American families are extended versus 20% of other ethnic groups. Some ethnic groups and some religions also include *fictive kin* in the basic family unit. Many Catholic Mexican Americans (and other Catholics) have godparents, close friends of the family who serve as the children's additional caregivers. You may also hear about **broken families,** consisting of divorced and/or single parents living with their kids. Each form of family relates to a different

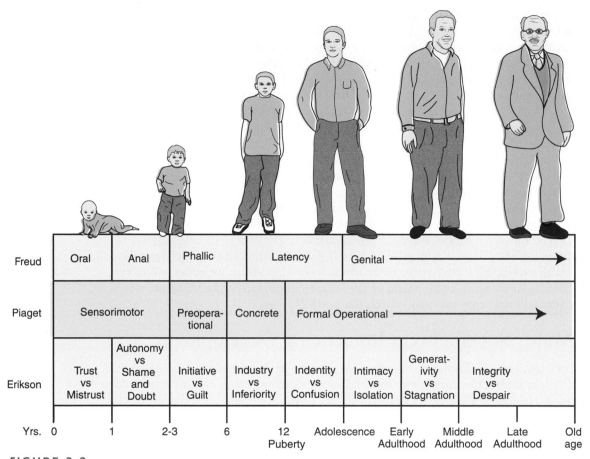

| Freud | Oral | Anal | Phallic | Latency | Genital ⟶ |
| | | | | | |

| Piaget | Sensorimotor | | Preopera-tional | Concrete | Formal Operational ⟶ |

| Erikson | Trust vs Mistrust | Autonomy vs Shame and Doubt | Initiative vs Guilt | Industry vs Inferiority | Indentity vs Confusion | Intimacy vs Isolation | Generat-ivity vs Stagnation | Integrity vs Despair |

| Yrs. | 0 | 1 | 2-3 | 6 | 12 Puberty | Adolescence | Early Adulthood | Middle Adulthood | Late Adulthood | Old age |

FIGURE 3.2

The Main Forms of Human Development

At each chronological age, we are undergoing a different form of social, cognitive, and psychosexual development.

family environment and can influence children's social and cognitive development. Some developmental psychologists study whether one type of family is better than another. Particular attention has been paid to gay families (children with two male or two female parents) and single parent families. At present, no clear evidence suggests that either of these two types of families is unhealthy for children (Patterson, Fulcher, & Wainright, 2002; Weinraub, Horvath, & Gringlas, 2002).

The composition of a family is less of a factor in development than is the quality of life in the family. Poor family environments can be unhealthy in their own right. Families in which a lot of arguing occurs between family members and in which relationships are cold, unsupportive, and neglectful, have been referred to as **risky families** (Repetti, Taylor, & Seeman, 2002). Biology and social environments interact as negative family characteristics (e.g., abuse, aggression, or conflict) create vulnerabilities that interact with genetically based vulnerabilities. The children then develop psychological problems (e.g., problems in expressing emotions), biological problems (e.g., disruptions in normal physiological stress responses), and poor health behaviors (e.g., especially substance abuse).

Parenting Styles

Within any family, the way parents treat their children plays a role in health behaviors and health. For example, problems with parenting early in a child's life, especially during times of high stress, have been linked to the development of childhood asthma (Mrazek et al., 1999). There are four main forms of parenting (Baumrind, 1991). **Authoritarian** parents expect unquestioned obedience and view the child as needing to be controlled. **Permissive** parents allow children to regulate their own lives and provide few guidelines. **Authoritative** parents are firm, fair, and reasonable. **Uninvolved** or neglectful parents are too absorbed in own lives to respond appropriately to kids who grow up to be indifferent to their parents. There are many interesting cultural differences in parenting. From a socioeconomic standpoint, working-class parents are more likely to stress obedience and respect for authority and to be more authoritarian than middle-class parents (McLoyd, 1990).

There are also some key ethnic differences. Authoritarian parenting styles are associated with strong positive parent-child relationships among African American families but are associated with weak and negative parent-child relationships among European American families (Boykin-McElhaney & Allen, 2001). African American children view their parents' use of physical discipline (not abuse) as a sign that the parents care (Deater-Deckard, Dodge, Bates, & Pettit, 1996). This is not the way European American children view a spanking. In a different study, Kelley and Tseng (1992) found that European American mothers scored higher on sensitivity, consistency, nonrestrictiveness, nurturance, and rule setting, whereas Chinese American mothers scored higher on physical punishment and yelling.

Socioeconomic Status, Development, and Health

SES is one of the most important factors that influence both development and health. A variety of mechanisms linking SES to child well-being have been proposed. Some involve differences in access to material and social resources; others involve reactions to stress-inducing conditions by both the children themselves and their parents. For children, SES impacts well-being at multiple levels. Living in a poor family and living in a poor neighborhood can both be problematic. The good news is that children's own characteristics, those of their family, and external support systems can compensate for low SES (Bradley & Corwyn, 2002). Still, children from low SES families also are more likely to experience growth retardation (DiPietro, Costigan, Hilton, & Pressman, 1999), be born prematurely, have an LBW, or be born with birth defects (U.S. Department of Health and Human Services, 2003). Neighborhood SES has also been linked to the development of childhood asthma (Huang & Joseph, 1999). Using an extensive data set from the Fullerton Longitudinal Study (FLS) to address several key questions about SES, parenting, and child development, Gottfried, Gottfried, Bathurst, Guerin, and Parramore (2003) found that SES is of immense importance to child development. In the FLS, a family's SES during a child's infancy predicted key aspects of that child's development through high school. The mother's education level had the most consistent relationship to child outcomes. Whether or not the mother was well educated had an influence on her style of parenting, largely accounting for SES effects on her child's behavioral outcomes during infancy. The SES-development-health relationship is seen in adolescents as well. Goodman (1999) found that SES correlated with depression, obesity, and overall health in adolescents, and poor teens are more likely to have stunted growth (Brooks-Gunn & Duncan, 1997). Many problems due to low SES in childhood and adulthood can create vulnerabilities and adverse health outcomes in adulthood.

Health across the Lifespan and Culture

Focusing on how we develop is also important in understanding why mortality and morbidity varies across age groups. The main causes of death are not the same at each point of the life cycle. Birth defects are the leading cause of infant deaths in the United States, accounting for 1,227 deaths out of every 100,000 live births in 2001. Other major causes in order of rate include complications from LBW, sudden infant death syndrome, and problems from labor, delivery, and other maternal complications (Figure 3.3) (National Center for Health Statistics, 2003). The trauma of losing a child and the way parents cope can vary with the ethnic group that the parents are from and the expectations they have, and many cultural variables can play a role. Many Mexican American mothers tend to have higher levels of stress during pregnancy. The idea that pregnancy is stressful is really ingrained in the culture: the Spanish word for labor is *dolor*, which also is the root for the words "sorrow" and "pain." Even without knowing the statistics, the expectation of giving birth can produce a great deal of fear. African and Latino Americans seem to rely on family ties more (Sagrestano et al., 1999). Other cultural variables beyond ethnicity can be important too. For example, prenatal care and nutrition vary by SES level and also influence development (Landry, Denson, & Swank, 1997). Many poor families do not have the health insurance or facilities to receive good prenatal care. Poor expecting mothers who are not well fed automatically have an increased chance of complications during labor and delivery (Giblin, Poland, & Ager, 1990; Sable, Stockbauer, Schramm, & Land, 1990).

Injury and accidents are the leading causes of death for children, adolescents, and young adults (Irwin, Cataldo, Matheny, & Peterson, 1992; National Center for Health Statistics, 2003), and many of the primary predictors of such deaths are psychosocial. For example, mothers with high levels of stress, who worked more than 15 hours a week outside the home, and who had a negative attitude toward medical care providers, were more likely to have children with serious injuries (Horwitz, Morgenstern, DiPietro, & Morrison, 1998). Adolescents also show high rates of binge drinking (Tucker, Orlando, & Ellickson, 2003) and may exhibit unhealthy weight-control behaviors (Neumark-Sztainer, Wall, Story, & Perry, 2003). Substance abuse and risky sexual behaviors are some of the other major predictors of adolescent mortality (Eisler et al., 1997). Many high school and college students experiment with drugs and tobacco. Longitudinal data from

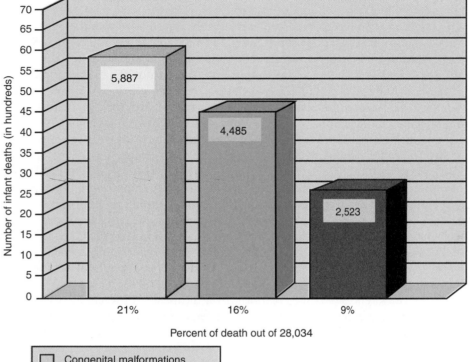

Main Causes of Infant Mortality for 2002 in the United States

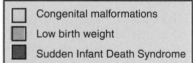

FIGURE 3.3
Infant Mortality Rates and Causes
Source: Deaths: Leading causes for 2002. National vital statistics report, 53(17) by R. N. Anderson and B. L. Smith, 2005. Hyattsville, MD: National Center for Health Statistics.

the Monitoring the Futures Studies (Johnston, O'Malley, & Bachman, 2001) indicate that although past month drug use by high school seniors fell in the late 1970s and stabilized in the 1980s, it rose steadily in the 1990s, peaking in 1997 with rates almost identical to those in 1975. Of those high school students in the class of 1999 who planned to finish four years of college, 31.4% had smoked at least one cigarette in the past 30 days (Johnston et al., 2001). Sadly, it may start with someone trying a joint of marijuana or a cigarette on a dare, but this may lead to the person trying and getting addicted to many other substances. Cigarettes and alcohol are thus referred to as **gateway drugs** because their use is the entrance to a host of other unhealthy and risky behaviors (Gerstein & Green, 1993).

Again, SES and ethnicity play key roles. Families living below the poverty line are more likely to live in high-crime areas where the risks to children increase and the accessibility to health care services decreases (Mayer & Jencks, 1989). During stages of adolescence as described earlier, the search for self is often accompanied by additional risk taking, including the initiation of smoking and drinking and risky sexual behavior, which can lead to early mortality.

As we age, we succumb to more diseases that are related to unhealthy behaviors. The top three killers of adults (ages 25 to 55) and older adults (ages 55 and older) are coronary heart disease, cancer, and stroke (National Center for Health Statistics, 2003), each exacerbated by eating badly, smoking, and overindulging in alcohol. Aging should not always be associated with illness and sickness either. A large-scale study conducted by researchers working with the MacArthur Foundation showed that eating well, getting physical activity, and giving and receiving a lot of social support are some of the factors that can provide many happy years of life for older adults (Berkman & Syme, 1994; Gurung, Taylor, & Seeman, 2003; Seeman et al., 1997). The physical deterioration of cells as discussed in the beginning of this chapter is related to specific diseases in adulthood. For example, many elderly adults experience marked problems in thinking and remembering or **dementia.** The most common problem is one that you will have heard about. Alzheimer's disease, a degenerative disease of the brain that leads to dementia, makes even simple everyday tasks like doing grocery shopping difficult. Other major causes of dementia include Parkinson's disease and stroke, which we shall discuss in greater detail in the chapter on chronic diseases.

These differences in causes of mortality indicate how different areas of health psychological research will be needed at different times of the life cycle. Prevention of injuries should be a major goal when intervening with children, a decrease in unhealthy behaviors is a pertinent goal for children and young adults, and help in coping with chronic and terminal disease is a critical goal for elderly persons.

Not as much attention has been paid to the role of different theories of human development in health psychology before. As you can see, the different factors that influence human development can play a major role in how we see the world. Our progress through the stages of cognitive and social development can be accelerated or retarded by biopsychosocial factors, most importantly parenting styles and our family's SES. The stage is set early in life. The groundwork for whether we smoke or not, how much we drink, how much physical activity we get, and what is our propensity to get sick, is all laid in the early parts of life. All of these health behaviors and our views of the importance of being healthy are directly tied to our developmental histories that in turn are directly influenced by our cultural backgrounds. One clear example of the link between culture and development is seen in the concepts of ethnic identity and acculturation.

Ethnic Identity

If I asked what you are (yes, a very general question), and if you are European American or White, you would probably reply "American." How you answer depends, of course, on context as I discussed in chapter 1, but this is a rather common answer. Non-Europeans sometimes also reply with "American," but more often they reply in ethnic terms (e.g., "I am Chinese American or Mexican American or Indian American."). This type of response is also what most European Americans are looking for when talking to non-European Americans (e.g.,

"Yes, I know you are American, but what type of American are you, what is your ethnicity?"). Of course, European Americans have ethnicities as well (e.g., Polish or Italian or German) but are not as likely to reply in ethnic terms. This is when the concept of ethnic identity becomes important.

Ethnic identity is an enduring fundamental aspect of a person's social identity that derives from his or her knowledge of membership in an ethnic group and feelings associated with that membership (Phinney, 1996). It refers to more than race and shared ancestry, referring also to beliefs, ways of communicating, attitudes, values, and behavioral norms shared by a culture (Knight, Bernal, Garza & Cota, 1993; Keefe, 1992). Ethnic identity has been measured differently for different ethnic groups and has been found to regulate behavior, serve as a reference point for evaluating oneself, and help to establish self-esteem (Phinney, 2002). Most importantly for our purposes, it can also influence mental and physical health (Balls Organista, Organista, & Kurasaki, 2002; Myers & Rodriguez, 2002; Porter & Washington, 1993). Theorists have often assumed that ethnic identity and acculturation influence the formation of the self-concept (cf., Gaines, 1997), but empirical findings have been mixed (Phinney, 1989; Rosenberg, 1986; Tiwari & Yanico, 1996). This area needs more focused study, especially given the role of ethnic identity, acculturation, and self-concept in healthy physiological functioning (Parham & Helms, 1985; Phinney & Rosenthal, 1996).

Acculturation

Ethnic identity formation is more of an issue for non-European Americans, as they are often made very aware of their not being White. For non-White children, the stress of forming one's ethnic identity is compounded by the fact that often parents are experiencing their own problems with the culture that surrounds them (Berrol, 1995). Immigrants, for example, often single-handedly enter a culture different from their own, leaving their families behind in their home cultures (Saran, 1985). They differ in the extent to which they acculturate, and while some remain steadfast in retaining the values and norms they were raised with, some subtly adapt to the different world around them (Helweg & Helweg, 1990). Acculturation is correspondingly an important variable. Being acculturated may mean different things to different people, and there have been many approaches to studying acculturation (Padilla, 1980). Roland (1990), who has studied and compared various cultures, sees the acculturation process as primarily entailing the adoption of one culture at the expense of the other. In contrast, Berry, Trimble, & Olmedo (1986) define four models of acculturation that directly pertain to the issues I have raised here. A strong identification with both groups is indicative of integration or biculturalism; a strong identification with only the dominant culture reflects assimilation; with only the ethnic group, separation; with neither group, marginalization.

Acculturation and ethnic identity formation are both factors that are critical aspects of human development, which are of much more significance to non-European Americans and that can influence health and health behaviors. Attending to acculturation and ethnic identity takes us beyond the basic cultural differences in health and can be seen in both mental and physical health. For example, African Americans have been found to have higher rates of mental disorders compared with European Americans and Mexican Americans, but these findings vary with acculturation level (Robins, Locke, & Regier, 1991; Ying, 1995). In many cases, greater acculturation is associated with better mental health (e.g., Balls Organista, Organista, & Kurasaki, 2002) although this is not the case for all ethnic groups or with physical health. Higher acculturated Mexican Americans, for example, have been found to be more depressed than recent immigrants with lower acculturation scores (Vega et al., 1998).

The acculturation-physical health link is just as fascinating. In general, recent immigrants are healthier than better-acculturated nonimmigrants (Myers & Rodriguez, 2002; Popkin & Udry, 1998). Cancer, diabetes, and risky sexual behavior are higher among most acculturated non-Europeans (Fujimoto, 1992; Hines, Snowden, & Graves, 1998; Harmon, Castro, & Coe, 1996), and there are only a few exceptions: acculturation is related to lower rates of diabetes among Mexican Americans (Hazuda, Haffner, Stern, & Eifler, 1988). The positive relationship can be seen across many cultural groups although as you can guess, the relationship is sometimes very complex when you add sex differences to the mix. More acculturated Mexican Americans are more likely to have high blood pressure than less acculturated Mexican Americans (Espino & Maldonado, 1990), but whereas less acculturated Latino American men drink more and are more likely to engage in risky sexual behavior, it is the more acculturated Latino women who drink more (Hines & Caetano, 1998). I will discuss more such ethnic and sex differences in later chapters.

Given that culture can be broadly defined as encompassing other factors such as religion, it is important to remember that acculturation may take place when any two or more cultural groups come into contact and that there is a lot of variance within each cultural group. When a Catholic dates or marries a Lutheran or someone from the South dates or marries someone from the North, acculturative pressure can influence both relationships, and the children of both couples can have problems forming their identities that could affect their health and health behaviors.

 FOCUS on Current Issues

Body Image and the Trials of Adolescence

You may have heard your parents or their friends comment on how things "aren't like they used to be." When *they* were young, they will go on to say, kids behaved differently, and no one got the types of things that kids of today ask for. In times of stress, when bills accumulate, work loads are up, and time is short, you may hear many adults talk differently. Then they wish for those carefree days of childhood, when things were easy and they did not have dependents to worry about. Your parents and many adults are right about one thing for sure: Kids today are NOT like kids were 20 or 30 years ago. On the flip side, they may not WANT to be a kid growing up today. Children today face a number of different issues, both from psychological and societal angles that influence their biology and their health.

Body image is one of the biggest issues that adolescents today have to deal with. Being thin is highly valued in our society (just take a look around you at billboards, television, and the movies), and thinness is often equated with at-

Teenagers Having a Good Time This stage of human development often involves many substantial risky behaviors. Many young adults (and unfortunately many adolescents as well) partake in a number of risky health behaviors such as excessive drinking.

tractiveness and popularity, particularly for women (Stice, Shaw, & Nemeroff, 1998). Muscularity is also valued; even toys are getting more muscular. The G.I. Joes and action figures of today could easily crush the action figures of your parents' youths. Even Barbie with her out-of-proportion curves, implants (no pun intended) many negative ideals about body image in young children. In a wonderful example of how the media and body image problems can cut across cultural lines and impact a variety of health behaviors, Edut (1998) compiled the stories of young women writing about body image and identity. The stories vividly portray the turmoil of adolescence, with girls being pressured by different aspects of culture—gender, religion, ethnicity, sexual orientation, and even the culture of athleticism—to try to be what they believe their different cultural groups want them to be. Included are writings from a Jewish girl who is ashamed of her nose, an African American woman who is ashamed of her large behind, and a female "jock" who is embarrassed by her muscularity. The psychological pressure causes them to act out and perform many negative health behaviors (disordered eating, overexercising, risky sexual behavior, and excessive drinking).

Children are not immune to media messages; even at the young age of 8, they are aware of the thin ideal, feel pressure to be thin, and respond to this pressure through disordered eating (Kelly, Ricciardelli, & Clarke, 1999) and increased exercising (Ricciardelli & McCabe, 2001). Harrison (2000) revealed that first through third grade children exposed to television showed increased symptoms of eating disorders. A growing girl looks around at the media and advertisements and sees that it is the thin women who are getting the attention and the good-looking guys. The heavier women are being made fun of and are often great for friends but are not really the people the guys want to date. Inaccurate messages like this surround the growing child and teenager and can exert severe psychological strain. The media's ideals of thinness, often portrayed to the extent of being emaciated, are frequently internalized by consumers and applied as personal standards (Cusumano & Thompson, 2001). The media fuels body image problems, and girls with image problems show increased depression and body dissatisfaction after being exposed to television commercials (Heinberg & Thompson,

1995). People with low self-esteem (David & Johnson, 1998) or people who are heavier (Henderson-King, Henderson-King, & Hoffman, 2001) also tend to be more vulnerable to the damaging effects of media. Females tend to display more harmful effects from media exposure. For example, the more hours ninth grade girls spent watching music videos, the more important they perceived appearance to be and the more weight concerns they had (Borzekowski, Robinson, & Killen, 2000). It is now becoming clear that these issues may now apply to boys as well (McCabe & Ricciardelli, 2003).

Ironically, the two most critical health issues for children are obesity and the rise in incidence of Type 2 diabetes, two biological outcomes resulting from overeating rather than insufficient eating driven by concerns with body image. We are a nation of people growing fat, and Americans can boast of having some of the heaviest and most unhealthy kids in the world. Obesity is currently the most prevalent nutritional disease of children and adolescents in the United States, affecting nearly one in five children (Dietz, 1998). An examination of the data from the Centers for Disease Control and Prevention's National Health and Nutrition Examination Surveys (NHANES) shows an alarming increase in the proportion of obese children. Between the times of the initial two survey cycles (1963 to 1965 and 1966 to 1970) and the NHANES III (1988 to 1991), overweight defined by the 85th percentile of body mass index (BMI) increased from approximately 15% to 22% for both 6- through 11-year-olds and 12- through 17-year-olds. When overweight was defined by the 95th percentile of BMI, the percentage rose from 5% to almost 11% for 6- through 11-year-olds and from 5% to approximately 12% for 12- through 17-year-olds. In general, the greatest increases in overweight prevalence occurred between 1976 and 1991. During those 15 years, the number of overweight children and adolescents nearly doubled (Troiano, Flegal, Kuczmarski, Campbell, & Johnson, 1995). Included in the many causes of the obesity epidemic are the consumption of prepackaged foods that are high in fat and low in nutritional value, the lack of family "sit-down" meals (even breakfast is now available in an eat-on-the-go package), and the widespread practice of providing large portion sizes. Everything is being "super-sized," and even schools market foods of minimal nutritional value. Although school meals actually deliver fewer calories than recommended, this fact is misleading because of the additional foods available to children from fast food restaurants both off and on campus. Advertising by fast food companies further encourages children to eat improperly. To add to this food issue, children are not getting enough physical activity: the average child spends approximately 20 hours a week in front of the television and computer (Muir, 2002).

Obesity is a critical risk factor for Type 2 diabetes, the form of diabetes in which the body loses its sensitivity to insulin. Type 2 diabetes, which was once considered a rare condition among children, now accounts for about 15% to 45% of all newly diagnosed cases of diabetes in children and teenagers (Fagot-Campagna et al., 2000). Again culture plays a critical role. Risk factors for the development of Type 2 diabetes in children and teenagers include racial background, family history of Type 2 diabetes, clinical evidence of insulin resistance, and female gender (American Diabetes Association, 2000). Girls are nearly twice as likely to develop diabetes as are boys, and its prevalence is especially high in ethnic minorities, including African Americans, Latinos, and American Indians (Levitsky, 2000). Despite the greater risk for the development of Type 2 diabetes among ethnic minorities, it has also increased in White children. About 25% of White children with newly diagnosed diabetes have Type 2 diabetes.

As you can see, it is no longer easy being a child. I already talked about how girls get their first menstrual cycle earlier than ever before. Is that another sign of the greater stress that teens are under today? There are many more health issues and pressures today than ever before, and health psychologists have to be more attuned to the specific issues of development. •

Chapter Summary

- Most health behaviors are learned when we are young and are strongly influenced by our cultural surroundings. Both cultural background and developmental processes correspondingly both influence health.
- Development can be divided into biological, social, and cognitive components. Each interacts with the other, and there are many different cultural factors that can influence the speed and success of each.
- The prenatal stage of human development is critical to the formation of a healthy physiological system, and the health behaviors of the mother, influenced by her culture, can strongly influence the development of the baby.
- There are different health risks at each stage of development—infancy, early childhood, adolescence, and adulthood. The major causes of death at each time point also vary. Puberty is a critical milestone in physical development with consequences for psychological well-being and health behaviors.
- A person's attachment style reflects his or her bond with the primary caregiver and can be an important basis for the development of later relationships. Securely attached children grow to have healthier relationships and show more adaptive coping skills.
- Theorists such as Erikson, Freud, and Piaget suggested key stages in development, each of which has major challenges for the growing individual.
- The family is perhaps the main way that most of us learn the rules of our culture, which include how to perform various health behaviors. There are four major parenting styles, each varying with culture.
- Socioeconomic status has a major cultural influence on both development and health. Children from low SES families often experience greater stress and do not practice the same level of health behaviors as children from high SES families.
- Ethnicity is another major cultural factor influencing development. Different ethnic groups have different child-rearing practices and different expectations for health behaviors. Ethnic identity and acculturation are two major concepts that clearly illustrate the role of culture in health behaviors.
- Adolescents are one of the most at-risk age groups in regard to health behaviors. Bad eating habits and high rates of tobacco use both jeopardize the health of this population.

Synthesize, Evaluate, Apply

- Given what you know about physical development, what recommendations do you have for parents?
- What are the psychosocial implications of the different physical milestones of development (e.g., puberty, menstruation, menopause)?
- What are the most different ways that psychosocial factors can hinder prenatal development?
- List the main stages of development and the major causes of death in each one.
- How does social development vary by culture?
- What are the main types of parenting styles and what implications do they have for health?
- Why is early parent-child attachment so critical for health across the lifespan?
- Why do you think the United States still has high infant mortality?
- Do Piaget's and Erikson's theories of development ring true for you? What problems do you see with each?
- How are attachment style, Erikson's ideas, and Piaget's stages related? How could they be combined to predict health outcomes?
- Using the different psychosocial crises of Erikson's stages, what unhealthy behaviors are more likely in each?
- How do the different levels of physical development relate to different levels of cognitive and social development?
- Why are social and cognitive development important to health psychology?
- How can low socioeconomic status cause poorer health?
- How does the media make it harder for people to perform healthy behaviors?
- At what stages of development are we more susceptible to the influences of the media and why?
- Diagram the key stages of human development and identify the different cultural influences on health at each stage.
- What do you think is the healthiest style of acculturation?
- Can there be cross-cultural prescriptions on healthy ways to raise children?
- Why should health psychologists be more aware of the nuances of human development?

KEY TERMS, CONCEPTS, AND PEOPLE

acculturation, 89
adolescence, 71
anal stage, 75
anxious-ambivalent
    attachment, 76
authoritarian, 85

authoritative, 85
autonomy, 78
avoidant attachment, 76
biopsychosocial, 67
blended family, 83
Bowlby, John, 76

broken families, 83
competencies, 78
concrete operational period, 81
dementia, 88
development, 67
developmental psychology, 67

ego-integrity, 80
Erikson, Erik, 77
erogenous zones, 74
ethnic identity, 88
extended family, 83
fixation, 75
formal operational period, 81
gateway drugs, 87
generativity, 80
genital stage, 75
gestation, 67
identity, 78

imprinting, 76
initiative, 78
intimacy, 79
irreversibility, 82
low birth weight, 67
menopause, 72
nuclear family, 83
object permanence, 81
oral stage, 75
parenting styles, 85
permissive, 85
phallic stage, 75

Piaget, Jean, 81
prenatal, 67
preoperational period, 81
preterm births, 67
psychosocial crises, 77
puberty, 71
risky families, 84
secure attachment, 76
sensorimotor period, 81
trust, 78
uninvolved, 85

ESSENTIAL READINGS

Chen, E. (2004). Why socioeconomic status affects the health of children. *Current Directions in Psychological Science, 13*(3), 112–115.

Pickin, C., & St. Leger, S. (1993). *Assessing health need using the life cycle framework.* Buckingham, England: Open University Press.

Siegler, I. C., Bastian, L. A., Steffens, D. C., Bosworth, H. B., & Costa, P. T. (2002). Behavioral medicine and aging. *Journal of Consulting and Clinical Psychology, 70*(3), 843–851.

Thomas, R. M. (1999). *Human development theories: Windows on culture.* Thousand Oaks, CA; Sage.

Williams, P. G., Holmbeck, G. N., & Greenley, R. N. (2002). Adolescent health psychology. *Journal of Consulting and Clinical Psychology, 70*(3), 828–842.

WEB RESOURCES

Visit the companion website at **http://psychology.wadsworth.com/gurung1e/,** where you will find online resources for this book, including chapter-by-chapter quizzes, weblinks, and more! You can also visit Wadsworth Psychology Resource Center at **http://psychology.wadsworth.com** to access additional resources.

**The National Institute of Child Health
and Human Development**
http://www.nichd.nih.gov

CHAPTER 4

Stress across Cultures

CHAPTER OUTLINE

Don't you just hate those times when you have to introduce yourself to a large group of strangers? Most of us do. Maybe it is a first day of class, and the instructor has everyone say something about themselves. Maybe it is a meeting where everybody has to share opinions. Your heart starts to beat a little faster as your turn approaches. You run over what you want to say in your head, while thoughts about how others will perceive you intrude on your planning ("How will this make me look? Will people think I'm cool?"). You barely notice what other people say before your turn. Your palms may become moist, and your face may turn red. The moment arrives when you must speak, and the drumbeat of your heart hammers away in a frenzied crescendo. Suddenly, when you finish, the world is a whole different place, and the birds start singing in the trees again.

Stress is a term that everybody uses freely and that we all seem to understand naturally. "Don't stress out" is often used interchangeably with other soothing advice, such as "Chill out" or "Don't freak out," all slang phrases related to those dreaded times when everything seems to go wrong or there is too much to do and too little time. There are many such stressful times in life. For example, when you have not even started on the large paper that is due the next day, or you have reached Sunday night after having wasted the entire weekend when you should have been studying for a test on Monday. How about having your car break down and getting sick and having a close family member have a major accident (all at the same time)? Almost everyone can recall a number of times when they have felt "stressed." However, *stress* has many meanings that we do not often acknowledge. There are many intriguing aspects to stress and how we experience it. Some things that caused you stress at one time (e.g., making sure you had the right clothes for a very important date, or giving a 5-minute presentation in a class) may amuse you today. Some things that are stressful for some people (such as getting up to sing at a Karaoke machine) are actually enjoyable for others. At its most extreme, stress can kill, severely hamper health, or drive someone to behave in risky, unhealthy ways.

What Is Stress?

What exactly is **stress**? Why do different people and cultures experience stress differently? What can we do to reduce stress? These are some questions that I answer in this chapter. I will start by defining the term and looking at how health psychologists study stress. You will notice that the factors that cause stress for people have varied historically. These varying factors map onto the main psychological theories that attempt to explain stress. Finally, I will look at how we can measure stress in an effort to control and manage it. In contrast to some early theories of stress, I will focus on the role of psychological processes, specifically thinking and behavior, and examine how different types of stress are associated

A Variety of Stressors Are Present in Everyday Life

with different cultures (e.g., socioeconomic status, age, and ethnicity), reviewing how different cultural beliefs influence the experience of stress.

Stress can be defined in many different ways. It has been studied using different approaches, and everyone has a different notion of what is stressful to them (Table 4.1). It is important that a definition of stress can be applied to many different people (and animals too). As an old adage says, "One man's meat is another man's poison." All negative events need not be stressful, and all positive events are not automatically free from stress. For example, losing your job may sound initially like a stressful event, but it may be a happy event if you hated your job and if this now opens up new opportunities for you. Similarly, although finding a romantic partner after a long period of being single sounds like a very positive event, you may worry about how to make sure the relationship lasts or whether your partner likes you or not. These worries could make this positive event stressful. As you can see, stress is subjective. What then is a convenient way to measure stress?

Most researchers argue that the best way to know when a person is stressed is to look at how his or her body responds to a situation. If the sympathetic nervous system activates in response to an event, then the person is under stress. This activation results in elevated heart rate, respiration, and circulation. Many early definitions of stress relied heavily on biological activity. Cannon (1929) viewed stress as the biological mobilization of the body for action, involving sympathetic activation and endocrine activity. Selye (1956) similarly saw stress as the activation of a host of physiological systems. Later theorists added more psychological components to the process of stress (e.g., Lazarus, 1966). The later and more psychological theories defined stress as being caused when the perceived demands on the organism exceeded the resources to meet those demands (e.g., Frankenhaeuser et al., 1989). Although these different definitions have all been well supported, the easiest way to define stress and a definition that allows for subjective differences and allows for physiological and psychological components is "stress is the upsetting of homeostasis" (Cannon, 1929).

TABLE 4.1

Definitions of Stress

A substantial imbalance between environmental demand and the response capability of the focal organism (p. 17)	McGrath (1970)
The response to the actual loss, threat of loss, or lack of gain of resources that all individuals actively seek to gain and maintain	Hobfoll (1989)
A condition or feeling experienced when a person perceives that demands exceed the personal and social resources the individual is able to mobilize	Lazarus (1966)
Psychosocial stress reflects the subject's inability to forestall or diminish perception, recall, anticipation, or imagination of disvalued circumstances, those that in reality or fantasy signify great and/or increased distance from desirable (valued) experiential states, and consequently, evoke a need to approximate the valued states (p. 196)	Kaplan (1983)
A perceptual phenomenon arising from a comparison between the demand on the person and his or her ability to cope. An imbalance in this mechanism, when coping is important, gives rise to the experience of stress, and to the stress response	Cox (1978)
The upsetting of homeostasis	Cannon (1929)

Each of our bodies has an optimal level of functioning for blood glucose level, body temperature, rate of circulation, and breathing. **Homeostasis** is the ideal level of bodily functions. Similar to the thermostat in homes, our body is designed to maintain its optimal level in all areas of functioning. We set our thermostats and if the temperature drops below the set level, the furnace starts. In this way a constant temperature is maintained. The hypothalamus in our brains similarly maintains set levels. Stress to our systems can thus be seen as something that upsets our ideal balance. This simple but effective definition of stress harkens back to the origins of the word stress.

Physicists have long studied the effects of large forces on solid structures, and stress was originally used to describe the force exerted on a body and resulting in deformation or strain. Stress has similar effects on our body. A **stressor** is *anything* that disrupts the body's homeostatic balance. The **stress response** is what is done to reestablish the homeostatic balance. This definition allows for subjectivity because stressors can vary among individuals. If an event does not activate your stress response or disrupt your system, it is just another event. If an event disrupts you, it is a stressor. One person's event can be another person's stressor. Likewise, even if talking in public is not stressful for you, remember it could be very stressful for someone else.

Stress over Time

Stressors today differ from what was perceived as stressful in the past. Common stressors today include relationships, too much work, not enough time, car problems, and not enough money. A list of common stressors can be seen in Table 4.2.

TABLE 4.2

Some of the Major Stressors as Assessed by the Hassles Scales

1. Death of a close family member	100
2. Death of a close friend	73
3. Divorce between parents	65
4. Jail term	63
5. Major personal injury	63
6. Marriage	58
7. Fired from job	50
8. Failed important course	47
9. Change in health of a family member	45
10. Pregnancy	44
11. Sex problems	44
12. Serious argument with family member	40
13. Change in financial status	39
14. Change of major	39
15. Trouble with parents	39
16. New girl or boy friend	38
17. Increased workload at school	37
18. Outstanding personal achievement	36
19. First semester in college	35
20. Change in living conditions	31
21. Serious argument with instructor	30
22. Lower grades than expected	29
23. Change in sleeping habits	29
24. Change in social habits	29
25. Change in eating habits	28
26. Chronic car trouble	26
27. Change in number of family get-togethers	26
28. Too many missed classes	25
29. Change of college	24
30. Dropped more than one class	23
31. Minor traffic violations	20

On the scale, you can determine your "stress score" by adding up the number of points corresponding to the events that you have experienced in the past 6 months or expect to experience in the coming 6 months.

If you review the list you will see that most of the examples are psychological in nature. They are not tangible threats such as impending invasion by a powerful army or being mauled by a wildcat but are things that we worry about or "stress over." There is also a range of stressful events that are tangible. For example, living in a loud neighborhood or a very cold environment can be stressful too.

Our current stress response is hypothesized to have developed in response to the stressors faced by primitive humans. Both early theorists such as Cannon (1929) and recent researchers such as Sapolsky (1998) suggested that the physiological responses to stress evolved many hundreds, even thousands, of years ago. Consider the early days of civilization before humans lived in cities and towns. Archaeological evidence suggests that humans, as we know them today, first flourished on the African continent (see Diamond, 1999 for a review of the archaeological evidence). Many wild animals roamed the African savannahs, including saber-toothed tigers, mammoths, and a host of other predators. Most of the early stressors were physical in nature and short term or **acute.** Imagine the early human going out of his or her cave looking for some fresh cactus flowers for lunch. Suddenly the roar of a nearby pack of lions looking for their lunch changes the stroll into an all out sprint for survival. The body had to be able to get ready to mobilize for sudden action in this fashion. Other than predatory animals, our ancestors probably also had to deal with marauding tribes who launched sneak attacks to steal food or mates. Again, the body had to be ready to fight at a moment's notice. Early stressors were most likely acute physical stressors.

With an acute physical stressor, your stress response either worked—you escaped the beast or defeated the ravaging tribes—or that was the end of your story. Those humans with better stress responses lived to reproduce. As civilization proceeded, humans started to live longer and experience more long-term, or **chronic,** stressors. Once agriculture flourished and humans traded nomadic lifestyles for village and town living, the types of stressors changed. Sometimes crops failed, and people would go hungry for long periods. At other times, weather conditions such as drought made food scarce. As the domestication of animals increased, large numbers of illnesses probably were caused from germs coming from these animals. All of these stressors could cause prolonged illnesses, but again the stressors were physical in nature. For much of human history, especially through the Middle Ages when thousands of people died of Bubonic Plague, the main stressors and causes of death were physical in nature. As described in chapter 1, medicine was not a successful cure of disease until the last hundred years, and diseases such as pneumonia, tuberculosis, and influenza caused great physical stress and death.

Today, stressors are very different. Yes, people in some countries still die of diseases due to viruses and bacteria, but the main physical killers in the United States, such as heart disease, are caused and made worse by the slow accumulation of psychological damage. Much of this damage is related to stress. Today, the major stressors in North America are psychological in nature. Our thoughts and the pressures we apply to ourselves generate stress. Few physical stressors exist here today. Except for people who live in countries with lots of political strife and civil war (e.g., large parts of Africa, India, and the Far East) or those living in high-crime neighborhoods (some North American inner cities), few of us in North America fear for our lives when we walk on the street. Yes, the occasional rabid dog gets out of control and mauls a person to death, but animals are not the physical threats they used to be. Instead, the bulk of our stress is self-generated and related to the pressures, frustrations, and changes of everyday modern life.

We can sit down on our behinds in a comfortable chair and *still* be stressed. Sometimes we do this because we want to. Do you like scary movies? Do you like action-blow-em-up movies? Do you like extremely sad "tear-jerker" movies?

Many movies make us experience physiological changes and change our homeostatic balances (for short periods in the safety of the theater). Sometimes even reading a well-written book can activate the same physiological mechanisms as a stressor. These few, mostly harmless, excursions aside, we humans show an alarming propensity to activate our stress responses by anticipating the bad things that could happen to us and worrying about all the things we have to do. Many people develop ulcers, slow-healing sores in the stomach, because of how much they worry (although 80% of ulcers are caused by bacterial infections, Tobin & Dusheck, 2001). Given that humans are most prone to thinking themselves to stress (there is insufficient evidence at present to suggest that animals think to stress themselves), it is not surprising that zebras and other animals do not naturally get ulcers (Sapolsky, 1998). Don't get me wrong, animals do experience stress (e.g., with a physical threat or parent-infant separation), but not in the many psychological ways humans do.

The pressures of modern society (see the section on Body Image and the Trials of Adolescence at the end of the last chapter, for example) and the expectations that parents and society have for us contribute to these higher levels of mental stress and anguish. Sadly, the bottom line is that stress, whether physical or psychological in nature, leads to a variety of poor health outcomes (e.g., Segrestrom & Miller, 2004). To better understand how this happens and to examine the physiological and psychological mechanisms at play, let's take a look at some critical physiology and the three main theories of stress.

Critical Physiology: The Nervous System

Understanding the physiological bases of stress provides us with a better understanding of how psychology can make a difference. The nervous system is the most critical physiological player although its functioning also influences the endocrine system together with which it modulates the functioning of the cardiovascular system, the respiratory system, the digestive system, and the reproductive system. I will discuss these secondary systems in greater detail later in the book where pertinent (e.g., see chapter 12 on Cardiovascular Disease for a discussion of the cardiovascular system).

The nervous system can be divided into two main parts: the central nervous system (CNS) (consisting of the brain and spinal cord), and the peripheral nervous system (consisting of all the nervous tissue and cells outside the brain and spinal cord).

The Central Nervous System

The primary function of the CNS is to process and coordinate information that it receives from the peripheral nervous system. In essence, the CNS is the command center of the body with the brain as the main coordinator. The brain coordinates every aspect of the stress response. In addition, the "psychological" part of health psychology has its physiological basis in different parts of the brain (Figure 4.1).

The vertebrate brain can be divided into three main parts. The hindbrain or rhombencephalon is located at the back of the brain and consists of the medulla,

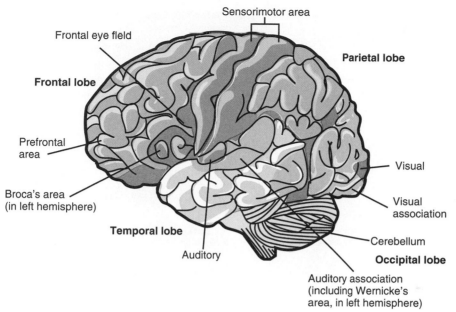

FIGURE 4.1
The Human Brain
Most of what we see is the forebrain with its four main lobes.

pons, and cerebellum. The medulla controls life-support functions (e.g., breathing), the pons relays information from the spinal cord to the higher brain areas, and the cerebellum controls motor coordination and movement in response to sensory stimuli. The midbrain or mesencephalon consists of structures that process visual information (superior colliculus) and auditory information (inferior colliculus) and those that play a key role in attention, pain control, and emotions (tegmentum, periaqueductal gray, and substantia nigra). The reticular formation plays a key role in the stress response handling emergency responses. It is a group of neurons that takes up a large portion of the midbrain but runs from the hindbrain to the forebrain.

The forebrain or prosencephalon is the part of the brain that you most likely associate with the word *brain,* that bean-shaped structure with grooves and fissures. This is the area where all that makes us human resides. Thinking, consciousnesses, talking, eating, and creating are all functions housed in the forebrain. Most of what you see or picture is only the cerebral cortex, the surface lobes of the brain. The cortex consists of four lobes. The frontal lobe contains the motor cortex and key command centers for the body. The parietal lobe processes sensory data from the body. The temporal lobe processes auditory, smell, and taste information. The occipital lobe processes visual information.

Under the cerebral cortex are other key forebrain structures. Perhaps the single most influential part of the brain is located in the forebrain. The hypothalamus directly controls the activity of the pituitary gland, which releases hormones and correspondingly regulates all of our motivated behaviors. Just above

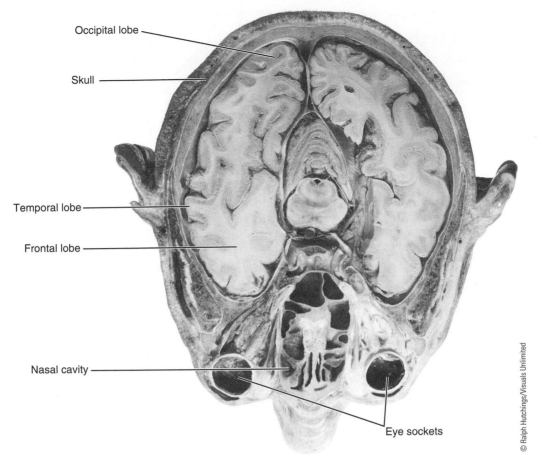

Occipital lobe

Skull

Temporal lobe

Frontal lobe

Nasal cavity

Eye sockets

© Ralph Hutchings/Visuals Unlimited

Physiology of the Brain A cross-sectional slice of a real human brain showing the compartments of the skull and brain matter.

the hypothalamus (*hypo* means *below* just like a *hyper* friend is *over*active) lies the thalamus, which relays information from the brain stem all over the cerebral cortex. The temporal lobe houses the hippocampus and amygdala, two structures making up what is called the limbic system. The hippocampus plays a pivotal role in emotions and memory, and the amygdala produces fear, escape, rage, and aggression. Many of these structures will feature prominently in the first major stress theory I discuss.

The spinal cord extends from the base of the skull to the tailbone and in cross-section resembles a gray "X." The gray matter consists of cell bodies of neurons and is surrounded by bundles of white axons. Bundles of axons are referred to as tracts (in the CNS) and nerves (in the peripheral nervous system). Bundles of cell bodies are referred to as nuclei (in the CNS) and ganglia (in the peripheral nervous system). Sensory information from the peripheral nervous system travels up the tracts in the CNS to the brain.

The Peripheral Nervous System

The peripheral nervous system transmits information to the entire body with 12 pairs of cranial nerves and 31 pairs of spinal nerves (one pair leaving the spinal cord at each of the vertebra in our spines). The two nerves comprising a pair serve each side of the body. The peripheral nervous system has two main divisions, the somatic nervous system and the autonomic nervous system. The somatic nervous system controls the skeletal muscles and is under conscious control. You can decide to move your arm to prop this book up higher, and then you can do it. The autonomic nervous system coordinates muscles not under your voluntary control and acts automatically in response to signals from the CNS. Your heart muscles, for example, are under autonomic control. One signal from the hypothalamus can lead to your heart rate jumping up. Another signal can make it slow down. An arm of the autonomic system called the sympathetic nervous system (SNS) produces the speeding up–type responses. Another arm of the system known as the parasympathetic nervous system (PNS) produces the slowing down responses. I will talk a lot more about these two arms of the autonomic system in the context of stress below.

Main Theories of Stress

Cannon's Fight-or-Flight Theory

Walter Cannon applied the concept of homeostasis to the study of human interactions with the environment (Cannon, 1914). Specifically, he studied how stressors affect the SNS. His basic idea is intuitive and can be remembered by a simple example. Imagine going to a Saturday night movie. You drove to the cinema by yourself and the only parking spot you found was far away from the theater doors. After the movie, you walk back to your car alone because the friends you met had closer parking spots. As you reach your car, you hear a crunching sound in the dark behind you. You stop. The crunching stops. You start walking faster, and the crunching speeds up. You scramble for your keys and in the reflection of your car window you see a hulking thug draw up behind you. He is masked and carries a very big stick. You can probably guess what your body is doing. Your heart pumps faster, your blood pressure rises, you breathe faster, you may be a little flushed, and your palms may be sweaty. And there you have it. All these reactions are caused by the SNS that prepares our body for action as described above (Figure 4.2). Activation of the SNS increases circulation, respiration, and metabolism, all factors that fuel your body to ready it either to fight the hoodlum or flee, escaping as fast as you can (those who run away live to fight another day). The higher respiration rate gets more oxygen into your lungs, the increased heart rate and blood pressure get the oxygenated blood to the muscles, and the increased metabolism breaks down energy for use by the fighting/fleeing muscles. The SNS also turns off certain systems in response to stress. Faced by a threatening mugger, you are probably not in a mood for two things: food and sex. Your body cannot be wasting resources and energy on these things. The SNS down-regulates (turns off) the digestive system and the reproductive system in times of stress.

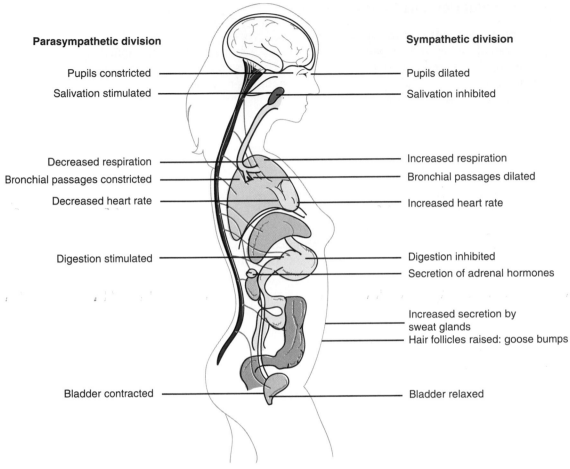

FIGURE 4.2
Major Components of the Autonomic Nervous System Involved in the Stress Response

The complete reversal of this process (the activating of some systems and the deactivating of others) is what helps your body recover from a stressor and is managed by the PNS. The PNS decreases circulation and respiration and increases digestion and reproduction. Correspondingly, most stress management techniques work to activate your PNS and slow down breathing and heart rate. The PNS and SNS are both parts of the autonomic nervous system and are coordinated by higher brain structures such as the hypothalamus.

Cannon (1914) was the first to sketch this pattern of responding to stress and to map out the full level of physiological activation. Cannon argued that when faced with a stressor, the SNS is activated (as just described), and in turn it activates the adrenal glands that secrete a class of hormones called **catecholamines**. The two major catecholamines are epinephrine and norepinephrine. Although these two names may seem strange to you, you may already know the main stress hormone. Epinephrine is also known as adrenalin (the British name). You have probably heard the phrase "my adrenalin was flowing" to suggest that someone was stressed or ready for action (the British hard rock band Def Leppard even titled one of their albums *Adrenalize* to signify how "pumped up" they were). The inner part of the adrenal glands, an area called the medulla, produces both these hormones. Consequently, Cannon's fight-or-flight theory of stress describes stress as leading to **sympathetic-adrenal-medullary (SAM) activation.** This fight-or-flight system has eight clear-cut effects (Guyton, 1977). Blood pressure, blood flow to large muscles, total energy consumption, blood glucose concentration, energy release in the muscles, muscular strength, mental activity, and the rate of blood coagulation all increase.

An intricate dance of chemical secretions leads to all these events. The hypothalamus orchestrates the SNS via the secretion of corticotropin-releasing factor (CRF). CRF stimulates the secretion of adrenocorticotrophic hormone (ACTH) from the anterior pituitary gland and stimulates the locus coeruleus (located in the pons area of the brain stem) to increase the levels of norepinephrine (or noradrenalin if you are in England or a Def Leppard fan) in the system. Epinephrine is what increases both the heart rate and blood pressure. With prolonged stress, there is a circular reaction and higher levels of epinephrine increase the secretions of ACTH. Research during the past 30 years has shown that the relative levels of epinephrine and norepinephrine vary with the type of emotion experienced with one being more of a "flight" chemical and the other being more of a "fight" chemical. Epinephrine is present in greater amounts when we are scared; norepinephrine is present in greater amounts when we are angry (Ax, 1953; Ward et al., 1983). The different physiological parts of SAM activation are heavily interconnected.

Selye's General Adaptation Syndrome

Hans Selye was a young assistant professor in search of direction when a colleague gave him some ovarian extracts. Selye set out to determine the role played by these extracts and, quite by chance, discovered another major explanation for the stress response. In his early experiments, he injected rats with the ovarian extract and observed them for changes. After months of study, he found that the rats had developed ulcers. Before running naked through town screaming excitedly (like Archimedes the Greek on discovering how to measure density) and as a good scientist, he decided to replicate his findings. He recreated the study and added a control group—a group of rats who got a placebo injection instead of the extract. Lo and behold, he found that his control group developed ulcers as well. What did this mean?

Well, Selye was not an established animal handler, and he had a lot of trouble weighing, injecting, and studying his rats. Through different forms of (unintended) mistreatment, he actually stressed both the experimental and control groups, resulting in both groups developing ulcers. The rats also had other physiological problems such as shrunken adrenal glands and deformed lymph nodes (Selye, 1956). On realizing the actual true cause of the ulcers, Selye exposed rats to a variety of stressors such as extreme heat and cold, sounds, and rain. He found that

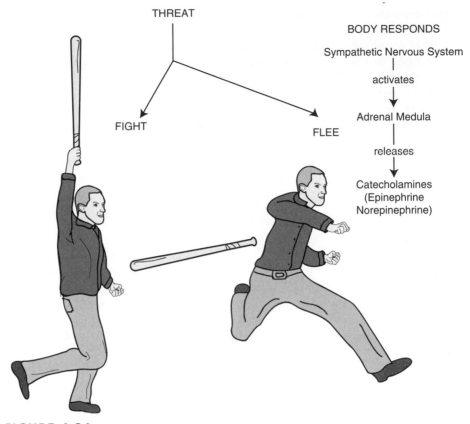

FIGURE 4.3A
The Basic Fight-or-Flight Response
Our body secretes hormones to prepare our body to deal with a stressor.

in every case, the rats developed physiological problems similar to those in his first groups of rats. Selye concluded that organisms must have a general nonspecific response to a variety of stressful events. Specifically, he hypothesized that no matter what the stressor, the body would react in the same way and theorized that these responses were driven by the **hypothalamic-pituitary-adrenal (HPA) axis.**

The first part of the HPA axis sequence of activation resembles the characteristics of SAM activation. The hypothalamus activates the pituitary gland that then activates the adrenal gland. The difference in Selye's theory is that a different part of the adrenal gland, the cortex, gets activated. The cortex is the outer part of the adrenal gland (the medulla in SAM activation is the inner part) and secretes a class of hormones called corticosteroids. The major hormone in this class is cortisol (hydrocortisone). Cortisol generates energy to deal with the stressor by converting stored glycogen into glucose, a process called gluconeogen-

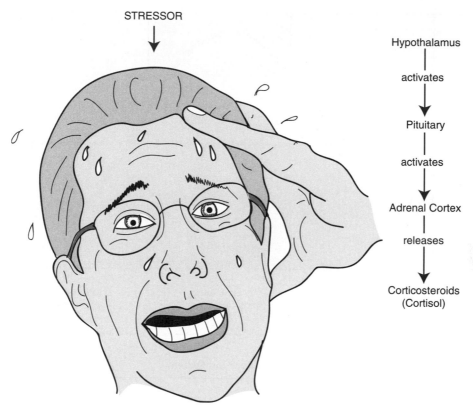

STRESSOR

Hypothalamus

activates

Pituitary

activates

Adrenal Cortex

releases

Corticosteroids
(Cortisol)

FIGURE 4.3B
The Main Physiological Pathway in Hans Selye's General Adaptation System

esis. Gluconeogenesis aids in breaking down protein, the mobilization of fat, and the stabilization of lysosomes. See Figures 4.3A and B for a summary of the basic physiological reactions to stress.

Selye argued that organisms have a general way of responding to all stressors, what he called a **general adaptation syndrome** (Figure 4.4). When faced with a stressor, whether a wild animal, a threatening mugger, or intense cold, the body first goes into a state of alarm. HPA axis activation takes place, and the body attempts to cope with the stressor during a period of resistance. If the stressor persists for too long, the body breaks down in a state of exhaustion. Many acute or short-term stressors can be successfully dealt with in the resistance stage. Chronic or long-term stressors drive us to exhaustion. Chronic stressors can exert true physiological and psychological damage on human bodies.

Cannon (1914) and Selye (1956) were the earliest theorists to offer physiological bases for stress. In summary, combining their models suggests that our SNS and the hypothalamus coordinate a physiological stress response that involves the pituitary and adrenal glands and the secretion of catecholamines and corticosteroids. Later stress researchers expanded and modified the early ideas.

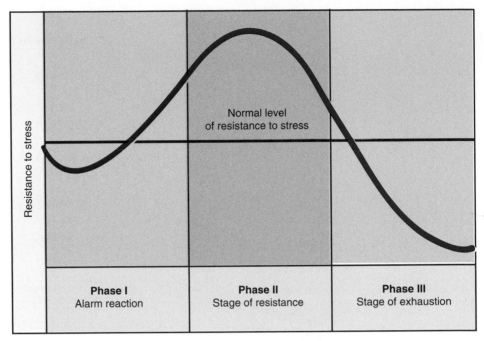

FIGURE 4.4
Main Stages in Hans Selye's General Adaptation System

For example, in contrast to Selye's theory of a general adaptation, Mason (1971) argued that stress responses are based on the type of stressor that we are dealing with. In all of these three theories, psychological aspects did not play major roles. Cannon suggested that organisms had threshold levels and that if stressors were below these limits, the fight-or-flight response did not activate. He also discussed emotional stressors, suggesting that mental processes played some role. Likewise, both Cannon and Selye believed that events had to be recognized as threatening to activate the response. However, neither scientist explained how this happened.

Lazarus' Cognitive Appraisal Model

Richard Lazarus (1966) devised the first psychological model of stress. Lazarus saw stress as the imbalance between the demands placed on the individual and that individual's resources to cope (Figure 4.5). He argued that the experience of stress differed significantly across individuals, depending on how they interpreted the event and the outcome of a specific sequence of thinking patterns called **appraisals.**

All of us are faced with demands. In school, you have papers to write and exams to take. At work, you may have projects and production deadlines to meet or a certain number of sales to make. Even in our personal lives, our family and friends rely on us and expect us to do various things. These different expectations, deadlines, and situations are all potential stressors. However, according to Lazarus, these expectations, deadlines, and situations are just events until we

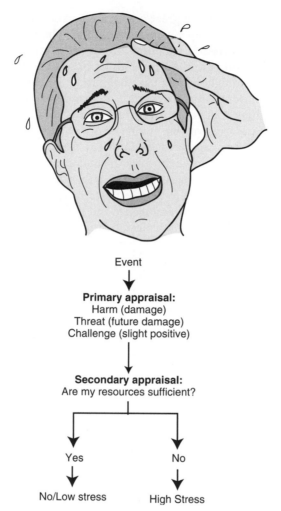

Event

↓

Primary appraisal:
Harm (damage)
Threat (future damage)
Challenge (slight positive)

↓

Secondary appraisal:
Are my resources sufficient?

Yes   No

↓   ↓

No/Low stress   High Stress

FIGURE 4.5
Main Stages of Lazarus' Cognitive Appraisal Model

deem them to be stressful. The main cognitive process at work here is making appraisals. On the *Antiques Road Show,* an informative and fairly entertaining program on PBS, people bring in artifacts or possessions that often look like junk and have been in their attics. Experts appraise the articles for how much they are worth, sometimes surprising the owners ("Did you know the table you bought at a garage sale for $50.00 is a colonial handmade collectable worth $15,000?"). When we appraise events, we follow essentially the same process. We set a value or judge the nature or quality of a situation or event.

Lazarus suggested that we make two major types of appraisals when we face any potentially stressful event. During **primary appraisals,** we ascertain whether the event is positive, negative, or neutral, and if negative, if it is harmful, threatening, or challenging. A harm (or harm-loss) appraisal is made when we expect to lose or actually lose something of great personal significance. For example, when we break up a close relationship we lose a confidant. The event can involve psychological aspects such as loss of support from the ex-partner or love of a parent who is dying, harm to one's self-esteem with the loss of a job, or even physical harm and loss from the diagnosis of a terminal illness. Threat appraisals are made when we believe the event will be extremely demanding and will put us at risk for damage. If you think that your bad performance on an upcoming project can severely ruin your reputation or that taking part in a certain race will hurt your body, you are seeing the project or race as a threat. Challenge appraisals occur in situations when we believe that we can grow from dealing with the event and may even look at the positive ways that we can benefit from an event. For example, you can view an exam as harmful to your self-esteem and a threat if you expect to do badly or as a challenge to your intelligence and how much you have studied. A primary appraisal can be heavily influenced by the stake we have in the outcome of the event (Lazarus, 1991).

After we make a primary appraisal, we assess whether or not we have the necessary resources to cope with the event. During **secondary appraisal** we essentially determine whether we can deal with the event and how we can cope. We may think about the social support we have, who can help us, and what exactly can be done. We are asking ourselves the question, "Do I have what it takes to cope?" The answer is critical. If the answer is "no," and we appraised the event as being harmful and threatening and determined that we do not have the resources to cope, then the event is a stressor. If we appraised the event as a challenge and feel that we have the resources to deal with it, the event remains just that, an event. All along this process there is often cognitive reappraisal taking place during which we can change how we view the situation. As Shakespeare said in Hamlet, "There is nothing either good or bad, but thinking makes it so."

Factors Influencing Our Appraisals

Many factors contribute to appraisals of events (Table 4.3). The duration of an event can play an important role in the process. Acute or short-term events may be appraised differently from chronic or long-term events. For example, you may not worry too much if you know that you will have houseguests for a weekend. You know that even though your routine is going to be disrupted, it will not be for too long. You will have an entirely different reaction if, on the other hand, you hear than your in-laws will be staying with you for 3 months (something in-laws of some ethnic groups in North America will often do). Similarly, acute physical

TABLE 4.3

Main Dimensions of Stress

Duration: Acute vs. chronic	**Predictability:** Predictable vs. unpredictable
Valence: Negative vs. positive	**Definition:** Ambiguous vs. clear cut
Control: Having control leads to longevity	**Centrality:** Proximity to cause

threats, such as taking a wrong turn and driving through a dangerous part of town, can have very different effects from chronic physical threats, such as living in a high-crime neighborhood.

Events can have either a positive or negative **valence**. This dimension of stress is more straightforward. Some events are automatically more threatening on the surface, such as having to speak in front of 500 people or being shot at by trigger-happy delinquents. Others can be positive on the surface, such as getting married. However, these positive events can involve a lot of demands on your mind and body such as planning and coordinating the event. The valence of an event often is colored by our emotional memories of similar events. We store emotional memories with other details of the event (Anderson, 1990), and these can influence future appraisals. A negative experience of public speaking in the past can influence our appraisal of doing it again in the future.

Control is another important feature in stress. When we believe that we have control over a situation, the situation is less likely to be stressful. Knowing that you are capable of changing the event is less stressful than not having any control over it. In a study demonstrating the positive effects of control, researchers gave 91 nursing home residents extra control over their day-to-day activities, their menus, and a little plant (they were told that they were completely responsible for the care of the plant). They were told that they were also responsible for themselves, and their day-to-day lives. In contrast, a similar group of residents was given a communication emphasizing that staff members were responsible for them and planned their activities. The comparison group had no control over aspects of their lives such as their menus. After 6 months, the group with control was significantly better off (Langer & Rodin, 1976).

Control can make a difference in how we cope with diseases, such as Type 2 diabetes and coronary heart disease. New research has shown that physical activity and good diets can reverse the effects of these potentially fatal diseases (Ornish et al., 1998). If you monitor what you eat and how much exercise you get, you reduce your chances of having a heart attack. Knowing that you can control the course of these diseases (based on your lifestyle choices) makes the diagnosis of coronary heart disease and diabetes less stressful.

Predictability is related to control. You will fear going to class less if you know that your professor gives a quiz in class every Friday. If you have no idea when a quiz or exam will be given, you would probably be more stressed. Think about sitting in a dentist's chair. If the dentist needs to use the drill but you have no idea how long the drilling is going to last, you will be stressed. Being able to predict the occurrence of exams or quizzes or even how long a drill is going to be used reduces stress. On a more serious note, research from the first Gulf War showed that when Israel was bombed, the citizens' ability to predict what the missiles held greatly reduced their stress. When the bombing first began, many people were hospitalized *just from the trauma*. They did not know whether the warheads contained chemical weapons or not (Wolfe & Proctor, 1996). When a signal preceded an oncoming missile attack in a similar wartime study, this predictability of stress led to a reduction in the number of stress-related problems reported (Rosenhan & Seligman, 1989).

Not having all the details about an event or not having the mental resources to fully understand what needs to be done in a certain case may make the outcome of the event unpredictable and stressful. For example, having scheduled medical examinations in a veterans' hospital was not perceived by the patients to be stressful when information about the medical procedures that were going to be used or needed was provided (Mischel, 1984). Hence the **definition** of the event is also important. Ambiguous events are a lot more stressful than are clear-cut ones.

Measuring Stress

A variety of tools can assess the different psychological and physiological aspects of stress. The easiest way to measure whether someone is stressed is to ask. If your colleague at work seems stressed, a simple question may confirm your observation. To make a valid and reliable measure of stress, health psychologists have devised a number of different forms of measurement. Most measures take the form of questionnaire checklists for which test subjects are given a number of different events (e.g., getting fired, having a fight with a romantic partner, or getting in trouble with the law). They are asked to indicate which of the events happened to them in a given period of time (e.g., the last 6 months). Adding the number of events that the person experienced provides an estimate of the demands placed on the individual and hence his or her level of stress. Examples of such questionnaires are the Life Experiences Survey (Sarason, Johnson, & Seigel, 1978) and the Social Readjustment Rating Scale (Holmes & Rahe, 1967) (Table 4.4).

Early stress research was focused primarily on major events in peoples' lives or **life events** (Brown & Harris, 1978; Coddington, 1972; Holmes & Rahe, 1967; Sarason et al., 1978). Holmes and Rahe (1974) read thousands of U.S. Navy medical records for events associated with injury or the onset of illness and asked a large independent group of people to identify the most stressful events. The researchers assigned values/weights to the events based on the group's ratings (more serious events were given a higher weight). The resulting scale was called the Social Readjustment Rating Scale (SRRS) (Holmes & Rahe, 1967) and consisted of 43 items, each with a different value called a Life Change Unit or LCU (a revised and updated version can be seen in Table 4.2). Holmes and Rahe conducted further studies with the SRRS and demonstrated that the experience of stress led to physical illness. For example, they asked a group of physicians to complete the SRRS, and then they tracked the physicians for a year. Holmes and Rahe found that physicians whose total number of LCUs was 300 or above had a 70% chance of falling ill in the following year (Rahe, 1972). For the most part, the association between life events, increased physical disease and injury, and psychological distress has been strong (Dohrenwand & Dohrenwand, 1974; Holmes & Rahe, 1967; Thoits, 1983), although the correlations have been moderate, rarely exceeding .40 (Ross & Mirowsky, 1979). Some researchers found little evidence of a connection between life events and illness (Schroeder & Costa, 1984).

Although the SRRS is one of the critical landmarks in the measurement of stress, it has been heavily criticized and is not as widely used today. Some critics argued that the scale does not distinguish between resolved events and unresolved events. Unresolved events, these critics argue, can be more harmful (Turner & Avison, 1992). Others point out that the SRRS combines events that vary in controllability and predictability (Gump & Matthews, 2000). In addition, you will

---

TABLE 4.4

The Life Experiences Scale

Listed below are a number of events which sometimes bring about change in the lives of those who experience them and which necessitate social readjustment. *Please check those events which you have experienced in the recent past and indicate the time period during which you have experienced each event.* Be sure that all check marks are directly across from the items they correspond to.

   Also, for each item checked below, *please indicate the extent to which you viewed the event as having either a positive or negative impact on your life* at the time the event occurred. That is, *indicate the type and extent of impact that the event had.* A rating of 23 would indicate an extremely negative impact. A rating of 0 suggests no impact either positive or negative. A rating of 13 would indicate an extremely positive impact.

Section 1	0 to 6 mo	7 mo to 1 yr	extremely negative	moderately negative	somewhat negative	no impact	slightly positive	moderately positive	extremely positive
1. Marriage			−3	−2	−1	0	+1	+2	+3
2. Detention in jail or comparable institution			−3	−2	−1	0	+1	+2	+3
3. Death of spouse			−3	−2	−1	0	+1	+2	+3
4. Major change in sleeping habits (much more or much less sleep)			−3	−2	−1	0	+1	+2	+3
5. Death of close family member:									
a. mother			−3	−2	−1	0	+1	+2	+3
b. father			−3	−2	−1	0	+1	+2	+3
c. brother			−3	−2	−1	0	+1	+2	+3
d. sister			−3	−2	−1	0	+1	+2	+3
e. grandmother			−3	−2	−1	0	+1	+2	+3
f. grandfather			−3	−2	−1	0	+1	+2	+3
6. Major change in eating habits (much more or much less food intake)			−3	−2	−1	0	+1	+2	+3
7. Foreclosure on mortgage or loan			−3	−2	−1	0	+1	+2	+3
8. Death of close friend			−3	−2	−1	0	+1	+2	+3
9. Outstanding personal achievement			−3	−2	−1	0	+1	+2	+3
10. Minor law violations (traffic tickets, disturbing the peace, etc.)			−3	−2	−1	0	+1	+2	+3
11. *Male:* Wife/girlfriend's pregnancy			−3	−2	−1	0	+1	+2	+3
12. *Female:* Pregnancy			−3	−2	−1	0	+1	+2	+3
13. Changed work situation (different work responsibility, major change in working conditions, working hours, etc.)									
14. New job			−3	−2	−1	0	+1	+2	+3
15. Serious illness or injury of close family member:									
a. father			−3	−2	−1	0	+1	+2	+3
b. mother			−3	−2	−1	0	+1	+2	+3
c. sister			−3	−2	−1	0	+1	+2	+3
d. brother			−3	−2	−1	0	+1	+2	+3
e. grandfather			−3	−2	−1	0	+1	+2	+3
f. grandmother			−3	−2	−1	0	+1	+2	+3
g. spouse			−3	−2	−1	0	+1	+2	+3
h. other (specify)			−3	−2	−1	0	+1	+2	+3

SOURCE: Sarason, Johnson, and Seigal (1978).

Continued

TABLE 4.4, CONT'D

The Life Experiences Scale

	0 to 6 mo	7 mo to 1 yr	extremely negative	moderately negative	somewhat negative	no impact	slightly positive	moderately positive	extremely positive
16. Sexual difficulties			−3	−2	−1	0	+1	+2	+3
17. Trouble with employer (in danger of losing job, being suspended, demoted, etc.)			−3	−2	−1	0	+1	+2	+3
18. Trouble with in-laws			−3	−2	−1	0	+1	+2	+3
19. Major change in financial status (a lot better off or a lot worse off)			−3	−2	−1	0	+1	+2	+3
20. Major change in closeness of family members (increased or decreased closeness)			−3	−2	−1	0	+1	+2	+3
21. Gaining a new family member (through birth, adoption, family member moving in, etc.)			−3	−2	−1	0	+1	+2	+3
22. Change of residence			−3	−2	−1	0	+1	+2	+3
23. Marital separation from mate (due to conflict)			−3	−2	−1	0	+1	+2	+3
24. Major change in church activities (increased or decreased attendance)			−3	−2	−1	0	+1	+2	+3
25. Marital reconciliation with mate			−3	−2	−1	0	+1	+2	+3
26. Major change in number of arguments with spouse (a lot more or a lot less arguments)			−3	−2	−1	0	+1	+2	+3
27. *Married male:* Change in wife's work outside the home (beginning work, ceasing work, changing to a new job, etc.)			−3	−2	−1	0	+1	+2	+3
28. *Married female:* Change in husband's work (loss of job, beginning new job, retirement, etc.)			−3	−2	−1	0	+1	+2	+3
29. Major change in usual type and/or amount of recreation			−3	−2	−1	0	+1	+2	+3
30. Borrowing more than $10,000 (buying home, business, etc.)			−3	−2	−1	0	+1	+2	+3
31. Borrowing less than $10,000 (buying car, TV, getting school loan, etc.)			−3	−2	−1	0	+1	+2	+3
32. Being fired from job			−3	−2	−1	0	+1	+2	+3
33. *Male:* Wife/girlfriend having abortion			−3	−2	−1	0	+1	+2	+3
34. *Female:* Having abortion			−3	−2	−1	0	+1	+2	+3
35. Major personal illness or injury			−3	−2	−1	0	+1	+2	+3
36. Major change in social activities, e.g., parties, movies, visiting (increased or decreased participation)			−3	−2	−1	0	+1	+2	+3
37. Major change in living conditions of family (building new home, remodeling, deterioration of home, neighborhood, etc.)			−3	−2	−1	0	+1	+2	+3

TABLE 4.4, CONT'D

The Life Experiences Scale

	0 to 6 mo	7 mo to 1 yr	extremely negative	moderately negative	somewhat negative	no impact	slightly positive	moderately positive	extremely positive
38. Divorce			−3	−2	−1	0	+1	+2	+3
39. Serious injury or illness of close friend			−3	−2	−1	0	+1	+2	+3
40. Retirement from work			−3	−2	−1	0	+1	+2	+3
41. Son or daughter leaving home (due to marriage, college, etc.)			−3	−2	−1	0	+1	+2	+3
42. Ending of formal schooling			−3	−2	−1	0	+1	+2	+3
43. Separation from spouse (due to work, travel, etc.)			−3	−2	−1	0	+1	+2	+3
44. Engagement			−3	−2	−1	0	+1	+2	+3
45. Breaking up with boyfriend/girlfriend			−3	−2	−1	0	+1	+2	+3
46. Leaving home for the first time			−3	−2	−1	0	+1	+2	+3
47. Reconciliation with boyfriend/girlfriend			−3	−2	−1	0	+1	+2	+3

Other recent experiences which have had an impact on your life. List and rate.

	0 to 6 mo	7 mo to 1 yr	extremely negative	moderately negative	somewhat negative	no impact	slightly positive	moderately positive	extremely positive
48. _____			−3	−2	−1	0	+1	+2	+3
49. _____			−3	−2	−1	0	+1	+2	+3
50. _____			−3	−2	−1	0	+1	+2	+3

Section 2: Student Only

	0 to 6 mo	7 mo to 1 yr	extremely negative	moderately negative	somewhat negative	no impact	slightly positive	moderately positive	extremely positive
51. Beginning a new school experience at a higher academic level (college, graduate school, professional school, etc.)			−3	−2	−1	0	+1	+2	+3
52. Changing to a new school at same academic level (undergraduate, graduate, etc.)			−3	−2	−1	0	+1	+2	+3
53. Academic probation			−3	−2	−1	0	+1	+2	+3
54. Being dismissed from dormitory or other residence			−3	−2	−1	0	+1	+2	+3
55. Failing an important exam			−3	−2	−1	0	+1	+2	+3
56. Changing a major			−3	−2	−1	0	+1	+2	+3
57. Failing a course			−3	−2	−1	0	+1	+2	+3
58. Dropping a course			−3	−2	−1	0	+1	+2	+3
59. Joining a fraternity/sorority			−3	−2	−1	0	+1	+2	+3
60. Financial problems concerning school (in danger of not having sufficient money to continue)			−3	−2	−1	0	+1	+2	+3

To Score LES

Negative Events

Add all scores for which subject has indicated a negative sign. Then use absolute value.

Positive Events

Add all scores for which subject has indicated a positive sign. Then use absolute value.

Total Events

Add absolute scores (i.e., disregarding sign) for positive and negative events together:

e.g., Positive = x, Negative = y Total = $x + y$

(disregarding sign)

notice that there are many positive events on the list (e.g., vacations and marriage) in keeping with the fact that even positive events can be stressful. This aspect was another issue raised when the SRRS was criticized because studies showed that some positive events can contribute to *reducing* morbidity instead of causing illness (Ray, Jefferies, & Weir, 1995). Because mood could skew your recollection of events in life and influence your reporting on the scale, ratings of life stress could also reflect a pessimistic outlook (Brett, Brief, Burke, George, & Webster, 1990). With later research the SRRS was tweaked to counter some of these problems.

Sometimes the occurrence of an event does not make it stressful. A number of more recent questionnaire measures of stress ask both if an event happened *and* how much distress it caused. Respondents are often asked to use a scale (e.g., ranging from 1 "happened but not distressing" to 6 "caused a lot of personal distress" to indicate just how much the event influenced them. In the Life Experiences Survey participants rate each event on a 7-point scale, ranging from extremely negative (−3) to extremely positive (+3). This form of measure compensates for the subjective aspect of stress and the fact that people's appraisals can vary by letting different individuals indicate how much each event influenced their well-being.

Together with major life events you probably know that small hassles can add up: the neighbor who is always noisy in the mornings, being stuck in traffic, or having too many things to do. There is a scale to measure even these little things. The Hassles and Uplifts Scale (Kanner, Coyne, Schaefer, & Lazarus, 1981) consists of 117 events. Small hassles have been shown to negatively affect health and aggravate the damage done by major life events (Weinberger, Hiner, & Tierney, 1987).

Although many of these measures tap into acute one-time events and daily hassles, other questionnaires assess major chronic stressors (Lepore, 1997). For example, Gurung, Taylor, Kemeny, and Myers (2004) demonstrated the utility of measuring chronic stress to predict depression in an ethnically diverse sample of low-income women at risk for contracting AIDS. Chronic stress or burden and low socioeconomic status were significant predictors of changes in depression for African American women and Latina women, respectively. Gurung et al. (2004) measured chronic burden using a 21-item scale developed from focus groups in which HIV-positive women discussed the life stresses that they faced. The researchers compiled a list of the most commonly mentioned stressors from the focus groups. Then participants in the study indicated whether or not they had experienced each stressor during the previous 6 months and the extent to which each stressor was a problem for them using a 4-point scale ranging from 1 "Not a problem for me in the last 6 months" to 4 "A major problem for me in the last 6 months." The final list, shown in Table 4.5, included financial difficulties, transportation problems, housing problems, childcare or caregiving difficulties, difficulties in personal relationships, work-related difficulties, exposure to accident or injury, immigration or citizenship problems, and exposure to crime and discrimination. This new measure of chronic stress promises to add to our ability to predict the effects of long-term stressors.

Most of the measures of stress discussed so far ask whether certain specific events actually took place or not. Whether hassles or life events, the assumption

---

TABLE 4.5

The Chronic Burden Scale

1. Not having enough money to cover the basic needs of life (food, clothing, housing)
2. Not having any savings to meet problems that come up
3. No reliable source of transportation (such as car that works or reliable bus service)
4. Housing problems (uncertainty about housing, problems with landlord)
5. Problems arranging child care
6. Being a caregiver for someone (taking care of someone sick, elderly, or infirm)
7. Divorce or separation from partner
8. Long-term, unresolved conflict with someone very important (child, parent, lover/partner, sibling, or friend)
9. Being fired or laid off
10. Trouble with your employer (in danger of losing job or being suspended/demoted)
11. Having work hours or responsibilities change for the worse
12. Partner's work hours or responsibilities change for the worse
13. Serious accident, injury, or new illness happening to you or a close family member/spouse/partner/close friend
14. You or a close family member/spouse/partner/close friend being the victim of a crime or physical assault
15. Chronic pain or restriction of movements due to injury or illness
16. Long-term medical problems
17. Either you or someone you are close to and depend on having immigration or citizenship problems
18. You or a close family member/spouse/partner/close friend being arrested or sent to jail
19. Living in a high-crime area
20. Losing the help of someone you depend on (person moved, got sick, or otherwise was unavailable)
21. Being discriminated against because of your race, nationality, gender, or sexual orientation

SOURCE: Gurung, Taylor, Kemeny, and Myers (2004).

is that if you experienced one of these, then you are likely to experience stress. A different type of assessment focuses on perceived stress. As the term suggests, this approach relies on what the individual feels. Cohen, Kamarck, and Mermelstein (1985) developed the Perceived Stress Scale that asks respondents how often they felt certain thoughts or feelings in the preceding month. One question asks how often the person was upset because of something that happened unexpectedly. Another asks how often the person felt angry because of uncontrollable things. Responses to the perceived stress scale reliably predict a range of health issues such as coronary heart disease (Strodl, Kenardy, & Aroney, 2003) and immune responses to vaccinations (Burns, Drayson, Ring, & Carroll, 2002).

Asking if someone is stressed can give us a good indicator of how stressed they really are. However, our perceptions of stress are not always accurate. Sometimes we may not be completely honest about our experiences (both to ourselves or to researchers who want to know). To compensate for these inaccuracies, a vast array of physiological measures can be used. It is difficult to trick your physiology. If you look back to the physiological effects of stress, you can see how you can get a measure of stress without asking questions. You can measure a person's blood pressure (systolic and diastolic), take his or her temperature, or measure his or her heart rate. When we become stressed, sympathetic activation increases all these physiological measures. Most laboratory studies of stress, especially experimental studies in which a person is stressed on purpose, use physiological measures. Some use galvanic skin responses, a measure of how our skin conducts electricity. We sweat more when we get stressed and even a minute increase in perspiration at the skin's surface increases the rate at which our skin conducts electricity. Measuring devices pick up this increase in conductance.

In many studies blood samples are taken for assessment of the levels of different chemical markers. The levels of stress chemicals in the blood, such as cortisol, epinephrine, and norepinephrine, increase when we are stressed. The number and types of different immune system cells vary when we become stressed. A small sample of blood, even a few tablespoons, helps researchers assess stress levels. For example, Janice Keicolt-Glaser and colleagues watch married couples fight and then use blood samples from them to assess how stressed the argument made them. For example, Kiecolt-Glaser, Glaser, Cacioppo, and Malarkey (1998) brought 90 newly married couples into their research laboratory and paid attention to how they managed disagreements while simultaneously measuring a range

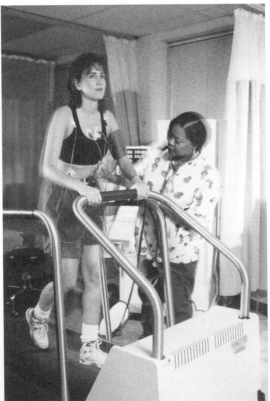

© Brand X Pictures/Alamy

A Modern Measure of Physiological Reactions to Stress: The Stress Test

of physiological measures such as blood pressure and levels of stress chemicals in their blood. Sure enough, negative or hostile behaviors were associated with increased levels of epinephrine and norepinephrine. Keicolt-Glaser et al. (1998) also found a significant sex difference. Wives demonstrated greater and more physiological changes related to marital conflict than husbands. A note of warning: many other activities besides stressful ones can also instigate some of these physiological responses so measures need to be interpreted with caution.

Culture-Specific Stressors

Culture influences both the appraisal of stress and the experience of stress. Given the central role of appraisal to the process of stress, anything that influences your appraisals correspondingly can influence how much stress you experience. One major influence on appraisals is culture. Different cultural groups have different expectations for various aspects of life, and these different expectations can make a low-threat event to one cultural group be a high-threat event to another group. For example, European Americans customarily look one another in the eye when speaking. This same behavior is considered rude among many Asian Americans. This difference between ethnicities also holds between different sexes. In many Asian cultures it is impolite for a woman to look a man directly in the eyes and converse or even to have the most basic physical contact. Cultural differences can lead to many stressful situations especially in the context of health care. Imagine a female European American doctor directly looking at a male Asian American. Interactions such as this between doctors and patients of different cultures (and sexes) can sometimes be strained, as we will discuss in more detail in chapter 8.

Culture also influences the experience of stress. Everyone in the United States is not treated the same way. Therefore, members of some cultural groups may experience more stress than others (Contrada et al., 2000). For example, many businesses are male dominated: oftentimes men are in higher positions of power and authority. It can be stressful for a female manager working around a group of all male managers. Age often interacts with gender to differentially influence how much stress someone experiences. Adolescent girls, for example, experience some of the highest levels of stress among children (Rudolph & Hammen, 1999).

Together with age and gender cultural differences, some of the most critical differences in the experience of stress are due to race and ethnicity. It may be stressful for a White European American to live in a predominantly African American neighborhood or for an African American to live in a predominantly White European American neighborhood. The United States of America has made many advances since the segregated days of the 1960s, but we still have a long way to go. Prejudice and stereotyping are often seen in our society. Many minority groups experience high levels of stress because of their ethnicity, race, or religious beliefs. Many cities in America are enclaves for certain ethnic groups that may make outsiders feel unwelcome. For example, driving through a Chinatown in New York, Toronto, or San Francisco and not being Chinese or strolling through little Havana in Miami and not being Cuban or through little Italy in Boston and not being Italian can be stressful to many. Of course, a large part of the stress may be in the mind of the perceiver (the Chinese Americans of Chinatown are not trying to stress you out), but as we know, real or not, a perception of stress is bad enough for our bodies.

Cultural differences in appraisal and in exposure to situations have led to the formulation of multicultural models of the stress process. Hobfoll (1998) points our attention to how the appraisal process can be biased by a range of conscious and nonconscious processes, such as cultural and familial norms. If your family has raised you to fear a certain group, pulling you out of the path of an approaching person of color, you are going to be conditioned to fear persons of that group. In a similar vein, Slavin, Rainer, McCreary, and Gowda (1991) expanded Lazarus and Folkman's (1984) cognitive appraisal model of stress to include a number of culture-specific dimensions (Figure 4.6). Slavin et al. (1991) argued that the occurrence of potentially stressful events can vary based on minority status, discrimination, or specific cultural customs. Furthermore, the primary appraisal of the occurring event can be biased by how the culture interprets the event. Similarly, the secondary appraisal, coping efforts, and final outcomes can be modified by the culture of the individual. For example, some cultural groups (e.g., Mexican and African Americans) have closer family ties and more active social support networks that could influence secondary appraisals. These cultural differences can even be seen at the level of the family (influenced by but not necessarily completely due to race or ethnicity). Some family cultural environments, based on the way parents raise their children, can be a lot more stressful than others. Families in which both parents are always fighting or low socioeconomic levels lead to hardships can be stressful (Repetti, Taylor, & Seeman, 2002).

Different Varieties of Stressors

Many different areas of life can be stressful. In today's world and in the health psychological literature on stress, we tend to focus on three main areas of stress that encompass the majority of life: relationships, work, and the environment. In addition, a number of physical stressors also are present in today's world. Millions of people around the world do not have enough food to eat or have insufficient shelter. Millions of people live in oppressed situations in which their every move is under the watchful eyes of tyrannical military regimes or rigid fundamentalist governments that forbid freedom of expression or the celebration of difference. Others live in constant fear of suicide bombings and terrorist acts. Most of us in North America do not experience these stressors but often create our own stressful worlds in our heads as we negotiate our situations of relationships and work.

Relationship Stress

At every stage of life, interacting with others can be potentially stressful. As discussed in chapter 3, developmental psychologists, such as Erikson and Piaget, and attachment theorists, such as Bowlby and Ainsworth, all identified how our interactions with others influence our social and cognitive development. When we are young, an insecure attachment with parents and parents who are indulgent or neglectful can cause anxiety (see chapter 3). As we grow older, we want to be

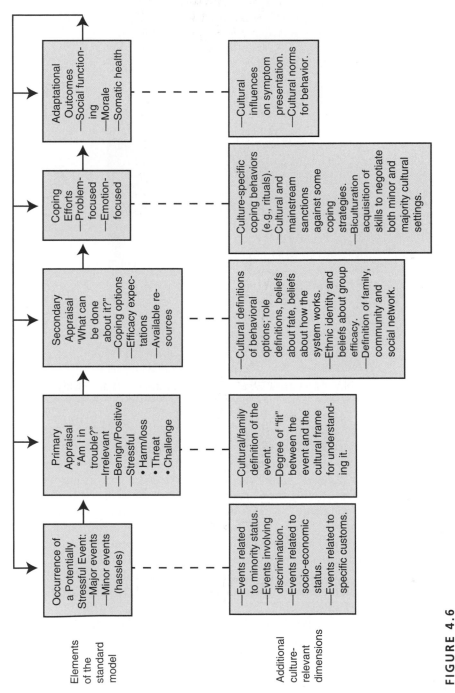

FIGURE 4.6
A Cultural Model of the Stress Response

Source: Adapted from Slavin, L. A., Rainer, K. L., McCreary, M. L., & Gowda, K. K. (1991). Toward a multicultural model of the stress process. *Journal of Counseling & Development. Special Multiculturalism as a fourth force in counseling, 70*(1), 156–163.

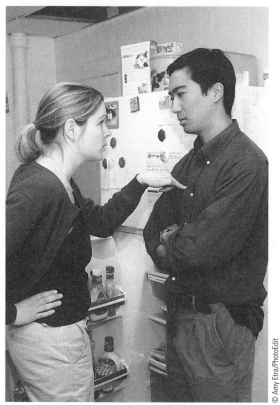

Conflictual Relationships Can Cause Wear and Tear on the Mind and Body

accepted by peers, partake in close relationships, and form satisfying relation-ships. These events can be stressful ordeals. The adolescence period in particular is a transitional period during which the importance of the peer group increases as the importance of the family decreases (Larson & Asmussen, 1991). Levels of conflict with parents and hence interpersonal stress rise (Laursen, 1996). The large number of divorces in North America also reflects the level of relationship conflict in adulthood. A number of health psychologists are actively studying the effects of marital conflict and divorce as stressors and their effects on health.

An unhealthy close relationship can be particularly problematic not just for your mental state of mind but for your physiology as well. Kiecolt-Glaser, Bane, Glaser, and Malarkey (2003) collected physiological measures from 90 couples during their first year of marriage (time 1) and found that these measures related to breakups and marital satisfaction 10 years later (time 2). Compared with those who remained together, the stress hormone levels (e.g., epinephrine) of divorced couples were 34% higher during conflict discussions and 22% higher throughout the day, and both epinephrine and norepinephrine levels were 16% higher at night. Couples whose marriages were troubled at time 2 produced 34% more norepinephrine during conflict, 24% more norepinephrine during the daytime, and 17% more during nighttime hours at time 1 than the couples with untroubled marriages.

The family is another area of focus in the context of stress and relationships. Stress on the family can come from within (e.g., conflictual relationships) or outside (e.g., living on the noisy flight path of an airport). If the home has a lot of stress because of marital conflict or poverty, each family member's health will suffer. The family cycle has distinct phases—partner selection, marital adjustment, raising and caring for children, having children leave, and retirement—each of which can be associated with stressors (Aldwin, 1994; Elkin, 1994; Patterson, 2002). The way our parents deal with stress can serve as critical models for how children deal with stress and can influence the children's own health as well (Kilmer, Cowen, & Wyman, 2001). If a child sees that when his or her father is stressed he locks himself up in his room away from others, the child is also more likely to cope with stress by withdrawing. Furthermore, a number of life events occur that can make family life stressful and force a change in the family social system. For example, events such as the death of a parent, divorce, the departure of a child to college or to the military, the loss of income, hospitalization, or a long-term chronic illness of a family member or even imprisonment, can be stressful and need to be adjusted to (McCubbin & Patterson, 1983). A number of stress theories have been devised, especially to focus on family dynamics and stress (e.g., Hill, 1949; Patterson & Garwick, 1994), that closely parallel Lazarus' (1991) cognitive appraisal model described before.

Abuse is one family stressor receiving great attention today. There is growing evidence of spouse and child abuse (e.g., McCauley, Kern, Kolodner, Dill, & Schroeder, 1997; Nabi & Horner, 2001) and growing literature on violence during pregnancy (e.g., Ballard et al., 1998). One study (McFarlane, Parker, & Soeken, 1996a) found that physical stress (i.e., abuse) during pregnancy was a significant risk factor for low birth weight as well as low maternal weight gain, infections, anemia, smoking, and use of alcohol and drugs (see also Parker, McFarlane, & Soeken, 1994). Disturbingly, many women face these types of stressors during pregnancy. Abuse and violence appear to be quite common. A review by Gazmararian et al. (1996) indicates that the prevalence of violence during pregnancy ranges from 9% to 20%. Similarly, McFarlane, Parker, & Soeken (1996b) found that the prevalence of physical or sexual abuse during pregnancy was high (16%). Estimates of violence against women in general are generally somewhat lower than these rates. In fact, family violence may be a more common problem for pregnant women than some conditions for which they are routinely screened and evaluated.

Work Stress

A 2000 Gallup Poll reported that 80% of workers feel stress on the job and nearly half say they need help learning how to manage stress. We spend much of our adult lives working. Finding and keeping a job have both direct and indirect consequences. Most directly, having a job ensures a steady flow of income to pay for the necessities of life such as rent, food, and clothing. As we grow, we add additional costs such as education and child rearing. Occupations also keep the mind and body active and engaged. However, any job can have many stressful

Workload Can Be a Major Form of Stress

elements. Job stress can produce physical health problems, psychological distress, and behavioral changes. On a physical level, there are many thousands of deaths on the job every year. For example, in addition to 8,786 work fatalities, a total of 5.2 million injuries and illnesses were reported in private industry workplaces during 2001 (U.S. Department of Labor, 2003). Day-to-day stress can make a person more likely to develop physical problems later.

Occupational stress even has an entry in the *Diagnostic and Statistical Manual of Mental Disorders* (DSM-IV) (American Psychiatric Association, 1994), the main tool used to diagnose clinical disorders. Some symptoms of work stress include feelings of frustration, anger, and resentment, lowered self-esteem, boredom, job dissatisfaction, mental fatigue, loss of concentration, loss of spontaneity and creativity, and emotional hyperactivity. Know anyone experiencing any of these? Maybe this person should look at how happy he or she is at work. Psychologically speaking, work stress can arise from a number of factors:

1. Cognitive overload: having too much to do
2. Role conflict: being unsure of one's job description
3. Ambiguity: not knowing what one is supposed to be doing
4. Discrimination: job ceilings that prevent one from rising in the ranks
5. Not getting promoted, because of sexism, ageism, or other prejudices
6. Poor social networks preventing outlets to process job stress
7. Lack of control over what one is doing and when it is done
8. Multiple roles that need to be balanced
9. Not being challenged enough

At first glance it may seem like the last item should not be a problem. Gosh, why would someone not want a comfortable, easy job? Everly and Girdano (1980) described and documented deprivational stress, a form of stress resulting from a job that fails to maintain the worker's interest and attention. The National Institute for Occupational Safety and Health even described assembly-line hysteria, a condition in which workers with boring repetitive jobs display symptoms of nausea, muscle weakness, headaches, and blurry vision, without any physical basis. These symptoms are more likely a psychological consequence of boredom because of this lack of physical cause.

If a person is unhappy or stressed at work there are consequences for both the individual and for people close to the individual. Work stress has been shown to spill over into family life and personal interactions (Perry-Jenkins, Repetti, & Crouter, 2002). In one of the strongest studies to show this effect, Repetti and Wood (1997) studied 30 mother and child pairs for 5 consecutive weekdays. They measured the mothers' reports of stress and how much they worked and videotaped a third of the mothers when they returned home to their children. Both the mothers and independent observers described mothers as more behaviorally and emotionally withdrawn (e.g., less speaking and fewer expressions of affection) on days when they reported having greater workloads or interpersonal stress at work. More recently, Doumas, Margolin, and John (2003) had 49 husbands and wives separately complete daily diaries addressing questions about work experiences, health-promoting behaviors, and marital interactions over 42 consecutive days. The researchers found that spouses reported more positive marital interactions on days when they worked less. This study is a testament to how patterns of spillover also differed for husbands and wives, suggesting that wives may be more reactive to their husbands' experiences and behaviors than vice versa.

Many different theories demonstrate the interconnectedness of the work and home spheres. This interconnectedness is referred to as a **stress contagion effect** (Edwards & Rothbard, 2000; Voydanoff, 2002). Bolger, DeLongis, Kessler, and Wethington (1989) first recognized and defined two specific types of stress contagion: spillover and crossover. **Spillover** refers to the intra-individual transmission of stress, when stress occurring in one domain of an individual's life affects other domains of life (Westman & Etizon, 1995). In comparison, **crossover** is the transmission of stress *between* individuals. Crossover occurs when stress or strain experienced by an individual affects the stress or strain of another individual (Westman & Vinokur, 1998). Crossover can occur between workers at a worksite or between an employee and his or her family.

The majority of studies on work stress have been cross-sectional, focusing on the crossover from the husband to the wife. Most studies show positive correlations between occupational stressors and spouse's stress or strain (Jones & Fletcher, 1993; Westman, 2001). Of note, crossover studies examining crossover from wives to husbands have not produced any consistent findings (Westman, 2001), and the literature suggests that women are more vulnerable to men's stress than husbands to their wives'.

The work stress contagion findings are explained by a combination of ecological theory and role theory. **Ecological theory** (Bronfrenbrenner, 1977) identifies different levels or systems in which the individual acts. Work and home domains are examples of **microsystems.** A microsystem includes the activities and roles the individual takes on in a particular setting. A **mesosystem** contains the relationships and interactions between microsystems at a specific point in time. Bronfenbrenner's concept of **reciprocity** recognizes that systems are not independent of one another but are in constant interaction. Consequently, elements of the work domain affect elements of the home domain and vice versa.

According to the **role theory** of Kahn, Wolfe, Quinn, Snoek, and Rosenthal (1964) stress contagion from work to home rises as a person's roles increase and if those roles lack definition. A role is the set of behaviors to be performed and is determined by one's own perceptions and the expectations of others. As an individual accumulates roles, the quantity and incompatibility of role demands increase. An individual experiences role strain that results in increased role conflict and ambiguity (Voydanoff, 2002). **Role ambiguity** is the degree to which required information regarding role expectations are available, clear, and communicated to the focal person. When companies establish new positions, the expectation for what someone in that position has to do is often undefined. Someone in this new position or in any position for which the job description is inadequate can experience role ambiguity. **Role conflict** is the incompatibility of expectations for a given role and between different roles. Sometimes a job may require a person to evaluate a member of his or her own work team when the evaluation also contributes to his or her own raise or bonus. In this case you have a conflict between making an accurate assessment and potentially hurting your own pay.

Environmental Stress

Working and living in a noisy environment can lead to many problems. Noise can even retard learning in children (Bronzaft & McCarthy, 1975). Children living close to an airport where constant roars of jet engines interrupt their daily lives were found to have higher levels of stress and more learning difficulties than students not living close to an airport (Cohen, Evans, Krantz, & Stokols, 1980). In a similar study, Cohen, Glass, and Singer (1973) showed that children living in noisy homes near busy roadways had greater difficulties with reading tasks than did children who lived in quiet homes. In a classic series of studies on the effects of noise, Glass and Singer (1972) had students work on different tasks and then exposed them to bursts of sound. Unpredictable bursts of sound hindered their performance the most, but those students who faced consistent background sounds during early tasks performed badly on later tasks. Noise can play a large role in how stressed we feel and is often implicitly influencing our well-being.

Just as noise can be a problem, crowding can also be stressful. If you grew up in a nice quiet city or town with a population of between 30,000 and 100,000 or less, your experiences with crowding are very different from mine. I grew up in Mumbai (previously Bombay), a city with a population tilting the scales at 20,000,000 (yes, 20 million). Overcrowding can often produce negative moods for men (Freedman, 1975), physiological arousal (e.g., higher blood pressure), increased illness, more aggression, and a host of other stressful outcomes. Even if you do not live in a big city, you can see the effects of crowding at large gather-

Natural Events Are a Form of Environmental Stress The 2004 Tsunami killed close to 200,000 people.

ings. Large rock concerts, state fairs, or amusement parks during holiday weekends can become overcrowded, making people feel stressed and frustrated.

Environmental stressors can be divided into three main categories: background stressors, natural disaster stressors, and techno-political stressors. **Background stressors** include crowding and noise, together with air pollution and chemical pollution (Fisher, Bell, & Baum, 1984). All of these can be long-term stressors and affect a large number of people. A second major category of environmental stressors is **natural disaster stressors.** These are short-term stressors and are often more severe than long-term stressors. For example, natural disasters such as flooding, earthquakes, and hurricanes can kill thousands of people and survivors often experience severe psychological consequences (Norris, Byrne, & Diaz, 2002). The tsunami that hit large portions of South Asia (especially Indonesia and Sri Lanka) in December 2004 killed close to 200,000 people. The survivors will probably experience the effects of this horrible event for many years to come. Sometimes the anxiety and fear from a natural disaster can last a lifetime (Leach, 1995). The third category of stressors can be called **techno-political stressors.** Although these types of stressors can be unpredictable and uncontrollable like natural disasters, they are directly linked to technological or political causes. Some examples are nuclear reactor accidents (e.g., Three Mile Island in Pennsylvania and Chernobyl in Russia), chemical plant accidents (e.g., the Union Carbide accident in Bhopal, India), and dam-related flooding (e.g., Buffalo Creek in West Virginia). Political tragedies, such as wars and acts of terrorism, are also extremely stressful. Life in the United States after the attack on September 11th, 2001, and life in Israel with the possibility of suicide bombings is very different today than it was before these events (Cohen Silver, Holman, McIntosh, Poulin, & Gil-Rivas, 2002).

A number of other factors are stressful even though they do not appear to be at first look. Many of us wish we had less to do and become stressed trying to complete everything that we have to do. However, not having enough to do can also be stressful. Bexton, Heron, and Scott (1954) paid students to just lie in bed and sleep. This seems pretty easy, right? Well, the twist was that they had to lie in a cubicle with their hands and arms padded and with glasses on that blocked their vision. They could not hear any outside sounds. No subject could do it for more than 3 days, and all reported extreme boredom, restlessness, and growing levels of stress, thus proving that boredom and low levels of sensory stimulation can be stressful too.

Consequences of Stress

In a nutshell, stress can make a person sick. Stress can have direct physiological effects on the body (e.g., suppression of the immune system and neuronal damage), direct cognitive and behavioral effects (e.g., distraction and memory loss), and secondary effects by exacerbating illnesses, making them worse and delaying recovery (see Dougall & Baum, 2002). Figure 4.7 illustrates some of the stress-related illnesses.

Most of the early major theories of stress (e.g., Selye and Cannon) paid a lot of attention to the physiological changes in the body that accompany the experience of stress. There is a good reason for that. A lot happens in our body when we get stressed. For example, the sympathetic nervous system has connections all over the body (nerves project all over the body from the brain and spinal cord) from sweat gland to muscles and hair follicles, all of which are stimulated to some extent during stress. We have also discussed the two main systems that are activated: the HPA axis releasing corticosteroids and SAM activation releasing norepinephrine and epinephrine. From a practical standpoint the activation of these systems is important and critical. They prepare our bodies to deal with stressors. A problem arises when we experience stress for a long time. Chronic, long-term stressors cause wear and tear on body systems, leading to tissue damage and irregular responding. How long is too long? The answer to that question depends on the individual. Let us not forget that the potentially stressful event can be acute or chronic, a person's appraisal and awareness of the stressor can be acute or chronic, and the actual mental and physiological consequences can be acute or chronic (Baum, O'Keefe, & Davidson, 1990).

Chronic stress can lead to other physiological consequences. Some people develop heart problems or loss of appetite. Others have sexual problems (e.g., men are unable to have or maintain an erection) or develop skin problems (e.g., rashes) or nervous ticks (e.g., uncontrollable jerky movements or winking). Chronic stress is a problem for many people and can be either objective (living in a noisy neighborhood) or subjective (overworking week after week and month after month). Health psychologists who focus directly on allostatic load or the effects of chronic stress have unearthed some disturbing findings (McEwen, 1998).

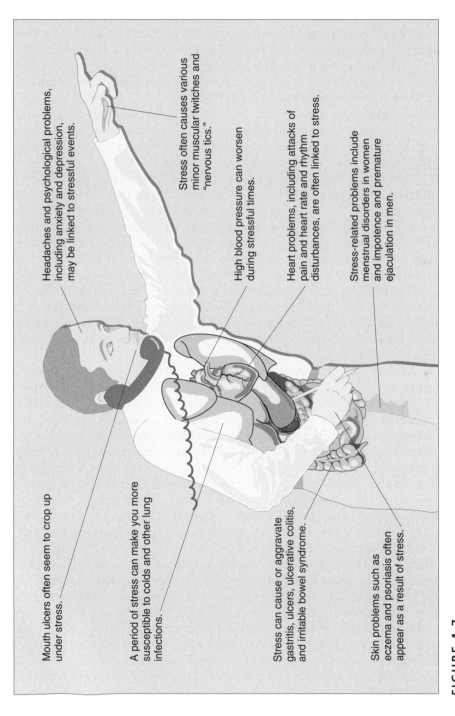

Mouth ulcers often seem to crop up under stress.

A period of stress can make you more susceptible to colds and other lung infections.

Stress can cause or aggravate gastritis, ulcers, ulcerative colitis, and irritable bowel syndrome.

Skin problems such as eczema and psoriasis often appear as a result of stress.

Headaches and psychological problems, including anxiety and depression, may be linked to stressful events.

Stress often causes various minor muscular twitches and "nervous tics."

High blood pressure can worsen during stressful times.

Heart problems, including attacks of pain and heart rate and rhythm disturbances, are often linked to stress.

Stress-related problems include menstrual disorders in women and impotence and premature ejaculation in men.

FIGURE 4.7
Stress-Induced Illness
SOURCE: *Diane Hales (2000). An Invitation to Health. San Francisco: Wadsworth.*

Allostasis is defined as the ability to achieve stability through change. Our environments keep changing, putting our body systems through various fluctuations to adjust to them. The different forces that shake our homeostatic balance stretch our systems to act like rubber bands. It is critical to our survival that our systems go back to their original shape and function like a taut rubber band does when it is released. With chronic stress, wear and tear on the body result from chronic overactivity or underactivity of allostatic systems (i.e., a load). Being under an allostatic load can have three main consequences.

Look at Figure 4.8. The first line represents normal responses to stress (a). For most acute stressors, our sympathetic system is activated before and during the event (say you have to make an oral presentation), and we adapt afterwards. Even if this acute stressor is repeated a few times (you have to give a number of talks in a month), the healthy stress response shows an activation followed by a return to baseline functioning. In the case of chronic stress (say living in a risky neighborhood where there are frequent stressors), allostatic load is seen when the poststress adaptation or the normal lessening of the response for repeat stressors is not seen (b). You still respond, but it is a lower activation each time. Correspondingly there is a prolonged exposure to the different stress hormones. This extra exposure can lead to a host of problems such as coronary heart disease. Another result of allostatic load takes place when our body is unable to shut off the stress response after the stressor stops. This again leads to extended exposure to stress hormones. The final case is system malfunctions in the response to stress. One system may not work, and other systems overcompensate. This also leads to extended exposure to stress hormones.

Bruce McEwen and colleagues have identified many markers of allostatic load (McEwen & Wingfield, 2003). Major markers include hypertension (high blood pressure), atherosclerosis (calcium deposits on arteries), fat staying in the system longer, higher waist-to-hip ratios (when fat goes to the waist not the hips), and sleep disruption. Extended stress also interferes with the immune system (more on this in chapter 13) and interferes with memory. Long-term stress actually destroys neurons in the hippocampus (they grow back if the stress is short term). Long-term stress and allostatic load as well as short-term stressors also have negative effects on our behavior, our thoughts or cognition, and our feelings. Going beyond physiology, stress makes us act, feel, and think differently.

Stress affects one's mood, behavior, problem solving, motivations, and goals and can cause distraction, memory lapses, and a host of other psychological consequences (Dougall & Baum, 2002). You are more likely to get depressed and be fearful when you are stressed, angry, or aggravated. People under stress often lose their tempers and are not as patient as they normally would be. In an interesting study about the effects of stress on memory, Cahill, Prins, Weber, & McGaugh (1994) told two groups of students a story. The experimental group heard about a boy who had an accident, lost his legs, and had them reattached (a very stressful situation). The control group heard a neutral version of the story in which the boy watched what was happening in a hospital. Half the participants in each group received a drug that blocked the action of norepinephrine, thereby reducing stress; the other half got a placebo. A week later all participants were asked to recall as many elements of the story as they could. The participants in the stress

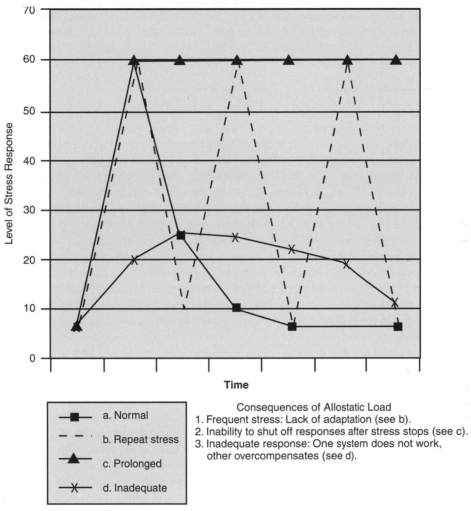

FIGURE 4.8
Main Effects of Allostatic Load

condition who received the placebo (and hence felt the effects of stress) remembered the least amount of information.

Stress also influences our behaviors. When we are stressed, we often are busy thinking about the cause of the stress and our attention to other tasks can suffer. Paying bills on time, remembering appointments, taking medicines, watering plants, or caring for a pet can all be negatively affected (Baba, Jamal, & Tourigny, 1998; Kompier & DiMartino, 1995; McNally, 1997). Obviously, the quality of work and the nature of interactions with friends and colleagues can also suffer. In some cases, people may not be able to sleep and may experience changes in their eating and drinking behavior (Conway, Vickers, Weid, & Rahe, 1981; Mellman, 1997).

Stress has many different causes, can be studied in different ways, and has many different effects. In the next chapter we shall examine the different ways to cope.

 ### FOCUS on Current Issues

Tend-and-Befriend or Fight-or-Flight?

Can menstrual cycles change the course of scientific research? As strange as it may sound, the fact that females have a menstrual cycle actually accounts for one of the strongest biases in scientific history. Before 1995, female subjects constituted only 17% of participants in laboratory studies of stress (Gruenewald, Taylor, Klein, & Seeman, 1999). In the 5 years between 1995 and 2000, that number improved to 34%. Nonetheless, still less than half of study participants were women. When asked to justify this skew in selection, scientists claimed that because females have more frequent hormonal fluctuations due to menstruation (female rats menstruate every 3 days), their data present a confusing and hard-to-explain pattern. This seemingly pragmatic exclusion accounts for perhaps one of the largest oversights in psychological theorizing and represents one of the most vivid examples of cultural differences in health psychology. In recognizing this difference and its implications, a new theory of stress was born.

A group of health psychologists suggested that men and women do not respond to stress in the same way. Shelley Taylor and colleagues (2000a, 2002) suggested that women **tend-and-befriend** in addition to fighting or fleeing. This theory started when Taylor and colleagues heard a lecture on the stress response in rats. The main stress theory discussed was Cannon's (1914) fight-or-flight model that you should now be very familiar with. The data presented, although consistent with the animal data, did not fit with data on some human stress responses and findings from a number of different areas (e.g., animal behavior studies). Taylor et al. realized that this discrepancy could be due to the fact that most stress response studies were being done on male animals. Diverse findings in the stress literature just did not fit with the fight-or-flight model. The fight-or-flight model assumes that men and women faced the same challenges in our evolutionary history. However, this was not true. Females have always been the primary caregivers of infants because of their greater investment in giving birth (a minimum investment of 9 months for women versus minutes for men). Men have easily been able to fight or flee, but women often had to look after infants. If women fought and lost, they would leave their infant defenseless. If women ran, they would either have to leave their infants behind or the weight of the infant would surely slow them down and lead to capture. Instead, the UCLA team argued that women developed additional stress responses aimed to protect, calm, and quiet the child, to remove the child from harm's way (i.e., tending), and to marshal resources to help. Essentially, women create social networks to provide resources and protection for themselves and their infants (i.e., befriending). This tend-and-befriend theory, thus, provides a more reasonable stress response for females than the basic fight-or-flight theory. This new theory builds on the brain's attachment/caregiving system, which counteracts the metabolic activity associated with the traditional fight-or-flight stress response—increased heart rate, blood pressure, and cortisol levels—and leads to nurturing and affiliative behavior.

Existing evidence from research with nonhuman animals, neuroendocrine studies, and human-based social psychology research supports this new theory. Neuroendocrine research shows that although women show the same immediate hormonal and sympathetic nervous system response to acute stress, other factors intervene to make fight-or-flight less likely in females. In terms of the fight response, whereas male aggression appears to be driven by hormones such as testosterone, female aggression is not. In fact, a major female hormone, oxytocin, actually counteracts the effects of stress chemicals such as cortisol and the catecholamines. Oxytocin inhibits flight and enhances relaxation, reduces fearfulness, and decreases the other stress responses typical of the fight-or-flight response. Supporting the role of oxytocin in befriending, blocking of oxytocin in women actually makes them spend less time with their friends (Jamner, Alberts, Leigh, & Klein, 1998).

Tending is observed in animal studies when rat pups are removed from their nest for brief periods—a stressful situation for pups and mothers—and then returned. The mothers immediately move to soothe their pups by licking, grooming, and nursing them (Meaney, 2001). Similar behaviors are seen in sheep (Kendrick et al., 1997) and monkeys (Martel, Nevison, Rayment, Simpson, & Keverne, 1993). In humans, breastfeeding mothers are found to be calmer (Uvnas-Moberg, 1996), and touch has been shown to soothe both the mother and infant (Field, 1999). In clear support of the theory (and relating to our earlier discussion of work stress), Repetti (1997) showed, on the one hand, that after a stressful day on the job, men want to be left alone and often fight with their spouses and children. Women, on the other hand, actually tended when stressed, spending more time with their children and having more physical contact with them.

The sex differences in social support strongly support the idea that women are more likely to develop social networks and befriend than men. Both studies of rodents and humans show that females prefer being with others, especially other females when they are stressed. Males prefer to be alone. Women are much more likely than men to seek out and use social support in all types of stressful situations, including health-related concerns, relationship problems, and work-related conflicts. Some other interesting support evidence is as follows: female rats caged together lived 40% longer than females housed alone (McClintock, 1998); under stress, female prairie voles turn to female "friends" (Carter, 1998); and female primates defend other female primates against males (Sapolsky, 2002).

It is too early to say whether this new theory should be emblazoned right next to the fight-or-flight idea. Good theories need to stand the test of time and rigorous empirical testing. A good case exists for females having a different stress response than males, but only direct tests of this theory will let us know for sure. Currently the tend-and-befriend theory is being actively researched.

Chapter Summary

- Stress is the physiological and psychological experience of disruption to our homeostatic balance. We are stressed any time excessive demands are placed on our body and mind. Stressors are factors that disrupt our homeostasis. Early stressors were acute and more physical in nature. Today stressors are long term and more psychological in nature.

- Stress activates the nervous system, especially the sympathetic nervous system, which in turn mobilizes the body for action. The parasympathetic system restores the body to rest after the stressor ends. The physiological stress response is characterized by the activation of different physiological pathways and the release of stress hormones.

- There are three major theories of stress. Cannon described the fight-or-flight response, which involves sympathetic adrenal medulla activation and the release of catecholamines. Seyle described the general adaptation syndrome involving hypothalamic-pituitary-adrenal axis activation and the release of cortisol. Lazarus described a cognitive appraisal model of stress with primary and secondary appraisals of events as determining stress.

- Many factors influence stress appraisal such as the duration, severity, valence, controllability, predictability, and ambiguity of the stressor.

- Stress can by measured by questionnaire and using physiological measures such as blood pressure, galvanic skin response, and analysis of stress chemicals in saliva and urine.

- Different cultural groups experience different stressors by how they appraise stress and by how they are treated (e.g., low socioeconomic status individuals experience higher stress levels). Different cultural models of stress exist to incorporate such factors.

- Research is conducted on three main varieties of stressors: work stressors, environmental stressors, and relationship stressors.

- Stress has serious physiological and psychological consequences on the body. Allostatic load, or the effects of chronic stress, can cause heart and memory problems.

- Recently, researchers have postulated a new theory of stress, the tend-and-befriend model, which suggests that men and women have evolved different stress mechanisms.

Synthesize, Evaluate, Apply

- What are the different factors that make it difficult to define stress?
- What are the pros and cons of the different theories of stress?
- How can you merge the different theories of stress?
- What are the key ways that culture can influence the experience of stress?
- Why may some cultural differences be more pertinent to the study of stress than others?

- List the biopsychosocial factors that can influence the appraisal of stress.
- Can you think of ways to counter the evolutionary origins of the stress response?
- What are the key dimensions in which stress can vary?
- How do you think the dimensions of stress can influence how you cope with stress?
- Does an event have to be consciously experienced to be stressful? Why or why not?
- What are the different ways to measure stress?
- What were the problems with the Social Readjustment Rating Scale (SRRS)? How were they resolved?
- Which of the different varieties of stress are most susceptible to cultural differences?
- What are the sociopolitical benefits and hazards to taking a cultural approach to stress?
- How can chapter 3's discussion of developmental theories and differences inform the study of stress?
- How can your knowledge of Lazarus' theory reduce relationship stress?
- What strategies and structures can employers use to keep work stress at a minimum?
- How can the results of spillover and contagion studies be applied to improving family life?
- What are the main ways that chronic stress can cause allostatic load?
- What do you think are the most potent consequences of stress?
- How would you evaluate the new tend-and-befriend theory?

KEY TERMS, CONCEPTS, AND PEOPLE

acute and chronic, 101
allostasis, 132
appraisals, 110
background stressors, 129
Cannon, Walter, 105
catecholamines, 106
cognitive appraisal model, 110
control, 113
crossover, 127
definition, 114
ecological and role theory, 127–128
fight-or-flight theory, 105
general adaptation syndrome, 109

Holmes and Rahe, 114
homeostasis, 99
hypothalamus-pituitary-adrenal (HPA) axis, 108
Keicolt-Glaser, Janice, 120
Lazarus, Richard, 110
life events, 114
McEwen, Bruce, 132
mesosystem, 128
microsystems, 128
natural disaster stressors, 129
predictability, 113
primary and secondary appraisal, 111–112
reciprocity, 128

role ambiguity, 128
role conflict, 128
Selye, Hans, 107
spillover, 127
stress, 97
stress contagion effect, 127
stressor, 99
stress response, 99
sympathetic-adrenal-medullary (SAM) activation, 107
Taylor, Shelley, 134
techno-political stressors, 129
tend-and-befriend, 134
valence, 113

ESSENTIAL READINGS

Cannon, W. B. (1963). *Bodily changes in pain, hunger, fear and rage.* Oxford, England: Harper & Row.

Cohen, S. (1980). Aftereffects of stress on human performance and social behavior: A review of research and theory. *Psychological Bulletin, 88,* 82–108.

Kemeny, M. E. (2003). The psychobiology of stress. *Current Directions in Psychological Science, 12*(4), 124–129.

Lazarus, R. S., & Folkman, S. (1984). *Stress, appraisal, and coping.* New York: Springer.

Taylor, S. E., Klein, L. C., Lewis, B., Gruenwald, T., Gurung, R. A. R., & Updegraff, J. (2000). The female stress response: Tend and befriend not fight or flight. *Psychological Review, 107,* 411–429.

 ## WEB RESOURCES

Visit the companion website at **http://psychology.wadsworth.com/gurung1e/,** where you will find online resources for this book, including chapter-by-chapter quizzes, weblinks, and more! You can also visit Wadsworth Psychology Resource Center at **http://psychology.wadsworth.com** to access additional resources.

Stressed At Work?
www.mayoclinic.com/invoke.cfm?id5WL00064

Handling Stress without Smoking
cis.nci.nih.gov/fact/10_3.htm

Relieving Trauma
www.nimh.nih.gov/publicat/reliving.cfm

Coping and Social Support

Y ou do not have to look far for examples of how to cope. Even popular music through the ages has provided us with examples of what we should do when we get stressed. Perhaps the most helpful chorus of all and one supported by substantial psychological research is by The Beatles, who illustrated the positive aspects of social support, showing we can "get by with a little help from our friends." Jump forward to the 1980s. A band called The Police suggested that, "when the world is running down, you make the best of what's still around." In another more recent example of good coping, the band REM suggested that even when it may seem like "it's the end of the world as we know it," you can still feel fine. Apart from reflecting life, music also provides a wonderful way to cope with stress. I know many people who listen to a number of specific songs when they feel unhappy or anxious. Of course, listening to music is just one way to cope, but these songs illustrate two major categories of coping with stress: you can cope by virtue of things you do as an individual that will vary with your personality and coping style (e.g., be optimistic or make the best of the situation) and you can cope by drawing on social networks for what you need to help you through the stressful situation (e.g., ask a friend to help you).

What Is Coping?

In this chapter I will review the major ways that we cope. **Coping** is defined as individual efforts made to manage distressing problems and emotions that affect the physical and psychological outcomes of stress (Somerfield & McCrae, 2000). If stress is a disturbance in homeostasis, coping is whatever we do to reestablish our homeostatic balances. Different factors can influence the severity of a stressor (termed moderators and mediators of stress) and influence coping as well. I will briefly summarize the most common ways of coping and also discuss different styles of coping across cultures. Given the central role of social support, we will spend some time getting a good feel for this powerful construct, highlighting how it varies across cultures.

Stress and coping research is one of the most exciting and most active areas in health psychology. I have already discussed the many different types of stress in chapter 4. As psychologists reached a better understanding of stress, research correspondingly studied how people coped with the stress. Given the impact stress can have on the mind and body, finding successful ways to cope is imperative. Unfortunately, finding the best ways to cope is not as easy as it may sound. Yes, you can observe people coping with various stressors and see which people get sick and which people do not. You can see who shows grace under pressure and who cracks. Finally you figure out why the successful people did not get sick or did not crack and there you have your answer. Oh, if only it were so simple.

There are two key issues. First, remember that people and situations vary a lot. What may work for one person may not work for another. Similarly, what works in one situation may not work well in another. If that is not enough variability, what works for one person in one situation may not work for another person in the same situation. Second, as human beings, we are tempted to look for direct causes of events. For example, we tend to think in very straightforward ways and believe that some factor, say personality, will directly lead to a certain outcome. If you are optimistic you will cope better and be less stressed. If you do not have a lot of social support, you will be more stressed and cope worse than if you had high social support. Although these statements are true in general, they greatly simplify the actual process of coping. A lot can influence what happens when you are stressed and what the result of your coping with the stressor will be.

To compensate for these two issues, that people and situations vary and that coping is a complex process, health psychologists consider a variety of factors surrounding stressful events. They measure different aspects of the person or organism coping to best account for individual differences in coping, and they also attempt to identify the different factors that influence the **coping process,** the process of reacting to a stressor and resulting in either a favorable (health and well-being) or unfavorable (sickness and unhappiness) outcome. These individual differences and the different factors that influence the process are referred to as moderators and mediators. As you will see, coping both moderates and mediates the relationship between stress and how you feel because of it. Getting a good feel for what these terms mean and how they are different from each other can be a challenge (nice primary appraisal), but I know you have the skill to do it (nice secondary appraisal).

Moderators versus Mediators

In life you will see that people who have a lot of a certain characteristic (are "high" on that variable) tend to behave and react differently than people who have a little of that characteristic (are "low" on that variable). The rich tend to be healthier than the poor. Older people tend to be more health conscious than younger people. People high in social support tend to cope better than people low in social support. In each of these cases the variables—income, age, and social support—are called moderators. A **moderator** is a variable that changes the magnitude (and sometimes the direction) of the relationship between an antecedent variable and an outcome variable. This is easier to understand in a picture. Look at Figure 5.1. In the example of social support, the number of stressors can

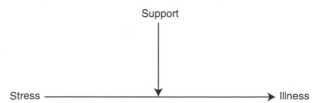

FIGURE 5.1
Moderation
People high in support show fewer negative effects when stressed than people low in support.

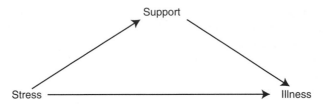

FIGURE 5.2
Mediation
Stress *makes* people activate their social support networks, which *then* influences how they feel. In this case social support is playing the role of a mediator.

be the antecedent variable and well-being is the outcome. A simple direct effect would be that people with more stressors are more unhappy (a positive correlation). However, as I said earlier, things are more complex than that. In any group of people, some people will have more social support than others. Let's measure social support and divide the people into a high support and a low support group. We would find that people with lots of support are happier than people with less social support (Cohen & Wills, 1985). Social support has moderated or buffered the relationship between stress and well-being.

Being high or low on some factor often moderates how we react to stress. In a nice laboratory demonstration of this effect, Roy, Steptoe, and Kirschbaum (1998) measured 90 young male firefighters' life events (within the past 12 months), social support, and cardiovascular responses to a variety of laboratory stressors. The researchers measured how long it took the men's blood pressure and heart rate to return to normal after they did some difficult math problems. Sure enough, the firefighters with more social support did not get as stressed as those with less social support in response to the stressful tasks and the high social support group showed faster recovery times from stress.

Coping is often what you do when you are stressed. What you do can either help or hurt. The response to a stressor and the factors that follow a stressor influence what the outcome is going to be. These responses and factors between the stressor and the outcome are called mediators. A **mediator** is the intervening process (variable) through which an antecedent variable influences an outcome variable. Coping behaviors in general and specific health behaviors are common mediators. Look at Figure 5.2. Instead of stress directly making you feel good or bad, it may influence your health behaviors (e.g., you sleep or eat more) that *in turn* influence whether you feel good or bad. Here, health behaviors have mediated the relationship (stress → mediated by health behaviors → health).

A large body of literature in health psychology concerns interventions aimed at improving well-being by enhancing coping, based on the assumption that the effectiveness of coping mediates the influence of stress on well-being (Coyne & Racioppo, 2000). As shown in Figure 5.3, it is easy to see whether mediation is taking place by comparing the correlation between the antecedent and outcome variables before and after the potential mediator is entered into the statistical

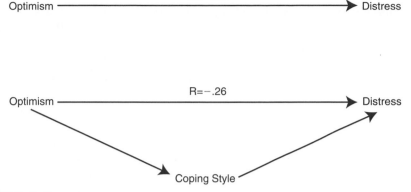

FIGURE 5.3

A Research Example of Coping

Optimism is directly related to distress as shown in the first relationship above. If you also consider coping style, you notice that optimism is related to coping style, which is related to distress. Once coping style is included in the analysis, the relationship between optimism and distress drops (Carver et al., 1993).

analysis. If the variable you are studying is a mediator, the relationship between the antecedent and outcome variable significantly changes (gets lower) once the mediator is in the analysis. If you are stressed and you take a nap, you will probably wake up feeling better. If you are stressed and you do not take a nap, you may feel worse. In this example sleep is said to mediate the relationship between your stress level and how you feel.

In an empirical example of mediation, Carver et al. (1993) tested whether coping mediated the relationship between optimism and well-being in a sample of 59 breast cancer patients. In their prospective study, they measured optimism, coping styles, and distress before surgery and 10 days, 3 months, 6 months, and 12 months after surgery. Optimism is a good quality to have, and when the researchers only looked at optimism and well-being, they found a strong positive relationship. The optimists were happier. After controlling for age, marital status, employment, education, stage of disease, and previous therapy, they found that even though optimism predicted happiness, this effect was due to how the optimistic women coped. Optimistic women tended to use more adaptive coping methods, and these more active coping strategies were what lessened their distress. Coping mediated the relationship. By looking for mediators, you get a clearer picture of the process that enables you to understand more clearly how distress can be changed. Figure 5.3 shows how the presence of coping mediated the relationship.

Although coping styles are most commonly discussed as a mediator of stress and well-being, other factors also mediate how one copes. For example, culture mediates coping styles. Bailey and Dua (1999) showed that some immigrant groups cope differently from others, and coping style can vary with acculturation and ethnic identity (discussed in chapter 3). Asian students moving to Australia showed high levels of perceived stress and tended to employ collectivist coping strategies more than any other group during their first 6 months away from home. Anglo Australians were lowest on measures of perceived stress and tended to use individualist coping styles. But an interesting thing happened. As the Asians became more Australian, they started using coping styles that were more similar to those of the other non-Asian Australians (Bailey & Dua, 1999).

Think about the different biopsychosocial variables we have discussed so far and see whether you can tell the difference between moderators and mediators. Most variables health psychologists study (e.g., coping styles and social support) can be both mediators and moderators. The role of the variable depends on the study (e.g., a cross-sectional study versus a prospective study), the statistical analyses used to test the variable, the situation, or the variable under study. As a rule, mediators are changed by the stressor and correspondingly change the outcome. If more stress leads to your asking for more social support, which leads to your feeling better, social support is a mediator. If a longitudinal study shows that those with more stress exercise more and this makes them feel better, then exercise is a mediator. If a correlational study shows that the group of people who exercise more are less distressed than a similar group of stressed individuals who exercise less, then exercise is moderator. In the first case (mediation) exercise follows the stressor, changing in level and influencing the outcome. In the second case (moderation), we are looking at two separate groups of exercisers. The only variables that cannot be both mediators and moderators are those that cannot change as a function of the stressor or antecedent variable. Age, ethnicity, and race are examples of moderators that cannot be mediators (e.g., being more stressed cannot change your race).

Coping Styles and Strategies

Coping includes anything people do to manage problems or emotional responses, whether successful or not (Carver & Scheier, 1994; Lazarus & Folkman, 1984; Pearlin & Schooler, 1978). We have both coping styles and coping strategies. **Coping styles** are general predispositions to dealing with stress. Similar to personality traits, coping styles are tools a person tends to use over and over again. The two most basic styles are **approach coping** and **avoidant coping.** An individual can approach a stressor and make active efforts to resolve it or try to avoid the problem (Moos & Schaefer, 1993). Many terms are used in studies of these two basic styles as shown in Table 5.1.

Coping strategies refer to the specific behavioral and psychological efforts that people use to master, tolerate, reduce, or minimize stressful events (Lazarus & Launier, 1978). Even though coping can refer to many different behaviors, it is easy to identify some main types of coping. You can either do something about the problem or you can ignore it. Researchers have particularly distinguished between problem-focused or emotion-focused coping strategies.

Problem-focused coping involves directly facing the stressful situation and working hard to resolve it. For example, if you have a demanding, aggressive boss

---

TABLE 5.1

Coping Styles

Approach	Avoidance	Reference
Monitoring	Blunting	Miller (1987)
Vigilance	Cognitive avoidance	Krohne (1993)
Problem-focused	Emotion-focused + appraisal-focused	Billings and Moos (1984)

---

at work, you may experience a lot of stress at your job. If you report the issue to your human resources department or have a direct conversation with your boss, you are taking concrete action to deal with the situation and following a problem-focused approach.

Sometimes the first thing you do is deal with the emotions surrounding the stressor. A person finding out that he or she is HIV positive or has test results showing cancer may experience a surge of fear and anxiety and is driven to cope with these feelings. The person may deny the test results or not want to talk about them for some time. This strategy of coping is referred to as **emotion-focused coping** because you use either mental or behavioral methods to deal with the feelings resulting from the stress. More often than not, problem-focused and emotion-focused styles are pitted against each other. Although conceptually distinct, both strategies are interdependent and work together, with one supplementing the other in the overall coping process (Lazarus, 2000; Tennen, Affleck, Armeli, & Carney, 2000).

What Is the Best Way to Cope?

One of these styles looks better than the other. In general, people who rely primarily on approach coping adapt better to life stressors and experience less negative affect than those who make use of avoidant coping (Aspinwall & Taylor, 1992; Folkman, Lazarus, Gruen, & DeLongis, 1986). A large body of work demonstrates the deleterious emotional impact of avoidant coping in a variety of populations (e.g., Aldwin & Revenson, 1987; Fleishman & Fogel, 1994; Stanton & Snider, 1993). Avoiding paying taxes can only cause more stress as you rush to complete the form at the last moment or face the consequences of being late. Waiting until the last moment to study actually makes those last moments even more stressful. Sure, not thinking about taxes until April 14 or not about the exam until the night before may seem like you are gaining some carefree days, but your avoidance has only accentuated your stress. Furthermore, the benefits from avoidance may be fewer than you think. In some samples, avoidance may exacerbate emotional distress. Ironically, people often become preoccupied with the thoughts that they attempt to suppress, and the inhibition of thoughts, feelings, and behaviors can cause physiological arousal (cf. Lobel, Yali, Zhu, & DeVincent, 1998). Also, the use of avoidant coping requires sustained effort to screen out stressor-relevant thoughts. If you do not want to think of the test that you have not studied for or the work assignment that you have not started on, a part of your cognitive processes are making sure that you are not thinking of the troubling aspect. You are using some mental energy just to make sure you do not think about something that troubles you.

It sounds like avoidant, emotion-focused coping may not be the best style, so is approach problem-solving coping the best? There is no real "best in show," "acme," or "voted number one" coping style. The situation is an important consideration. The style to use depends on the severity, duration, controllability, and emotionality of the situation (Aldwin, 1994; Auerbach, 1989). Even when you consider the type of situation, it is critical to be specific about it. People may want to know the best way to cope with breast cancer or diabetes. You may want to know the best way to cope with the loss of a loved one. Just referring to breast cancer or diabetes in general may not be as helpful as discussing coping with different stages of breast cancer or different problems areas of diabetes such as managing episodes of hypoglycemia (Maes, Leventhal, & de Ridder, 1996).

There is over-reliance on the "problem-focused coping is good, emotion-focused coping is bad" dichotomy. This can be dangerous because sometimes using the seemingly better problem-focused coping style can be associated with poorer psychological outcomes (Bolger, 1990; Coyne & Gottlieb, 1996). It is sometimes hard to define what style of coping a certain behavior is. Coyne and Racioppo (2000) use the example of "seeking social support." Seeking social support can be either problem- or emotion-focused coping, and its success depends on the timing and circumstances of the seeking, how, what, and from whom the support is sought, and the actions to which support seeking refers. For example, wanting your doctor to spend more time with you to tell you about a diagnosis is a form of seeking support that gives you emotional support and information on how to deal with the issue.

It is essentially best to match the type of coping you use with the situation and with your comfort level. If you work in a hospital and you are stressed by how many hours you work and how many patients you see, you have some control over the situation. Finding a way to be scheduled for better hours is a problem-focused way to cope. In the short term, avoidant, emotion-focused coping may be beneficial because this coping style gives your body time to recover from the shock of and physiological responses to the stressor. If you were diagnosed with cancer and you are so anxious that you cannot function, it may be better to be emotion-focused and first cope with your emotions and ignore the issue because it stresses you. At some point, however, you must face the problem, get more information about it, and learn what you should do to deal with it.

Who Copes Well?

Some people cope with stress by buying and consuming a pint (or a gallon!) of their favorite ice cream. Others go for a fast run. Still others sleep extra hours and do not eat. You may have some friends or coworkers who are not fazed even when everything seems to be going wrong. Other individuals fall apart and get "freaked out" by the most minor negative events. As you read in chapter 4, how a person appraises an event can determine the extent to which that person thinks it

© K. Beebee/Custom Medical Stock Photo

Indulgence One way of coping is to indulge in something that you know is not great for you. Too much snack food and watching television all night is bad for your health, but it seems so soothing when we are stressed.

is stressful. According to Lazarus and Folkman's (1984) framework, cognitive appraisals and coping are two critical mediators of responses to stressful events. A person's subjective perception of stress will depend on the objective features of the situation (e.g., potentially stressful life events) and the way that person appraises the events. Your feeling of stress depends both on how many things you really have due and on how serious or demanding you think the assignments or deadlines are. Even if you do not really have too much to do, just believing that you have too much to do or that what you have to do is very difficult can be stressful. A person experiences distress when primary appraisals of threat exceed secondary appraisals of coping ability (Folkman, Lazarus, Gruen, & DeLongis, 1986). One's secondary appraisal will depend in large part on the personal resources a person brings to the situation, such as personality factors (e.g., optimism) and perceived resources for coping with the situation. Many factors influence how someone appraises a situation and correspondingly copes with stress. In this section, we will examine some of the factors that influence appraisals and coping and make the difference between weathering the storm and falling to pieces.

Personality and Coping

A person's personality characteristics provide some of the best clues as to how they will cope with a stressor (Cosway, Endler, Sadler, & Deary, 2000; Penley & Tomaka, 2002). **Personality** is defined as an individual's unique set of consistent behavioral traits, where traits are durable dispositions to behave in a particular way in a variety of situations. When you described yourself in the "Who am I?" task in chapter 1, you probably used a number of trait terms to describe yourself (e.g., honest, dependable, funny, or social). One of the earliest personality psychologists, Gordon Allport (1961), scoured an unabridged dictionary and collected more than 4,500 descriptors used to describe personality. Later personality theorists such as Cattell (1966) used statistical analyses to measure correlations between these different descriptors. Cattell found that all 4,500 descriptors can be encompassed by just 16 terms. It gets better. McCrae and Costa (1987) further narrowed these 16 terms down to a core of only 5 as part of their five-factor model of personality. Often referred to as the "Big Five," a wealth of research suggests that personality can be sufficiently measured by assessing how conscientious, agreeable, neurotic, open to experience, and extraverted a person is (John & Srivastava, 1999; Wiggins & Trapnell, 1997). For an easy way to remember them, I like to use the acronym CANOE or try OCEAN if you are live on the coast). Clear definitions and examples of each trait are listed in Table 5.2.

The Type A behavior pattern was perhaps the first and most controversial aspect of personality that was thought to relate to stress and coping. The cardiologists Friedman and Rosenman (1959, 1974) identified the **Type A coronary-prone behavior pattern** based on their observations of heart patients who showed a sense of time urgency (always doing more than one thing at the same time), competitiveness, and hostility in their interactions with other people. People with this constellation of personality characteristics were found to have a higher risk for coronary heart disease and stress. Early interventions helped such individuals

TABLE 5.2	
The Big Five Personality Traits	
Trait	Characteristics
Conscientiousness	Ethical, dependable, productive, purposeful
Agreeableness	Sympathetic, warm, trusting, cooperative
Neuroticism	Anxious, insecure, guilt-prone, self-conscious
Openness to experience	Daring, nonconforming, imaginative
Extraversion	Talkative, sociable, fun-loving, affectionate

cope better. There were problems replicating Friedman and Rosenman's hypothesized link between cardiovascular disease and Type A personality, and it later became clear that the critical personality risk factor was hostility (Dembrowski, MacDougall, Williams, Haney, & Blumenthal, 1985). Hostility was the component that reliably predicted heart attacks. Having a sense of time urgency and being competitive is all right, but being hostile is most dangerous to your health. Remember that the next time you feel like snapping at someone or giving in to traffic road rage.

Does it follow then that people with different personalities will use different methods to cope with stress? For the most part this is true. It is probably no surprise that some personality types use different coping styles than others, and empirical tests mostly confirm this assumption. For example, in a study of 298 outpatients with depression, those patients with less-adaptive coping strategies (i.e., emotion-focused coping) had less-adaptive personality traits (i.e., neuroticism) and were more depressed. The reverse was found for adaptive problem-focused coping strategies (McWilliams, Cox, & Enns, 2003). In another study, neuroticism was highly related to avoidant coping, agreeableness was negatively related to problem-focused coping, and conscientiousness was positively related to problem-focused coping and negatively related to avoidant coping (McCormick, Dowd, Quirk, & Zegarra, 1998). Clearly, personality styles can predict what coping style a person is likely to use, but there is not always a direct relationship.

One thing to keep in mind is that coping styles are not merely reflections of personality but mediate the relationship between personality and well-being. So although having a high level of optimism or a low level of neuroticism is associated with feeling less stressed in general, people with these personality characteristics are more likely to use more adaptive coping styles and hence decrease their stress. A study of college students illustrates this process. The students completed measures of perceived stress, social support, optimism, and coping in their first semester of college. The optimists had smaller increases in stress and depression over the course of the first semester of college, but mediational analyses showed that the optimists were more likely to use adaptive coping styles, such as positive reinterpretation and growth (Brissette, Scheier, & Carver, 2002). So the personality style led to the favoring of a specific coping style, which then influenced well-being. The personality style did not directly influence the outcome. Similarly, knowing the coping styles of heart failure patients in addition to just knowing their personalities enabled researchers to better predict their depression (Murberg, Bru, & Stephens, 2002). Again, coping style mediated the relationship between personality and well-being.

Beyond these core aspects of personality, people vary on a number of other characteristics that can influence their coping. For example, health psychologists suggest that we pay close attention to the concepts of optimism, mastery, hardiness, and resilience.

Optimism refers to generalized outcome expectancies that good things, rather than bad things, will happen (Carver & Scheier, 1999; Carver, Scheier, & Weintraub, 1989). Optimists are the people who can always find the positive aspects of any situation and always seem to look on the bright side of life no matter how bad things are. This personality trait is associated with a number of health-related factors. Optimists tend to cope better with stress and practice better health behaviors (Scheier et al., 1989; Taylor, Kemeny, Aspinwall, Schneider, Rodriguez, & Herbert, 1992). Optimism is strongly and positively correlated with problem-focused coping strategies and strongly negatively correlated with avoidant coping strategies (Scheier, Weintraub, & Carver, 1986). Optimists, in general, show good psychological well-being (Armor & Taylor, 1998), suggesting that optimism may moderate depression. Optimism relates to the presence of active potent natural killer cells during stress (Segerstrom, Taylor, Kemeny, & Fahey, 1998) and serves as protection against HIV exposure by decreasing intentions to engage in unsafe sex (Carvajal, Garner, & Evans, 1998). Measures of AIDS-related optimism have been related to a slower disease course (Taylor, Kemeny, Reed, Bower, & Gruenewald, 2000). Optimists differ significantly from pessimists in secondary (but not primary) appraisal, coping, and adjustment. In addition, knowing a person's level of optimism adds significantly to predictions of that person's adjustment, beyond what was accounted for by knowing about how the person makes appraisals and copes (Chang, 1998).

Mastery is a relatively stable tendency of an individual and another variable that can influence the appraisal of stress and help people cope (Dweck & Sorich, 1999). Mastery is defined as the extent to which one regards one's life chances as being under one's own control (Pearlin & Schooler, 1978, p. 5). Someone with a high level of mastery believes that he or she has the capability to succeed at whatever task is at hand. Conceptually similar to perceived control, locus of control, and self-efficacy, mastery has proved useful in many studies of stress and appraisal (Cox & Ferguson, 1991; Frone, Russell, & Cooper, 1995; Herman-Stahl & Petersen, 1996; Pearlin & Skaff, 1995; Skaff, Pearlin, & Mullan, 1996; Wallston, 1992). For example, Hemenover and Dienstbier (1996) showed that mastery predicted stress appraisals for an intellectual task in a group of college students in various situations, including academic stressors. Students with high levels of mastery reported lower levels of stress. Similarly, Aldwin, Sutton, and Lachman (1996) demonstrated a strong relationship between mastery, coping, depression, and stress in three studies using large community samples. Again, people high in mastery coped better and were less depressed in the face of stress than people with low levels of mastery. In the realm of parent-child interactions, feelings of mastery among parents improve their coping with stressful events and have indirect beneficial effects on their children, teaching them to develop a sense of control by striving to confront stressful events actively (Rogers, Parcel, & Menaghan, 1991). The effects of mastery also vary by age. Ben-Zur (2002) measured the coping styles and mastery levels of 168 young and old community residents and found that older people with elevated feelings of mastery used more efficient coping strategies.

Two other personality characteristics that moderate the effects of stress and aid coping are hardiness and resilience. People who are strongly committed to their lives, enjoy challenges, and have a high level of control over their lives are high on the trait of **hardiness** (Maddi & Kobasa, 1991). In general, being hardy is related to better adjustment to a range of health issues (Kobasa, Maddi, & Kahn, 1982; Pollack, 1986). Resilience closely relates to hardiness. If you see a person who has encountered a tremendous number of stressful events but always seems to bounce back into action and still do fine, he or she is said to be resilient. Like hardiness, resiliency accompanies adaptive coping strategies that lead to better mental and physical health. Although early studies of this concept were conducted with children, there is now a wealth of research on resilience across the life course (see Ryff & Singer, 2003a, 2003b, for reviews).

Social Support

How we cope with stress often is influenced by how much support we receive from others around us. Even more importantly, just the perception that support would be available if we need it can greatly enhance our coping strategies. Not surprisingly then, social support is one of the most important factors in the study of stress and coping.

The sociologist Durkheim (1897/1951) first provided empirical evidence of the importance of social support and showed that a lack of social relationships increased the probability of a person committing suicide. The connections of social support to health were strengthened by the work of Cassel (1976) and Cobb (1976) who demonstrated that the "presence of other members of the same species" was a critical ingredient to good health. This social support–health connection was supported later by the now classic 9-year epidemiological study done in Alameda County, CA, where men and women who were socially integrated lived longer (Berkman, 1985; Berkman & Syme, 1979). In fact, the age-adjusted

Support Network Our social networks, friends, and colleagues can be a major source of social support.

relative risk for mortality for the men and women with weak social connections (e.g., marriage, contact with family members and close friends, and memberships in religious and volunteer organizations) was almost twice as high as the risk for the participants with strong social connections.

The evidence showing the usefulness of social support is astounding. **Social support,** generally defined as emotional, informational, or instrumental assistance from others (Dunkel-Schetter & Bennett, 1990), has been tied to better health, more rapid recovery from illness, and a lower risk for mortality (House, Umberson, & Landis, 1988; Sarason, Sarason, & Gurung, 2001; Uchino, Cacioppo, & Kiecolt-Glaser, 1996). Social support also reduces psychological distress during stress (Cohen & Wills, 1985; Fleming, Baum, Gisriel, & Gatchel, 1982). Epidemiological studies document increased risk for depression among people who lack social support (George, 1989; Stanfeld, Rael, Head, Shipley, & Marmot, 1997). Studies of people with HIV infection suggest that social support from peers is critical for emotional well-being and, in periods of crisis, family support may become an especially important determinant of emotional well-being (Crystal & Kersting, 1998; Miller & Cole, 1998).

Types of Social Support

Beware of loose definitions! The statement, "social support is helpful," is really too general to be practical. Social support undoubtedly is an effective aid to health and coping with stress. However, the majority of research findings available mask an important fact: there are many different types of social support. Table 5.3 provides an overview of the main ways in which social support can differ. The most basic division is between **network measures** and **functional measures.** The earliest research looked at a person's networks (e.g., Berkman, 1985), asking whether the person was married or not or asking how many people the person saw on a weekly basis. The measurement of networks also varied. Some researchers just asked for the number of people in a network whereas others also assessed the relationship of the support provider to the support recipient.

Even greater variety exists in the functional measures of support. Functional support is assessed in two main ways. You can measure the social support the person reports was provided to him or her, called **received support,** or the social support the person believes to be available to him or her, called **perceived support.** These two forms of support vary further in the function that they serve. If you think about when you are stressed, the type of support that you get and that will be helpful will depend to a large extent on the type of stress you are experiencing. If you are stressed because you have a big assignment due at school, but you do not even know how to begin, any information that you obtain about how to do it will be helpful. If you are stressed because your car broke down and you do not know how you will go to work, then someone giving you a ride will best help you cope. If someone close to you passes away or you have trouble in a close relationship, people who show you that you are esteemed, loved, and cared for will be the most supportive. These are the three main types of received support, and each has its counterpart form of perceived support. Received or perceived support can be (1) instrumental (also called tangible or material support, e.g., the loan of the car),

---

TABLE 5.3

Main Forms of Social Support and How It Can Be Measured

I. Networks	Structure and existence of social relationships
	Frequency contacts; composition (who-friend, family, coworker)?
	Perceived: If something happens you will get help (if needed it will be there)
	Are you loved, valued and esteemed?
	Satisfaction: Was what you got enough?
	Received: When something happened, how much did you get?
II. Sources	Relationship partner, family, friends, fellow workers, doctors, nurses.
III. Types	*Emotional:* Empathy, caring, concern.
	Esteem: Confidence building, encouragement.
	Instrumental/Tangible: Direct assistance, cash, etc.
	Informational: Advice, directions, feedback.
IV. Specificity	*Global* (for stressor and source, e.g., all stressors or from everyone?).
	Specific (for this event *or* in this relationship?).
	Time: Over last year, last month, last week.

(2) informational (or advice, e.g., how to do your assignment), and (3) emotional (e.g., being told that people care for you).

Other distinctions become important in the measurement of support and are essential to maximizing its predictor power. For example, you can measure global support, a person's sense of support from people in general or specific support, support from a specific person or relationship. The recipient or perceiver's satisfaction with social support can be studied. Finally, you can create categories by focusing on who is providing the support, the source of support (e.g., spouse, family, friends, doctors, or medical staff). These different categories can fit into a hierarchy with the general approach (received or perceived) as the primary dimension (Table 5.3). Within each of these, the source of support can be distinguished, and finally, different types or functions of support can be embedded within each source (Schwarzer, Dunkel-Schetter, & Kemeny, 1994). The most effective and theoretically compelling model combines received and perceived support measures but separates them by source (Dunkel-Schetter, Gurung, Lobel, & Wadhwa, 2001).

The way support is measured in a study can also influence the types of effects it can show. Social support is a moderator when you measure perceived support. People who are stressed and high in perceived support do better than people who are stressed and low in perceived support. Evidence for a **direct effect** is found when the support measure assesses a person's degree of integration in a large social network. Across the board, having more friends and better connected networks is beneficial whether you are stressed or not. Both conceptualizations of social support are correct in some respects, but each represents a different process through which social support may affect well-being (Cohen & Wills, 1985).

A study of social support provided during pregnancy provides an example of how different forms of social support can be studied. The major comparison is between support transactions at the level of a couple or dyad (e.g., support provided to the baby's mother from the baby's father) versus at the level of a network or group (e.g., support provided by friends and family). Another set of studies focused on the impact of support from professional sources (e.g., nurses and doctors) (Blondel, 1998). How do the effects of support from these three different sources compare? In a study designed to answer this question, Gurung, Dunkel-Schetter, Colins, Rini, & Hobel (2005) compared the support a woman received from her baby's father with the support received from her friends and family. The ethnically diverse sample consisted of 480 women (African American, Latin American, and non-Hispanic White). Various types of support measures were assessed at multiple time points before the birth, together with standard measures of depression and anxiety. Different sources of support were associated with different outcomes. Specifically, social support from the baby's father predicted significantly less anxiety but not significant differences in depressed mood. Support from the mother's friends and family was a significant predictor of the mother's depressed mood but did not predict her anxiety (cf. Kalil Gruber, Conley, & Sytniac, 1993). Social support from the baby's father predicted maternal changes in anxiety independent of sociodemographic variables such as age, ethnicity, and socioeconomic status and individual difference measures such as mastery and coping. This difference in support effects by source is consistent with the theory and some results in the social support literature showing that support is most effective when the type of support a person needs matches the type of support provided (e.g., Cutrona, 1990). Others discuss the existence of an optimal support provider for different specific needs (Cantor, 1979; Litwak, 1985).

Cultural Variables in Social Support

Culture shapes beliefs about health and illness and provides the context by which an individual evaluates his or her situation and decides whether he or she needs social support and how much. Not surprisingly, strong cultural differences exist in social support (Burleson & Mortenson, 2003; Norris, Murphy, Kaniasty, Perilla, & Ortis, 2001; Goodwin & Giles, 2003; Hyun et al., 2002; Taylor, Sherman, Kim, Jarcho, Takagi, & Dunagan, 2004).

How about a truly different sample example for a change? Pines, Ben-Ari, Utaso, and Larson (2002) studied what predicted burnout and asked Israeli, Israeli Arab, Hungarian, and North Americans to rate the importance of six types of social support and to indicate the extent to which each was available to them in their lives. Results showed both universal and culture-specific effects. From a universal viewpoint, respondents in all four countries viewed the six forms of support as very important, but burnout was correlated more with the availability of support than with its importance. Respondents felt burnout if support was not available. Different types of social support had different importance and availability ratings and different correlations with burnout in the four countries.

Gender is one of the most robust predictors of use of social support (Taylor et al., 2000; Unger, McAvay, Bruce, Berkman, & Seeman, 1999). Women receive and give more support over the life course (e.g., Rook & Schuster, 1996), and women experience greater benefits from social network interactions (see Antonucci & Akiyama, 1987; Berkman, Vaccarino, & Seeman, 1993; Flaherty & Rich-

Social Support among Women Women often turn to other women for social support and to share their emotions.

man, 1989; Shumaker & Hill, 1991, for reviews). Some studies have shown that for men, friendships and nonfamily activities decline with age, whereas women's friendships outside the home do not change (Field, 1999).

Strong gender differences exist in social support. Luckow, Reifman, and McIntosh (1998) analyzed gender differences in coping and found that the largest difference arose in seeking and using social support. Of the 26 studies that tested for gender differences, one study showed no differences and 25 favored women. None of the studies favored men (Luckow et al., 1998). Indeed, so reliable is this gender effect that, following the early studies on affiliation in response to stress by Schachter (1959), most subsequent research on affiliation under stress used only female participants.

Across the entire life cycle, females are more likely to mobilize social support, especially from other females, in times of stress. They seek it out more, they receive more support, and they are more satisfied with the support they receive. Adolescent girls report more informal sources of support than do boys, and girls are more likely turn to their same-sex peers for support than are boys (e.g., Copeland & Hess, 1995; see Belle, 1989, for a review). Female college students report having more available helpers and receiving more support than males do (e.g., Ptacek, Smith, & Zanas, 1992; see Belle, 1989, for a review). Adult women maintain more same-sex close relationships, mobilize more social support in times of stress, rely less heavily on their spouses for social support, turn to female friends more often, report more benefits from contact with their female friends and relatives (although they are also more vulnerable to network events as a cause of psychological distress), and provide more frequent and more effective social support to others than men (Belle, 1989; McDonald & Korabik, 1991; Ogus, Greenglass, & Burke, 1990; Taylor et al., 2000). Although females give help to both males and females in their support networks, they are more likely to seek help and social support from other female relatives and female friends than from males (Belle, 1989; Wethington, McLeod, & Kessler, 1987).

Women are also more engaged in their social networks. They are significantly better at sharing what is going on in their networks than men. For example, a woman is more likely to discuss the major illnesses of her children with others and is more likely to report being involved if there is a crisis event in the network (Wethington et al., 1987). In an extensive study of social networks, Veroff, Kulka, and Douvan (1981) reported that women were 30% more likely than men to have provided some type of support in response to network stressors, including economic and work-related difficulties, interpersonal problems, death, and negative health events. Gender also affects social support receipt: Men receive emotional support primarily from their spouses, whereas women draw more heavily on their friends and relatives and children for emotional support (Gurung, Taylor, & Seeman, 2003).

So consistent and strong are these findings that theorists have argued for basic gender differences in orientation toward others, with women maintaining a collectivist orientation (Markus & Kitayama, 1991) or connectedness (Clancy & Dollinger, 1993; Niedenthal & Beike, 1997; Kashima et al., 1995) and men maintaining a more individualistic orientation (Cross & Madson, 1997). These findings appear to generalize across cultures. In their study of 6 cultures, Whiting and Whiting (1975) found that women and girls seek more help from others and give more help to others than men do, and Edwards (1993) found similar sex differences across 12 cultures.

Let's go back to social support in pregnancy to highlight some more specific cultural differences. Studies of ethnic minority groups in the United States show that for some groups (e.g., African Americans and Latinas), the family, particularly female relatives, are a critical source of support in pregnancy (Knouse, 1991; Zuniga, 1992). Mexican American families tend to live in close units with tight bonds to other family units and with the extended family serving as the primary source of support (Chilman, 1993; Keefe, Padilla, & Carlos, 1979). Similarly, the family is the most important source of support to African Americans (Cauce, Felner, & Primavera, 1982; Miller, 1992). In one of the most cited studies of ethnic differences in support, Norbeck and Anderson (1989) measured life stress, social support, anxiety state, and substance use at mid- and late pregnancy in Hispanic, European American, and African American low-income women. This study found that none of the social support measures was a significant predictor of gestational age, birth weight, or gestation and labor complications when the sample was analyzed as a whole. However, for African American women, lack of social support from the woman's partner or mother was a significant predictor of gestational complications and of the likelihood of prolonged labor and cesarean section complications. For European Americans, social support was significantly related to length of labor and to drug use. None of the support measures was a statistically significant predictor of complications or birth outcomes for the Hispanics. Analyzing ethnic groups separately has yielded similar differences in social support in a number of other studies and samples (e.g., Gurung, Dunkel-Schetter, Collins, Rini, & Hobol, 2005; Gurung, Taylor, Kemeny, & Myers, 2004).

In a direct test of ethnic differences in social support, Sagrestano, Feldman, Rini, Woo, and Dunkel-Schetter (2000) analyzed data from two multiethnic prospective studies of African American, Latina, and non-Hispanic White pregnant women and found strong ethnic differences in support from family and friends. Statistical analyses that simultaneously included multiple variables assessing ethnic differences while controlling for sociodemographic variables showed that African American women reported receiving the most support from family. Latinas and European American women reported receiving support from the next levels. However, White women reported more family members in their social networks than did Latinas. Furthermore, Latinas reported higher-quality interactions with family. Similar differences in the context of coping with a natural disaster can be seen in Norris et al. (2001).

Theories of Social Support Change

How do our social networks change over time? Are you still friends with the people you were friends with when you were in grade school? Do you call the same people for help today as you did 10 years ago? There are two main theories of how our networks change (Gurung & Von Dras, in press). The **social convoy model** (Antonucci, 1991) provides a conceptual framework for studying age-related changes in structural and compositional characteristics of social networks (Figure 5.4). This model suggests that people are motivated to maintain their social network sizes as they themselves age, despite changes in the composition of the networks. Individuals construct and maintain social relationships while becoming increasingly aware of specific strengths and weaknesses of particular members. This knowledge allows them to select different network members for different functions (e.g., certain people are relied on for emotional support and others for instrumental support) and possibly avoid members who are not supportive. Empirical support for the model (Kahn & Antonucci, 1984) clearly identifies the importance of simultaneously looking at different sources when studying changes in age-related social support. Although specific nonsupportive network members may drop out over time, the social convoy model suggests that general levels of support will be constant or even increase, given that social support is coordinated to optimize support receipt. We work to make sure we get the most out of our networks and that our networks contain those who will give us what we need.

Socioemotional selectivity theory (Carstensen, 1987; Carstensen & Fisher, 1991) proposes that people prune their social networks to maintain a desired emotional state depending on the extent to which time is perceived as limited. Basic functions of social interaction, such as maintaining a good mood, differ in respect to their relative importance for determining social preferences across the lifespan. When we get older, we believe that we have less time and want to maximize the time we have. We do not want to waste time on people or things that are not worth it. Emphasis in old age is placed on achieving short-term emotional

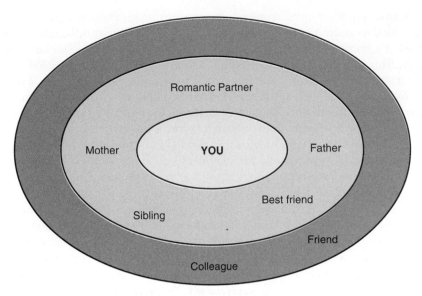

FIGURE 5.4
A Social Convoy
You are in the center, the people closest to you are in the first circle, and the people not as close are in the outer circles. As we age we should maintain our convoy to keep emotionally healthy.

goals. Correspondingly, whereas older adults' social networks may be smaller than those of younger adults, the numbers of close relationships are comparable (Lang & Carstensen, 1998). Lang and Carstensen (1994) examined the interrelationships among age, network composition, and social support in a representative sample of 156 community-dwelling and institutionalized adults aged 70 to 104 years and found that the social networks of older people were only half as large as those of younger people, but the number of very close relationships did not differ across age groups.

Both theories have empirical evidence supporting them (Antonucci & Akiyama, 1995; Carstensen, Isaacowitz, & Charles, 1999; Lansford, Sherman, & Antonucci, 1998). The evidence indicates that it is not necessarily the size, membership, or particular structure of the network, but the quality of transactions (i.e., perceived and received social support) that is critical to mental and physical health.

Is there clear evidence of whether support increases or decreases in time? Using longitudinal, community-based data from the MacArthur Studies of Successful Aging, Gurung et al. (2003) examined determinants of changes in social support receipt among 439 married older adults. Men and women in the sample were surveyed over a period of 6 years, and support received was assessed at the beginning and end of the study. In general, social support increased over time, especially for those with many preexisting social ties, but those experiencing more psychological distress and cognitive dysfunction reported more negative encounters with others.

One last point on social support. At the start of this chapter I mentioned that there are many individual differences in coping. This is true for social support as well. We are active managers of our social networks and play a role in determining how much support we get. In addition to experiencing changes in who we have in our networks due to nonelective events such as death of network members, people differ in their propensity to prune or augment their own networks and in their likelihood of being pruned from or added to others' networks. Referred to in the support literature as "evocative qualities," personal characteristics may be critical determinants of whether support transactions increase or decrease over time (Pierce, Lakey, Sarason, & Sarason, 1997).

Common Measures of Coping

Can specific styles of coping be identified across individuals and settings? Although there are not necessarily a "big five" of coping as there are for personality, people cope in some clear-cut ways. Each of the two main styles discussed previously, problem-focused and emotion-focused coping, have many separate subcomponents, each of which can be assessed by questionnaires. Two of the most commonly used measures are the Ways of Coping Questionnaire (WCQ) (Folkman & Lazarus, 1988) and the COPE (Carver et al., 1989).

Ways of Coping Questionnaire

The WCQ first started as the Ways of Coping Checklist (WCC) (Aldwin, Folkman, Schaefer, Coyne, & Lazarus, 1980). Devised from a pool of 68 items with a yes-no response format, the original checklist yielded two main factors with the majority (40) of the items forming a problem-solving subscale and the rest an emotion-focused subscale. Over time the use of the scale with different populations yielded varying numbers of major factors. The current version of the WCQ consists of 50 items with 16 filler items and has a 4-point Likert rating scale for responses. Scientists ask participants to think of a real-life stressor (e.g., a conflict at work) and respond to each question. The WCQ has 8 different subscales reflecting problem-focused and emotion-focused coping:

1. Confrontive Coping (e.g., I stood my ground and fought for what I wanted)
2. Distancing (e.g., I went on as if nothing had happened)
3. Self-Controlling (e.g., I tried to keep my feelings to myself)
4. Seeking Social Support (e.g., I talked to someone to find out more about the situation)
5. Accepting Responsibility (e.g., I criticized or lectured myself)
6. Escape Avoidance (e.g., I hoped a miracle would happen)
7. Planful Problem Solving (e.g., I made a plan of action and followed it)
8. Positive Reappraisal (e.g., I changed or grew as a person in a good way).

As you can tell, using one of these coping styles (e.g., seeking support) can automatically involve using another one (e.g., problem solving). This is not something theoretically controlled for with this measure and has been cited as one of its major problems (Schwarzer & Schwarzer, 1996). Different researchers have adapted the WCQ to directly correspond to specific stressors. For example, Dunkel-Schetter, Feinstein, Taylor, and Falke (1992) rewrote the WCQ to measure how patients coped with cancer.

The COPE

In contrast to the WCQ whose subscales were devised using primarily empirical methods (e.g., factor analysis), Carver et al. (1989) used a rational scale construction procedure. They first created different subscales (versus using statistical procedures to determine the subscales) and tested them on a sample of 978 undergraduates. Furthermore, instead of asking for coping responses to a specific stressor, the students were asked what they usually do when they are experiencing considerable stress. This procedure yielded the **COPE** inventory (Carver et al., 1989) containing 13 scales with 4 items each. The main subscales representing different forms of problem-focused and emotion-focused coping are the following:

1. Active Coping (e.g., I do what has to be done, one step at a time)
2. Planning (e.g., I make a plan of action)
3. Suppression of Competing Activities (e.g., I put aside other activities to concentrate on this)
4. Restraint Coping (e.g., I force myself to wait for the right time to do something)
5. Seeking Social Support for Instrumental Reasons (e.g., I talk to someone to find out more about the situation)
6. Seeking Social Support for Emotional Reasons (e.g., I talk to someone about how I feel)
7. Positive Reinterpretation and Growth (e.g., I learn something from the experience)
8. Acceptance (e.g., I learn to live with it)
9. Turning to Religion (e.g., I put my trust in God)
10. Focus and Venting of Emotions (e.g., I let my feelings out)
11. Denial (e.g., I refuse to believe that it has happened)
12. Behavioral Disengagement (e.g., I just give up trying to reach my goal)
13. Mental Disengagement (e.g., I daydream about things other than this)

Later versions included additional items relating to the use of humor and alcohol as coping mechanisms. Notice that the COPE has separate subscales for different types of social support seeking: problem-focused and emotion-focused support seeking. Five of the above subscales were designed to encompass each main style (problem-focused or emotion-focused), but this design was not supported by statistical analyses (Zeidner & Hammer, 1992).

Other measures of coping, including scales by Amirkhan (1990) and McCrae (1984), are variations on the WCQ and the COPE. Many of these scales are targeted for special populations, such as the Life Events and Coping Inventory for Children (Dise-Lewis, 1988), the Adolescent Coping Orientation for Problem Experiences Inventory (Patterson & McCubbin, 1987), and the Life Situations Inventory (Feifel & Strack, 1989), which is aimed at assessing coping with real-life circumstances in middle-aged and elderly men.

Be warned, some researchers lament the overuse of coping instruments (e.g., Coyne & Racioppo, 2000), and others report few consistent positive associations between the use of any particular coping style and positive outcomes (Coyne & Gottlieb, 1996; Watson & Hubbard, 1996). The main problem seems to be that some of the questions are too general, and researchers tend to utilize one standard measure across many different situations, thereby ignoring the unique aspects of different stressors. In addition, the summary scores achieved by adding together the responses to the different questions on the scales dilute and omit important information such as timing, sequencing, and appropriateness of a specific behavior (Coyne & Racioppo, 2000). Finally, many of the coping styles are closely related to personality characteristics and also correlate strongly with distress, both variables that serve to confound coping results. These problems notwithstanding, the coping scales allow health psychologists to study large numbers of people using limited time and money and allow for a quantification of the coping process (Lazarus, 2000). To compensate for some of the problems of scale measures, most contemporary coping researchers also include detailed interviews and observations to assess coping (Folkman & Moskowitz, 2000).

Keys to Coping with Stress

Suggestions such as "chill out" and "just relax" may sound trite, but if you can successfully relax, you can bring about psychological and physiological changes that will help you deal well with stress. Even though it may seem easy, relaxing well requires some practice and some know-how. Health psychological research has identified two major types of strategies that are useful to help people cope better and relax. The first broad category is called relaxation-based approaches and includes methods such as mindfulness, meditation, yoga, biofeedback, hypnosis, and the relaxation response. The second major category is cognitive-behavioral approaches and includes the use of learning theory (i.e., classical and operant conditioning) and other means designed to help a person label the problem, discuss the emotions associated with it, and find a way to solve it.

Relaxation-Based Approaches

In relaxation-based approaches, the goals are to reduce the cognitive load or number of thoughts a person is experiencing and to activate the parasympathetic nervous system to help the body recover from the activation of the sympathetic system. Most stressors that we experience today are stressors relating to thinking. It is our worrying about problems and anticipating threats that cause the most havoc. We can sit around and think ourselves into a frenzy. Right now, you can let your mind wander to how much money you owe, to all the different things that you have to do, to a performance you have to give, or to the kids you have to pick up or feed, and so on. The generation and fixation on all these thoughts can activate the stress response (mediated by the specific primary and secondary appraisals we make, of course). Relaxation-based approaches stop or at least reduce our fixation on these different stressful thoughts, thereby automatically lessening the stress response.

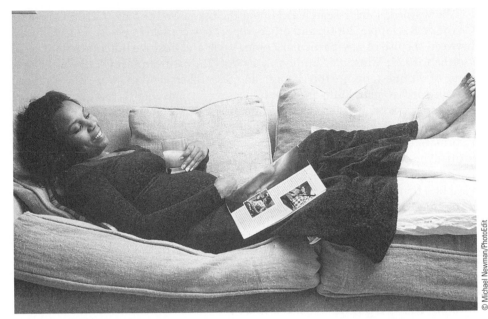

© Michael Newman/PhotoEdit

Relaxation There are many forms of meditation that can be very relaxing. Here a person listens to soothing music and tries to relax.

Most relaxation-based techniques ask a person to focus on a specific thought, word, image, or phrase. By focusing on just one item and giving it complete attention, the person is not thinking about all the things that are stressful. Together with the focus on a single object comes a slowing down of the breathing and the lowering of heart rate, respiration, circulation, and essentially all the functions of the body supervised by the parasympathetic nervous system. Most importantly, the different stress chemicals (catecholamines and cortisol) are no longer released. Most practices such as mindfulness, meditation, and yoga use this slowing down of the breath and the clearing of the thoughts to bring about stress relief. Mindfulness, in particular, involves intentionally bringing one's attention to the internal and external experiences occurring in the present moment and is often taught through a variety of meditation exercises. It has been empirically demonstrated to result in increased immune activity (Davidson et al., 2003), stress reduction (Carlson, Speca, Patel, & Goodey, 2003), and a host of other positive health outcomes (Baer, 2003; Kabat-Zinn, 2003).

Sometimes guided imagery, imagining different peaceful scenarios, or aromatherapy, the use of calming smells and scents, can also aid in relaxation. Table 5.4 gives you something you can try at home. Similarly, progressive muscle relaxation, in which you focus your attention on specific muscle groups and alternately tighten and relax them (Sarafino, 2001), can be beneficial.

Biofeedback involves the use of an electronic monitoring device that tracks physiological processes (e.g., pulse) and provides feedback regarding changes. If you are stressed, your high pulse is indicated by either a sound (e.g., pinging) or an image on a screen (e.g., a large circle). The goal is to make your pulse slow

---

TABLE 5.4

Guided Imagery Instructions: Have a friend read these out to you slowly.
Find a comfortable position and listen to the words and try to picture what is being said.

Picture yourself right now in a log cabin somewhere high up in the mountains. . . . It's wintertime, but even though it is very cold outside, you can enjoy the comfort of being in that cabin . . . for inside of the cabin is a large fireplace with a brightly blazing fire providing plenty of heat and warmth . . . and now you can go up to one of the windows and notice the frost on the windowpane . . . you can even put your warm hand on the cold, hard glass of the windowpane feeling the heat from your hand and fingers melting the frost . . . And then to get a view of the outside, you can begin to open the window, feeling it give way against the pressure of your hand; as the window opens, you take a big breath of that pure, fresh, cool mountain air and feel so good. Looking outside you can see the snow on the ground and lots of tall evergreen trees. And then looking off in the distance and seeing a wonderful view . . . perhaps of a valley down below or other mountain peaks far, far in the distance. . . . And now you can close the window and walk over to the fire feeling its warmth as you get closer. . . . Go ahead and sit back in a comfortable chair facing the fire . . . or if you wish, you can lie down next to the fire on a soft bearskin rug . . . feeling the soothing warmth of the fire against your skin . . . letting your body absorb the warmth bringing deep relaxation and comfort. . . . You can also enjoy looking at the fire, seeing the burning logs, hearing the crackling of the logs and hissing sound from the sap encountering the fire . . . smelling the fragrant smoke from the burning logs. You can even look around noticing the room as it is illuminated by the light from the fire . . . noticing the flickering shadows on the walls . . . noticing the furniture and any other objects in the room . . . just look around and take it all in . . . all the sights and sounds and smells . . . feeling so peaceful in this place . . . . so calm and completely tranquil. And you can be reminded that even though the cold wind is howling outside, you can feel so warm and comfortable inside . . . letting that comfort spread to all parts of your mind. And in this place you have absolutely nothing to worry about . . . for all that really matters is that you just allow yourself to enjoy the peacefulness, enjoy the deep comfort of being in this place right now . . . as a relaxed, drowsy feeling comes over you . . . and all the sights and sounds and smells gradually fade far away . . . while you drift . . . and float and dream in that cabin far off in the mountains. (Pause) And now, whenever you are ready, you can bring yourself back to a normal, alert, and wide-awake state by counting slowly from 1 to 3, so that when you reach the number 3 you will open your eyes feeling completely refreshed and comfortable.

---

down (and hence make the pinging slow or the image on the screen smaller). By trying different methods, such as slowing down your breathing, you see the results directly on the machine. The machine reinforces your attempts to calm down by producing less pinging. You are more likely to do whatever it was you did to reduce the pinging, and operant conditioning helps you develop a way to cope.

Another form of conditioning, classical conditioning, lies between relaxation and behavioral therapy. **Systematic desensitization** is a form of classical conditioning in which stressful thoughts or events are paired with relaxation. According to classical conditioning, whenever two events are linked enough times, responses that came naturally in response to one event now are found to occur in response to the second event. Let's say that you are scared to speak in public. Your first step is to create a hierarchy of the things about public speaking that scare you with the scariest thing at the top of the list (e.g., the moment just before you start and are facing 50 strangers) and the least scary aspect at the bottom (e.g., a month before you have to speak). Then, while thinking about the thing at the bottom of your list you practice relaxing. You do this until you can think about the speech a month away and still feel the conditioned response, relaxation. You now pick the next scary event in your hierarchy and pair that one with relaxation. In this way you move up your list until you can think about being in front of people and still feel relaxed. Once this link between the thought and the relaxation has been

© Spencer Grant/PhotoEdit

Biofeedback Biofeedback helps you monitor your pulse and heart rate and use your mind to slow it down.

strengthened, the next time you are in front of a group of people you should feel the relaxation that you conditioned (Figure 5.5).

Cognitive-Behavioral Approaches

Cognitive-behavioral therapies that treat clinical disorders can easily be adapted to cope with stress. For example, **cognitive restructuring** can be used to replace stress-provoking thoughts (e.g., "everyone is going to be looking at how I perform") with realistic, unthreatening thoughts (e.g., "everyone is too busy to see what I am do-ing"). Similarly, Ellis' (1987) rational-emotional therapy is often used to identify and change irrational beliefs that a person may have that can cause stress. In a similar fashion, Beck's (1976) cognitive therapy involves the identification and change of maladaptive thought patterns that can often be automatic and cause stress (e.g., you always assume that people do not believe you). Another cognitive approach, Mei-chenbaum and Cameron's (1983) stress-inoculation training provides people with skills for reducing stress such as having the person (1) learn more about the nature of the stressor and how people react to it, (2) learn and practice things to do when they do get stressed (separately referred to as proactive coping by Aspinwall & Taylor, 1997), and (3) practice the new skills in response to a real or imagined stressor.

Emotional expression is one of the most widely researched forms of cognitive-behavioral therapies in recent history (Niederhoffer & Pennebaker, 2002; Smyth & Pennebaker, 2001) (Table 5.5). Although most therapies involve the sharing and discussion of a troubling issue, emotional expression involves disclosure in

An Anxiety Hierarchy for Systematic Desensitization	
Degree of fear	
5	I'm standing on the balcony of the top floor of an apartment tower.
10	I'm standing on a stepladder in the kitchen to change a light bulb.
15	I'm walking on a ridge. The edge is hidden by shrubs and treetops.
20	I'm sitting on the slope of a mountain, looking out over the horizon.
25	I'm crossing a bridge 6 feet above a creek. The bridge consists of an 18-inch-wide board with a handrail on one side.
30	I'm riding a ski lift 8 feet above the ground.
35	I'm crossing a shallow, wide creek on an 18-inch-wide board, 3 feet above the water level.
40	I'm climbing a ladder outside the house to reach a second-story window.
45	I'm pulling myself up a 30-degree wet, slippery slope on a steel cable.
50	I'm scrambling up a rock, 8 feet high.
55	I'm walking 10 feet on a resilient, 18-inch-wide board, which spans an 8-foot-deep gulch.
60	I'm walking on a wide plateau, 2 feet from the edge of a cliff.
65	I'm skiing an intermediate hill. The snow is packed.
70	I'm walking over a railway trestle.
75	I'm walking on the side of an embankment. The path slopes to the outside.
80	I'm riding a chair lift 15 feet above the ground.
85	I'm walking up a long, steep slope.
90	I'm walking up (or down) a 15-degree slope on a 3-foot-wide trail. On one side of the trail the terrain drops down sharply; on the other side is a steep upward slope.
95	I'm walking on a 3-foot-wide ridge. The slopes on both sides are long and more than 25 degrees steep.
100	I'm walking on a 3-foot-wide ridge. The trail slopes on one side. The drop on either side of the trail is more than 25 degrees.

FIGURE 5.5
A Stress Hierarchy
The most stressful event is at the bottom. You pair relaxation with the first event and then move down until you can imagine your most stressful event and be relaxed.

writing. A number of studies have shown that just writing out your feelings can lead to a range of positive outcomes. The basic procedure is simple. Participants write about extremely important emotional issues, exploring their deepest emotions and thoughts. They are asked to include their relationships with others (parents, lovers, and friends), their past, present, and future, and their goals and plans. All their writing remains completely confidential, and they are asked not to worry about spelling or grammar.

The only rule is that once they begin writing they are to continue until the time (often 15 minutes) is up. People following this simple exercise are less likely to get sick (Greenberg & Stone, 1992; Pennebaker & Beall, 1986; Richards, Pennebaker, & Beall, 1995) and report reduced levels of stress, less negative moods, and less depression (Murray & Segal, 1994; Rime, 1995).

TABLE 5.5

Key Examples of Emotional Expression Studies

Author/Date	Sample	Duration	Result
Francis and Pennebaker (1992)	University employees	1/week 4 weeks	Lower absenteeism
Pennebaker et al. (1991)	College students	3/week	Better grades
Spera et al. (1994)	Unemployed professionals		Quicker reemployment
Pennebaker et al. (1988)	College students		Improved immune functioning
Petrie et al. (1995)	Negative hepatitis B patients		Higher antibody levels to hepatitis B
Petrie et al. (2004)	HIV-infected patients	4 days (30 minutes each)	Increased lymphocyte count
Ullrich and Lutgendorf (2002)	College students	1 month	Increased meaning finding
Zakowski et al. (2004)	Cancer patients	3 days (20 minutes each)	Reduced stress

A separate way to cope with stress is to increase your physical activity. People who exercise on a regular basis tend to be less depressed and less stressed (Norlander, Bood, & Archer, 2002; Salmon, 2001). If you are wondering if this is just a correlation and guessing that people who are less stressed may exercise more (notice how many people skip their workouts when they have a lot of things due?), fear not. In addition to correlational studies, a number of experimental manipulations have established that exercise helps individuals cope with stress (Babyak et al., 2000; Kerr & Kuk, 2001). For example, Brown (1991) tested the stress-buffering effect of fitness with subjective and objective indicators of exercise, fitness, and physical well-being on 110 undergraduates. He found that both self-reports of exercise and objective measures of fitness showed the **buffering effect,** with the objective fitness levels buffering stress even when visits to a health facility were measured. Exercise helps mainly by influencing the release and metabolism of stress hormones and varying the way that the sympathetic nervous system reacts to stress. For example, 53 members of the Austin Fire Department were randomly assigned to an exercise or no exercise condition and then stressed with a fire drill. Before training, the groups did not differ in their cardiovascular response to the fire drill. Significant group differences were observed after training. Exercise-trained participants reacted with significantly lower pulse and mean arterial pressure than their counterparts in the control condition (Throne, Bartholomew, Craig, & Farrar, 2000). The next time you feel stressed with work, it may be worth the effort to exercise even if you only take a quick paced walk outside.

How do you know when coping works? You feel better, your heart rate, pulse, and breathing are normal, your thinking is clearer, and your general sense of well-being improves. Consistent with the emerging movement in psychology to focus on the positive outcomes in life, referred to as the **positive psychology** movement (Seligman & Csikszentmihalyi, 2000), health psychologists have begun to investigate an arena of positive outcomes. In their review of trends in coping research, Somerfield and McCrae (2000) identified outcomes such as stress-related growth (Park, Cohen, & Murch, 1996), positive personal change (Curbow,

Exercising Exercising can prove to be a great stress reliever.

Somerfield, Baker, Wingard, & Legro, 1993), meaning-making (Park & Folkman, 1997), benefit-finding (Tennen & Affleck, 1999), growth-oriented functioning and crisis growth (Holahan, Moos, & Schaefer, 1996), and meaning-based coping (Folkman & Moskowitz, 2000).

FOCUS on Current Issues

May God Help You

Millions of people around the world turn in the same direction when they are stressed. It is not a point on the compass; it is toward God. It may not be the same God, but for many people religion and religious institutions provide a major way to cope with stress. After being neglected in the field of psychology for many years, religion and prayer have received a lot of attention in the last decade. Does believing in God cure diseases and help you live longer? I review the empirical literature in health psychology on this topic in chapter 10.

To some extent, world events forced religion onto center stage. The September 11, 2001, attack by Islamic terrorists in the United States, the clashes between Palestinians and Israelis in the Middle East and Hindu and Muslims in India, and the sex abuse scandals in the Catholic church are just some examples. More importantly, religion is a focus of study because most people who are stressed or who face seemingly insurmountable problems pray. In fact, religious beliefs and practices appear to be especially important in stressful situations that push people to the limits of their resources (Pargament, 2002). Religious coping has been found to help people deal with a range of problems such as living in stressful neighborhoods (Krause, 1998) and dealing with lack of sexual gratification (Wallin & Clark, 1964). Religion is more helpful in some situations than others. For example, the degree and recency of loss (Mattlin, Wethington, & Kessler, 1990; Maton, 1989) make a difference (religion moderated high-loss situations and recent loss of a child).

Are you religious? To some, the answer is as simple as saying whether they believe in God or not. To others and to the researchers who study it, **religiosity** is measured by looking at the frequency of temple/church/mosque/synagogue attendance, the average frequency of prayer, and the commitment to religious rituals. Many people classify themselves as followers of a certain denomination but rush to add that they are not "practicing." Such people may identify themselves as being of a certain religion (e.g., Hindu), but still not stick to the rules of that religion (e.g., being vegetarian). No matter what your religious background, you probably use some form of religious coping at some time or the other. Different world religions such as Christianity, Islam, and Hinduism include different beliefs, rituals, practices, and standards, but they all share the idea that we have entities or higher powers who created us and who are in some way involved in our lives. Turning to the higher powers in times of stress is as natural as a young child turning to his or her parent when she is scared or threatened.

An interesting example of the use of religion and faith as a coping mechanism can be seen in a movie called *Signs*. In it, hunky Australian Mel Gibson plays a priest who lost his faith after his wife was killed in an accident. Strange crop circles turn up on his Pennsylvania farm and around the world. Suddenly, aliens invade the earth (the circles are the signs of contact). People are terrified. Mel's brother in the movie needs reassurance, and Mel replies that there are two kinds of people. Some people see scary things like the aliens and recognize them as signs from God. These are the people who believe in miracles and have faith. They see these signs as evidence that God exists, trust that God will save them, and are calm. The other kind of people are nonbelievers and, seeing the invasion, realize that they have no one to turn to or no one to watch out for them and are terrified. Which type you are determines how you cope. Although not scientifically tested (this is a Hollywood production after all) that basic dichotomy is at the heart of the role of religion in coping.

As you read in our discussion of coping styles, the COPE does have a subscale to assess the use of religion, but the study of religious coping has been much more intensive than that. Pargament (1997), in his book on religion and psychology, documents an array of cases in which religion is used as a coping mechanism and notes that our tendency to turn to God intensifies as situations become more critical. Of course, people use religion in different ways. You can turn everything over to God (deferring religious coping—"whatever happens is God's will, what will be will be"), you can engage God's help and work with what God has provided (self-directed religious coping—"God helps those who help themselves"), or you can work with God (collaborative religious coping—"with God on my side how can I lose?"). This is no big surprise, because, similar to the emotion-focused strategies discussed earlier in the chapter, deferring religious coping is not optimal (Schaefer & Gorsuch, 1991).

In addition to these three styles, Pargament, Smith, Koenig, and Perez (1998) also identified two major dimensions of religious coping: positive and negative religious coping. Positive religious coping methods (e.g., seeking spiritual support from God and using collaborative coping) have helped a wide range of people including refugees (Ai, Peterson, & Huang, 2003), victims of natural disasters (Smith, Pargament, Brant, & Oliver, 2000), older hospitalized patients (Koenig, Pargament, & Nielsen, 1998), and students (Pargament, Koenig, & Perez, 2000). Negative religious coping methods (e.g., questioning the power of God and expressing anger toward God) have been related to poorer adjustment among many groups such as medical rehabilitation patients (Fitchett, Rybarczyk, DeMarco, & Nicholas, 1999), students (Exline, Yali, & Lobel, 1999), and victims of natural disasters (Pargament, Smith, Koenig, & Perez, 1998).

Religious coping in general can be such a great aid that the lack of it can be problematic for some. For example, Strawbridge, Shema, Cohen, Roberts, and Kaplan (1998) found that although personal and organizational religiosity buffered the effects of stressors, such as financial problems, poor health, and disability or depression, the lack of personal religiousness amplified the effects of child problems and the lack of organizational religiousness amplified the effects of marital problems and abuse.

Chapter Summary

- Coping is defined as individual efforts to manage distressing problems and emotions that affect the physical and psychological outcomes of stress. A coping response may be anything we do to reestablish our homeostatic balance.
- Many different cultural factors buffer or moderate and mediate the effects of stress and influence coping. Our age, sex, socioeconomic status, religion, and ethnicity are some of the key cultural buffers.
- The two primary coping styles are problem-focused or approach coping and emotion-focused or avoidant coping. The efficacy of each depends on the nature of the stressor, especially its duration and controllability.
- A variety of personality traits are associated with more effective coping. People high in self-esteem, who are conscientious, low in neuroticism, optimistic, hardy, and resilient and have a sense of mastery, cope better with stress.
- Social support is one of the most important factors influencing coping. Commonly defined as emotional, information, or instrumental assistance from others, social support has been associated with a variety of positive health outcomes.
- Social support can be received or perceived, global or specific, or vary in function. It can be emotional, informational, or tangible. Support works best when it matches the needs of the individual.
- Some cultural groups have higher levels of support than others, depending on the context. African Americans tend to derive more support from their families than do other ethnic groups. Individuals with strong religious ties perceive having more support than those with weak religious ties. Women also give and receive more social support than men.

- Coping is commonly measured by questionnaire and is divided into many categories. Major types of coping are confrontative, distancing, self-controlling, accepting responsibility, seeking social support, escape avoidance, positive reappraisal, suppression, planning, turning to religion, venting of emotions, denial, and the use of humor.
- Two major categories of coping are relaxation-based (meditation, yoga, biofeedback, hypnosis, guided imagery, and progressive muscle relaxation) and cognitive-behavioral (using learning theory, systematic desensitization, psychoanalysis, and emotional expression).

Synthesize, Evaluate, Apply

- What are the main coping styles? Generate situations in which each would be optimal.
- What are some biopsychosocial mediators and moderators of stress and coping?
- What are the major drawbacks to current coping research?
- How do different personality styles/traits relate to coping?
- What are the key cultural factors involved in coping?
- What are the coping styles inherent to emotional expression interventions (disclosure)?
- What are the main types of social support?
- Which dimensions/types are more related to distress?
- What are the buffer and direct hypotheses of the effects of social support and which is right?
- What are some factors to bear in mind to provide effective social support?
- Do you cope in ways not discussed in this chapter on coping?
- How do the different ways of coping apply to the different theories of stress?
- How would you design a stress management program for people at a local company using what you know about coping?
- How can focusing on your breathing (e.g., during meditation) provide both cognitive and physiological stress relief?
- What would you rate as the most effective measure of coping?
- How would you evaluate your own coping mechanisms?
- How can religion be just another form of social support?
- How are the different physiological components of stress counteracted by the different coping methods?

KEY TERMS, CONCEPTS, AND PEOPLE

ESSENTIAL READINGS

Compas, B. E., Connor-Smith, J. K., Saltzman, H., Thomsen, A. H., & Wadsworth, M. E. (2001). Coping with stress during childhood and adolescence: Problems, progress, and potential in theory and research. *Psychological Bulletin, 127*(1), 87–127.

Lazarus, R. S. (2000). Toward better research on stress and coping. *American Psychologist, 55*(6), 665–673.

Skinner, E. A., Edge, K., Altman, J., & Sherwood, H. (2003). Searching for the structure of coping: A review and critique of category systems for classifying ways of coping. *Psychological Bulletin, 129*(2), 216–269.

Somerfield, M. R., & McCrae, R. R. (2000). Stress and coping research: Methodological challenges, theoretical advances, and clinical applications. *American Psychologist, 55*(6), 620–625.

Uchino, B. N., Cacioppo, J. T., & Kiecolt-Glaser, J. K. (1996). The relationship between social support and physiological processes: A review with emphasis on underlying mechanisms and implications for health. *Psychological Bulletin, 119*(3), 488–531.

WEB RESOURCES

Visit the companion website at **http://psychology.wadsworth.com/gurung1e/**, where you will find online resources for this book, including chapter-by-chapter quizzes, weblinks, and more! You can also visit Wadsworth Psychology Resource Center at **http://psychology.wadsworth.com** to access additional resources.

**Critically Assess This Commercial Product
Designed to Help Coping Using Biofeedback**
www.wilddivine.com

Models of Behavior Change

What are five health behaviors that you could improve on? Do you know the extent to which doing them or not doing them influences your risk of an early death? Most of us know what it takes to live a long and healthy life—at least we think we know. Eat well. Don't drink too much alcohol. Don't smoke. Get some exercise. These are some of the most common actions considered to make someone healthy. You can also hope that you do not inherit any dangerous conditions from your parents. However, it is not that easy. You may want to eat well, but what exactly does "eating well" mean? You may think you know, but research and the media suggest that the "right" things to eat are always changing. One day, eating a lot of meat is thought to be bad for you; the next day eating a little meat is bad. For years, eggs and milk were considered to be essential for a growing child. Then, for many years we were warned not to eat too many eggs. Gosh, even if you do figure out what is good for you through all the mixed messages in the media, it is still one thing to know what the good thing to do is, and a completely different thing to actually do it. Likewise, you may know that exercise is important, but do you manage to exercise as often as you should? Do you plan on exercising but don't because you are too tired or you do not have enough time? Join the club, and I don't mean the YMCA or your local health club (just being a member of a health club does not always mean you will exercise more anyway). Millions of people would like to exercise, plan on exercising more than they do currently, but just do not manage to do it.

In this chapter I will show you how health psychologists explain why we don't do all that we should and why we do some of what we should not. Even though people know that it is important to get physical activity, why do some people not exercise? If smokers know the risks of tobacco addiction, why do they still smoke? What are the different stages that people goes through as they consider changing a behavior and then try to do it? Health psychologists have devised many theories to explain the performance of health behaviors and ways to institute change. I will first summarize the key theories on health behavior performance and change and then describe how psychologists intervene to change behaviors.

What Are Healthy Behaviors?

Healthy behaviors are defined as any specific behaviors that maintain and enhance health. These can range from the mundane (e.g., brushing your teeth and flossing) to the critical (e.g., not practicing unsafe sex with multiple partners). Many of our daily behaviors can influence our health and how long and how happily we live. Do you wear your seatbelt when you drive? You should. A majority of road fatalities are due to the drivers or passengers not wearing seatbelts. Wearing a seatbelt is a health behavior. The sad fact is that many of the most common health problems that plague us today are worsened and in some cases even caused by unhealthy behaviors. For example, eating a lot of fatty foods and

© IT Stock Free/PictureQuest

Physical Activity Being physically active is one of the most beneficial health behaviors you can perform. Most individuals use gyms or clubs to get their work-outs, but even walking and climbing stairs at work can burn enough energy to keep one healthy.

not getting enough physical activity increase the likelihood of developing Type 2 diabetes and coronary heart disease. One specific unhealthy behavior, smoking, can be tied to a range of negative health outcomes such as lung cancer and heart disease. Practicing healthy behaviors is so critical that it is estimated that 50% of all deaths could have been postponed or avoided by changing the health behaviors practiced. Behavioral factors such as tobacco use, diet and activity patterns, and avoidable injuries are among the most prominent contributors to mortality (Mokdad, Marks, Stroup, & Gerberding, 2004).

Before health psychology was a field of study in its own right, health educators stressed the relevance of political, economical, and social factors as determinants of health (Derryberry, 1960; Nyswander, 1966). For example, Griffiths (1972) urged health educators to focus on the institutions and social conditions that impede or facilitate individuals reaching optimal health instead of focusing on just individuals and their families. Correspondingly, policy, advocacy, and organizational change have been the central activities of public health and health education (Glanz, Rimer, & Marcus-Lewis, 2002). **Health education** attempts to close the gap between what is known about optimal health practices and what is actually done (Griffiths, 1972). The goal of health education is to teach people to limit behaviors detrimental to their health and increase behaviors that are conducive to health (Green, Kreuter, Partridge, & Deeds, 1980; Simonds, 1976). Closely paralleling the biopsychosocial approach, health educators pay attention

---

TABLE 6.1

Healthy People 2010: Goals and Main Areas of Focus

Overarching goals
   1. Increase quality and years of healthy life.
   2. Eliminate health disparities.

Focus areas

1. Access to Quality Health Services	15. Injury and Violence Prevention
2. Arthritis, Osteoporosis, and Chronic Back Conditions	16. Maternal, Infant, and Child Health
3. Cancer	17. Medical Produce Safety
4. Chronic Kidney Disease	18. Mental Health and Mental Disorders
5. Diabetes	19. Nutrition and Overweight
6. Disability and Secondary Conditions	20. Occupational Safety and Health
7. Educational and Community-Based Programs	21. Oral Health
8. Environmental Health	22. Physical Activity and Fitness
9. Family Planning	23. Public Health Infrastructure
10. Food Safety	24. Respiratory Diseases
11. Health Communication	25. Sexually Transmitted Diseases
12. Heart Disease and Stroke	26. Substance Abuse
13. HIV	27. Tobacco Use
14. Immunization and Infectious Diseases	28. Vision and Hearing

to a range of factors including the individual, interpersonal relationships, institutions, community, and public policy (Smedley & Syme, 2000). Health psychologists essentially follow the same agenda but with more of a focus on individual factors such as attitudes, beliefs, and personality traits.

Different health behaviors are important for different people. If people smoke and are overweight, the most important behaviors for them to change probably are their smoking, eating, and exercise habits. Nonsmoking and fit, but very overworked, nurses may need to change their sleeping habits. Otherwise healthy college students practicing unsafe sex may have sexual behavior as their key change behavior. The most important health behaviors are outlined as **Leading Health Indicators** established by U.S. Department of Health and Human Services' Healthy People 2010 Program. Table 6.1 lists the main objectives for this program.

Healthy People 2010

Healthy People 2010 is the prevention agenda for the United States. It is a statement of national health objectives designed to identify the most significant preventable threats to health of Americans and to establish national goals to reduce these threats. Healthy People 2010 was developed by the Healthy People Consortium, an alliance of more than 350 national membership organizations and 250 state health, mental health, substance abuse, and environmental agencies. Additionally, through a series of regional and national meetings and an interactive website, more than 11,000 public comments on the draft objectives were received. This provided the American public with a say and provided input from all levels of society. The Leading Health Indicators will be used to measure the health of

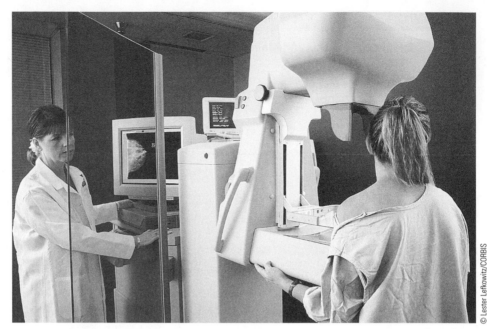

Mammogram Machine Women being tested place their breasts between the plates, which then are clamped down to squeeze the breast tissue. Although playing a key role in the prevention of breast cancer, mammograms can be painful and cause discomfort. Tests for testicular cancer do not involve any such machine squeezing.

people in the United States of America over the next 10 years. As a group, the Leading Health Indicators reflect the major health concerns in the United States at the beginning of the 21st century (Healthy People 2010, 2003). The Leading Health Indicators are physical activity, overweight and obesity, tobacco use, substance abuse, responsible sexual behavior, mental health, injury and violence, environmental quality, immunization, and access to health care. Correspondingly, physical activity, eating well, smoking, alcohol and drug use, and sexual behavior are some of the health behaviors studied most by health psychologists.

Living a healthy life entails more than just doing the right things on a personal level. Many health behaviors necessitate the help of medical institutions and trained professionals. For example, although you control what you buy and eat, whether or not you exercise or smoke, and how much you drink, it is also important to have medical check-ups. Cancers, such as breast cancer and testicular cancer, begin as tiny lumps. Whereas personal self-examinations catch many lumps in their early stages, it is important for both men and women to schedule regular check-ups for a thorough examination. Scheduled check-ups for prostate or breast cancers are more important for older men and women, respectively, but even young children need to visit medical institutions for vaccinations and immunizations.

Health psychologists aim to get people to improve personal health behaviors and to remember to get the various check-ups that their cultural demographics (i.e., age, sex, and ethnicity) may require. Health psychologists use **interventions,**

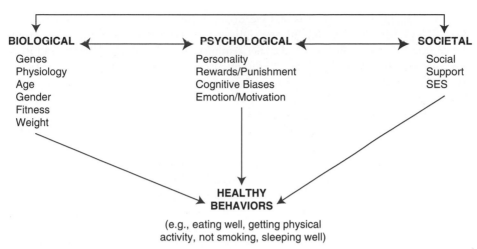

FIGURE 6.1
Healthy Behaviors
There are biological, psychological, and social factors that determine healthy behaviors. These are just some of the many ingredients that contribute to good health.

specific programs designed to assess levels of behaviors, introduce ways to change them, measure whether change has occurred, and assess the impact of the change. The ultimate goal of health psychological interventions is to decrease the number of deaths due to preventable diseases, delay the time of death, and improve quality of life (especially for the elderly). Increasing the numbers of positive health behaviors practiced also saves money. When more money is spent on increasing healthy behaviors, the nation (via health care costs) and employers spend less money. An ounce of prevention really is worth a pound of cure.

What Determines Health Behaviors?

In chapter 3 we discussed many different ways that our developmental history shapes who we are. Our developmental history—comprising both our physiological and psychological make-up—plays a major role in the health behaviors we practice. Why do you smoke if you do? Why don't you smoke if you don't? Why don't you get enough exercise? Are you likely to eat well? An examination of our developmental history and our cultural backgrounds using the biopsychosocial perspective can answer all these questions (Figure 6.1).

Biologically, we are born with many predispositions that can influence the types of health behaviors that we practice. For example, if both your parents are very overweight, there is a good chance that you will be overweight or have a propensity to put on weight. From our parents we inherit metabolic rates, which determine how we break down and process what we eat. We also inherit the type of muscle definition we can have. For example, if you have always wanted a flat stomach with each separate muscle block clearly defined ("the six-pack"), you must watch what you eat and do many sit-ups. Unfortunately, that is not the end of the story. Some of us will not be able to achieve well-defined "washboard abs" no matter how many sit-ups we do because we may not have the specific muscle type for this. Yes, having the right muscle type in the abdominal region is determined by your biology and genetic inheritance. Similarly, the likelihood of becoming addicted to smoking or drinking also has been shown to have a biological basis. For example, the dopamine D_2 receptor gene plays a role in alcoholism. People (and animals) who have more copies of this gene show a higher likelihood of becoming addicted to alcohol (Finckh, 2001).

In examining the psychological predictors of health behaviors, many of the usual suspects are seen again. Similar to my discussion of stress in chapter 4, personality traits and characteristics play a large role in determining health behaviors (Friedman, 2000; Salovey, Rothman, & Rodin, 1998; Wasylkiw & Fekken, 2002). The Big Five personality traits (discussed in chapter 5) are good indicators of a person's likelihood to practice a specific behavior. For example, Jerram and Coleman (1999) measured neuroticism, extraversion, and openness together with medical problems, perceived health status, positive health behaviors, and frequency of visits to general practitioners (GPs). Neuroticism was associated with a higher number of reported medical problems, negatively perceived health status, and a higher frequency of visits to the GP. Extraversion was associated with positive health behaviors. Openness to experience and agreeableness were associated with positive health perceptions. There were interesting sex differences as well. Agreeable women reported fewer medical problems and less frequent visits to the GP than antagonistic women, whereas conscientious men reported more positive health perceptions and more visits to the GP than nonconscientious men. Other studies show similar associations between personality traits and health behaviors. Conscientiousness and agreeableness were particularly noteworthy as predictors of health behaviors and cognitive attitudes and tendencies (Bogg & Roberts, 2004; Lemos-Giraldez & Fidalgo-Aliste, 1997). Because associations are evident for each of the personality traits, all of the Big Five personality traits should be included in research on health behaviors to investigate their relevance for clinical practice. Positive traits are not always associated with positive health behaviors. Extraverts are also more likely to participate in risky behaviors such as drinking (Theakston, Stewart, Dawson, Knowlden-Loewen, & Lehman, 2004).

Ways of interacting with others are also key aspects of personality that can be important. For example, **agency** and **communion** are broad dimensions of personality that reflect a focus on the self and a focus on others, respectively. People with high levels of agency require mastery, status, power, and achievement, whereas people high in a communion orientation place more value on interpersonal relatedness, friendship, caring, and love. Helgeson and Fritz (2000) distinguished unmitigated agency, a focus on the self to the exclusion of others, from agency, and distinguished unmitigated communion, a focus on others to the exclusion of self, from communion. They showed that unmitigated agency and unmitigated communion are linked to domains of problem behavior, in particular relationship difficulties, a lack of support from others, a reluctance to ask others for help, and a range of poor health behaviors.

In another demonstration of the long-term impact of personality, Caspi et al. (1997) followed babies until they were 21. At age 3, observational measures were used to classify the children into distinct temperament groups. At age 18, the researchers assessed 10 distinct personality traits with the Multidimensional Personality Questionnaire (MPQ). At 21, the adolescents were separated into groups based on their involvement in each of four different health-risk behaviors: alcohol dependence, violent crime, unsafe sex, and dangerous driving habits. Results showed that a constellation of adolescent personality traits (with developmental origins in childhood) are linked to different health-risk behaviors at 21. Associations between personality and different health-risk behaviors were not seen because the same people engaged in different health-risk behaviors. Instead, the associations implicated the same personality type in different but related behaviors. In planning campaigns, health professionals may need to design programs that appeal to the unique psychological makeup of persons most at risk for particular behaviors (Caspi et al., 1997).

The "social" part of the biopsychosocial model is very important as well. Think back to when you were young. Did your parents ever hassle you about what you watched on television, which movies you went to, or (depending on how old you are) which websites you surfed to on the Internet? If you complained about the restrictions they placed on what you were exposed to, here is something to think about. The fact is that the media messages we are exposed to have a strong impact on the types of health behaviors we perform. The culture we live in and what we are surrounded by give us a lot of information about what is acceptable and what is not. As we grow and look out at the communicators of culture (e.g., magazines, movies, or television) what we see can influence what we do. This sounds feasible, right?

To prove this association Sargent, Dalton, Heatherton, and Beach (2003) first counted the occurrences of smoking in each of 600 popular movies. They gave teens a list of 50 recent popular films selected randomly from a pool of 600 recent popular films that they had analyzed for tobacco depictions. Based on the films each student reported seeing from the list of 50, the researchers tallied the total number of times that a teen would have been exposed to smoking or other tobacco use. More than 31% of teenagers who saw 150 or more instances of actors smoking on film tried smoking themselves, compared with about 5% of teens who saw 50 or fewer tobacco-related scenes. The prevalence of susceptibility to smoking increased with higher categories of exposure: 16% among students who viewed 0 to 50 movie tobacco occurrences; 21% among students who viewed 51 to 100 occurrences; 28% among students who viewed 101 to 150 occurrences; and 36% among students who viewed more than 150 occurrences. The association remained statistically significant after controlling for gender; grade in school; school performance; school; friend, sibling, and parent smoking; sensation-seeking; rebelliousness; and self-esteem (Sargent et al., 2002). Similar relationships between movie watching and drinking have also been found (Dalton et al., 2002).

Psychological and social factors also interact. Jessor, Turbin, and Costa (1998) tested the role of psychosocial factors on a wide range of adolescent health-enhancing behaviors—healthy diet, regular exercise, adequate sleep, good dental hygiene, and seatbelt use. The researchers assessed the perceived effects of health-compromising behavior, the presence of parents or friends who model health behavior, involvement in prosocial activities, and church attendance among 1,493 Hispanic, White, and Black high school students in a large, urban school district.

© RKO Radio Pictures Inc./Photofest

© Kobal Collection/Twentieth Century Fox

Smoking in the Movies One of the major social factors influencing adolescent smoking is the movies. In the early days of filmmaking (e.g., Jimmy Stewart above) actors were often sent cartons of 'smokes' so they would smoke on screen. Later, movie companies were paid to show cigarettes on screen.

Both individual difference factors and social factors (e.g., church attendance and behaviors of social networks) predicted adolescent health behavior.

Key Theories of Health Behavior Change

Health psychologists' approaches to understanding and changing the extent to which health behaviors are practiced nicely illustrate the scientific method. Look at a real world problem, devise a theory of why it occurs, design research to test it, and then apply successful theory to help intervene and solve the problem. There have been and continue to be a number of different theories to explain why we practice some behaviors and fail to practice others. The next section of this chapter introduces you to the major health psychological theories of behavior change.

The Health Belief Model

The **Health Belief Model** (HBM) represents one of the first theoretical approaches to studying why we behave the way that we do. The basic contention of the HBM is that our beliefs relating to the **effectiveness,** ease, and **consequences** of doing (or not doing) a certain behavior will determine whether we do (or not do) that behavior. It is one of the most widely used frameworks and has been used for both behavior change and maintenance. It was developed when a group of social psychologists were brought together at the U.S. Public Health Service to try to explain why people did not participate in programs to prevent or detect disease (Hochbaum, 1958; Rosenstock, 1960). The HBM was then extended to explain people's responses to illness symptoms (Kirscht, 1971) and also to explain what influences whether someone will adhere to his or her prescribed treatments (Becker, 1974).

The formulation of the HBM provides a good illustration of how social psychology and cognitive and behaviorist views influenced health psychology. For example, learning theorists such as Skinner (1938) believed that we learned to do a certain behavior if it was followed by a positive outcome (a reinforcement). So if exercising made us feel healthy we would be more likely to exercise. Cognitive theorists added a focus on the value of an outcome (e.g., health) and the expectation that a particular action (e.g., exercise) will achieve that outcome. The HBM is a value-expectancy theory in which the values and expectations were reformulated from abstract concepts into health-related behaviors and concepts. A big issue in the 1950s was that a large number of eligible adults did not undergo screening for tuberculosis (TB) although TB was a big health problem and the screenings were free. Beginning in 1952, Hochbaum (1958) conducted surveys of more than 1,200 adults to understand why this was the case. He found that 82% of the people who believed they were susceptible and who believed early detection worked had at least one voluntary chest x-ray. Only 21% of the people who had neither beliefs had an x-ray.

How does the HBM explain health behavior? The model, built on Hochbaum's surveys, suggests that individuals will perform healthy behaviors if they believe they are susceptible to the health issue, if they believe it will have severe

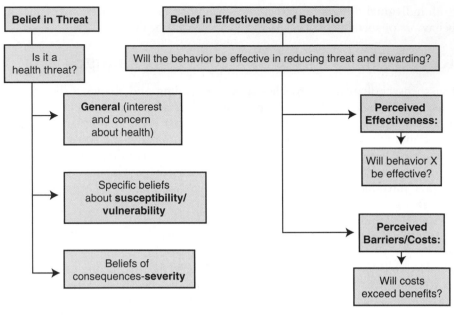

FIGURE 6.2
Main Components of the Health Belief Model

consequences, if they believe that their behavior will be beneficial in reducing the severity or susceptibility, and if they believe that the anticipated benefits of the behavior outweigh its costs (or barriers). In addition, the original model included "cues to action," which suggested that things such as a news story on television or in a newspaper or even finding that your pants no longer fit because of how heavy you have become can serve to get you started on changing your behavior. This component was never empirically studied and has not been featured in the bulk of work using the HBM. The main components are described in Figure 6.2.

Another factor that was added to the model with great success was the concept of **self-efficacy**. Self-efficacy is defined as the conviction that one can successfully execute the behavior required to produce the outcome (Bandura, 1977) and was added to the HBM by Rosenstock, Strecher, and Becker (1988). This suggests that it is not enough just to know what behaviors *will* efficiently reduce severity and susceptibility, but one has to be confident that one can actually do that behavior.

Is one more component more important than the others you may ask? There is a problem with answering that question. The measurement of HBM components has been inconsistent and a majority of studies conducted with it did not use reliable or valid measures of constructs. Part of the reason is that researchers fail to adequately control for the relationship between different components. Another reason is that health beliefs and health behaviors have often been measured simultaneously, contaminating the findings. If I first ask you whether you believe drinking is dangerous and then immediately ask you if you drink, your answers may not be the same as if I asked you each question at a different time. There are good examples of HBM measures when you look at specific actions for certain illnesses such as cancer screening (Champion, 1999; Rawl, Champion, Menon, & Foster, 2000).

Here is an example of how you can take a theory and put it into action. An intervention study targeting the susceptibility, benefits, and barriers components of the HBM may be performed as follows. Champion, Ray, Heilman, and Springston (2000) had counselors speak to more than 300 low-income African American women. Counselors (1) clarified misconceptions and provided information to (2) increase the perceptions of benefits, (3) increase perceptions of susceptibility, and (4) reduce the perceptions of barriers of getting mammograms. For example, many women were scared of the procedure (it involves the breast tissue being squeezed between the steel plates of a machine). The most frequently mentioned barriers were the fear of finding something wrong, the fear of pain, and the fear of what the radiation used by the machine could do. Almost half the women in the experimental group, who did not have a mammogram before, got one. Only 18% of the women in the control group got one. Even phone counseling targeting HBM components had similar effects (Duan, Fox, Derose, & Carson, 2000).

In general, a number of empirical studies have established the utility of the HBM (Becker, 1974; Janz & Becker, 1984). Perceived barriers is the most powerful component of the model across studies. Although perceived susceptibility and benefits are both important, knowing how susceptible one feels is a better predictor of that person's health prevention behavior and knowing the person's perceptions of benefits is a better predictor of his or her sick-role behaviors (Janz, Champion, & Strecher, 2002).

Culture and the Health Belief Model

The HBM has also been used in different cultural settings. Together with scales and interventions being designed for specific populations such as the African American women mentioned above, numerous studies have investigated the usefulness of the HBM in multicultural settings. Fulton, Rakowski, and Jones (1995) compared Latino, non-Latino Black, and non-Latino White women and found that Latino women were less likely than others to perceive themselves as susceptible to breast cancer and less likely to perceive breast cancer as curable. Similarly, Byrd, Mullen, Selwyn, and Lorimor (1996) found that Latino women were more likely to have the following barriers to getting prenatal care in the later stages of pregnancy: embarrassment with the physical examination, long waiting times for the doctor, and poor patient-practitioner interactions. Lee (2000) also found embarrassment to be a significant barrier for Korean American women seeking cervical cancer screenings. Research has even found differences between age groups within ethnicity (i.e., between young and old Chinese Americans; Tang, Solomon, & McCracken, 2000) and provides us with ways to adopt health care delivery to best suit different populations. For example, Dignan et al. (1995) found that American Indian women were reluctant to talk openly about their personal health to physicians (a barrier) and so lay health educators, project guides, were used to present the screening education program.

Theory of Planned Behavior

Another way to try to predict whether someone is going to do something is to see if he or she *intends* to do something. Let's say we go to dinner together at a restaurant that has great desserts. If you want to predict whether or not I am going to get some dessert, all you have to do is ask. If my intentions are to get some dessert, I will probably get some (I love dessert). Behavioral intentions play a major role in many models of health behavior change such as the Theory of Reasoned Action (Fishbein & Ajzen, 1975), the Theory of Planned Behavior (TPB) (Ajzen, 1988), the Protection Motivation Theory (Rogers, 1983), and the previously mentioned concept of self-efficacy (Bandura, 1977).

So what is an **intention?** Fishbein and Ajzen (1975) defined an intention as a person's subjective probability that he or she will perform the behavior in question. It is essentially an estimate of the probability of your doing something. If you ask me if I want dessert at the start of a meal when I am hungry, the probability that I will say "yes" will be higher than that after a meal when I have stuffed myself. Thus, to get a good measure of intentions they need to be measured with a high degree of specificity regarding the attitude toward the exact action (e.g., eating dessert), the target (e.g., chocolate cake), the context (e.g., on that day), and the time (e.g., right after the meal). The TPB, an extension and updating of the Theory of Reasoned Action, assumes that people decide to behave a certain way on the basis of their intentions that are dependent on their attitude toward the behavior and their perceptions of the social norms regarding the behavior.

Similar to the HBM, attitudes toward the behavior are based on what the person believes are the consequences of the behavior and how important these consequences are (both costs and benefits). Will eating dessert make me put on weight? One of the most useful components is the one assessing perceived norms. This assesses what *you* think others think about the behavior or the **normative beliefs.** Do the people you know support eating sweet things? If you believe that everyone around you thinks that eating dessert is an acceptable thing, you are more likely to want to do it. Of course, you may not care what people around you think. Your **motivation to comply** with others' preferences is also part of the perception of social norms. If you care about the people around you *and* they support dessert eating, you are more likely to eat dessert. The full model with its components is shown in Figure 6.3.

Culture and the Theory of Planned Behavior

The TPB has been used in many different settings. For example, Montano, Kasprzyk, von Haeften, and Fishbein (2001) used questionnaire data to identify TPB measures that best predicted condom use among African American, Latino, and European American women. They recruited participants from the Seattle

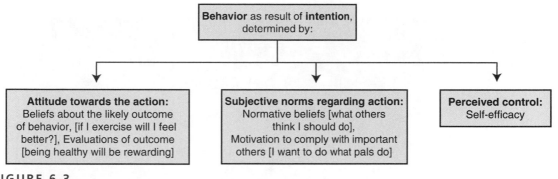

FIGURE 6.3
Major Components of the Theory of Planned Behavior

area and interviewed them at two time points 3 months apart. Participants were asked about their condom use, their beliefs about the consequences of the condom use, their intentions to use condoms, and their attitudes toward condom use. The researchers also measured the participants' perceptions of the subjective norms about condom use. Specifically, Montano et al. (2001) had participants rate whether 15 different friends and relatives thought they should use condoms. The researchers also assessed the participants' motivation to comply with what their friends said. There was a strong significant correlation between intending to use a condom and actually using one, as measured by self-report. Similarly, in support of the TPB model, subjective norms and attitudes toward condom use and perceived behavioral control were also significant predictors of the behavior.

Although tested in multiethnic samples (Montano et al., 2001), it is becoming clear that models such as the TPB do not apply in the same way across cultural groups. For example, ethnic differences are seen in the relative effects of peers and parents on adolescents' substance use. Peers exert a stronger influence on cigarette use among Whites and Latinos than among African Americans (Gottfredson & Koper, 1996). On the other hand, parents have a greater impact on the use of alcohol among African American children than among White children (Clark, Scarisbrick-Hauser, Gautam, & Wirk, 1999). Thus, although the TPB might predict tobacco use among both African American and White children, the relative contribution of the key components (especially of the subjective norm factor) differs among cultural groups.

Transtheoretical Model

Every December, as the New Year approaches, it is New Year's resolution time. Men and women around the nation vow to do more of this or less of that. The newspapers provide tips on how best to make and keep resolutions. You often see extensive mention of the **Transtheoretical Model** (TTM) (Prochaska & DiClemente, 1983) of behavior change. It was developed to identify common themes across different intervention theories (hence *Trans*theoretical) and notes

Choose Your Cover Skin Cancer Prevention Campaign/Centers for Disease Control and Prevention

College-Based Interventions A number of college-based interventions have used the Theory of Planned Behavior Model to increase the use of sun screen and reducing skin cancer. This poster uses credible, attractive role models to make sun protection more normative.

that we process through different stages as we think about, attempt to, and finally change any specific behavior.

Different psychological traditions had different processes to account for why people changed their behaviors. The behaviorists argued that people changed to manipulate the contingency of reward and punishment, the humanists believed that helping relationships spurred change, and the psychodynamic theorists suggested that change came about due to consciousness raising. DiClemente and Prochaska (1982) assessed whether a group of smokers who were trying to quit used any of these processes. The researchers found that smokers used different processes at different times in their quest to quit smoking and first identified that behavior change unfolds in a series of stages. From smoking, the stage model was extended to study a variety of behaviors with health consequences including alcohol and substance abuse, delinquency, eating disorders and obesity, consumption of high-fat diets, unsafe sex with the risk of HIV/AIDS, and sun exposure (Prochaska, Redding, & Evers, 2002).

The TTM sees change as a process occurring through a series of six stages. The main stages are summarized in Table 6.2. If you know what stage a person is in, you will need to tailor your intervention to fit the state of mind that the stage

---

TABLE 6.2

Stages of Change: The Transtheoretical Model

1. Precontemplation
   —Not aware of behavior, no intention to change
2. Contemplation
   —Aware that problem exists, thinking about change
   —Weighing pros and cons
3. Preparation
   —Intend to change, modified but not committed
4. Action
   —Modified and commitment to time and energy
5. Maintenance
   Working to prevent relapse
6. Termination Phase

---

describes. When people are not aware that they are practicing a behavior that is unhealthy or do not intend to take any action to change a behavior (especially not in the next 6 months), they are said to be in the **precontemplation** stage. People could have tried to change before, failed, and become demoralized to change, or they may just be misinformed about the actual consequences of their behavior. Some teenage smokers are so confident about their own health that they do not believe smoking is a problem for them and have no intention of quitting. People in this stage avoid reading, thinking, or talking about their unhealthy behaviors. Health promotion programs are often wasted on them because they either do not know they have a problem or do not really care.

When people recognize they may be doing something unhealthy and then intend to change (within the next month), they are said to be in the **contemplation** stage. Here they are more aware of the benefits of changing and are also very cognizant of the problems that changing may involve. For the dieter it may be avoiding the foods that he or she has grown to love. For the smoker it may mean not spending time with the buddies he or she always used to smoke with. The ambivalence associated with knowing the pros and cons of the behavior change often keeps people in this stage for a long time and calls for unique interventions.

Preparation is the stage in which the person is ready to take action to change the behavior. He or she generates a plan and has specific ideas of how to change. Someone who wants to lose weight may go out and buy new workout clothes and a gym membership. Someone who wants to drink less may give away all the alcohol in his or her house or have a talk with his or her doctor to get help. In essence these people make a commitment to spend time and money on changing their behaviors. As you can guess, this is the stage in which people should be if an intervention is going to have any effect.

Once people are actually changing their behavior, they are in the **action** stage. The change has to have taken place over the last 6 months and should involve active efforts to change the behavior. For example, frequent trips to the gym characterize someone who is in the action stage of trying to lose weight. Does any attempt to change behavior no matter how small count as being in the action stage? No, it does not. People must reach a criterion that health professionals can agree is sufficient to reduce the risk for disease (Prochaska et al., 2002), for example, losing enough weight to no longer be classified as obese or abstaining from smoking for a significant period of time.

Maintenance is the stage in which people try to not fall back into performing their unhealthy behaviors or relapsing. They may still be changing their behaviors and performing new behaviors, but they are not doing them as often as someone in the action stage. In this stage, the temptation to relapse is reduced, and there is often confidence that the new behavior changes can be continued for a period of time. For example, maintenance of abstinence from smoking can last from 6 months to 5 years (U.S. Department of Health and Human Services, 2000).

Finally, people may reach a stage in which they are no longer tempted by the unhealthy behavior they have changed. The ex-smoker who no longer craves a cigarette, the ex-fast food addict who now no longer feels like eating a burger and fries, and the once-couch potato who cannot think of not getting regular physical activity. If a person reaches this point he or she is said to be in the **termination** stage. Can this stage be achieved? Snow, Prochaska, and Rossi (1992) found that less than 20% of former smokers and alcoholics reached this zero-temptation stage. For the most part, this part of the model has been loosely interpreted as representing a lifetime of maintenance.

The most helpful contribution of the TTM is that it clearly identifies how interventions can be successful. Interventions need to be tailored according to the stage of change that a person is in. The most common application involves the tailoring of communications to match the needs of the individual. For example, individuals who are in the precontemplation stage could be given information that would make changing their behavior more of a pro and hence move themselves into the contemplation stage (Kreuter, Strecher, & Glassman, 1999). Of course, just knowing what stage a person is in is not enough. Abrams, Herzog, Emmons, and Linnan (2000) tested whether knowing a smoker's TTM stage or knowing the extent of addiction would better predict cessation over 12 to 24 months. They found that addiction-related variables such as number of cigarettes smoked and the duration of prior quit attempts were better predictors that the TTM.

Comparing the Models

These three models are the most widely cited models of health behavior change in health psychology (Glanz, Rimer, & Lewis, 2002). They have each received strong support but also have some limitations (Ogden, 2003). For example, the HBM has not been as rigorously quantified as the TPB, but its components have received considerable empirical support (Mullen, Hersey, & Iverson, 1987). Some of its components still need to be better understood and others, such as beliefs about severity, have low predictive value (Rimer, 2002). Similarly, the TPB and the TTM do not necessarily include all the elements responsible for behavior change and can each be supplemented with additional concepts. The TPB does not recognize emotional elements such as the perceived susceptibility to illness as does the HBM. Consequently, a combination of these three models may produce the best predictor of behavior (e.g., Garcia & Mann, 2003). In addition, a host

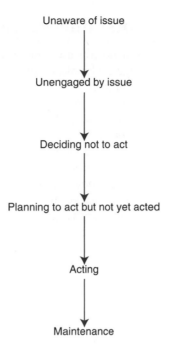

FIGURE 6.4
The Precaution Adoption Process Model

of relatively new theories/models are garnering attention. For example, Weinstein and Sandman (1992) formulated the Precaution Adoption Process Model (PAPM) that identifies seven stages along the path from lack of awareness to action (Figure 6.4). Similarly, Schwarzer (1992) introduced the Health Action Process Approach (HAPA) that distinguishes between two main phases: when a decision to act is made and when the action is carried out. During the initial phase of the HAPA, people develop an intention to act based on beliefs about the risk and outcomes and their self-efficacy. After a goal has been established within this phase, people enter a volition phase in which they plan the details of action, initiate action, and cope with the difficulties of successfully completing the action.

Few studies have pitted more than one theory against another. In a notable exception, Garcia and Mann (2003) tested the ability of several social-cognitive models to predict intentions to engage in two different health behaviors (resisting dieting and performing a breast self-examination). All constructs from the HBM (with and without self-efficacy), the TPB (with and without perceived behavioral control), and the motivational process of the HAPA (Schwarzer, 1992) were measured simultaneously in two samples. The authors hypothesized that models that included self-efficacy (or the related construct of perceived behavioral control) would be more effective than the models that do not include it. Their results supported this prediction. The HAPA was the best predictor of intentions to engage in both behaviors. Additional comparative research will continue to provide health psychologists with practical theories.

Changing Behaviors: Interventions

Understanding why we do or do not do something is important because it provides us with a way to change and make a difference in our health. Armed with the knowledge about what determines behavior, health psychologists attempt to intervene to change behaviors. As you can see from the preceding discussion, our behavior is determined by the attitudes, beliefs, and intentions we have toward it and on the stage that we are in.

Health psychologists have tried different techniques to get people to do what is healthy. In the 1950s, the most common advertisements to change behavior tried to scare the viewer into changing. To some extent you still see some fear appeals today. Many high schools use posters of blackened lungs or rotten teeth to get students to not smoke. Together with using scary visuals, early interventions also tried to provide information about different health hazards. The theory was that if you knew more about the dangers of doing a certain behavior, you may be more likely to not do it. With the advances in television and technology in the 1970s and 1980s, these

Billboards Billboards like these two sponsored by the California antismoking campaign is a form of intervention that reaches many thousands of people.

fear and information appeals were broadcast via mass media. Most mass media appeals have the benefits of reaching a large number of people relatively easily. Together with alerting people to health risks, these forms of interventions can have a cumulative effect over time and can also reinforce other change techniques.

Different interventions focus on different antecedents of behavior. Some health psychologists choose to change a person's attitudes to change his or her behavior; others attempt to change his or her beliefs or intentions. The way an intervention is designed can depend on the specific behavior that needs to be changed, the funding available for the behavior change, and the number of people that the intervention has to reach. To put all these different factors into order, let's look at some of the basic principles of intervention design. Some additional suggestions from a review summarizing effective interventions (Rotheram-Borus & Duan, 2003) are shown in Table 6.3.

Top Ten Prescriptions

1. Interventions Should Be Based on Theory. Having a theory is important for many reasons. First, it helps focus attention on the most important factors that need to be addressed for the behavior change at hand. For example, the application of the TPB to change specific behaviors involves identifying underlying beliefs that determine one's attitude, subjective norms, and perceived behavioral control and having the intervention address these components. Far too often researchers try to address as many different aspects of behavior as they can in an intervention. They fill posters with arguments and information that tackle these different aspects. If such interventions do result in changing behavior, it is hard to identify what the actual reason was because the contents of the intervention were not based on a theory. Thus, it is hard to replicate the findings and difficult to focus on and identify what actually worked. This "throw in everything including

---

TABLE 6.3

Additional Success Strategies for Interventions

1. Use private enterprise models of product development to increase the dissemination of the intervention to the general public.
2. Initiate interventions by teams committed to a specific problem.
3. Provide investigators with training in management.
4. Establish the acceptability of the program's design features to consumers, providers, and funding agencies before the development and evaluation of the program.
5. Use data from national marketing surveys to tailor intervention designs and delivery formats for different subgroups.
6. Identify essential ingredients of the intervention to facilitate adaptation of the program.
7. Implement the program with a goal to maintain change over extended periods of time.
8. The implementation plan should include program evolution over time, rather than replication with fidelity.
9. The intervention should be branded and certified by a credible agency.

SOURCE: From Rotheram-Borus, M. J., & Duan, N. (2003). Next generation of preventive interventions. *Journal of the American Academy of Child and Adolescent Psychiatry, 42*(5), 518–526.

the kitchen sink" approach to interventions can lead to change but more often than not involves the use of money without the promise of successful replication of the behavior or prolonged success. Interventions based on theory have a better chance of being useful over the long run.

2. Intervene at the Appropriate Level. When designing an intervention, the researcher has to decide what the best unit of intervention is. You can design an advertising campaign to target an entire city, state, or part of the country. You can also decide to target areas of a city or town, neighborhood, or community. You can get even more specific and target families or specific individuals in a family. The level at which you intervene should be appropriate to the problem at hand. If the issue is something like obesity, and people in specific states are more at risk than others, a statewide campaign may be better. If the issue is something like smoking and only members of a specific cultural group, say high school students, are at risk, then targeting that group is critical. Interventions can also be targeted to policy makers. Changing the superstructure of government and policies toward specific health behaviors can also result in behavior change. Many state governments have raised the tax on cigarettes and have seen a corresponding drop in cigarette purchases among young adults.

3. Size Matters. The size of the intervention is closely related to the extent of behavior change seen in response to it. Size can refer to the duration of the intervention and to the intensity of the intervention. Sustained interventions are more likely to lead to sustained behavior change. Furthermore, in many studies, rates of high-risk behavior increase when interventions are withdrawn. Having an intervention continue over a long period of time, even if it is not too involving, can still ensure that the unhealthy behavior is kept at bay. For example, if you want to have a group exercise more, having them complete weekly exercise logs that are turned in (increasing accountability and involvement) is likely to make them be active. More intense interventions are more likely to result in greater risk reduction. For example, Rotheram-Borus and colleagues (2003) designed a successful intervention called Street Smart for runway children. Street Smart provided these children with access to health care and condoms and delivered a 10-session skill-focused prevention program based on social learning theory. The more sessions conducted, the better the success rate was. Finally, the effect size of an intervention is another good indicator of success. Effect size is a statistical measure of the power of any experimental manipulation. Even if there is a small sample, looking at the effect size can provide a useful estimate of the effectiveness of the intervention.

4. Interventions Should Target People at Risk. When researchers do not take pains to intervene at the appropriate level, large numbers of people are exposed to the intervention with the hope that those who need it are included in the exposed group. This shotgun approach can waste a lot of time and money. In some cases it may be difficult to find out who is most in need of the intervention, but attempting to do so can lead to better, more directed interventions. Investigators can find out who is at risk by identifying risk factors. For interventions to increase the use of mammograms, investigators can identify groups of women who have high rates of breast cancer and find measures to identify them. Culture comes in handy here. There may be people in a specific part of the country, a specific ethnic group, a religious group, or an age group who are more likely to perform an unhealthy behavior or be at risk for a specific disease. Identifying that group, finding out where they are located, and going to them are effective ways to intervene.

5. Interventions Should Be Appropriate for the Risk Group/Risk Factor. Once a risk group is identified the intervention should be designed to be appropriate for that group. If you are targeting a specific age group, sex, ethnic group, or member of a specific sexual orientation, format the intervention in a way that appeals to and is understandable by the target group. If you want to target bad eating behaviors of seventh grade students, the language of the intervention should not be set at the level of the college freshman. If the intervention is to appeal to a certain ethnic or religious group, it should use terminology, images, or styles familiar to that group. In addition, it is important to remember that not everyone speaks English. Interventions aimed to change the behaviors of people from different ethnic groups in which different languages are spoken should be designed in the language of the target population.

6. Be Sure Your Intervention Does Only What You Want It to Do. Sometimes an intervention can have unintended effects. Interventions to curb eating disorders provide a sad example. Prevention programs for eating disorders attempt to simultaneously prevent new occurrences (primary prevention) and encourage students who already have symptoms to seek early treatment (secondary prevention), even though ideal strategies for these two types of prevention may be incompatible with each other. In a study to assess the effectiveness of such programs, Mann et al. (1997) evaluated an eating disorder prevention program. In the intervention, classmates who had recovered from eating disorders described their experiences and provided information about eating disorders. Paradoxically, at follow-up, intervention participants had slightly more symptoms of eating disorders than did control subjects instead of fewer symptoms. Mann et al. (1997) hypothesized that the program may have been ineffective in preventing eating disorders because by reducing the stigma of these disorders (to encourage students with problems to seek help), the program may have inadvertently normalized them. Similarly, researchers should be sure that their control group is not receiving anything special. If an intervention consists of providing social support over the phone but the control group also receives phone calls (for information gathering), control group participants may still rate the calls as being supportive.

7. Preventing Dropouts Should Be a Priority. Not everyone in a longitudinal research study stays in the study until the end. Similarly, not everyone who enrolls in an intervention study attends all the sessions. Although dropouts are a fact of life for most longitudinal research studies, they can be especially problematic for interventions. First, the participant is not getting the entire treatment. Second, the presence of dropouts hinders a thorough assessment of the intervention. This is akin to having a cold and getting prescribed a course of antibiotics only to stop taking the medicine once you start feeling better. Just like colds, unhealthy behaviors can return once the intervention/treatment has been stopped. Researchers need to devote resources to preventing attrition and simultaneously collect data to be sure they can assess the effects of attrition.

8. Be Ethical. Although interventions are designed to get people to perform healthy behaviors and reduce unhealthy behaviors, these notable ends do not justify unethical means. It is important for the researchers to respect participants' rights and refrain from using deception or making false claims about the ills of unhealthy behaviors or the virtues of healthy ones. There are enough facts about most health behaviors so that researchers should not be tempted to exaggerate details for a stronger effect. In interventions that include a control group and an intervention group, it is critical that members of the control group participate in the intervention after the study is over. This way they too can get the benefits of the intervention. Health professionals should also be thinking of what will happen once the intervention is removed. Will the behavior go back to what it was before the intervention? Will an unhealthy behavior get worse because the intervention is seen as a crutch, the removal of which is detrimental?

9. Be Culturally Sensitive. Some models of health behavior change are automatically culturally sensitive, but most theories are designed to apply to any cultural group. Researchers must pay close attention to the symbols and language used because the same symbol may mean different things to different cultures. A great example is the swastika, a cross made up of four L's. For centuries it was a good luck emblem (and is still considered a good luck emblem by Hindus), but its meaning was corrupted when it became the symbol of Hitler's Nazi Germany. Thus, its use for good luck by some cultures (e.g., Hindus) may offend others (e.g., Jews). Similarly, researchers cannot assume that everyone speaks English, and language differences should be kept in mind. Interventions that apply at the community level often take cultural differences into account. For example, the Community Organization and Development model for health promotion in communities of color involves community-controlled coalitions that undertake their own community assessment and design culturally relevant interventions (Braithewaite, Bianchi, & Taylor, 1994). In other cases, general theories are revised for use with culturally diverse populations. Gilliland and colleagues (1998) tweaked Social Learning theory ideas into an intervention especially designed to reduce the incidence of Type 2 diabetes among American Indians and Native Hawaiians. Their programs use problem-solving approaches and involve family and social networks to fit the different circumstances and values of each cultural group. Such culturally based interventions have increased movement along stages of change for fat intake and physical activity (Mau et al., 2001). Some researchers do not believe that a general, one-size-fits-all-cultures theory is valid and suggest that new culturally sensitive models need to be developed and used (Oomen, Owen, & Suggs, 1999). Given the increase in cultural diversity in North America today, much more research needs to be applied to designing culturally valid interventions.

10. Prevent Relapse. Sometimes it is not enough to intervene to change behavior, see the behavior change, and then walk away. One of the biggest problems in health behavior change involves fostering maintenance of the new behavior (Marlatt & George, 1990). Be aware that smoking a single cigarette after quitting, eating one slice of pizza if you are on a diet, or skipping one day of exercise may not constitute relapse. Relapse occurs when the behavior that was changed reoccurs on a consistent basis. The person's failure to change can be demoralizing and can sometimes lead to increased levels of the original unhealthy behavior. Good interventions should strive to ensure that relapse does not occur by providing participants with the cognitive and behavioral skills to maintain the behavior change.

Together with these main points, health professionals designing interventions should strive to compensate for individual differences as much as possible. A smoking intervention that works on one campus may not necessarily work in exactly the same way on another campus even if it is in the same state. People's personalities vary as well, and not everyone in an intervention is going to react in the same way. A good way for you to assess how well you understand the 10 key aspects is to use them. Pick a health issue—e.g., secondhand smoke in the workplace or binge drinking on campus—and see if you can design an intervention using these 10 principles. Fine-tune your intervention according to the demographics of your location. You know your peers best, and your intervention can be as powerful (if not more powerful) than those designed by the experts. In the next chapter I will discuss some of the main health behaviors that interventions attempt to influence and give you some examples of interventions to compare yours with.

Changing Personal Behavior

On an individual level you can change health behaviors as well. If your reading of this book highlights your health behaviors that need to be modified then there are some easy things for you to do. First, take a week or two and closely monitor the behavior that you want to change. If it is eating better, write down everything you eat or drink for a week (including times, places, and hunger). If you want to stop smoking, similarly write down every time you smoke (the urge, the company, and so on). Self-observation or self-monitoring is the first and most important step. Then use what you have learned from this chapter. List the barriers that are preventing you from changing the unhealthy behavior or adding the healthy behavior. Think about your susceptibility and vulnerability to the consequences of not changing. Think about the severity of the health problem that could result if you do not change. Also assess what stage you are in. Using this information you can develop a plan to change in an organized manner. Use principles of operant conditioning (reinforcement and punishment) to make sure you keep on track and set achievable goals. By paying close attention to the different biopsychosocial correlates of health behaviors as discussed here, you should be able to develop the behavioral and cognitive skills to change any behavior you desire.

FOCUS on Applications

Smoking Interventions in College

Interventions to reduce smoking by college students have focused on the use of antismoking advertising campaigns and educational material. Greenberg and Pollack (1981) tested what was then a new strategy for motivating college students to not smoke. They divided 342 undergraduates into an experimental and a control group. The experimental group received educational material on smoking and topics such as social approval, academic achievement, and career success and significantly changed their thoughts and attitudes about smoking in general. Nonsignificant but positive changes occurred in smokers' motivation to attempt to quit smoking as well (Greenberg & Pollack, 1981). In a similar study, Freeman, Hennessy, and Marzullo (2001) showed smoking and nonsmoking college students several antismoking videos and compared smoking status, rate, duration, recent attempts to quit, endorsement of the smoker stereotype, and importance of smoking behavior as an identity within the self-concept. Smoking status, current smoking identity, and long-term future smoking identity were significantly associated with a defensive evaluation of the antismoking messages (Freeman et al., 2001).

Even when the message that smoking is harmful is broadcast loud and clear, many college students still choose to smoke. Some inventions have attempted to change behavior by changing smoking policies. For example, Apel, Klein, McDermott, and Westhoff (1997) theorized that limiting the areas in which students were allowed to smoke on campus would cut down on the prevalence of on-campus smoking. A new policy was imposed at the University of Koln, Germany, limiting smoking to separate, designated areas in School of Education buildings. Although the majority (77%) of the 1,223 students surveyed did not expect the changed policy to affect their smoking habits, approximately 28% of the men and 30% of the women said they were smoking less at the university after the change went into effect. Surprisingly, 91% of the nonsmoking students and 68% of the smoking students actually supported the new policy. According to researchers, the

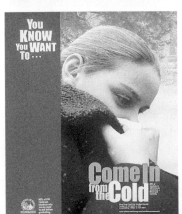

Courtesy Student Health Center, University of Wisconsin Oshkosh

Posters Posters are often a cheap way to convey a message, whether in workplaces or across college campuses. This series of posters was designed to curb college smoking by highlighting all the different rewards of not smoking. By quitting, people can save money, are more kissable, and do not have to go out in the cold in the winter to smoke (more on this specific series in the next chapter).

findings in this study indicate that campus-wide policy changes may result in a decrease in the number of cigarettes smoked, at least on campus (Apel et al., 1997).

Research consistently shows that teenagers and college students misperceive and overestimate their peers' use of tobacco. Perkins, Meilman, Leichliter, Cashin, & Presley (1999) analyzed data from more than 100 college campuses and found that more than three-quarters of the students believed that the typical student used tobacco almost weekly and almost half believed that the typical student used tobacco every day. Although it is true that more college students are smoking now than in the past decade, it is also true that most college students do not smoke. Historically, antismoking campaigns have focused on the short- and long-term health effects of smoking and paid little attention to the fact that smoking is not a normative behavior. Outcome evaluations of these common smoking and health campaign strategies have shown mixed results (Fiori et al., 1993; Goldman & Glantz, 1998). Although research with high school and middle school children documents misperceptions that indicate norms correction might be a beneficial strategy (Sussman, 1998; Hansen, 1993), until recently there have been few published studies related to correcting tobacco use misperceptions (see Perkins, 2003, for a review).

Approaches changing *social norms* have been effective in reducing binge drinking on college campuses (Haines, 1996). For example, reductions of 18% to 21% in binge drinking rates among college students have been achieved over a 2-year period by a number of campuses including Northern Illinois University, Hobart and William Smith Colleges, Western Washington University, and the University of Arizona (Perkins et al., 1999). Simply because changing social norms is effective for alcohol use reduction, it does not automatically mean that it will be effective for tobacco use prevention and cessation. Changing social norms might impact a variety of issues related to tobacco use including prevention of initiation, cessation promotion, policy change, and basic cultural change concerning the acceptance of tobacco use. The use of this approach in an attempt to reduce smoking on campuses has been somewhat successful in getting students to seek smoking cessation treatment (Hancock, 2000).

Chapter Summary

- Health behaviors are specific behaviors that maintain and enhance health. The most important are getting physical activity, limiting the consumption of alcohol, not smoking, and eating well, all described as Leading Health Indicators. Health educators close the gap between what is known as optimal health practices and what is actually done. Interventions are specific programs designed to assess levels of behaviors, introduce ways to change them, measure whether change has occurred, and assess the impact of the change.
- There are biopsychosocial determinants of health behaviors. Biologically we have genetic predispositions that can influence the types of health behaviors we practice and our metabolic rates or risk of addiction. Psychologically, personality traits, self-esteem, and social support are some key factors influencing health behaviors. Social aspects such as the culture we are raised in also predict healthy behaviors.

- Three major theories predict the extent to which we perform health behaviors. The Health Belief Model suggests that our beliefs relating to the effectiveness, ease, and consequences of performing or not preforming a behavior will influence whether or not we do or do not do it. Our perception of susceptibility, the consequences of the illness, and the extent to which we believe behavior change is effective and worthwhile all contribute to the likelihood of performing the behavior.
- The Theory of Planned Behavior suggests that our intentions to perform a behavior are the most important predictors of whether we do it and are influenced by our attitudes toward the behavior and the perceptions of the social norms regarding the behavior.
- The Transtheoretical Model of behavior change suggests that we pass through key phases in regard to a behavior. We move from not thinking about changing or precontemplation to contemplating change, to preparing to change, to changing (action stage), and then to maintenance of the change.
- There are several prescriptions to keep in mind when one is designing interventions to change behavior. Interventions should be based on theory, be at the appropriate level, be at the right level of severity, target people at risk, be appropriate for the risk group, only do what they are designed to do, be ethical, be culturally sensitive, and be designed to minimize dropouts and relapse.

Synthesize, Evaluate, Apply

- Pick a healthy behavior that you do not perform sufficiently. Use each of the three main theories of health behavior change to explain why.
- Which of the three health behaviors do you think best explains peoples' behaviors?
- What are the pros and cons of the Healthy People 2010 approach to changing health behaviors (look at www.healthypeople.gov for more details)?
- What are the main biopsychosocial factors determining why you get the physical activity that you do?
- Compare and contrast each of the three models of health behavior change.
- Are there any factors that need to be added to the models of behavior change?
- How would you use the Transtheoretical Model to refine interventions to decrease smoking?
- Can you think of any additional factors to optimize the delivery of interventions?
- What are the major weaknesses of a "shotgun" approach to interventions?
- Given how personality traits influence a number of different behaviors, how can you best use knowledge of someone's personality to predict his or her likelihood of performing health behaviors?
- Design a study that would incorporate the best aspects of all the models of health behavior change.

- Let us say you want to get all your friends to eat better. You have read about the Health Beliefs Model in class and think that is an interesting model to use. Write one question that you would ask your friends to assess each component of the model.
- What biopsychosocial factors do you think can predict relapse?

KEY TERMS, CONCEPTS, AND PEOPLE

action, 187
agency, 178
Bandura, 182
communion, 178
consequences, 181
contemplation, 187
effectiveness, 181
Fishbein and Ajzen, 184
Health Belief Model, 181

health education, 174
Healthy People 2010, 175
healthy behaviors, 173
intention, 184
interventions, 176
Leading Health Indicators, 175
maintenance, 188
motivation to comply, 184
normative beliefs, 184

precontemplation, 187
preparation, 187
Prochaska and
   DiClemente, 185
Rosenstock and
   Hochbaum, 181
self-efficacy, 182
termination, 188
Transtheoretical Model, 185

ESSENTIAL READINGS

Bellg, A. J., Borrelli, B., Resnick, B., Hecht, J., Minicucci, D., Ory, M., et al. (2004). Enhancing treatment fidelity in health behavior change studies: Best practices and recommendations for the NIH behavior change consortium. *Health Psychology, 23*(5), 443–451.

Prochaska, J. O., DiClemente, C. C., & Norcross, J. C. (1992). In search of how people change: Applications to addictive behaviors. *American Psychologist, 47,* 102–1114.

Rosenstock, I. R. (1990). The Health Beliefs Model: Explaining health behavior through expectancies. In K. Glantz et al. (Eds.), *Health behavior and health education: Theory, research, and practice* (pp. 39–62). San Francisco: Jossey-Bass.

Schwarzer, R. (2001). Social-cognitive factors in changing health-related behaviors. *Current Directions in Psychological Science, 10,* 7–51.

Weinstein, N. D. (1993). Testing four competing theories of health-protective behavior. *Health Psychology, 12*(4), 324–333.

WEB RESOURCES

Visit the companion website at **http://psychology.wadsworth.com/gurung1e/**, where you will find online resources for this book, including chapter-by-chapter quizzes, weblinks, and more! You can also visit Wadsworth Psychology Resource Center at **http://psychology.wadsworth.com** to access additional resources.

Food and Nutritional Information
http:// www.nalusda.gov/fnic/index.html

CHAPTER 7

Health Behaviors: Eating, Physical Activity, Smoking, and Drinking

"**E**at, drink, and be merry," sounds like a simple plan for being content. Of course, we need to do the first two things to survive. The last one has been tied to longer life as well. Unfortunately, being merry is associated too often with eating too much (or eating unhealthy foods), drinking too much, smoking, and a host of other unhealthy activities. The extent to which people perform each of the main health behaviors can vary dramatically. Some people eat too much. Others eat too little. Some people rarely move from the couch, whereas others spend too much time working out. Many people have never smoked a cigarette in their lives (puffing but not inhaling still counts as smoking). A little over one-fifth of people in the United States smoke regularly. There are even trends and fads within each of these behaviors. In the early 1990s and 21st century, yoga centers started appearing around the

© (Royalty-Free) BananaStock/PictureQuest

Behaviors That Can Influence Our Health Eating can be a lot of fun, but one should not eat too much, too little, or the wrong variety of food. If you eat too much and do not get the physical activity to burn off the extra calories, you have even more problems. Do you drink alcohol with your meals? Do you smoke? All these behaviors have serious health consequences.

country and millions of Americans tried this form of physical activity. Simultaneously, many thousands of people tried specialized diets, cutting out all carbohydrates from their systems (e.g., the Atkins and South Beach diets). What is healthy eating? How much physical activity is appropriate? When does substance use become substance abuse and have unhealthy consequences? In this chapter I take a closer look at the different behaviors that can influence our health.

Every health behavior, and particularly what and how much we eat and how much physical activity we do, is strongly influenced by a range of sociocultural factors. Health problems relating to bad eating and not getting enough exercise are more prevalent in some cultures than others. For example, African Americans have high rates of hypertension, and American Indians have high rates of diabetes. Let's determine why these cultural differences exist and what can be done about them. In the previous chapter, I described some of the main psychological theories that predict the performance of health behaviors and theories of behavior change. In this chapter I will focus on three major categories of health behaviors: eating, physical activity, and substance abuse, especially smoking and drinking. I will describe the factors influencing each behavior and how they vary across cultures. We will pay close attention to the developmental precedents of unhealthy behaviors where appropriate and discuss the unhealthy consequences related to each.

Eating

More than 20% of Americans were obese at the beginning of the 21st century (Mokdad et al., 2004). Just 10 years earlier, only 13% of Americans were obese. That is a big difference, and does not even include the 65% of people who are overweight. Understanding more about food and nutrition can go a long way toward turning this weight increase trend around.

What percentage of your daily intake of food is carbohydrates, proteins, and fat? How much do you eat? Are you eating a balanced diet? What *is* a balanced diet? These are some of the most common questions asked about food and eating. The answers are critical for determining your health. Unfortunately, some of the answers seem to change every week, varying with new research or media coverage of new fads. My aim in this section is to provide you with facts relating to these issues and to provide a background for why we eat what we do, when we eat, and how much we eat. I also will discuss the main health problems that arise when we do not eat well and types of eating disorders.

Eating is something we all must do. Together with sleeping, eating is perhaps one health behavior that everybody participates in. Most of us do not pay enough attention to what and how we eat. Many of us do other activities while we eat such as watch television, read newspapers or magazines, or drive (not a good idea). Assess what you eat. Think about the last few days. How many times did you eat yesterday? What did you eat? How much did you eat? What determined

Obesity Obesity is one of America's greatest health concerns today. Even children are getting larger, and the health consequences of being overweight are increasing.

what and how much you chose to eat? Why did you eat what you ate? Use Table 7.1 and list everything that you have eaten in the past 24 hours. Try to identify why you ate what you did. Your list will provide a reference point to think about the material in this chapter.

What Should We Be Eating?

Sixty percent of Americans are familiar with the U.S. Department of Agriculture's (USDA) **Food Guide Pyramid** (Escobar, 1999). Are you? The USDA's earliest attempts to inform consumers about how much protein, fats, and carbohydrates to consume date back to the early 1900s. The first food guide, as we know it today, was published in 1916 and consisted of five major groups (Welsh, Davis, & Shaw, 1993). The economic problems of the Depression in the 1930s greatly influenced families' buying habits as they had to balance price and nutrition. Affordable foods were often low in nutritional value. To alleviate this situation, the USDA released buying guides with 12 food groups in the 1930s. Over the next several decades the number of food groups changed from seven in the 1940s to four in the 1950s and 1960s and then back to five in 1979 with the "Hassle-Free" Foundation diet. The Food Guide Pyramid as seen on bread packages and cereal

---

TABLE 7.1

Examine the factors that affect your eating habits: Choose one day of the week that is typical of your eating pattern. In the table below, list all the food and drinks that you consumed on that day. Then list the other information asked for. Use these symbols: Taste (T), Convenience (C), emotion (e), availability (a), advertising (ad), weight control (WT), hunger (h), family values (FV), peers (p), nutritional value (NV), cost ($), and health (Ht) as reasons for choice. You may be surprised by what you see.

Eating Habits Survey

Time of Day	Minutes Spent Eating	Meal/ Snack	Degree of Hunger (0–5)	Activity While Eating	Food and Quantity	Others Present?	Reason for Food Choice

---

boxes through the middle of 2005 was introduced in 1984 with six food groups. This configuration was revised in the early 1990s based on the U.S. Department of Health and Human Services' (DHHS) Surgeon General's Report on Nutrition and Health. The report included the recommendations of a panel of nutritional experts selected by the USDA and the DHHS. This pyramid established the basic principles of a balanced diet designed to help people maintain or improve their general health and reduce the risk of diet-related diseases. The Pyramid, although well recognized, was not well used. Given the problems with understanding the traditional Pyramid, cultural variations needed for it to apply to all Americans, along with a large amount of new nutritional research, it should be no surprise that the Pyramid as we knew it went extinct. The DHHS released an updated set of nutritional guidelines for Americans in January 2005, complete with a new pictorial guide revamping the pyramid, now called MyPyramid (DHHS, 2005). Key changes include explicitly urging the consumption of more whole grains, a variety of fruits and vegetables, and an increase in physical activity. As you can see in the figure, the pyramid now has a staircase on one side to remind Americans that exercise is an important complement to good eating. Instead of the horizontal bands of the old pyramid, there are now rainbow-colored bands streaming down. Food groups are represented by six different colors: Orange for grains, green for vegetables, red for fruits, yellow for oils, blue for milk products, and purple for meat and beans. The bands are wider for grains, vegetables, fruit, and milk products to remind people to eat more of them. There is no longer just one for all. There are 12 individually tailored models for different age groups and men versus women.

The Food Guide Pyramid shows foods typically eaten by North Americans to illustrate the USDA and DHHS recommendations. This Pyramid suggests the types

GRAINS	VEGETABLES	FRUITS	MILK	MEAT & BEANS
Eat 6 oz. every day	Eat 2½ cups every day	Eat 2 cups every day	Get 3 cups every day for kids aged 2 to 8, it's 2	Eat 5½ oz. every day

FIGURE 7.1
The USDA MyPyramid
Oils are also included (the narrow band between fruits and milk).

and amount of foods to eat each day. Four factors were considered in establishing the serving sizes (e.g., eat two to three servings of fruit): typical portion sizes from food consumption surveys, ease of use, nutrient content, and traditional uses of foods (Herring, Britten, Davis, & Tuepker, 2000). Although a single serving of one type of fruit may have more calories than a single serving of another, the number of different serving sizes was kept to a minimum to make the Pyramid easy to use. I hope that the phrase "traditional uses of food" made you think. Don't different cultural groups have different traditional foods? Absolutely they do! To compensate for this, Oldways Preservation and Exchange Trust of Cambridge, MA, developed food pyramids for different cultural groups. Mediterranean, Asian, and Latino Diet Pyramids as seen in Figure 7.2 incorporate habits of various cultural groups in the United States. There is even an American Indian food pyramid. The main difference between these pyramids and the standard USDA Pyramid is that the culturally diverse pyramids illustrate proportions of food to be consumed and not exact serving sizes. Furthermore, the Oldways pyramids show foods specific to the different

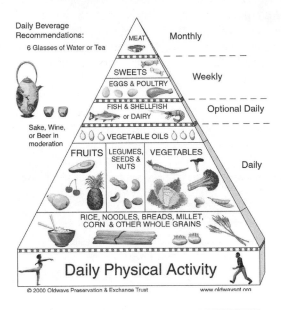

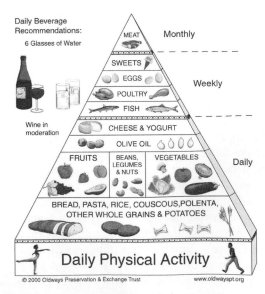

FIGURE 7.2
Food Pyramids for Different Cultural Groups
Copyright © 2000 Oldways Preservation & Exchange Trust. Reprinted by permission.

cultures and suggest consumption amounts over a period of 2 to 3 days, weeks, or even months, in contrast to the USDA guide.

These different guides highlight the fact that what we eat often is deeply tied to our cultural backgrounds. Throughout history, many cultures have ascribed health-promoting powers to certain foods, and many religions have followed specific dietary practices. Chinese "herbs of immortality" were a popular fad among the ancient Egyptians. These herbs have a modern manifestation in Chinese herbs promoted to bodybuilders in health food stores. Different cultures have different beliefs about what should be eaten. As described in chapter 1, many cultures including the Chinese believe that some foods are hot and others are cold. This belief refers to a food's influence on health and well-being, not to the temperature or spiciness of foods. Cold foods include most vegetables, tropical fruits, dairy products, and inexpensive cuts of meat (e.g., rump). Hot foods include chili peppers, garlic, onion, most grains, expensive cuts of meat, oils, and alcohol. Just as the USDA Food Guide Pyramid balances nutritional value, cultures such as the Chinese and the ancient Indians suggested eating foods to balance energy levels. Most non-Western cultures believe that the type of food eaten needs to balance the type or condition of the person. For example, pregnancy is considered a "hot" condition during which many Latinos typically avoid hot foods, believing this will prevent the infant from contracting a "hot" illness, such as a skin rash. In contrast to the Hispanic beliefs, the Chinese believe that pregnancy is a "cold" condition during which the expectant mother should consume hot foods to keep in balance and remain healthy.

Development of Food Preferences

Have you wondered why you like certain foods and dislike others? A part of our **food preferences** are biologically programmed into us. There are two completely innate preferences. Humans innately prefer sweet tastes and are adverse to sour tastes. In general, our experiences and exposure to food determine the bulk of our preferences. If the context in which you were given broccoli was positive, you probably will develop a preference for broccoli. If you always were forced to eat your beans, you probably will develop an aversion to beans. If you were raised near a cheese factory, you probably will develop a preference for cheese. Basic reward and punishment and sociocultural factors also play a large role in the development of our food preferences. Foods used as rewards (e.g., clean your room and you get your ice cream) or paired with fun social events or holidays (e.g., Mom's spice cake at Christmas) automatically become preferred.

Obesity

You often hear about the weight problem in the United States and the alarming rise in obese and overweight children and adults. What exactly do the terms obese and overweight mean? There are established norms for body weight. As seen in Table 7.2, research has established the weight range for healthy living for people of different heights. If a person weights more than his or her normal range he or she is referred to as being overweight. **Obesity** is defined as having a **body mass**

TABLE 7.2

Body Mass Index

BMI Height (ft. in.)	Normal						Overweight					Obese					
	19	20	21	22	23	24	25	26	27	28	29	30	31	32	33	34	35	36
	Body Weight (pounds)																	
4'10"	91	96	100	105	110	115	119	124	129	134	138	143	148	153	158	162	167	172
4'11"	94	99	104	109	114	119	124	128	133	138	143	148	153	158	163	168	173	178
5'	97	102	107	112	118	123	128	133	138	143	148	153	158	163	168	174	179	184
5'1"	100	106	111	116	122	127	132	137	143	148	153	158	164	169	174	180	185	190
5'2"	104	109	115	120	126	131	136	142	147	153	158	164	169	175	180	186	191	196
5'3"	107	113	118	124	130	135	141	146	152	158	163	169	174	180	186	191	197	203
5'4"	110	116	122	128	134	140	145	151	157	163	169	174	180	186	192	197	204	209
5'5"	114	120	126	132	138	144	150	156	162	168	174	180	186	192	198	204	210	216
5'6"	118	124	130	136	142	148	155	161	167	173	179	186	192	198	204	210	216	223
5'7"	121	127	134	140	146	153	159	166	172	178	185	191	198	204	211	217	223	230
5'8"	125	131	138	144	151	158	164	171	177	184	190	197	203	210	216	223	230	236
5'9"	128	135	142	149	155	162	169	176	182	189	196	203	209	216	223	230	236	243
5'10"	132	139	146	153	160	167	174	181	188	195	202	209	216	222	229	236	243	250
5'11"	136	143	150	157	165	172	179	186	193	200	208	215	222	229	236	243	250	257
6'	140	147	154	162	169	177	184	191	199	206	213	221	228	235	242	250	258	265
6'1"	144	151	159	166	174	182	189	197	204	212	219	227	235	242	250	257	265	272
6'2"	148	155	163	171	179	186	194	202	210	218	225	233	241	249	256	264	272	280
6'3"	152	160	168	176	184	192	200	208	216	224	232	240	248	256	264	272	279	287
6'4"	156	164	172	180	189	197	205	213	221	230	238	246	254	263	271	279	287	295

TABLE 7.2

Body Mass Index—cont'd

BMI Height (ft. in.)	Obese									Extreme Obesity								
	37	38	39	40	41	42	43	44	45	46	47	48	49	50	51	52	53	54
	Body Weight (pounds)																	
4'10"	177	181	186	191	196	201	205	210	215	220	225	229	234	239	244	248	253	258
4'11"	183	188	193	198	203	208	212	217	222	227	232	237	242	247	252	257	262	267
5'	189	194	199	204	209	215	220	225	230	235	240	245	250	255	261	266	271	276
5'1"	195	201	206	211	217	222	227	232	238	243	248	254	259	264	269	275	280	285
5'2"	202	207	213	218	224	229	235	240	246	251	256	262	267	273	278	284	289	295
5'3"	208	214	220	225	231	237	242	248	254	259	265	270	278	282	287	293	299	304
5'4"	215	221	227	232	238	244	250	256	262	267	273	279	285	291	296	302	308	324
5'5"	222	228	324	240	246	252	258	264	270	276	282	288	294	300	306	312	318	324
5'6"	229	235	241	247	253	260	266	272	278	284	291	297	303	309	315	322	328	34•
5'7"	236	242	249	255	261	268	274	280	287	293	299	306	312	319	325	331	338	344
5'8"	243	249	256	262	269	276	282	289	295	302	308	315	322	328	335	341	348	354
5'9"	250	257	263	270	277	284	291	297	304	311	318	324	331	338	345	351	358	365
5'10"	257	264	271	278	285	292	299	306	313	320	327	334	341	348	355	362	369	376
5'11"	265	272	279	286	293	301	308	315	322	329	338	343	351	358	365	372	379	386
6'	272	279	287	294	302	309	316	324	331	338	346	353	361	368	375	383	390	397
6'1"	280	288	295	302	310	318	325	333	340	348	355	363	371	378	386	393	401	408
6'2"	287	295	303	311	319	326	334	342	350	358	365	373	381	389	396	404	412	420
6'3"	295	303	311	319	327	335	343	351	359	367	375	383	391	399	407	415	423	431
6'4"	304	312	320	328	336	344	353	361	369	377	385	394	402	410	418	426	435	443

Source: National Heart, Lung and Blood Institute.
The BMI score is valid for both men and women but it does have some limits: It may *overestimate* body fat in athletes and others who have a muscular build; and it may *underestimate* body fat in older persons and others who have lost muscle mass.

index (BMI) of 30 or greater. A BMI of between 25 and 29.9 qualifies a person as overweight. To calculate your BMI, multiply your weight by 703 and divide it by the square of your height measured in inches [BMI = (Wt × 703)/(Ht × Ht)].

Although the BMI score is commonly used, there is an important caveat in its use, and it should not be used as the only indicator of a person's being at a healthy weight because it misrepresents weight in different cultural groups. This misrepresentation also helps explain some inconsistencies in the eating behavior literature by demonstrating the impact of controlling for BMI when BMI and eating behaviors are compared in individuals from different racial/ethnic backgrounds. Gluck and Geliebter (2002) demonstrated this in a study of European, African, and Asian American women who completed an Eating Habits Questionnaire (EHQ) and other measures of body image and eating. European Americans had greater body dissatisfaction (as measured by a higher difference between current and ideal image) than Asian Americans and higher EHQ scores than both Asian Americans and African Americans. African American women chose a larger body size as their ideal than the other groups. Now here is the caveat. Asian American women had a significantly lower BMI than both other groups. However, after controlling for BMI, ideal body size differences were minimized. Also after controlling for BMI, both European Americans and Asian American had greater body discrepancy and EHQ scores than African Americans (Gluck & Geliebter, 2002).

Half of the people in the United States are either overweight or obese (Flegal, Carroll, Kuczmarski, & Johnson, 1998). Our weight increases (not counting the weight gain with pregnancy) as a natural part of the aging process (Figure 7.3). The weight of infants usually doubles in the first 6 months, and older adults gain weight as their metabolic system naturally slows with age. For important reasons, pregnant women add 30 to 35 pounds of weight on average to sustain a pregnancy. Obesity, however, is more than a normal addition of weight needed for growth or health. The chance of being obese increases with age, and obesity occurs more commonly in women than in men, especially among non-European American women. Approximately 55% to 60% of African American and Mexican American women 40 to 60 years of age are overweight (Wing & Polley, 2002).

Being obese means a lot more than just not looking good. Obesity increases the chances of having a chronic disease, exacerbates conditions such as coronary heart disease, and correspondingly shortens life. As the number of overweight and obese people increases, the prevalence of problems such as Type 2 diabetes, gallbladder disease, coronary heart disease, high blood cholesterol levels, high blood pressure, and osteoarthritis also increases. The chance of having two or more health conditions increases with weight in all racial and ethnic subgroups (DHHS, 2005). Gaining extra weight in adulthood even increases the risk of heart attacks (Willett & Singer, 1995). In the Second National Health and Nutrition Examination Survey (NHANES II), overweight adults were three times more likely to develop diabetes and high blood pressure (Van Itallie, 1985). In fact, there is almost a direct negative correlation between BMI and mortality. The higher your BMI, the sooner you may die. One study, the Nurses' Health Study, followed 115,000 women aged 30 to 55 for 16 years (Manson et al., 1995). Women with

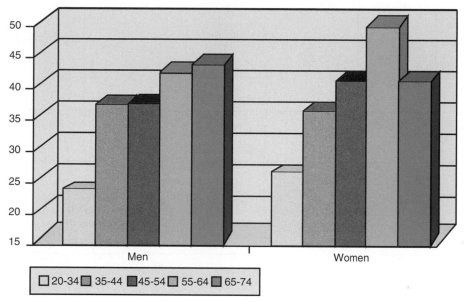

FIGURE 7.3
Being Overweight Increases with Age
The percentage of overweight people increases with age. As you get older, you are at risk for gaining weight. As the body's metabolic rate slows down, you need to increase your physical activity level and pay more attention to what you eat to ensure that you do not add pounds.

BMIs of 19 to 21 showed the lowest mortality rates. Women with a BMI of 32 or greater were almost four times more likely to die from cardiovascular disease and twice as likely to die from cancer compared with women who had BMIs less than 19. There is currently a controversy regarding the exact levels of BMI that are unhealthy. It is possible that being a little overweight (e.g., BMI between 25 and 30) may serve a protective function, but it is clear that being obese, especially BMIs over 35, is very unhealthy (Flegal et al., 2005; Katzmarzyk, 2001). In case you were wondering, you CAN be too thin. Research also shows that BMIs of under 18 put a person at risk for health problems (Flegal et al., 2005).

Many different factors cause obesity. A person may be obese or have excess body fat for a number of reasons. The most direct reason is a combination of bad eating habits (eating too much or too many high-calorie foods) with lack of enough physical activity. In addition, if calorie intake is greater than calorie output you are going to gain weight. Both genetic and environmental factors also are at work. Clearly genetics plays a role in obesity (Bouchard, 1995). Twin studies show that identical twins when overfed are both likely to gain similar amounts of weight, whereas fraternal twins do not show this relationship (Bouchard et al., 1990). There are even specific genes linked to obesity. The *ob* gene, which codes for the protein leptin, has been linked to obesity (Campfield, Smith, & Burn,

FIGURE 7.4
A Handy Guide to Serving Sizes
Lay your fist next to your food (e.g., your pasta or potatoes or vegetables) to see how much you need. How much is a serving size? Use your hands: most adult fists = 1 cup (single serving). Your easy guide to serving sizes: Serving sizes are smaller than most people think.

1996). Leptin signals satiety and people with mutated *ob* genes do not have as much leptin, which possibly leads to overeating. Of course, dramatic increases in obesity are not necessarily due to dramatic mutations of the *ob* gene. Many environmental factors are at play as well.

Changes in food marketing and availability are the most recent and blatant environmental factors influencing eating. The fast food industry has been "supersizing" its offerings. For a small increase in costs, fast-food chains generate a large profit from the public, many of whom like to get large servings. The influence of larger servings in restaurants is seen as one component of a Western way of life because it tends to be localized to developed countries. As proof of the ills of "Western living," Ravussin, Valencia, Esparza, Bennett, and Schulz (1994) compared Pima Indians in the United States with Pima Indians living in a rural part of Mexico. The U.S. Pima Indians had a mean BMI of 35.5. The Mexican Pima Indians had an average BMI of 25.1. Similarly, Alvord and Van Pelt (2000) have also documented rising cases of gallbladder infection and other diet-related problems in the Navajo Indians of New Mexico. How much food does a person really need? The actual amount of food in a recommended serving may surprise you (Figure 7.4).

Most overweight people eat more than normal weight people and often do not even realize the quantities they consume (Lichtman et al., 1992). That said, overweight people do not just eat more of anything. Taste and quality are important. One study suggests that overweight individuals actually prefer (and eat) more fat than normal weight people (Rolls & Shide, 1992). Be warned though, most people eat more in the presence of others. Furthermore, a greater variety of foods presented leads to greater quantities consumed by individual eaters. Hetherington and Rolls (1996) showed that if only one type of food is available at a meal, people eat a moderate amount of it. If a second food is then introduced, the amount of the new food eaten will be more than if it was presented by itself. This phenomenon is called sensory specific satiety. Simply changing the cost of foods makes a difference too. The cheaper the food is, the more people will eat, which even applies to healthy items such as fruits (Jeffery, French, Raether, & Baxter, 1994).

Eating Disorders

Many people have psychological problems, such as low self-esteem, that contribute to an unhealthy relationship with food. For others, being overweight leads to disorderly eating. For example, obesity has been associated with binge eating disorder, in which obese individuals consume large quantities of food and experience a lack of control over their lives (Marcus, 1993). Problems with low self-esteem coupled with pressures to be like slim models or actresses and actors on television, in the movies, or in magazines and bad role models often drive some young girls and boys to starve themselves. Young girls, in particular, are at risk for developing anorexia nervosa or bulimia nervosa. Anorexia involves an intense fear of gaining weight, a disturbed body image, a refusal to maintain normal weight, and extreme measures to lose weight. People with anorexia often exercise 2 to 3 hours a day, take weight loss pills or appetite suppressants, and skip meals. No matter how thin they get, anorexics are only happy when they lose more weight. This condition can sometimes be fatal. Bulimia involves habitually overeating followed by self-induced vomiting, fasting, and excessive exercise. The eating is usually done in secret and is then accompanied by intense guilt and weight gain concerns. Given the strong psychological and social components to eating disorders and possible genetic predispositions, the biopsychosocial approach of health psychologists to illness can be a great aid in preventing eating disorders and helping those with them.

Cultural Variations in Eating Behaviors

There are some significant cultural differences in eating disorders and with the body image problems that cause them. Most of the previous research on body image has focused on European Americans, and it is unclear how models developed to understand body image disturbances apply to diverse populations (Thompson, 2001). Cultures vary in their concepts of ideal body shape, and sociocultural models of body image suggest that the prevalence of eating disorders and body image disturbance in Western countries is partially attributable to cultural ideals of beauty that value thinness. Furthermore, most assessment tools have been validated only on samples of European Americans, lack specificity in defining cultural groups, and show biases in detecting and reporting eating disorders in women of color (Gilbert, 2003). Eating disorders are no longer clearly just a European American problem. For example, Edman and Yates (2004) found no cultural differences in eating disorder symptoms or self-dissatisfaction or body dissatisfaction scores between Asian American and European American women.

Some cultural groups may have higher rates of eating disorders than others. Caballero, Sunday, and Halmi (2004) compared Latino and European American patients with anorexia nervosa or bulimia on severity and types of preoccupations and rituals related to eating disorders and the motivation to change. Patients were interviewed with the Yale-Brown-Cornell Eating Disorder Scale (YBC-EDS). All YBC-EDS scores were higher for the Latino group who also had more preoccupations and rituals. Latinos were also more likely to have rituals in many measured categories. Exactly how culture contributes to eating disorders is still unclear, but researchers are beginning to explicitly look at the role of culture in the development of eating behaviors and the formation of body image (Markey, 2004).

Physical Activity

Most people know that exercise is good for their health. Unfortunately, few people manage to successfully adopt and maintain an exercise habit (Marcus et al., 2000). Researchers are aware of many physical and psychological benefits of physical exercise, including lowered blood pressure, weight loss, stress reduction, and increased self-confidence (Brownson, Chang, Davis, & Smith, 1991; Taylor, Doust, & Webborn, 1998; Calvo, Szabo, & Capafons, 1996; Fontane, 1996). **Physical activity** is any bodily movement produced by contraction of the skeletal muscles that results in energy expenditure (Caspersen, Powell, & Christenson, 1985). How physically active are you? Do you exercise regularly? Do you take an elevator when you could use the stairs?

How much physical activity is needed? In 2003, a study suggested that at least 60 minutes of physical activity per day is optimal for a healthy life. This information was particularly depressing for people who had trouble exercising

Physical Activity You do not have to go to a gym to get your daily requirement of physical activity. Even walking can burn energy. A brisk 20-minute daily walk has been found to be enough to prevent weight gain.

even 20 minutes a few times a week. What exactly is physical activity? First, here is some good news: A common prescription is that people should aim to exercise at a moderate level (e.g., walking) for at least 30 minutes on at least 5 days per week or at a vigorous level (e.g., running) for at least 20 minutes on at least 3 days per week (Eden, Orleans, Mulrow, Pender, & Teutsch, 2002). An hour a day may be optimal, but even 30 minutes is healthy.

So much for how much we need. What should you do? It is important to remember that there are numerous ways that you can expend energy and be physically active. When people think about the recommendations for physical activity, they often translate that to mean exercise and picture going to a gym, running, biking, or lifting weights. About 50% to 70% of the total amount of energy we use relates to the working of our different cells and organ systems, referred to as our basal metabolic rate. Another 7% to 10% of energy is used to break down the food we eat, called the thermic effect of food (Ravussin & Rising, 1992). The rest is physical activity, including the things we have to do every day, such as bathing, grooming, and moving around the house or office, and the things that we choose to do, such as playing sports, dancing, and walking as a leisure time activity. The more physical activities we choose to do, the more energy we expend. The amount of energy used in different daily activities is shown in Table 7.3.

Exercise is defined as activity planned with the goal of improving one or more aspects of physical fitness (Caspersen et al., 1985). Exercise contributes to our level of fitness, defined as the ability to perform daily tasks with vigor and alertness without undue fatigue, enjoy leisure time activities, and meet unforeseen challenges (Phillips, Kiernan, & King, 2002). Are you fit? Several different components can assess whether you are fit or not. Cardiovascular endurance, often referred to as aerobic fitness, refers to the body's capacity to take in, transport, and utilize oxygen. A common measure of aerobic fitness is the volume of oxygen (VO_2) a person uses during different tasks. Muscular strength, muscular endur-

TABLE 7.3

Energy Used in Various Physical Activities

Activity	Calories Burned in 5 Minutes (Typically*)	
	Woman	Man
Walking fast	20	30
Washing a car	20	30
Having passionate sex	20	30
Doing yard work	20	30
Painting	20	30
Mowing the lawn	25	35
Biking to work	30	40
Walking up stairs	35	45
Running up stairs	75	100

*Calories estimated for a 132-pound woman and a 176-pound man. Adjust proportionally to your weight if needed.

ance, muscular power, speed, flexibility, agility, balance, good reaction times, and a low percentage of body fat are other components used to assess fitness (Phillips et al., 2002). Generally, most national studies of health behaviors use "physical activity" rather than "exercise levels" to assess health although both are important components of a healthy lifestyle.

Most commonly used measures of physical activity assess leisure time activities that require energy use above the level of daily living. This type of measurement works well in countries such as the United States and in the study of other populations with high socioeconomic status (SES) because most jobs in these economic environments do not require the expending of too much energy. Sitting at a desk or standing in one spot in a production line does not use as much energy as working in a field. In developing countries and among population with lower SES, a lot more energy is spent on the job (Pereira et al., 1998).

Cultural Variations in Physical Activity

Ethnic, socioeconomic, age, and sex differences all account for cultural differences in physical activity. Minority groups in the United States consistently are found to have relatively lower physical activity levels than majority group members (Kriska, 2000). Minority women are among the least active subgroups in American society (Brownson et al., 2000). A cross-sectional study conducted in 1996 and 1997 among 2,912 African American, American Indian, Alaskan Native, Latina, and White women aged 40 years and older showed that physical activity was lowest among African Americans, American Indians, and Alaskan Natives (Brownson et al., 2000). In three national surveys, the **National Health Interview Survey** (NHIS, 1991), the **Third National Health and Nutritional Examination Survey** (NHANES III, 1988–1991), and the **Surgeon General's Report** (DHHS, 1996), physical activity was found to be lowest among people with low incomes and lower levels of education.

In general, people are more active when they are younger. For example, 64% of students in grades 9 to 12 engaged in vigorous physical activity 3 or more days per week for at least 20 minutes versus only 16% of people aged 18 and older (CDC, 2003). Age and ethnicity also have an effect. Pima Indian, Latino, African American, and Asian American children are less active than European American children (Aron, 1993; Stevens, 1996). A school-based survey of 551 girls showed that more minority girls reported getting less than 1 hour of strenuous activity per week than nonminority girls. Minority girls also watched on average 5 hours more television per week than nonminority girls (Wolf, 1993). Ethnic differences are seen in adulthood as well. Older African Americans score lower on various measures of physical activity compared with European Americans (Clark, 1995).

Physical Consequences of Physical Activity

Being physically active and exercising daily are good for physical health. As mentioned earlier, there is some debate about how much exercise is needed, but no debate about whether it is needed. As early as the mid-twentieth century, physically active individuals were shown to be less likely to develop coronary heart disease (Kahn, 1963; Morris, Heady, Raffle, Roberts, & Parks, 1953). Physical activity not only relates to reduced mortality from different diseases (Bouchard, 2001; Kohl, 2001) but also increases life expectancy (Blair, Kohl, Gordon, & Paffenbarger, 1992; Lee & Skerrett, 2001; Paffenbarger, Hyde, Wing, & Hsieh, 1986). In particular, physical activity (controlling for the ill effects of a bad diet or smoking) has been identified as an independent risk factor in development of diseases such as cardiovascular disease (Berlin & Colditz, 1990; Pate, 1995). Evidence is accumulating that shows connections between physical activity and cancers (Thune & Furberg, 2001). In general, higher levels of both occupational and leisure time physical activity relate to lower levels of prostate, lung, testes, colon, rectal, and breast cancers, although evidence in some of these cases is inconsistent. In addition, being physically active relates to lower incidence of Type 2 diabetes (Hu et al., 2001; Manson, Shore, Baron, Ackerson, & Neligh, 1992; Wannamethee, Shaper, & Alberti, 2000), osteoporosis or loss of bone density (Greendale, Barrett-Conner, Edelstein, Ingles, & Halle, 1995; Mussolino, Looker, & Orwoll, 2001), strokes (Wannamethee & Shaper, 1992), and hypertension (Reaven, Barrett-Conner, & Edelstein, 1991).

Psychological Consequences of Physical Activity

Being physically active is probably beneficial for psychological health as well. Why do I say only "probably"? At this point few methodologically sound longitudinal studies have been performed to test the causal relationship between physical activity and mental health (Morgan, 1997; Phillips et al., 2002). Nevertheless, a strong body of correlation work suggests that there is a link. In chapter 4, you read that exercising can be a great stress reliever. This is just one of the many positive associations between physical activity and mental health. Numerous epidemiological studies and reviews of research link higher levels of physical activity with reduced symptoms of depression (Farmer et al., 1988; Paffenbarger, Lee, & Leung, 1994). Dunn, Trivedi, and O'Neal (2001) reviewed 37 studies published between 1970 and 2000. They found that greater amounts of occupational and leisure time physical activity generally were associated with reduced symptoms of depression. Quasi-experimental studies also showed that exercise of light, moderate, and vigorous intensity reduced symptoms of depression. Both quasi-experimental and randomized controlled trials showed that resistance training and aerobic exercise reduced symptoms of depression. Physical activity also reduces anxiety (Bhui & Fletcher, 2000; Raglin, 1997) and increases self-esteem (Sonstoem, 1997). Covey and Feltz (1991) highlighted the role of physical activity in development, concluding that physically active high school girls report significantly healthier self-image and coping characteristics than physically inactive girls. Similarly, Wankel and Berger (1990) showed that physical activity is significantly related to personal growth, social integration, and positive social change. However, these associations may not hold for elderly persons (Brown, 1992).

To some extent, finding links between physical activity and mental health can be frustrating. The link appears to make sense. You may notice that you feel better after a run, walk, or bicycle ride, but robust demonstrations of this association are difficult to find. The bulk of the research linking psychological well-being and physical activity is correlational in nature, and the scientific community is hesitant to declare physical activity as an unqualified balm for the mind. This ambivalence can be seen in examinations of why physical activity can be helpful. Neither biological nor psychological mechanisms of the physical activity and well-being link have been clearly established. Physical activity could lead to better mental health because activity increases monoamines, such as norepinephrine, epinephrine, dopamine, and serotonin, or releases endorphins. Unfortunately, evidence for each of these possibilities is spotty (Phillips et al., 2002). What can we be sure of? Physical activity prevents excessive weight gain (the dangers of which are described above) and is linked clearly to physical well-being. The assumed links to psychological well-being have yet to be demonstrated causally.

Smoking and Drinking

Both smoking and drinking are commonly considered to be vices. Although tobacco and alcohol are both potentially addictive substances, the body metabolizes alcohol and nicotine differently. Alcohol is a liquid, absorbed in the stomach, from where it then travels to the heart, the lungs, and finally to the brain. The active elements (e.g., nicotine) of tobacco are usually inhaled, resulting in a rapid transmission to the brain. Smoking has quick effects. Whereas a drinker may consume alcohol several times a week or a day, a pack-a-day smoker experiences about 200 puffs or "behavioral reinforcers" in a wide variety of social settings. The majority of regular smokers are addicted, although many people can use alcohol socially and not become addicted (Russell, 1990). This difference in social use and the amount of behavioral cueing, for example, people who always smoke at a bar are tempted to smoke when they are at a bar, explains, in part, why the relapse rates for tobacco addiction is higher than those for alcohol **addiction.** Many alcoholics can quit drinking but have more difficulty in quitting smoking.

Our society has social and cultural differences in how we treat the use of each substance. Tobacco use is legal for the vast majority of college age students, whereas alcohol use is illegal for those younger than 21. Alcohol use is also prohibited during work hours and class activities and has been relegated to certain "social" events (except for alcoholics), which usually occur in the evening. Tobacco use, on the other hand, is a more accepted daily behavior, often occurring at any time of the day in a variety of settings. Circumstances may make smoking appear more common than it actually is. Because of current trends in indoor air policies, smokers are forced to stand outside building entrances, which further increases their visibility and fuels misperceptions of the prevalence of smoking.

Smoking

In 2003, almost a quarter of all North Americans admitted to regularly putting a flame to little paper-covered cylinders of dry leaves, and sucking the bitter smoke into their lungs (CDC, 2003). Tobacco contains roughly 500 chemicals, and tobacco smoke contains about 4,000 (Dube & Green, 1982). Yet, 23% of adults in the United States smoke. Anyone knowing that cigarettes contain chemicals, cancer-causing black tar, and an addictive substance called nicotine may wonder why smokers persist. Many smokers who know the same information wonder why they persist as well, and many try to quit.

Who smokes more? If you have followed the trends in prevalence of smoking in America you know there is good news and bad news. During the 7 years from 1993 to 2000, the numbers of smokers substantially decreased for all age groups, except those between 18 and 24 (CDC, 2003). Correspondingly, the reduction of smoking or the cessation of tobacco use among college students is a critical public health priority. Between 1993 and 1997, cigarette smoking increased 28% among U.S. college students (Wechsler, Kelley, Seibring, Kuo, & Rigotti, 2001), and these numbers could get a lot worse. Although 29% of college students are current smokers, 53% have tried smoking and 38% have smoked in the past year (Rigotti, Lee, & Wechsler, 2000).

Tobacco use is the leading cause of preventable morbidity and mortality in the United States (DHHS, 2002). Yet, smoking continues in the broader culture as well as on high school and college campuses (Hilts, 1996; Glantz et al., 1996). Longitudinal data from the Monitoring the Futures Studies (Johnston, O'Malley, & Bachman, 2001) indicate that although past month use by high school seniors fell in the late 1970s and stabilized in the 1980s, it rose steadily in the 1990s. Smoking rates in high school peaked in 1997 with rates almost identical to those in 1975. Of those high school students in the class of 1999 who planned to finish 4 years of college, 31.4% had smoked at least one cigarette in the past 30 days (Johnston et al., 2001). One may be tempted to believe that this lack of change and increase in smoking can be attributed to students not having enough information about tobacco or to demographic issues, but this is not the case. At the college level, no significant differences are found between smokers and nonsmokers and year in college, sex, age, race, or having attended public or private high schools (DeBernardo et al., 1999). DeBernardo et al. also showed that whereas 98% of those who responded felt that they understood the harmful effects of smoking on their health, just 39.1% of smokers seriously considered stopping, and 11.5% of nonsmokers intended to start smoking. These data prove that knowledge alone is insufficient to change behavior.

Cultural Variations in Smoking

When looking at the population in general, we see some clear-cut cultural differences in who smokes. Men smoke more than women (DHHS, 2003). People earning less and who are not well educated smoke more than people higher on the socioeconomic ladder (CDC, 2003). In fact, in more deprived neighborhoods (i.e., those with higher crime rates and less access to health care), people are more likely to smoke (Duncan, Jones, & Moon, 1999). In general, people with lower status (e.g., lower ranked military personnel) smoke more than higher status individuals (e.g., ranked officers) (Hebold, 1987). Geography also accounts for differences in smoking rates. In 2003, Kentucky had the highest number of smokers in the United States. Smoking rates for different states are shown in Table 7.4.

The most pronounced differences in smoking are racial and ethnic (Figure 7.5). The American Lung Association reports that American Indians have the

TABLE 7.4

Prevalence of Current Cigarette Smoking* Among Adults, by Area and Sex—Behavioral Risk Factor Surveillance System, United States, 2000

Area	Men %	Men (95% CI†)	Women %	Women (95% CI)	Total %	Total (95% CI)
Alabama	29.0	(±3.8)	22.0	(±2.5)	25.3	(±2.2)
Alaska	26.8	(±4.1)	23.1	(±3.6)	25.0	(±2.8)
Arizona	18.4	(±4.4)	18.8	(±4.6)	18.6	(±3.1)
Arkansas	26.2	(±2.9)	24.2	(±2.2)	25.2	(±1.8)
California	20.1	(±2.4)	14.4	(±1.6)	17.2	(±1.5)
Colorado	19.5	(±2.9)	20.6	(±2.7)	20.1	(±2.0)
Connecticut	20.5	(±2.4)	19.5	(±1.8)	20.0	(±1.5)
Delaware	25.8	(±3.4)	20.3	(±2.6)	23.0	(±2.1)
District of Columbia	22.1	(±3.6)	19.9	(±2.7)	20.9	(±2.2)
Florida	24.5	(±2.1)	22.1	(±1.7)	23.2	(±1.4)
Georgia	26.5	(±2.7)	21.0	(±2.0)	23.6	(±1.7)
Hawaii	22.9	(±2.2)	16.5	(±1.7)	19.7	(±1.4)
Idaho	22.9	(±2.1)	21.9	(±1.8)	22.4	(±1.4)
Illinois	24.9	(±2.5)	20.0	(±1.9)	22.3	(±1.6)
Indiana	28.5	(±2.8)	25.5	(±2.4)	27.0	(±1.8)
Iowa	25.9	(±2.6)	20.9	(±2.1)	23.3	(±1.7)
Kansas	24.2	(±2.3)	18.2	(±1.7)	21.1	(±1.4)
Kentucky	33.4	(±2.5)	27.9	(±2.0)	30.5	(±1.6)
Louisiana	26.7	(±2.2)	21.8	(±1.6)	24.1	(±1.4)
Maine	24.6	(±3.4)	23.1	(±2.7)	23.8	(±2.2)
Maryland	22.0	(±2.4)	19.2	(±1.8)	20.6	(±1.5)
Massachusetts	20.2	(±1.7)	19.8	(±1.4)	20.0	(±1.1)
Michigan	26.0	(±2.9)	22.5	(±2.5)	24.2	(±1.9)
Minnesota	20.7	(±2.5)	18.9	(±2.2)	19.8	(±1.7)
Mississippi	25.3	(±3.4)	21.9	(±2.8)	23.5	(±2.2)
Missouri	30.1	(±3.1)	24.6	(±2.2)	27.2	(±1.9)
Montana	18.0	(±2.7)	19.7	(±2.4)	18.9	(±1.8)
Nebraska	22.1	(±2.6)	20.7	(±2.2)	21.4	(±1.7)
Nevada	28.7	(±3.6)	29.5	(±4.2)	29.1	(±2.8)
New Hampshire	26.9	(±3.7)	23.9	(±2.9)	25.4	(±2.3)
New Jersey	23.5	(±2.5)	18.6	(±1.8)	21.0	(±1.5)
New Mexico	26.2	(±2.6)	21.2	(±2.2)	23.6	(±1.7)
New York	22.5	(±2.6)	20.9	(±2.0)	21.6	(±1.6)
North Carolina	28.4	(±3.2)	24.1	(±2.3)	26.1	(±1.9)
North Dakota	25.9	(±3.3)	20.7	(±2.7)	23.3	(±2.1)
Ohio	26.7	(±3.5)	26.0	(±2.8)	26.3	(±2.2)
Oklahoma	23.7	(±2.4)	23.0	(±2.1)	23.3	(±1.6)
Oregon	22.3	(±2.4)	19.3	(±1.9)	20.8	(±1.5)
Pennsylvania	25.4	(±2.7)	23.3	(±2.0)	24.3	(±1.6)
Puerto Rico	16.8	(±2.6)	9.9	(±1.6)	13.1	(±1.5)
Rhode Island	23.8	(±2.6)	23.2	(±2.1)	23.5	(±1.7)
South Carolina	28.5	(±3.2)	21.3	(±2.3)	24.7	(±1.9)
South Dakota	22.6	(±2.1)	21.4	(±1.7)	22.0	(±1.4)
Tennessee	27.7	(±3.1)	23.8	(±2.1)	25.7	(±1.8)
Texas	25.3	(±2.1)	18.8	(±1.5)	22.0	(±1.3)
Utah	14.5	(±2.5)	11.4	(±2.0)	12.9	(±1.6)

TABLE 7.4

Prevalence of Current Cigarette Smoking* Among Adults, by Area and Sex—Behavioral Risk Factor Surveillance System, United States, 2000—cont'd

Area	Men %	Men (95% CI[†])	Women %	Women (95% CI)	Total %	Total (95% CI)
Vermont	21.8	(±2.5)	21.2	(±2.1)	21.5	(±1.6)
Virginia	24.4	(±3.4)	18.8	(±2.5)	21.5	(±2.1)
Washington	21.7	(±2.4)	19.7	(±1.9)	20.7	(±1.5)
West Virginia	27.8	(±3.1)	24.7	(±2.4)	26.1	(±1.9)
Wisconsin	24.4	(±2.8)	23.9	(±2.4)	24.1	(±1.8)
Wyoming	23.2	(±3.8)	24.3	(±2.8)	23.8	(±1.9)

*Persons aged ≥18 years who reported having smoked ≥100 cigarettes and who reported smoking every day or some days.
[†]Confidence interval.
SOURCE: *Morbidity and Mortality Weekly Report, 50,* 1103. Center for Disease Control (2001).

highest rates of smoking (36%), followed by African Americans (26%), European Americans (24%), and then Asian and Pacific Islanders (17%).

Smoking and culture have some interesting interactions. African Americans who are more traditional are more likely to smoke than African Americans acculturated to mainstream European American ways (Klonoff & Landrine, 2001). In contrast, some Asian Americans and Latinos are less likely to smoke if they are more traditional in their ways (Lafferty, Heaney, & Chen, 1999). In another interaction of smoking and ethnicity, Llabre, Klein, Saab, McCalla, and Schneiderman (1998) found that when African Americans are exposed to stress (demonstrated in an experimental setting), they show greater changes in the functioning of their blood vessels than in the functioning of their heart muscles. This has implications for the development of cerebrovascular disease for African Americans who are smokers.

Why Do People Smoke?

In keeping with the biopsychosocial approach of health psychology, biological, psychological, and social factors contribute to the initiation of smoking. Biologically, nicotine has some pleasing effects on the brain and body, and it works extremely fast. The moment a smoker puffs a cigarette, the nicotine is absorbed through the fine inner lining of the cheek and reaches the brain within 15 seconds. In general, nicotine causes good moods, reduced feelings of hunger, and increased alertness and attention (Grunberg, Faraday, & Rahman, 2002).

In addition to these biological effects, there are some clear genetic components to smoking (Pomerleau & Kardia, 1999). If one member of an identical twin set chooses to smoke, the other will probably smoke as well. Is a specific gene involved? Lerman et al. (1999) showed that versions of the dopamine transporter gene *SLC6A3* and the dopamine receptor gene *DRD2* are associated with the likelihood of smoking. People who had specific versions of these genes were

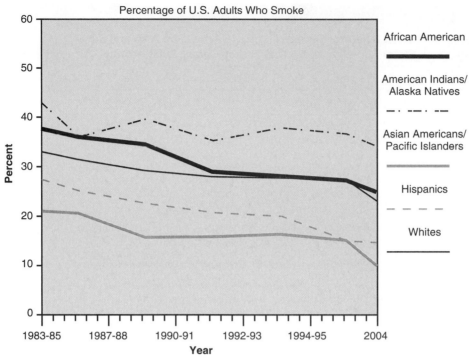

FIGURE 7.5
Percentage of U.S. Adults Who Smoke
There are significant differences in smoking rates across cultural groups.
Source: National Health Interview Survey, National Center for Health Statistics, Centers for Disease Control and Prevention, 1978–1995. Health, United States (2004).

more likely to start smoking before age 16 than those individuals who did not have them. Of note, the genotype most related to addictive behavior, *DRD2-A1*, was most commonly found in African Americans, the ethnic group with high smoking rates. Another clue to the physiological reasons for smoking comes from studies showing how people are addicted to nicotine. Smokers may not even be conscious of the extent of their physiological addiction. For example, when unknowing smokers were given cigarettes that had lower levels of nicotine, they automatically puffed longer and took more puffs (Schachter, 1980). Consequently, they smoked more low-nicotine cigarettes to get amounts of the nicotine comparable to those that they were used to.

Psychological Causes of Addiction

People start smoking for a host of psychological reasons. Some personality types such as individuals with low self-esteem who can be easily influenced or extroverts who savor the stimulation of nicotine are more likely to smoke. Extroverts find the nicotine arousal rewarding and smoke to increase this arousal. Some of the developmental theories discussed in chapter 3 also have been invoked to explain initiation. For example, Erikson's theory of human social development suggests that the struggle both to overcome inferiority and establish an identity can make a person more likely to smoke. Others have extended Erikson's theory to explain adolescent deviant behavior. Turbin, Jessor, and Costa (2000) see problem behaviors such as smoking as special cases of the transition process experienced by all adolescents. Although difficult to measure and not conclusively linked to smoking, some theorists and many advertisers have used psychoanalytical theory to explain smoking. These groups argue that a smoker has experienced difficulties during Freud's theorized psychosocial oral stage. Because the pleasure-causing erogenous zone (see chapter 3) is the mouth, the smoker derives pleasure from the mouth and the placement of the cigarette in it. Many suggestive advertisements also use Freudian ideas to attract people to smoking.

People start smoking for many social and cultural reasons. Movies are very relevant in this regard. An extensive body of research has shown a strong correlation between the number of people shown smoking in the movies and the number smoking in the population. Many people imitate the heroes and heroines of the big screen. Even cartoons are not off limits to tobacco companies for product placements. Goldstein, Sobel, and Newman (1999) found that more than two-thirds of animated children's films made between 1937 and 1997 by five of the major production companies (e.g., Walt Disney, Universal, and 20th Century Fox) featured tobacco in story plots without clear verbal messages of any negative long-term health effects associated with its use.

Sometimes social pressure leads people to smoke. Rebellious adolescents may smoke to appear more adult or to distinguish themselves from others. Paradoxically, many children start smoking because they want to be like others, and thus they imitate their peers or family members who are smoking. Perhaps the key social factor is advertising. Cigarettes are some of the most heavily advertised products in the media (DHHS, 1994) with advertising budgets reaching more than 1 billion dollars per year. Until recently, younger children were the key targets. Camel cigarettes had a cartoon character named Joe Camel that was recognized second to only Mickey Mouse among North American children (Grunberg, Brown, & Klein, 1997). Consequently, close to 40% of adolescent smokers began smoking with Camels or Camel Lights.

Physiological Consequences of Smoking

There is no doubt that smoking can kill. A smoker has a 100% greater chance of dying earlier than a nonsmoker, and this mortality ratio increases with the amount smoked, the length of time one has smoked, and the tar and nicotine contents of the cigarettes (Grunberg et al., 1997). The longer one smokes, the greater is the risk of dying prematurely. The overall risk of dying also increases for smokers who inhale smoke versus those who only puff it in and out. Smokers are most likely to die prematurely from coronary heart disease, related cardiovascular diseases, or a range of cancers of the respiratory tract. Common smoking-related cancers are cancers of the lung, larynx, oral cavity, pancreas, and esopha-

Image courtesy of The Advertising Archives

© Bettmann/CORBIS

Smoking Early media campaigns (before media advertising was regulated by the Surgeon General) used celebrities to get people to smoke. Here the then Hollywood actor and later President Ronald Reagan and President Roosevelt appear in ads and press photos with cigarettes lit.

TABLE 7.5

Smoking and Cancer Mortality Table

Type of Cancer	Gender	Relative Risk Among Smokers	Relative Risk Among Smokers	Mortality Attributable to Smoking	Mortality Attributable to Smoking
		Current	Former	Percent	Number
Lung	Male	22.4	9.4	90	82,800
	Female	11.9	4.7	79	40,300
Larynx	Male	10.5	5.2	81	24,000
	Female	17.8	11.9	87	700
Oral Cavity	Male	27.5	8.8	92	4,900
	Female	5.6	2.9	61	1,800
Esophagus	Male	7.6	5.8	78	5,700
	Female	10.3	3.2	75	1,900
Pancreas	Male	2.1	1.1	29	3,500
	Female	2.3	1.8	34	4,500
Bladder	Male	2.9	1.9	47	3,000
	Female	2.6	1.9	37	1,200
Kidney	Male	3.0	2.0	48	3,000
	Female	1.4	1.2	12	500
Stomach	Male	1.5	?	17	1,400
	Female	1.5	?	25	1,300
Leukemia	Male	2.0	?	20	2,000
	Female	2.0	?	20	1,600
Cervix	Female	2.1	1.9	31	1,400
Endometrial	Female	0.7	1.0	—	—

Not all cancers are equally influenced by smoking. Notice the differences in relative risk from smoking for the different types of cancers and the sex differences.

gus. Table 7.5 shows how the rates of cancer vary for men and women and how the risks are lower for nonsmokers.

Smoking has a synergistic effect on many health issues. Women who use oral contraceptives and who smoke have an increased risk of dying from ovarian, cervical, or uterine cancers (Vessey, Painter, & Yeates, 2003). Teenage girls who smoke have an increased risk of developing breast cancer before they reach menopause (Band, Le, Fang, & Deschamps, 2002). Similarly, people who have coronary heart disease and who smoke are more likely to die from a heart attack than are nonsmokers with coronary heart disease (Goldenberg et al., 2003). Howard et al. (1998) found that cigarette smoking increases plaque formation around arteries by as much as 50% in a 3-year period. This atherosclerosis can increase blood pressure and hasten the occurrence of a stroke or cardiac arrest. Among women undergoing treatment for early breast cancer, those who smoke are more than twice as likely to die from their cancer as nonsmoking women. In a study examining the effect of smoking on long-term outcomes of breast cancer patients treated with conservative surgery and radiation, researchers found that women who continue to smoke during therapy are 2.5 times more likely to die from the cancer than are women with no history of smoking (American Cancer Society, 2005). The study examined 1,039 nonsmokers and 861 smokers who underwent conservative therapy for breast cancer from March 1970 to December 2002. In addition, smoking correlates with increased occurrences of a wide host of diseases from sexual impotence to seeing and hearing problems and ovarian cysts to multiple sclerosis and even the common cold (American Cancer Society, 2005).

Although still debatable because of conflicting studies, the evidence weighs in against **secondhand smoke** or **environmental tobacco smoke** (ETS). ETS is the tobacco smoke inhaled by nonsmokers who are in the presence of smokers. This passive smoking is linked to lung cancer (Kreuzer, Krauss, Kreienbrock, Jockel, & Wichmann, 2000) and cardiovascular disease (He et al., 1999; Kawachi et al., 1997). Infants and children are probably most at risk from ETS. Early exposure to ETS has been linked to an increased risk of asthma (Larsson, Frisk, Hallstrom, Kiviloog, & Lundback, 2001). All in all, it is clear that any amount of tobacco use is detrimental to health.

Drinking

When health psychologists talk about drinking, they are probably referring to alcohol consumption. Drinking water seems to be good for you (although the "drink 8 glasses of water a day" prescription was recently found to have no scientific basis—everybody promotes the prescription, but nobody is sure where it came from). In contrast, alcohol is responsible for 100,000 deaths each year, the third leading cause of death after tobacco and insufficient physical activity/poor diet (McGinnis & Foege, 1993). Be aware that whether drinking alcohol is a good thing or a bad thing has probably stimulated more spirited conversations than any other health behavior topic. Smoking is dangerous, no question, but is drinking? The government recommendation is that men can "safely" consume two drinks per day (but only one for women) (USDA, 2000). You have also probably had friends justify their drinking by citing research concluding that a drink per day is actually *better* than no drinks at all. Is this true? How much, if any, alcohol is healthy? First let's get familiar with usage.

Who Drinks, How Much, and Why?

Patterns for drinking and causes for initiation of drinking are similar to those for smoking, and I will outline only some of the major differences here. Alcohol is the drug of choice among high school youth with 51% of high school seniors having used alcohol in the past 30 days (NIDA, 2000). Given that many sources suggest that some drinking is all right, it is important to distinguish between use and misuse. **Alcohol abuse** is characterized by one or more of the following as a result of alcohol use: (1) failure to fulfill major role obligations; (2) recurrent physically hazardous use; (3) recurrent alcohol-related legal problems; or (4) continued use despite persistent alcohol-related social or interpersonal problems (Wood, Vinson, & Sher, 2002). At most colleges, alcohol abuse is pretty evident. Nearly half

Drinking and Addiction The British painter William Hogarth had some strong opinions of what could happen if people drank too much strong liquor. In Gin Lane (1751) he represents the horror of what could happen if people became addicted to gin.

of college students are binge drinkers, men who have consumed five or more and women who have consumed four or more drinks in a row at least once during the previous 2 weeks (Wechler, Moeykens, Davenport, Castillo, & Hansen, 2000). In the general population, approximately 13.8 million people abuse alcohol or are dependent on it (Grant et al., 1994). Alcohol abuse is 2.5 to 5 times higher in men than in women, but this sex difference is least pronounced in people aged 18 to 24 (Grant et al., 1991). Like smoking, many cultural differences are manifested in drinking, especially across ethnic, SES, religious, and geographical lines. Beer is the most common form of alcohol (57% of drinkers) followed by hard liquor (e.g., gin, rum, and vodka, 29%) and wine (13%) (Williams, Stinson, Sanchez, & Dufour, 1998).

As with many other health behaviors, it is important to take a biopsychosocial approach to understanding why people drink. From a biological angle there are some genetic predictors of alcoholism. Alcohol misuse tends to run in families (Merikangas, 1990), and identical twins have a much higher concordance of both alcohol use and misuse than fraternal twins (Ball & Murray, 1994; McGue, 1999). This shows that there are genetic predispositions to starting to drink. Research has even identified different markers at the genetic level. For example, people with certain genes (e.g., the beta-subunit of alcohol dehydrogenase) are more sensitive to alcohol. The presence of this gene varies across ethnic groups (McGue, 1999; NIAAA, 1993). Some false alarms have also been sounded along the way. For example, since the early 1990s researchers were certain that the dopamine DRD2 receptor gene was one of the best markers for severe alcoholism (Blum et al., 1990). Later research showed this not to be the case (Gelernter, Goldman, & Risch, 1992). All things considered, there is considerable optimism that we are close to identifying the key genes that place a person at risk for alcoholism (McGue, 1999). Some significant nongenetic biological markers of vulnerability to alcoholism are known. Children of alcoholics, a vulnerable group, have different brain wave activity in response to the presentation of alcohol-related stimuli material (reduced P3 waves) (Polich, Pollock, & Bloom, 1994), show lower activity levels of the enzyme monoamine oxidase (von Knorring, Oreland, & von Knorring, 1987), and are less sensitive to the subjective intoxicating effects of alcohol (Schucklit, 1994). The lower sensitivity to alcohol (i.e., they do not feel as shaky on their feet after drinking) may lead them to drink greater amounts.

Psychologically, three broad personality characteristics are linked to alcoholism. People who are high in neuroticism, impulsive, and extroverted are more likely to become alcoholic (Sher & Trull, 1994). Given the many behaviors that these traits are associated with, they are seen more as mediators or moderating variables within larger psychosocial etiological models of alcoholism (Wood et al., 2002). They are not direct causes of alcoholism. Research has also identified patterns of thinking that could put a person at risk for alcoholism. Maisto, Carey, and Bradizza (1999) reviewed the ways that social learning theories have been applied to alcohol use. This review showed that there are a number of specific beliefs that people have about the behavioral, cognitive, and emotional effects of drinking (alcohol outcome expectancies) which can predict their likelihood of drinking (see also Goldman, DelBoca, & Darkes, 1999). For example, if young adults have a positive alcohol expectancy—they expect good outcomes from drinking—before the first time they drink, then they are more likely to drink more subsequently (Smith, Goldman, Greenbaum, & Christiansen, 1995).

Blending biological and psychological causes of drinking, alcohol also seems to be used to reduce stress (Cappell & Greeley, 1987). The consumption of alcohol serves as a reinforcement: the positive feelings after alcohol consumption increase the behavior of drinking, and drinking is associated with a decrease in stress. For example, students in a study were told that they were taking part in a taste test to obscure the true intent of the researchers (to test effects of alcohol). These students drank more when they were experimentally stressed than when they were not (Statsiewicz & Lisman, 1989).

Who people spend their time with makes a difference in how much they drink. From a psychosocial standpoint, children of alcoholics are more likely to drink (Chassin, Rogosch, & Barrera, 1991), as are people with friends who drink (Wills & Cleary, 1999). Curran, Stice, and Chassin (1997) also showed that drinkers do not just pick friends who drink, but drinkers can make nondrinkers start drinking. Sometimes, just believing that it is normal to drink can make a person drink even if this perceived norm is completely inaccurate. Baer, Stacy, and Larimer (1991) found that college students nearly always perceived that their close friends consumed alcohol more frequently than they did. Finally, as with smoking, the media and advertising also play a large part in getting people to start drinking (Grube & Wallack, 1994).

Consequences of Alcohol Abuse

Drinking too much has been shown to negatively impact most organ systems and to be a major cause of injuries, many of them fatal (NIAAA, 1997). For many of the injuries, age is a critical factor because consequences of drinking are different across the lifespan. Prenatal infants often suffer the consequences of alcohol. Of course, they are not doing the drinking. Mothers who drink during pregnancy can influence the development of their fetuses. Fetal alcohol syndrome, described in chapter 3, results in developmental abnormalities and is a major result of mothers drinking (NIAAA, 1997; Streissguth et al., 1994). Alcohol-related motor accidents are the leading consequence of drinking for underage drinkers. The 21-year age limit is more than an arbitrary line drawn by the government (although it may have originally been one). A report compiling several studies on brain damage and alcohol concluded that underage drinkers face a greater risk of damage to the prefrontal regions of their brains. Double the amount of alcohol is required to do the same damage to someone older than 21. The development of the frontal lobes continues until age 16 after which point the brain maintains a high rate of energy expenditure that does not decrease until age 20 (Hoover, 2002). Consequently, underage drinking does retard brain cell growth.

Liver disease is one of the most common consequences of drinking excessively for older drinkers (Crabb, 1993). Problems range from excess fat in the liver to a swelling of the liver or to permanent and progressive scarring, referred to as cirrhosis of the liver. The risks of developing cirrhosis vary by sex; women are more likely to develop the problem (Lieber, 1994). Drinking too much—more than six drinks per day (for most, less for some)—also increases the risk of cardiovascular problems (Richardson, Wodak, Atkinson, Saunders, & Jewitt, 1986) and stroke (NIAAA, 1997). Drinking three to four drinks per day and drinking frequently have both been linked to hypertension (Marmot et al., 1994; Russel, Cooper, Frone, & Welte, 1991; Thadhani et al., 2002). Other health consequences include problems with the pancreas (Steinberg & Tenner, 1994), blackouts (Vinson, 1989), memory loss (Parsons, 1994), and chronic brain disease (Victor, 1993).

Together with its interactions with other health behaviors, alcohol use also relates to many different psychological problems and negative social behaviors. Families in which the parents abuse alcohol are often uncomfortable environments to grow up in. More fighting and conflict, less cohesion and expressiveness, and more children being injured are reported in alcoholic families (Bijur, Kurzon, Overpeck, & Scheidt, 1992; Sher, 1991). People who abuse alcohol are also more likely to partake in risky sex (Leigh & Stall, 1993), drive dangerously (Yi, Stinson, Williams, & Bertolucci, 1998), and be involved in crimes such as assault (Murdoch, Pihl, & Ross, 1990) and especially sexual assault (Roizen, 1997). People who drink too much alcohol or drink too often are also more at risk for a range of psychological disorders, such as anxiety and mood disorders (Kessler et al., 1997). Note, however, that in many of these cases, it is hard to establish causal links because of the many other factors that may have been involved.

The possibility of the benefits of some alcohol consumption has received a lot of press attention in the last few years. Some evidence of health benefits for small or moderate amounts of alcohol consumption has been demonstrated (Albert et al., 1999; Friedman, Armstrong, Kipp, & Klatsky, 2001). In fact, people who consume two standard drinks per day have a 20% lower risk for coronary heart disease than those who do not drink (Corrao, Bagnardi, Vittadini, & Favilli, 2000). What is a **standard drink?** The medical field agrees that a 12-ounce serving of beer (a standard bottle or can), a 5-ounce glass of wine, or a 1.5-ounce of gin, vodka, rum, or scotch, is a standard serving.

Moderate alcohol consumption is hypothesized to be the answer to the **French paradox,** the fact that most people in France have a diet that is high in fat but still have lower rates of heart disease. For example, Renaud, Gueguen, Siest, and Salamon (1999) studied 36,250 healthy French men between 1978 and 1983 and found that both those who drank beer (28% of the sample) and those who drank wine (61%) had a lesser risk for cardiovascular diseases. The reduction in mortality risk varies, depending on what is consumed. People who drink a glass of wine each day show a lower risk for mortality than those who drink spirits or beer (Gronbaek at al., 1995; Renaud et al., 1999). This lowered risk may be due to the other positive health behaviors that wine drinkers perform (Mortensen, Jensen, Sanders, & Reinisch, 2001; Wannamethee & Shaper, 1999). Wine drinkers may be better off economically, may eat better, and may exercise more. The main benefits of moderate alcohol consumption are tied to the ability of alcohol to reduce the risk for coronary heart disease by raising the drinker's levels of high-density lipoprotein (HDL) cholesterol. Higher levels of HDL cholesterol help to keep the arteries free of clogs. Should nondrinkers older than 21 now start drinking? The answer is probably no. Remember, other health behaviors can lower the risk of coronary heart disease, and moderate drinkers face the risk of becoming heavy drinkers, which will truly be detrimental to their health. Furthermore, the French eat smaller serving sizes than Americans, which could partially explain the paradox (and wine may not be your answer to overeating).

FOCUS on Applications

You Know You Want To . . . : Changing Social Norms

Let's go down into the trenches to take a closer look at one of the most dangerous health behaviors out there: smoking. One of the most exciting places to see health psychologists changing this health behavior is at colleges. As I described in the section on smoking, a significant cultural group that does not show a decrease in their unhealthy health behaviors is college and high school students. Smoking rates for this group are not dropping as are the rates for most other age groups. Let me tell you about one way some researchers are trying to change this fact.

Researchers at the University of Wisconsin in Oshkosh, WI, began their research by studying the different psychological reasons for smoking. They noticed that one of the most common reasons for students starting to smoke was that they thought that it was actually a pretty normal thing to do. Students believed that many of their peers were smoking. The researchers knew that this was not the case. They also realized that if the college could show that this was not really the case, students may decrease their smoking behavior. This approach is called a **social norms approach.**

Social norming research has shown that college students often believe that those engaging in healthy behavior are in the minority when, in fact, they are not. Health psychologists acknowledge that norms are important predictors of health behaviors. For example, the Theory of Planned Behavior discussed in chapter 6 (Ajzen & Madden, 1986) holds that health behaviors directly result from behavioral intentions that are composed of attitudes toward the specific action, perceived behavioral control, and subjective norms regarding the action. If people who smoke believe that smoking is normative or if they believe that their friends do not believe that not smoking is the norm, these people are less likely to change their behavior. An inaccurate perception of the norms could also cause nonsmokers to try smoking. If impressionable students believe that most students their age smoke, these distorted perceptions of group behavior and attitudes may lead them to comply with inaccurate peer pressure. In a comparison of college smokers, nonsmokers, and occasional smokers, regular smokers perceived more approval for their smoking and believed that their peers smoked more frequently than the nonsmokers and occasional smokers perceived (Grube, McGree, & Morgan, 1986). The smokers perceived more positive social and physiological consequences of smoking (e.g., feeling more relaxed and fewer negative consequences (e.g., feeling sick). Smokers valued the concept of "health" less than did nonsmokers or occasional smokers (Grube et al., 1986).

So what did the research team do? They assessed the actual and perceived behaviors and attitudes of the students and developed a social marketing campaign to modify misperceptions. The multimedia campaign used posters, an "art car" (a car painted with antismoking information), television and radio ads, a mannequin (covered with messages about the dangers of smoking), information tables, varsity sport promotions, and other promotional items (e.g., plastic piggy banks) to convey the message collected from the campus-wide surveys. The primary message was that few students smoked and that those who did wanted to quit smoking. Media and special events utilized the theme "You know you want to" because it tested well with students and captured the power of positive norming. "You know you want to . . ." promoted cessation services and directed smokers and nonsmokers to resources to learn more about the health benefits of not smoking. Advertisements extended the "You know you want to" message. One ad, "You know you want to . . . be kissed" highlighted the statistic that most students want to quit and that most students, all things being equal, prefer to kiss a nonsmoker. Another ad, "You know you want to . . . get out of the cold" included the statistics of quitting and the finding that nearly three of four students wanted to help a friend quit smoking (and get out from the cold where smokers who cannot smoke indoors have to go). A third ad, "You know you want to . . . be true" used the fact that a majority of students think that tobacco companies manipulate people to become smokers. Posters with these messages were placed around campus. A marketing survey completed 3 months after the introduction of the campaign showed that 91% of students reported seeing the "You know you want to . . ." posters.

Did the social norms approach work? The intervention was a resounding success. At the start of the intervention, 34% of students on campus smoked. When the students were surveyed 1 year after the media campaign, the number of smokers had dropped to 27%. Research is currently under way to replicate the campaign at different campuses around the state of Wisconsin, the state with a high level of smoking. In a twist on the old adage, it is not so much what you do not know that can hurt you, but what you think you know that actually is wrong may hurt even more.

Chapter Summary

- Obesity is one of America's greatest health threats. Few Americans eat a balanced diet or get a sufficient amount of nutrients. Obesity increases the chances of developing a chronic disease and increases the chances of developing coronary heart disease. Obesity can be caused by both genetic and environmental influences. The Food Guide Pyramid illustrates the USDA recommendations for a healthy diet and has been modified for different cultural groups.
- Food preferences develop at an early age and are strongly influenced by the ways parents feed infants and children. There are innate preferences, but the majority of our tastes come about because of exposure to various foods as we grow.
- Physical activity is any bodily movement that results in energy expenditure. People should get at least 30 minutes of physical activity five times per week to maintain a healthy lifestyle. Ethnic, socioeconomic, age, and sex differences all account for cultural differences in physical activity. Physically active individuals are less likely to develop coronary heart disease and are more likely to live longer. Physical activity has also been associated with better mental health.
- Smoking is most common among college-aged individuals. Rates of smoking are dropping across most age groups except the 18- to 24-year range. The most pronounced differences are ethnic and racial, followed by SES. Evidence is building to support a genetic component to smoking, whereas a number of different personality traits such as low self-esteem and extroversion are associated with increased addiction to smoking. The media and movies are also linked to rates of smoking.
- Smokers are much more likely to die younger than nonsmokers. Smokers are more likely to die prematurely from coronary heart disease and a range of cancers, although they are significant sex differences in rates of cancer due to smoking.
- Alcohol consumption is responsible for more than 100,000 deaths each year although some research suggests that drinking moderate levels of alcohol can actually have health benefits. Like smoking, there are genetic and environmental reasons for alcohol abuse. People who are extroverted, neurotic, and impulsive are most likely to abuse alcohol. Drinking too much has been shown to negatively impact most organ systems and to be a major cause of injuries.

Synthesize, Evaluate, Apply

- Take a close look at your own health behaviors. Monitor your physical activity and dietary patterns and compare them to prescribed levels for good health.
- What are the main reasons for people not eating a balanced diet?
- What are the differences between the cultural food pyramids?
- What are the pros and cons of having different pyramids?
- What are the biggest factors influencing the development of food preferences?
- Apply what you know about food and exercise to develop a plan for optimal health.
- Evaluate the literature on the psychological effects of exercise. Design an empirical study to resolve the ambiguities.
- Describe how eating and physical activity can interact with each other.
- What are the biopsychosocial determinants of smoking and drinking?
- What are the common elements underlying the performance of health behaviors?
- What are other behaviors that could influence the performance of the four behaviors described in this chapter?
- How would high levels of stress influence each of these behaviors and why?
- What are possible causes for the cultural differences seen in the performance of each behavior?
- What should the priorities for future research on health behaviors be?
- What aspects of 21st century society accentuate the performance of unhealthy behaviors?
- How can family, developmental differences, and child-rearing influence health behaviors?
- Apply your knowledge to design an intervention to reduce bad eating habits in the workplace.

KEY TERMS, CONCEPTS, AND PEOPLE

addiction, 218
alcohol abuse, 226
body mass index, 207
eating disorders, 213
exercise, 215
food preferences, 207
Food Guide Pyramid, 203
French paradox, 230

National Health Interview
  Survey, 216
obesity, 207
physical activity, 214
secondhand smoke/
  environmental tobacco
  smoke, 226

social norms approach, 231
Third National Health and
  Nutritional Examination
  Survey, 216
standard drink, 230
Surgeon General's Report, 216

ESSENTIAL READINGS

Dubbert, P. M. (2002). Physical activity and exercise: Recent advances and current challenges. *Journal of Consulting and Clinical Psychology, 70*(3), 526–536.

Marlatt, G. A., & Witkiewitz, K. (2002). Harm reduction approaches to alcohol use: Health promotion, prevention, and treatment. *Addictive Behaviors, 27*(6), 867–886.

Niaura, R., & Abrams, D. B. (2002). Smoking cessation: Progress, priorities, and prospectus. *Journal of Consulting and Clinical Psychology, 70*(3), 494–509.

Prochaska, J. O., Velicer, W. F., Rossi, J. S., Redding, C. A., Greene, G. W., Rossi, S. R., et al. (2004). Multiple risk expert systems interventions: Impact of simultaneous stage-matched expert system interventions for smoking, high-fat diet, and sun exposure in a population of parents. *Health Psychology, 23*(5), 503–516.

Wadden, T. A., Brownell, K. D., & Foster, G. D. (2002). Obesity: Responding to the global epidemic. *Journal of Consulting and Clinical Psychology, 70*(3), 510–525.

 ## WEB RESOURCES

Visit the companion website at **http://psychology.wadsworth.com/gurung1e/,** where you will find online resources for this book, including chapter-by-chapter quizzes, weblinks, and more! You can also visit Wadsworth Psychology Resource Center at **http://psychology.wadsworth.com** to access additional resources.

**Take a Closer Look at the Food Pyramid
and What Is Right for You**
www.MyPyramid.gov

Factors Surrounding Illness

What do you do if you have a headache? Most of us wait some time to see if it goes away and then take a pill if it does not. What if you sprain your ankle or pull a muscle? Most of us have heard that you first use cold (e.g., ice cubes wrapped in a towel) and then hot (e.g., a store-bought pack heated in a microwave oven), and then wrap the ankle and rest. Now it is a little trickier if you notice aches or pains or signs that you have not noticed or experienced before. What if you develop a rash or your skin turns different colors? What if you have a deep throbbing pain in your stomach that does not seem to go away? What if you find a lump under your skin? Do you go to your doctor immediately? Do you use a homemade family remedy and see if the problem goes away? Would you have a local shaman sacrifice a chicken for you? Being physically, mentally, emotionally, and spiritually healthy is a positive thing, but even the luckiest among us cannot always be without problems. Different cultures have different ways of coping and reacting to symptoms of illness. This chapter describes what we do when we do not feel good. I will focus primarily on physical health and describe what we do when we get sick. If you are seriously considering a career in the health care profession, especially as a doctor or nurse, this chapter is especially important for you.

Culture and Illness Behaviors

Many factors surround illness, and culture influences every one of them (Loue, Lane, Lloyd, & Loh, 1999). Before we get treated, we have to recognize that we have a problem. Then we have to report it. Once we get a diagnosis, we have to adhere to the course of treatment prescribed for us. Recognition, reporting, and adhering, collectively referred to as illness behaviors, are three main stages influenced by our cultural backgrounds. **Illness behaviors** are the varying ways individuals respond to physiological symptoms, monitor internal states, define and interpret symptoms, make attributions, take remedial actions, and utilize various forms of informal and formal care (Mechanic, 1995). A number of sociodemographic variables such as age, sex, ethnicity, and socioeconomic status can influence peoples' illness behaviors. For example, a study of 2,168 households in five New York and Pennsylvania counties showed that age was one of the most important predisposing factors in seeking health care (Wan & Soifer, 1974). Latinos do not utilize in-patient mental health services as much as other ethnic groups (Escobar, Randolph, & Hill, 1986). Even when there may be few superficial differences, a closer analysis reveals some of the complexity of culture. For example, Berkanovic and Telesky (1985) found few differences between African, European, and Mexican Americans in terms of reporting illnesses but African Americans were less likely to define short-term physical sensations as illnesses and were more likely to consult physicians if it was easy to do and they felt a particularly high risk for illness. African Americans were also less likely than Mexican Americans and European Americans to consult others in deciding whether to go to the doctor. You will see many other cultural differences throughout this chapter.

There is a marked underutilization of mental health resources by many non-White groups, which suggests an increased focus on the availability and preferences for alternate medicine (Balls Organista, Organista, & Kurasaki, 2002; Sue, Nakamura, Chung, & Yee-Bradbury, 1994). Regardless of the significant increase in the use of Western medicine among minority patients, traditional medicine continues to be important, and many minority groups report the use of a dual health system (Chung & Lin, 1994; Chan & Chang, 1976; Higginbotham, Trevino, & Ray, 1990; Lin & Lin, 1978). Ayurvedic medicine, an ancient Indian tradition rooted in the humoral theory of health in which the proper balance of bodily humors indicates health, is especially popular among Indians (Ramakrishna & Wiess, 1992). Acculturation and ethnic identity (discussed in more detail in chapter 3) can play an important part in the use of Western mental health resources and health services. For example, Chan and Chang (1976) found in a sample of Chinese patients that the number of years individuals spent in America was negatively correlated to the use of Chinese medicine. Whereas this is good to know in itself, the acculturation and ethnic identity of the health providers may be even more important, given the way the American health system is set up. Doctors are seen as credible people in powerful positions, whose advice can have an important impact on the health behaviors of their patients. This perception suggests that it is important to look at the ethnic identity and acculturation and, more importantly, the beliefs and preferences of the doctors, because these factors may influence their referrals and their prescriptions. Minority doctors with strong ethnic identities who are well assimilated or integrated may be more likely to be comfortable prescribing alternate medicine or serving minority patients (Gurung & Mehta, 2001). Although suggested by Sue et al. (1994), the contribution of the medical services by under-referral to underutilization of medical resources by Asian Americans has yet to be fully studied.

Some basic social psychological theories influence interpersonal interactions. These mostly hold across cultures. I will first discuss these theories and then extend them to demonstrate how different cultural beliefs can influence the use and utility of health care services.

Recognizing Symptoms

With physical problems, it is often clear when you need to see a doctor. A serious car or bike accident immediately brings medics to the spot. Other physical accidents such as those from sports-related activities (e.g., sprains or breaks) are also taken care of immediately. The limited movement caused by a sprain or the pain from a potential broken bone leads people to go to a hospital for an x-ray or to have the injury examined by a doctor. With other injuries, if symptoms at first do not seem to be life threatening, people may ignore them or delay going to a doctor. Why is this the case? There are many psychological factors that help us understand some of these reasons.

© AP/Wide World Photos

Sports Injuries An injury from a sports activity is one of the most common reasons people go to emergency rooms. With sprains or twists, it is often clear that some treatment is needed.

The Confirmation Bias

Once we believe something is true we often change the way we interpret new information and the way we look at the world because of it. We tend to try to confirm our belief and have a bias in how we process information. This is a **confirmation bias.** Social psychologists have shown that if there is any ambiguity in a person's behavior, people are likely to interpret what they see in a way that is consistent with their bias (Olson, Roese, & Zanna, 1996). If we believe that a change in our bodies is not a symptom of illness we will probably look for information to support that belief (Figure 8.1). For example, if you have spent too long in the sun and have pale skin there is a chance that you may develop some forms of skin cancer (Stack, 2003). The first signs are often discolorations of the skin that are round in nature (i.e., without irregular outlines). You could look at one of these developing spots and believe that it is a blemish or a growing pimple or that it was always there. You may now look at your skin and try to draw attention to parts that look great, ignoring the developing skin spots. You confirm your bias that you are right and cancer free by thinking that you have always had those spots off and on and they never meant anything before. You may even think that you have actually been feeling especially great recently so the spots could not be the beginning of a problem.

This confirmation bias can lead to misperceptions of the social world and an accentuation of symptoms that do get attention. If you believe that you do not

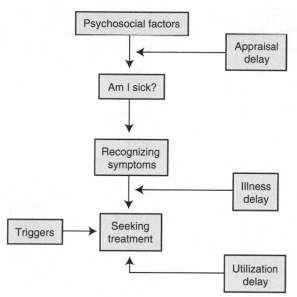

FIGURE 8.1
Overview of the Main Stages of an Illness and Some of the Critical Delays in Seeking Treatment

need to go to a doctor to seek treatment for flu-like symptoms or a cold and you have managed without seeing a doctor on past occasions or if you see others who do not seem to go when they have symptoms, you may begin to overestimate how successful you can be by not going to a doctor. We not only find confirmation for what we expect to see, but we also tend to overestimate how often we are right (Shavitt, Sanbonmatsu, Smittipatana, & Posavac, 1999). The belief that our expectations have been correct more times than they actually have been is referred to as an **illusory correlation.** A partial explanation for why confirmation biases occur is that we ignore disconfirmations of our biases and selectively remember information to support our biases (Fiske, 1998).

Attributions and Misattributions

Another social psychological process that can influence the recognition of symptoms is related to how we determine the cause of events. The cognitive process of assigning meaning to a symptom or behavior is referred to as making **attributions** (Jones et al., 1972). Many factors influence our attributions (Miller & Diefenbach, 1998). If your stomach hurts you may attribute the pain to what you just ate. If you have not eaten anything different recently, you are more likely to worry about a stomach pain than if you have just tried something that is very different (spicier or oilier than you are used to). How you attribute a pain in your chest may depend on physical factors such as your age or psychological factors such as beliefs that you hold about illness in general. A teenager may be likely to think of a chest pain as gas or a cramp of sorts. An older person may worry about a heart attack. The cause you attribute your symptoms to can influence whether you seek treatment for them or not.

Attributions vary across cultures as well. Mexican American children may consider hearing voices to be evidence of a religious experience (Padilla & Ruiz, 1973) whereas most European Americans may consider it a sign of mental imbalance. Hmong Americans consider epilepsy the mark of a shaman (Fadiman, 1997). Beliefs about the cause of a disease will directly correspond to how it will be dealt with. If the spirits mean that you should have a certain pain, then it would be angering them and risking further pain if you tried to do something to alleviate it. Sometimes, we mistakenly label our physiological experiences based on external factors (Schachter & Singer, 1962). If you feel tired and there are a lot of people at work with you who have a cold, you are likely to **misattribute** your tiredness to your developing a cold, when it could be due to your not getting enough sleep. This misattribution can increase your anxiety and in combination with a confirmation bias (that you have a cold), you may soon find yourself accumulating more evidence to support your theory. Your belief that you are getting sick will, in fact, make you sick (a self-fulfilling prophecy). Such self-fulfilling prophecies can contribute to the continual use of folk medicines and treatments. If you are biased against Western biomedicine you will probably not try to get better after a visit to a doctor. If you are biased toward shamanism, you are probably going to feel a lot better after a shamanistic ritual is performed over you (see chapter 2 for more). Sometimes your doctor does not even have to support your attribution to help you feel better. Snell (1967) found that African Americans who believed they have been "hexed" could be treated effectively by a psychiatrist using hypnosis, even when the psychiatrist did not believe in hexing.

Personality

Before we look at cultural levels of difference, let's take a look at key individual factors. Perhaps the most common individual factor that influences the recognition of symptoms and the seeking of treatment is personality. As described in chapter 5, personality is what defines each one of us. We have a unique and stable set of characteristics that relate to consistent patterns of behavior across situations. In general, different personality styles are related to a number of health outcomes (Contrada & Guyll, 2001), but there are many personality characteristics that relate to seeking treatment.

Studies have shown that people who are relatively high in anxiety tend to report more symptoms of illness than others do (Feldman, Cohen, Gwaltney, Doyle, & Skoner, 1999; Leventhal, Hansell, Diefenbach, Leventhal, & Glass, 1996). Neuroticism is another key personality trait in this regard. People who are high in neuroticism experience higher levels of anxiety and tend to be "high-strung." This characteristic often translates into oversensitivity to symptoms and to more complaining about ill health (Brown & Moskowitz, 1997). In fact, a thorough review of the personality and health literature suggested that people with chronic negative affect show a disease-prone personality (Friedman & Booth-Kewley, 1987).

Some people's personality types make them more attentive to bodily sensations, and they report more symptoms than others (Barsky, 1988). People who monitor their symptoms to an extreme may be **hypochondriacs.** Hypochondriasis or hypochondria is a psychological disorder characterized by excessive preoccupation with one's health and constant worry about developing physical illnesses. Hypochondriacs believe that any minor change in their condition could be the sign of a major problem. They are constantly going to their physicians to be checked. Even when they are told they are all right, they do not believe the diagnosis and may change doctors (Holder-Perkins & Wise, 2001).

Other personality traits such as optimism and self-esteem normally buffer us against stress and illness but may delay us from seeking treatment. For example, look at people with high self-esteem. They believe that they are very healthy and are optimistic in their outlook. They may also believe that their bodies can fight off infections or heal without any specific medical treatment. These people may wait to see if they get better.

Other specific individual differences influence how patients fare in the health care process. Patients vary in how much they want to be involved in their treatment and how much information they want. **Behavioral involvement** includes the patient's attitude toward self-care, specifically an active involvement in treatment. **Informational involvement** measures how much the patient wants to know about his or her illness and specific details of its treatment. Each form of involvement has different implications in the health care setting (Auerbach, 2000; Christensen, Smith, Turner, Holman, & Gregory, 1990). Mahler and Kulik (1991) measured these two variables with male coronary bypass patients. The researchers found that patients who had a high compared with a low desire for behavioral involvement experienced less ambulation dysfunction, fewer social interaction problems, and less emotional upset immediately after release from the hospital. Patients who had a high compared with a low desire for information involvement experienced more social interaction and emotional problems during this period. At final follow-up, these involvement group differences disappeared, and no differences in cardiac health were found (Mahler & Kulik, 1991). Nonetheless, these results suggest these variables should be taken into account to improve patient recovery in the period right after surgery.

Some individuals are more sensitive to their health states than others (Arntz & de Jong, 1993). Referred to as **private body consciousness,** this increased vigilance over the body may also cause the patient to feel more discomfort than the patient with low vigilance. Differences in vigilance may underlie a major sex difference in symptom reporting. Women both perceive and report more physical symptoms than men (Goldberg, DePue, Kazura, & Niaura, 1998), which could be due to women being higher in private body consciousness.

Seeking Treatment

Once you recognize you have a problem, you have to decide to seek treatment. DiMatteo (1991) has identified a number of different reasons why people do not seek treatment. She suggested that (1) people often misinterpret and underestimate the significance of their symptoms, (2) they worry about how they will look

TABLE 8.1

Major Reasons for Delays in Seeking Treatment

Misinterpretation of symptoms	Interference with social plans
Fear of false alarms	Packing and rescheduling before going to the
Concerns with troubling health care	hospital
professionals	

if the symptoms turn out to be nothing, (3) they are concerned about troubling their physicians, (4) they do not want to change their social plans by having to see a doctor, and (5) they tend to waste time on unimportant things, such as getting their personal belongings together, before going to the hospital.

A substantial area of health psychology examines why people delay in seeking treatment. There are three main components of delay. People sometimes take a lot of time to recognize they have symptoms; this is **appraisal delay,** and many psychological factors discussed previously can prevent symptom recognition. Appraisal delay can lead to **illness delay,** the time between the recognition that one is ill to the decision to seek care. Finally, there are often **utilization delays** between the decision to seek care and the actual behaviors to obtain medical health care. Beyond the absence of the main triggers described above, a host of other psychological reasons explain why people delay. Sometimes the delay in seeking treatment results from the symptoms of a problem being misattributed. For example, many heart attack patients do not immediately call 911 for assistance because they believe the pains they are experiencing may be due to other, less serious problems such as indigestion or the flu that are not potentially fatal (Scherck, 1997).

The different psychosocial barriers to recognizing symptoms and reporting them notwithstanding (Table 8.1), some factors increase the likelihood that a person will seek treatment (Figure 8.2). Health psychologists refer to these as **triggers** (Verbrugge, 1985). There are five triggers that will increase the likelihood that a person will seek treatment (Zola, 1964). First, the degree to which you are frightened by symptoms is critical. If the symptoms are out of view, say on your back, or if they do not cause too much pain, they may be easy to ignore. You may tell yourself that you will do something about the problem if it gets worse but not otherwise. If your symptoms do cause a lot of pain or are noticeable or if you believe they may be indicative of a serious illness, you may worry about them, and your anxiety will increase, possibly prompting you to go to a doctor. Correspondingly, the second trigger is the nature and quality of symptoms. The more symptoms you have and the worse they are, the more likely you are to go to a doctor. Sometimes, symptoms get so severe that your interactions with your romantic partner, spouse, friends, and family may suffer. If you are in too much pain to attend social events or have had low energy for some time, and your symptoms interfere with relationships, this interpersonal crisis is likely to trigger a visit to the doctor. This interference with life can go beyond your personal relationships and extend to your job or to plans that you have made. Social interference, when your occupation or vacation is threatened by symptoms, is the fourth trigger.

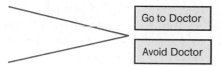

Social interference
Interpersonal crisis
Number and severity of symptoms
Fear of symptoms
Social sanctioning

Go to Doctor

Avoid Doctor

FIGURE 8.2
Main Triggers in Seeking Treatment

Finally, even if you do not want to seek treatment, your employer could pressure you to get treatment or return to work. Many businesses have noticed that their insurance rates are much higher for smokers. To cut health insurance costs, employees are provided with incentives to get treatment to quit smoking and in many cases face implicit and explicit pressure to quit smoking. **Social sanctioning** such as this can also trigger a visit to the doctor.

In addition to the various psychosocial factors influencing treatment seeking, a number of explicit cultural variables play a role. To begin, there are consistent age and sex differences. Women and elderly persons use health services at a significantly higher rate than do men and younger individuals (Cockerham, 1997; Fuller, Edwards, Sermsri, & Vorakitphokatron, 1993; National Center for Health Statistics, 2004). Part of this difference is due to the fact that these two groups have more specific issues that need care such as pregnancy and childbirth for women and chronic and terminal illnesses among elderly persons. In addition, women have been shown to be more sensitive to changes in their bodies than men (Leventhal, Diefenbach, & Leventhal, 1992) and may find it more socially acceptable to report symptoms than men. Men may not report symptoms as much so as not to appear weak ("boys don't cry") or report pains.

Treatment seeking varies by ethnicity as well. In one of the most systematic studies of ethnic differences, Suchman (1965) studied ethnic groups in New York and found that many non-European Americans tended to form close, exclusive relationships with friends, family, and members of their ethnic group and to show a skepticism of medical care. These groups were more likely to rely on a **lay-referral system**—nonprofessionals such as family, friends, and neighbors—in coping with illness symptoms instead of seeking biomedical treatment. Beyond relying on a lay-referral system, some ethnic groups refrain from seeking treatment from biomedically trained physicians in hospitals, relying instead on folk medicine (as discussed in chapter 2). Although there are few recent studies on the treatment-seeking behavior of different ethnic groups, older studies of groups such as Mexican Americans show them as being reluctant to visit physicians (Andersen, Lewis, Giachello, Aday, & Chiu, 1981). Having close-knit networks or having strong religious beliefs does not always prevent someone from seeking treatment. In contrast to Suchman's data, Geertsen, Kane, Klauber, Rindflesh, and Gray (1975) showed that members of the close-knit Mormon community in Salt Lake City were actually more likely to seek treatment than members of loosely knit communities.

Perhaps the biggest cultural factor predicting the seeking of treatment is socioeconomic status (SES). In fact, many conditions that may at first appear to be a function of ethnicity may actually be due to poverty. Early sociological studies describe a culture of poverty in which poverty over time influences the development of psychological traits and behaviors including the utilization of health services (Koos, 1954; Rundall & Wheeler, 1979). This lack of utilization is directly correlated with financial barriers to medical care as demonstrated by the increase in utilization of health care by low-income groups after the introduction of national insurance programs such as Medicaid and Medicare in the 1960s. SES may also influence the type of care sought. Kleinman (1980) showed that only upper middle-class families treated all illnesses with Western biomedicine and only lower-class families treated all illnesses at home. The opposite pattern was seen with wealthier Puerto Ricans in New York who were more likely to consult spiritual healers than were poorer individuals (Garrison, 1977).

The Hospital Setting

Once people decide to utilize medical services, they have to face the bureaucracies of a hospital. There are both for-profit and nonprofit hospitals, and cities with many hospitals find each hospital competing for patients. Sometimes this can benefit the patient as hospitals offer discounts and special services to be more appealing. Many hospital administrators view health care primarily as a business (Knox, 1998). Unfortunately, this attitude contributes to patient dissatisfaction with the process of getting treatment. Even for most emergencies, people still have to pro-

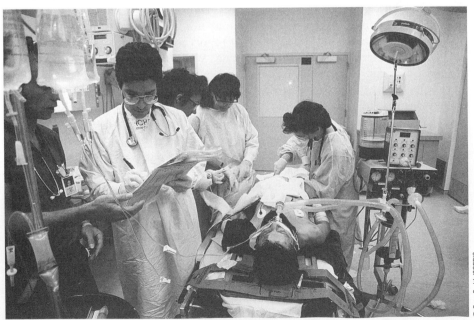

© Greg Smith/CORBIS

Going to the Hospital Hospitals can be intimidating places. There is much activity, and a lot of equipment often is involved.

vide evidence of ability to pay the bill. This may take the form of health insurance from a job or may sometimes be personal insurance. Many millions of American citizens do not have health insurance of any form, a factor that can prevent them from going to the hospital except for the most extreme situations. Most hospital visits begin with the filling out of forms and the gathering of information and are often accompanied by long waiting periods. For these two reasons and a host of others, most people dread having to go to a hospital.

The majority of the tedium of going to a hospital is hard to avoid. Medical visits have to follow a certain pattern. A health care professional, usually a physician's assistant or a nurse practitioner, first gathers basic information from the patient (e.g., medical history and main symptoms). Then a medical examination of the relevant areas of the body is conducted. Further medical tests are recommended or a diagnosis is made followed by the prescription of a treatment regimen. The physician may only spend a very brief time with each patient, and this is often one of the major causes of dissatisfaction with the treatment-seeking process (Chung, Hamill, Kim, Walter, & Wilkins, 1999). Doctors would like to spend more time with their patients (Probst, Greenhouse, & Selassie, 1997), but they cannot because most have a quota (set by the hospital resulting from a complex interplay of health maintenance organization and insurance billing requirements) of patients that they need to see in a day (Waitzkin, 1985).

Staff Relations

Health psychologists have begun to pay attention to another level of interaction in hospitals. Going beyond the interaction between a doctor and a patient, the diversity within hospital staff compels a look at staff relationships as well. Not only are patients culturally diverse, but hospital staffs are also. In addition to European American staff, hospitals frequently have large numbers of doctors of East Indian, Chinese, and Middle Eastern descent and nurses from Mexico, the Philippines, and other non-White ethnicities (Galanti, 2004). Different cultures have different expectations of the roles played by the different levels of hospital staff. For example, some East Indian male physicians tend to be sexist and are not as respectful of European American nurses (Gurung & Mehta, 2001). The doctor-nurse relationship can be strongly influenced by the culture of each person. Some cultures are more respectful of authority than others, and have a greater desire to maintain harmony and avoid conflict. Nurses of Asian or Latino backgrounds are sometimes reticent to stand up to questionable behavior by European American doctors.

Gender and culture also influence interdoctor and internurse relationships. Some East Indian female physicians often feel intimidated by their male counterparts. Male nurses sometimes have discordant interactions with their female counterparts. Medicine is a hierarchical profession in which orders are followed by rank and not sex, but this hierarchy can often cause problems for men from male-dominant cultures. Medical staff members also face conflicts between their roles as health care providers and their own religious beliefs. Galanti (2004) recounted a case study in which a nurse who was a Jehovah's Witness refused to aid in a blood transfer in an emergency room because blood transfusions were

Doctors and Nurses Come from Different Cultural Backgrounds

against her faith. In another case, a devout Catholic nurse refused to participate in an abortion. An interesting side note is that the Hippocratic Oath sworn by doctors actually directly addresses abortion—doctors have to swear not to do it (see chapter 1 for the Oath).

Patient-Practitioner Interactions

When a patient has recognized that he or she has symptoms of an illness and has sought treatment from a health care professional, it is only the beginning of the journey toward recovery. Many things occur as the patient interacts with the health care system, negotiating the paperwork of insurance and registration at the hospital to begin and then actually seeing a doctor and getting a diagnosis. When you do see a doctor, the quality of your interaction with him or her can play a big role in how you feel and the extent to which you adhere to the prescribed treatment.

Patient-practitioner interactions can vary around some basic themes (Ballard-Reisch, 1990; Roter & Hall, 1992). Szasz and Hollender (1956) describe three major models of interaction. In the active-passive model the doctor plays a pivotal role, making the majority of the decisions because the patient is unable to do so (because of his or her medical condition). Here the patient has little to no say in what is done. In the guidance-cooperation model the doctor still takes the primary role in diagnosis and treatment, but the patient plays a part by answering questions although he or she does not take part in decision making regarding treatment. In the mutual cooperation model, the doctor and patient work together at every stage, consulting each other on the planning of tests for diagnosis and in decisions regarding treatment. Obviously the optimal model of interaction, the mutual co-operation model is characterized by effective patient-practitioner communication and an open exchange of ideas and concerns. Good communication is perhaps one of the most critical ingredients in successful patient-practitioner interactions. Let's take a closer look at factors that influence these interactions.

Communication

Conversations between doctors and their patients can range from being narrowly biomedical, in which the doctor uses a lot of medical jargon and limits conversation using closed-ended questions, to consumerist, in which the patient is primarily the one doing the talking and getting answers to his or her questions (Roter et al., 1997). The extent to which doctors discuss psychological or social issues varies greatly, especially across cultures. Many factors influence the quality of communication between doctors and patients (Ong, DeHaes, Hoos, & Lammes, 1995). Different cultures have different expectations for communication. In the West it is very common for people to use small talk, for example, "How are you doing?" It is rare that the speaker really wants to know the answers to questions such as this. Non-Western cultures rarely engage in small talk to the same extent (Triandis, 1996). Sometimes it may seem like doctors are from Venus and patients are from Mars (to borrow the analogy from a pop psychologist's attempt to characterize male and female interactional patterns). It is not uncommon to see a patient looking goggle-eyed at a doctor while the doctor is trying to explain a procedure or diagnosis using technical terms, with the patient understanding only a fraction of the conversation. Psychologists have identified many key ways that communication can go wrong.

One of the major cultural dimensions influencing patient-practitioner communication is individualism and collectivism. As described in chapter 2, people in different cultures vary in the level to which they are self-focused or independent/individualistic or other-/group-focused or collectivistic. When it comes to communication between the doctor and patient, a patient's level of collectivism can be a key factor. Collectivists tend to communicate all but the most important piece of information, which the doctor is supposed to supply to make the whole message comprehensible (Triandis, 1996). This strategy has the advantage of allowing a collectivist to monitor another's feelings and avoid disrupting harmony (Armstrong & Swartzman, 2001). The individualist on the other hand, who is not as concerned with maintaining social harmony, is more likely to get straight to the point. Combine an individualist doctor and a collectivistic patient and you have a recipe for frustration because the doctor wants the point and the patient is offended by the doctor's drive for the point.

Doctors have been found to do many things that inhibit communication. Some doctors may not listen to everything the patient says (Probst et al., 1997), often talking too much. A look at the statistics makes some doctors almost seem rude. Beckman and Frankel (1984) found that on average, doctors cut off their patients after only 18 seconds. In talking to patients, doctors may use too much medical jargon that the patient does not understand (Cormier, Cormier, & Weisser, 1984). Given the Greek roots of many disease classifications and the technical terms used to describe many procedures and even different parts of the body, it is not surprising that a layperson may be confused by medical jargon. Although providing a common language for doctors to communicate with each other and being valid ways to describe aspects of illness, the inappropriate use of medical terminology can confuse, frustrate, and even anger patients (Frankel, 1995). Phillips (1996) found that patients are particularly dissatisfied with treatment when doctors appear to deliberately use jargon even when it does not seem to be needed. Conversely, some doctors "dumb down" the message or talk down to patients, assuming that they do not understand.

Patients contribute to communication problems with doctors as well. Patients are often very anxious when they go to a doctor (Graugaard & Finset, 2000). This anxiety may make them not describe all their symptoms or have difficulty concentrating on the doctor's questions. Sometimes patients from lower socioeconomic backgrounds or those who speak a different language may not understand what is being asked of them. Language problems can even occur between people who speak English. I was raised in Bombay, India, where the English spoken is of the British variety (the "Queen's English"). In India and Britain, a *rubber* is an eraser. In America, a rubber is a condom. In college I quickly learned that difference (much to my embarrassment) after the first time I made a mistake on an exam and needed to erase it. In a health care setting, simple word usage can play a big role in the context of conversations about birth control. Another example is the word *positive*. In most everyday contexts, positive connotes a good thing.

Many Psychological and Social Factors Influence Patient-Practitioner Communication

In the context of an HIV test, however, having positive test results is not a good thing at all. To make matters worse, the same English word may mean different things in other languages. If someone told you that he or she got a stomachache from eating a puto, the language the person speaks makes a big difference. The word *puto* means "rice cake" in the Philippines but "male prostitute" in Spanish. Similarly, to *douche* is to shower in Dutch, but it has a very different meaning in English (i.e., feminine hygiene).

Additionally, different symptoms may mean different things in different cultures, making some patients hesitant to describe a symptom that they believe relates to a very personal or private bodily function.

Cultural Stereotyping

We all hold various stereotypes. For example, you may believe that Asians are good at math, or women are bad at math. **Stereotypes** are widely held beliefs that people have certain characteristics because of their membership in a particular group. Many stereotypes may have a kernel of truth to them, but human beings treat stereotypes as if they are always accurate for all members of the group. Social psychologists have argued that we use stereotypes as a shortcut. When we do not have the cognitive time or energy to find out more about somebody, we fall back on what we have heard about the cultural group that he or she belongs to.

Stereotypes of doctors or patients based on their sex, ethnicity, or religion are one of the biggest factors influencing the quality of patient-practitioner communication and interactions. In the limited time that doctors and nurses have to interact with patients, their behavior may often be influenced by their stereotypes of their patients instead of realities. Many such stereotypes exist and play a role in the hospital setting. For example, Americans of Middle Eastern and Indian descent are often believed to be demanding and to express their pain freely and loudly (Galanti, 2004). Mexican Americans stereotypically have large families. Asian American men and women are stereotypically very quiet and stoic. If doctors see older patients or female patients, they may make assumptions about how the patients will behave or about their pain tolerance or behaviors based on ageist or sexist stereotypes (Hall, Epstein, DeCiantis, & McNeil, 1993; Haug & Ory, 1987). It is important to remember, as discussed in chapter 1, that even though there may be some individuals who do fit a certain cultural stereotype, there is a lot of variance within cultures. Generalizations based on stereotypes can be inaccurate, may be offensive, and can sometimes result in malpractice claims. Sadly, there is empirical evidence showing that some cultural groups (e.g., African Americans, Latinos, or low SES individuals) are given less information and are treated worse than other groups (Hooper, Comstock, Goodwin, & Goodwin, 1982). An extreme case of the problems with cultural stereotyping is discussed in the focus on clinical application section at the end of this chapter.

Adherence to Treatment

Once the patient and practitioner interact and a diagnosis is made, the patient has to follow the doctor's prescription and recommendations. The extent to which a patient's behavior matches with his or her practitioner's advice is referred to as **adherence** (Kaplan & Simon, 1990). Nonadherence can cause morbidity and influence clinical diagnosis of treatment plans, the cost-effectiveness of health care, and the effectiveness of clinical trials (Shearer & Evans, 2001). Studies suggest that adherence ranges from 15% to 93% (Haynes, McKibbon, & Kanani, 1996). A large number of patients do not completely adhere to medical treatment (Myers & Midence, 1998; Rand & Weeks, 1998). Various psychosocial factors, including many cultural forces, influence the extent to which ill patients adhere to treatments.

There are many practical concerns that influence adherence. As you can guess, adherence rates vary according to the type of treatment prescribed and to the disease or illness a patient has. Rapoff (1999) showed that about 33% of patients do not adhere to prescriptions for acute illnesses whereas around 55% of patients do not adhere to treatments for chronic illnesses. Some treatments are easier to adhere to than others. You are much more likely to not do something that you dislike (it is easy to avoid eating Brussels sprouts if you did not like them before) than to stop doing something that you do like (avoid sweets). Some treatments are long term and complex, severely interfere with life, and impact desirable behaviors. Such treatments automatically are associated with low levels of adherence. Patients' intentions to adhere, their understanding of the treatment, and their satisfaction with their practitioners can also influence how likely they are to adhere. In fact, many of the health behavior change models described in chapter 6 (e.g., the Health Belief Model) also help predict which patients will adhere to their treatments.

Nonadherence can take many different forms. Ryan (1998) showed that villagers in Cameroon did not directly follow their doctor's advice, but they did still make an effort to do things that would improve their health. For example, they chose treatments that were less expensive and easier to perform than what the doctor ordered. Other individuals may go overboard. Reis (1993) found that patients with asthma used their sprays for relief more often than prescribed. Sometimes patients indirectly disobey their doctors' orders. Referred to as **creative nonadherence,** patients sometimes modify and supplement their treatment plans. For example, patients may save a dose for later or skip or discontinue a course of medicine if they are feeling good.

In addition to the psychological reasons that explain nonadherence, culture, by itself, can also be a major explanatory force. As described in chapter 2, different cultural groups have different beliefs. Ethnic groups, racial groups, people from different geographical regions, and even men and women—all of these members of different cultures—may have beliefs that are barriers to adherence. For example, most European American women are often back at work after the births of their babies. In contrast, many Asian American women believe that a week or a month lying-in period is needed during which the mother spends time in bed to recover. Anderson (1993) suggested that the health care system might be organized to favor the majority culture. Social, political, and economic bar-

© AP/Wide World Photos

Hmong American Women in Traditional Festive Clothes Seeing someone in non-western outfits can enhance how they are stereotyped.

riers prevent minority group members from complying with their practitioner's prescriptions.

One large area in which cultural beliefs interfere with adherence to treatment involves dietary practices. Many treatments involve either food restrictions or prescriptions to eat certain foods. These prescriptions may not fit with some cultural beliefs. For example, Muslims are forbidden to eat from sunrise to sunset during the month of Ramadan, an important Muslim festival. Orthodox Jews follow kosher dietary laws that forbid eating pork, shellfish, and nonkosher red meat and poultry, or mixing meat and dairy products (no cheeseburgers allowed). Hindus do not eat beef. Many Catholics do not eat meat on Fridays during the season of Lent. There are many documented cases in which hospital staffs unknowingly attempt to feed patients certain foods that are against the patients' cultural beliefs (Galanti, 2004).

As you can see, many different steps are involved in the process of getting sick and recovering. Many individual difference factors and major cultural differences can influence the extent to which patients recognize their symptoms, report them, seek treatment, and adhere to their treatments. Understanding and incorporating these differences are critical to optimizing the success of a health care system.

FOCUS on Applications

When the Spirit Catches You, Cultures Clash

BAAAM!!! When a door slams hard, you may jump back, startled at the sound. Your ears may ring and you may even direct a harsh stare in the direction of the person who did it. Would you worry about what the slamming could mean for your soul? Most probably you would not, yet that is exactly what Foua Lee worried about when her elder daughter Yer Lee slammed the front door of the family apartment. Within seconds, Foua's youngest daughter and Yer's younger sister, Lia, fainted. The Lees had little doubt about what happened. The sound of the slamming door had been so alarming that little Lia Lee's soul had fled her body and become lost. What followed as the Lee family struggled to cure Lia is a tragic story of how the clash of two sets of cultural beliefs, in this case those of Western biomedicine and Hmong folk beliefs, can have fatal consequences. Cultural differences led to innumerable complications, deplorable patient-practitioner interactions, and delays in the recognition, reporting, and adequate treatment of Lia Lee's epilepsy or *quag dab peg,* literally translated from the Hmong language to mean "the spirit catches you and you fall down" (Fadiman, 1997).

The Hmong people originally lived in the hills of Laos in Southeast Asia (right next to Vietnam). In 1975, Laos fell to Communist forces, and 150,000 Hmong fled to refugee camps in Thailand and then to America. In fact, the American government promised the Hmong asylum in exchange for their help in fighting the Vietnam War. Correspondingly, thousands of Hmong men, women, and children immigrated to America and settled primarily in California, Minnesota, and Wisconsin. Most of the Hmong immigrants do not speak English, and all the Hmong hold a belief system very different from that of Western culture. The Hmong believe that illness can be caused by a variety of different factors such as eating the wrong food, having sinful ancestors, being cursed, having one's blood sucked by a spirit or *dab*, touching a newborn mouse, and having bird dropping fall on one's head. The most common cause of illness is soul loss. When Lia Lee convulsed and collapsed, the family automatically thought that her soul was lost. And that's not all. The seizures were paradoxically seen as a mixed blessing. To the Hmong, *quag dab peg* is a special illness and often the sign of a shaman. You can guess how that belief was received when they took Lia to the local hospital.

In the hospital, almost all of the issues described in this chapter became factors. Initially, none of the doctors or nurses could really understand what had happened to the little girl because none of the health practitioners spoke Hmong, the Lee family spoke very little English, and there were no interpreters on hand. Lia had stopped convulsing by the time she had reached the hospital so the only symptoms she showed were a cough and a congested chest. The resident on duty did what he could with the limited information, and Lia was sent home after her parents signed a paper acknowledging the receipt of instructions for care. But the Lees could not read. Needless to say, the prescription was not followed. To accentuate the dangers of nonaherence, the Lee family decided to use their own treatment for the soul loss based on their own cultural beliefs. Lia Lee was soon back in the emergency room a second and then a third time. On the third arrival the consulting physician deemed her to have meningitis and ordered a spinal tap, but Lia's parents resisted only to be finally convinced.

Lia had repeated seizures over the next few years, and there were problems with every step of her treatment. When she was checked into the hospital, her father and many other members of the family stayed with her, often ignoring the posted visiting hours and interfering with the treatment. At one time, the nurses had used restraints on Lia to prevent her from hurting herself when she had a seizure. Lia's father could not understand why this was being done to his daughter, and no one could speak Hmong to tell him. When the nurses were out of the room he untied Lia's restraints and placed her on the floor, much to the disapproval of the hospital staff who had to restrain her again. Most of the time the Lee parents were uncertain of what medicines to give Lia, and in another form of nonaherence, they just skipped giving her medications when the drug regimen became too complex, substituting folk remedies instead.

The Lee family sacrificed a cow, cut the heads off chickens, and attempted a number of different shamanistic remedies, but none worked. Still the family worked hard to keep Lia happy, even opting to keep her at home and take care of her instead of having her be in the hospital. Unfortunately, although many Hmong see epilepsy as a sign of divinity and are content to just care for the person with it without necessarily trying for a cure, this approach is not approved by Western society, and a family services agency removed Lia Lee from her loving parents and placed her in a foster home. The Lees got their daughter back, but it was not the end of Lia's problems. Sadly, the plot thickened. After a further series of miscommunications between the Western doctors and this Hmong family, Lia Lee went into a coma and never regained consciousness.

What started out as a straightforward case of epilepsy spiraled out of control. Were the Lees to blame? Yes, they did not give Lia the medicines they were supposed to, but this nonadherence was a combination of their not understanding why and what they had to do and not wanting to do it because of their own beliefs. Was the Western medical system to blame? Yes, many assumptions and guesses were made about what the problem was and often the Lees were stereotyped and mistreated because of it, but the language barrier was a large part of the problem again and, as in many cases throughout our nation, the health practitioners did not have the time or the necessary cultural education to know better. Although this is an extreme case, the travesty of Lia's vegetative state resulting from the collision of these two cultures is, nonetheless, an important reminder of how important cultural differences are to the patient-practitioner interaction and the seeking and delivery of medical treatment.

Chapter Summary

- Illness behaviors are the varying ways individuals respond to physiological symptoms, monitor internal states, define and interpret symptoms, and essentially work toward getting better. The first main step in coping with an illness is to recognize the symptoms. Then we need to report them and adhere to treatment prescriptions. Delays can occur at each of these steps.

- Many psychological factors such as confirmation biases, personality styles, and attributional problems compounded by cultural differences interfere with accurate symptom recognition. Delays in appraising illness can lead to delays in seeking help and utilizing health care. A number of different triggers increase the likelihood that people will seek treatment. Socioeconomic status is perhaps the largest cultural factor that predicts the seeking of treatment. People living in poverty are less likely to have sufficient health care or utilize it effectively.

- The bureaucracies of the hospital setting sometimes make it difficult for patients to have their illnesses dealt with. A variety of factors influence staff relationships with patients. Staff often stereotype patients based on SES, sex, age, and ethnicity. In particular, stereotyping and prejudice, language barriers, use of jargon, and time pressure influence communication between patient and practitioners.

- Adherence to treatment varies based on the complexity of the treatment, the extent to which the treatment interferes with social functioning, and the duration and severity of the treatment. A large number of patients do not fully adhere to doctor's prescriptions. Nonadherence is compounded by different cultural factors.

Synthesize, Evaluate, Apply

- What are the cultural factors that influence your use of health care?
- Develop a personality profile of the person most likely to seek treatment at the optimal time.
- How do the different psychological processes interact to delay the seeking of treatment?

- What recommendations do you have to make the hospital environment more patient friendly?
- Given the time constraints faced by hospital staff, what can be done to improve patient treatment?
- What are the main psychological processes that underlie the recognizing and reporting of symptoms?
- How can triggers be utilized to ensure all who need treatment get it?
- What are the socioeconomic barriers to health care?
- Summarize how cultural differences create conflict between patients and practitioners and between staff members. What are key solutions?
- What can be done to prevent cultural stereotyping?
- How could the different approaches to health described in chapter 2 influence each of the three main stages of the health care process described in this chapter?
- How would developmental differences play a role in the factors surrounding illness?
- When do you know when to go to a doctor? What are your triggers?

KEY TERMS, CONCEPTS, AND PEOPLE

adherence, 250
appraisal delay, 242
attributions, 239
behavioral involvement, 241
confirmation bias, 238
creative nonadherence, 251
hypochondriacs, 241

illness behaviors, 236
illness delay, 242
illusory correlation, 239
informational involvement, 241
lay-referral system, 243
misattribute, 240

private body consciousness, 241
social sanctioning, 243
stereotypes, 249
triggers, 242
utilization delays, 242

ESSENTIAL READINGS

DiMatteo, M. R. (2004). Social support and patient adherence to medical treatment: A meta-analysis. *Health Psychology, 23*(2), 207–218.

Galanti, G. (2004). *Caring for patients from different cultures: Case studies from American hospitals.* Philadelphia, PA: University of Pennsylvania Press.

Kleinman, A., Eisenberg, L., & Good, B. (1978). Culture, illness, and cure: Clinical lessons from anthropologic and cross-cultural research. *Annals of Internal Medicine, 88,* 250–258.

Nilchaikovit, T., Hill, J. M., & Holland, J. C. (1993). The effects of culture on illness behavior and medical care: Asian and American differences. *General Hospital Psychiatry, 15,* 41–50.

Ong, L. M. L., DeHaes, J. C. J. M., Hoos, A. M., & Lammes, F. B. (1995). Doctor-patient communication: A review of the literature. *Social Science and Medicine, 40*(7), 903–918.

WEB RESOURCES

Visit the companion website at **http://psychology.wadsworth.com/gurung1e/,** where you will find online resources for this book, including chapter-by-chapter quizzes, weblinks, and more! You can also visit Wadsworth Psychology Resource Center at **http://psychology.wadsworth.com** to access additional resources.

An Example of a Site for Increasing Cultural Awareness in Health Care

http://www.culturediversity.org/index.html

Pain

The world seems like such a different place when we are in pain. Whether it is a mild headache from a stressful day, the ache from a twisted ankle from a misstep, a stomachache from spoiled food, or the burn of a fall during basketball, pain is uncomfortable and is something we want to avoid. In the midst of a painful experience, we long for the time when the pain will be gone. We try anything we can to escape pain. For common pains such as headaches we may reach for aspirin or maybe take a nap, hoping that the pain will be gone when we awake or once the pill takes effect. There are many cultural differences in how we cope with pain, and many cultural explanations for why we feel pain. What is pain? Why do we experience it? How is it caused? Maybe most important of all: What are the ways to relieve it? In this chapter I shall describe the phenomenon of pain and answer each of these questions. First I shall discuss the different types of pain and take a look at how pain has been explained over the centuries. After a look at contemporary views on pain, I shall discuss some of the major ways we can cope with pain, making the distinction between short-term and long-term pain management. Then I shall highlight the many ways different cultures cope with pain.

© Uriel Sinai/Getty Images

Experiencing Pain Pain is a multifaceted experience that is hard to bear. Pain can by physiological or psychological and is experienced to different extents by different age groups and sexes.

What Is Pain?

At the most basic level, pain can be referred to as **nociception,** the activation of specialized nerve fibers that signal the occurrence of tissue damage. Nociception is often accompanied by cognitive, behavioral, and affective states. Your thoughts are influenced by pain, your behaviors change when you are in pain, and your feelings are influenced by pain. Of course, pain can also be purely emotional in nature, without nociception, and is often described as suffering. Pain is a phenomenon that clearly exemplifies how important taking a biopsychosocial approach can be. Whereas pain can have direct biological causes, for example, I punch you on your arm and you will feel pain, the experience of pain is strongly influenced by psychological and cultural factors.

In a clear example of psychological factors influencing pain, Beecher (1955) compared World War II soldiers' experiences of pain on the battlefield with the pain experienced by civilians. He found that for injuries of similar severity, approximately 80% of the civilians requested painkillers whereas only 33% of the soldiers did. Even the self-reports were different. Whereas only 42% of the soldiers reported that their pain was in the severe to medium range, 75% of civilians reported their pain to be in this range. The stress of battle and possibly the realization that their injuries meant they were returning home seemed to lessen the

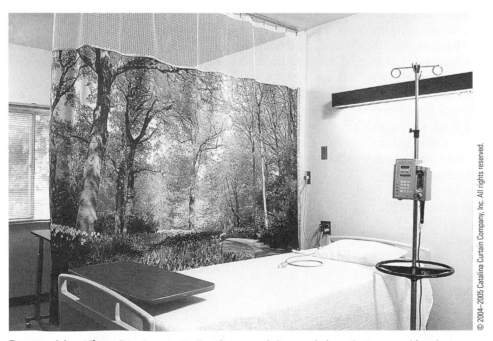

Room with a View Based on the finding that a good view can help patients cope with pain, you can now buy curtains with scenic views on them. Now even if a patient does not get a room with a view or if the hospital does not have a good location to provide views, patients can still reap some of the benefits of natural vistas.

soldiers' pain. In another fascinating example, Ulrich (1984) found that patients recovering from gallbladder surgery differed in how much pain they experienced based on the view from their hospital beds. The patients whose windows faced greenery and trees, requested significantly fewer painkillers than patients who did not have a view! Consider that next time you have to recuperate from an illness.

Cultural Variations in the Experience of Pain

Many cultural factors influence the perception and experience of pain, but two of these stand out: sex and ethnicity. In large part, the cultural variations are due to differences in socialization and expectations across different cultural groups. Boys are socialized to bear pain whereas girls are socialized to express pain. If a man cries in pain, he is seen as being less masculine, but it is perfectly acceptable for a woman to cry because of pain. There are also different expectations for pain tolerance across ethnicities and races. Middle Eastern women are more likely to scream during pregnancy than are Japanese women.

Sex Differences

A growing body of research suggests that there are sex differences at every level—biological, psychological, and social—in the experience of persistent pain (Bernabei et al., 1998; Fillingim, 2003; Rollman, 2003). For example, Berkley (1997) found that for experimentally delivered stimuli to the body, females have lower thresholds, greater ability to discriminate, higher pain ratings, and less tolerance of noxious stimuli than males. Of note, these differences only existed for some forms of painful stimulations and varied based on situational factors such as the experimental setting. For internal pains, Berkley (1997) found that women report more multiple pains in more areas of the body than men. Similar to studies of depression and anxiety, women are more likely to report pain to a doctor and to experience more frequent episodes of pain (Muellersdorf & Soederback, 2000).

Some painful diseases are more prevalent among females and others among males, and, for many diseases, symptoms differ between females and males (Barsky, Peekna, & Borus, 2001). In terms of types of pain, the only significant sex differences relate to headaches (including migraine), facial, and back pain (Breslau & Rasmussen, 2001). There are also sex differences in attitudes toward pain (Liddell & Locker, 1997). Men report less pain, cope better with pain, and respond to treatment for pain differently from women (Walker & Carmody, 1998), although there are perhaps more within-group differences than between-group differences.

Ethnic Differences

Members of different ethnic groups, similar to members of the two sexes, give very different meanings to the experience of pain. These differences take the form of when pain should be expressed, how the pain should be expressed (e.g., verbally and behaviorally), what the expression of the pain signifies about the individual, and how long the pain should be expressed (Bates, Edwards, & Anderson, 1993; Bates, Rankin-Hill, & Sanchez-Ayendez, 1997).

A look at the clinical literature on ethnicity and pain suggests that the picture is straightforward and black and white. It is also very focused on two ethnic groups, African Americans and European Americans, and the differences are clear. For example, Edwards, Fillingim, and Keefe (2001) reviewed the pain literature and found that studies show greater sensitivity to experimental pain stimuli among African Americans compared with European Americans. Clinical studies of acute and persistent pain also showed higher levels among African American patients compared with European Americans. Similarly, Riley et al. (2002) tested for ethnic differences in processing of chronic pain in 1,557 European and African American chronic pain patients. Results showed that after controls for pain duration and education were applied, African Americans reported significantly higher levels of pain unpleasantness, emotional response to pain, and pain behavior but not pain intensity than did European Americans. African Americans with chronic pain report significantly more pain and sleep disturbance as well as more symptoms consistent with post-traumatic stress disorder and depression than White Americans (Green, Baker, Sato, Washington, & Smith, 2003).

Other ethnic groups show differences as well. Studies have documented differences among different groups in America (Faucett, Gordon, & Levine, 1994; Lipton & Marbach, 1984) as well as across different nationalities (Sanders et al., 1992). In an experimental design (the researchers actually manipulated how much pain participants felt), Lawlis, Achterberg, Kenner, and Kopetz (1984) studied the experience of chronic back pain in Mexican, European, and African Americans. They induced pain in participants and collected reports of how much pain could be tolerated and when the induced pain matched the chronic pain. The authors also collected observer ratings of pain behavior to match self-reports. In a clear demonstration of how culture can cover up differences, Mexican Americans reported the highest level of pain when the induced pain matched the chronic pain, but they were judged as not presenting with an "exaggerated" pain response. European Americans reported less chronic pain but had a lower pain tolerance than Mexican Americans, and the African American group did not differ from either of the other groups on any measures of pain.

Moving to a larger scale, interesting differences in pain perception are seen when geographical areas are compared. Bates et al. (1997) compared participants living in New England with those living in Puerto Rico. Participants were European American and Latino in New England and Puerto Rican in Puerto Rico. New Englanders held Western biomedical beliefs and felt high levels of control of their pain. Both New England patients and practitioners shared this view, but these patients experienced high treatment-related stress. The Puerto Ricans with more holistic beliefs preferred biopsychosocial approaches to the treatment of pain. Interestingly, here too patients and practitioners shared the same values, but the patients experienced less treatment-related stress.

Other cultural factors are important in the context of pain. Some ethnic groups may have language barriers that influence the success with which the patients convey their level of pain or understand the doctor's instructions. Many ethnic groups experience disproportional levels of stress due to acculturation (see chapter 3) or lower socioeconomic status. Prolonged experiences of stress could result from unemployment or family issues relating to changes in roles or the process of acculturating to a new dominant society. For example, Latinos are the fastest growing ethnic group in North America but have experienced decreasing economic and educational levels and are underrepresented in those who have health insurance (Betancourt & Fuentes, 2001). All these factors represent significant psychological factors for Latinos and those in other cultural groups coping with chronic pain.

Before you assume that if someone is from a different culture he or she has to experience pain differently, remember that there are also big individual differences within cultures. In addition, a number of studies have failed to find significant differences in pain perceptions (Flannery, Sos, & McGovern, 1981; Pfefferbaum, Adams, & Aceves, 1990). The different studies compared different ethnic groups and different measures of pain, making it tougher to understand the basic phenomenon. The samples are often not heterogeneous and are not always chosen by random sampling (Korol & Craig, 2001). Future health psychological research should aim to have bigger groups for comparison to produce a more thorough understanding of cultural differences. An increased focus on cultural influences in pain can already be seen in some areas of health care. For example, home care clinicians have been urged to be aware of the impact of various ethnic and even religions backgrounds on the perception of pain and subsequent acceptance of treatment regimens (Callister, 2003). Reviews of home care procedures suggest that when the clinician deals with different cultures, a continuum of characteris-

Cultural Differences in the Perception of Pain Some cultural rituals, such as fire walking, look very painful but the participant reports no pain at all. This is a great example of how cultural beliefs, expectations of pain, and context interact to influence our pain perceptions.

tics is seen ranging from stoicism, denial, and a reluctance to accept treatment to loud exclamations of pain (Ondeck, 2003). There is a particular need for a better understanding of some of the cultural healing techniques used for pain.

Developmental Differences

Sex and ethnic differences interact, and this interaction changes as we grow older. As we age our pain thresholds increase, but we get less and less tolerant of pain and tend to report it more (Lautenbacher & Strian, 1991; Skevington, 1995). This is not because young children do not know the words for pain or because they do not have fully developed nerve endings for pain, but probably reflects the extent to which pain is influenced by cognitive and psychological factors. Pain also tends to increase in frequency as we age. The older adult complaining about more aches and pains (or middle-aged people concluding that they "must be getting old" because they hurt more) reflects the natural changes in pain occurrences. Lack of language and cognitive development makes it difficult to measure pain in young children, forcing researchers to rely more on facial reactions and other pain behaviors (Anand & Craig, 1996). For the longest time doctors believed that infants do not feel pain (hence the lack of resistance to the perceived sanitary benefits of performing circumcisions on male infants). This belief has been reassessed, and much contemporary pain research is taking a developmental approach to determining specific age-related differences in the experience of pain.

Why Feel Pain?

As signified by the technical definition of nociception, pain is essential to survival. Different cultural groups may experience it to different levels and may have different ways to cope with it, but in all cases it serves the same purpose. Pain warns us of bodily danger and provides feedback of bodily functions. If you are hiking up a hill and you place your foot on a rock in the wrong way, your foot may hurt before you put all your weight on it. You automatically place it down in the right way. If you break a finger or your arm, the pain in the limb is a reminder to you to refrain from using it to give it time to heal. When you get too close to a fire, the pain from the heat reminds you to keep a safe distance from the fire. When you experience pain you are more likely to go to a doctor. Unfortunately, the opposite is also true. Finnegan et al. (1995) found that heart attack victims who did not experience too much pain delayed seeking care for their symptoms. Let's take a closer look at the different types of pain that we can experience.

Types of Pain

Think about how you describe your sensations of pain. After running into a wall or a corner of the table, you may experience a numbing pain. A headache throbs. A tooth aches. A burn smarts. There are many different causes for the sensation we refer to as pain. In addition, many different words can be used to describe pain. Pain has been classified in many different ways: it can be short term, referred to as **acute** pain, or it can be experienced for a long period of time, termed

chronic pain. If the chronic pain is associated with a disease such as cancer, it is referred to as chronic malignant pain. If it is not associated with a malignant state, such as lower back pain, it is referred to as chronic noncancer pain (Turk, 2001). Acute pain can last for minutes, hours, or even days or weeks. Chronic pain often persists for months or even years. Pain can be limited to a small area, say your lower back, or spread out over a large area, for example, your entire body when you have the flu.

In addition to terms based on the duration of the pain (e.g., acute and chronic), pain can be described based on its origins. For example, purely psychological pain without a physiological basis is referred to as **psychogenic pain.** Pure nociception without significant psychological pain is referred to as **neuropathic pain.** Similarly, physiological pain without specific tissue damage is referred to as **somatic pain** (Turk, 2001).

The Biology of Pain

Before we explore the elements of the gate control theory of pain we need to understand some basic information. There are four distinct physiological processes critical to understanding pain: transduction, transmission, modulation, and perception (Fields, 1987). **Transduction** takes place at the level of the receptors where chemical (e.g., caustic fumes), mechanical (e.g., a pinprick), or thermal (e.g., a flame) energy is converted in electrochemical nerve impulses. This electrochemical energy is then transmitted or relayed from the sensory receptors to the central nervous system. Substance P is a neurotransmitter that plays a role in transmission. The sensory nerve fibers transmitting signals from the receptors to the spinal cord are called afferent fibers and are part of the peripheral nervous system. The spinal cord neurons that relay the signal up to the brain are part of the central nervous system and ascend to the brainstem. In the brain, neurons transmit impulses between the thalamus and the various parts of the cortex. **Modulation** refers to the neural activity leading to the control of pain transmissions between the various parts of the brain. The main parts of nervous system involved in modulation are the frontal cortex, hypothalamus, periaqueductal gray matter, reticular formation, and medulla in the brain and the areas of the spinal cord to be described shortly. The end result of these three processes is perception of pain when the neural activity of transmission and modulation results in a subjective experience (Figure 9.1).

Measuring Pain

Given the multifaceted nature of pain, it is particularly difficult to measure. Can we objectively measure tissue damage? No, we really cannot. Furthermore, the same physical problem may cause different amounts of pain to different people. A broken limb may hurt Nikhil much more than the same break may hurt Nathan. Given the number of words that one can use to describe pain, we also encounter major language issues when we try to ask someone if he or she is in pain or what sort of pain he or she is experiencing. These issues make measuring pain difficult.

Most hospitals in North America now consider pain to be a **vital sign,** one of five basic measures that doctors get from patients (temperature, pulse, blood

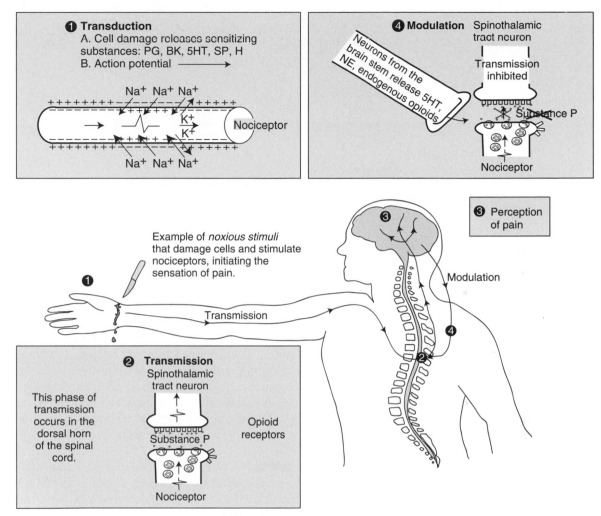

① Transduction
A. Cell damage releases sensitizing substances: PG, BK, 5HT, SP, H
B. Action potential ⟶

Na⁺ Na⁺ Na⁺
Nociceptor
K⁺
K⁺
Na⁺ Na⁺ Na⁺

④ Modulation Spinothalamic tract neuron
Neurons from the brain stem release 5HT, NE, endogenous opioids
Transmission inhibited
Substance P
Nociceptor

③ Perception of pain

Example of *noxious stimuli* that damage cells and stimulate nociceptors, initiating the sensation of pain.
❶

Modulation

Transmission

② Transmission
Spinothalamic tract neuron

This phase of transmission occurs in the dorsal horn of the spinal cord.

Opioid receptors
Substance P
Nociceptor

FIGURE 9.1
Four Basic Processes Involved in Understanding Pain
The location where each process takes place is shown with the corresponding numbers on the diagram.
Source: From McCaffery and Pasero, Pain: Clinical Manual, *p. 21. Copyright © 1999 Mosby, Inc. Reprinted by permission of Elsevier.*

pressure, and respiration are the other four). Given that pain has to be measured right away, how do you do it if the patient does not speak English and no interpreter is available? How do you do it if the patient is a young child who cannot comprehend the question?

Basic Pain Measures

Hospitals have a variety of simple ways to assess pain that can be used across cultures. Regardless of the race, ethnicity, or age of the patient, illustrations of different levels of pain can help in pain assessment (Jensen & Karoly, 2001). A

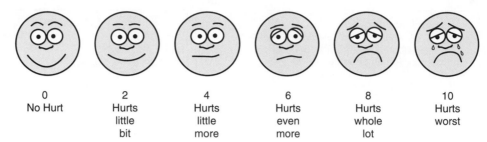

0	2	4	6	8	10
No Hurt	Hurts little bit	Hurts little more	Hurts even more	Hurts whole lot	Hurts worst

FIGURE 9.2
Sample Pictorial Measure of Pain
A pictorial measure of pain can be used by young children and people from different cultures (labels are translated to different languages).

sample pictorial measure of pain is shown in Figure 9.2. The young patient is shown a series of 6 to 10 descriptive faces. At one end of the spectrum is a smiling face (representing no or low pain). At the other end of the spectrum is a frowning face (representing lots of pain). The patient indicates which face best represents how he or she is feeling. This measure is also used with patients from different cultural backgrounds with simple instructions printed in different languages beneath it (McGrath & Gillespie, 2001). For example, in many hospitals ranging from Green Bay, WI, to Los Angeles, CA, color clipboards or posters with the scale shown in Figure 9.2 are accompanied by instructions in Spanish. Together with this simple pictorial measure, hospitals also use a continuous measure of pain. Patients are instructed to pick how much pain they are feeling on a scale of 0 to 10 with 0 meaning no pain and 10 signifying extreme pain.

The McGill Pain Questionnaire (MPQ) A number of validated pain questionnaires are used in addition to the preceding simple measures of pain. The MPQ is one of the earliest and most frequently used questionnaires and draws on the fact that we use words to describe pain (Melzack, 1975). It consists of three main dimensions, sensory, affective, and evaluative, with each tapping into different aspects of pain. The sensory aspect captures the frequency, location, and sensory quality of pain (e.g., spreading, burning, pulsing, or crushing). The affective aspect captures more emotional qualities (e.g., annoying, terrifying, exhausting, or sickening). The evaluative aspect captures the experience or pain (e.g., agonizing or excruciating). In addition, patients can indicate where exactly they feel pain on two outlines of the human body as shown in Figure 9.3.

The Multidimensional Pain Inventory (MPI) The MPI is a longer measure consisting of 52 questions and divided into three main sections (Kerns, Turk, & Rudy, 1985). Using a more biopsychosocial approach, the first section assesses the intensity of pain, the patient's view of his or her own functioning with pain and other aspects such as the extent to which pain interferes with the patient's life. The second section measures the patient's views of how those with close relationships respond to him or her. The third section assesses the extent to which the

ST. VINCENT HOSPITAL
GREEN BAY, WISCONSIN
www.stvincenthospital.org
PAIN ASSESSMENT FORM

Date:_____

Patient's Goal_____

Age_____

1. Current Intensity:

—10   Worst pain imaginable
— 9
— 8
— 7
— 6
— 5
— 4
— 3
— 2
— 1
— 0

2. How and when did pain begin? Did something trigger your pain?

_____

_____

3. Where is the pain located? I = Internal, E = external. Use drawing.

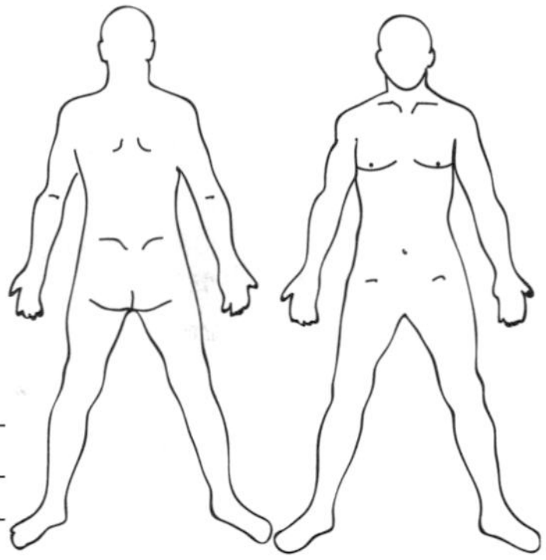

4. Is pain:
Continuous Intermittent
Describe patterns/changes:

_____

_____

_____

_____

5. Describe in your own words what your pain feels like. _____

_____

6. What makes the pain better/what has helped in the past?_____

_____

7. What makes the pain worse/what has not helped in the past?_____

_____

8. What other symptoms accompany your pain?_____

9. How does pain affect your:

Sleep _____

Appetite _____

Physial Activity _____

Concentration _____

Emotions (Anxiety Factor) _____

Social Relationships _____

What would you like to do that you are not able to now? _____

10. What do you think is causing your pain?_____

11. Current analgesics and nonpharmacologic regimes:_____

12. Plan/comments:_____

_____

_____

_____

_____Signature/Date_____

FIGURE 9.3
A Hospital Measure of Pain
Notice the many different aspects of the phenomenon of pain that are assessed.
Copyright © 2005 St. Vincent Hospital. Used by permission of the author.   *Continued*

1. Medical History

Diabetes	Depression	Peptic Ulcer	Gout
Liver Disease	Renal Disease	Osteoarthritis	Cardiac Disease
Fibromyalgia	Rheumatoid Arthritis	Neuromuscular Disease	HTN
Migraines	Wounds	Spondylolisthesis	Other_____

2. Previous Treatments

Pain Clinic Injections	Chronic Pain Clinic	Spiritual Consult	Guided Imagery
Massage Therapy	Herbal Treatment	Psychotherapy	Body Mechanics
Vocational Rehab	Aquatic Therapy	Physical Therapy	Other_____
Occupational Therapy	Dietary Consult	Relaxation	

3. Other Physician Consults:

Chiropractic	Neurosurgeon	Addictionologist
Rehab Physiatrist	Orthopod	Pain Physician
Rheumatologist	Neurologist	Other_____

4. Tobacco, Alcohol, Nonprescription meds. Explain_____

5. Allergies:_____

6. Liver Function: _____AST _____ALT _____ Alk. Phos.

7. Renal Function:_____Creat. _____BUN

8. Other medications: _____
_____

9. Side effects of analgesics/adjuvants:
Constipation   Xerostomia   Drowsiness   Twitching   Other_____

10. History of accidents:_____
_____

11. History of previous surgeries:_____
_____

12. Results of scans, x-rays, cultures, etc. _____
_____

13. Other consultants and their recommendations:_____
_____
_____

14. Follow-up visits and recommendations:
Date   Comments   Signature
_____
_____

FIGURE 9.3, cont'd
A Hospital Measure of Pain

pain prevents the patient from taking part in daily life by measuring how often the patient partakes in 30 different daily activities. This form of measurement of the patient's perceptions and behaviors is seen in other pain measures as well. For example, the Multiaxial Assessment of Pain (MAP) (Turk & Rudy, 1986) measures both psychological and behavioral aspects of pain.

The Short Form with 36 Questions (SF-36) Some general measures of health include measures of pain. Ware, Snow, Kosinski, and Gandek (1993) developed the (pedestrian, but precisely named) SF-36, a health status questionnaire with eight scales assessing most of the important dimensions of health status. Together with measuring aspects such as physical and social functioning, the SF-36 also has a measure of Bodily Pain. The Bodily Pain scale has a range of 0 to 100 and has been suggested as a good tool for busy primary care clinicians because its use facilitates and focuses listening and the result can be viewed as a vital sign (Wetzler, Lum, & Bush, 2000).

Other Measures Other psychological tests such as the Minnesota Multiphasic Personality Inventory (MMPI) and the Beck Depression Inventory (Beck, Ward, Mendelson, Mock, & Erbaugh, 1961) are also used to get a sense of a person's pain. For example, patients who are likely to experience chronic pain are also likely to score high on the MMPI subscales of hypochondriasis, depression, and hysteria (referred to as the neurotic triad) (Bradley & Van der Heide, 1984).

In addition to paper and pencil measures and interviews, you can also assess the extent to which people are in pain by just observing their behaviors. Even for something as mundane as sleeping in an odd way and getting a crook in your neck, your behaviors change. You walk with a slightly different step because of the pain in your neck, and you may grimace as you turn your head. For patients with chronic pain, the pain can impact many aspects of their lives. They may moan and groan in pain, walk with trouble, and even avoid doing things that they have to do, such as picking up a bag of groceries. Likewise, even if patients report not feeling a lot of pain, a doctor can get a sense of their pain levels by watching how they sit, stand, move, and talk (Fordyce, 1990).

Although the physiological measures such as electroencephalography, electromyography (EMG), and skin conductance are often used to assess pain (Blanchard & Andrasik, 1985), they have not always been found to be very helpful (Flor, 2001).

Theories of Pain

Early Physiological and Psychological Approaches

So how did humankind explain pain in first place? Healers, shamans, and physicians throughout history encountered people with pain and were driven to help them get rid of it. To treat pain, one must have a sense of how it is caused. There have been many explanations for pain over the last 3,000 or so years. Table 9.1 summarizes the main theories of pain. Going back as far as we can to the Greeks, we find that pain was considered an experience subject to rational thinking just

TABLE 9.1

Main Theories of Pain from a Historical Perspective

3000 B.C.	Evil spirits
1000 B.C.	God's will
500 B.C.	Irrational thinking—Greeks
1664 A.D.	Specific stimuli—Descartes
1886	Pattern theory
1884	Specificity theory
1959	Pain-prone personality—Engel
1965	Gate control theory—Melzack and Wall
1974	Cognitive-behavioral model—Brewer
1990	Diathesis-stress theory of pain (Turk et al.)
1999	Neuromatrix theory of pain—Melzack

like any other experience or behavior. Centuries later, Descartes (1664) provided one of the first theories of how we experience pain. He argued that pain is the result of specific stimuli acting on the body: the stronger the stimuli, the stronger the pain. Descartes hypothesized the existence of long nerves that extended through the body from the brain to the sense organs. Sensations at the skin's surface, for example, the bite of a dog, would be relayed to the brain, which would then coordinate a response (i.e., pulling your hand away).

This unidimensional model of pain used a **specificity** concept, later made explicit by Von Frey (1894). Pain was thought to be a specific independent sensation such as heat or touch, with specialized receptors responding to specific stimuli. Specialized centers in the brain would then stimulate actions to avoid further harm. Concurrent with the formulation of the specificity theory, Goldschneider (1886) suggested that pain results from a combination of impulses from nerve endings. According to this **pattern theory,** different patterns of stimulations caused different types of pain. No separate pain system was needed and instead of the intensity of the stimulus, strong, mild, and medium levels of pain resulted in how impulses were integrated in the dorsal horn of the spinal cord.

Although prevalent for many years, neither model explained some basic observations. For example, patients with similar objectively determined injuries vary greatly in their reports of pain severity (Turk, 2001a). Similarly, patients experiencing the same reports of pain who are treated in similar ways do not experience similar relief. Furthermore, surgery designed to alleviate pain by severing the neurological pathways responsible for it often does not work (Turk & Nash, 1996).

In contrast to both these physiological theories (neither of which had any place for psychological influences on pain), Engel (1959) proposed one of the first models to allow for the role of emotions and perceptions. Having a **pain-prone personality** was thought to predispose a person to experience persistent pain. Expanded on by Blumer and Heilbronn (1984), the pain-prone person tends to deny emotional and interpersonal problems, is unable to cope with anger and hostility, and has a family history of depression, alcoholism, and chronic pain. Not only

Descartes' (1664) Model of Pain and Suffering According to Descartes there was a specific system for pain that was responsible for the sensation of the stimulus and the experience of the pain.

was there little empirical support for this theory (Turk & Salovey, 1984), but it did not account for how pain itself can produce changes in personality. Nonetheless, there is something intuitively satisfying about individual differences in pain perception. In recognition of the fact that psychological factors can predispose one to pain, the American Psychiatric Association created two psychiatric diagnoses: pain associated with psychological factors either with or without a diagnosed medical condition (Turk, 2001b).

Biopsychological Theories of Pain

So far, the different theories we have discussed were primarily physiological or psychological in nature. In lieu of purely psychological predispositions to pain, many researchers attempted to link these two aspects (e.g., Pilowsky & Spence, 1975; Waddell, Main, Morris, DiPaola, & Gray, 1984). One of the earlier models, the cognitive-behavioral model (e.g., Brewer, 1974; Turk, Meichenbaum, & Genest, 1983) suggested that people get conditioned to experience pain on the basis of learned expectations. For example, you hear that dentist office visits can be painful and you condition yourself to fear going to the dentist and then experience more pain when you do go. People with pain are thought to have negative expectations about their own ability to function normally without experiencing pain and believe they have limited ability to control pain. Similar to the cognitive-behavioral model and as a variation on the pain-prone personality idea, theorists proposed that some individuals may have physiological predispositions to pain that interact with psychological factors to cause pain. Referred to as the **diathesis-stress model,** Flor, Birbaumer, and Turk (1990) proposed that predisposing factors, such as a reduced threshold of nociception, precipitating stimuli, such as an injury, and maintaining processes, such as the expectation that the pain will persist, are all important in explaining pain. Although this theory provides a compelling model for the etiology of many forms of pain, the most widely accepted theory of pain is one first published in 1965.

The Gate Control Theory of Pain

The most effective biopsychosocial theory of pain comes from Melzack and colleagues (Melzack & Casey, 1968; Melzack & Wall, 1965). Referred to as the **gate control theory** (GCT) of pain, this model proposed that the bulk of the action takes place in the dorsal horn substantia gelatinosa of the spinal cord and is influenced by the brain. The diagram in Figure 9.4 shows the key components of this model.

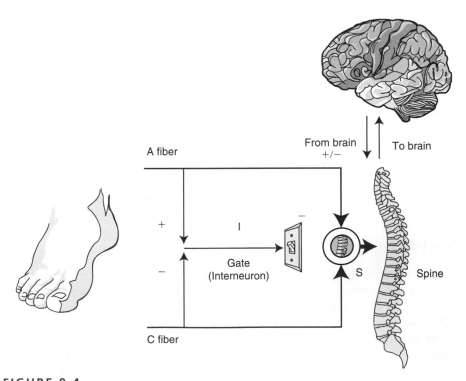

FIGURE 9.4
Key Components of the Gate Control Theory
Pain receptors on the surface of our bodies (e.g., on our feet) are connected to the brain via A and C fibers, interneurons, and the spinal cord.
Positive sign (+) signify activation.
Negative sign (−) signify deactivation.

Some basic features of the GCT are consistent with older theories of pain. For example, we start with pain receptors located throughout the body. Some are on the surface just under the skin. These receptors inform us when we are poked, scratched, cut, or scraped. Other receptors are deeper in the muscles and among the glands and organs, telling us about muscular strains and pulls and changes in normal functions. In partial support of specificity theory, some receptors only convey pain information. Others also report on general sensations such as contact and temperature. All of these receptors send nerve projections to the spinal cord to the aforementioned dorsal horn. Now here is where the GCT was innovative. Instead of these nerves from the receptors sending impulses directly to the brain, the GCT proposed that the neural impulses from the peripheral nervous system are modulated by a "gate-like" mechanism in the dorsal horn before they flow into the central nervous system up to the brain. What exactly is going on in the dorsal horn?

Three main types of nerve fibers are involved: A fibers, C fibers, and the "gate" interneurons (see Figure 9.4). Melzack and Wall (1965) found that the diameters of the fibers of the peripheral nervous system varied in size. A-beta fibers have a large diameter and are myelinated (insulated with a protein sheath), resulting in quick transmission of impulses. C fibers are smaller in diameter and are not myelinated, resulting in slower transmission of impulses. A-delta fibers, another form of A fiber, are also small in diameter and have a function similar to that of C fibers. Each of the different fibers (A-beta, A-delta, and C) synapse on both the interneuron and on to the central nervous system neurons going up to the brain (see I and S in Figure 9.4). The interneurons are hypothetical gates that are located in the spinal cord and do not allow pain sensations to be relayed up to the brain if they are stimulated by the A-beta fibers (i.e., they close the gate). If they are not stimulated or if they are inhibited by the action of the C fibers or A-delta fibers, they allow pain sensations to be sent up to the brain (i.e., the gate remains open). The interneuron is thus an inhibitory neuron. The status of the gate depends on the balance of activity between small diameter (A-delta and C) and large diameter (A-beta) fibers.

The Psychology of Pain

Where does psychological control fit in, you may ask? Melzack and Wall (1965) also proposed that descending pathways from the brain also modulate activity at the level of the dorsal horn. In addition to the afferent activity from the receptors in the periphery, this efferent activity also influences pain sensations. Different psychological states such as anxiety or fear can increase the levels of pain experienced. In such scenarios, the descending pathway activates the C fibers that turn the interneuron off and increase the pain sensations making their way up to the brain. On the other hand, when someone is happy or optimistic, these positive affective states also influence the transmission of pain because the descending pathways now activate the interneurons and shut the gate, lessening the pain sensation. For this reason a football player may not feel the pain of a violent tackle if it is in the middle of an important game, and he is excited or focused on winning. Similarly, if a person is bleeding from a cut but has not noticed she was hurt, she may not feel any pain. A lot depends on how we appraise an event. Similar to Lazarus' cognitive appraisal theory of stress (see chapter 4), if we appraise a wound or illness to be severe, descending pathways from the brain to the dorsal horn can accentuate the level of pain experienced.

In addition to appraisal, many other psychological factors can modulate the experience of pain via the descending efferent pathway. Bandura (1969) first highlighted the role of observational or social learning in many areas of human life. Social learning can even influence pain. If a young child sees her mother receive an injection without a reaction, the child will probably not react as much to receiving an injection herself. If the same child sees her mom scream and yell in pain when receiving an injection, this child may expect to feel a lot of pain as well. A number of studies have documented the role of social learning (e.g., Craig, 1988). Pain and pain behaviors can be modified by other basic learning and behaviorist theories as well. Psychological pain can be operantly conditioned. For example, if complaining a lot when one is in pain results in getting a lot of attention, the pain behavior can be reinforced and strengthened. Flor, Kerns, and Turk (1987) found that chronic pain patients reported more pain when they had spouses who were considerate and caring.

Pain can also be classically conditioned. If every visit to the dentist's office is accompanied by pain (e.g., a lot of drilling), one is likely to experience fear at just the thought of going to the dentist. This classically conditioned fear can predispose a person to experience more pain when he or she actually goes to the dentist. Even if you have not experienced pain at a dentist's office, just believing a visit can be painful can be enough to activate those descending pathways and increase your experience of pain. A large body of research documents the fact that patients' beliefs about pain, their attitudes, the context in which the pain is experienced, expectancies, and perceptions all affect their reports of pain (Jensen, Turner, & Romano, 1994; Meagher, Arnau, & Rhudy, 2001; Slater, Hall, Atkinson, & Garfin, 1991; Turk, 2001a).

Consequently, there is now a new theory that builds on the GTC and focuses more on the neural modulation in the brain. Empirical support is now slowly accumulating for the neuromatrix theory of pain (Melzack, 1999), and we will undoubtedly hear more about it in years to come.

Using the Gate Control Theory to Explain Pain Relief

The theorized combination of large fiber, small fiber, interneuron, and descending neuron activity has many implications for when and how we experience pain. First, it nicely explains why some pains are short lived whereas others persist for long periods of time. Whenever we experience sharp pains for a short period of time (e.g., we step on a nail), the A-beta fibers are activated and (1) send a fast message up to the brain via the central nervous system and (2) activate the interneuron, shut the gate, and turn the pain experience off. This is why we only feel the pain for a short period. When we experience slow, aching, burning pains with greater motivational and affective components, the C or A-delta fibers have probably been stimulated. They not only pass on the impulse to the brain, but they also inhibit the firing of the interneuron closing the gate. Some chronic conditions may cause long-term pain by deactivating the A-beta fibers. Herniated discs, tumors, and some injuries may decrease the firing of large fibers, making even mild stimuli that are not typically painful cause severe pain for extended periods of time (Turk, 2001a).

The GTC also explains some of the behaviors that we use to relieve pain. We often try to shut the gate ourselves. If we have a sharp pain in a certain spot, even something small like a bug bite, we often scratch around the pain or pinch ourselves close by to reduce the pain. This **counterirritation** serves to activate the large fibers that stimulate the interneuron, shutting the gate and providing temporary relief (Zimmerman, 1979). Counterirritation is sometimes achieved with the delivery of minute bursts of electricity to nerve endings right under the skin near the painful area or near the spinal cord near the painful area (Nashold, Somjen, & Friedman, 1972). This transcutaneous electrical nerve stimulation has been found to produce relief for a variety of diverse pains (Kim & Dellon, 2001). Together with psychological ways to activate the descending efferent pathways and close the gate described above, researchers have found that electrically stimulating the brain can also reduce pain (Reynolds, 1969), a process referred to as **stimulation-produced analgesia.** Let's take a look at some of the other ways to control pain.

Pain Management Techniques

There are three main categories of pain management techniques. The entire list is summarized in Table 9.2. The use of each of these will depend on the duration of the pain, the tolerance levels of individuals, and their pain thresholds. Some of us have high **thresholds** for pain. This means it takes a lot of painful stimuli for us to perceive something as being painful. Even if we have a low threshold for pain and perceive pain easily, we may still have a high **tolerance** level. Tolerance is the amount beyond which pain becomes unbearable, and we cannot accept any more. The main cultural differences that I discussed previously relate more to pain tolerance than to pain threshold. Men and women or members of different ethnicities tend to have different tolerance levels based on their expectations and cultural backgrounds.

We will examine some primarily physiological ways to reduce pain and also a wide variety of psychological techniques. Methods in each of these two categories can be used to cope with either acute or chronic pain although they are all used primarily for short-term treatment. The discussion of the third category of tech-

---

TABLE 9.2

Major Pain Management Techniques

Chemical—Aspirin, acetaminophen, ibuprofen	Hypnosis
Chemical—Morphine	Biofeedback
Stimulation-produced analgesia	Relaxation
Acupuncture	Guided imagery
Surgical—Transcutaneous electrical nerve stimulation	Meditation
Distraction	Long-term self-management programs

niques will focus specifically on chronic pain and will include self-management programs. Our goal is to understand analgesia or pain relief.

Physiological Treatments

Chemical   For most common pains, such as twisted ankles, headaches, bruises, and body aches from colds or flu, most individuals turn to over-the-counter medications. In most countries around the world, a number of tablets are available to alleviate pain. You have probably taken an aspirin, a Tylenol, or a Motrin at some point (or many) in your life. The use of these quick-shot pain relievers is so common that you can even buy pills with the active chemical ingredients (e.g., aspirin, acetaminophen, or ibuprofen) in bulk packages of 500 to 1,000 pills. These medications act locally, often at the site of the pain.

For pain associated with surgery and for chronic pains, patients are often given stronger medications such as morphine. Morphine binds to receptors in the periaqueductal gray area of the midbrain and produces pronounced analgesia and pleasant moods. Because of its effectiveness, there is a tendency for patients to want to use it regularly. This can lead to tolerance, drug dependence, and addiction (Hill, 1993; Julien, 2001). Morphine is part of a class of chemicals referred to as opiates, drugs made from plants that regulate pain in the body by mimicking the effects of opioids, chemicals made by the body that regulate pain. First discovered by Akil, Mayer, and Liebeskind (1976), opioids (more technically, endogenous opioid peptides) can be divided into three main classes: beta-endorphins, proenkephalin, and prodynorphin. Each class exerts its pain-relieving effects in different parts of the body.

Our body sometimes releases opioids when we are stressed, a state that can be induced by motor activity such as physical activity. You have probably heard of a phenomenon known as the "runner's high," referring to a positive mood state achieved by approximately 20 minutes of physical activity such as running (Heitkamp, Schulz, Rocker, & Dickhuth, 1998). This is a form of **stress-induced analgesia** (SIA) and has also been documented in a variety of experimental settings (Helmstetter & Bellgowan, 1994). For example, rats who are stressed by repeated immersions in cold water show SIA and higher pain tolerance when their tails are placed on a hot plate (no, this is not a pretty picture). Research now suggests that in addition to physical activity, even meditation can release beta-endorphins (Harte, Eifert, & Smith, 1995). The occurrence of SIA is not definite though. There is some controversy about what exactly causes SIA because some studies have not replicated the effect (e.g., Kraemer, Dzewaltowski, Blair, Rinehardt, & Castracane, 1990).

Acupuncture   This Chinese traditional medicine treatment, discussed in chapter 2, is often used to relieve pain. The acupuncturist inserts fine metal needles into the skin at predetermined points. These points, charted from the work of Chinese physicians over centuries, are thought to stimulate energy flow. Disruptions in energy flow can cause pain. Western biomedicine interprets the effectiveness of acupuncture as being due to the needles stimulating large fibers that close the gate. Acupuncture can produce such high levels of analgesia that even entire

© Courtesy Columbus Instruments, OH

Studying Stress-Induced Analgesia in a Rat Using Excessive Exercise

surgical procedures in China have been performed without the use of anesthetics. Not only has acupuncture been empirically shown to reduce pain, but also it does so without the side effects of many other medications (Berman et al., 1999; Leng, 1999). Although some studies suggest that acupuncture works because of a placebo effect (e.g., White & Ernst, 1999), it has been found to produce endorphins because the injection of naloxone, an endorphin blocker, also reduces the effectiveness of acupuncture. Furthermore, if the location of the needle is moved by even millimeters from where it is supposed to be, there is no analgesic effect, supporting a valid physiological basis for this treatment.

Surgical   Sometimes pain can be so intense that a person may just want to cut out that part of his or her body to get rid of the pain. Some version of this macabre scenario did take place hundreds of years ago when surgeons cut off infected limbs for which there was no cure, but this is not something considered today. Yet, given our understanding of the physiological pathways of pain, some treatments for pain do involve the severing of nerves that transmit pain or lesioning of sections of the brain responsible for pain perceptions. Unfortunately, although this method sounds great in theory, practical usage is limited because pain relief from surgery tends to be short lived as nerve pathways grow back and reconnect.

Psychological Treatments

A wide variety of psychological ways can be used to reduce pain. As discussed in the previous chapter and earlier in this chapter, our expectations of hospitals, injuries, or treatments can influence our experience of pain and discomfort. If you think a certain wound or procedure is going to be painful, you will probably experience more pain. You can use this same psychological angle to your advantage. If you expect a certain method of pain relief to work, it probably will. This power of expectation is often referred to as a placebo effect. Beyond expectations influencing pain, our psychology can influence our experience of pain in a variety of other ways.

Psychological States and Cognitive Styles   Given those descending pathways from the brain, our moods can influence our pain. As discussed in the section on the GCT, if we are anxious, depressed, tense, fearful, or sad, we are likely to experience more pain. Often these negative mood states can lead to biased forms of thinking. These cognitive biases can accentuate the feelings of pain and need to be modified. For example, people often exaggerate the extent of an injury (catastrophize), believe the pain will last forever (stable attributional style), believe they have no control over the pain (external locus of control), or just give up and fail to try to alleviate their pain (learned helplessness). Other pain patients feel victimized by the situation and cannot get past the fact that the pain is happening to them. They often blame themselves and feel worthless, sometimes excessively dwelling on the pain. Changing these detrimental cognitions can aid pain relief.

Distraction   Another way to vary psychological states to lessen pain is to distract the person from the pain (Eccleston, 1995). If you have a headache or a stomachache and are not doing anything but sitting and thinking about how bad you are feeling, chances are you will not feel much better anytime soon. Instead, if you distract yourself from the pain by reading, watching television or a movie, or even surfing on the Internet, you can alleviate some of the pain. Cognitive distraction can also take the form of guided imagery in which patients immerse themselves in an involving and pleasing scenario (Fors, Sexton, & Gotestam, 2002; Sheikh, 2003) or the use of music (MacDonald et al., 2003; Magill, 2001).

Hypnosis   One method that combines distraction with relaxation and a self-fulfilling prophecy is hypnosis (from the Greek word for sleep). It was first popularized by the Austrian Mesmer who hypnotized patients (this treatment later became known as mesmerization) to effect cures in eighteenth century Europe and then later was practiced by the Scottish physician Braid who used it as anesthesia for surgery and then by Freud in his treatment of psychopathology. Under hypnosis, some patients have been found to be able to withstand treatments that would otherwise cause considerable pain (Patterson, Adcock, & Bombardier, 1997). In hypnosis, a patient is induced into a relaxed state, often by being told to focus on an object or the calming voice of the doctor, and is then given a suggestion (e.g., the pain is fading) that is recalled when the patient comes out of the "hypnotic trance" (Hilgard, 1978). Although the exact mechanism by which hypnotism works is still unclear, hypnosis can influence both affective and sensory components of pain (Lang et al., 2000; Rainville, Carrier, Hofbauer, Bushnell, & Duncan 1999; Sellick & Zaza, 1998).

General Cognitive Methods   Other cognitive methods to treat pain are similar to those used to cope with stress. As described in chapter 5, biofeedback, relax-

Franz Anton Mesmer Hypnotizing a Patient

ation, guided imagery, and meditation are all forms of cognitive therapy that can alleviate pain. Biofeedback allows a person to get more control over his or her autonomic activity and together with relaxation and meditation helps to reduce anxiety and muscle tension. This facilitates the redirection of blood flow away from the painful areas.

Self-Management of Chronic Pain

Many of the methods discussed in the preceding section are used extensively to treat acute pain. Some of them, such as imagery and hypnosis, are used with chronic pain as well. Still, chronic pain is different and calls for unique strategies. One category of pain relief therapy differs from the straightforward medical model in terms of its goals for change and in terms of who is responsible for change. **Self-management** programs (e.g., Hanson & Gerber, 1990) make the patient with chronic pain the one with the major responsibility for making the change rather than the doctor or the health professional staff. These programs have fewer side effects because psychological change, ways of thinking and behaving, are emphasized over the use of medications. In most cases, physicians refer patients to such programs only after medications have been tried. Correspondingly, there is less use of physical procedures and medication and more use of cognitive-behavioral change.

These programs focus on many different elements of the pain experience: the emotional, cognitive, and sensory experiences of pain; the behaviors and actions influenced by pain; and the social consequences of pain, such as the balance of work and play, daily physical activity, and interactions with the social environment. The patient is trained to attend to and modify many of the cognitive processes that can influence pain perception as discussed earlier, for example, the focus of attention, memories of previous experiences with pain and events related to the pain condition, perceived coping alternatives, expectations regarding impact of chronic pain on well-being, and attitudes and beliefs regarding oneself and others. The main goals of such programs are to:

1. Provide skill training to divert attention away from pain.
2. Improve physical condition (via physical reconditioning).
3. Increase daily physical activity.
4. Provide ways to cope more effectively with episodes of intense pain (without medication).
5. Provide skills to manage depression, anger, and aggression.
6. Decrease tension, anxiety, stressful life demands, and interpersonal conflict.

After an intensive interview staff evaluate pain and pain behaviors and take a medical history. The medical staff then assesses the patient's functional status (e.g., his or her actual physical, emotional, and mental status). The patient and staff together develop program goals, and the patient signs a contract agreeing to work toward the goals. The specific components include some medication but are primarily geared toward patient education. The patient gets skills training, learns relaxation, and learns how to change maladaptive cognitions and maladaptive behaviors (e.g., poor nutritional habits). Finally, the program includes relapse prevention and follow-up.

Pain is something that we all will experience at some point in our lives. There are a number of different ways that we can cope with pain, and our cultural backgrounds may favor some over others. Given the complexity and the potential severity of the pain experience, the more ways that you know about how to cope with pain, the better off you will be.

FOCUS on Applications

A Hospital Case Study

Pain assessment is a growing focus in hospitals around America. In this chapter I discussed many physiological and psychological ways that pain is managed, but what do patients actually use? This section will give you a view from the ground up and will discuss a clinical assessment of patient satisfaction with pain management and the varying preferences for different types of pain management.

Many hospitals pay close attention to how successful they are in helping patients cope with pain. In Green Bay, WI, there are three major not-for-profit hospitals in town, and representatives from each hospital gather once a month to evaluate how pain is being treated. This Pain and Comfort Team (PACT) reviews the latest research on pain management and holds training sessions for health care professionals to pass on new information. PACT also periodically assesses patient satisfaction with pain treatment. This description of one of their studies provides a rich picture of what patients go through in a hospital (Triest-Robertson, Gurung, Brosig, Whitfield, & Pfutzenreuter, 2001).

Patients in short-term stay, postsurgery wards, and a cancer ward completed a short one-page questionnaire either before leaving the hospital or at home. All together 445 patients participated in the study. The questionnaire asked what their worst pain experience was, how often this pain was experienced, and which of a number of pain relief methods was used to cope with the pain. Patients were also asked how satisfied they were with the health care professionals they interacted with.

The worst pain experienced by patients on a standard 10-point scale was 6.28. Of great pragmatic significance, location of completion of the questionnaires was a significant factor: satisfaction with pain management was significantly higher when forms were completed in the hospital. Once patients went home, it is likely that their recollection of their experiences was not as fresh as when they were still in the hospital. Of course, the reason for the pain also made a difference. As you may expect, satisfaction with pain relief significantly differed by floor. Patients who were in short-term stay were the most satisfied with their pain management. The differences were significant even when controls were added for severity of pain (i.e., worst pain) and the number of times worst pain was experienced (both of these variables were significant factors).

So how do patients cope with pain? People use many different ways to cope with pain. The study found that although medication was the most commonly chosen pain relief method, with 50% of the respondents saying they used pills or morphine when they felt pain, a significant number of different methods were also used. Close to 20% of the patients also used prayer and relaxation, 14% used breathing techniques and other forms of distraction, and 8% used music. Which of these was the most effective? Although medications again came out a clear winner (8.9 on a 9-point scale with 9 being most relief), other forms of pain management were very effective as well. Relaxation and prayer were both rated 6.8, and breathing and distraction rated in the high 5s. Music was only rated a little more than 1.

The predictors of satisfaction with pain management also varied by floor. The most significant predictors of satisfaction were the number of times worst pain was experienced, how often patients were asked what their acceptable level of pain was, and how much control they perceived they had. Assessment studies such as this can provide hospitals with clear-cut ways to improve the services they provide and to decrease their patients' experiences of pain.

Chapter Summary

- Pain has physiological and psychological components and behavioral, cognitive, and affective states. Two of the largest cultural variations in pain are due to ethnicity and sex, both influenced by socialization. Females have lower thresholds and less tolerance for pain than males. When and how pain should be expressed varies among ethnic groups.
- Pain can be acute or chronic and can get worse with time or stay stable. It is measured by simple pictorial measures or by questionnaire. One of the most

common questionnaire measures, the McGill Pain Questionnaire, assesses sensory, affective, and evaluative aspects of pain.

- Early theories of pain attributed causes to spiritual sources. Various models of pain have been formulated, ranging from the unidimensional specificity theory hypothesizing specialized receptors for pain to the heavily psychological pain-prone personality idea, which suggested that certain personality types were more likely to experience pain. The most commonly used theory is the gate control theory, which posits that pain can be modulated at the level of the spinal cord and can also be influenced by impulses coming from the brain.

- Four basic physiological processes critical to the experience of pain are transduction, transmission, modulation, and perception. Psychologically, classical conditioning, operant conditioning, and observational learning can influence pain.

- Some ways to relieve pain include counterirritation, transcutaneous electrical nerve stimulation, and stimulation-produced analgesia. A range of physiological and psychological treatments are available. Physiological treatments include the use of medication, acupuncture, and surgery. Psychological treatments include distraction, hypnosis, biofeedback, relaxation, guided imagery, and progressive muscle relaxation.

- The management of chronic pain often calls for additional techniques. The most common are self-management programs for pain in which patients are empowered to control their experiences to alleviate their pain.

Synthesize, Evaluate, Apply

- Generate a list of different causes of pain and classify them using the system described in this chapter.
- What are some personality factors that can influence the perception of pain?
- What are other possible reasons to explain the results of Beecher's study with soldiers and Ulrich's study of patients with a view?
- What cultural factors influence your experience of pain?
- How would people with different approaches to health (as described in chapter 2) experience pain differently?
- Compare and contrast the main theories of pain.
- Are there any types of pain that the gate control theory would not be able to explain?
- Combine the different measures of pain to generate an optimal measure of pain.
- What are the biopsychosocial bases of the different pain management techniques?
- How does the cognitive appraisal model of stress relate to pain perception?
- Describe a technique to use both classical and operant conditioning to alleviate pain.
- What guidelines would you recommend for the use of morphine, a potentially addictive pain reliever?

- What aspects of the hospital setting (described in chapter 8) can negatively influence the experience of pain?
- Evaluate the pros and cons of each of the different pain management techniques.
- Why do acute and chronic pains have to be dealt with differently?

KEY TERMS, CONCEPTS, AND PEOPLE

acute, 263
chronic, 264
counterirritation, 275
diathesis-stress model, 272
gate control theory, 272
McGill Pain
    Questionnaire, 266
Melzack, Ronald, 272
Melzack and Wall, 273

modulation, 264
neuropathic pain, 264
nociception, 259
pain-prone personality, 270
pattern theory, 270
psychogenic pain, 264
self-management, 279
somatic pain, 264
specificity, 270

stimulation-produced
    analgesia, 275
stress-induced analgesia, 276
thresholds, 275
tolerance, 275
transduction, 264
Turk, Dennis, 270
vital sign, 264

ESSENTIAL READINGS

Fordyce, W. E. (1988). Pain and suffering: A reappraisal. *American Psychologist, 43*(4), 276–282.
Gatchel, R. J. (2005). *Clinical essentials of pain management.* Washington, DC: American Psychological Association.
Haley, W. E., Turner, J. A., & Romano, J. M. (1985). Depression in chronic pain patients: Relation to pain, activity, and sex differences. *Pain, 23,* 337–343.

Melzack, R., & Wall, P. D. (1965). Pain mechanisms: A new theory. *Science, 150*(3699), 971–979.
Turk, D. C., & Okifuji, A. (2002). Psychological factors in chronic pain: Evolution and revolution. *Journal of Consulting and Clinical Psychology, 70*(3), 678–690.

WEB RESOURCES

Visit the companion website at **http://psychology.wadsworth.com/gurung1e/,** where you will find online resources for this book, including chapter-by-chapter quizzes, weblinks, and more! You can also visit Wadsworth Psychology Resource Center at **http://psychology.wadsworth.com** to access additional resources.

The American Pain Society
http://ampainsoc.org

The American Pain Foundation
http://www.painfoundation.org

Chronic Illnesses and Death

Colds, sniffles, runny noses, body aches, and fevers are not experiences anyone looks forward to (even if it means not having to go to work or school). Headaches are no fun either. When we have headaches, we long to be free of them. Most aches and pains nag us and keep us from our daily activities, but such ailments are temporary. Unfortunately, not all poor health issues are short term. There are a large number of illnesses, referred to as **chronic illnesses,** that persist over long periods of time, mostly ending with death. You have heard of most of them: cancer, cardiovascular disease (CVD) and coronary heart disease (CHD), back pain, diabetes, and arthritis (I will discuss CVD and cancer in more detail in chapters 12 and 13). Each condition is accompanied by a unique set of symptoms and involves some form of impairment to the individual. In most cases the physiological damage is irreversible, and the person never again resembles the person he or she was before contracting the illness.

Some chronic illnesses occur early in life, such as asthma, and last for a lifetime. Others, such as cancers, may strike at midlife or in old age. All chronic illnesses are accompanied by severe physiological, psychological, and social changes for the individual. A large percentage of North Americans have such illnesses at any given time,

© (Royalty-free) Digital Vision/Getty Images

Back Pain Is One of the Most Commonly Reported Chronic Pains

and they cope with them in a variety of ways. Again, culture makes a difference, men and women cope differently, the old and the young cope differently, and different ethnic and religious groups cope differently. In this chapter I take a close look at some of the common themes surrounding chronic illnesses. How do you react when you find out you have a chronic illness? What does having a chronic illness do to your life? What can you do to cope? How *do* different people cope?

Prevalence Rates of Chronic Illnesses

What are the most common chronic illnesses and just how common are they? In the early days of our evolutionary histories, people died young and the end came pretty quickly (see chapters 1 and 4). Archaeological evidence suggests that men and women lived only until their early 20s and the main causes of death were predation by animals and other hostile humans. There were few, if any, long, drawn out chronic illnesses. Most illnesses resulting from viruses or bacteria were short lived because there were few cures. If you got sick, you died. Even during the Roman Empire (around A.D. 100) life expectancy was between 22 and 25 years. Current estimates suggest that women born in 2001 will live 79.8 years and men will live until about 74.4 years (Centers for Disease Control and Prevention [CDC], 2003). Even compared with 100 years ago, this represents a big change: Women born in 1900 lived on average 48.3 years and men lived 46.3 years. This change in life expectancy is due to the immense improvements in medicine that can postpone death. What this means is that people who get sick will still have a fair amount of time to live and have to cope with the illness.

Today the major causes of death are CVDs, cancer, lower respiratory diseases, diabetes, influenza, and pneumonia. The important thing for us to focus on in this chapter is that everyone who dies of one of these illnesses spends a large portion of his or her life coping with it first. The different causes of death all correspond to chronic illnesses in that they can be experienced for a very long period of time. At any given time close to 50% of Americans have one chronic illness or the other. The numbers are truly staggering. Currently, more than 64 million North Americans have a CVD (the total population of the United States is 281 million). Fifty million have high blood pressure. Close to 5 million have had strokes (American Heart Association, 2004), and 1.5 million men and women have some form of cancer (American Cancer Society, 2004). Diabetes, an illness that can hasten the onset of CVDs, is also a very common chronic illness and more than 18 million Americans are estimated to have one type of it or the other. In fact, heart disease and stroke account for approximately 65% of deaths due to diabetes (CDC, 2004). Figure 10.1 shows you the incidence of different chronic diseases.

Asthma

Asthma is a chronic illness that requires a lot of coping, but it is not always thought of as being in the same category as CVDs, stroke, and diabetes, because it is rarely fatal by itself. Deaths from asthma range from 1.4 per 100,000 for Eu-

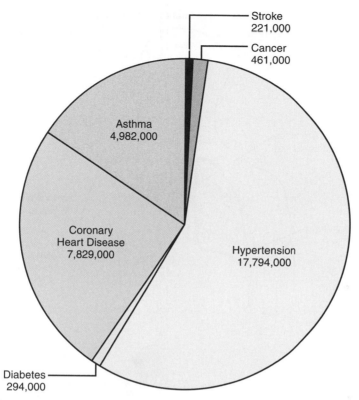

FIGURE 10.1
The Incidence of Different Chronic Illnesses in North America (2005 Estimates)
SOURCES: *Center for Disease Control, Summary Health Statistics for US Adults, National Center for Health Statistics. Estimates based on data from 2000–2004.*

ropean Americans to 3.4 per 100,000 for African Americans (National Center for Health Statistics, 2003). Asthma affects approximately 15 million Americans, including approximately 10% to 12% of children younger than age 18. Asthma may occur at any age, although onset is more common in individuals younger than age 40. During 1980 to 1999, asthma prevalence, morbidity, and mortality increased among North American adults. These annual rates were higher among certain ethnic groups. For example, 11.6% of American Indians and 9.3% of African Americans versus 7.6% of European Americans reported cases of asthma. Some ethnic groups have significantly low levels of asthma (e.g., 2.9% of Asian Americans). In addition, racial/ethnic minority populations reported higher use of emergency departments and doctors' offices for asthma treatment than European Americans (CDC, 2002). Slight geographical variations are seen. Within the United States, current asthma prevalence is 7.5%, ranging from 5.8% in South Carolina to 10.0% in Maine.

Asthma is a disease of the airways of the lungs, characterized by tightening of these airways. If you have asthma, you may cough or wheeze (a whistling sort of

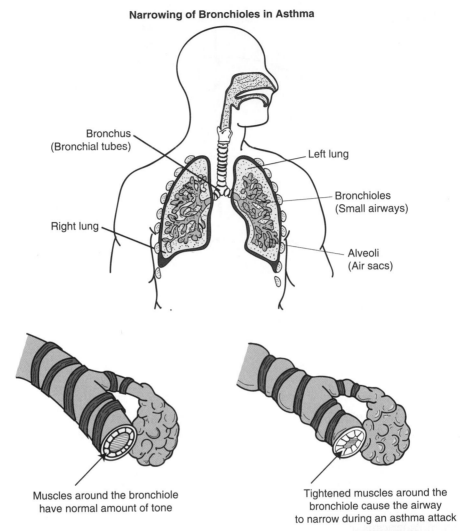

Narrowing of Bronchioles in Asthma

Bronchus
(Bronchial tubes)

Left lung

Bronchioles
(Small airways)

Right lung

Alveoli
(Air sacs)

Muscles around the bronchiole
have normal amount of tone

Tightened muscles around the
bronchiole cause the airway
to narrow during an asthma attack

Asthma Asthma is also a chronic illness. The diagram shows the main physiological problems causing asthma.

breathing), feel out of breath, and have chest pains. The tightening of the airways and inflammation, referred to as an asthma attack or episode, can be triggered by tobacco smoke, excessive exercise, allergies, some weather conditions (high humidity or cold air), and even extreme emotional experiences. For example, some people with asthma have been known to have an episode during very exciting movies. However, coping with asthma has not received much attention in the health psychology literature because of asthma's significantly lower association with mortality, and in the bulk of this chapter I will focus instead on coping with the other major chronic illnesses and death.

Varieties of Chronic Illnesses

Something to remember about chronic diseases in general is that although they are often referred to collectively, there is great variation within each type of disease. As you will see in later chapters, even though you may have often heard of one disease, there are many variations of it. For example, there are many different types of cancer (e.g., lung, breast, and prostate) and the biological and psychological correlates of one type may not be the same as those for the others. Chronic illnesses also vary in other ways. The illness can be progressive, getting worse with time, or remitting (one that ends). Treatments can vary in duration and invasiveness and the extent to which they interrupt daily life. Whereas some treatments may require checking into the hospital, others may require medications that one can self-administer. Prognoses vary. Some cancers can be cured, but as of now there is still no cure for AIDS. The pain from the disease and the side effects of treatment often vary tremendously from illness to illness and even from person to person (within the same illness). Consequently, the clinician needs to consider many different biopsychosocial factors when trying to understand how people cope with and adjust to chronic illnesses.

Coping with Chronic Illnesses

Improving one's diet, not smoking, and keeping drinking to a minimum (see chapter 7) may go a long way toward preventing chronic illnesses, but as you can see from the preceding section, a good subset of those reading these words will still get a chronic illness.

Goals of Treatment

Before we discuss how one can adjust to chronic illnesses, it is important to consider some goals for the treatment of chronic illnesses. Of course, the absolute goal would be to cure the illness. Being able to cure cancer and other chronic illnesses would save many lives, but we are not there yet. Science has made many advances in the treatment of cancer and HIV infection, and some research suggests that illnesses such as CHD and diabetes can be reversed (e.g., Ornish et al., 1998), but we still cannot cure these illnesses. If we cannot cure them, helping people cope with them is the next best thing. Health psychologists have studied different forms of adjustment to chronic illness. Five major forms of adjustment are the successful performance of daily tasks, the absence of psychological disorders, low levels of negative affect and high levels of positive affect, good functional status, and the experience of satisfaction in different areas of life (Stanton, Collins, & Sworowski, 2001). Of all of these, the most common psychological outcome studied is the quality of life.

Quality of Life

Rising above the different forms of adjustment, the most commonly used measure of how someone is coping with a chronic illness is a measure of his or her **quality of life** (QOL). Important for planning further treatment, QOL was originally a measure made by the physician, purely by whether the disease was present or absent. If the disease presence was strong, it was assumed that QOL would be low. It is now clear that patients are the best judges of their own QOL. Asking patients how much pain they are experiencing and how they feel (e.g., assessing depression and anxiety) is a valuable way to determine how they are coping. QOL includes several components. Similar to measures of adjustment, QOL includes a measure of physical status and functioning, psychological status, social functioning, and the presence of the disease- or treatment-related symptoms. Using a patient's subjective view can be problematic because the way persons assess their own QOL may change as they compare themselves with others and as they go through treatment (Sprangers, 1996). Nonetheless, QOL is still the primary measure of adjustment to chronic illnesses. A common measure of QOL is shown in Table 10.1. Let's take a look at the different biological, psychological, and sociocultural factors that can influence QOL and adjustment.

TABLE 10.1

The World Health Organization Quality of Life Brief Measure (Commonly administered in an interview)

The following questions ask how you feel about your quality of life, health, or other areas of your life. I will read out each question to you, along with the response options. **Please choose the answer that appears most appropriate.** If you are unsure about which response to give to a question, the first response you think of is often the best one.

Please keep in mind your standards, hopes, pleasures and concerns. We ask that you think about your life **in the last four weeks.**

	Very poor	Poor	Neither poor nor good	Good	Very good
1. How would you rate your quality of life ?	1	2	3	4	5

	Very dissatisfied	Dissatisfied	Neither satisfied nor dissatisfied	Satisfied	Very satisfied
2. How satisfied are you with your health?	1	2	3	4	5

The following questions ask about **how much** you have experienced certain things in the last four weeks.

	Not at all	A little	A moderate amount	Very much	An extreme amount
3. To what extent do you feel that physical pain prevents you from doing what you need to do?	5	4	3	2	1
4. How much do you need any medical treatment to function in your daily life?	5	4	3	2	1
5. How much do you enjoy life?	1	2	3	4	5
6. To what extent do you feel your life to be meaningful?	1	2	3	4	5

TABLE 10.1

The World Health Organization Quality of Life Brief Measure (Commonly administered in an interview)—cont'd

The following questions ask about how much you have experienced certain things **in the last four weeks.**

	Not at all	A little	A moderate amount	Very much	Extremely
7. How well are you able to concentrate?	1	2	3	4	5
8. How safe do you feel in your daily life?	1	2	3	4	5
9. How healthy is your physical environment?	1	2	3	4	5

The following questions ask about how completely you experienced or were able to do certain things in the last four weeks.

	Not at all	A little	Moderately	Mostly	Completely
10. Do you have enough energy for everyday life?	1	2	3	4	5
11. Are you able to accept your bodily appearance?	1	2	3	4	5
12. Have you enough money to meet your needs?	1	2	3	4	5
13. How available to you is the information that you need in your day-to-day life?	1	2	3	4	5
14. To what extent do you have the opportunity for leisure activities?	1	2	3	4	5

	Very poor	Poor	Neither poor nor good	Good	Very good
15. How well are you able to get around?	1	2	3	4	5

	Very dissatisfied	Dissatisfied	Neither satisfied nor dissatisfied	Satisfied	Very satisfied
16. How satisfied are you with your sleep?	1	2	3	4	5
17. How satisfied are you with your ability to perform your daily living activities?	1	2	3	4	5
18. How satisfied are you with your capacity for work?	1	2	3	4	5
19. How satisfied are you with yourself?	1	2	3	4	5
20. How satisfied are you with your personal relationships?	1	2	3	4	5
21. How satisfied are you with your sex life?	1	2	3	4	5
22. How satisfied are you with the support you get from your friends?	1	2	3	4	5

TABLE 10.1

The World Health Organization Quality of Life Brief Measure (Commonly administered in an interview)—cont'd

The following questions ask about how completely you experienced or were able to do certain things in the last four weeks.

	Very dissatisfied	Dissatisfied	Neither satisfied nor dissatisfied	Satisfied	Very satisfied
23. How satisfied are you with the conditions of your living place?	1	2	3	4	5
24. How satisfied are you with your access to health services?	1	2	3	4	5
25. How satisfied are you with your transport?	1	2	3	4	5

The following question refers to how often you have felt or experienced certain things in the last four weeks.

	Never	Seldom	Quite often	Very often	Always
26. How often do you have negative feelings such as blue mood, despair, anxiety, depression?	1	2	3	4	5

Do you have any comments about the assessment?

_____

_____

[The following table should be completed after the interview is finished]

Equations for computing domain scores	Raw score	Transformed scores* 4–20	0–100
27. **Domain 1** $(6-Q3) + (6-Q4) + Q10 + Q15 + Q16 + Q17 + Q18$ □ + □ + □ + □ + □ + □ + □	a=	b:	c:
28. **Domain 2** $Q5 + Q6 + Q7 + Q11 + Q19 + (6-Q26)$ □ + □ + □ + □ + □ + □	a=	b:	c:
29. **Domain 3** $Q20 + Q21 + Q22$ □ + □ + □	a=	b:	c:
30. **Domain 4** $Q8 + Q9 + Q12 + Q13 + Q14 + Q23 + Q24 + Q25$ □ + □ + □ + □ + □ + □ + □ + □	a=	b:	c:

*See Procedures Manual, pages 13–15

Biopsychosocial Components of Adjustment

The bad news is that most of us will contract a chronic illness at some point in our life. There are two main forms of good news. First, it is clear that changing health behaviors can greatly reduce the chance of contracting some chronic illnesses (Nicassio, Meyerowitz, & Kerns, 2004; Smith, Orleans, & Jenkins, 2004). For example, Blanchard et al. (2004) had cancer survivors complete a survey that included lifestyle behavior questions and a measure of health status. The survivors who practiced more than one of the recommended levels of lifestyle behaviors had a significantly better QOL than those who only met one recommendation (Blanchard et al., 2004). Second, there are many psychological strategies that can help one cope with chronic illness. For example, Wright, Barlow, Turner, and Bancroft (2003) studied the efficacy of self-management skill training for patients with chronic illnesses. Adjusting for baseline values and sex, significant increases were found on cognitive symptom management, self-efficacy in fighting the disease and its symptoms, and communication with doctors. Similar significant decreases were found on fatigue, anxiety, and depression, although there were no changes in the use of health care resources or on self-reported exercise behavior (Wright et al., 2003).

Adjustment to chronic illnesses has many different components. People have to deal with their own affect, behaviors, and cognitions in regard to the illness, and they also have to cope with how others in their social networks treat them because of their illness. They may experience many different feelings including anxiety, depression, and frustration and may not be able to do many of the things that they are normally used to such as working as normal or in some cases even getting their own groceries. Let's look at some of the different components of adjustment using the major approach in health psychology.

Biological Issues

From a biological standpoint, different chronic illnesses will have different courses. For example, in the case of the two major causes of death, cancer and CHD, major changes in the physiology of the body occur. In cancer, cells begin to grow uncontrollably, harming surrounding tissue and limiting normal functioning. In CHD, the blood vessels around the heart get clogged with plaque and fat, changing blood flow and eventually leading to a heart attack. Other chronic illnesses such as diabetes and asthma similarly have physiological correlates, such as changes in insulin sensitivity and the blocking of breathing channels. I will discuss the physiological details of some illnesses more specifically in later chapters. The slow physiological changes limit functioning in many domains and are often accompanied by an increase in pain. Consequently, physical rehabilitation is a big component of any treatment of chronic illnesses. The loss of functioning and pain also have major consequences for how the patient views the world, and major psychological issues need to be considered as well.

Psychological Issues

Psychological Aspects of Coping   In a recent review of both theoretical and empirical literature on adjusting to chronic illnesses, Stanton, Collins, and Sworowski (2001) identified two key multidimensional psychological aspects. First, the individual has to go through an adjustment, which includes cognitive aspects such as intrusive thoughts and changing views of the self, emotional aspects such as depression and anxiety, and behavioral and physical aspects such as dealing with pain or not being able to perform daily activities. Second, there is also an interpersonal adjustment during which the sick person has to negotiate personal relationships with friends and family as well as professional relationships with health care providers.

Perhaps one of the most effective psychological resources that a person with a chronic illness has is his or her mental approach to the situation and **appraisals** (Maes, Leventhal, & de Ridder, 1996). Most theories of adjustment to chronic illness use the cognitive appraisal model of stress discussed in chapter 4 (Lazarus & Folkman, 1984). Patients' primary and secondary appraisals of the illness can correspondingly influence how they fare. If the illness is seen as a challenge (primary appraisal) and they believe they have a lot of social support to cope with it (secondary appraisal), they will probably have a higher QOL (Gatchel & Oordt, 2003b). A number of health psychologists have modified the theory from its original context (i.e., stress) and have adapted it to help explain coping with chronic illnesses such as arthritis (Smith & Wallston, 1992), breast cancer (Stanton & Snider, 1993), and AIDS (Pakenham, Dadds, & Terry, 1994).

A person's **goals** are important too. The moment the patient expects to continue to live his or her life to the fullest even in the face of the illness, he or she is more likely to use active or approach coping and fare better (Scheier & Bridges, 1995). Similarly, having successful coping as a goal and appraising the situation as something that can be dealt with is critical to healthy and effective psychological coping with chronic illness (Affleck et al., 1998; Gatchel & Oordt, 2003a).

Psychological Responses to Chronic Illness There are some common psychological responses to chronic illnesses. **Denial** is one of the psychological reactions first felt the moment a person is informed that he or she has a chronic illness (e.g., the doctor gives them test results). The person may feel unbalanced and consciously or unconsciously attempt to block out reality and the implications of the test. Denial may be beneficial for a very short period early in the process because it reduces anxiety, but it is harmful in the long run because it decreases adherence to treatment and is associated with delays in reporting and seeking treatment. Another common psychological reaction to a positive test result or even experiencing symptoms of a chronic illness is **anxiety**. Anxiety interferes with healthy functioning, causing a person to cope poorly and also delay the recognition and reporting of symptoms. Anxiety is often high when the patient is waiting for test results, receiving a diagnosis, and awaiting invasive medical procedures. Not knowing about the course of the illness or not having enough information about what the illness entails is especially anxiety provoking. Such lack of information–induced anxiety is more pronounced in populations of lower socioeconomic status and in some ethnic groups.

The most common reaction to a chronic illness tends to be **depression** (DeVellis, 1995; Cox & Gonder-Frederick, 1992; van't Spijker, Trijsburg, & Duivenvoorden, 1997). Some estimates suggest that approximately one-third of patients experience long-term psychological problems, especially depression (Ell & Dunkel-Schetter, 1994). The depression can be either biological or psychological in nature, and the symptoms often get camouflaged by the symptoms of the chronic illness and are not diagnosed. When patients get depressed they are less motivated to cope actively with the illness, tend to interpret any bodily change in a negative fashion, and sometimes are even driven to suicide. That said, most individuals adjust fairly well to chronic illnesses and over the long term their lives are not significantly different from those of the general population or of people with psychological disorders (without chronic illnesses). Unlike anxiety, depression tends to be more of a long-term reaction and increases as pain and disability increase.

The form of psychological reaction also varies depending on the illness (HIV infection versus diabetes versus cancer) and also varies considerably across individuals with the same illness. Personality factors, the amount of social support one receives or perceives to have, and cultural beliefs surrounding the illness can all influence coping with the illness and alleviate depression and anxiety. Chapter 5 includes details about the ways different personality factors influence coping, and the same relationships that link stress and coping necessarily link chronic illnesses (a stressor after all) and coping. The Big Five personality variables (conscientiousness, agreeableness, neuroticism, openness, and extraversion; see chapter 5) have been linked to coping in general (Bolger, 1990) and coping with chronic illnesses in particular (Affleck, Tennen, Urrows, & Higgins, 1992; Friedman et al., 1995; Smith, Wallston, & Dwyer, 1995).

Optimism is another powerful personality characteristic in coping with chronic illnesses (Affleck, Tennen, & Apter, 2001; Fournier, de Ridder, & Bensing, 2003). Carver et al. (1993) first convincingly demonstrated the role of optimism in women coping with breast cancer. When measured before surgery, the optimistic women were those using more active coping and facing the disease, and also those with less distress. This pattern held for three further assessments at 3, 6, and 12 months after the surgery. Optimism is also helpful in coping with diabetes mellitus, rheumatoid arthritis, and multiple sclerosis (Fournier, de Ridder, & Bensing, 2002a, 2000b), coronary bypass surgery (Scheier et al., 2003), and HIV infection (Lutgendorf, Klimas, Antoni, Brickman, & Fletcher, 1995).

Another important component of psychological coping is related to how patients compare themselves with others with the disease and how much meaning they derive from the illness. For example, the social psychological literature on upward and downward social comparison shows that people can sometimes compare themselves with those better off than they are ("Boy, my coworker has the same problem, and he is doing so much better than I am") or worse off than themselves ("Oh, at least I am doing better than my neighbor who has the same illness"). In a study of breast cancer patients, Wood, Taylor, and Lichtman (1985) found that, in general, the women who coped better made comparisons with people who were inferior or less fortunate than they were to enhance their self-esteem. Finding meaning in your illness can often be beneficial, but in some cases it can be detrimental to well-being as well. Originally, research documented that finding meaning in your experience can lead to positive well-being and better adjustment to the disease (Taylor, 1983). Newer research is showing some important qualifications to this finding. Tomich and Helgeson (2004) examined the consequences of finding meaning (they called it "benefit finding") on QOL in 364 women diagnosed with stage I, II, or III breast cancer. Benefit finding and QOL were measured 4 months postdiagnosis (T1), 3 months after T1 (T2), and 6 months after T2 (T3). Women with lower socioeconomic status, minority women, and those with more severe disease perceived more benefits at baseline. Benefit finding was associated with more negative affect at baseline and also interacted with stage of disease, such that negative relationships to QOL across time were limited to those with more severe disease. Findings suggest that there are qualifiers as to whether "finding something good in the bad" is good or bad (Tomich & Helgeson, 2004). I will discuss this issue in more detail in chapter 12.

Culture and Chronic Illness

A person's sociocultural environment has many implications for how he or she copes with chronic illnesses. Jose, who lives with a large extended Mexican-American family, is going to cope with a diagnosis of cancer in a very different fashion from Joshua, who lives alone and far away from his European American family. Jessica, a devout Catholic, may face breast cancer very differently from Carmel, a nonbeliever. Friends and family and the society around a person can make a big difference in how he or she copes. If you get a chronic illness that is disdained in society, you are likely to be discriminated against for having the disease, and this discrimination can negatively influence your ability to cope with it. When the AIDS epidemic began in the early and mid-1980s homosexual men were the most likely people to get this disease (although not the only ones as you will see in chapter 11). AIDS was often referred to as a "gay disease," and gay men were subjected to even more societal wrath. Men who were infected with HIV and at risk for AIDS were often shunned. Hollywood star Tom Hanks illustrated the prejudice and discrimination experienced by gay men, both in the workplace and in everyday life, in his Oscar-winning performance in the movie *Philadelphia* (1993). You see how his coworkers and even some of his friends started to treat him differently once his symptoms started showing.

Family and Neighborhoods

The environment that you live in can accentuate a disease or help control it (Gurung, Taylor, Kemeny, & Myers, 2004; Holahan, Moos, Holahan, & Brennan, 1997). If there are many stressful events happening around you, your anxiety will also increase, thereby influencing adjustment to the disease (Evers, Kraaimaat, Geenen, & Bijlsma, 1997; Lepore & Evans, 1996). In a major review of the ways that sociocultural factors can annoy you, Taylor, Repetti, and Seeman (1997) traced the different ways that unhealthy environments—stressful work or family situations, living in a crime-ridden neighborhood, being unemployed, or having multiple chronic burdens—can reduce social support and hurt adaptation to illness. As shown in Figure 10.2, each of these different elements plays a role in influencing perceptions and the availability of coping resources.

The importance of social factors such as the family and community structures increases when the person with the chronic illness is a child (Obeidallah, Hauser, & Jacobson, 2001). For example, the diagnosis of diabetes in a child will require a substantial reorganization of family dynamics and adds new twists to the already complex developmental issues taking place (see chapter 3). Some families become even more protective and controlling when an adolescent has diabetes (if you thought an early curfew was bad when you were young, imagine your par-

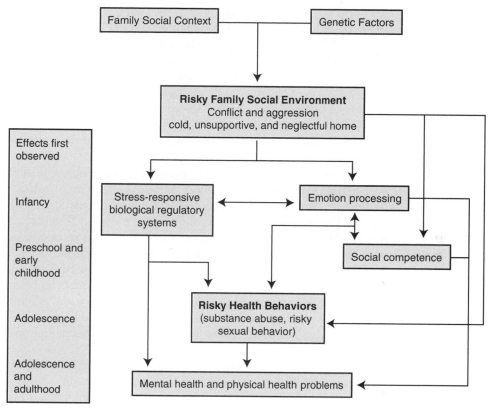

FIGURE 10.2
Various Aspects of the Environments We Live in Can Influence How We Cope With Chronic Illnesses
Source: Taylor, Repetti, & Seeman (1997)

ents wanting complete control over what you eat and drink). In such situations, families may get overtaxed and reach out to for help from the extended family, neighbors, or the community (Stack & Burton, 1993). It is important to have neighborhoods and communities that can assist the family coping with chronic illnesses. Adolescents living in dangerous neighborhoods are more susceptible to engaging in risky behaviors, hence accentuating the course of their chronic illnesses (Obeidallah et al., 2001).

Culture and Ethnicity

Your cultural environment is important as well. The experience of illness is shaped by cultural factors that influence how it is perceived, labeled, and explained and how the experience is valued. We actually learn ways of being ill that depend on our cultural backgrounds (see chapter 2). Someone coming from a self-reliant farm family may be taught to downplay illness and put up a brave face and keep on working. Someone else who grew up in a city may be more likely to follow the complete bed-rest prescriptions of a doctor. Both the patients' and the providers' cultural approaches to the source of disease and illness affect patients' care-seeking behavior and treatment opinions, choices, and compliance (Turner, 1996).

Some cultural groups react to chronic illnesses differently from others (Galanti, 2004; Gurung et al., 2004). Many collectivist groups see chronic illnesses as something that an entire family or community and not just the individual has to cope with. In the last section of chapter 8 you saw how the Hmong family rallied around the sick child with epilepsy and endured severe personal hardships to take care of her. There are similar cultural patterns across different religious and ethnic groups. For example, many church groups have organized programs to take care of chronically ill worshippers.

Are there differences in how different cultural groups cope with specific illnesses? Not as much is known about how members of different ethnic groups cope with experiences such as diagnosis and treatment of breast cancer although research in this area is growing. For example, Culver, Arena, Wimberly, Antoni, and Carver (2004) tested for differences in coping responses in middle-class African American, Latinos, and European American women with early-stage breast cancer. They found only two differences in coping (controlling for medical variables, education, and distress). Compared with European American women, the other two groups both reported using humor-based coping less and religion-based coping more. There was one difference in how coping related to distress. Venting related more strongly to elevated distress among Latinas than among non-Latinas (Culver et al., 2004).

Religion (as seen in coping with breast cancer) plays a key role in understanding cultural differences in coping with chronic illnesses. In a study directly testing the role of religion in coping with pain and psychological adjustment, Abraido-Lanza, Vasquez, and Echeverria (2004) found that Latinos with arthritis reported using high levels of religious coping. Further analysis indicated that religious coping was correlated with active but not passive coping and directly related to psychological well-being. Passive coping was associated with greater pain and worse adjustment. Findings such as this, together with similar work in other ethnic groups (e.g., African American) (Farran, Paun, & Elliot, 2003), suggest that interventions and community-based outreach approaches should embrace an appreciation for expressions and experiences of spirituality for both patients and caregivers.

The cultural group's beliefs about health and illness are important as well. For many chronic medical problems a patient's coping behaviors and adherence to treatment will depend on the quality of the patient-practitioner interaction (see chapter 8). Some early work actually suggests that improvement may be better when patients whose cultural beliefs favor folk medicine go and see folk healers rather than biomedical doctors (Kleinman, Eisenberg, & Good, 1978). In part, this could be because the greater matching of belief systems (and cultural matching) is reassuring in addition to there being a smaller social class difference between patient and practitioner. In other cases, it may be because the doctor's own cultural identity may influence how he or she treats a patient from a similar culture (Gurung & Mehta, 2001). In many folk and traditional medical systems a greater emphasis is also placed on communication and ex-

Chapels in Hospitals Many hospitals have chapels such as the one shown here. Caregivers can come and pray for their loved ones and even patients who are too sick to go to church can go say a prayer.

planation that can increase patient satisfaction and adherence to treatment (see chapter 2).

Social Support

Social support is the sociocultural factor that has garnered the most research attention (Stanton et al., 2001). In general, a large number of empirical studies and reviews show that people with more social support have more positive adjustment to chronic illnesses. Illnesses studied ranged from cancer (Blanchard, Albrecht, Ruckdeschel, Grant, & Hemmick, 1996) and CVD (Shumaker & Czajlowski, 1994) to rheumatic diseases (DeVellis, Revenson, & Blalock, 1997). Having a socially supportive environment often makes the patient more likely to use active coping and take a role in dealing with the illnesses versus disengaging and getting worse (Schreurs & de Ridder, 1997). You will learn more about the role of social support in chronic illnesses in the next three chapters.

Interventions

Health psychologists are invaluable in providing important interventions and guidance to help primary care physicians with patients who are chronically ill (Gatchel & Oordt, 2003a). Interventions to help patients with chronic illnesses serve to alleviate the different biopsychosocial problems they experience. I will provide a brief overview of different treatments for chronic illnesses here. Each treatment will be covered in greater detail in chapters 11 to 13.

Physicians prescribe a treatment regimen to counter the physiological aspects of illnesses, and these necessarily vary with the illness. Illnesses such as CHD often require surgery of some form if the blockages to the arteries are too severe. CVD patients are often given medications such as statins to reduce their cholesterol levels and slow down the clogging of their arteries. Illnesses such as cancer and HIV infection often require medications designed to slow down the growth of the cancerous cells or viral activity. In many cases, patients are also given pharmacological agents to help with psychological problems such as depression and anxiety or reduce pain to increase motor activity.

Psychological interventions are primarily designed to change health behaviors that influence the progression of disease or to help the patient cope with the stress and other negative affect related to the illness. Interventions may aim to reduce smoking behavior, to improve nutrition and dietary choices, or to increase physical activity. Psychological help may be provided in the form of individual or family therapy, in which the patient or the patient's caregivers are provided with cognitive and behavioral skills to better cope with the illness.

A large number of interventions are designed to provide social support (Helgeson & Cohen, 1996). These can take the form of individually delivered support messages via health care worker visits, the telephone, or the Internet, but more often are support groups. Support group members discuss issues of mutual concern, which helps to satisfy unmet needs, and provide support in addition to that provided by friends and family members. Also you have often heard it said that "misery loves miserable company," an adage borne out by early work on the social psychology of affiliation (Schachter, 1959). Groups also provide a form of public commitment to adhere to and change behaviors to help cope with the illness.

Groups do not always work, nor do they work for everyone. Helgeson, Cohen, Schulz, and Yasko (2000) determined the extent to which individual difference variables moderated the effects of an information-based educational group and an emotion-focused peer discussion group helped women with breast cancer. Women who really needed support (e.g., did not have strong personal ties) benefited the most from the educational group, and peer discussion groups were helpful for women who lacked support from their partners or doctors. However, here is a surprise: getting a lot of support if you already have a good amount may not always be beneficial. Helgeson et al. (2000) found that the discussion groups were harmful for women who had high levels of support. You will find more on support and illness in chapter 5 and information on specific interventions in chapters 11 to 13.

Death

The course of chronic illnesses may span many years, and some people may even have to cope with one from childhood until adulthood. Although not all chronic diseases are necessarily fatal (e.g., asthma), most do not provide any hope for recovery, and many of them reach a stage in which the patient gets progressively worse. Some chronic illnesses such as cancer or AIDS are often referred to as advancing or **terminal illnesses** because people with these diseases often die after a relatively short time (although this time can range from months to a few years). Not only is coping with a weakening body difficult, but also facing the reality of approaching death is an even bigger psychological challenge. Different cultural groups face death differently, whether it is one's own death or the death of a close friend or family member (Irish, Lundquist, & Nelsen, 1993). In addition, it matters how and when death arrives. As described in chapter 3, the major causes of death vary across the lifespan. Whereas accidents are one of the top killers of adolescents, middle-aged men and women are more likely to die from a heart attack. How death occurs automatically influences how survivors cope. It is next to impossible to prepare for the loss of a child due to a sudden car accident. More can be done both mentally and physically to prepare for the death of a person who has a long, drawn out chronic illness. Let's take a look at some of the key biopsychosocial factors associated with death and dying.

The Path to Death

As the moment of death approaches, some explicit physiological changes accompany the different psychological stages. Dying patients often experience incontinence, losing control of their bladder and other bodily functions (e.g., bowels). In particular, old, sick patients may be unable to control their salivation and will not be able to feed themselves or even eat solid food as their digestive systems reduce functioning. With cancer or CHD, there is often an increase in pain and medical practitioners prescribe high doses of morphine, even putting the delivery of morphine under the patient's own control. In this way patients can self-medicate to alleviate their pain and suffering. Patients will now experience severe memory problems and also have problems concentrating. Interactions with caregivers and hospital staff can become difficult, and there is an increased occurrence of misunderstandings and miscommunication. Friends and family have trouble facing the patient in this state, and the patient may not want to be seen by anyone. Given that talking about death is taboo among many North Americans, the last few days of a patient's life can be very difficult as visitors and even medical personnel do not always know how to approach the topic.

Facilitating Death

In the final stage of death one of the thorniest ethical issues arises. If a patient is in tremendous pain, is extremely uncomfortable, or is unconscious (e.g., in a coma), should his or her life be terminated? **Euthanasia, physician-assisted suicide,** and the withdrawing of life-sustaining treatment are some of the most difficult moral and ethical dilemmas we face today. Euthanasia is the termination of life by the injection of a lethal drug. Assisted suicide involves a physician supplying the actual drug although not actually administering it. When life-sustaining treatment is withdrawn, the underlying disease takes its own course. All are subjects of intense national debate.

Consider this scenario. By 2005, Terri Schiavo, a Florida woman, had been in a persistent vegetative state for 15 years. Her husband, Michael Schiavo, had been in a battle with her parents over whether his wife should be allowed to die. He argued that because she was "brain dead," it would not be fair to keep her alive. Terri Schiavo suffered heart failure from a potassium imbalance in 1990. Her husband said his wife told him that she would not want to be kept alive artificially. Doctors who testified on behalf of Michael Schiavo said that his wife had no hope for recovery. She was fed through a tube, but breathed on her own. Terri Schiavo's parents, Bob and Mary Schindler, maintained that their daughter could be helped with therapy. After years of litigation and appeals, Terri Schiavo's feeding tube was removed in October 2004, only to be reinserted 6 days later after the Florida Legislature, in emergency session, passed a law that affected only Terri Schiavo. The legislation gave Governor Bush the power to intervene in the case, and he ordered the feeding tube reinserted. In early 2005 the tube was removed again and Terri Schiavo died on March 31, 2005, of starvation and dehydration. What should have been done here? Should she have been kept alive? Was Terri conscious of the world around her? Did she experience psychological pain by being kept alive? Her vegetative state made it difficult to answer any of these questions.

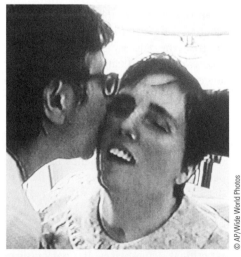

Terri Schiavo Terri Schiavo from Florida had been in a coma for 15 years. Her husband wanted to turn off life support but her family wanted to keep her alive. She died in March 2005. What information can help decide what should have been done?

Apart from this more recent case, the most publicized event that put these procedures into public consciousness was Dr. Jack Kevorkian's defiant assistance in 44 suicides since 1990. This Michigan doctor helped patients end their own lives even in the face of threats to his own life. Three juries refused to convict him despite a Michigan statute established for that purpose. The furor surrounding his case led to intense political movements with advocates on both sides of the issue, and Kevorkian is now in prison. In 1994 Oregon became the first state to legalize euthanasia.

There are interesting arguments on both sides. On one hand, one of the most important ethical principles in medicine is that the patient has autonomy (Angell, 1997). Terminally ill patients may spend months in pain and experience excruciating pain and discomfort in the process of dying. The extent of pain felt and the amount of cognition present are criteria that can be used to argue for allowing, or even mandating, a person to end his or her own life. It is still very hard to draw a line. Even if a person is in extreme pain, **palliative care** (a form of treatment aimed at alleviating symptoms without necessarily affecting the cause) could be used (see the Focus section at the end of this chapter). If a person is in a coma and has no measurable cognitive functioning, there is still no guarantee that cognition will not return or that the person is not thinking or feeling. Sometimes the decision to cut off life support is made easier by the patient's having filled out a *living will* in which he or she clearly specifies the conditions under which life support should be switched off. A sample of a living will is shown in Table 10.2.

Families also play a major role in this issue. However, research shows that surrogate preferences can inaccurately reflect patients' treatment wishes (Haley et al., 2002). Families provide the majority of care for individuals with chronic illness for many reasons, including a sense of attachment, cultural expectations, and preferences for avoiding institutional care. Although it is optimal for the families, patients, and health care providers to have ongoing discussions about goals of care, it is often only when the patient's condition worsens that decisions regarding end-of-life care take place. Research suggests that family members are often key decision makers for end-of-life issues regardless of patients' prior preferences concerning end-of-life care. Doctors tend to consult with family members even in the presence of written advance directives from their patients (Haley et al., 2002). Because of family and ethical issues surrounding physician-assisted suicide and euthanasia, many doctors argue for an increase in ways to provide more competent care for the dying (Foley, 1997).

Are There Stages?

Many in the lay population have heard of the concept of stages of death and that people who are dying experience a series of emotions. This somewhat inaccurate belief stems from work published by Elisabeth Kübler-Ross (1969). Kübler-Ross interviewed more than 200 dying patients and concluded that the process of dying involves five stages that vary in their emotional content and intensity. First comes denial, an initial reaction to the thought of death. This stage lasts around 2 days, can be a form of emotional coping (see chapter 5), and can mask anxiety without necessarily removing it. Next comes **anger,** a stage in which patients are upset that

TABLE 10.2

North Carolina Statutory Form, G.S. 90-321

NORTH CAROLINA COUNTY OF _____
DECLARATION OF A DESIRE FOR A NATURAL DEATH
I, _____, being of sound mind, desire that, as specified below, my life not be pro-
longed by extraordinary means or by artificial nutrition or hydration if my condition is determined to be terminal and
incurable or if I am diagnosed as being in a persistent vegetative state. I am aware and understand that this writing au-
thorizes a physician to withhold or discontinue extraordinary means or artificial nutrition or hydration, in accordance
with my specifications set forth below:
(Initial any of the following, as desired):
____ If my condition is determined to be terminal and incurable, I authorize the following:
    ____ My physician may withhold or discontinue extraordinary means only.
    ____ In addition to withholding or discontinuing extraordinary means if such means are necessary, my physi-
    cian may withhold or discontinue either artificial nutrition or hydration, or both.
____ If my physician determines that I am in a persistent vegetative state, I authorize the following:
    ____ My physician may withhold or discontinue extraordinary means only.
    ____ In addition to withholding or discontinuing extraordinary means if such means are necessary, my physi-
    cian may withhold or discontinue either artificial nutrition or hydration, or both.

This the _____ day of _____
Signature: _____

I hereby state that the declarant, _____, being of sound mind signed the above dec-
laration in my presence and that I am not related to the declarant by blood or marriage and that I do not know or have
a reasonable expectation that I would be entitled to any portion of the estate of the declarant under any existing will or
codicil of the declarant or as an heir under the Intestate Succession Act if the declarant died on this date without a will.
I also state that I am not the declarant's attending physician or an employee of the declarant's attending physician, or
an employee of a health facility in which the declarant is a patient or an employee of a nursing home or any group-care
home where the declarant resides. I further state that I do not now have any claim against the declarant.

Witness: _____
Witness: _____

CERTIFICATE

I, _____, Clerk (Assistant Clerk) of Superior Court or Notary Public (circle one as appropriate) for _____ County hereby certify that _____, the declarant, appeared before
me and swore to me and to the witnesses in my presence that this instrument is his/her Declaration Of A Desire For A
Natural Death, and that he/she had willingly and voluntarily made and executed it as his/her free act and deed for the
purposes expressed in it.

I further certify that _____ and _____, witnesses, appeared before me and
swore that they witnessed _____, declarant, sign the attached declaration, believing
him/her to be of sound mind; and also swore that at the time they witnessed the declaration (i) they were not related
within the third degree to the declarant or to the declarant's spouse, and (ii) they did not know or have a reasonable expectation that they would be entitled to any portion of the estate of the declarant upon the declarant's death
under any will of the declarant or codicil thereto then existing or under the Intestate Succession Act as it provides at
that time, and (iii) they were not a physician attending the declarant or an employee of an attending physician or an
employee of a health facility in which the declarant was a patient or an employee of a nursing home or any group-care
home in which the declarant resided, and (iv) they did not have a claim against the declarant. I further certify that I am
satisfied as to the genuineness and due execution of the declaration.

death is happening to them. In many ways the fact that they are dying violates a sense of the world being just. Most people believe that they do not deserve to die because they have been good or at least have not been bad enough to be punished with death. There is often misplaced resentment and a lot of irritability. Next comes the **bargaining** stage. Patients try to restore their belief in a just world and may promise to be good or live life better (e.g., give a lot to charity) in exchange for life. This trading for life then gives way to depression. The patient feels a lack of control and now grieves in expectation of his or her death, a process known as **anticipatory grief.** The depression is often driven by a realization that a person will be losing his or her past and will also be losing all that was possible in a future. Finally, the patient may reach a stage of **acceptance** in which he or she fully acknowledges that death cannot be avoided. At this point the patient is often very weak and faces death with a peaceful calm.

Although these stages sound appropriate, and you probably can nod your head and see how a dying person could go through them, there is little empirical evidence for these stages. Kübler-Ross only used cross-sectional research and did not follow patients as they got closer to death. The fact is that people may experience these stages but not necessarily in the order just described. One constant feature in Kübler-Ross's stages of death is that most people will experience some depression just before death. How someone experiences death is going to vary based on his or her culture, how much social support he or she has, the physiological progression of his or her disease, and other factors. Consequently, other researchers have attempted to explain the experience of dying (e.g., Pattison, 1977; Shneidman, 1980), although they hypothesize variations on Kübler-Ross's five stages. The five emotions seem to represent the most relevant experiences of the dying patient.

Helping People Cope with Terminal Illnesses

What can be done to make ending of life easier? I discussed some of the problems of hospitalization in chapter 8. Problems with communication and visiting hours and too many administrative details can make an already difficult time even more so. Care is highly fragmented in a hospital and up to 30 people pass through a room daily, monitoring the patient and performing different tests. In general, care should be taken to counter the effects of hospitalization. Patients and their families arrive with anxiety, and emotions are high if death is imminent. Health care practitioners need to be explicitly prepared to address these issues. In particular, informed consent procedures should be closely followed whereby patients are told of their condition and the treatments available, if any. Patients should also be helped to accept their situation and prepare for death. This normally means helping patients to use their remaining time well.

Psychological counseling should be made available for both the patient and his or her family. The patient may need help in facing death and in making sense of life. The family may need help to cope both with their grief and with the strain of caregiving. Both the patient and his or her family may also need help dealing with each other, in saying goodbye, and in dealing with sometimes conflicting needs (the patient fearing death and the family unable to imagine living without the patient). One of the alternatives to dying in a hospital are hospices, described in detail at the end of this chapter.

Cultural Variations in Death and Dying

When the time of death draws closer and it is clear that little can be done for the dying patient, it is important to help the person and his or her family prepare for death. I have already discussed some of the traditional ways this has been done (e.g., psychological counseling). There is an important additional dimension to consider when you look beyond the biology and psychology surrounding dying: culture. From a psychological perspective fear, depression, and even denial of death may be common for patients and their families, but the exact experiences vary significantly across cultural groups (Galanti, 2004; Parry & Ryan, 1995; Rosenblatt, 1993).

European American health practitioners are often unintentionally ethnocentric and this ethnocentricity makes it difficult for them to fully comprehend the experiences of people from other cultures. With an emotionally charged situation such as dying, this issue becomes even more important. Cultural differences become more evident from even a basic level of definition of key terms. It may seem pretty clear what being "dead" is, but do not take death for granted. In many

Cultural Rituals for Death and Dying Different cultures have very different rituals for death and dying. The caskets shown above are part of the burial rituals of the people of Ghana who use different shapes of coffins for different individuals.

cultures people are considered officially dead when Western biomedicine would consider them living and vice versa (Rosenblatt, 1993). There are correspondingly some significant differences in the expression and experience of emotions such as grief and loss. In some cultures it is normal for people to cut themselves or otherwise hurt themselves to express their loss. Some East Indians, for example, fast for weeks as a sign of grieving. There are also cultural differences in the fear of death. African Americans report higher levels of death anxiety than European Americans (Depaola, Griffin, Young, & Neimeyer, 2003).

Some of these cultural variations are seen in the rituals that accompany death. Making sure that the adequate ritual is conducted for the bereaved person is often critical to the health and coping of those left behind. Although they are not given any attention in the health psychological literature to date, cultural differences in dealing with the dead may have important implications for psychological adjustment. Many cultural beliefs may clash with the beliefs of Western biomedicine, and hospital policies may prohibit certain practices, but they are important practices nonetheless. For example, in the American Indian culture, the burning of sage and other herbs is often part of many religious ceremonies and is also used to prepare the soul of the dying person for the afterlife. Hospitals have nonsmoking policies and lighting a fire may seem clearly out of the question. But if sage is not burned, it could jeopardize the happiness of the dying patient's soul and greatly hurt his or her family. Health care professionals have to be aware of such cultural practices and negotiate a way to satisfy all concerned. For Muslims, there are also clear-cut practices that have to be followed at the time of death. As soon as a relative sees that the person is dead, he or she must turn the body to face Mecca (the site in the middle east of the *Kaaba,* the Muslim's holy ground), have someone sitting close by to read the Koran (the word of God as channeled through the prophet Mohammed), close the body's mouth and eyes and cover the face, and quickly bathe the body and cover it with white cotton (Gilanshah, 1993).

Being sensitive to different cultural traditions can make health practitioners more effective when helping individuals during the difficult time of coping with death. Many of the specific considerations needed are difficult for members of different ethnic groups to bring up themselves. In the middle of coping with loss, it may be too much to expect a member of a different cultural group to explain exactly what is needed. It is likewise difficult for health care workers to know all the different cultural idiosyncrasies surrounding death, but both groups need to work toward ensuring an adaptive experience for all concerned.

For some groups, this sharing and explaining of cultural routines may be especially difficult. For example, given the negative points in the history of African Americans and American Indians in North America, both these ethnic groups have particularly strained relationships with European Americans and the health care institution in particular (Barrett, 1998). Many African Americans still remember the painful incident of the Tuskegee Syphilis Study in which treatment was withheld from nearly 400 African American farmers. Consequently, there is an increase in the development of separate models to understand how different cultural groups understand death and dying. Barrett (1995, 1998), for example, has derived a list of special considerations for caregivers working with African Americans who experience loss (Table 10.3). Although devised for African Amer-

TABLE 10.3

Critical Considerations for Helping African Americans Cope with Death and Dying

1. Understanding the sociocultural influences from both Western and African traditions that combine to influence the attitudes, beliefs, and values.
2. Acknowledge and appreciate the uniqueness of the subgroups of African Americans (when in doubt, ask).
3. Be sensitive to basic differences in quality of life and differences in death rates and causes for African Americans versus European Americans.
4. Understand the impact of collective losses that African Americans often grieve for.
5. Include a consideration of socioeconomic status as well as religion and spirituality.
6. Acknowledge the role of cultural mistrust regarding health.
7. Be sensitive to the value placed by African Americans on expressions of condolence.
8. Understand the role played by and expectations for the clergy and spiritual leaders (often higher expectations than for the medical community).

SOURCE: Barret (1998).

icans, these models serve as good reminders for health professionals working with any cultural group.

Sex, Gender, and Death

In the context of culture, it is also important to look at sex differences relating to the experience of death. Scholarship in death studies suggests that the different perceptions and experiences of men and women must also (in addition to cultural differences) be taken into consideration to best help those dying as well as those caring for the dead and grieving (Noppe, 2004). Martin and Doka (2000) remarked that the benchmark for grieving is normally set as how women handle loss. Women tend to show emotion, seek social support, talk about loss, and allow time to grieve openly, things not normally done by men (Cook, 1988). In a major review of gender differences in adjustment to bereavement, Stroebe, Stroebe, and Schut (2001) reported that women express their emotions more than men, although they found little evidence for the hypothesis that working through grief helps them recover faster. Of note is the fact that men suffer relatively greater health consequences when grieving than women (possibly because widowers get less support than widows) (Stroebe & Stroebe, 1983). Specifically, widowers are significantly more distressed and depressed than widows and also have a higher incidence of mental illnesses. Widows have been found to suffer from fewer physical health problems and illnesses than widowers and are less likely to die during the period of acute grief after the loss of a spouse (Stroebe et al., 2001). Keeping these ethnic and sex differences in mind is clearly important in understanding how different subgroups of people experience the certainty of death. Another cultural factor that transcends ethnicity and sex is religion.

Terminal Illnesses and Religion

A sizable body of research supports the link between religiosity and health (Hill & Pargament, 2003; Miller & Thoresen, 2003; Powell, Shahabi, & Thoresen, 2003). One of the most salient aspects of culture, religion is intrinsically tied to the other major elements of culture such as race and ethnicity. Different races often have different religious beliefs. Even though North America is primarily Christian, there are still a significant number of North Americans who have non-Christian beliefs. Turning to religion is a form of coping (see the Focus section of chapter 5) and can also be a form of pain management (see the Focus section of chapter 9). But this link is also a classic case study for the differences between a correlational study and an experiment (see chapter 1). Just because people who are religious are also the people who cope better with illness does not allow us to conclude that religiosity causes better health. Nonetheless, what is important is that religion can help, and in the context of chronic and terminal illnesses, health psychologists should use any tool that can make a difference.

One of the growing number of studies of different ethnic groups illustrates this point well. Abraido-Lanza et al. (2004) tested for the link between religious, passive, and active coping, pain, and psychological adjustment among a sample of 200 Latinos with arthritis. The participants reported using high levels of religious coping that was correlated with active but not with passive coping. Religious coping was directly related to psychological well-being. Passive coping was associated with greater pain and worse adjustment (Abraido-Lanza et al., 2004). Traditional Latinos tend to be very religious, practicing Catholicism, curanderismo, or more often, a blend of both (as discussed in chapter 2). With the growing number of North Americans who are Latino, findings such as these suggest a greater focus on the role of ethnicity and religion on coping.

A person's religious beliefs can play an even bigger role when death draws near. Each religion has a different view of the role of pain and of the role and significance of death. Different religions even have different ways to treat death and distinct ways to treat the lifeless human body. The more entrenched you are in your religion the more likely are you to turn to it if you or someone you love is dying. The way death is treated can influence how well you cope. For example, for devout Catholics, suffering is related to original sin and a Catholic has to face suffering like Christ did. Death is freeing of the soul to the father who is in heaven. A righteous, well-lived life serves as preparation for death. As death draws near, the family and the terminally ill patient can draw solace from the visitation of a priest who will help the patient wind up his or her earthly affairs. There is a final confession of sins, receiving of Holy Communion (a piece of bread or wafer that represents the body of Christ), an anointing and a last blessing, known as the *last rites*. This scripted ritual goes a long way to helping the terminally ill patient and family try to come to terms with the impending loss.

Different religions deal with death differently. Muslims, or followers of Islam, see death as the termination of the soul's attachment to body. Death is a blessing and a gift for the believer. To prepare, the person must do penance, and be careful to not be under obligation to any other human being—the patient should make sure that he or she pays any dues or debts owed. Cleanliness at the time of death is more important than at any other time. Of special importance is the edict that the seriously ill must die at home. To Hindus, suffering is part of *maya* or illusion. The only way to transcend suffering is to be free from the cycle of birth and death and rebirth. The Hindu tries to work off bad karma from an early point in life and a measure of where you stand in the karmic cycle is indicated by your status in the world; for example, if you sinned in your past lives you will be reborn as an animal or even worse as a worm. This belief in predetermined fate helps reduce the anxiety of death. Other Eastern religions share some of these beliefs. Buddhists speak of and contemplate death often, in stark contrast to many non-Buddhists. Pain is unavoidable, but attitudes and behavior influence suffering. The only way to avoid suffering is to free the self from desire, which is the cause of suffering. The Buddhist believes that as long as there is fear of death, life is not being lived to its fullest. Contemplating death can free us from fear, change the way we live and our attitude toward life, and help us face death right.

The sense that death can be joyous is also reflected in different religious traditions. The Irish funeral is often a rousing celebration of the recently departed's life and is accompanied by drinking and dancing. To the Sikhs of India, death is seen as a great opportunity to do something we put off all our lives. It is a chance to cleanse the soul of psychic fantasy, and life is an opportunity to practice dying, until one dies a death that will not have to be repeated. Death is not sad; friends chant and sing hymns near the dying to set a peaceful vibration and inspire the dying person to be in the best frame of mind. Hence many religions downplay the sadness of death and play up the happiness coming from freedom and the unification with the creator.

FOCUS on Applications

Hospice

When it is clear that the end is fast approaching, how would you like to die? Yes, I know this is a morbid thought, but thinking about it now rather than later could influence how much discomfort you experience at life's end. For most terminal illnesses, the signs that death is near are relatively well established (e.g., breathing and blood pressure changes and cognitive impairment). When the signs are seen, patients are normally admitted into a hospital where they are monitored until they stop breathing. Sometimes patients die in their sleep at home; sometimes even hospitalized patients choose to be sent home to receive home care so that they can die in their own houses. Another choice that has gained popularity recently is hospice.

Hospice is a form of care that has its origins in medieval times. In the early nineteenth century hospices were places where pilgrims, travelers, the homeless, and the destitute were offered lodging, usually by a religious group. In 1967, an English doctor, Cicely Saunders, felt that the terminally ill persons needed better care and began a new movement. The word **hospice** is derived from the words for hospitality and guesthouse, and hospices are also referred to as nursing homes for the dying. The hospice movement spread to the United States in the next 10 years, and today there are hospices in every state and also around the world. They tend to be small residential institutions where the treatment is focused on the patient's QOL rather than on curing the illness.

Unlike in a hospital, hospices do not attempt to cure the patient or prolong life (Kastenbaum, 1999). The dying are comforted, and their pain and other symptoms are alleviated. Unlike hospitals, patients are urged to customize their surroundings and make them seem like home. Patients can wear their own clothes (no uncomfortable hospital gowns) and bring in pictures, paintings, or other personal effects. The patient and family are included in the care plan, and emotional, spiritual, and practical support is given based on the patient's wishes and family's needs. Similar to church-affiliated hospitals, some hospices have been started by churches and religious groups (sometimes in connection with their hospitals), but hospices serve a broad community and do not require patients to adhere to any particular set of beliefs. Most hospice patients are cancer patients, but hospices accept anyone regardless of age or type of illness.

Patients can be asked to move to a hospice at any time during a terminal illness, although it is often the case that patients in a hospice do not have more than 6 months to live (and often much less). In North America, the decision belongs to the patient although many people are not comfortable with the idea of stopping active efforts to beat the disease in the switch to palliative care. Hospice staff members are highly sensitive to this debate and facilitate discussions of the same with the patient and family. As you can guess the decision-making process for hospice care has many components. In a study of patients with advanced cancer, Chen, Haley, Robinson, and Schonwetter (2003) found that patients receiving hospice care were significantly older, were less educated, and had more people in their households. Hospice patients had multiple health conditions and worse activities of daily living scores than nonhospice patients and were also more realistic about their disease course than their nonhospice counterparts.

Once the patient decides to go to hospice, the hospice program contacts the patient's physician to make sure he or she agrees that hospice care is appropriate for this patient at this time. The patient then signs consent and insurance forms, similar to the forms patients sign when they enter a hospital, acknowledging that the care is palliative (aimed to provide pain relief and symptom control) rather than curative. A hospice team then prepares an individualized care plan addressing the amount of caregiving needed by the patient, and staff visit regularly and are always accessible. Unlike in a hospital, in a hospice family and friends deliver most of the care, but hospices provide volunteers to assist the families and to provide the primary caregivers with support. Hospice patients are also cared for by a team of physicians, nurses, social workers, counselors, hospice-certified nursing assistants, clergy, therapists, and volunteers—and each provides assistance based on his or her own area of expertise. In addition, hospices provide medications, supplies, equipment, and hospital services related to the terminal illness.

There is considerable empirical evidence for the efficacy of hospices. The National Hospice Work Group and the National Hospice and Palliative Care Organization conducted one of the most comprehensive assessments of hospice. The two groups spearheaded a detailed 2-year study of the efficacy of end-of-life care and studied more than 3,000 caregivers and patients. Some of the key results were that the majority of patients entering hospice in pain were made comfortable within days of admission, and caregivers' confidence in the care of their loved ones increased because of hospice services (Ryndes et al., 2001).

The hospice emphasis on palliative care can be seen in comparisons of pain relief. Hospice patients are twice as likely as nonhospice patients to receive regular treatment for daily pain (Miller, Mor, Wu, Gozalo, & Lapane, 2002). For example, Miceli and Mylod (2003) looked at how satisfied family members were with the end-of-life care their loved ones received. Family satisfaction with hospice care was generally quite high, although the timing of the referral was critical. It was critical to get patients into hospice earlier rather than later. Families rated services lower almost across the board when the referral to hospice was deemed "too late."

Experiments comparing hospices to hospitals are hard to do and unethical (randomly assigning a dying loved one to a condition is clearly unpalatable), but some studies have compared the experiences of patients in each setting. Compared with patients in hospitals, patients in hospices and their families report more piece of mind and greater satisfaction with care (Ganzini et al., 2002; Kastenbaum, 1999; Lynn, 2001). Note that in most cases there are few significant differences in pain symptoms and activities of daily living, although hospice patients report more overall psychological well-being (Gatchel & Oordt, 2003a; Viney, Walker, Robertson, Lilley, & Ewan, 1994). Patients in hospices do not necessarily live longer nor do they have significantly fewer physician visits (Kane, Klein, Bernstein, & Rothenberg, 1986).

There are some significant cultural differences in hospice use as well. Colon and Lyke (2003) found that African Americans and Latinos both used hospice services at significantly lower rates than European Americans. In addition, African American use of hospices declined significantly during the study (1995 to 2001), whereas European American use increased.

Chapter Summary

- Chronic illnesses are illnesses that persist over a long period of time. The most common chronic illnesses are cancer, cardiovascular disease, AIDS, back pain, diabetes, and arthritis. Some of these such as cardiovascular disease are reversible, but most end with death. Most chronic diseases show varying incidence rates across different cultural groups.
- To help patients and their families cope with the changes in lifestyle from chronic illnesses, health psychologists often focus on improving the quality of life (QOL) of the individual. QOL is measured by assessing physical and psychological status together with functioning.
- Patients' cognitive appraisals of their situation and their own personal goals are critical components of coping with chronic illnesses. Common responses to the diagnosis of a chronic illnesses are denial, anxiety, and depression. Optimism is a powerful tool in coping with illness.
- Sociocultural factors play a major role in coping with chronic illnesses. The quality of one's close relationships, interactions with family and friends, and even the

neighborhood one lives in can all influence QOL. Patients with strong religious beliefs or from certain ethnic groups may have different coping responses.

- A majority of health psychological interventions are designed to provide chronically ill patients with social support. Although many interventions show success, not all group support interventions work or work for everyone.

- The proximity of death brings its own specific challenges. Together with physiological and psychological deterioration, patients often experience denial, anger, depression, acceptance, or anticipatory grief and sometimes bargain (not always in this order).

- Physician-assisted suicide, euthanasia, and the withdrawal of life support are hotly contested issues in terminal care. Patients are urged to complete living wills that specify what they would like to be done if they are nonresponsive, in a coma, or receiving life support. Palliative care and hospice care are both commonly used forms of care that do not include c attempts to cure the illness and prolong life.

- Not all cultures define death in the same way. Based on varying cultural philosophies regarding the purpose of life and the nature of the afterlife, different cultures have different behaviors and procedures for coping with the impending death of a loved one.

Synthesize, Evaluate, Apply

- What are the most common chronic illnesses?
- What sociocultural factors explain the most common causes of death and chronic illness?
- What are the different ways illnesses within the category of chronic illnesses vary?
- Evaluate the main goals of treatment. Should there be more?
- What suggestions do you have for change?
- Why is it important to have a valid and reliable measure of quality of life?
- How do the main biopsychosocial components of adjustment to chronic illness compare with the factors for adjustment to stress? Identify the similarities and differences.
- How would you apply the different biopsychosocial models to the design of an intervention to help people cope with chronic illnesses?
- How do you think different personality characteristics (e.g., optimism) will change how one reacts to a chronic illness?
- Map out the relationship between different sociocultural factors and coping with a chronic illness.
- Using the broad discussion of culture described in chapter 1, what cultural groups do you think would cope better with chronic illnesses and why?
- How does religion play a role in chronic and terminal illnesses and coping with death?
- Are there biopsychosocial factors that could be used to justify when euthanasia is appropriate?

- How can cultural variations in death and dying be translated into better health care?
- Compare and contrast the biopsychosocial differences in care between hospitals and hospice.

KEY TERMS, CONCEPTS, AND PEOPLE

acceptance, 305
anger, 303
anticipatory grief, 305
anxiety, 294
appraisals, 294
asthma, 286
bargaining, 305

chronic illnesses, 285
denial, 294
depression, 294
euthanasia, 301
goals, 294
hospice, 310
Kevorkian, Jack, 303

optimism, 295
palliative care, 303
physician-assisted suicide, 301
psychological aspects of coping, 293
quality of life, 289
terminal illnesses, 301

ESSENTIAL READINGS

Gatchel, R. J., & Oordt, M. S. (2003). *Clinical health psychology and primary care: Practical advice and clinical guidance for successful collaboration.* Washington, DC: American Psychological Association.

Irish, D. P., Lundquist, K. F., & Nelsen, V. J. (Eds.). (1993). *Ethnic variations in dying, death, and grief: Diversity in universality.* Philadelphia, PA: Taylor & Francis.

Ornish, D., Scherwitz, L. W., Billings, J. H., Gould, K. L., Merritt, T. A., Sparler, S., et al. (1998). Intensive lifestyle changes for reversal of coronary heart disease. *Journal of the American Medical Association, 280*(23), 2001–2007.

Stanton, A. L., Collins, C. A., & Sworowski, L. (2001). Adjustment to chronic illness: Theory and research. In A. Baum, T. A. Revenson, and J. E. Singer (Eds). *Handbook of health psychology* (pp. 321–657). Mahwah, NJ: Lawrence Erlbaum.

 ## WEB RESOURCES

Visit the companion website at **http://psychology.wadsworth.com/gurung1e/,** where you will find online resources for this book, including chapter-by-chapter quizzes, weblinks, and more! You can also visit Wadsworth Psychology Resource Center at **http://psychology.wadsworth.com** to access additional resources.

Association for Death Education and Counseling
http://www.adec.org

Psychoneuroimmunology and HIV

O pen your mouth, breathe in, chew. Chew? You have probably heard stories about how we are surrounded by millions and millions of bacteria. You may have seen those television specials that show you just how many living things are harbored by your mouth or on a patch of your skin or on the surface of your pillow or in the carpet. Well, these are more than just stories. A microscopic examination of the air we breathe, the water we drink, and the world around us reveals a teeming multitude of life. Bacteria, viruses, and germs of various sorts cohabit our world. Many of these viruses and bacteria can cause us to get sick. The common cold and the flu are some examples of what happens to the body when we are infected by viruses. Yet, we clearly do not get sick as much as we should given how many infectious agents we are exposed to. Why is this the case? The answer is that we have a specialized arrangement of cells, organs, and processes that is designed to ward off such threats and protect the body from infection: the immune system.

When our immune system is strong we are sickness free. When we are stressed or otherwise psychologically challenged and our immune system is weakened, we are more susceptible to disease and illness. In addition, some diseases such as lupus and AIDS can debilitate our immune defenses and threaten our health and our lives regardless of our psychological makeup. In this chapter I will introduce you to the key components of the immune system, discuss how the immune system works, and recount what happens when it fails or is compromised. As with other areas of health psychology, you will see that once again cultural factors play a major role, and there are many striking differences in immune-related diseases across cultural groups. In particular, you will see how sex and ethnicity, two major cultural aspects, play large roles in the experience and incidence of HIV infection and AIDS.

The Physiology of Immunity

The **immune system** is the component of our bodies that protects us from threats, mostly in the form of bacteria and germs. The components of the immune system serve two main functions: (1) to discriminate what constitutes our bodies from what are foreign substances, and (2) to destroy and clear those foreign substances and infected cells. I shall first give you an overview of the main components of the system, and then we will take a closer look at exactly how immunity works.

The immune system is composed of a collection of cells and organs. Similar to the circulatory and nervous systems, the immune system has a network of capillaries, the **lymphatic system,** and small oval bodies called lymph nodes (Figure 11.1). The lymphatic capillaries lie along blood vessels and carry a colorless fluid called lymph that is composed of fats, proteins, and water and holds the key cells of the immune system, white blood cells (WBCs) or **leukocytes.** Lymph nodes serve as a filtering system and are packed with leukocytes. Leukocytes filter microorganisms and other particles from the lymph and greatly reduce our risks of

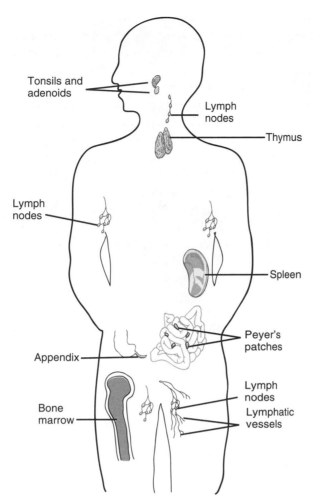

FIGURE 11.1
The Main Components of the Immune System

infection. There are three main types of leukocytes. The most common, comprising between 50% and 70% of leukocytes, are polymorphonuclear granulocytes. You will not hear too much more about them here because they have been hard to study and as far as researchers can tell, play a minor role in psychoneuroimmunology. The most important leukocytes are lymphocytes, which comprise 20% to 40% of leukocytes. These are the true fighters of the immune system.

There are three main types of lymphocytes, two of which, **T cells** and **B cells,** are further subdivided in more types. T cells and B cells are both formed in the bone marrow, but each one is conveniently named on the basis of where they mature. T cells mature in the thymus gland, an organ situated at the base of the neck. Although you rarely hear much about the thymus (unlike the liver

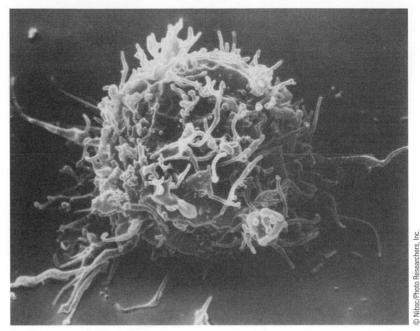

© Nibsc/Photo Researchers, Inc.

A T Cell

or kidneys or heart), it is the main site for T-cell development. It is prominent when we are young but shrinks after we reach puberty. There are three main types of T cells. The workhorses are the T cytotoxic cells or T_C cells. These cells are responsible for killing virally infected cells. A second kind of T cell is the helper T cell or T_H cell. These cells enhance the functioning of other T cells and also play a role in the maturation of B cells. They serve as sentinels, prowling through our bloodstreams looking for invaders. When they encounter foreign cells, germs, or bacteria, they secrete chemical messengers that draw other types of immune cells to the location and destroy the invaders. T_H cells are some of the most common T cells, comprising 30% to 60% of T cells. The third kind of T cell is the suppressor T cell or T_S cell. These cells slow down the functioning of the immune system and prevent the body from damaging itself. In particular, once foreign germs have been eliminated, the T_S cells secrete chemicals to turn off the action of T_C and T_H cells.

B cells are both born in and mature in the bone marrow. One type of B cell, the antibody-producing B cell, forms specific substances earmarked for specific germs or **antigens** (*anti*body *gen*erators, more on this later). The other form of B cell, the memory B cell, is the one that explains why so many of us are subjected to immunizations and vaccinations during childhood. Memory B cells are cells that form a template or identification for invading antigens. Memory B cells circulate in the body for many years after an antigen has been eliminated, ready to identify it if it were to invade the body again. By having this indicator of the

---

TABLE 11.1

Main Cells of the Immune System

Key components
1. Bone marrow (origin of white blood cells [WBCs]) or leukocytes (three types)
    i. 50%–70% polymorphonuclear granulocytes (PMNs)—hard to study, minor role in psychoneuroimmunology
    ii. 20%–40% lymphocytes
        T (mature in thymus)
          T cytotoxic (TC) (CD8): kill virally infected cells
          T helper (TH): enhance functioning; moderate maturation of B cells (30%–60% of T cells)
          T suppressor (TS): slow down the immune system
        B (mature in bone marrow)
          B antigen-producing
          B memory
        Natural killer (NK)
    iii. 2%–8% monocytes (circulating)/macrophages (in tissue)
        Their chemical messengers are interleukin-1 and -2; interferon
2. Lymph vessels (lie along blood vessels) and lymph node—filtering system (packed with WBCs)
    thymus (T-cell school where T cells differentiate)
    spleen (filter for blood)

---

antigen, we are less likely to become sick from the same antigen again because the moment we are infected by it, the memory B cells recognize it and activate our bodies' defenses before the invader has a chance to establish a foothold.

The third kind of lymphocyte is the **natural killer (NK) cell.** These cells circulate in the body, playing a role in different immune responses and especially in destroying diseased cells by injecting them with toxic chemicals. Table 11.1 shows a nice summary of the different components of the immune system (I know how confusing discriminating among all these types of cells can be).

There are other hard-working immune cells as well. The foot soldiers of the effort and often those at the forefront of defenses are monocytes (circulating in the lymphatic system) and macrophages (a type of monocyte found in the tissue). These cells are the first to attack germs or foreign invaders, destroying them by engulfing and devouring them. In fact, if you want to joke with a friend of yours who eats a lot, you can call him or her a "macrophage" because the word translates literally from its Greek origins to mean "large eater" (yes, this is somewhat nerdy humor but fun nonetheless). Other important immune system components are the chemical messengers, especially interleukin-1 and -2, and interferon, a chemical that prevents viral infections from spreading. Another component of the immune system is the spleen, a ductless organ in the upper left of our abdomen, which serves as a filter for blood. The least common cells are the monocytes and macrophages. Last and perhaps least important (given that many people have them removed) are the tonsils. The tonsils are oval tissue masses in the mouth (open up and say ah and you can see them). Their primary function is the storage of lymphocytes.

Measures of Immune Response

How do you know how active your immune system is? Well, we could make you sick and see how quickly you recover, but there are easier ways to find out. Researchers measure immunity by using blood or saliva samples. A common technique is that an antigen (germ) is added to the sample and then cell activity is measured. First you can look for **differentiation** or how much the immune cells divide up into the different types of cells (e.g., T_C or T_H or T_S). You can also look for **proliferation** or the extent to which the immune cells multiply. A strong immune response is characterized by great differentiation and proliferation. Immune functioning can also be measured by the extent or levels of chemical messengers (e.g., interferon) present in the sample in response to the antigen. Finally, and perhaps most directly, you can measure **cytotoxicity** or the extent to which the antigens are killed or destroyed. If there are no antigens left in the sample shortly after they are introduced, the person probably has a strong immune system.

Although seemingly straightforward, assessing immune functioning is associated with many problems. First, no single test is available, and it is hard to compare reports from different tests. There is also a lot of variability among assays; results vary from laboratory to laboratory, depending on the technician who does the tests and the serum used. The time of the day and the season can also influence results. Paradoxically, it is not always clear what a "good direction" of immune functioning is. Sometimes a lot of differentiation may suggest strong immunity (the body is reacting); at other times a lot of differentiation may suggest low immunity (the first lines of defense are inadequate). Finally, tests of immunity are available only for blood and not lymph, making a good measurement difficult.

The Process of Defense

Our primary foes are microorganisms such as bacteria and viruses. As I mentioned at the start of this chapter, germs surround us. The doorknobs you touch, the chairs you sit on, and the air that you breathe are all filled with germs. Sometimes germ transmission is more direct; for example, when people with a cold hand something to you after blowing their nose, they are probably passing on the cold virus. Most directly, you can be infected by the bite of another living creature that carries the virus (e.g., an insect, animal, or fellow human being).

The main lines of entry for foreign invaders are the skin and the different openings of the body: the nasal passage and mouth (the upper respiratory system) the walls of the stomach and intestine (the gastrointestinal tract), and the sexual and excretory organs (urogenital tract). We have a number of basic processes that protect us at each of these points. We secrete mucus (e.g., in the lining of the nose) that serves to trap germs and prevent their entry. We cough to get germs out of our lungs. Our skin also has a number of glands that secrete a mild oily substance called sebum that also serves to prevent microorganisms from breaking the skin barrier or from growing on the skin. Most microorganisms do not get past the barrier of the thick pile of cell layers that make up the epidermis. As shown in Figure 11.2 the outer layer consists of nondividing cells, many of which are dead or dying, that protect the dividing skin cells beneath. Even when germs do enter

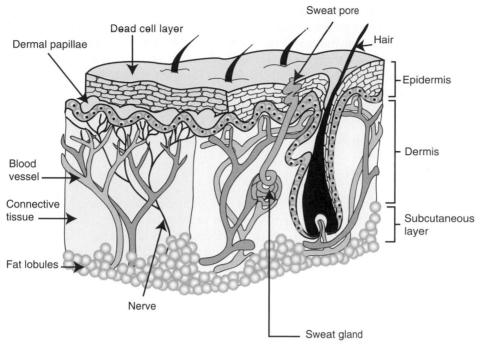

FIGURE 11.2
Cross-Section of the Skin Showing the Different Layers That Serve as Our Body's First Line of Defense

the body on particles of food or dust, they usually die due to exposure to lysozyme, an enzyme found in saliva and tears, which digests the cell walls of many microorganisms. These barriers do not rely on the cells of the immune system and are referred to as **nonimmunologic defenses.**

Nonspecific or Natural Immunity

In addition to these defenses on the body's surface, we also have internal processes that similarly do not differentiate between different types of invaders. These **nonspecific immune** defenses work on a wide variety of disease-causing microorganisms. In the body, macrophages, described above, circulate in the immune system on the lookout for external cells not recognized as being the body's own. When such cells are identified, the body may respond by getting inflamed and swelling. You may notice this if you fall and skin your knee. The area around the injury swells from an increase in blood flow to the area. The immune cells stream into the damaged site to destroy and inactivate germs potentially present in the dirt or dust you have in the wound. The secretion of chemicals such as **histamine** instigates the swelling or **inflammatory response.** If you have allergies you are probably familiar with the effect of histamines, which can cause the itching in the eyes, nose, and throat that accompanies the swelling. When the pollen count is too high or you find your allergies being active, your immune system is essentially reacting to all the substances in the air (as taken in through your nasal passage and mouth) and secreting histamine. The inflammation is often accompanied by an increase in temperature, the fever being a clear sign of your body's combating the germs; bacteria cannot survive in high temperatures. The actual destruction is accomplished by macrophages that engulf the antigens by **phagocytosis** (the name given to the engulfing process). NK cells and T_C cells may also join the fray. This form of immunity is also referred to as natural or innate immunity.

Acquired Immunity

Do you wonder why we give babies a large number of injections? Those immunizations function as a proactive step to prevent future infection. How does that work? We have another form of immunity, which is referred to as **acquired immunity** and is a form of a specific immune response. This immunity involves the activation of a unique group of cells, the lymphocytes, which are designed to respond to specific microorganisms that the body has run into before. Acquired immunity is distinguished from nonspecific or natural immunity by five characteristics (Kusnecov, 2002):

1. *Specificity.* Each foreign particle generates only one specific immune response. In this form of immunity the body is only responding to specific antigens that it has encountered before.
2. *Diversity.* Different immune cells recognize different antigens.
3. *Memory.* Each lymphocyte that bonds to a specific antigen the first time it invades the body will recognize the same antigen if it returns again. In subsequent attacks of the same antigen, its matching lymphocyte will be higher in intensity and faster.
4. *Self-Limitation.* After an antigen is destroyed the responding cells will be turned off or suppressed (T_S cells).
5. *Self/Nonself-Discrimination.* An essential capability of the lymphocytes of the immune system is their ability to discriminate cells from our own body from those that originated outside our body.

Acquired immunity takes place either in the blood or in cells. The form of immunity orchestrated by immune cells circulating in the blood is also referred to as **humoral-mediated immunity.**

Here is how humoral-mediated immunity works (Figure 11.3). When a bacterial or viral cell enters the bloodstream, the macrophages identify the antigens on the cell's surface and bind to the cell. This bond causes the macrophage to release the chemical transmitter interleukin-1 that alerts T_H cells. The T_H cells proliferate or multiply and release a second chemical messenger, B-cell growth factor. This chemical causes B cells to proliferate. The B cells form structures named antibodies that are designed to bond to the specific invader, hence immobilizing it and targeting it for destruction. Different B cells produce different antibodies, depending on the type of antigen they are faced with. Every antigen contains one or more epitopes, a specific shape and charge distribution recognized by antibodies.

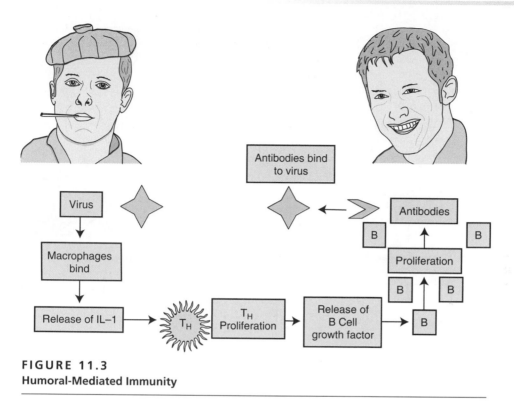

FIGURE 11.3
Humoral-Mediated Immunity

Epitopes are small parts of molecules on each antigen, and it is estimated that the immune system can make antibodies to recognize more than 100 million different epitopes. In addition, memory B cells save a copy of the antibody and remain circulating in the blood after the attack has been completed. These memory B cells have a print, as it were, of the invader and so are ready to sound the alarm if the same invader is seen again. When we are immunized as babies, our body produces a large number of memory B cells in response to a small amount of the injected germ (e.g., smallpox), hence protecting us from getting that same sickness later in life. Of course, we also acquire this form of immunity when we actually have (not just been vaccinated for) certain illnesses. For example, if you had chickenpox as a child you are not likely to get it again because of you have circulating B memory cells for chickenpox.

Humoral-mediated immunity is one form of specific immunity. Another form takes place at the level of the cell. **Cell-mediated immunity** involves T cells although the first few stages are similar to the process for humoral-mediated immunity. In this case, the antigen is first recognized by macrophages, which activate T_H cells. T_H cells then release interleukin-1, which stimulates the proliferation of more T_H cells. The multiplying T cells now release interleukin-2, which leads to T_C cell proliferation. The T_C cells then attack and destroy the antigens. Figure 11.4 shows both forms of immune responses.

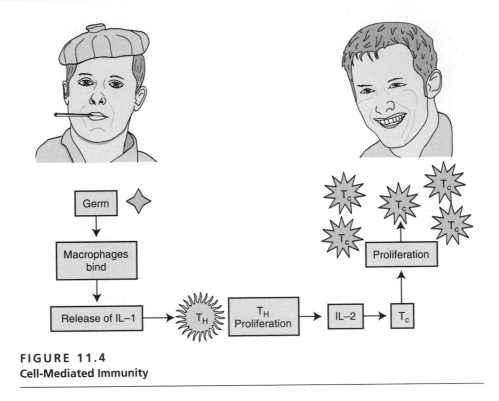

FIGURE 11.4
Cell-Mediated Immunity

Psychoneuroimmunology

What biopsychological science has only discovered relatively recently is that the immune system is strongly influenced by the nervous system and correspondingly by our minds and thinking (Ader, Felten, & Cohen, 1991; Dunn, 1989). The influence of psychological processes on immune functioning (the "biopsycho" connection) can be seen in many ways. For example, Futterman, Kemeny, Shapiro, and Fahey (1994) had an actor imagine that he was rejected for a part or had just won an acting award (they conducted this experiment in Los Angeles so there was no problem finding participants for the study). Even the faked feelings of intense sadness led to an increase in immune cells in the bloodstream whereas the happy act led to a decrease. Findings such as these are all encompassed by the fascinating area of psychoneuroimmunology.

The field of **psychoneuroimmunology** (PNI) evolved out of the disciplines of biology and psychology and is dedicated to understanding the interplay between these disparate systems. PNI developed in response to research findings highlighting the fact that both psychological and physical factors (especially stress) can affect the functioning of the immune system. As the name implies, PNI researchers study interactions between the nervous system (discussed in chapter 4), the endocrine system, the immune system, and psychological activity and behavior. This collaboration of researchers is needed because the cells of the immune, endocrine, and nervous systems each bear receptors that respond to the same neurotransmitters, neurohormones, and neuropeptides.

Behavioral Conditioning and Immunity

From a health psychological perspective, there are two main pillars of PNI research. The first pillar is the observation that alterations of immune function can be linked to a conditioned stimulus (CS), such that the CS becomes able to instigate immune changes similar to those instigated by the unconditioned stimulus (UCS) with which it has been paired (Kusnecov, 2002). Whereas the UCS would be some immunosuppressive drug, the CS could be a sound, a light, or, more commonly, flavored water. Thus, similar to how Pavlov conditioned a dog to salivate to the sound of a bell, researchers found that they could condition the body's immune system to also respond to a CS. Ader and Cohen (1975) conducted the classic study in this area when they demonstrated a conditioned immune response in rats. They paired a novel-tasting solution (sweet water, the CS) with an illness-inducing drug (cyclophosphamide, the UCS). The drug served to suppress the immune system. After learning trials (pairing the CS and UCS), they gave one group of animals the CS only, gave another group plain water, and gave a third group the UCS again. All animals were then immunized with sheep red blood cells and the immune responses were measured. As predicted, both the groups that got the UCS and the one that got the CS showed a suppressed immune system demonstrating that the body could be conditioned to react as if it received a drug. Similar studies have been conducted in humans as well. For example, Buske-Kirschbaum, Kirschbaum, Stierle, Lehnert, and Hellhammer (1992) gave college students sherbet (the CS) paired with epinephrine (the UCS). The UCS caused an unconditioned response of increasing the number of NK cells. Sure enough, when given sherbet a few days later (without the UCS), the students experienced a similar increase in NK cell activity. An active area of PNI research has fine tuned these processes (Ader et al., 1991).

Stress and Immunity

The second major pillar of PNI research is the association between the immune system and stress (Cohen & Herbert, 1996). Knowledge of a stress-immune link can be traced back to the work of Hans Selye (discussed in chapter 4). Selye found that immune tissues such as the thymus atrophied in rats that were subjected to stress. For slightly longer than the past 10 years, health psychologists have accumulated significant evidence that stressful life events and psychological distress predict biologically verified infectious illnesses by impacting the immune system (Marsland, Bachen, Cohen, & Manuck, 2002). Upper respiratory infections such as the common cold have been the primary disease model used in the literature (Cohen et al., 1998), and a variety of inventive studies have provided insights into stress-immunity interactions (Stone et al., 1992; Turner, Cobb, & Steptoe, 1996). For example, Sheldon Cohen and colleagues have inoculated healthy individuals (volunteers for the study) with common cold or flu viruses after assessing for stress. The volunteers are kept in quarantine and monitored for the development of the illness. Sure enough, the volunteers who were more stressed (and consequently had a challenged immune system) were more likely to develop a cold (Cohen et al., 1998).

Stress in general has been reliably associated with the functioning of the immune system (Bachen, Marsland, Manuck, & Cohen, 1998; Herbert & Cohen, 1993; Kiecolt-Glaser & Glaser, 1991). Stress is inversely related to circulating lymphocytes such that the more stress we experience, the fewer lymphocytes are produced by our bodies (McEwen et al., 1997). Stress is also accompanied by a redistribution of lymphocytes and extended stress has been linked to the shrinking of the thymus (Sapolsky, 1991). In a particularly gruesome relationship, stress has been shown to kill T cells by a form of "suicide killing," in which cortisol damages the DNA of the T cell, mutating it and causing it to eat itself up from the inside out (Wyllie, 1980; Compton & Cidlowski, 1986). Acute stressors such as final exams and sleep deprivation have been found to suppress immune function, causing an increase in illness (e.g., Kiecolt-Glaser et al., 1984; Marshall et al., 1998) and even slower wound healing (Kiecolt-Glaser, Page, Marucha, MacCallum, & Glaser, 1998). Many life events are associated with immune system changes, such as job stress and unemployment (Arnetz et al., 1987), loss of a partner (Goodkin et al., 1996; Kemeny et al., 1995), separation (Kennedy, Kiecolt-Glaser, & Glaser, 1988), the strain of caregiving (Kiecolt-Glaser et al., 1987; Light & Lebowitz, 1989), and natural disasters (Solomon, Segerstrom, Grohr, Kemeny, & Fahey, 1997).

Note also, however, that acute stress may sometimes jump-start the immune system. In an inventive study, Schedlowski et al. (1993) wired 45 first-time parachutists and gathered measures of their stress chemicals and immune cells from $\frac{1}{2}$ hour before their first jump, all the way through their jump, and then for some time after the jump. The numbers of both lymphocytes and NK cells significantly increased just after they jumped and then decreased greatly (to numbers below where they were before the whole process) 1 hour later. Thus, our immune responses are heavily tied to the context and chronicity of the stress.

Why does chronic stress suppress the immune system? The best answer is that suppression prevents overaction and consequently autoimmune diseases. Remember that one of the functions of the immune system is to distinguish "self" from "non-self." If this process fails, problems ensue. Sometimes it does fail. With multiple sclerosis, for example, part of the nervous system is attacked. In lupus, the cartilage around joints is attacked. One of the most fatal autoimmune diseases is AIDS.

HIV and AIDS

These are two short acronyms, but each is associated with large amounts of pain, fear, death, and sadness. AIDS or **acquired immunodeficiency syndrome** is one of the most well known of all the illnesses that cause death from problems with the immune system. "AIDS" was thought to be a suitable name because people acquired the condition rather than inherited it, because it resulted in a deficiency within the immune system, and because it was a syndrome, with a number of manifestations, rather than a single disease. Since the beginning of the epidemic in the late 1970s, it is estimated that more than half a million people have died of AIDS in the United States, and many millions have died worldwide (Centers for Disease Control and Prevention [CDC], 2003; World Health Organization, 2004). In this disorder, the immune system is gradually weakened and finally disabled by the **human immunodeficiency virus** (HIV). HIV infection is now clearly a world pandemic, and although great strides are being made in understanding the epidemiology of the disease, the number of infected people worldwide continues to grow at an alarming rate (Janeway & Travers, 1996). AIDS is now one of the five leading causes of death among women aged 15 to 44, and it strikes poor and minority women disproportionally (Rosenberg & Biggar, 1998). Table 11.2 shows the number of people with AIDS worldwide.

TABLE 11.2

Regional HIV and AIDS Statistics and Features, End 2002 and 2004

	Adults and Children Living with HIV	Adults and Children Newly Infected with HIV	Adult Prevalence (%)	Adult and Child Deaths Due to AIDS
Sub-Saharan Africa				
2004	25.4 million	3.1 million	7.4	2.3 million
	(23.4–28.4 million)	(2.7–3.8 million)	(6.9–8.3)	(2.1–2.6 million)
2002	24.4 million	2.9 million	7.5	2.1 million
	(22.5–27.3 million)	(2.6–3.6 million)	(7.0–8.4)	(1.9–2.3 million)
North Africa and Middle East				
2004	540,000	92,000	0.3	28,000
	(230,000–1.5 million)	(34,000–350,000)	(0.1–0.7)	(12,000–72,000)
2002	430,000	73,000	0.2	20,000
	(180,000–1.2 million)	(21,000–300,000)	(0.1–0.6)	(8,300–53,000)
South and Southeast Asia				
2004	7.1 million	890,000	0.6	490,000
	(4.4–10.6 million)	(480,000–2.0 million)	(0.4–0.9)	(300,000–750,000)
2002	6.4 million	820,000	0.1	430,000
	(3.9–9.7 million)	(430,000–2.0 million)	(0.1–0.2)	(260,000–650,000)
East Asia				
2004	1.1 million	290,00	0.1	51,000
	(560,000–1.8 million)	(84,000–830,000)	(0.1–0.2)	(25,000–86,000)
2002	760,000	120,000	0.2	37,000
	(380,000–1.2 million)	(36,000–360,000)	(0.1–0.3)	(18,000–63,000)
Oceania				
2004	35,000	5,000	0.2	700
	(25,000–48,000)	(2,100–13,000)	(0.1–0.3)	(<1,700)
2002	28,000	3,200	0.6	500
	(22,000–38,000)	(1,000–9,600)	(0.5–0.8)	(<1,000)

SOURCE: Joint United Nations Programme on HIV/AIDS December 2004 Update.

Continued

TABLE 11.2

Regional HIV and AIDS Statistics and Features, End 2002 and 2004—cont'd

	Adults and Children Living with HIV	Adults and Children Newly Infected with HIV	Adult Prevalence (%)	Adult and Child Deaths Due to AIDS
Latin America				
2004	1.7 million (1.3–2.2 million)	24,000 (170,000–430,000)	0.6 (0.5–0.8)	95,000 (73,000–120,000)
2002	1.5 million (1.1–2.0 million)	190,000 (140,000–320,000)	0.6 (0.4–0.7)	74,000 (58,000–96,000)
Caribbean				
2004	440,000 (270,000–780,000)	53,000 (27,000–140,000)	2.3 (1.5–4.1)	36,000 (24,000–61,000)
2002	420,000 (260,000–740,000)	52,000 (26,000–140,000)	2.3 (1.4–4.0)	33,000 (22,000–57,000)
Eastern Europe and Central Asia				
2004	1.4 million (920,000–2.1 million)	210,000 (110,000–480,000)	0.8 (0.5–1.2)	60,000 (39,000–87,000)
2002	1.0 million (670,000–1.5 million)	190,000 (94,000–440,000)	0.6 (0.4–0.8)	40,000 (27,000–58,000)
Western and Central Europe				
2004	610,000 (480,000–760,000)	21,000 (14,000–38,000)	0.3 (0.2–0.3)	6,500 (<8,500)
2002	600,000 (470,000–750,000)	18,000 (13,000–35,000)	0.3 (0.2–0.3)	6,000 (<8,000)
North America				
2004	1.0 million (540,000–1.6 million)	44,000 (16,000–120,000)	0.6 (0.3–1.0)	16,000 (8,400–25,000)
2002	970,000 (500,000–1.6 million)	44,000 (16,000–120,000)	0.6 (0.3–1.0)	16,000 (8,400–25,000)
Total				
2004	39.4 million (35.9–44.3 million)	4.9 million (4.3–6.4 million)	1.1 (1.0–1.3)	3.1 million (2.8–3.5 million)
2002	36.6 million (33.3–41.1 million)	4.5 million (3.9–6.2 million)	1.1 (1.0–1.2)	2.7 million (2.5–3.1 million)

SOURCE: Joint United Nations Programme on HIV/AIDS December 2004 Update.

The History of AIDS

Today, most people have heard of HIV or AIDS (even if they do not know what the letters stand for). In fact, the terms are so ubiquitous that it is strange to think that they are only about 25 years old. The CDC coined the term *AIDS* in 1982, and HIV was discovered and named in 1984. Like most new diseases (the 2003 outbreak of the severe acute respiratory syndrome [SARS] virus is another example), the medical community first realized that something different was going on when groups of people began to get sick with a similar set of symptoms, fever, and pneumonia. In 1978 gay men in the United States and Sweden and heterosexuals in Tanzania and Haiti began showing symptoms of what would later come to be known as AIDS.

The Faces of Those Impacted by AIDS Not just a gay man's disease, AIDS can kill men, women, and children, and everyone is influenced by it.

The year 1981 was perhaps the year that marked the true start of the epidemic. In June of that year, the CDC reported that five young men, all active homosexuals were treated for a special type of pneumonia (caused by *Pneumocystis carinii*) at three different hospitals in Los Angeles. At around the same time reports of 26 cases of a unique form of cancer (Kaposi sarcoma) were also reported among gay men. Kaposi sarcoma was a rare form of relatively benign cancer that tended to occur in older people. Because there was so little known about the transmission of what seemed to be a new disease, there was concern about contagion and whether the disease could by passed on by people who had no apparent signs or symptoms. For a long time, people believed that AIDS was just a disease seen in gay men and something that would not harm heterosexuals or women. The medical journal *Lancet* even called it the gay compromise syndrome, whereas at least one newspaper referred to it as GRID (gay-related immune deficiency). They were

*The National Library of Medicine's Profiles in Science program has made every effort to secure proper permissions for posting items on the web site. In this instance, however, it has not been possible to determine the current copyright owner. If you have information indicating who the copyright owner may be, please contact the NLM at profiles@nlm.nih.gov.

wrong. When it began turning up in children and transfusion recipients, public perceptions began to change. Until then it was entirely an epidemic seen in gay men, and it was easy for the average person to think it would not happen to him or her. The number of people who could become infected was to widen again at the beginning of 1983, when it was reported that the disease could be passed on heterosexually from men to women.

Worldwide, researchers searched frantically to identify the cause. At the CDC researchers had been continuing to investigate the cause of AIDS through a study of the sexual contacts of homosexual men in Los Angeles and New York. They identified a man as the link between a number of different cases and they named him "patient O" for "Out of California" (some who read the published article on him misread the "O" as a "0" and referred to him as patient zero). He was a Canadian flight attendant named Gaetan Dugas, whose job and sexual habits caused him to spread the virus. A large number of individuals infected early in the epidemic had some sort of contact with Dugas. Between 1983 and 1984, researchers at the Pasteur Institute in France and at the CDC and National Cancer Institute managed to crack the mystery and identified two viruses they believed caused AIDS, lymphadenopathy virus (LAV) and human T-lymphotropic virus type III (HTLV-III). In 1985 it was clear that both viruses were the same and were referred to as HIV. For a great account of the history of AIDS, read *And the Band Played On* (Shilts, 2000).

Where did this virus come from in the first place? During the early years of the epidemic it was assumed that HIV made the transition from animals to humans at some time during the 1970s. It was not until 1999 that research suggested HIV had "crossed over" into the human population from a particular species of chimpanzee, probably through blood contact that occurred during hunting and field dressing of the animals (Gao et al., 1999).

HIV is transmitted primarily through the exchange of bodily fluids (not by sitting on toilet seats that have been used by HIV carriers as was once believed). Blood contains the highest concentration of the virus, followed by semen, followed by vaginal fluids, followed by breast milk. The most common ways of passing on HIV are by unprotected sexual contact, particularly vaginal or anal intercourse, and direct blood contact including injection drug needles, blood transfusions, accidents in health care settings, or certain blood products. This is why blood donation centers are very careful about how they collect blood and why every needle is only used once and then discarded. For many years people did not give blood because they feared getting infected by HIV.

The Difference between HIV and AIDS

Remember that HIV is the virus that causes AIDS and that HIV and AIDS are not synonymous. A person can be HIV positive for a long time before developing AIDS. Currently, the average time between HIV infection and the appearance of signs that could lead to an AIDS diagnosis is 8 to 11 years. This time varies greatly from person to person and can depend on many factors including a person's health status and behaviors. Today medical treatments that can slow down the rate at which HIV infection weakens the immune system are available. You may have heard about "protein cocktails," combinations of medications that slow down the progression of the disease. Considered to be one of the best treatments available, the cocktail or **highly active antiretroviral therapy** (HAART) involves many different anti-HIV drugs that keep the virus from replicating. The utility of a combination of drugs is that if one does not work, one of the others should. One of the most commonly used components of HAART is zidovudine (AZT). Other treatments can prevent or cure some of the illnesses associated with AIDS. As with other diseases, early detection offers more options for treatment and preventative health care. Primary HIV infection is the first stage of HIV disease, when the virus first establishes itself in the body. Some researchers use the term acute HIV infection to describe the period of time between when a person is first infected with HIV and when antibodies against the virus are produced by the body (usually 6 to 12 weeks).

Even with successful treatments the disease is still unpredictable. In early 2005 a gay methamphetamine user in New York City was found to have a new strain of HIV that was resistant to treatment. He died in months. Is this a new strain of the virus or an anomaly? The answer is not known, but the implications are disturbing.

Physiological Correlates of HIV/AIDS

HIV is a retrovirus, an RNA virus that secretes an enzyme that injects its own RNA into DNA inside the cells that it infects. DNA is what our genetic code is stored in. When the HIV RNA manipulates the DNA of the host cell, the host cell functions improperly. HIV infects the cells of the immune system, specifically T_H. About 60% of T_H cells have a receptor known as CD4 whereas another large chunk have CD8 receptors (each have specific activation and suppression functions in the system). Two of the main physiological symptoms of AIDS are low numbers of CD4 T cells and higher than average numbers of CD8 cells. If you are healthy you probably have about 1,000 CD4 T cells per milliliter of blood. The sickest AIDS patient will have an average of less than 50 of these cells. The lack of these cells corresponds to the AIDS patient being unable to mount an effective immune defense. This invasion of HIV into the system proceeds through four main stages as shown in Figure 11.5.

Some people newly infected with HIV experience some "flu-like" symptoms. These symptoms, which usually last no more than a few days, might include fevers, chills, night sweats, and rashes (not cold-like symptoms). Other people either do not experience "acute infection" or have symptoms so mild that they may not notice them. Given the general character of the symptoms of acute infection, they can easily have causes *other* than HIV, such as a flu infection. For example, if a person had some risk for HIV a few days ago and is now experiencing flu-like symptoms, it might be possible that HIV is responsible for the symptoms, but it is *also* possible that he or she has some other viral infection. Often some people with HIV have no symptoms, and studies of the effects of HIV normally include additional analyses to control for illness severity. HIV-positive patients can be either asymptomatic or symptomatic with or without an AIDS diagnosis. Classification as HIV/symptomatic requires the presence of at least one of the following

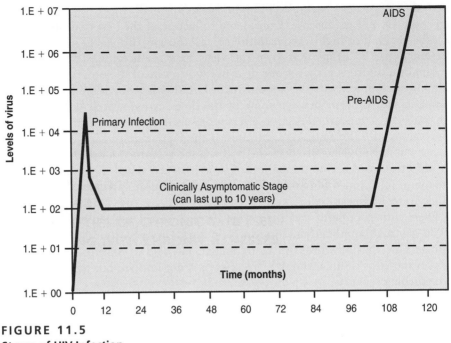

FIGURE 11.5
Stages of HIV Infection

symptoms in the last 6 months: diarrhea (1 to 6 times per week or more), night sweats (1 to 6 times per week or more), fevers (1 to 6 times per week or more), yeast infections (2 or more), weight loss of more than 10 pounds, thrush, or hairy leukoplakia, a precancerous condition that is seen as small thickened white patches, usually inside the mouth or vulva.

There are no common symptoms for individuals who have AIDS. Classification as having AIDS requires the presence of fewer than 200 CD4 T cells and/or an AIDS-defining condition (e.g., toxoplasmosis or cryptococcosis). When immune system damage is more severe, people may experience **opportunistic infections** (called opportunistic because they are caused by organisms that cannot induce disease in people with normal immune systems, but take the "opportunity" to flourish in people with HIV infection). Most of these more severe infections, diseases, and symptoms fall under the CDC's definition of "full-blown AIDS." The median time to receive an AIDS diagnosis among those infected with HIV is 7 to 10 years.

Psychological Correlates of HIV/AIDS

The utility the biopsychosocial approach of health psychology is especially clear when one is dealing with illnesses such as AIDS because both severe physiological and psychological problems are seen with the development of full-blown AIDS.

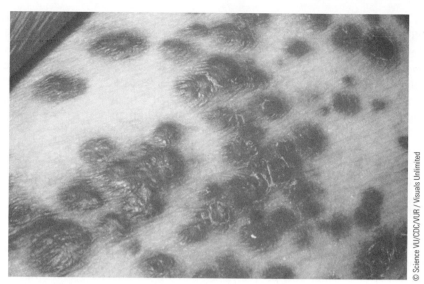

© Science VU/CDC/VUR / Visuals Unlimited

Skin Rashes Such as This Are a Common Symptom of HIV Infection

Psychological factors can influence the acquisition of HIV, the development of HIV infection into AIDS, and the progression of AIDS. As with other chronic illnesses (as discussed in chapter 10), HIV/AIDS is influenced by a variety of psychological factors. Some psychological factors help a person cope with HIV infection and AIDS whereas others can shorten the time one lives with AIDS. For example, optimism, social support, and coping styles are three of the most important psychosocial resources that have been consistently associated with good psychological and physical outcomes and that have been directly associated with lower emotional distress in patients with HIV infection (Commerford, Gular, Orr, Reznikoff, & O'Dowd, 1994; Kaplan, Marks, & Mertens, 1997; van Servellen et al., 1998).

Optimism refers to generalized outcome expectancies that good things, rather than bad things, will happen and is associated with boosts in immune systems in the presence of HIV infection (Littrell, 1996; Kalichman & Ramachandran, 1999), higher NK cell cytotoxicity during stress (Segerstrom, Taylor, Kemeny, & Fahey, 1998), and in some patients, protection against HIV exposure by decreasing intentions to engage in unsafe sex (Carvajal, Garner, & Evans, 1998). Optimists tend to cope better with stress, experience less negative mood effects, and may practice better health behaviors (Taylor, Kemeny, Aspinwall, Schneider, Rodriguez, & Herbert, 1992). Optimism is strongly and positively correlated with active coping and emotional regulation coping strategies and strongly negatively correlated with avoidant coping strategies (Scheier, Weintraub, & Carver, 1986). Optimists, in general, show better psychological well-being (Armor & Taylor, 1998), suggesting that optimism may be an important moderator of the likelihood of depression in response to a stressor such as HIV infection.

As discussed previously (see chapter 5), the presence of social support has been found to be health promoting and health restoring and is also associated with a decrease in mortality risk and progression of AIDS (Chesney & Darbes, 1998; Hays, Turner, & Coats, 1992; Kalichman, Heckman, Kochman, Sikkema, & Bergholte, 2000). Studies of populations with HIV infection suggest that social support from peers is critical for emotional well-being and, in periods of crisis, family support may become an especially important determinant of emotional well-being (Crystal & Kersting, 1998). In a clear example, Metts, Manns, and Kuzic (1996) showed that higher levels of emotional support from both friends and family made independent contributions to lower depression in a sample of persons infected with HIV. Furthermore, in a 5-year study of HIV-positive patients, Theorell et al. (1995) found that participants who had more emotional support and reported better social networks showed significantly lesser declines in their T-cell counts over the course of the study.

The amount of social support one has can also influence the transition from being HIV positive to actually developing AIDS (Leserman et al., 2000). Paradoxically, social support is one thing that persons with HIV infection or AIDS find is harder to get because the label of being HIV positive or having AIDS often becomes stigmatizing, and people tend to avoid the patient (sometimes for the misplaced fear that HIV infection can be transmitted in the air or through casual contact).

Coping strategies, as described in chapter 5, refer to the specific efforts, both behavioral and psychological, that people use to master, tolerate, reduce, or minimize stressful events (Lazarus & Launier, 1978). Among the coping strategies believed to relate to coping with HIV infection, three types of strategies stand out. Problem-solving strategies include planning to confront the stressor and taking action. Avoidance strategies include efforts to distract oneself from, ignore, or forget the stressor, and social support–seeking strategies include attempts to obtain emotional and information support. The first two categories map directly onto two major types of coping as analyzed in the literature, approach and avoidant coping (Lazarus & Folkman, 1991). An individual can approach a stressor and make active efforts to resolve it or try to avoid the problem (Moos & Schaefer, 1993). The third category emphasizes and incorporates the need for and importance of social support in the coping process (e.g., Sarason, Sarason, & Gurung, 2001). In general, patients with HIV infection who rely more on approach coping and who seek support tend to have a higher quality of life and experience less negative affect than those who make use of avoidant coping (Mulder, de Vroome, van Griensven, Antoni, & Sandfort, 1999; Reed, Kemeny, Taylor, & Visscher, 1999).

Despite the differences in health and health risk factors between minority and nonminority populations (Siegel, Karus, Raveis, & Hagan, 1998; Sikkema, Wagner, & Bogart, 2000; Sue, 2000), very few studies test for differences in psychosocial factors among ethnic groups. Some studies show that different ethnic groups vary in how social support is provided and utilized (Gant & Ostrow, 1995; Ulbrich & Bradsher, 1993), others show that different ethnic groups vary in coping styles in response to HIV infection (Heckman et al., 2000; Kaplan et al., 1997). Given that social support and coping have been shown to influence depression as discussed previously, any ethnic differences in these psychosocial factors could have significant implications for the life expectancy of HIV-positive individuals. For example, Schutte, Valerio, and Carrillo (1996) examined the relationship between optimism and socioeconomic status (SES) in European and Mexican Americans and found significant correlations between optimism and SES for European Americans, but not for Latinos.

Psychological Factors Influencing Progression

Understandably, there is intense anxiety and maybe even some denial when a person first finds out he or she may be HIV positive, which is often followed by depression. AIDS patients who deny the reality of their being HIV positive often experience a more rapid development of symptoms (Ironson, Schneiderman, Kumar, & Antoni, 1994). There are some curious exceptions. Reed, Kemeny, Taylor, Wang, and Visscher (1994) found that HIV-positive men who denied their diagnosis actually survived longer than those who accepted their fate. Conflicting evidence such as this clearly demonstrates the need to better understand the ways different psychological constructs interact to influence coping. One psychological outcome of HIV infection and AIDS is unequivocally dangerous: depression. Depression is a critical psychosocial risk factor for individuals with compromised immune systems (Boland, 1997). It is a common experience of AIDS patients (Griffin, Rabkin, Remien, & Williams, 1998) and is related to physical symptomatology, number of days spent in bed, and progression of HIV infection (e.g., Cole & Kemeny, 1997). I will use the example of depression to highlight some important cultural differences in the experience of HIV infection and AIDS, especially focusing on the cultural components of sex and ethnicity.

Cultural Variations in AIDS

Women and AIDS

Despite the fact that depression is more prevalent among women than men with HIV infection (Moore et al., 1999), few studies have focused on depressed women at risk for HIV infection. Much of what is known about the psychosocial concomitants of AIDS has been provided by studies of gay men, and such studies may not be enlightening with respect to women. AIDS was originally seen as a disease of White gay men (Mays & Cochran, 1987), and a large portion of studies focus on this group. Gay men infected with HIV tend to be more economically advantaged, better educated, likely to be European American, and often have no dependents, relative to women infected with HIV (Siegel, Karus, Ravies, & Hagan, 1998). Women account for an increasing percentage of new cases of HIV infection (CDC, 2004; Siegel et al., 1998), and low-income women of color are especially at risk (Wyatt, 1994). Hispanic women are seven times more likely to get AIDS than European American women (Klevens, Diaz, Fleming, Mays, & Frey, 1999). Women account for 44% of all estimated HIV infections worldwide, and the proportion of women infected is rapidly increasing in every geographical area (Ickovics, Thayaparan, & Ethier, 2002).

Some key physiological differences between men and women increase women's likelihood to be infected. Women are more likely than men to be infected with HIV via heterosexual sex, and male to female transmission of HIV is eight times more likely than female to male transmission (Padian, Shiboski, Glass, & Vittinghoff, 1997). Whereas vaginal fluids can be easily washed off the male anatomy after sex, seminal fluids can reside within the female vagina for a long period, increasing the chance of infection. Furthermore, the tissue lining the walls of the vagina is fragile and prone to injury and related infection (Royce, Sena, Cates, & Cohen, 1997). Psychological power differentials are important as well (Thorburn, Harvey, & Ryan, 2005). It is also harder for women to raise the issue of condom use than it is for men, given the traditional power differentials in the sexes, the possibility of abuse, or cultures in which women are not "supposed" to admit to sexual knowledge (Abel & Chambers, 2004).

Women with HIV infection and chronic depressive symptoms are up to 2.4 times more likely to die even after controls were added for other clinical features known to be associated with morbidity and mortality (Ickovics et al., 2001). Such differences in incidence and in the responses (e.g., depression) compel a closer look at this group of individuals.

Ethnicity and AIDS

Together with gender, ethnicity may also be a critical variable in the relationship between depression, HIV status, and health. There are some clear-cut differences in mortality patterns, health status, and health risk factors between ethnic minorities compared with each other and with the European American population (Sikkema et al., 2000; Sue, 2000). For example, African American and Latina women account for approximately 77% of AIDS cases diagnosed among women in the United States (Wortley & Fleming, 1997). African Americans and Hispanic Americans have been disproportionately affected by HIV infection, as is demonstrated by HIV seroprevalence and in the numbers of reported cases of AIDS (CDC, 1996; Jillson-Boostrom, 1992; Karon et al., 1996). Among women, as of 1995, African American women had the highest incidence rate of AIDS (60 per 100,000), compared with 5 per 100,000 for European American women (Rosenberg & Biggar, 1998). Figure 11.6 shows the differences in prevalence of HIV across ethnicities.

Ethnic and sex differences in HIV infection and AIDS interact. Are psychological problems such as depression a greater risk factor for ethnic minority HIV-positive women? Additional knowledge on the concomitants of depression in women with HIV infection across different ethnic groups is sorely needed (Sikkema et al., 2000). To fill this need, Gurung, Taylor, Kemeny, and Myers (2004) studied an ethnically diverse sample of low-income women at risk for AIDS. The prospective design followed 350 African American, Latina, and European American women over a 6-month period to assess the relationship of HIV status, SES, and chronic burden to depression and examine the moderation of these effects by psychosocial resources (social support, optimism, and coping style). HIV status and ethnicity were significantly associated with depressed mood at each point, but not with changes over time.

Gurung et al. (2004) paint a graphic picture of the how ethnicity, SES, and sex can influence coping with HIV infection. Being seropositive for HIV was a

Race or Ethnicity	# of Cumulative AIDS Cases
White, not Hispanic	364,458
Black, not Hispanic	347,491
Hispanic	163,940
Asian/Pacific Islander	6,924
American Indian/Alaska Native	2,875
Unknown or multiple race	887

FIGURE 11.6
Cases of HIV Infection Broken Down by Ethnicity
Source: CDC (2003).

significant stressor associated with depression, but it was also associated with a substantially greater number of chronic burdens affecting all aspects of life, including money, housing, work, vulnerability to crime, and relationships. The fact that these differences were found between the HIV-seropositive and -seronegative women after controlling for SES suggests that seropositivity confers risk for these additional burdens and highlights how biology and the social world directly interact. HIV infection thus increases vulnerability to depression both in its own right and secondarily by expanding the range of chronic burdens to which low-income seropositive women are vulnerable. Moreover, although HIV-positive women were significantly more depressed than HIV-negative women, changes in depression over the 6-month period of the investigation were more strongly predicted by changes in the chronic burdens the women faced that are frequently associated with low SES (see chapter 4 for more information on chronic stress). This study provides another clear example of why a biopsychosocial approach to understanding chronic illnesses such as HIV infection is critical.

Other Cultural Issues

Race and ethnicity also influence the extent to which **sexual mixing** takes place (Catania, Binson, Dolcini, Moskowitz, & van der Straten, 2002). Sexual mixing, which has been found to have a central influence on HIV transmission rates (Garnett & Anderson, 1993), is defined as the extent to which people engage in sexual activities with sexual partners from other sexual networks (dissortative mating) versus partners from their own network (assortative mixing). Heavy mixers form an important link in the spread of HIV infection. Laumann, Gagnon, Michael, and Michaels (1994) examined sexual mixing in a national sample of heterosexual adults aged 18 to 49. Their data indicated that for respondents with multiple sexual partners, women are more likely than men to be heavy mixers (14% versus 11%) and that Hispanic males (59% versus 17% African American and 5% White) and females (33% versus 4% African American and 15% Whites) are more likely than other males and females to be heavy mixers with African American males and White females reporting moderate levels of mixing. Developmental state is important (as discussed in chapter 3), and these patterns vary by age group. Young adult Hispanic males and females report the most heavy mixing.

Advances in genetic research and the ability to hone in on specific parts of genes are providing new insights into cultural differences in diseases such as HIV infection and AIDS (Just et al., 1992; Kilpatrick, Hague, Yap, & Mok, 1991; Martin et al., 1998). For example, Mays et al. (2002) suggested that one useful area to consider in identifying ethnic differences in HIV infection is in the distribution of human leukocyte antigen (HLA). HLA molecules serve to initiate the immune response by how they present antigens to T cells, which, as described above, then clear the virus from the body. Ethnic variations in the genes encoding HLA molecules can affect antigen presentation and, correspondingly, how the host responds. Variations in aspects of HLA molecules (the specific details of which are technically beyond the scope of this text) have been found across racial groups. Some aspects of HLA were four times more likely to be found in African Americans than in European Americans (Dunston, Henry, Christian, Ofosu, & Callendar, 1989). Osborne and Mason (1993) have found aspects of HLA unique to the Hispanic population. The new discoveries are paving the way for the design of new genetic therapies targeting specific gene variations among individuals (McNicholl, 1997).

The great ethnic discrepancies in incidence and prevalence of HIV and AIDS compel more cross-cultural research, but this has been slow in developing. Much research continues to be conducted using European American men (Mays et al., 2002) although researchers such as Wyatt et al. (2002) and Sikkema, Hansen, Kochman, Tate, and Difranciesco (2004) are focusing on mixed ethnic samples of women. African Americans, who made up 34% of all AIDS cases (Fahey & Flemming, 1997), previously made up only 7% of National Institutes of Health HIV studies (Ready, 1988). Similarly, Hispanics represented 17% of AIDS cases but were only represented by 9% of research participants (Mays et al., 2002).

Health Psychological Models Relating to HIV/AIDS

Given that one of the major ways of contracting HIV infection is via unprotected or risky sexual activity, you may think that one easy way to curtail the spread of AIDS is to get people to have safe sex. Of course, that is easier said than done. For years, researchers have been trying to get men and women to have safe sex. These efforts range from educating individuals on the proper use of condoms to changing behavioral intentions. In a general sense, practicing safe sex can be considered analogous to any other health behavior and consequently most of the health behavior models that we discussed in chapter 6 apply here as well. For example, researchers have used the Health Belief Model and the Theory of Planned Behavior to influence beliefs and intentions in regard to condom use and safe sex (Abraham, Sheeran, Spears, & Abrams, 1992; Aspinwall, Kemeny, Taylor, Schneider, & Dudley, 1991; Jemmott, Jemmott, & Hacker, 1992; Winslow, Franzini, & Hwang, 1992).

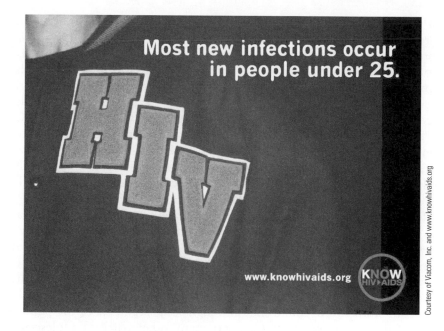

Courtesy of Viacom, Inc. and www.knowhivaids.org

Courtesy of Viacom, Inc. and www.knowhivaids.org

Examples of Posters Designed to Cut Down on the Spread of the HIV Virus

Some models are specific to AIDS. For example, Catania, Kegeles, and Coates (1990b) proposed the AIDS Risk Reduction Model (ARRM), which states that people must first understand the threat of HIV infection and recognize that their behaviors put them at risk for infection with the virus and consequently developing the disease.

Attitudes toward the protective behavior matter too. Using condoms can significantly reduce the risk of contracting a sexually transmitted disease, but many people believe that condoms reduce sexual pleasure, and this belief decreases condom use (Albarracin et al., 2000). Others may not be confident in their ability to properly use condoms (Catania, Kegeles & Coates, 1990a; Rosario, Nahler, Hunter, & Gwadz, 1999). As suggested by the social norms component of the Theory of Planned Behavior, people's attitudes toward condom use will also be influenced by what they think the norms are and what they believe their friends and partners think about it (Fischer, Fisher, & Rye, 1995). Other factors influencing condom use include concurrent alcohol or drug use (Gordon, Carey, & Carey, 1997; Leigh, Schafer, & Temple, 1995), level of commitment between the people having sex (Katz, Fortenberry, Zimet, Blythe, & Orr, 2000), level of sexual arousal (more arousal leads to less use of condoms) (Galligan & Terry, 1993), and the type of relationship (women are more likely to practice safer sex in casual sexual relationships) (Morrill, Ickovics, Golubchikov, Beren, & Rodin, 1996).

The first line of attack is most often education. If you can increase a person's knowledge about an illness, automatically their beliefs about their own susceptibility or vulnerability to it as well as their sense of the severity of the disease (factors from the Health Belief Model) will change. There are many misperceptions about HIV infection and who is most likely to get it. I already mentioned that people tend to believe that it is something just homosexuals get. In general, studies have found that although some segments of the population are well informed about AIDS (e.g., gay men), others such as adolescents are not (LeBlanc, 1993). Similarly, Murphy, Mann, O'Keefe, and Rotheram-Borus (1998) found that single, inner-city women often have little knowledge of AIDS or what behaviors place them at risk. Methods for providing education vary. General interventions that provide counseling about HIV infection seem to be effective to curtail the activity of those already infected with HIV, but are not as effective for those who are not (Weinhardt, Carey, Johnson, & Bickman, 1999). Instead, more targeted interventions (e.g., those aimed at very specific populations) have proved to be more effective (Jemmott, Jemmott, & Fong, 1992; Nyamathi, Stein, & Brecht, 1995).

Beyond education about AIDS, health psychological interventions have also targeted sexual activity. For most health behaviors, the best predictor of future behavior is past behavior. Old habits die hard. If a person has used condoms and practiced safe sex before, he or she is more likely to do it in the future. Modifying sexual behavior becomes especially difficult because it is linked to ideas of freedom and spontaneity. For many young men and women, being independent translates into not having to do anything (e.g., particularly have sex) in any specific way (even safely). Modification of sexual behavior has been found to be a threat to identity (McKusick, Horstman, & Coates, 1985). Consequently, many interventions are designed to vary different aspects of the process of indulging in sexual behavior. Some teach people how to exercise self-control and not rush into sex (which is more often unsafe) (Miller, Bettencourt, DeBro, & Hoffman, 1993). Other interventions model skills to avoid high-risk behaviors (van der Velde & Van der Pligt, 1991). Targeting sexual activity seems to work. Kalichman, Carey, and Johnson (1996) reviewed behavioral interventions conducted with a wide variety of participants and found them to be useful. However, this approach is not as commonsensical as it may seem, because a number of interventions do not result in any changes whatsoever.

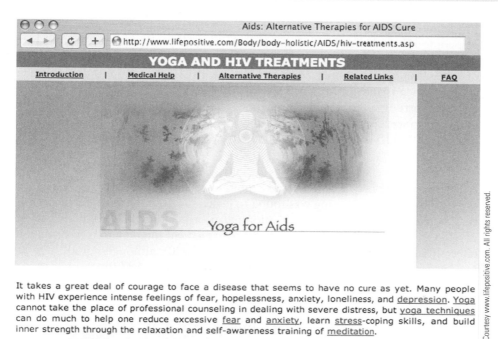

It takes a great deal of courage to face a disease that seems to have no cure as yet. Many people with HIV experience intense feelings of fear, hopelessness, anxiety, loneliness, and depression. Yoga cannot take the place of professional counseling in dealing with severe distress, but yoga techniques can do much to help one reduce excessive fear and anxiety, learn stress-coping skills, and build inner strength through the relaxation and self-awareness training of meditation.

Yoga for AIDS More and more groups are offering yoga classes specifically designed for people with AIDS. The postures and movements serve to relieve many of the physical symptoms, ease anxiety, and help with coping. The upper panel shows a screenshot of a website specifically designed for AIDS patients.

Being HIV positive does not signify the end of sexual activity. More than 70% of people infected with HIV continue to be sexually active (Kline & VanLandingham, 1994), and a large number of interventions seek to increase disclosure of status. Such interventions empower those with HIV infection to disclose their status to friends and family. Not only does this disclosure provide the patient with more opportunities for social support, but it also allows their sexual partners to make informed decisions about sexual activity with them. In addition, men who disclose their HIV status are more likely to practice safe sex (DeRosa & Marks, 1998).

Some interventions aimed at reducing the ill effects of HIV infection and AIDS have used physical activity and cognitive-behavioral approaches. For example, aerobic exercise training was found to lessen the drop in immune functioning that normally accompanies being informed of a positive HIV test (La Perriere et al., 1991). Cognitive-behavioral stress management interventions have similar effects (Antoni et al., 1991, 2000; Cruess et al., 2000), although not all such attempts are successful (Coates, McKusick, Kuno, & Stites, 1989).

FOCUS on Applications

Yoga and Coping with Illnesses Such as AIDS

Scientists are working hard to find the cures for chronic and terminal illnesses such as cancer and AIDS, and although advancements are being made, there are no absolute cures as yet. A large focus then is on how best to help the patient cope with the pain and discomfort of the illness. Health psychologists are very useful in this regard. Many cognitive and behavioral approaches are used (e.g., distraction), but a majority of techniques involve some form of relaxation training (e.g., guided imagery or meditation). One particular technique that has become popular with the North American general public and one that is growing in utility in the treatment of chronic illnesses as well is yoga. In keeping with an increase in the use of complementary and alternative treatments, a recent survey of more than 30,000 Americans showed that 5% used yoga for health reasons (Barnes, Powell-Griner, McFann, & Nahin, 2004). Another study determined that yoga use was closer to 8% (Saper, Eisenberg, Davis, Culpepper, & Phillips, 2004).

Up to a few years ago (and maybe in the minds of some of you today as well) yoga conjured up images of people bent into twisted, uncomfortable shapes and was a lifestyle associated with hippies, flower children, and pacifism. There are many stereotypes about yoga, and this is a good time to look at the facts. Practices such as yoga are likely to become more accepted in public consciousness as the utility of using the mind to calm and relax the body gets even stronger empirical validation. To the millions of practitioners of yoga, the benefits are clear, and many people practice yoga daily. Given that a complete yoga lifestyle does include the practicing of many healthy behaviors (e.g., not smoking, limiting drinking, physical activity, relaxation and meditation, good eating, and getting enough sleep), the practice of yoga shows a potential for enhancing the quality of life of those with chronic illnesses.

Yoga originated in India approximately 4,000 years ago, and the word is derived from Sanskrit (an ancient Indian language), meaning "to unite." There are many different aspects in the practice of yoga. The physical postures are just one aspect. Derived from Hinduism and Buddhism, the practice of yoga has as its basic goal the transformation of the self and diminished cravings. Yoga is a part of the ayurvedic approach to health (see chapter 2). Traditionally practitioners believed that a universal spirit pervades everything and used yoga to clear the mind and release this spirit. A stressed mind was compared with a turbid lake and yoga calmed the waters. There are four main types of yoga. Hatha yoga stresses purification, postures, relaxation, and diet. Hatha yoga and variations of it are the most common forms of yoga in North America. The most common variation is Iyengar yoga, which is characterized by precise poses often with the aid of various props, such as cushions, benches, wood blocks, straps, and even sand bags. Other variations are Astanga yoga (involving synchronizing of breath with a progressive series of postures) and Bhikram yoga (in which postures are done in a 100° F heated room). Other forms of yoga include Jnana yoga (yoga of wisdom involving a study of literature and striving for attainment of right views), Bhakti yoga (yoga of devotion, finding inner change through prayer or religious ecstasy), and Karma yoga (yoga of action and the pursuit of a higher social purpose).

Yoga involves a lot more than just striking poses. Traditional yoga has eight parts (angas or limbs). There are four practices and four experiences that one should strive for. The practices involve (1) attitude toward the world (abstinence, truthfulness, and chastity), (2) attitude toward self (purification and contentment), (3) posture (or asana, which is what you probably have heard of), and (4) breath regulation (pranayama). The four experiences are (1) withdrawal of senses (pratyaha), (2) fixed attention (dhyana), (3) contemplation (dharana), and (4) absolute concentration (superconsciousness/samadhi). A true yoga practitioner would not only do the physical components but also strive to live life in accordance with the moral and psychological components. Only a small number of the many Americans who practice yoga strive for (or even know about) the complete scope of the practice.

The use of yoga for the treatment of chronic illnesses is increasing, and empirical studies of its effectiveness for a range of illnesses have slowly begun to be reported. For example, patients with multiple sclerosis in a yoga class showed significant improvement in measures of fatigue compared with a control group of patients with similar levels of the disease (Oken et al., 2004). Similar successes have been found with cardiovascular functioning (Harinath et al., 2004) and diabetes (Manyam, 2004). Yoga has begun to be implemented in a number of different health care programs. For example, the Stanford Cancer Supportive Care Program (SCSCP) at the Center for Integrative Medicine at Stanford Hospitals offers yoga to both cancer patients and their families. A recent assessment showed that more than 90% of the patients using the SCSCP felt there was benefit to the program, and yoga was one of the classes with the highest number of participants (Rosenbaum et al., 2004).

In the context of HIV infection and AIDS, a number of AIDS patients use yoga to ease their pain and negative feelings. AIDS patient Steve McCeney (quoted in the *Yoga Journal,* 2001) provides a glimpse of what it is like. He said, "Sometimes I don't know what it's like to feel normal anymore, but I do know that after an hour of restorative poses, I feel like a new person mentally, spiritually, and physically." An international group of yoga therapists provides a variety of special resources and information for AIDS patients, and studies of the effects of yoga on HIV infection are being conducted.

Some yoga postures are thought to activate the hormonal system of the body, the ductless glands of the body, to start to balance their activities. For example, I talked earlier about the role of the thymus gland in the immune system. Open-chested poses such as Supta Baddha Konasana (reclining bound angle pose) or Setu Bandha over bolsters or a bench (bridge pose) stimulate the thymus gland (Kout, 1992). Yoga also can be a psychological booster, helping patients to strengthen their minds and build their resolve. In the words of another AIDS patient:

Yoga is the main thing that makes me feel good, besides emotional things I can do with a partner or being in love. I really feel it if I don't have it every week. It is a big security blanket. Yoga does more for me than anything else I do. It makes so much sense, especially now that I am studying massage and learning about the organs. I'm feeling more in touch with my body than I thought I ever could. It helps me to slow down and look at life week by week, day by day; using what I have, not always wanting more; learning to live in the moment (Kout, 1992).

Chapter Summary

- The immune system comprises our body's protection system. The cells and organs of this system filter out bacteria and viruses that infiltrate our bodies and break down infected cells.
- The main components of the immune system are the lymph nodes, lymph fluid, and leukocytes or white blood cells. Lymphocytes are T cells and B cells, the primary defensive cells of the system along with macrophages. There are many types of lymphocytes, each with specific immune functions. The strength of an immune response can be determined by measuring cell differentiation, proliferation, or cytotoxicity.
- Natural immunity is brought about by circulating macrophages and the secretion of histamines, which instigate inflammatory responses. Macrophages engulf antigens or invading germs by phagocytosis. Acquired immunity is the response of lymphocytes to specific microorganisms and takes place in the blood or in the cells and tissue.
- Psychoneuroimmunology is a field that focuses on how psychological factors influence immune functioning. Research in PNI includes that done on behavioral conditioning of the immune response and the association between the immune system and stress. Stress has been reliably associated with the functioning of the immune system, mostly having a negative effect (e.g., in the long run) but sometimes activating it as well (in the short run).
- Acquired immunodeficiency syndrome (AIDS) and the human immunodeficiency virus (HIV), first noticed in the early 1980s, are a worldwide threat to health. Al-

though a cure is yet to be found, health psychologists can be influential in helping change behaviors that can cause the spread of this disease. Originally thought to be a disease affecting only homosexual men, AIDS is now known to strike both heterosexuals and homosexuals alike. Low socioeconomic status individuals and those from some minority groups have a disproportionate risk for contracting this disease.

- Many psychological factors such as optimism and social support can be useful in helping a person with AIDS live a longer life. Similarly, problem-solving, avoidance, and support-seeking strategies all relate to coping with HIV infection.

- Specific health behavior change models such as the AIDS Risk Reduction Model (ARRM) have been designed to help combat the spread of AIDS, and research is now addressing understudied cultural populations such as women and minority groups.

Synthesize, Evaluate, Apply

- Describe the pros and cons of the body's way of protecting itself from illness.
- What functions do the various cell differentiations serve?
- What are the basic nonspecific immune responses?
- Given what you know about the immune system, what health behaviors would you recommend to best keep a person healthy?
- How are cell- and humoral-mediated immunity different?
- Why do people start sniffling during an allergic reaction?
- How can conditioning be used to create an immune response greater than that stimulated by a certain dose of a drug?
- What are the different ways stress and coping can influence the immune response?
- What is the most feasible pathway linking psychological coping with immunity?
- What factors in the history and nature of AIDS are most responsible for the worldwide health epidemic of this disease today?
- Compare and contrast coping with AIDS with coping with stress. What techniques would be more beneficial in this context?
- In what ways does the delivery of social support have to be modified in the context of AIDS?
- How do cultural factors influence the behaviors that put someone at risk for HIV infection and for its spread?
- Given the fatal course of HIV infection, what psychological factors could explain why people would still continue to engage in unsafe sexual practices/drug use?

KEY TERMS, CONCEPTS, AND PEOPLE

acquired immunity, 322
acquired immunodeficiency
 syndrome, 326
antigens, 318
B cells, 317
cell-mediated immunity, 323
cytotoxicity, 320
differentiation, 320
highly active antiretroviral
 therapy, 331

histamine, 321
human immunodeficiency
 virus, 327
humoral-mediated immunity,
 322
immune system, 316
inflammatory response, 321
leukocytes, 316
lymphatic system, 316
natural killer (NK) cell, 319

nonimmunologic
 defenses, 321
nonspecific immunity, 321
opportunistic infections, 332
phagocytosis, 322
proliferation, 320
psychoneuroimmunology, 324
sexual mixing, 337
T cells, 317

ESSENTIAL READINGS

Ader, R., Felten, D. L., & Cohen, N. (2001). *Psychoneuroimmunology*. San Diego, CA: Academic Press. (This edited volume has a collection of some of the best empirical work in the field of psychoneuroimmunology. Pay especially close attention to the chapter by Cole and Kemeny.)

Cohen, S., & Herbert, T. B. (1996). Health psychology: Psychological factors and physical disease from the perspective of human psychoneuroimmunology. *Annual Review of Psychology, 47,* 113–142.

Reed, G. M., Kemeny, M. E., Taylor, S. E., & Visscher, B. R. (1999). Negative HIV-specific expectancies and AIDS-related bereavement as predictors of symptom onset in asymptomatic HIV-positive gay men. *Health Psychology, 18*(4), 354–363.

Segerstrom, S. C., & Miller, G. E. (2004). Psychological stress and the human immune system: A meta-analytic study of 30 years of inquiry. *Psychological Bulletin, 130*(4), 601–630.

WEB RESOURCES

Visit the companion website at **http://psychology.wadsworth.com/gurung1e/,** where you will find online resources for this book, including chapter-by-chapter quizzes, weblinks, and more! You can also visit Wadsworth Psychology Resource Center at **http://psychology.wadsworth.com** to access additional resources.

National Institute of Health AIDS information
http://www.aidsinfo.nih.gov

Cousins Center for Psychoneuroimmunology
http://www.cousinspni.org

Culture and Cancer

If you are reading this in a public place, take a good slow look around you. If you are reading this alone, think of the faces of your colleagues, students, or coworkers. Want to know some sobering facts? A good percentage of the people you see or the people you are thinking of have had a close encounter with cancer. They either know someone who has been diagnosed with it or may have been diagnosed with it themselves. Close to half of us are predicted to develop some form of cancer in our lifetimes. More than 1 million new cases of cancer are diagnosed every year, and cancer is the second leading cause of death in the United States (after heart disease). Cancer accounts for approximately one-half million deaths a year. You may know someone with cancer yourself—your mother, father, uncle, aunt, brother, or sister. You have probably heard of the cyclist Lance Armstrong, the golfer Arnold Palmer, the master chef Julia Child, the actresses Shirley Temple, Suzanne Somers, and Kate Jackson (star of *Charlie's Angels*), former first ladies Betty Ford and Nancy Reagan, the writer Gloria Steinem, and politicians Bob Dole (go beyond his Viagra commercials), Colin Powell, John Kerry, and Rudy Guliani. All of them had cancer.

Even saying the word *cancer* conjures up images of sadness or dread. Having cancer is not something people want. It is not even something you wish on those you dislike (unless you really have a very mean streak in you). The fear of cancer has been so pervasive that finding a cure for it is often seen as the pinnacle of achievement,

Lance Armstrong—Cancer Survivor

© Doug Pensinger/Getty Images

the truly ambitious child's dream. People jest about how the epitome of an impressive resume would be "found a cure for cancer" rating equally with "brokered world peace." The good news is that health psychology is demonstrating how preventative measures can greatly reduce the incidence of cancer. What you do (and how much attention you paid to chapters 6 and 7 on health behaviors) can predict your likelihood of getting cancer. Want to hear some even better news? Health psychological research designed to improve cancer screening and increase early detection is helping more people survive what was once a completely fatal disease. Most breast cancers, for example, are diagnosed at an early stage and up to 96% of those with localized disease survive 5 years (American Cancer Society, 2004).

What exactly is this dreadful disease? How do you get it? Who gets it? How is it treated? How can one survive it? These are just some of the questions I will answer in this chapter. Consistent with the theme of this book and the health psychological approach, we will also examine how cancer varies across cultural lines and is strongly influenced by psychological factors.

Prevalence of Cancer

Unfortunately, the chances of our developing some form of cancer in our lifetime are pretty high, and the chances get higher as we get older. For people between the ages of 60 and 70 there is a 1 in 3 chance (if you are male) or 1 in 4 chance (if you are female) of getting cancer (Figure 12.1). This incidence drops to a 1 in 12 and 1 in 11 chance for men and women between the ages of 40 and 59, respectively, and a 1 in 52 chance for men between the ages of 1 and 39 (1 in 73 for women in the same category). Every year, a large number of new cases of cancer are diagnosed, and many people lose their lives to cancer. Some estimates suggest that one person dies of cancer every 90 seconds (Parker, Tong, Bolden, & Wingo, 1997). In 2004 it was estimated that there were 1,368,030 new cases of cancer and 563,700 persons died of cancer (American Cancer Society, 2004).

We are making large strides in the fight against cancer. New results on the incidence of cancer show that it is not as common as it was before, although the good news is limited to European American populations. Jemal et al. (2004) collected cancer morbidity and mortality data from several government organizations (e.g., the Centers for Disease Control and Prevention [CDC]), evaluated trends in cancer incidence and death rates, and compared survival rates over time and across racial/ethnic populations. The good news is that incidence rates for all cancers combined decreased from 1991 through 2001, but stabilized from 1995 through 2001 when adjusted for delay in reporting. The incidence rates for female lung cancer decreased and mortality leveled off for the first time after increasing for many decades. Colorectal cancer incidence rates have also decreased. Death rates decreased for all cancers combined and for many of the top 15 cancers occurring in men and women. The rate at which patients with cancer survived also improved for all cancers combined and for most, but not all, cancers over two diagnostic periods (1975 to 1979 and 1995 to 2000).

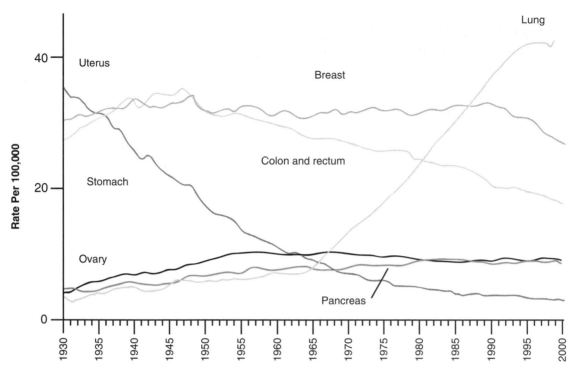

FIGURE 12.1

Cancer Death Rates for Women in the United States, 1930 to 2000

Rates age-adjusted to the 2000 U.S. standard population.

SOURCE: *U.S. Mortality Public Use Data Tapes 1960–2000, U.S. Mortality Volumes 1930–1959, National Center for Health Statistics, Centers for Disease Control and Prevention, 2003.*

The bad news from a cultural perspective is that cancer-specific survival rates were lower, and the risk of dying from cancer, once it was diagnosed, was higher in most minority populations compared with the White population (Table 12.1) (Jemal et al., 2004). The relative risk of death from cancer (all types combined) compared with that for European American men and women was higher for both Hispanic men (1.16) and American Indian men (1.69). Another study showed that the breast cancer rate for Asian American women rose 6% per year from 1993 to 1997 compared with only 2% per year for European American women (Deapen, Lui, Perkins, Bernstein, & Ross, 2002).

What Is Cancer?

Similar to stress and pain, two other things that nobody wants even a little of, cancer is something that we often just use one word for but actually has many different forms and meanings. The word *cancer* is derived from *carcinos* and

---

TABLE 12.1

Cancer Sites in Which African American Death Rates Exceed White Death Rates for Men in the United States, 1996 to 2000

Site	African American	White	Ratio of African American/White
All sites	356.2	249.5	1.4
Larynx	5.7	2.4	2.4
Prostate	73.0	30.2	2.4
Stomach	14.0	6.1	2.3
Myeloma	9.2	4.5	2.0
Oral cavity and pharynx	7.9	4.0	2.0
Esophagus	12.2	7.3	1.7
Liver	9.3	6.0	1.6
Lung and bronchus	107.0	78.1	1.4
Pancreas	16.4	12.0	1.4
Small intestine	0.7	0.5	1.4
Colon and rectum	34.6	25.3	1.4

Rates per 100,000, age-adjusted to the 2000 U.S. standard population.
SOURCE: Surveillance, Epidemiology, and End Results Program, 1975–2000, Division of Cancer Control and Population Sciences, National Cancer Institute, 2003.

---

carcinoma, terms first used by the Greek Hippocrates (see chapters 1 and 2) to describe nonulcer-forming and ulcer-forming tumors. The shape of a spreading cancer cell resembles the outstretching legs of a crab to which these words refer (in Greek the word for crab is *cancer;* a good clue is the zodiac signs for which cancer is the crab as well). Although typically discussed as one illness, cancer is a group of diseases that vary in terms of incidence and mortality rates, epidemiology, risk factors and causes, and treatments (American Cancer Society, 2004; Meyerowitz, Bull, & Perez, 2000). In fact, understanding cancer and its effects is perhaps one of the areas of health psychology most illustrative of the need of the use of a cultural approach because a comprehensive understanding of cancer requires a consideration of sex, gender, ethnicity, geographical location, sexual orientation, and all the other aspects of what makes up culture.

First, let's look at basic biology and some terminology. Cancer is the name given to the illness or condition caused by the presence of a malignant tumor. A malignant tumor or cancerous cell is identified as one showing uncontrollable cell growth that destroys healthy tissue. Cells that show abnormal growth are also referred to as **neoplasms.** Normally our cells grow, divide, and die in an orderly fashion, and cell growth is more pronounced when we are young. As we grow older, cells in most parts of the body divide only to replace worn-out or dying cells and to repair injuries. Because cancer cells continue to grow and divide, they are different from normal cells. Instead of dying, they outlive normal cells and continue to form new abnormal cells.

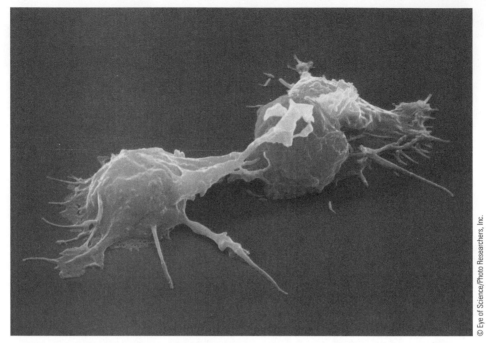

A Cancer Cell (Center) Being Attacked by Immune System Killer T Cells Scanning electron microscope shows killer T cells attacking the cancer cell (with crab-like tentacles).

When a normal cell turns cancerous, it is often the result of a mutation in the cell's DNA that alters it and makes it grow uncontrollably, disrupting surrounding tissue and often spreading to organs all around the body (Hanahan & Weinberg, 2000). Most of the time when DNA becomes damaged, the body is able to repair it. In cancer cells, the damaged DNA cannot be repaired. Such genetic mutations can also be inherited, which accounts for why risk for cancer increases if someone in a person's family has had cancer. Many times though, a person's cancerous cell mutations occur because of exposure to environmental toxins such as cigarette smoke or other **carcinogens** (cancer-causing substances). The branch of medicine that deals with the study and treatment of cancer is referred to as oncology, and this is the term used more frequently in hospitals (e.g., the oncology ward or floor).

Types of Cancer

There are more than 100 different types of cancer, and even tumors within each type show a lot of variability. However, note that not all tumors are cancerous or **malignant. Benign** or noncancerous tumors do not **metastasize** or spread to other parts of the body and, with very rare exceptions, are not life threatening. Some cancers, such as leukemia, do not form tumors. Instead, these cancer cells involve

TABLE 12.2

Sites of Cancer and Incidence

2004 Estimated US Cancer Deaths*

		Men 290,890	Women 272,810		
Lung and bronchus	32%			25%	Lung and bronchus
Prostate	10%			15%	Breast
Colon and rectum	10%			10%	Colon and rectum
Pancreas	5%			6%	Ovary
Leukemia	5%			6%	Pancreas
Non-Hodgkin lymphoma	4%			4%	Leukemia
Esophagus	4%			3%	Non-Hodgkin lymphoma
Liver and intrahepatic bile duct	3%			3%	Uterine corpus
Urinary bladder	3%			2%	Multiple myeloma
Kidney	3%			2%	Brain/ONS
All other sites	21%			24%	All other sites

SOURCE: American Cancer Society, 2004

the blood and blood-forming organs and circulate through other tissues where they grow. The course of the disease and the likelihood of survival vary greatly with each type of cancer so if someone just says he or she has cancer, you should not make any generalizations about his or her experiences until you have more details. Some cancers show very little deviation in patterns of disease course, and psychosocial influences on coping and treatment are minimal (Henderson & Baum, 2002).

The key variables that influence the interaction between biological, psychological, and social factors and the role each plays in cancer mortality or morbidity are cancer site, type, and severity. The most common sites for cancer are the lungs, breasts, prostate gland, colon, and rectum (the latter two are often affected together, which is referred to as colorectal cancer). The top 15 cancer sites and related incidence and mortality statistics for each are shown in Table 12.2.

There are four main types of cancer. The most common are **carcinomas** that start in the surface layers of the body or epithelial cells. This form of cancer accounts for the bulk of cancer cases and is seen in the most common sites. **Sarcomas** are cancers of the muscles, bones, and cartilage. **Lymphomas** are cancers of the lymphatic system (see chapter 11) and are referred to as Hodgkin's disease if the cancer spreads from a single lymph node (non-Hodgkin lymphomas are found at several sites). **Leukemias** are cancers that are found in the blood and bone marrow. In leukemia, white blood cells proliferate to displace red blood cells, which causes anemia (a shortage of red blood cells), bleeding, and other immune system problems.

The severity of cancer is determined by a multifactor assessment of stage. The **TNM system** is the most common method used to stage cancer (American Cancer Society, 2004). It provides three main pieces of information. The T describes the size of the tumor and whether cancer has spread to nearby tissues and organs. The N describes how far the cancer has spread to nearby lymph nodes. Given that the lymph nodes are critical components of the body's immune system, they are often heavily involved in fighting cancer cells. The M indicates the extent to which the cancer has metastasized. Letters or numbers after the T, N, and M give more details about each of these factors. For example, a tumor classified as T1, N0, M0 is a tumor that is very small, has not spread to the lymph nodes, and has not spread to distant organs of the body. Once TNM descriptions have been established, they can be grouped together into a simpler set of stages, stages 0 through IV. In general, the lower the number, the less the cancer has spread. A higher number, such as stage IV, indicates a more serious, widespread cancer (American Cancer Society, 2004).

Cultural Variations in the Incidence of Cancer

Similar to the ethnic differences in incidence of HIV infection described in the previous chapter, there are large differences in the cultural makeup of people who have cancer (Gotay, Muraoka, & Holup, 2001; Meyerowitz, Richardson, Hudson, & Leedham, 1998). In fact, there is a growing body of research clarifying the link between cancer and membership in certain ethnic groups (Elmore, Moceri, Carter, & Larson, 1998; Perkins, Cooksley, & Cox, 1996). Before looking at possible biological reasons why one ethnicity may be more at risk than another, let's first look at the different patterns of cancer across diverse ethnic groups.

There are two main statistics to bear in mind when studying the prevalence of cancer. The first is **incidence** or rates of newly diagnosed cases of the disease. The second is actual mortality. Keeping the two numbers separate is important because there are many people who are diagnosed with cancer who live (remember there was good news), and the number of survivors varies across cultural groups. So even if there are two cultural groups who both have the same incidence levels for a certain type of cancer, they may not show the same mortality rates. Figure 12.2 shows the incidence and mortality rates for the main types of cancer broken down by two main cultural variables, sex and ethnicity.

As you can see, different ethnic groups and the two sexes do not get cancer or die from it in the same ways. African Americans have the highest general cancer incidence rates and mortality rates of any population in the United States, with this difference being driven more by higher rates of cancer among African Ameri-

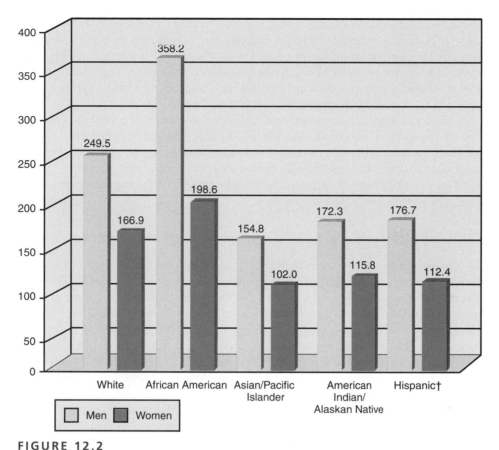

FIGURE 12.2
Cancer Death Rates* by Race and Ethnicity, 1996 to 2000
*Per 100,000, age-adjusted to the 2000 U.S. standard population.
†Hispanic is not mutually exclusive from Whites, African Americans, Asian/Pacific Islanders, and American Indians.
Source: Surveillance, Epidemiology, and End Results Program, 1975–2000, Division of Cancer Control and Population Sciences, National Cancer Institute, 2003.

can men. Illustrating the difference between incidence and mortality, American Indians have greater mortality rates relative to their incidence rates, suggesting that if they have cancer they are more likely to die of it. Separating total cases of cancer from individual types of cancer is important too. Although Asian Americans show much lower rates of cancer than European Americans in general, their rates of colorectal cancer diagnoses are about the same. In contrast to some other ethnic differences, European American men are four times more likely to have testicular cancer than are African American men (Hawkins & Miaskowski, 1996).

In addition to these ethnic differences, there are significant sex differences in cancer incidence as well. Men experience higher incidences of cancer in general (American Cancer Society, 2004). The most common sites for male cancer are the prostate gland, the lungs, the colon, and the rectum (American Cancer Society, 2004). Testicular cancer is relatively uncommon among men in general, but it is one of the most common forms of cancer in younger men aged 15 to 35. Male cancers have not received as much research attention as have female cancers and less is known about the etiology of most male cancers and men's psychological and social experiences with cancer (Gordon & Cerami, 2000).

The most common sites for female cancer for women of most ethnic groups are the breasts, lungs, colon, and rectum. In case you were wondering, men do get breast cancer although the rates are infinitesimal (and no, women cannot get testicular cancer although they do get ovarian cancer). Other common cancers tend to vary by ethnicity but usually include cancers of the reproductive organs (e.g., the uterus, cervix, and ovaries).

Cultural Differences in Beliefs and Knowledge about Cancer

In line with a biopsychosocial approach, biological, psychological, and societal differences can also account for cultural differences in cancer incidence. The most prominent cultural differences pertain to the beliefs held about cancer, people's attitudes toward cancer, and knowledge of cancer. Many studies have shown that low socioeconomic groups, those lower in income and education, are less knowledgeable about cancer regardless of their sex, ethnicity, or religion (e.g., Breslow, Sorkin, Frey, & Kessler, 1997). Ethnically diverse groups have shown different levels of knowledge as well. African Americans (Miller & Champion, 1997), Hispanics (Hubbell, Chavez, Mishra, & Valdez, 1996), Chinese Americans (Mo, 1992), Vietnamese Americans (Pham & McPhee, 1992), Native Hawaiians (Blaisdell, 1998), American Samoans (Mishra, Luce-Aoelua, & Hubbell, 1998), and Korean Americans (Kim, Yu, Chen, Kim, & Brintnall, 1998) have all been found to have lower levels of knowledge about risk factors and cancer symptoms than European American groups.

Sometimes these cultural differences are linked to cultural beliefs and misconceptions about disease in general. Many strong religious minded individuals may believe that cancer is just punishment for sins or that cancer has spiritual meaning (Ashing-Giwa & Ganz, 1997; Martinez, Chavez, & Hubbell, 1997; Perez-Stable, Sabogal, Otero-Sabogal, Hiatt, & McPhee, 1992). The misperceived causes of cancer may also be more tangible. Vietnamese, Chinese, and Hispanic Americans (Garcia & Lee, 1989; Hubbell et al., 1996; Martinez et al., 1997; Pham & McPhee, 1992) reported poor hygiene or dirt as a cause for breast and cervical cancer. Another common cultural cancer belief is **fatalism,** the belief that a person with cancer cannot live a normal life and will die (Gotay et al., 2001). High levels of fatalism has been found in African American men, women, and adolescents, Vietnamese Americans, and Hispanics (Champion & Menon, 1997; Demark-Wahnefried, Rimer, & Wimer, 1997; Perez-Stable et al., 1992; Pham & McPhee, 1992).

A vivid example of how culture influences perceptions is seen in the views of American Indians. Many American Indians see cancer as a "White man's" disease and something that is a punishment for one's actions or the actions of a family member (Alvord & Van Pelt, 2000). Some see cancer as a natural part of life's pathway and as providing a lesson to learn from. Many also see cancer as penance and a person with cancer must "wear the pain" to protect other members of the community (Burhansstipanov, 2000). A diagnosis of cancer is equivalent to a doctor shooting a hole through the spirit and thus results in depression and fear of the doctor instead of trust. Beliefs about how you can get cancer may seem outlandish to the ethnocentric non-Indians. Some American Indians believe cancer can result from a curse or from violating tribal mores (e.g., stepping on a frog or urinating on a spider). Others believe that it is contagious and that it can be caught from a mammography machine or from the child of someone who has cancer (Burhansstipanov, 2000). Some American Indians do not want to even talk about cancer for fear of catching the cancer spirit. Regardless of the extent to which you think these beliefs are far-fetched they have to be respected and anticipated to optimize helping the American Indians who do hold them.

Developmental Issues in Cancer

You are more likely to get cancer as you get older. The rates for cancer increase dramatically over the lifespan. Incidence rates range from less than 15 per 100,000 for those younger than 15 years of age, but balloon to more than 2,000 per 100,000 for those older than 75 (Ries, 1996). Age is a cultural variable as well, and one that also needs to be attended to in understanding cancer.

Cancer can be considered a developmental disease (Meyerowitz et al., 2000). Why is this so? Although cancer is primarily diagnosed in older adults, cancers actually develop when people are younger. Because there typically is a large gap between when a tumor starts to grow and when it is large enough to be diagnosed, exposure to many of the risk factors for cancer (described below) at a young age necessarily predict the occurrence of cancer at an older age. Significant risks for cancer are also associated with the different developmental milestones (as described in chapter 3). There is a risk associated with girls starting to menstruate early (Colditz & Frazier, 1995) and dietary problems during the reproductive years have been linked to the development of oral and other cancers in older women years later (Muscat, Richie, Thompson, & Wynder, 1996). There are also risks associated with menopause and the ways that women cope with it. The biggest risk factor for cancer, smoking, also has a strong developmental link: smoking almost always begins in the teenage years; few adults initiate a regular smoking habit (Berman & Gritz, 1991).

Developmental age also influences how people, especially children, will cope with a cancer diagnosis. For example, Barrera et al. (2003) recruited preschool, school age, and adolescent patients and measured their psychological adjustment and quality of life (QOL), 3, 9, and 15 months after cancer was diagnosed. The children's age at diagnosis significantly affected both their adjustment and QOL. At 3 months after diagnosis, preschoolers had more externalizing behavior problems than did adolescents. Preschoolers had better QOL than adolescents at all three assessments, suggesting that preschoolers with cancer are at risk for behavior problems and adolescents are at risk for poor QOL. Studies such as these are gentle reminders that the psychological reactions to cancer experienced by adults may be very different from those of children (Katz, Kellerman, & Siegel, 1980). A developmental approach also helps us understand how family interactions change when one family member has cancer (Johnson, 1997; Weihs & Reiss, 1996).

Physiological Correlates of Cancer

The physiological symptoms of cancer will depend on the size, location, and stage of cancer. If a cancer has reached a later stage and metastasizes, then symptoms may occur at different locations in the body. As the mutant cells divide, they exert pressure on the surrounding organs, blood vessels, and nerves that will be consciously felt by the individual. Some cancers, such as pancreatic cancer, are not felt until the cell has reached an advanced stage of development. Some of the general symptoms of cancer are fever, fatigue, pain, changes in the skin, and weight loss. Remember that having these symptoms does not necessarily mean a person has cancer but suggests that something is not right (there are many other reasons for these same symptoms). Sometimes, cancer cells release substances into the bloodstream that cause symptoms not generally thought to result from cancers (American Cancer Society, 2004). For example, some cancers of the pancreas can release substances that cause blood clots to develop in veins of the legs. Some lung cancers produce hormone-like substances that change blood calcium levels, affecting nerves and muscles and causing weakness and dizziness.

Together with general symptoms some symptoms are more specifically indicative of cancer. Any changes in your excretory functions could signify cancer of the colon (e.g., constant diarrhea) or bladder/prostate gland (e.g., painful urination or blood in the urine). Sores that do not heal, especially in the mouth or on sexual organs, are signs of skin cancers. As a rule, the appearance of blood in fluids in which you do not normally see it (e.g., saliva, urine, stool, nonmenstrual vaginal fluids, or breast fluid) should be reported to a doctor immediately. The appearance of lumps (e.g., in the breast, testicles, or lymph nodes) may also be a sign of cancer. In general, it is clear that the better you know your body, the more aware you will be of changes that may signify problems with it.

Psychological Correlates of Cancer

You can divide up the reality of cancer into three main phases: the period leading up to a diagnosis, the diagnosis and reactions to it, and the period following it. Psychological factors may play a role in all three although the research evidence on how psychology influences progression is clearer than that on its role in the development of cancer.

Psychological Factors in Cancer Incidence

There is presently little unequivocal proof that psychological factors cause cancer, except for the case of stress (more on this later). At least three general pathways through which psychological factors may influence the development of cancer have been identified: (1) direct effects of psychological processes on bodily systems, (2) healthy and unhealthy behaviors, and (3) responses to perceived or actual illness, such as screening behaviors or adherence to treatment recommendations (Henderson & Baum, 2002). The main psychological processes studied have been personality, social support, depression, stress, and health behaviors. Stress and health behaviors are perhaps the most pervasive and will be discussed later in the chapter.

Although receiving a lot of attention in the mid-1980s, the role of *personality* in cancer has been somewhat exaggerated. Morris, Greer, Pettingale, and Watson (1981) first found an association between breast cancer and anger suppression, leading to the hypothesis of a cancer-prone or **Type C personality.** A Type C person was described as cooperative, appeasing, unassertive, and compliant and as someone who did not express negative emotions (Temoshok, 1987). Some later reviews (McKenna, Zevon, Corn, & Rounds, 1999) supported these early findings, but not very strong results and some contradictory findings (e.g., Persky, Kempthorne-Rawson, & Shekelle, 1987) suggest that personality plays only a small role in cancer etiology.

Similarly, social support has not been found to have a strong protective effect against cancer development (Fox, 1998). To be fair, the social support research has been thwarted by the fact that there are many different types of social support (as described in chapter 5), and it has been operationalized in different ways, making study comparisons difficult (Sarason, Sarason, & Gurung, 2001). If your intuition says that social support must do something, you are right (although don't let intuition get in the way of empirical evidence to the contrary). Women who were socially isolated were found to have a higher cancer incidence, although this relationship was not found in men (Reynolds & Kaplan, 1990).

There is slightly more evidence for the role of depression in cancer incidence than that for social support. Two literature reviews have shown depression to be a marginally significant risk factor for cancer (McGee, Williams, & Elwood, 1994; McKenna et al., 1999), and at least two prospective studies strengthen this conclusion (Gallo, Armenian, Ford, Eaton, & Khachaturian, 2000; Penninx et al., 1998). Gallo et al. (2000) used a large population-based sample in Baltimore, following approximately 2,000 individuals for 13 years. Although there was no link between cancer and depression across the board, there was a significant association between depression and cancer for women. In conjunction with similar sex differences for social support, it is clear that the link between psychological factors and cancer may be very different for men and women. This difference may be linked to biological pathways or may be indicative of greater cultural differences between the sexes that have biopsychosocial components (e.g., Taylor, Kemeny, Reed, Bower, & Gruenewald, 2000).

Psychological Responses to Cancer Diagnosis

Even being screened for a potential cancer can be a fearful experience (Wardle & Pope, 1992). A positive diagnosis (i.e., that cells are cancerous) can be devastating and has been referred to as causing an "existential plight" (Weisman & Worden, 1972). In addition to anxiety, denial, and depression, the major responses to learning you have a chronic illness as covered in chapter 9, a cancer diagnosis and its treatment result in stress and a lowered QOL (Anderson, Kiecolt-Glaser, & Glaser, 1994). The high emotions experienced right after diagnoses do lessen with time, and emotions actually improve as recovery begins after the end of treatment (Edgar, Rosberger, & Nowlis, 1992). Two other highly psychologically disturbing times occur during treatment, whether it be surgery or radiotherapy (Anderson & Tewfik, 1985; Gottesman & Lewis, 1982).

In general, depression is more common in those patients undergoing active treatment, rather than those in follow-up, and those experiencing pain or with a history of stressors or low social support (Holland, 1989). Approximately half of cancer patients meet the American Psychiatric Association's criteria for having a psychological disorder, the majority of them being related to emotional and/or behavioral problems resulting from having to adjust to cancer (Tope, Ahles, & Silberfarb, 1993). Over half of those treated for cancer experience fear, pain, insomnia, and related anxiety disorders (Derogatis et al., 1983).

Psychological Factors in Cancer Progression and Coping

Similar to HIV infection and other chronic illnesses, some psychological characteristics help one cope better with cancer and also influence the course of the disease. Similar to the factors associated with incidence, a person's personality, social support, depression, stress, and health behaviors again figure prominently (Helgeson, Snyder, & Steltman, 2004; Henderson & Baum, 2002).

Personality In the late 1970s, the first positive links between personality and cancer progression were seen. How people coped with cancer seemed to be one of the most important factors. Patients who denied the cancer had higher disease recurrence rates (Greer, Morris, & Pettingale, 1979). Other studies followed and have established that avoidant, repressive, or unexpressive personalities or coping styles are associated with poorer disease courses (Epping-Jordan, Compas, & Howell, 1994; Jensen, 1987). Other personality characteristics are important, too. For example, optimism is strongly and positively correlated with active coping and emotional regulation coping strategies and strongly negatively correlated with avoidant coping strategies (Scheier, Weintraub, & Carver, 1986). Optimists, in general, show better psychological well-being (Armor & Taylor, 1998). In the context of cancer, Carver et al. (1994) showed that optimism predicts adjustment to early-stage breast cancer over several time points, with optimistic women showing higher subjective well-being and satisfaction with their sex life and lower levels of intrusive thoughts.

Social Support The case for social support and survival of cancer patients is very strong (Helgeson, Cohen, Schulz, & Yasko, 1999). Garssen and Goodkin (1999) reviewed 38 prospective studies assessing the role of psychological factors in cancer initiation and progression, including recurrence and survival and found that low levels of social support consistently promoted cancer progression. In terms of specific aspects of social support, having a high number of confidants to discuss personal problems (Maunsell, Brisson, & Deschenes, 1995), having a high number of social connections (Reynolds & Kaplan, 1990), having more contact with friends and supportive others (Waxler-Morrison, Hislop, Mears, & Kan, 1991), and believing that you have a lot of emotional support (Ell, Nishomoto, Mediansky, Mantell, & Hamovitch, 1992) all have been linked to slower progression of cancer and higher survival rates. A small, but growing body of work also suggests that spiritual sources (e.g., belief in God and prayer) also provide social support and aid in adjustment and slowing of cancer progression (Gall & Cornblat, 2002).

Depression has also been linked to cancer progression (Spiegal, 1996) with a number of studies suggesting that depression and lower QOL in general have adverse effects on survival (Butow, Coates, & Dunn, 1999). I will come back to the role of social support and depression when I discuss interventions later in this chapter.

Finding Meaning   One of active areas of psychosocial research in coping with cancer revolves around the notion of finding meaning or **benefit finding.** Taylor (1983) first reported that 53% of women in whom breast cancer was diagnosed reported that they experienced positive changes in their lives since their diagnosis, a finding since replicated (Antoni et al., 2001; Cordova, Cunningham, Carlson, & Andrykowski, 2001). Most of the research that followed linked benefit finding to positive outcomes (e.g., Davis, Nolen-Hoeksema, & Larson, 1998; Taylor, Lichtman, & Wood, 1984). This seems to make intuitive sense. If, unexpectedly, you find that you have cancer and then if you can see a positive meaning you should do better. But now here's a twist. Recent longitudinal studies of benefit finding (most of the previously cited work was cross-sectional) are suggesting that benefit finding may not be always good. Tomich and Helgeson (2004) followed 364 women for a 6-month period and found that benefit finding was associated with more negative emotions although the negative associations with QOL were limited to those women with more severe disease. Some interesting cultural variations were found as well. Lower socioeconomic status (SES) women and African American and Hispanic women (independent of SES) were more likely to find benefit in their cancer than European American women (Tomich & Helgeson, 2004). If it is useful to be optimistic, shouldn't finding benefit be good too? Research is under way to unravel this contradiction because nothing in the data collected offered a definite resolution (Tomich & Helgeson, 2004).

Cancer, Stress, and Immunity

Stress has been shown to influence both the incidence of cancer and its progression (although again, the link for the latter is stronger). A cancer diagnosis sets up a negative cycle of experiences between stress and illness (see chapter 11 for another example). The diagnosis and treatment cause stress that in turn influences the course of the disease by affecting the immune system. Stress has a direct effect on the activity of natural killer (NK) cells, which themselves are critical in the body's fight against cancer (Anderson et al., 1998). Patients with a variety of cancers have lowered NK cell activity in the blood to begin with (Whiteside & Herberman, 1994). Low NK cell activity in cancer patients is significantly associated with the spread of cancer and in patients treated for metastases, the survival time without metastasis correlates with NK cell activity. Correspondingly, the experience of any additional stress can have direct effects on the development of the cancer, complementing and antagonizing the low NK cell levels. Stress can also increase unhealthy behaviors that can accelerate illness progression. The patient may increase drug, tobacco, or alcohol use, get less sleep or physical activity, or eat badly, all behaviors that may further affect immunity (Friedman, Klein, & Specter, 1991).

It may be no surprise that cancer can stress you but can stress actually give you cancer? I have talked about the negative impact stress can have on our minds and bodies before (see chapter 4) so this is clearly a possibility. In fact, this question has been actively debated. Retrospective studies of stress and the onset of cancer have shown mixed results and are heavily criticized (Cooper, Cooper, & Faragher, 1986; Delahanty & Baum, 2001), but prospective studies show that, in general, patients with a subsequent diagnosis of cancer reported more severe stressful events than control groups (Cooper, 1989; Geyer, 1993). Stress has been shown to damage DNA, and this has been suggested as a general pathway through which stress can influence the development of cancer (Forlenxa & Baum, 2000; Pettingale, 1985). In a meta-analysis of 46 studies, McKenna et al. (1999) found that the relationship between stressful life events and cancer was only modest.

Health Behaviors and Cancer

As mentioned in the introduction to this chapter, many things can predict your likelihood of getting cancer. Figure 12.3 lists some of the main health behaviors that put you at risk for getting cancer. Take a moment to see how you fare. To some extent the results may surprise you ("You mean doing *that* puts me at risk for cancer?" Yes, it may.). The usual unhealthy behaviors turn up again (see chapter 7) and, not surprisingly, cultural differences in the practice of some of these behaviors are significant in explaining cultural differences in cancer.

Tobacco Use

Do you want an easy way to decrease your risk of getting cancer? Make sure you do not smoke. Probably the most clear-cut cause of cancer is tobacco use (American Cancer Society, 2004; CDC, 2004). Smokers have nine times the risk of getting lung cancer compared with nonsmokers (Lubin, Richter, & Blot, 1984). Note that this risk is nine times—not double, not triple—but nine times. Talk about really playing with fire! Cigarette smoking accounts for at least 30% of all cancer deaths. As shown in Table 12.3 smoking is a major cause of cancers of the lung, larynx (voice box), oral cavity, pharynx (throat), and esophagus and is a contributing cause in the development of cancers of the bladder, pancreas, liver, uterine cervix, kidney, stomach, colon and rectum, and some leukemias.

The link between smoking and cancer is best illustrated when we look at populations that increased tobacco use. Smoking rates among women rose dra-

Answer the following questions:

1. Do you protect your skin from overexposure to the sun? _____
2. Do you abstain from smoking or using tobacco in any form? _____
3. If you're over 40 or if family members have had colon cancer, do you get routine digital rectal exams? _____
4. Do you eat a balanced diet that includes the RDA for vitamins A, B, and C? _____
5. If you're a woman, do you have regular Pap tests and pelvic exams? _____
6. If you're a man over 40, do you get regular prostate exams? _____
7. If you have burn scars or a history of chronic skin infections, do you get regular checkups? _____
8. Do you avoid smoked, salted, pickled and high-nitrate foods? _____
9. If your job exposes you to asbestos, radiation, cadmium, or other environmental hazards, do you get regular checkups? _____
10. Do you limit your consumption of alcohol? _____
11. Do you avoid using tanning salons or home sunlamps? _____
12. If you're a woman, do you examine your breasts every month for lumps? _____
13. Do you eat plenty of vegetables and other sources of fiber? _____
14. If you're a man do you perform regular testicular self-exams? _____
15. Do you wear protective sunglasses in sunlight? _____
16. Do you follow a low-fat diet? _____
17. Do you know the cancer warning signs? _____

Making Changes
Cutting Your Cancer Risk
You may not be able to control every risk factor in your life or environment, but you can protect yourself from the obvious ones.

- *Avoid excessive exposure to ultraviolet light.* If you spend a lot of time outside you can protect your skin by using sunscreen and wearing long-sleeve shirts and a hat. Also, wear sunglasses to protect your eyes. Don't purposely put yourself at risk by binge-sun-bathing or by using sunlamps.

- *Avoid obvious cancer risks.* Besides ultraviolet light, other environmental factors that have been linked with cancer include tobacco, asbestos, and radiation.

- *Keep yourself as healthy as possible.* The healthier you are, the better able your body is to ward off diseases that can predispose you to cancer. Get regular exerciser; eat a balanced, high-fiber, low-fat diet; and avoid excessive alcohol use.

- *Be alert to changes in your body.* You know your body rhythms and appearance better than anyone else, and only you will know if certain things aren't right. Changes in bowel habits, skin changes, unusual lumps or discharges—anything out of the ordinary may be clues that require further medical investigation.

- *Don't put off seeing your doctor if you detect any changes.* Procrastination can't hurt anyone but you.

FIGURE 12.3
Are You at Risk for Cancer?
If you answered no to any of the questions, your risk for developing various kinds of cancer may be increased.
Source: Hales (2000).

matically between the 1960s and the 1990s, and deaths due to lung cancer in women increased correspondingly (Berman & Gritz, 1991). Shopland (1996) showed that the risk of contracting lung cancer for women who smoke is 1,200% greater than that for women who do not smoke, and one-quarter of all cancer deaths among women can be attributed to smoking (Shopland, Eyre, & Pechacek, 1991). In men, almost 85% of lung cancers are related to cigarette smoking (Holland, 1989). The fact that men smoke more than women accounts for ap-

TABLE 12.3

Cancer and Smoking

Smoking and Cancer Mortality Table

Type of Cancer	Gender	Relative Risk Among Smokers	Relative Risk Among Smokers	Mortality Attributable to Smoking	Mortality Attributable to Smoking
		Current	Former	Current	Former
Lung	Male	22.4	9.4	90	82,800
	Female	11.9	4.7	79	40,300
Larynx	Male	10.5	5.2	81	24,000
	Female	17.8	11.9	87	700
Oral Cavity	Male	27.5	8.8	92	4,900
	Female	5.6	2.9	61	1,800
Esophagus	Male	7.6	5.8	78	5,700
	Female	10.3	3.2	75	1,900
Pancreas	Male	2.1	1.1	29	3,500
	Female	2.3	1.8	34	4,500
Bladder	Male	2.9	1.9	47	3,000
	Female	2.6	1.9	37	1,200
Kidney	Male	3.0	2.0	48	3,000
	Female	1.4	1.2	12	500
Stomach	Male	1.5	?	17	1,400
	Female	1.5	?	25	1,300
Leukemia	Male	2.0	?	20	2,000
	Female	2.0	?	20	1,600
Cervix	Female	2.1	1.9	31	1,400
Endometrium	Female	0.7	1.0		

Not all cancers are equally influenced by smoking. Notice the differences in relative risk from smoking for the different types of cancers and the sex differences.
Source: Centers for Disease Control, 2003.

proximately 90% of the sex differences in lung cancer mortality (Waldron, 1995). As men's and women's smoking rates become similar, their lung cancer rates also become similar. See Figure 12.4 for an illustration of how lung cancer rates and smoking rates have paralleled each other over the last 100 years.

Differences in tobacco use also highlight many of the cultural differences in cancer rates. Different ethnic groups have had different historical relationships with tobacco, serving to either increase or decrease their exposure to it. African Americans, for example, had heavy exposure to tobacco from the early 1600s when Africans were first brought to the Americas and were employed in southern tobacco-growing plantations and in tobacco manufacturing during the colonial period (Gotay et al., 2001). Tobacco was used in South America and Latin America even before the European colonization and the *curanderismos* (see chapter 2) often used tobacco in religious and healing practices. Even today, cigarette smok-

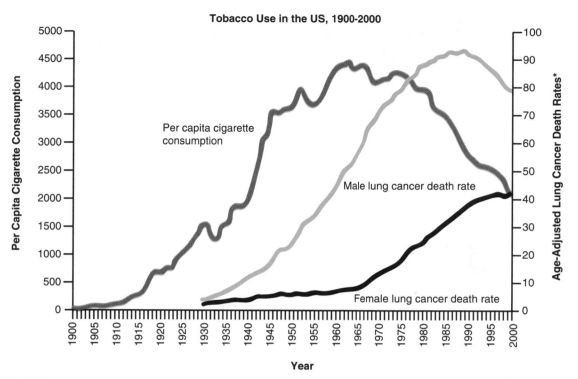

FIGURE 12.4
Tobacco Use in the United States, 1900 to 2000
*Rates age-adjusted to the 2000 U.S. standard population.
SOURCE: *U.S. Mortality Public Use Data Tapes 1960–2000, U.S. Mortality Volumes 1930–1959, National Center for Health Statistics, Centers for Disease Control and Prevention, 2002. Cigarette consumption: U.S. Department of Agriculture, 1900–2000.*

ing is considered a "social activity" for Latinos, consistent with cultural values of *personalismo* (importance of personal relations) (Marin, Marin, Perez-Stable, Sabogal, & Otero-Sabogal, 1990). Many Asian groups also have had a long history of smoking. In China, tobacco was mixed with opium and smoked and then was also used medicinally. In India, the end of a hard day in the fields was often marked by the smoking of a *hookah,* a contraption that bubbled tobacco through water. Use of a hookah to smoke also has become a trendy habit in many New York and Los Angeles bars.

Diet

For the majority of Americans who do not smoke, eating a nutritionally balanced diet and being physically active are the most important ways to reduce cancer risk. Evidence suggests that one-third of the 550,000 cancer deaths that occur in the United States each year are due to unhealthy diet and insufficient physical activity (Byers & Doyle, 2004). Different cultural groups have different eating habits (see chapter 7), which can accentuate their risk for cancer. There are a number of dietary features that are linked to an increased risk for cancer (Willett & Trichopoulos, 1996). For example, eating too much fat and not getting enough fiber have been associated with increased cancer incidence (Steinmaus, Nunez, & Smith, 2000; Wynder et al., 1997). On the other hand, diets with high consumption of fruits and vegetables are associated with a lower risk for several types of cancer (Potter & Steinmetz, 1996). In Hawaii, native Hawaiians have the shortest life expectancy of any ethnic group because of their bad diets, including high consumption of cholesterol-containing foods and red meat, animal fat, eggs, milk, and cheese (the traditional roast pig at a luau is a mouth-watering example).

The data for some cancers are stronger than those for others. Eating a lot of animal fat is strongly linked to colon cancer. There are some fats, such as omega-3 polyunsaturated fat found in salmon, that may actually prevent cancer and are associated with lower rates of breast cancer and colorectal cancer (Gogos et al., 1998; Greenwald, Clifford, Pilch, Heimendinger, & Kelloff, 1995), but evidence supporting this finding is still mixed.

The diet-cancer link is probably mediated by obesity. Bad diets and eating too much make people overweight and obese. Obesity may promote breast cancer because of the effects of adipose tissue on epithelial cell growth (Guthrie & Carroll, 1999) or on the production and functioning of hormones such as estrogen (Mezzetti et al., 1998). Obesity has also been linked to a higher incidence of colon, endometrial, and gallbladder cancers (Ford, 1999; Pi-Sunyer, 1998).

A wide variety of foods are supposed to help prevent cancer and also to cure it. Only a small percentage of the foods touted as curative have stood the test of scientific research (Table 12.4). Be warned that there are a lot of television and Internet reports of so-called cancer-busting foods for which there is no scientific basis. For example, eating grapes is supposed to be good, but the effects have not been proven. That said, eating a diet with high amounts of fruits and vegetables, especially those containing antioxidants, does seem to increase the cancer-fighting capacity of the body (Cao, Booth, Sadowski, & Prior, 1998). Also, eating soy products and broccoli actually does seem to help prevent some cancers (Fahey, Zhang, & Talalay, 1997; Moyad, 1999), and vegetarianism similarly has been linked to lower incidence of cancer (Hebert et al., 1998). For the rest of the things you may hear about, for example, vitamin A or C, the mineral selenium, and flavonoids (effective antioxidants, you'll hear more about these in the next chapter), there is enough research to suggest that each is a potential cancer fighter (Knekt et al., 1997; Young et al., 1997), but we are far from having a guaranteed "perfect anticancer" diet. We are getting close though, as more and more nutrients are proving to be viable cancer fighters (Freeman et al., 2000; Norrish, Jackson, Sharpe, & Skeaff, 2000). As always, you should be a critical consumer of what claims you hear or read about.

Physical Activity

The reasons for staying in shape (or getting in shape) continue to increase. A large body of evidence suggests that physical activity, especially during our younger years, can reduce the risk of breast cancer in women (Bernstein, Henderson,

TABLE 12.4

Foods Supposed to Help Prevent and Treat Cancer

Component	Food	Cancer Link
Fiber	Carrots, beets, onions and potatoes	Prevents colon, stomach
Folate and folic acid	Leafy vegetables, grains and legumes	Prevents breast
Antioxidants	Fruits, vegetables, nuts, grains	Potential
Beta-carotene	Carrots, cantaloupe, other orange foods	Potential
Vitamin E	Nuts, broccoli, corn oil	Potential
Vitamin A	Liver, egg yolks and milk, cabbage	No clear link
Vitamin C	Citrus fruits and leafy vegetables	No clear link
Selenium	Meat and bread	No clear link
Vitamin B	Brussels sprouts	No clear link
Flavones/Indoles	Broccoli, artichokes, celery	No clear link
Phytochemicals	Soy products	Potential
Omega-3 fatty acids	Fish oils, salmon	No clear link
Aspartame	Artificial sweetener	No clear link
High-fat diets		Increased risk of breast, colon, rectum, prostate, endometrium

Hanisch, Sullivan-Halley, & Ross, 1994) and colon cancer in men (Longnecker, Gerhardsson, le Verdier, Frumkin, & Carpenter, 1995). Getting regular physical activity also lowers the risk for breast cancer for both pre- and postmenopausal women (Gilliland, Li, Baumgartner, Crumley, & Samet, 2001). Being active is good for men too. Physical activity reduces the rate of prostate cancer in men (Lee, Paffenbarger, & Hsieh, 1992) and could protect both men and women from colon cancer (Batty & Thune, 2000). The relationship between physical activity and testicular cancer though is a little inconsistent and for lung cancer a relationship has yet to be fully established (Thune & Furberg, 2001).

Sun Exposure

Few people lying on the beach soaking in the sun's rays are thinking about the fact that they have almost tripled their chances of getting squamous cell skin cancer (American Cancer Society, 2004). Did you know that 45% of Americans who live to 65 years of age get skin cancer at least once? Prevention is again the key: 78% of skin cancers reported could have been prevented if people younger than age 18 had put on sunscreen. Even tanning booths are carcinogenic. A 15- to 20-minute session is equivalent in **ultraviolet (UV) ray** exposure to one full day at the beach. Although tanning salons often advertise that sun bed tanning is safer than sunbathing outside, the intensity of light in tanning beds is actually much greater. The customer not only has light rays above his or her body but also below it. Many of the older tanning beds emit short-wave UV rays, which burn the outer layers of the skin. The majority of the tanning beds used today, however, use long-wave UV rays, which actually penetrate deeper and weaken the skin's inner connective tissue. Tanning salon rays also increase the damage that is done by the sunlight, because the UV light from the tanning beds thins the skin, making it less able to heal. Both the sun and tanning beds produce a tan from UV rays. UV rays cause the skin to protect itself from burning by producing additional pigmentation and coloring. Overexposure to these UV rays can lead to eye injury, premature wrinkling, light-induced skin rashes, and increased chances of skin cancer. To get that nice tanned look without the risk, consumers are now flocking to risk-free tanning booths that use sprays.

So should you stay out of the sun altogether? No, that's not right either. Although overexposure to sunlight can be very detrimental to one's health, we still need some amount of exposure to sunlight for both physical and psychological reasons. A lack of sunlight is associated with poor mood, as well as with a condition called seasonal affective disorder. Sunlight is also a major source of vitamin D in humans, because it produces vitamin D in the skin after exposure to UV radiation (Weinrich, Ellison, Weinrich, Ross, & Reis-Starr, 2001). Without vitamin D, diseases such as rickets occur.

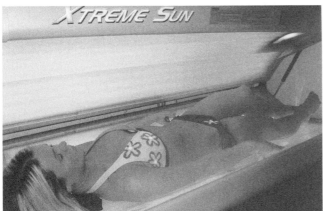

Photo courtesy Lacey Moore

Photo courtesy Lacey Moore

Tanning A tanning booth (left) in which even a single visit can expose you to carcinogenic ultraviolet rays. A safer alternative for a "tanned" look is a spray-on tan (right) where you just step into the shower-like set-up and nozzles all around you coat you with a fine mist.

Treatment Options

Cancer need no longer be a death sentence, although many people still believe it is. Although earlier cancer detection increases its chances of being completely treated, even some cancers in their later stages can be successfully treated. Because cancer is essentially cells that are out of control, the main goal of treatment is to get the cells out of the body. There are three major ways to treat cancer.

Surgery

The oldest and most straightforward way to treat cancer is *surgery,* during which the surgeon can remove the tumor. Surgery is most successful when the cancer has not spread because this provides the best chance of removing all the mutant cells. Surgery also has other uses in cancer. **Preventative surgery** is performed to remove tissue that is not malignant as yet but has a high chance of turning malignant. This happens in the case of women with a family history of breast cancer who also have a mutant breast cancer gene (*BRCA1* or *BRCA2*). Preventative surgery may also be used to remove parts of the colon if polyps, small stalk-shaped growths (not the little marine animals), are found. **Diagnostic surgery** is the process of removing a small amount of tissue to either identify a cancer or to make a diagnosis. If the patient does receive a positive diagnosis of cancer, sometimes **staging surgery** is needed to ascertain what stage of development the cancer is in. This form of surgery helps determine how far the cancer has spread and provides a *clinical stage* for the growth. If the cancer has been localized to a small area, **curative surgery** can be used to remove the growth. This is the primary form of treatment for cancer and is often used in conjunction with the other treatments. If it is not possible to remove the entire tumor without damaging the surrounding tissues, **debulking surgery** reduces the tumor mass. Finally, **palliative surgery** is used to treat complications of advanced disease (not as a cure), and **restorative surgery** is used to improve a person's appearance after curative surgery (e.g., after a **mastectomy** or breast removal).

Chemotherapy

The second major form of treatment for cancer involves taking medications with the aim of disabling the cancer growth, a process referred to as **chemotherapy.** The medications are either given in pill form, in the form of an injection, or in the form of an intravenous injection (medication delivered through a catheter right into a vein). The type of cancer and its severity determine the frequency of chemotherapy, and it can range from daily to monthly medication. This form of treatment often has very strong side effects but often results in successful outcomes. Patients who undergo chemotherapy (or "chemo" for short) often lose all their hair (not just the hair on their head as is commonly believed), experience severe nausea, and have a dry mouth and skin. Chemotherapy also has biopsychosocial effects. Biologically, the treatment lowers both red and white blood cell counts. Fewer red blood cells make a person anemic and feel weak and tired. A reduced number of white blood cells makes a person more prone to infection, and a person undergoing chemotherapy needs to take special care to not be exposed to germs (e.g., visitors with colds) or sources of contamination (e.g., undercooked food). Psychologically, the fatigue can lead to low moods and also a loss of sexual desire and low sociability. Social interactions become strained as well. The patient often feels embarrassed by not having any hair and may not want to be seen by other people or may be too tired to interact. Simultaneously, many visitors and friends feel uncomfortable at the sight of the hairless, fatigued patient. As with most chronic illnesses it is important for the patient's support networks to be prepared for and compensate for the effects of treatment.

Radiation Therapy

The third major form of treatment for cancer involves the use of radioactive particles aimed at the DNA of the cancer cells, a process referred to as **radiation therapy.** Radiation used for cancer treatment is called ionizing radiation because it forms ions as it passes through tissues and dislodges electrons from atoms. The ionization causes cell death or a genetic change in the cancerous cells (American Cancer Society, 2004). There are many different types of radiation treatments (e.g., electron beams, high-energy photons, protons, and neutrons), each sounding like something out of a science fiction movie and varying in intensity and energy. The process for getting radiation therapy is a little more complex than that for chemotherapy and surgery, although the preliminary stages are the same. Medical personnel first need to identify the location and size of the tumor and then pick the correct level of radiation. The key is to be able to do the most damage to the cancerous cells without damaging the normal cells. This is hard to do because the radiation stream cannot differentiate between types of cells, and normal cells often end up being affected as part of the process, resulting in side effects of treatment. The total dose of radiation, a rad, is often broken down into fractions, and delivered over several weeks. Radiation therapy is perhaps the most involved type of therapy, with treatments usually being given daily, 5 days a week, for 5 to 7 weeks (American Cancer Society, 2004). The main side effects are fatigue and irritation of the body areas close to the radiation site, often accompanied by some disruption of functioning. For example, radiation to the throat area can cause difficulty in swallowing and a redness of the neck and surrounding areas.

Other Treatments

In addition to these three main forms of treatment, there are also a variety of other possible ways to treat cancer. For example, **immunotherapy** involves the activation of the body's own immune system to fight the cancer. There are also a number of alternative and complementary therapies that help people cope with cancer (some of which are believed to keep cancer at bay as well). These include aromatherapy, music therapy, yoga, massage therapy, meditation to reduce stress, special diets (e.g., peppermint tea for nausea), and acupuncture.

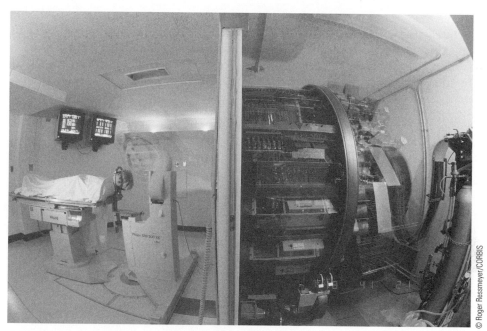

A Person Preparing to Undergo Radiation Therapy

There is growing public interest, especially among those living with cancer and/
or the relatives of people with cancer, in obtaining information about complementary and alternative medicine (CAM) (discussed in chapter 2) and methods of treatment. This interest is even more prevalent among individuals from
different cultural groups who may have approaches and beliefs about cancer
and its treatment that vary greatly from the view held by Western biomedicine.
Very often cancer patients do not tell their doctors that they are also trying
other treatments. Although there may be many treatments for cancer used by
other cultures that are actually beneficial, very few methods have been tested
by Western science and correspondingly North American health practitioners
recommend very few alternative methods.

The stance of Western biomedicine is reflected particularly well in how the
American Cancer Society refers to alternative and complementary medicine. The
American Cancer Society (2004) defines alternative methods as "unproved or
disproved methods, rather than evidence-based or proven methods to prevent,
diagnose, and treat cancer" and complementary methods as "those supportive
methods used to complement evidence-based treatment." The American Cancer
Society acknowledges that more research is needed to determine the safety and
effectiveness of many of these methods and advocates for peer-reviewed scientific
evidence of the safety and efficacy of these methods. Health care practitioners
recognize the need to balance access to alternative and complementary therapies
while protecting patients against methods that might be harmful to them. For ex-

ample, the American Cancer Society supports patients having access to CAM but strongly encourages more oversight and accountability by governmental, public, and private entities to protect the public from harm. Part of the problem arises from the fact that harmful drug interactions may occur and must be recognized. In addition, sometimes use of the other treatments causes delays in starting standard therapies and are detrimental to the success of cancer treatment.

Behavioral Interventions

The main way to reduce the death rates from cancer is to increase the practice of healthy behaviors and decrease other behavioral contributions to cancer risk (Hiatt & Rimer, 1999). The general approaches to improving common behaviors—reduce tobacco use, eat a nutritionally balanced meal, and get physical activity—have been covered in some detail in chapters 6 and 7. Although challenging, interventions to get people to change old habits, such as what they eat, are beginning to be successful (Kumanyika et al., 2000). Another major health behavior not covered in as much detail before is getting routine screenings.

Aiding Prevention: Increasing Screening Behaviors

One of the strongest contributions of health psychological research has been to increase health behaviors that will ensure the early detection of cancer. The most direct early detection behavior is **screening**, and a number of interventions have attempted to increase cancer screenings especially for breast, cervical, and colorectal cancer (Rimer, 1994; Snell & Buck, 1996). Early detection ensures that the cancer can be treated in an early stage, almost literally "being nipped in the bud." Screening can take two main forms: screening that needs help from professionals and medical equipment (e.g., mammograms), and screening that you can do at home (e.g., testicular or breast self-examinations). The American Cancer Society has a clear set of recommendations for when and how often a person should be screened/should check for cancer (Table 12.5). The big question here is: Even if you know how often you should get screened, will you do it?

The **Health Belief Model (HBM)** (Rosenstock, 1974, see chapter 6) has been the model used most often to guide interventions to increase screening behavior (Aiken, Gerend, & Jackson, 2001; Henderson & Baum, 2002). According to this model, the extent to which you see yourself as being susceptible to cancer, the extent to which you believe cancer to have severe consequences, the perceived barriers keeping you from getting screened, and the perceived benefits to getting screened all combine to predict your screening behavior. A number of interventions have included components especially designed to influence different parts of the HBM (e.g., Aiken, West, Woodward, Reno, & Reynolds, 1994). The Focus section at the end of this chapter gives you a concrete example of an intervention aimed at increasing screening.

The model works well. Even increasing people's knowledge about cancer severity and the benefits of screening increases the likelihood that people will get screened (DiPlacido, Zauber, & Redd, 1998). Factors that influence percep-

Screen for Life: National Colorectal Cancer Action Campaign. Centers for Disease Control and Prevention

A Campaign to Increase Screening for Colorectal Cancer Colorectal cancer is another cancer that can be successfully treated if it is detected early enough. This is one of the posters in a national campaign to increase screenings.

tions of susceptibility or risk are important as well (Cole, Bryant, McDermott, Sorrell, & Flynn, 1997). Factors related to and probably influencing susceptibility are linked to screening. People with a family history of breast cancer and those who had breast problems are more likely to get screened (McCaul, Branstetter, Schroeder, & Glasgow, 1996). Susceptibility is not as predictive of self-examinations (Miller et al., 1996). Having strong perceived barriers to screening are some of the strongest predictors of self-examinations (Wyper, 1990). Other significant barriers to getting screened are the costs of tests, the lack of health insurance, the lack of time, and an inconvenient test location (Friedman, Hall, & Harris, 1995; Maxwell, Bastani, & Warda, 1998; McPhee et al., 1997).

TABLE 12.5

Screening Guidelines for the Early Detection of Breast Cancer, American Cancer Society, 2005

- Yearly mammograms are recommended starting at age 40 and continuing for as long as a woman is in good health.
- A clinical breast examination should be part of a periodic health examination, about every 3 years for women in their 20s and 30s and every year for women 40 and older.
- Women should know how their breasts normally feel and report any breast changes promptly to their health care providers. Breast self-examination is an option for women starting in their 20s.
- Women at increased risk (e.g., family history, genetic tendency, and past breast cancer) should talk with their doctors about the benefits and limitations of starting mammography screening earlier, having additional tests (i.e., breast ultrasound and MRI), or having more frequent examinations.

Paradoxically, believing yourself to be extremely susceptible to cancer (e.g., taking a genetic test showing you have a mutated gene) or having a strong knowledge of severity and the fact that the disease could be fatal sometimes keeps people from getting screened (Sutton, Bickler, Sancho-Aldridge, & Saidi, 1994). The fear of actually finding something can keep people from even getting the test (Bastani, Marcus, & Hollatz-Brown, 1991). This problem is amplified in some cultural groups. Fatalism, discussed previously, among older, low-income Mexican American women is associated with lower Pap smear rates (a test for uterine cancer) (Suarez, Rouche, Nichols, & Simpson, 1997).

Cultural Differences in Screening

Cultural differences arise once more in the use of preventative measures for cancer. Low SES women are less likely to get mammograms (National Center for Health Statistics, 1997). Non-European American groups do not use routine screening tests as frequently as European American groups and, consequently, have more severe cancer at diagnosis (Gotay et al., 2001). Hiatt et al. (1996) collected some of the best detailed information on ethnic differences in screening from a study of 4,228 individuals in the San Francisco Bay area. Illustrative data from Hiatt et al. (1996) and from the National Center for Health Statistics at the CDC collected around the same time are shown in Table 12.6.

As you can see, there are significant differences between African Americans, Hispanics, European Americans, and Asian Americans. In terms of ever having a screening test for both breast and cervical cancer, Asian Americans reported significantly lower rates. Similar patterns can be seen for adherence to recommendations to get screening tests. Why is this the case? The main barriers to getting screened, described above, particularly affect low SES men and women across all ethnic groups (Hoffman-Goetz, Breen, & Meissner, 1998). For some

TABLE 12.6

Cultural Difference in Screening

Screening Test	African Americans	American Indians	Asian Americans	Latino	European American
Clinical breast examination	96		60	89	98
Mammogram	90		61	80	93
Pap test	98		56	76	99
Mammogram or Pap test in past 2 years	56	53	46	50	56
Pap test in past 3 years	84	73	66	74	76

Sources: Hiatt, R. A., Pasick, R. J., Perez-Stable, E. J., McPhee, S. J., Engelstad, L., Lee, M., et al. (1996). Pathways to early cancer detection in the multiethnic population of San Francisco Bay area. *Health Education Quarterly, 23* (Suppl.), S10–S27; Gotay, C. C., Muraoka, M. Y., & Holup, J. (2001). Cultural aspects of cancer prevention and control. *Handbook of Cultural Health Psychology,* 163–193.

cultural groups the embarrassment of having the test keeps them away. Asian American and Hispanic women, for example, are embarrassed when undergoing breast and cervical cancer screenings (Jennings, 1997; Maxwell et al., 1998). Cultural beliefs about modesty and who is allowed to see the naked body also have an influence. For members of many cultures it is inappropriate for an unknown member of the opposite sex, such as a doctor or nurse, to see the person's body (Galanti, 2004). Such issues are seen in the preferences of Vietnamese, Chinese, and Hispanic women to request service from a female physician (Galanti, 2004; Gotay et al., 2001).

The previously mentioned paradox between fear and screening (more fear of having cancer leads to avoiding the screening) has also been shown in both Hispanic and African American women (Friedman et al., 1995; Lobell, Bay, Rhoads, & Keske, 1998). In fact, the fear that the radiation from a mammogram is dangerous is higher among Asian and Hispanic women than among European American women (Dibble, Vanomi, & Miaskowski, 1997). African American and Hispanic women also report more fear of the pain associated with mammograms (Stein, Fox, & Murata, 1991). Finally, non-European American ethnic groups also report higher levels of incorrect knowledge about screening and cancer in general (Sung, Blumenthal, Coates, & Alema-Mensah, 1997; Yi, 1998). Some of this could be due to recent immigration-related issues, including a combination of inadequate English proficiency, acculturation problems, and potentially male-dominated family structures, which prevent some women from receiving community-based public health information (McPhee et al., 1996; Wismer et al., 1998; Yi, 1994).

Inhibiting Progression and Helping Patients Cope

Going beyond the prevention of cancer, another category of interventions has been designed to prolong life after diagnosis and to reduce patients' treatment anxiety (Anderson, 1992; Helgeson & Cohen, 1996; Meyer & Mark, 1995; Spiegel, 1996; Wallace, Priestman, Dunn, & Priestman, 1993). Social support again figures prominently (Helgeson et al., 1999). In the classic demonstration of the effectiveness of social support, Spiegel, Bloom, Kraemer, and Gottheil (1989) had women with breast cancer attend weekly supportive group therapy meetings. This group lived on average 36.6 months after the start of the intervention. In contrast, survival of the control patients who only received standard cancer care averaged 18.9 months. More recently, Fawzy et al. (1993) used a structured social support group to reduce distress and enhance the immune functioning in patients with newly diagnosed cancer. The group involved health education, illness-related problem solving, and relaxation, and members met weekly for 6 weeks. By 6 months, the intervention group showed lower levels of emotional distress, depression, confusion, and fatigue than the control group. Even their immune activity was higher. In general, such support groups are designed to promote the development of supportive relationships among group members and encourage expression of patients' feelings or disease-related anxieties (Henderson & Baum, 2002).

Other potentially useful psychological interventions involve relaxation training or hypnosis (Sims, 1987; Spiegel et al., 1989) although neither method has received solid empirical support. For example, although relaxation is often recommended for cancer-related pain (Millard, 1993) and has been found to be a useful tool in pain management in general (see chapter 9), a recent review found only two studies that used a controlled randomized design to directly examine the effectiveness of relaxation training (Redd & Jacobsen, 2001). Sloman, Brown, Aldana, and Chee (1994) used both progressive muscle relaxation and mental imagery to reduce patients' pain. Randomly assigned hospital patients were trained to relax by either a nurse or with the use of an audiotape. The intervention group reported significantly less pain and requested less pain medication. A similar study by Syrjala, Donaldson, Davis, Kippes, and Carr (1995) compared relaxation training with cognitive-behavioral coping training and found that both methods worked.

Keeping cultural differences in beliefs about cancer in mind, some interventions build on cultural values to change health behaviors that could cause cancer. For example, Lichtenstein and Lopez (1999) developed a program to reduce smoking in American Indian tribes in the Northwest by using American Indian staff to ensure the target population that the intervention was at least partly Indian-owned. Distinctions were made between social uses of tobacco and ritualistic uses and tribal representatives were closely involved in the process of developing American Indian–specific materials on smoking cessation.

In general, a number of psychosocial interventions have shown promise for alleviating the pain and discomfort of cancer. When used in conjunction with medications, these interventions can help in making life bearable and even enjoyable for the patient with cancer.

FOCUS ON APPLICATIONS

Increasing Cancer Screening

A number of adages support the importance of early intervention for cancer. There is truth to the adages, "A stitch in time saves nine," "An ounce of prevention is worth a truckload of cure," and so on. Many chronic illnesses take a long time to develop and are not always detectable in their early stages. That said, as described earlier in this chapter, cancer is a disease that can be cured if it is caught early enough. Consequently, one of the most common clinical applications of health psychological theory is in the design of interventions to increase health screening behaviors (Aiken et al., 2001). Interventions provide a wonderful window to look at theory in action. Let's take a close look at one intervention in particular to give you a better sense of the problem and a feel for how interventions are done.

A prototypical example of a screening intervention is one conducted by Leona Aiken and colleagues (Aiken et al., 1994). Their main goal was to increase mammography screening rates in accordance with American Cancer Society guidelines (i.e., women should have a baseline mammogram between 35 and 39 years of age and then have a mammogram every year or two and yearly after age 50). There have been a lot of very public debates about these recommendations and about the effectiveness of screening in general. Health experts agree that women in their 50s should get mammograms. The debate centers on whether the tests reduce the risk of breast cancer for women in their 40s. Another factor is that mammograms can sometimes be inaccurate: nearly 1 in 4 women who regularly have a mammogram will have at least one false-positive result (Christiansen et al., 2000), but the benefits do seem to outweigh the costs.

Breast cancer has received some of the highest levels of funding of all cancer research, and, consequently, the majority of cancer research in the field of health psychology involves studies on the incidence and progression of this disease. Breast cancer is a malignant tumor that starts from cells of the breast. The breast itself is made up of lobules, ducts, fatty and connective tissue, blood vessels, and lymph vessels. When breast cancer cells reach the underarm lymph nodes and continue to grow, they cause the nodes to swell. Once cancer cells have reached these nodes they are more likely to spread to other organs of the body as well. There are several types of breast tumors. Most are abnormal benign growths. Some lumps are not really tumors at all. These lumps are often caused by the formation of scar tissue and are also benign. To detect the growth of cancers as early as possible, women in their 20s and 30s should have a clinical breast examination (CBE) as part of a regular physical examination by a health expert preferably every 3 years (American Cancer Society, 2004). Women are also urged to conduct regular breast self-examinations (BSE) to also detect abnormalities in changes. Unfortunately, growths have to be relatively large to be felt by BSEs or even CBEs. Mammograms, on the other hand, can detect extremely small particles in the breast and, consequently, it is important for women to go get screened.

The theory used by Aiken et al. (1994) was the HBM (see chapter 6). They designed an intervention that targeted each of the four components of the HBM: perceived susceptibility, severity, benefits, and barriers.

The sample comprised 295 primarily middle-class European American women. The authors sent out letters of invitation to 253 female support groups around the state of Arizona asking them if they would like to participate in a study. Forty-four groups replied. Each volunteer was given a pretest (before the intervention) and an assessment right after the intervention and was also contacted 3 months later during the time when actual compliance was measured. At each assessment, the women's intention to get a screening and questions based on the model were used (e.g., What prevents you from getting a mammogram? [barriers] or How susceptible do you think you are to getting breast cancer? [vulnerability]).

There were three experimental groups. One group received an educational program. This group was given information about prevalence rates of breast cancer and its risk factors to increase perceived susceptibility. The pathological course of the disease and survival rates were described to increase severity, and the advantages of early screening were described to increase perceived benefits. To decrease barriers, the authors stressed the minimal nature of the risks (women feared the radiation from the mammography machine could be dangerous) and low costs and presented a slide show of the procedure so it was clear what exactly was done.

The second experimental group received the educational program plus psychological training. The women were presented with counterarguments against mammography, actors modeled the process with a role-play, provided action steps for women to take (gave them the addresses and phone numbers of where to go to get a mammogram), made the women commit to calling and making an appointment by signing a form, and then mailed the women copies of the signed form and action steps 2 weeks later. The control group only completed the preintervention questionnaire.

What was the result? Not surprisingly, two to three times more women in the intervention groups went to get screened than women in the control group. In assessing the exact reasons behind the increase in compliance, Aiken et al. (1994) conducted a mediational analysis (a statistical procedure that illustrates links between chains of variables and tests for mediation; see chapter 5). Essentially they asked whether the HBM variables (susceptibility, severity, benefits, and barriers) served to mediate the connection between the intervention and the change in behavior (West & Aiken, 1997). In keeping with the predictions of the HBM model, strong mediational pathways were found between perceived susceptibility and perceived benefits to intentions, and there was a strong link between intentions to get screened and actually going in for a screening. Aiken et al. (1994) also found that perceived susceptibility played a substantial role in predicting behavior. In fact, the authors found that perceived susceptibility played both an indirect role in influencing behavior (intervention → susceptibility → benefits → intentions) and a direct role as well (intervention → susceptibility → intentions).

Such psychological interventions nicely demonstrate the effectiveness of health psychological research and the role it plays in health behavior change and the prevention of illness.

Chapter Summary

- Cancer is the second leading cause of death, and the chances of being diagnosed with cancer increase with age. Cancer is the name given to a category of illnesses in which the main problem is the presence of a malignant tumor. Cancer cells form because of cell mutations in DNA caused by exposure to environmental toxins and unhealthy behaviors such as smoking.

- Tumors vary in where they are found, can be malignant or benign, and can vary in severity. The four main types of cancer are carcinomas (starting in surface layers of the body), sarcomas (in muscles, bones, or cartilage), lymphomas (in the lymphatic system), and leukemias (in the blood or bone marrow).

- There are large differences in the cultural makeup of people who have cancer. Both incidence rates and mortality rates vary across cultures. African Americans have the highest general cancer rates. Men experience higher incidences of cancer than women. These cultural differences also extend to beliefs and knowledge about cancer.

- Cancer can be considered a developmental disease because the chances of getting it increase as you age, and health behaviors at different stages of development may put one more at risk for having cancer.

- Psychological factors play a part in both the incidence of cancer and in responding to diagnosis although the effects are stronger for the latter. Personality traits such as optimism, the presence of social support, and finding meaning in the illness are all associated with coping with cancer and its progression.

- The key health behaviors associated with a higher incidence of cancer are tobacco use, poor diets, and a lack of physical activity. Sun exposure and the use of tanning beds also are associated with cancer incidence.

- The main treatments for cancer are surgery, chemotherapy, radiation therapy, and immunotherapy. A number of alternative and complementary therapies such as yoga, massage, meditation, and acupuncture are also being used to help patients cope with cancer.

- Health psychologists aid in the prevention of cancer by designing behavioral interventions to increase screening behaviors. There are a number of cultural differences in screening behaviors with low socioeconomic status individuals being the most likely to not get screened consistent with American Cancer Society guidelines. There are also significant differences in screening behaviors among African Americans, Latinos, European Americans, and Asian Americans.

- Some interventions are designed to inhibit the progression of cancer and help patients cope.

Synthesize, Evaluate, Apply

- What are the benefits and problems with celebrities going public to talk about their cancers?
- What can be done to demystify "cancer"?
- How can coming from a different cultural background influence your risk of getting cancer?
- How are different cultural beliefs and knowledge levels about cancer related to broader sociocultural differences (e.g., cross-cultural approaches to health)?
- Why should cancer be conceptualized as a "developmental disease"? How can this concept change how it is studied and treatments for it?
- What personality characteristics interact with health behaviors to influence risk of cancer?
- How are the biopsychosocial pathways and associations for cancer incidence different from those for the progression of cancer?
- Evaluate the benefits and problems with benefit finding. At what stage do you think this process can be most helpful? When can it hurt and why?
- Health behaviors play a large role in putting someone at risk for cancer. How does each behavior interact with the others?
- Map out how each behavior can synergistically influence a person's biology, psychology, and sociocultural background.
- What factors should go into the choice of a treatment?
- How would you design an intervention to reduce risks for cancer?
- Pick a health behavior change model and use it to increase screening behaviors.
- What can be done to reduce the delay between identification of cancer symptoms and going in to a doctor?

KEY TERMS, CONCEPTS, AND PEOPLE

benefit finding, 361
benign, 352
carcinogens, 352
carcinomas, 353
chemotherapy, 369
curative surgery, 369
debulking surgery, 369
diagnostic surgery, 369
fatalism, 356
Health Belief Model (HBM), 372

immunotherapy, 370
incidence, 354
leukemias, 354
lymphomas, 353
malignant, 352
mastectomy, 369
metastasize, 352
neoplasms, 351
palliative surgery, 369
preventative surgery, 369
radiation therapy, 370

restorative surgery, 369
sarcomas, 353
screening, 372
Spiegel, David, 376
staging surgery, 369
TNM system, 354
Type C personality, 359
ultraviolet (UV) rays, 367

ESSENTIAL READINGS

Anderson, B. L., Kiecolt-Glaser, J., & Glaser, R. (1994). A biobehavioral model of cancer stress and disease course. *American Psychologist, 49,* 389–404.

Meyerwitz, B. E., Richardson, J., Hudson, S., & Leedham, B. (1998). Ethnicity and cancer outcomes: Behavioral and psychosocial considerations. *Psychological Bulletin, 123,* 47–70.

Persky, V. W., Kempthorne-Rawson, J., & Shekelle, R. B. (1987). Personality and risk of cancer: 20-year follow-up of the Western Electric study. *Psychosomatic Medicine, 49,* 435–449.

Spiegel, D., Sephton, S. E., Terr, A. I., & Stites, D. P. (1998). Effects of psychosocial treatment in prolonged survival may be mediated by neuroimmune pathways. *Annals of New York Academy of Science, 840,* 674–683.

WEB RESOURCES

Visit the companion website at **http://psychology.wadsworth.com/gurung1e/,** where you will find online resources for this book, including chapter-by-chapter quizzes, weblinks, and more! You can also visit Wadsworth Psychology Resource Center at **http://psychology.wadsworth.com** to access additional resources.

The American Cancer Society
www.cancer.org

Culture and Cardiovascular Disease

"Quick! Call 911. I think Pat is having a heart attack!" Try to picture the scene. You have probably seen enough movies to imagine what this scenario must look like: a person writhing in agony on the floor, chest clutched between sweaty fingers. Horrified onlookers debate the best course of action. Maybe the person was eating at a restaurant and in a terrified wave of panic has swept the cutlery off the table. Bits of broken china and half-eaten food are strewn over the floor. People are standing with jaws gaping. Someone or some people are screaming. You get the idea. Now for the key question. What does Pat look like in your scene? I can bet that in your mind's eye, you see Pat as an old or middle-aged White man, probably someone's grandfather or uncle named "Patrick". Heart problems are often expected of older men, but this stereotype is not accurate. In fact not only are heart-related diseases more common in older women than older men (yes, it was probably Patricia), but heart-related diseases are also the third most common cause of death for children younger than age 15. Yes, Pat could be a young boy or an older woman having a heart problem. But that's not all. Heart attacks are not always as dramatic as the scenario described here either.

In this chapter I will get to the "heart" of the matter (pun almost unavoidable). I will describe the class of diseases that affect the heart and circulatory system and then review the main biopsychosocial determinants as well as the factors that alleviate the illness. The core causes of most of the cardiovascular diseases (CVDs) are very similar. To make the discussion easier, I will focus on the most common CVDs, namely coronary heart disease, stroke, and hypertension (Figure 13.1). I will also highlight the many cultural factors that influence the effects and progression of this set of diseases.

Prevalence of Cardiovascular Diseases

Heart problems and those related to the circulatory system are the leading causes of death not only in North America (Figure 13.2), but also all around the world. Problems due to this set of diseases do vary from country to country (Anand & Yusuf, 1998), and there is no underplaying of the magnitude of the problem. One-fifth of all deaths in developing countries such as India and Mexico and 40% of all deaths in developed countries such as the United States, Britain, and Canada are attributable to heart diseases (Murray & Lopez, 1997). The number of deaths from CVDs for men and women is shown in Figure 13.3.

One of the biggest catalysts to our understanding of heart disease is a longitudinal study that is unique is size, scope, and impact. Much of what is discussed in this chapter and what is known about heart disease comes from or is aided by a monumental study started in the late 1940s. More than 50 years ago, the town of Framingham, MA, was selected by the U.S. Public Health Service as the site of a large-scale study to understand why heart disease had become North America's

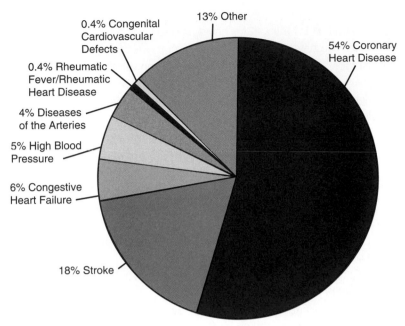

FIGURE 13.1
Percentage Breakdown of Deaths from Cardiovascular Diseases in the United States in 2001
SOURCE: *Third National Health and Nutrition Examination Survey (1988–1994).*

number one killer. A total of more than 5,000 healthy residents between 30 and 60 years of age, both men and women, were enrolled as the first cohort of participants. Every 2 to 4 years, study participants are given extensive medical examinations including a medical history, blood tests, and other tests of current health status. The **Framingham study** was the first in which a relationship was established between levels of cholesterol and high blood pressure and the risk for disease (Apel at al., 1997), and the researchers also found that a lifestyle typified by a bad diet, sedentary living, smoking, and unrestrained weight gain accelerated the occurrence of cardiovascular problems. Let's take a closer look at these often fatal diseases.

Diseases resulting from problems with the heart and the circulatory system are all gathered under the general heading of **cardiovascular disease** or CVD. The most common are coronary heart disease (CHD) (also referred to as coronary artery disease [CAD]) and heart failure (both commonly referred to as heart attacks), strokes, and hypertension or high blood pressure (medically referred to as essential hypertension). Others include abnormal heart rhythms, congenital heart disease, heart valve failure, heart muscle disease (cardiomyopathy), rheumatic fever, pulmonary heart disease, cerebrovascular disease, and diseases of the veins, arteries, and lymph nodes (the last three collectively are called vascular diseases). To get a better feel for how CVDs develop, let's first take a look at some of the basic biology involved. A good place to start is with the circulatory system (illustrated in Figure 13.4).

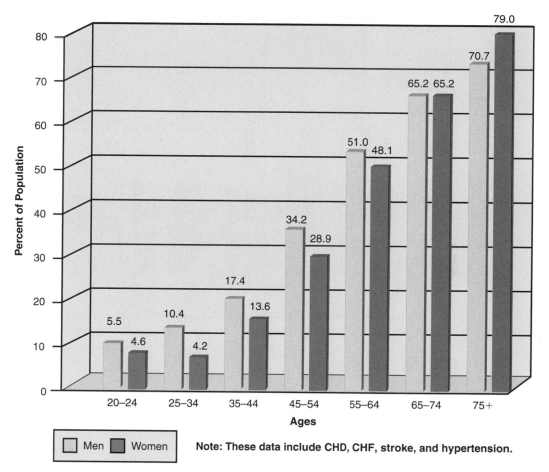

FIGURE 13.2
Prevalence of Coronary Heart Diseases in the General Population and Broken Down by Sex and Age
Source: *Third National Health and Nutrition Examination Survey (1988–1994).*

The Circulatory System

Some History

The circulatory system had many people guessing for centuries. Today we understand the mechanisms that provide every cell in our body with life-giving oxygen, but this was not always the case. At first, it was believed that life was maintained not so much by the constituents of blood, but by a vital spirit or *pneuma*. The Greek Empedocles of Agrigentum who lived around 500 to 430 B.C. was the first to postulate that the heart was the center of the circulatory system although he believed it to be the seat of life-giving pneuma. This pneumatic theory held a long time. Later Greeks added to our knowledge of circulation, but pneumaticism still

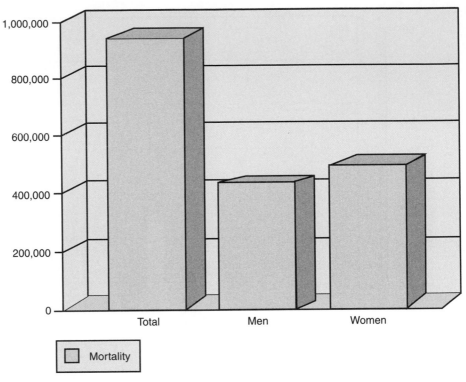

FIGURE 13.3
Mortality from Coronary Heart Diseases in the General Population and Broken Down by Sex (2003)
SOURCE: *Centers for Disease Control and Prevention/National Center for Health Statistics (2005).*

reigned. For example, Erasistratus (around 300 B.C.) identified the role played by veins and arteries and even traced them down to the limits of his vision, to the fine branches that later came to called capillaries. The greatest early contributor to our understanding was Galen (around 150 B.C.; see chapters 1 and 2) who through his animal dissections clarified the functions of the arteries and veins. His only mistake, apart from also accepting the pneumatic theory, was in believing the heart was a form of heater that warmed the blood instead of recognizing it as a pump. He believed blood flowed because of the pulsing of the arteries and moved back and forth like the tides (not in a circular fashion). It was not until the work of English physician William Harvey in 1628 that we got a complete understanding of the circulatory system. The Italian Marcello Malphighi discovered capillaries in 1689, the only component that Harvey could not see but had correctly hypothesized about.

Circulatory System

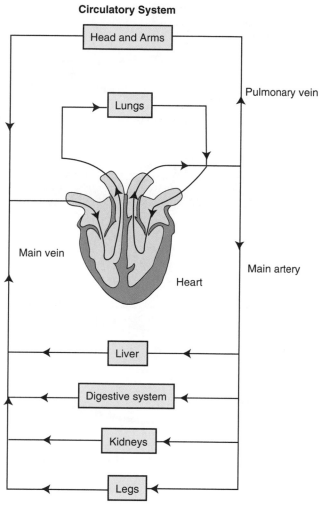

FIGURE 13.4
The Circulatory System

Key Components

The circulatory system is so named because the blood flows in a circle (from the Latin, *circus*—the next time the circus is in town notice that it plays in the middle of a big circle as well). The heart, arteries, veins, and capillaries are the key components of the system.

The human heart with its muscular myocardium walls is about the size of a clenched fist, sits just beneath our breastbone, and is protected by a fibrous sac called the pericardium. The heart has two main halves (see Figure 13.4). The

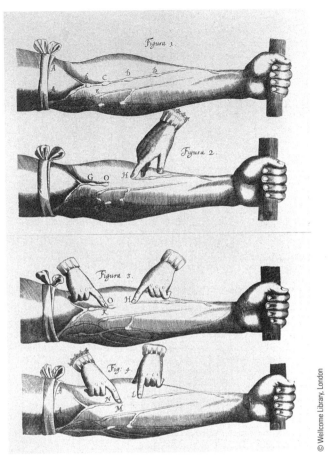

© Wellcome Library, London

Illustration of William Harvey's Experiments in His *On the Circulation of the Blood* (1628) Venal valves had already been discovered, but here Harvey shows that venal blood flows only toward the heart. He put a ligature on an arm to make the veins and their valves obvious and then pressed blood away from the heart and showed that the vein would remain empty because it was blocked by the valve.

right half receives blood low in oxygen from all over the body and pumps it to the lungs. The left half receives blood rich in oxygen from the lungs and pumps it back all over the body. Each half of the heart is further divided into two chambers. The upper and thinner-walled chambers on each side are called the **atria;** the lower, thicker-walled chambers on each side are called **ventricles.**

Blood vessels that carry blood away from the heart are called arteries, and the vessels that carry blood to the heart are called veins. Two large veins, the superior (from the upper parts of the body) and the inferior (from the lower parts of the body) venae cavae, carry deoxygenated blood into the heart. A large artery carries oxygenated blood to the rest of the body. Two other vessels carry blood between the heart and the lungs. The **pulmonary artery** carries deoxygenated blood from the

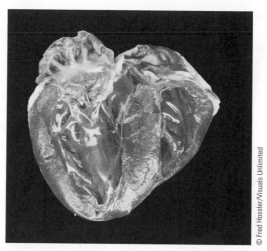

A Real Mammalian Heart (Pig) Notice the thick muscular lining of the walls. These muscles contract and expand to pump blood.

heart to the lungs, and the **pulmonary vein** carries blood from the lungs to the heart. What keeps everything separate? Its valves. A system of valves ensures that the blood flows in one direction only (a nice idea that would work great to keep backwash to a minimum when one is sipping from a can or bottle). Each valve consists of flaps of connective tissue and the actual sound of a heart beat is the sound of the valves closing. The first "buh" is when the valves between the atria and ventricles close. The second "bub" is when the valves between the ventricles and the arteries shut. The heart, the valves, and its main vessels and chambers are shown in Figure 13.5.

The Mechanics of Circulation

As Harvey first clearly showed, humans have what is called double circuit circulation. Deoxygenated blood from all over the body flows into the heart, from where it is pumped to the lungs. In the lungs the carbon dioxide in the blood is removed and oxygen flows into the blood in the tissues and air sacs of the lungs. The blood then flows back to the heart and is pumped to the rest of the body. The circuit between the heart and the lungs is called pulmonary circulation (pulmo is Latin for "lung"). The circuit around the rest of the body is called systemic circulation. As the arteries leave the heart they get narrower and branch out many times into smaller vessels called arterioles. They then narrow into even finer vessels called **capillaries.** Veins similarly branch into smaller vessels, called venules, and into even smaller vessels also called capillaries. Is this the same word? Yes, it is, and the same location too: because the blood vessels all form one giant circle, they must meet someplace, and that place is the capillaries. Like a neighborhood recycling center where metal cans are turned in and the material is reused, oxygen slips out of the capillaries and into the surrounding cells and tissues, and carbon dioxide and other cell wastes slip in. The blood then moves from the capillaries into the veins and back to the heart to be rejuvenated.

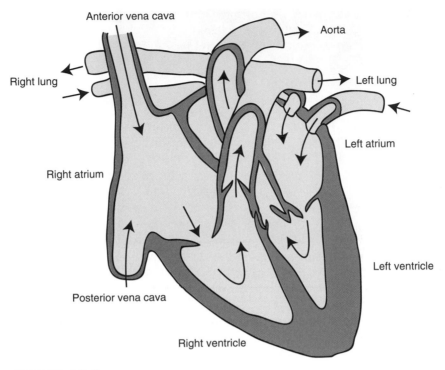

FIGURE 13.5
The Mammalian Heart The arrows describe the pathways of blood into the heart, to and from the lungs, and then back out to the rest of the body.

The main function of the heart is to help put oxygen into the blood and to push the blood around the body to the places where it is needed. When the heart beats, it pumps blood to the arteries. Because the diameters of the vessels near the heart are much larger than the diameters of the arteries that the blood is being pumped into, there is pressure in the arteries. The arteries also influence this blood pressure as they resist the blood flow. Healthy arteries are muscular and elastic. They stretch when your heart pumps blood through them, with more stretching being produced by stronger pumping. The pressure rises with each beat and falls in between beats as the heart muscles relax. The actual process of pumping is a two-stage process consisting of a cycle of contractions by different parts of the heart. In the first stage the atria contract and the ventricles relax. In the second stage the reverse takes place.

The heart beats between 55 and 85 times per minute when you are at rest, but the rate of beating can change dramatically with each different move. Break into a run, and the rate will increase to get oxygen to the organs and muscles that need it. Take a nap, and it will slow down. It can even change from minute to minute, depending on what you are thinking. If you are watching a movie and a scary bit comes on, your heart will speed up (or even skip the proverbial beat, which really reflects an irregular beat and not really missing one). Blood pressure is described using two numbers, the **systolic** pressure when the heart is beating and the **diastolic** pressure when the heart is resting and is measured in millimeters of mercury (mm Hg) (the height in mm of Hg that that pressure could support). A healthy adult's blood pressure should be less than 120/80 mm Hg.

A Biological Primer

You may have noticed that medical journals tend to be filled with a lot of big words. Those of you in premedical programs or in medical school or those working toward degrees in occupational or physical therapy have probably already had your encounters with medical terminology (it pays to know some Latin, doesn't it?). If you are truly term phobic then skip the next paragraph (and lose the chance to impress your friends with your erudition and M.D.-like medical know-how).

In discussing CVDs and reading the medical literature you will probably encounter many technical terms that you need to be familiar with. Chest pain, a common symptom of heart attacks or **myocardial infarctions** (or cardiac arrest/ CHD/CAD), is referred to in medical circles as **angina pectoris**. The myocardium is the medical term for the muscle of the heart. You may also read about **ischemia,** a term for the condition in which blood flow is limited in a certain part of the body. Heart attacks are also sometimes referred to as myocardial ischemias, although more specifically, heart attacks result from ischemias to the cardiac region. Many millions of Americans have ischemias without even knowing it; these are referred to as silent ischemias. Because silent ischemias are not accompanied by angina, individuals who have them may also have a heart attack without warning (American Heart Association, 2004).

Cultural Variations in the Incidence of Cardiovascular Disease

Whenever you see cultural differences in a phenomenon, they can be due to many factors. As with other chronic illnesses, there are some significant cultural differences in the incidence of CVDs. As shown in Figure 13.6, American Indians show the lowest numbers of deaths due to CVD followed by Asian Americans and Latinos and then by African and European Americans who do not show large differences. For strokes, all the different ethnic groups have a significantly higher risk for stroke than European Americans. The differences in incidence are often due to differences in the levels of health behaviors and risk factors among different cultural groups. They can also be due to the psychological experiences of different groups that relate to CVD (Baker, Richter, & Anand, 2001). For example, hostility, anger, and social support, each of which plays a key role in the development of CVD, also vary across cultures and map onto larger cultural dimensions (see chapter 1).

Anger and other components of the Type A personality such as competitiveness and time urgency are closely tied to the individualistic/collectivistic dimension of culture. People in individualistic cultures are more competitive, and competition is actually seen as a desirable trait. Those in collectivistic cultures are more cooperative, and competition against members of one's group is often frowned

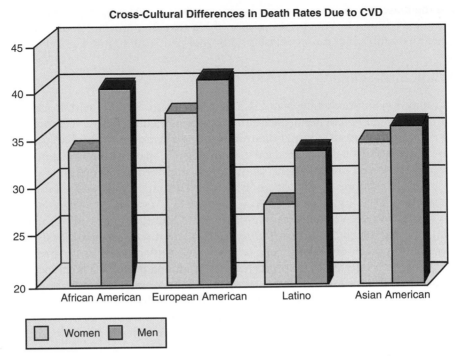

FIGURE 13.6
Cross-Cultural Differences in Death Rates Due to Cardiovascular Disease (Percentage)
Source: *American Heart Association, 2004.*

on. Social support, similarly, is seen more in collectivistic cultures (Sagrestano et al., 1999). Time orientation varies with another cultural dimension: **fluid versus fixed time.** In most cultures in North America, time is fixed in that when you say you will meet someone at 10:00 A.M., you mean exactly that. In fluid-time cultures such as those in India and also among American Indians, meeting someone at 10:00 really means you will show up anywhere between 10:15 and 10:30. This is understood and expected, and no one is frustrated when someone is late. In fact, in many East Indian American communities people set appointments and specify whether they mean an exact time or Indian Standard Time (I.S.T.). Accelerated blood pressure due to time constraints is generally less common in such cultures, and the stress of being late accordingly is different as well.

Two other cultural dimensions can also influence CVD. In the **control versus constraint** dimension (Trompenaars, 1997), some cultures believe that they have absolute control of their outcomes (similar to having an internal locus of control). People in constraint cultures believe everything is in the hands of God or is fate. Those in control cultures may have higher levels of anxiety and stress and correspondingly have more risk for heart problems (Baker et al., 2001). Similarly, the level of emotionality may make a difference as well. **Neutral cultures** such as that of Japan do not sanction the open display of emotions. **Affect cultures** such as that of Italy in contrast place a premium on the display of emotions. Not expressing emotions could also lead to higher levels of CVD.

Developmental Issues in Cardiovascular Disease

As we age we have a greater risk for developing CVDs. A large part of this risk is due to wear and tear on our arteries and the accumulation of plaque that increases with time, but this risk also has psychosocial correlates. As discussed in chapter 3, humans go through different stages of physical, social, and cognitive development. Erikson, for example, hypothesized that we progress through eight different stages, and each has its challenges and milestones. The life changes that accompany social development can serve as stressors that in turn can lead to higher risks for CVDs. Some milestones include puberty, graduation from high school or college, a first job, and perhaps losing a first job. Even relationships, dating, and marriage can be important correlates of CVDs. Satisfying relationships can provide social support, and acrimonious relationships or divorces could raise blood pressure and otherwise negatively impact health. Important negative life events corresponding to developmental stages increase in frequency in the months before a heart attack (Welin et al., 1992). Although heart disease has been studied more extensively in men, studies of women also show that heart disease patients experience a significantly larger number of negative life changes, many of them related to family life (Orth-Gomer, Chesney, & Wegner, 1998).

Beyond developmentally related life events, it is also important to factor in development and take a lifespan approach to CVD because one of the main psychosocial correlates of CVD, social support, changes over time. Younger women with poor social networks have higher levels of heart problems (Orth-Gomer & Johnson, 1987). Surprisingly, older retired women with more extensive social networks also had a higher incidence of cardiac problems. The additional networks for older women could have come with more mental burdens. To understand conflicting data such as these it is important to look at how social support changes over the lifespan (see chapter 5 and Gurung, Taylor, & Seeman, 2003).

Physiological Correlates of Cardiovascular Disease

The primary physiological antecedent for the incidence of CVDs is **atherosclerosis,** the accumulation of fatty substances in the blood vessels (American Heart Association, 2004; Krantz & Lundgren, 1998). Microscopic accumulations of fats within artery walls progress to visible fatty streaks as early as childhood (Strong et al., 1999). This accumulation of fat, often in the form of plaque, reduces and sometimes blocks the arteries supplying blood to the heart. The plaque buildup can get so great as to tear the artery, creating a "snag" in which a blood clot can form to block the artery. Lesions are sometimes observed in adolescents and become increasingly common with age. This interference to blood flow to the heart is what causes heart attacks. A related condition is the hardening of the arteries, or **arteriosclerosis,** in which the arteries lose their elasticity and are more susceptible to blockages from clots or plaques.

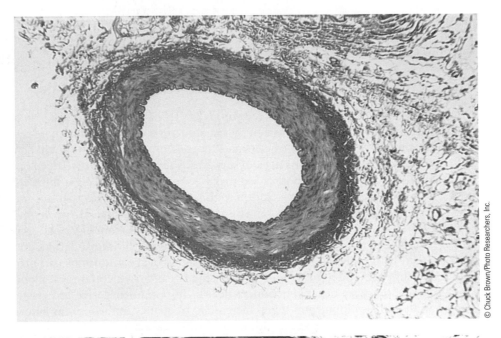

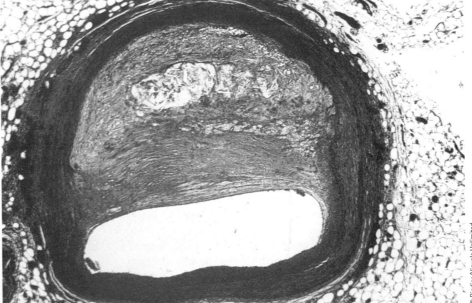

Cross-Sections of Human Arteries The artery on the top is normal (clear wide opening). The artery on the bottom has a much smaller bore due to the accumulation of plaque (atherosclerosis).

Some of the main physiological risk factors cannot be changed: age, sex, and family history. The risk for having a CVD increases as a person gets older, and men younger than 50 are more likely to develop a problem. At around 50 years of age, corresponding to when women reach menopause (see chapter 3), they have a greater risk for CVDs than men. It is also clear that having a parent or relative with a CVD greatly increases the incidence rates of CVDs (Nicolosi & Schaefer, 1992). Other physiological factors predicting the incidences of CVDs are high blood pressure, diabetes, high cholesterol level, inactivity, and overweight or obesity (Ockene, Kristeller, Goldberg, & Ockene, 1992). Men with diabetes, for example, are twice as likely to develop CVD whereas women with diabetes are up to 7 times as likely to develop CVD (American Diabetic Association, 2004). As you can see this second group can all be modified depending on a person's health behaviors (more on this later).

Another important issue in the modifiable physiological risk factors is the fact that different cultural groups vary in their genetic predispositions. Some ethnic groups are more prone to high blood pressure. Some groups are more prone to be overweight. These underlying differences in risk factors could explain cultural differences in CVD. For example, laboratory studies measuring participants' cardiovascular reactivity to different stressors have found that African Americans show higher blood pressure and epinephrine responses to tasks compared with European American participants (Mills, Berry, Dimsdale, & Neleson, 1993). **Cardiovascular reactivity,** changes in heart rate and blood pressure in response to stress, varies greatly between individuals and is a key physiological risk factor for the development of CVD (Rozanski, Blumenthal, & Kaplan, 1999).

As discussed previously (chapter 6) there are also significant ethnic and geographical differences in obesity, tobacco use, diet, and activity levels.

Psychological Correlates of Cardiovascular Disease

There is strong evidence for a link between psychological characteristics and the development of CVDs (Orth-Gomer, Rosengren, & Wilhelmsen, 1993), making this set of diseases a prime candidate for use of the biopsychosocial approach of health psychology. Of all the chronic diseases, CVDs are perhaps most illustrative of the importance of focusing on psychological factors together with biological factors. Psychological factors, such as personality traits (e.g., hostility), anger, depression, social support, and stress, and health behaviors, such as dietary habits and physical activity, have all been intrinsically tied to the incidence and progression of CVDs (Krantz & Manuck, 1984; Suchday, Tucker, & Krantz, 2002).

Perhaps the best-known controversy in regard to the psychological causes of heart attacks revolves around a constellation of personality characteristics called the Type A personality (see chapter 3). Friedman and Rosenman (1974) noted that heart patients who showed a sense of time urgency (always doing more than one thing at the same time), competitiveness, and hostility in their interactions with other people were found to have a higher risk for CHD. In contrast, the Type B personality is relaxed, patient, and easygoing. The original finding that was greeted with much hoopla did not stand up to further examination (Shekelle et al.,

1985), although to this day a number of people still believe that having a Type A personality, in general, is not a good thing. What seems more accurate is that being *hostile* is the problem (Scherwitz, Graham, & Ornish, 1985; Williams, 1987). Hostility and anger are negative emotions that can trigger a heart attack and even sudden death among individuals who are at risk (Muller, 1999; Willich, 1995). For example, in a study of patients at risk, Mittleman et al. (1995) found that anger episodes occurred within 2 hours before the beginning of the heart attack.

Other negative emotions play a role in cardiac arrest too. Feeling sad and depressed may also increase your likelihood of heart problems and the progression of CVD (Hance, Carney, Freedland, & Skala, 1996). Anda et al. (1993) studied the relationship of both depressed affect and hopelessness to CHD incidence using data from a large cohort of 2,832 North American adults. The participants had no history of CHD or serious illness at baseline. Anda et al. (1993) found that people who were depressed were significantly more likely to have a fatal heart attack (relative risk 1.5). Depression was also associated with an increased risk of nonfatal heart attacks. In other studies of survivors of heart attacks, depression was found to be related to increased mortality in the 6-month period after the first heart attack (Frasure-Smith, Lesperance, & Talajic, 1995). Similarly, feeling hopeless, an emotion often accompanying depression, can independently predict the incidence of CVD as well (Everson, Goldberg, Kaplan, & Cohen, 1996).

A variety of different types of social supports also relate to CVD (Berkman, 1995; Seeman & Syme, 1987; Shumaker & Cjakowski, 1994), and social support is often a moderating factor (Orth-Gomer et al., 1993). Social support could influence the development of CVD by buffering the person from the effects of stress (the moderator role), consequently safeguarding the person from the deleterious effects that stress has on the circulatory system (Krantz & Lundgren, 1998). Supportive networks also ensure that a person is more likely to get help and to comply with doctor's orders. If a man is at risk for a heart attack and he is not supposed to eat fatty foods, smoke, or drink too much, a supportive partner and good friends are likely to make sure that he does not. In support of this link, studies of unmarried patients without close confidants showed them to be more likely to die over a 5-year period (Case, Moss, Case, McDermott, & Eberly, 1992).

In a recent study of the power of social support, Sundquist, Lindstrom, Malmstrom, Johansson, and Sundquist (2004) examined whether low social participation predicted incidence rates of CHD. They followed 6,861 Swedish women and men for almost 10 years and found that persons with low social participation (as measured by an interview) had the highest risk of CHD. They were more than twice as likely (relative risk 2.15) to have another heart attack than those with high social participation. This increased risk remained even after controls were added for education and smoking habits (Sundquist et al., 2004).

Not having enough social support is often related to not having enough resources in general and is strongly linked to socioeconomic status (SES). Especially in developing countries, SES is negatively correlated with the risk of CVD (Adler et al., 1994; Kaplan & Keil, 1993). In a much cited study of the relationship between socioeconomic status and CVD, Marmot et al. (1991) studied British civil servants in the Whitehall part of London (hence their research is referred to as the Whitehall Studies). They showed that higher rates of CVD were seen in men of lower employment grade. At every rung of the bureaucratic ladder, men in the lower positions were worse off.

Stress

You may have heard of the television show *Sex and the City,* but have you considered that a show might be called *Stress and the City*? Studies in different cultures have shown that the stress from living in an urban environment can make you nine times more likely to develop CVD compared with living in a rural area (Gupta, Gupta, Jakovcic, & Zak, 1996). A little stress can go a long way. Not only does being stressed influence your health behaviors (as described in chapter 7), but it also increases your likelihood of developing a number of diseases. In chapter 4 I described how our body's reactions to short-term physical stressors are thought to have evolved to get us out of danger. You should also remember that these same responses, when activated for a long period of time (chronic stress), can begin to break down the body's systems (e.g., allostatic load). Cardiovascular problems are some of the most common ways that the body breaks down.

Superficially, the relationship is pretty intuitive. What happens when we get stressed? At the physiological core of the response, the catecholamines and cortisol pumped into the bloodstream increase blood flow, thus raising blood pressure. The heart is pumping faster, and blood is shunting around the body faster. There are also changes in how we metabolize food for energy (details in chapter 4). This constellation of factors that accompany the experience and process of stress take a toll on the circulatory system and aid in the incidence of CVD. A sizeable body of research documents how various stressors, particularly those at work, accentuate CVD via effects on blood pressure (Brisson et al., 1999). Together with the work front, environmental stress (especially that caused by low SES) and stress from interpersonal relationships at home have also been associated with the incidence of CVD.

Acute stress (e.g., a person's being the victim of an assault or having to deliver a very difficult presentation) can also trigger heart problems if the individual already is at risk because of atherosclerosis (Gottdiener et al., 1994; Muller, Tofler, & Stone, 1989). Early work showed that catastrophic events such as earthquakes and the death of a spouse could also initiate a heart attack (Cottington, Matthews, Talbott, & Kuller, 1980; Muller et al., 1989; Meisel et al., 1991). After the big Northridge earthquake outside Los Angeles, CA, in 1994, a significant increase in heart attacks was seen compared with the incidence in the previous week (Kloner, Leor, Poole, & Perritt, 1997).

The work-stress and CVD relationship has garnered the most research attention (Schnall, Landsbergis, & Baker, 1994; Smith & Ruiz, 2002; Theorell & Harenstam, 2000). We can all acknowledge the fact that working can be stressful. Even if you enjoy your job, having to work can still challenge the body. The stress from work can be even more dangerous if you are overworked, have too many roles to fulfill, are not clear what your job role is, are bored with your job, or do not have support at work (see chapter 4). No matter what the exact cause, work stress can accentuate the chances of developing CVD. Even job status is important. For example, Wamala, Mittleman, Horsten, Schenck-Gustafsson, & Orth-

Gomer (2000) used data from the Stockholm Female Coronary Risk Study, a population-based case-control study comprising 292 women with CHD aged 65 years or younger and 292 age-matched healthy women, and found that unskilled women had 4 times the risk for CHD compared with the executive/professional women. Simultaneous adjustment for traditional risk factors and job stress lowered this risk to 2.45. Similar findings are found for men (Schnall et al., 1994).

There are also some interesting cultural differences in the work-stress relationship. Higher job strain was a major explanation for why Lithuanian men had 4 times the risk for CVD than Swedish men (Kristensen et al., 1998). In Japan, there is even a term for "death from overwork" (Nishiyama & Johnson, 1997).

Researchers have only recently begun to look at the interaction of work stress and home stress. Orth-Gomer et al. (2000) followed women for an average of 5 years after hospitalization in one of the first studies to look at the longitudinal effects of marital stress and work stress in women patients. They found that stressful experiences from marital relationships may seriously affect prognosis in women with CHD, whereas living alone without a partner had no effect.

Health Behaviors and Cardiovascular Disease

Tobacco Use

The number one behavior to avoid if you want to minimize your risk for cardiovascular diseases is smoking. You can see why we spent so much time on this topic before (see chapter 7). Together with being an important risk factor for other chronic diseases such as cancer (see chapter 12), cigarette smoking has also been identified as an important factor in the development of CVD (Woodward, Oliphant, Lowe, & Tunstall-Pedoe, 2003). In one of the clearest demonstrations of this link, Doll, Peto, Boreham, and Sutherland (2004) followed approximately 35,000 British doctors from 1951 to 2001 and found that the dangers of smoking varied with cohorts. Men born in 1900 through 1930 who smoked only cigarettes and continued smoking, died on average about 10 years sooner than lifelong nonsmokers. Quitting was a good thing regardless of the age at which it was attempted. Men who quit when 60, 50, 40, or 30 years of age gained, respectively, about 3, 6, 9, or 10 years of life expectancy (Doll et al., 2004). The risk of CVD is almost 3 times as high for smokers as it is for nonsmokers, and the risk for smokers is higher if they are younger (Baker et al., 2001).

People around the world smoke. Smoking is more common in some cultures than in others, and the link between CVD and smoking is not the same across cultures. For example, although there are relatively high rates of smoking in countries such as Japan and China, CVD mortality and morbidity are not proportionally as high (WHO, 2000). In other countries, high levels of other unhealthy behaviors also accompany high smoking rates. Europeans tend to smoke more than do Americans in general and also consume diets higher in saturated fats (Baker et al., 2001). Recent attention has turned to the presence of risk factors that accentuate the effect of smoking, and some of the most important are dietary factors and cholesterol.

Dietary Recommendations to Minimize CVD
• Eat a variety of fruits and vegetables. Choose 5 or more servings per day.
• Eat a variety of grain products, including whole grains. Choose 6 or more servings per day.
• Include fat-free and low-fat milk products, fish, legumes (beans), skinless poultry, and lean meats.
• Choose fats and oils with 2 grams or less saturated fat per tablespoon, such as liquid and tub margarines, canola oil, and olive oil.
• Balance the number of calories you eat with the number you use each day. (To find that number multiply the number of pounds you weigh now by 15 calories. This represents the average number of calories used in one day if you're moderately active. If you get very little exercise, multiply your weight by 13 instead of 15. Less-active people burn fewer calories.)
• Maintain a level of physical activity that keeps you fit and matches the number of calories you eat. Walk or do other activities for at least 30 minutes on most days. To lose weight, do enough activity to use up more calories than you eat every day.
• Limit your intake of foods high in calories or low in nutrition, including foods like soft drinks and candy that have a lot of sugars.
• Limit foods high in saturated fat, trans fat, and/or cholesterol, such as full-fat milk products, fatty meats, tropical oils, partially hydrogenated vegetable oils, and egg yolks. Instead choose foods low in saturated fat, trans fat, and cholesterol from the first four points above.
• Eat less than 6 grams of salt (sodium chloride) per day (2,400 milligrams of sodium).
• Have no more than one alcoholic drink per day if you're a woman and no more than two if you're a man. "One drink" means it has no more than 1/2 ounce of pure alcohol. Examples of one drink are 12 oz. of beer, 4 oz. of wine, 1–1/2 oz. of 80-proof spirits or 1 oz. of 100-proof spirits.

FIGURE 13.7
Dietary Recommendations to Minimize Cardiovascular Disease
Source: American Heart Association (2005).

Diet

Your food choices play a large role in your overall health and well-being. What you eat determines the levels of nutrients available for your cells and ensures the smooth and healthy functioning of your bodily symptoms. There are many dietary factors that influence the incidence and progression of CVD (Figure 13.7), and diet is a factor that affects the interaction between culture, psychology, and behavior. Your diet can influence your cholesterol level, your blood pressure, your tolerance for glucose (and consequently your risk for diabetes), your likelihood to be overweight, and even how your blood coagulates. Each of these factors is associated with the development of CVD (Kesteloot, Sasaki, Xie, & Joossens, 1994).

One of the most important risk factors for CVD is cholesterol level. Cholesterol is found in most animal products and is an important component of cell walls and membranes. It is also a main component of plaque. As discussed in chapter 7, we have high-density lipoprotein and low-density lipoprotein (HDL) and LDL cholesterol), and if you want to prevent heart disease you need to keep your total cholesterol level below 200 milligrams per deciliter (American Heart Association, 2004). As the level of cholesterol in the blood increases, the risk of CVD increases as well (Ballantyne, 2004; Dean, Borenstein, Henning, Knight, & Merz, 2004). LDLs seem to be the primary factor and a number of treatments (e.g., statins) aim to reduce the LDL levels in the bloodstream. A high cholesterol level is even more likely to cause CVD in people with other health issues such as diabetes (Tanasescu, Cho, Manson, & Hu, 2004). One other major risk factor is a diet high in saturated fat.

Diets including fish (Whelton, He, Whelton, & Munter, 2004) and high levels of whole grains and fiber (Singh et al., 2002) are particularly good for you. In a recent intervention, Singh et al. recruited 1,000 patients with angina pectoris and myocardial infarctions and had half of them eat a diet rich in whole grains, fruits, vegetables, walnuts, and almonds (referred to as an **Indo-Mediterranean diet**). The control group ate a diet suggested by the National Cholesterol Education Program (NCEP). Interestingly, the intervention group had fewer heart problems, including heart attacks (both fatal and nonfatal) and showed lower cholesterol levels than the control group. The Indo-Mediterranean diet is one of the protective factors of culture: people in and from the southern part of Europe who follow it show lower incidence of CVD (Trichopolou & Lagiou, 1997).

A related cultural diet component is alcohol. For example, the French have relatively low levels of CVD even though French food is known to be rich in saturated fats. This "French paradox" (see chapter 7) has been linked to moderate consumption of alcohol. One or two glasses of wine per day seem to reduce the incidence of CVD (Rimm & Ellison, 1995).

Physical Activity

In terms of physical activity, not only is exercising useful in reducing the risks of CVD, but being physically inactive actually increases the risks. In this respect, standing still actually makes you slide backward on the continuum of health. For example, Yeager, Anda, Macera, Donehoo, and Eaker (1995) found a strong association between CHD mortality rates and the prevalence of a sedentary lifestyle that remained significant even after controls were added for the prevalence of diagnosed hypertension, smoking, and overweight.

A key component of treatment and many behavioral interventions to reduce CVD hence includes some form of physical activity. Taylor, Lerner, Sage, Lehman, and Seeman (2004) presented a recent review of the effectiveness of exercise-based cardiac rehabilitation in patients with CHD. Their study included 48 trials with a total of 8,940 patients and found that compared with control subjects, exercise was associated with both fewer deaths from all causes and from heart attacks. Patients who exercised also showed greater reductions in total cholesterol level, systolic blood pressure, and smoking. In a specific example, Blumenthal et al. (2004) examined the link between physical exercise and CVD mortality and morbidity among 2,078 heart attack patients who were participating in the Enhancing Recovery in Coronary Heart Disease (ENRICHD) multicenter clinical trial. Patients reporting regular exercise had less than half the events of those patients who reported no regular exercise. The most commonly recommended form of exercise is cardiovascular training, especially walking and increasing movement (American Cancer Society, 2005).

Hypertension and Stroke

Although the bulk of this chapter has focused on CVDs as a category and coronary heart/artery disease more specifically, two closely related conditions and subtypes of CVD bear some individual attention as well.

Hypertension or high blood pressure is a condition in which the blood pressure remains chronically elevated. Blood pressure that stays between 120 and 139/80 and 89 mm Hg is considered prehypertension and blood pressure above this level (140/90 mm Hg or higher) is considered hypertension. Hypertension increases the risk for heart attack and stroke. The two most common risk factors for hypertension beyond age and family history are too much salt in the diet and obesity. Hypertension shows strong cultural differences and is found at a higher rate in African Americans (Ng-Mak, 1999). Some evidence suggests an intriguing sociobiological reason. Gleiberman, Harburg, Frone, Russell, and Cooper (1995) showed that high blood pressure is positively correlated to dark skin color, which could induce more discrimination (i.e., because of being darker skinned) as a genetic marker of some sort.

Stroke is the third leading cause of death in the United States behind CHD and cancer and is the leading cause of disability among adults. About 550,000 people have strokes each year, and 150,000 of them die of the strokes within a year. Stroke is a type of CVD that affects the arteries leading to and within the

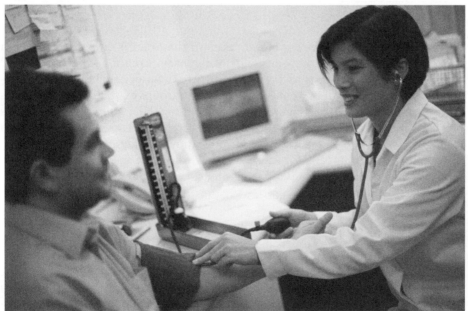

Measurement of Blood Pressure High blood pressure is one of the easiest ways to detect a risk for heart problems and is associated with obesity, bad diets, and not enough physical activity.

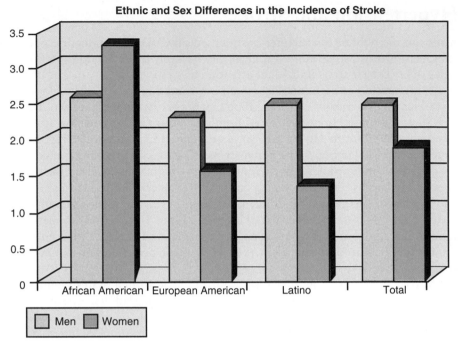

FIGURE 13.8
Ethnic and Sex Differences in the Incidence of Stroke (Percentage)

brain. A stroke occurs when a blood vessel to the brain is either blocked by a clot or bursts. When that happens, part of the brain cannot get the blood (and oxygen) it needs, so it starts to die (American Stroke Association, 2004). Men experience more strokes than women, and all ethnic groups experience more strokes than European Americans (Figure 13.8). Similar to CHD, a lower risk of stroke has been related to the intake of fruits and vegetables (Hak et al., 2004). In an analysis of data from the Physicians' Health Study, a study of 22,071 U.S. male physicians, Hak et al. (2004) found that men who were in the bottom fifth for intake of antioxidants (such as alpha-carotene, beta-carotene, and lycopene) had the highest risk of stroke.

Treatment Options

The specific treatment for CVD is determined by the severity of the symptoms, the size and quantity of areas with ischemias (reduced blood flow), how well the left ventricle of the heart is pumping, and other medical factors such as severity of chest pain (American Heart Association, 2004). As you can tell from the previous sections, unhealthy lifestyles (e.g., bad eating habits and not getting enough physical activity) are key determinants of whether or not you will develop a CVD. Correspondingly, changing health behaviors is one of the most critical treatment options to prevent the development of symptoms, relieve the symptoms, and lower the risk of heart attack and death. The primary goal will be to change unhealthy behaviors. The patient is normally admitted to a **cardiac rehabilitation program.** Rehabilitation programs educate patients on the best way to change their lifestyles and use a combination of physical activity and social support to improve their overall functioning and prevent death (Dafoe & Huston, 1997; Dusseldorp, van Elderen, Maes, Meulman, & Kraaij, 1999). If the person smokes, a smoking cessation program will be prescribed. He or she will also receive consultations on how to change diet, reduce salt intake, and eat more nutritionally balanced meals. If excessive drinking or not enough physical activity is the issue, it is critical to tackle each of these problems. Patients may even be told to start taking aspirin. Aspirin, you say? That's right, not just any headache or pain killer, but aspirin. Many studies have shown that aspirin reduces the risk of heart attack in people with known CHD (Hayden, Pignone, Phillips, & Mulrow, 2002). In fact, for people at increased risk for CHD, studies have shown that aspirin therapy reduced the risk by 28%, although there are some risks associated with taking aspirin (Hayden et al., 2002). Major risks of aspirin therapy include bleeding inside the brain or gastrointestinal tract, and this treatment is not recommended for individuals with a low risk for CVD. It may be necessary to help restore the blood flow to the affected parts of the heart if the ischemias are serious or the disease continues to worsen despite measures to slow it down (sometimes because the person continues the unhealthy behaviors). In patients with critical conditions surgery is often needed.

Surgery

There are two main forms of invasive surgery to deal with blockages: angioplasty and cardiac bypass surgery. **Angioplasty** is a procedure done to open a partially blocked blood vessel so that blood can flow through it more easily (Figure 13.9). It is most often done on arteries that deliver blood to the heart (coronary arteries) when they are narrowed by atherosclerosis. The procedure involves the insertion of a thin, flexible tube (catheter) through an artery in the groin or arm, which is carefully guided into the artery that is narrowed. This is not a comfortable procedure. Once the tube reaches the narrowed artery, a small balloon at the end of the tube is inflated. The balloon may remain inflated from 20 seconds to 3 minutes. The pressure from the inflated balloon pushes the plaque against the wall of the artery opening up the passageway to improve blood flow. Once the fat and calcium buildup is compressed, a small, expandable wire tube called a stent is sometimes inserted into the artery to keep it open.

Another way to deal with the blockage is to just go around it. If you are driving to work, and you hear that there is a traffic jam ahead, you may take an alternative route. In the circulatory system there are few alternative routes for blood to take, so medical personnel create one. Cardiac bypass surgery involves taking a blood vessel from elsewhere in the body (usually the chest or leg) and using it to redirect blood flow around a severely blocked artery. Blood is redirected through the new blood vessel, bypassing the blocked artery and restoring blood flow to the affected portion of the heart muscle.

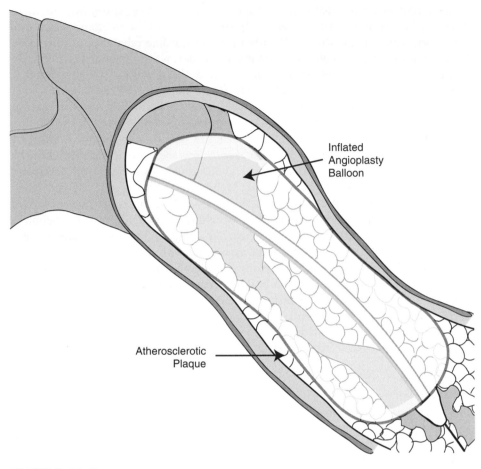

FIGURE 13.9
Balloon Angioplasty

Behavioral Interventions

Most health psychological behavioral interventions for CVD take the form of cardiac rehabilitation programs. These programs are hard to assess because they have many different components. If there is a change in risk, a decrease in mortality, or an increase in quality of life, any one of the components could have caused it (or even an interaction of several components). That said, meta-analytical studies have shown that rehabilitation programs in general have accounted for reductions in mortality compared with that for control groups (Fletcher, 1996). Programs building physical activity have been particularly effective (O'Conner et al., 1989).

Given the number of psychological factors involved in CVD, a number of interventions to reduce stress and negative emotions have also been tried, and the news is good (Linden, Stossel, & Maurice, 1996; Rozanski et al., 1999). Linden et al. (1996) reviewed studies that collectively evaluated 2,024 patients who received psychosocial treatment versus 1,156 control subjects and found that the psychosocially treated patients showed greater reductions in psychological distress, systolic blood pressure, heart rate, and cholesterol level. Patients who did not receive psychosocial treatment were more likely to die earlier and had heart attacks reoccur during the first 2 years of follow-up. The most common interventions attempted to modify personal characteristics such as hostility, stress, and social support.

One of the earliest and most ambitious such interventions was conducted by Friedman et al. (1986). They observed 1,013 heart patients for $4\frac{1}{2}$ years to determine whether their Type A behaviors could be altered. There were three experimental groups: a control section of 270 patients received group cardiac counseling, an experimental section of 592 patients received both group cardiac counseling and Type A behavioral counseling, and 151 patients served as a comparison group. The results were startling. At the end of the study, 35.1% of participants given cardiac and Type A behavior counseling reduced their Type A behavior compared with 9.8% of participants given only cardiac counseling, and the heart attack recurrence rate was only 12.9%. The recurrence rate in the control group was 21.2%, and the comparison group fared worse (recurrence rate of 28.2%). There was also a significant difference in the number of cardiac deaths between the experimental and control participants, clearly showing that altering Type A behavior reduces cardiac morbidity and mortality (Friedman et al., 1986). Given that the critical component of Type A behavior is hostility, you should expect that interventions designed specifically to reduce hostility should work even better, and you're right (Friedman et al. 1996).

Interventions to improve stress management and increase social support also reduce the effects of CVD (Blumenthal et al., 2002a). Blumenthal et al. (2002b) examined the effects of exercise and stress management training over a 5-year follow-up period in 94 male patients with established CVD. Patients either exercised (3 times per week) or partook in a $1\frac{1}{2}$ hour weekly class on stress management. Blumenthal et al. (2002b) found that stress management was associated with a significant reduction in heart attack episodes over each of the first 2 years of follow-up and after 5 years. The stress management was even significantly cheaper than the exercise program.

FOCUS on Applications

The Lifestyle Heart Trial

For many years the first twangs of heart pains, evidence of atherosclerosis, and the eventual heart attack signified the end of life. The prognosis was bad, and life would never be the same for the many thousand men and women who discovered that they had heart disease. Medical research had come up with ways to ease the pain and prolong life, but CHD was mostly seen to be a dead end street—you venture down it and you will not be returning. Health psychologists helped engineer a number of interventions to help, for example, the Ischemic Heart Disease Life Stress Monitoring Program (Frasure-Smith & Prince, 1987) and the Recurrent

Coronary Prevention Program (Friedman et al., 1986), but these were primarily designed to increase social support and decrease the stress of patients with CHD. Alleviation of suffering is a good thing, but could CHD actually be reversed? Dean Ornish surprised the health community by showing that it could.

Ornish et al. (1998) conducted one of the first multiple component interventions designed to change peoples' behaviors to reverse heart disease. Patients with CHD are especially susceptible to the effects of bad eating and insufficient exercise. If you can get people who have CHD to change these behaviors, will the physiological disease change as well? To test this, Ornish et al. randomly sampled 48 patients with moderate to severe CHD and randomly assigned them to one of two groups.

The 24 patients in the experimental group, an intensive lifestyle change group, were given special prescriptions of how to change their behaviors. As the name of the group implies, membership in this group was no walk in the park (although walks in the park were involved). This experimental group was told to severely restrict how much meat they ate and switch to an essentially vegetarian diet. They were not to eat more than 10% of fat (in contrast to the Atkins diet you may have heard a lot about that was discussed in chapter 7). The rest of the diet was divided into 12% to 20% proteins and 70% to 75% carbohydrates, predominantly complex. All caffeine-containing beverages were eliminated, and alcohol consumption was discouraged. No animal products were allowed in the vegetarian diet except egg white and 1 cup per day of nonfat milk or yogurt. Patients were also told to stop smoking (if they were smokers) and were helped with smoking cessation. Physical activity also had to be increased, and they were given a program of moderate levels of aerobic exercise to do. Each patient was told to exercise at least 5 times a week for a total of 5 hours. They could either walk or jog.

Together with these important health behaviors (nonsmoking, eating well, and getting physical activity), the Ornish program also aimed to reduce stress levels. I have talked about how emotional stress plays an important role in just about all illnesses. In CHD, stress makes arteries constrict and increases blood clot speed, both of which cause heart attacks. To make matters worse, stressed people are more likely to smoke, overeat, drink too much, and overwork hard. The Lifestyle trial included yoga exercises (primarily stretching), relaxation techniques involving breathing, meditation and mental imagery training, and social support groups. Patients in the control group were not asked to make lifestyle changes other than those recommended by their cardiologists (often similar though not in magnitude and not backed up by trained professionals with follow-ups).

The results were astounding. After 1 year, patients in the experimental group showed a significant overall reduction of coronary atherosclerosis as measured by x-rays of heart blood vessels injected with radioactive chemicals (coronary angiography). The arteries went from being 40.0% blocked (stenosis) to 37.8% in the experimental group, but blockages increased from 42.7% to 46.1% in the control group. Overall, 82% of experimental patients experienced reduced blockages. The experimental group was able to make and maintain the lifestyle changes and also showed a 37% reduction in low-density lipoprotein level and a 91% reduction in cardiac problems. The control group showed a 165% increase in cardiac problems. Given that the control group was not doing as well, you would be right in wondering if it was ethical for the experiment to continue. The researchers did not explicitly address this, but one can assume that time period was a critical component in the intervention.

Was this a fluke? As good scientists should, Ornish et al. extended the study to confirm the findings and see if they persisted. One concern was that the lifestyle change was too drastic and would be difficult to maintain. Skip ahead 4 years. When assessing the health and behaviors of the original sample 5 years from the start of the original study, Ornish et al. (1998) found there was even more reduction and continued improvement. In the experimental group, the average percent diameter stenosis was 7.9% relative improvement after 5 years. In contrast, the average percent diameter stenosis in the control group was 27.7% relative worsening after 5 years. Twenty-five cardiac events occurred in the experimental group versus 45 events in the control group during the 5-year follow-up. Even better, the people in the lifestyle change group showed better results than the people in the control group who were taking fat-lowering medications (none of the experimental group was taking any).

Similar positive effects of lifestyle change have also been shown in the Nurses' Health Study that followed 85,941 healthy women from 1980 to 1994. The women who did not smoke, were a healthy weight, ate well, and got sufficient physical activity had an 83% less risk of a heart attack (Stampfer et al., 2000). Other studies also varied dietary intake or increased exercise with similar results.

It is undoubtedly difficult to live a healthy life, and it definitely takes a lot of willpower and help to keep to a healthy regimen such as the one prescribed by the Lifestyle Heart Trial, but the results are clear. Not only can healthy behaviors keep heart disease from worsening, but can actually reverse it as well. Given that some people may not be able to tolerate lipid-lowering drugs, the fact that participants in this study showed improvement without the drugs is extremely important. It may be that the extremely rigorous levels of change are not needed, but why take a chance on your health? Be well aware of your behaviors and don't forget how many different benefits eating well, not smoking, and being physically active can have.

This is a wonderful example of how health behaviors can be changed to reverse heart disease, but there are a few caveats. It can be argued that these findings cannot easily be generalized to the population at large because the participants of Ornish et al. were highly motivated and compliant, both important attributes for a demanding intervention. Nevertheless, the point they make is clear: What you do with your lifestyle will determine how long you will live.

Chapter Summary

- Cardiovascular diseases result from problems with the heart and the circulatory system. The most common are coronary heart disease or cardiovascular disease (CVD), heart failure, strokes, and high blood pressure or hypertension. Others include abnormal heart rhythms, pulmonary heart disease, and diseases of veins, arteries, and lymph nodes.

- The heart is made up of four chambers, two atria, and two ventricles. Arteries carry oxygenated blood away from the heart and veins carry deoxygenated blood to the heart. Blood pressure is described as systolic and diastolic pressure for when the heart is beating and resting, respectively.
- American Indians show the lowest instances of deaths due to coronary heart disease followed by Asian Americans and Latinos. In contrast, all non-European ethnic groups have a higher risk for strokes. Anger, competitiveness, and time urgency are some of the main psychological differences among ethnic groups that could account for the differences in CVD.
- The accumulation of wear and tear on the circulatory system as we age accounts for significant developmental differences in the incidence of CVD. Social support networks also change as we age although the exact relationship is still unclear.
- The accumulation of fatty substances in the blood vessels and the thickening of the arteries are the most common precursors to CVD. The main physiological risk factors are age, sex, family history, obesity, diabetes, hypertension, high cholesterol levels, and inactivity. The main psychological predictors of CVD are stress, hostility, negative emotions, depression, and low social support.
- Changing unhealthy lifestyles is critical to preventing and treating CVD. Patients normally join cardiac rehabilitation programs to reduce stress and improve health behaviors such as quitting smoking, increasing physical activity, and eating better. Patients with severe CVD may need surgery, ranging from angioplasty to open blocked blood vessels to cardiac bypass surgery in which blood flow is redirected around blocked areas.
- Behavioral interventions such as the program of Dean Ornish and colleagues and those conducted by Friedman and colleagues demonstrate that CVD is reversible.

Synthesize, Evaluate, Apply

- What psychosocial factors explain why heart diseases are one of the biggest health issues in the twenty-first century?
- Evaluate the pros and cons of basing a lot of information on studies such as the Framingham study. What concerns with the study do you have?
- Trace the connections between different health behaviors and different heart diseases.
- How can the different cultural variations that you have been exposed to in other chapters also explain differences in the incidence and progression of cardiovascular diseases?
- Each culture has factors that make people less or more likely to get CVD. Can you think of some examples from your own culture?
- What are the main cross-cultural similarities in risk for heart disease? Is one major factor to blame?
- How can the different ways we cope with stress influence our risk for CVD?

- Identify the personality characteristics that will interact heavily with societal and cultural factors.
- Design your optimal intervention to reduce risk for CVD.
- Using what you know of the causes and types of stress, which forms of stress do you think best explain CVD and which theory of stress would be most useful for this?
- How would you make people more aware of the risks of smoking, bad eating, and not exercising in relation to CVD?
- Use the Health Belief Model and the transtheoretical model to design an intervention to reduce risks for CVD.
- What specific areas of research do you think are most needed in the context of CVD?

KEY TERMS, CONCEPTS, AND PEOPLE

affect cultures, 393
angina pectoris, 391
angioplasty, 403
arteriosclerosis, 393
atherosclerosis, 393
atria, 388
capillaries, 389
cardiac rehabilitation
 program, 403
cardiovascular disease, 384

cardiovascular reactivity, 395
control versus constraint, 392
diastolic, 391
fluid versus fixed time, 392
Framingham study, 384
hypertension, 401
Indo-Mediterranean diet, 400
ischemia, 391
Lifestyle Heart Trial, 405

myocardial infarctions, 391
neutral cultures, 392
Ornish, Dean, 406
pulmonary artery, 388
pulmonary vein, 389
stroke, 401
systolic, 390
ventricles, 388

ESSENTIAL READINGS

Baker, B., Richter, A., & Anand, S. S. (2001). From the heartland: Culture, psychological factors, and coronary heart disease. In S. S. Kazarian & D. R. Evans (Eds.). *Handbook of cultural health psychology* (pp. 141–162). San Diego, CA: Academic Press.

Linden, W., Stossel, C., & Maurice, J. (1996). Psychosocial interventions for patients with coronary artery disease: A meta-analysis. *Archives of Internal Medicine, 156*(7), 745–752.

Ornish, D., Scherwitz, L. W., Billings, J. H., Gould, K. L., Merritt, T. A., Sparler, S., et al. (1998). Intensive lifestyle changes for reversal of coronary heart disease. *Journal of the American Medical Association, 280*(23), 2001–2007.

Smith, T. W., & Ruiz, J. M. (2002). Psychosocial influences on the development and course of coronary heart disease: Current status and implications for research and practice. *Journal of Consulting & Clinical Psychology, 70*(3), 548–568.

WEB RESOURCES

Visit the companion website at **http://psychology.wadsworth.com/gurung1e/,** where you will find online resources for this book, including chapter-by-chapter quizzes, weblinks, and more! You can also visit Wadsworth Psychology Resource Center at **http://psychology.wadsworth.com** to access additional resources.

American Heart Association
www.americanheart.org

American Stroke Association
www.strokeassociation.org

The Future of Health Psychology

Y ou may have heard people say, "don't miss the forest for the trees," referring to how we often miss the big picture when we focus too much on the small details. I trust that by this point of the book, you have a very good sense of the many species of "trees" there are in the "forest" that is health psychology. This is a good time to step back and look at some of the bigger issues. We can actually take the forest analogy a long way. The field of health psychology is so vibrant, exciting, and sometimes wild (there are areas that still need a lot of cultivation), an invitation to learn more about it is akin to saying "welcome to the jungle." Like a forest, some areas of health psychology, such as stress and coping, are the old oaks that have been studied for many years. Other areas such as psychoneuroimmunology are the young saplings, new and still growing. Different parts of the forest can be used for many different purposes: the basic research in health psychology can be applied in many different ways and translated into interventions and programs that can be life saving as well as increasing the quality of life. There are also areas of the forest that are enjoyable to be in, the research findings that help us understand complex psychosocial issues and alleviate the pain and suffering of those with chronic illnesses. Some parts of the forest are dark and uninviting, the areas of health psychology that are rife with ethical concerns and difficult implications such as genetic testing and the design of some interventions or suggestions for policy change that may be perceived as compromising individual freedoms. There are also many areas of the forest yet to be discovered. What's next for the field of health psychology? What are the opportunities available for you as a health psychologist? What do you do next?

Looking to the Future

Health psychology has come a long way. In chapter 1 I sketched the history of health psychology and the different organizations that cater to people using the health psychological approach. The Division of Health Psychology (**Division 38**) of the American Psychological Association (APA) recently celebrated 25 years of existence. The Society for Behavioral Medicine and the American Psychosomatic Society are even older (founded in 1978 and 1942, respectively). Times are changing, and the awareness of the role of psychology in health and well-being has become explicit and prominent. Even the APA recently modified its mission statement to include the advancement of psychology as a "means for promoting health, education, and human welfare" (APA, 2004).

You know an area of study has come a long way when there are published articles and special conferences designed to take stock of the field and set the agenda for its future growth. This has been the case for health psychology. In 2000, Wallston and Kiecolt-Glaser, the past President and President of Division 38, presided over a conference to examine the state of the field. The proceedings of the conference resulted in many researchers taking a critical look at what health psychologists have achieved and what critical issues needed to be addressed. The results of this directed focus was a special issue of *Health Psychology* (Smith &

Suls, 2004). Not too long ago, the *Journal of Consulting and Clinical Psychology* (Smith, Kendall, & Keefe, 2002) published a special issue on behavioral medicine and clinical health psychology that also gives us a good sense of what the important issues for the field are. Let's take a look at some of these.

A Greater Focus on Sociocultural Issues

This book was written with the explicit goal of increasing awareness of sociocultural issues. In looking back over the different chapters you may have noticed that some chapters included a lot more "culture" in them than others. You may have thought I had swayed off course in the chapters without too much culture, but that's not so. The shortage of information on culture in some areas mirrors a sad lack of information of cultural differences in some areas of health psychology (Keefe, Buffington, Studts, & Ramble, 2002). To be fair, cultural research is not always easy to do and there are many barriers. Often language barriers necessitate the hiring of translators or bilingual researchers. English questionnaires have to be translated into the different languages and then translated back into English to establish reliability and validity. Many non-White ethnic groups are wary of White researchers and non-Christian individuals are often hesitant to share spiritual or folk medicinal practices. An examination of articles and books in the field show that *culture* and *health psychology* have not been common key words (Kazarian & Evans, 2001), and even reviews of *Health Psychology* (the journal) have shown a limited number of articles on culture and health (Landrine & Klonoff, 1992; Klonoff & Landrine, 2001), although the numbers are increasing.

One of the most pressing needs for health psychology is to spend more time and energy on examining how cultural differences influence health and behavior. A number of health psychologists have drawn attention to this problem (Kazarian & Evans, 2001; Landrine & Klonoff, 2001; Smith & Suls, 2004; Yali & Revenson, 2004). Many groups in addition to Division 38 are recognizing the need for a greater focus on culture. In 1995 a special issue of the *Journal of Behavioral Medicine* included the recommendations of the eight task groups of the National Conference on Behavioral and Sociocultural Perspectives on Ethnicity and Health that called for "future research, research funding and research training relevant to sociocultural and behavioral perspectives on ethnicity and health" (Anderson, 1995, p. 649). Similarly, Krantz (1995), in an editorial for *Health Psychology,* strongly encouraged the inclusion of women and minority groups in research.

Why has there not been enough cultural research? The limited focus on cultural differences arises from a number of different factors. One reason is that the majority of theories used by health psychologists were developed within other areas of psychology (Marks, 1996). Mainstream psychology has tended to be blind to culture, not so much because of some explicit prejudice (although it has been argued that the primarily European American male researchers were biased) (Guthrie, 2003), but because of the belief that there are commonalities to human behavior that transcend culture. Early health psychological research also strove for depth versus breath, something necessary for a new field to establish itself (Kazarian & Evans, 2001). Furthermore, the field has had a tendency to focus on individuals out of context. Conceivably a function of the individualistic bias of mainstream psychology, health psychology has only recently begun to consider the theoretical implications of a focus on the collective context, the family, peers, community, and culture, of the individual.

In a move toward a greater focus on culture, certain key problems need to be avoided. There appears to be a considerable amount of ambiguity surrounding the use of race and ethnicity in health research (Kazarian & Evans, 2001). For example, Williams (1995) identified 10 different terms used to refer to the concept of ethnicity (e.g., color, race or origin, racial and ethnic minority groups, and minority status). Race and ethnicity are often used interchangeably (see chapter 1 for why this is a problem). Many different cultural groups are often subsumed under single categories with little recognition of inherent differences (Phinney, 1996). For example, there are many different Asian Americans and Japanese Americans and East Indian Americans who will not necessarily behave in the same way or have the same beliefs regarding health (see chapter 2).

Other problems relate to how culture is presently used. Most often ethnicity or race is used as a grouping variable in statistical analyses. As Wyatt (1994) has noted, large epidemiological studies often use traditional **grouping variables,** such as race, in studies of health and disease. Because ethnicity and socioeconomic status are correlated, when economic status is controlled, ethnic group comparisons sometimes suggest a high level of similarity (Murray, 1992; Zuckerman, 1990). The results of recent research (Gurung, Taylor, Kemeny, & Myers, 2004; Gurung, Dunkel-Shetter, Collins, Rini, & Hobel, 2005) suggest that controlling for ethnicity may obscure important group differences. For example, in analyses of changes in depression, Gurung et al. (2004) found that chronic burdens of African American women (when analyzed alone) predicted their depression over time, but when ethnicity was included as a control variable in analyses on the entire sample, it was not significantly related to depression. The separate analyses by ethnicity highlighted the fact that the African-American women are vulnerable to socioeconomic status-related stressors (especially not having enough money to cover basic needs of life). Additionally, using social support to cope was not a significant variable when the entire sample was used but was significant for African American women. Likewise, optimism was not a significant predictor of changes in depression for the entire sample but was significant for the Latina sample. Findings like these, which are obscured in overall analyses controlling for race, have important implications for understanding the particular circumstances that may be faced by different ethnic groups.

Why is this problem in urgent need of rectification? Now more than ever, health psychologists need to focus on cultural differences. As described in chapter 1, North America today looks very different from the North America of even 20 years ago. The population is rapidly becoming more ethnically diverse and older. With major changes in population demographics come major changes in patterns of health (Whitfied, Weidner, Clark, & Anderson, 2002; Yali & Revenson, 2004). There is a sizeable amount of research already providing some answers (as the many chapters in this book bear testimony to), but much more is needed.

A Focus on Developmental Issues and the Lifespan

Older adults are the largest consumers of health care, and the number of older adults is increasing every year. As the population grows older and life expectancy increases, it becomes even more important to identify and change the behaviors that increase the incidence of chronic illnesses of middle and later adulthood (Smith et al., 2002; Siegler, Bastian, Steffens, Bosworth, & Costa, 2002). Increased longevity affects men and women differently. Women tend to live longer, and this has its own unique implications. For example, there will be a large number of older women living with chronic but not life-threatening illnesses (e.g., arthritis). Ways to manage pain and stress are going to be especially important (Keefe et al., 2002).

For each of the major chronic illnesses described in the preceding chapters, but especially for cancer and coronary heart disease, age is one of the biggest predictors of incidence. There are clear age-related increases in incidence for each. Research on the determinants of health behaviors among older adults will become even more important to complement similar research being conducted on younger age groups (Smith, Orleans, & Jenkins, 2004). The illnesses that manifest in adulthood often start to develop early in the lifespan and are accelerated by risky health behaviors (again more prominent in younger age groups). A developmental context is critical for a thorough understanding of chronic diseases (Williams, Holmbeck, & Greenley, 2002).

There are already large collections of research literature on aging and lifespan development and different parts of the life cycle are receiving specific attention. For example, adolescence is a pivotal period of development in respect to health and illness because this is the time that healthy behaviors are consolidated and unhealthy behaviors first become evident (Williams et al., 2002). Additionally, nearly 20% of adolescents have chronic physical conditions that will call for approaches to treatment that are different from those used with adults (Gortmaker, 1985). On the other end of the spectrum, older adults have unique needs and problems as well. Decreases in physical mobility and cognitive ability together with increases in pain severely influence the quality of life of the aging population (Siegler, Bastian, Steffens, Bosworth, & Costa, 2002). A key future direction for health psychology is to pay more attention to these different collections of literature as optimal approaches to behavior change will obviously vary across the lifespan (Wilcox & King, 1999).

Fine-Tuning the Biopsychosocial Model

By now you should be comfortable with the main health psychological approach, the biopsychosocial model (Matarazzo, 1980). Since its inception in the late 1970s, the biopsychosocial model has served as a guiding principle and has fueled dramatic advances in health psychological research (Suls & Rothman, 2004). Clearly a useful and accurate model, it has been supported by a variety of research (Anderson 2002; Niaura & Abrams, 2002; Smith & Ruiz, 2002). The success of the approach can also be seen in the number of organizations that serve and collect researchers and practitioners from biological and psychological perspectives and the increase in governmental support for health-related behavioral and psychological research. However, there is still a way to go.

Suls and Rothman (2004) calculated the frequency of citations of *biopsychosocial* in Medline (the database for medical science) and specifically in major medical journals such as *The New England Journal of Medicine* and *The Journal of the American Medical Association* (JAMA) and found that citations constituted only a small proportion of the absolute number. Even within health psychology, Suls and Rothman (2004) reported that although the *bio* and *psycho* components of the model are well represented, the *social* component is the least measured. Furthermore, assessments of people's social environments focused on subjective experiences of their relationships, or social information was restricted to demographic data and only used to describe the sample (and not as variables in the study). To fully capitalize on the strengths of a multidimensional approach it is critical for health psychologists to pay more attention to the links between the different subsystems and improve the data collected to assess each subsystem. This may mean collecting physiological, self-report, and sociological data, possibly over a long period of time. There is a clear need to work toward greater applications of the biopsychosocial model and move it from the theoretical realm into a more practical one, while also ensuring that practice informs research and both (practice and research) inform policy changes (Keefe et al., 2002).

A Multidimensional Approach

Another aspect of fine-tuning the biopsychosocial model comes from the recognition and need for **multidimensional approaches** and more collaborative research. When you do try to include a consideration of biological, psychological, and societal processes you are automatically talking about different levels of measurement, different research methods, and different statistical analyses. No matter what illness you choose to study, you can see that many different bodily systems are involved and often more than one health behavior can influence the incidence or progression of the disease. Coronary heart disease, for example, can be influenced by what you eat and drink and whether you smoke or not. Your levels of physical activity can also influence it. Each of these health behaviors can vary based on the sociocultural environment the person lives in as well as with biological factors such as metabolic rates and family histories. Stress can also play a role in the development of heart disease, so now you have the interaction between your nervous system (stress) and circulatory system (heart disease) together with many other factors.

To complicate matters even more, some variables such as culture can play multiple roles within an investigation (Kelty, Hoffman, Ory, & Harden, 2000; Penn et al., 2000; Yali & Revenson, 2004). For example, a certain ethnic group may have biological predispositions for a certain illness (a biological component), and they may also experience more stress from prejudice or discrimination (a psychological component), but they may also have stronger social networks (a social component). Consequently, the researcher has to balance multiple systems, variables, and levels. One individual is rarely trained in all the necessary areas, and it is hence important for researchers with different areas of expertise to collaborate. Each person contributes a different part of the puzzle so that the big picture can be made clearer. The complexity of the challenge can also be made more manageable with better tools. Fortunately, there have also been a number of methodological and technological innovations that are now available for health psychologists.

Technical Innovations

Medicine and health technology have been advancing at a rapid pace. We now have a good idea of constituents of the human genome, and techniques for the assessment of biological states and processes are giving us insights we could never have imagined possible. There are correspondingly a variety of implications of such advances for health psychology (Keefe et al., 2002; Saab et al., 2004).

The biggest area of innovation is in an area referred to as **behavioral telehealth** (Suleiman, 2001; Jerome et al., 2000; Whitten, Kingsley, Cook, Swirczynski, & Doolittle, 2001) in which health care is delivered over the telephone or through other technical means such as the Internet. Although it means no or little face-to-face contact with a health care provider, it still allows individuals in remote locations a means to receive treatment. Procedures currently used include online treatment for weight management, pain relief, and smoking cessation, self-help chat rooms for cancer, assessments, strategies to increase adherence, and consultation services (Saab et al., 2004). Are these methods as effective as face-to-face contact? Research is currently under way to assess this question.

An associated issue for health psychologists to be aware of is people's use of the Internet to get health information. If someone experiences a certain symptom or seems to be developing a certain illness, he or she can log onto the Internet and using sites such as WebMD, get a good idea of what he or she may (or may not) have. Health care providers and health management organizations (HMOs) are also setting up sites where members can access personalized health information before even seeing their primary care providers. This situation can be good and bad. The benefits are that patients can be forewarned and maybe learn enough to reduce treatment-seeking delays. The problem is that the same information can also increase some delays (see chapter 8) because it may increase anxiety. Furthermore, not all health-related websites, and there are many (it took my computer 0.32 seconds to come up with 14,100,000 sites that mention "health information"), have reliable information. Inaccurate or misleading information can pose a risk by also undermining confidence in a provider's recommendations (Robinson, Patrick, Eng, & Gustafson, 1998).

The Internet can also greatly expand research opportunities and increase accessibility to personal medical information. Researchers can now conduct major surveys online with very little associated time or money, and large databases can be made available to research collaborations (more on this later). Even patients are going to have more control over their health information. The Health Insurance Portability and Accountability Act (HIPAA) that took effect in 2003 has regulations that allow patients to examine their computerized medical records to correct mistakes and seek action against misuse of their records.

Two advances in medical science have direct implications for the work of health psychologists. First, living organ and tissue transplants are getting more and more common and more effective in treating diseases (Niklason & Langer, 2001). Are you willing to be an organ donor? Would you give up your organs if you died (do you have an organ donor sticker on your driver's license)? There are many psychosocial factors that predict the answer to that question. In some cultures it may not be appropriate to donate organs or touch the deceased. Some individuals are not aware of the factors surrounding donations. Correspondingly, the aim of a body of psychological research is to identify transplant candidates and help people make donation decisions (Olbrisch, Benedict, Ashe, & Levenson, 2002). Second, more and more individuals now have access to genetic tests that can inform them of possible risks for chronic illnesses such as cancer. In the future, testing for risk may be as common as getting a cholesterol test, but it has a lot more implications (Collins & McKusick, 2001). A high cholesterol level is not as anxiety provoking as finding out you have a high risk for cancer. What are the psychosocial consequences of being able to know? Consequently, health psychologists need to better understand the individual differences surrounding coping with the results of genetic testing (Saab et al., 2004).

Interventions

It is clear that psychosocial interventions are valuable additions to traditional health care (Meyerowitz & Kerns, 2004; Smith et al., 2002; Smith et al., 2004). The good news is risky behaviors can be changed, and the large number of psychological and economical gains of using psychology to prevent illness and slow down the progression of illness means competition between health psychological interventions and medical treatments for attention and research funding. The development of both forms of interventions, preventative and those that restrict progression, now need more focused attention. It is becoming more important to be able to evaluate the clinical significance of each intervention (Kendall, 1999), and there is greater consideration of the associated costs (Kaplan & Groessl, 2002; Tovian, 2004).

In keeping with the refining of the biopsychosocial model, the design of interventions must also integrate interdisciplinary approaches and include different levels of analysis (Nicassio et al., 2004). Determinants of health behaviors, often the primary targets of interventions, range from biological processes and individual level processes to family and small-group processes as well as larger community and societal factors. A more comprehensive approach to interventions will be one that has at least four different dimensions: (1) recognition of the time course of the disease, including the stage of disease risk, disease development, and health outcome; (2) different levels of analysis; (3) consideration of cultural differences, and (4) a focus on risk and health threat across the lifespan (Nicassio et al., 2004; Smith et al., 2004). Already, interventions explicitly designed for women, the elderly, and minority groups have been implemented (Antoni et al., 2001; Lichstein, Riedel, Wilson, Lester, & Aguillard, 2001). Even more are needed.

There are also barriers that prevent interventions from reaching the clinical populations for whom they have been designed. Nicassio et al. (2004) suggested that the key barriers to be overcome are (1) researchers not always understanding the clinical applicability of their basic research; (2) a reluctance of clinicians to accept the value of basic research-driven interventions; and (3) various institutional-level constraints such as lack of time, training, or funding. The empirical evidence for the effectiveness of psychological interventions is strong; now the task is to disseminate the findings more and reach out to more people who need them.

Enhanced Training

Training in the areas of cultural competency and awareness of lifespan issues will also have to be enhanced. As discussed earlier, these are two critical areas for health psychologists to be cognizant of. Henderson and Springer-Littles (1996) have indicated that therapists often graduate ill prepared for their role within a culturally diverse society and could consequently do great harm. The same can be said of health psychologists. To keep up with the increasing diversification of the United States, health psychologists are going to need to be informed and aware of not only lifespan development issues (due to the aging population), but also culturally appropriate research methods (Smith & Suls, 2004). Present training programs give trainees very limited exposure to these two very important areas but, as with this book, the awareness and inclusion of these areas are growing.

Of course, sometimes it is not possible to train someone in all the needed areas of expertise to best use the biopsychosocial model. Most medical programs and psychological programs are already busy enough. Just getting through the medical school or psychology graduate school can be very demanding. Where do you fit in developmental and cultural information? Where can you fit in the statistical training that is needed for dealing with complex multivariable data sets? The answer again is collaboration. Although postdoctoral training and special practicum experiences can give individuals exposure to the different areas needed for a comprehensive study of illness, it is more productive to have different researchers working together, each sharing their experience. Unfortunately, only a few existing programs provide the necessary training to facilitate the development of health collaborations (Suls & Rothman, 2004), and this is another key training area for the field to incorporate.

It is also going to be important for health psychologists to be able to spread the word about the effectiveness of a biopsychosocial approach. Health psychological content needs to make its way into the curricula of related areas such as medicine, public health, and health education. Even the public needs to be made more aware of the rich findings from the field.

To ensure that there is adequate funding for the continuing advancement of health psychological research, time and effort need to be allocated to the education of policymakers. This could lead to increased support for health psychological training and research. Some governmental changes are already under way, as you shall see in the next section.

Related Developments

Mirroring the innovations and advancements within the field of health psychology, many different changes are taking place on national and international levels that will influence the health psychological agenda. On the national front, the National Institutes of Health (NIH) began a new initiative (first introduced in 2003) to speed up the process of improving public health. Director Zerhouni, together with more than 300 scientists, government and business representatives, and feedback from the public, mapped out a path of scientific discovery. In keeping with the need for multilevel investigations described above, the key goal of this initiative was to give scientists new ways to perform molecular-level research and translate the results from the same into clinical applications. Known as the **NIH Roadmap,** the plan sketches out 28 cross-institutional projects especially designed to tackle multifaceted issues such as obesity that result from a variety of different biopsychosocial factors. The plan includes the creation of "molecular libraries," publicly accessible databases documenting the properties and functions of minute organic compounds that can help the design of behavioral research conducted at the molecular level. The plan also includes the creation of a **National Electronic Clinical Trials and Research (NECTAR)** network, which will make the results of clinical trials easy to find and utilize. Because studies involving physiological measurement are expensive and time-consuming and require trained personnel, this sharing of data will reduce duplication among researchers and facilitate greater collaboration. These two collections of information will undoubtedly also speed the rate of health psychological research. One more thing is needed—money helps the world go around, not to mention making major studies possible. The NIH Roadmap also includes an incentive for researchers to collaborate: Directors of various suborganizations at NIH (e.g., the National Institute on Aging) are committed to funding more collaborative research.

Another form of collaboration is important: the collaboration between mind and body. To a large extent, even suggesting that the mind and body collaborate is to assume that the two are separate entities. The underlying and implicit assumption used by most health psychologists today is that the two are actually one; that is, the psyche of the mind is a creation of the physiology of the body. Mind-body medicine, the name often used for complementary and alternative medicine (CAM) (described in detail in chapter 2), and treatments are growing in popularity in America. In one study, more than half of the patients with depression and anxiety reported using alternative treatments (McFarland, Bigelow, Zani, Newsom, & Kaplan, 2002). As more and more alternative treatments such as acupuncture, yoga, and meditation are subjected to scientific tests, it is likely that more and more of them will be prescribed for and used by the general public. This use is going to call for a new series of interventions. Many CAM techniques are already components of the belief systems of different cultural groups. Many Chinese Americans are not waiting for research to demonstrate the effectiveness of Tai Chi or Qi Gong. They just do it. Once such health behaviors receive empirical validation, more and more individuals will want to practice them. Alternatively, if CAM is found to be effective, health psychologists will have the new challenge of finding the best ways to incorporate the techniques into people's lives to prevent unhealthy behavior.

Finally, let us go back to the question of money. Not being reimbursed by insurance has been one of the biggest reasons for not enough attention being paid to psychological factors and treatment. That situation is in the process of changing. In early 2002, the American Medical Association's **Current Procedural Terminology (CPT) Manual** was updated with new billing codes designed to capture behavioral services provided to patients to address physical health problems. The introduction of the health and behavior assessment and intervention codes and their acceptance by the federal Medicare program marked years of work by the APA Practice Organization (APAPO) and its members to advance the concept of psychologists as practitioners whose knowledge can help patients deal with physical as well as mental health issues (Richmond, 2004). The first year of implementation was a time of transition, with much work being done to ensure that Medicare carriers were properly reimbursing psychologists for health and behavior services. With Medicare carriers across the country reimbursing for the codes, the APA is expanding its work to get private insurance carriers to increase coverage as well. As more and more behavioral and psychological treatments are reimbursed (e.g., smoking cessation), the financial barriers to prevention will be eliminated.

Biopsychocultural Health Psychology

Taken as a whole, health psychologists have made gigantic strides in the prevention of illness and in aiding those of us who do get sick. There is still more to be done, but the utility of a taking a biopsychosocial approach has already paid dividends. Now all we need is to expand our focus across the lifespan and to better incorporate diverse cultural backgrounds. The fact is that there really is not enough of a "social" focus in the biopsychosocial approach (Keefe et al., 2002). Indeed, what we do and why we do it are shaped by a variety of factors, and our health and well-being are no exceptions. A **biopsychocultural** approach might provide health psychology with stronger direction that not only incorporates the social nature of our interactions, but also explicitly acknowledges the role that culture plays in our lives.

FOCUS on Applications
Careers and Graduate Training in Health Psychology

So now that you have read about the spectrum of what constitutes health psychology, what do you do next? I hope that the research you have read has inspired you to consider working in this fascinating field. Well, then, what are your main options?

Most health psychologists work in either basic research settings or in applied settings. The former are academic psychologists who may be affiliated with a university or research center. The latter are clinicians who may be affiliated with hospitals or clinics. Researchers aim to determine the biopsychosocial factors involved in the many areas that we have discussed in this book such as stress, cardiovascular diseases, cancer, and HIV. Clinical activities include the conducting of a variety of tests such as cognitive and behavioral assessments, psychophysiological assessments, clinical interviews, demographic surveys, objective and projective personality assessments, and various other clinical and research-oriented protocols (*Health Psychology,* 2005). Health clinicians also implement interventions to change health behaviors, reduce stress, help people cope with chronic illnesses, and increase adherence to treatment. Many psychologists work in health care settings and many HMOs include psychologists as well. Health psychologists have also been employed in governmental agencies, rehabilitation centers, medical schools, and pain centers.

Although few undergraduate institutions offer specialized programs in health psychology, a growing number of graduate programs offer a degree or at least an emphasis in health psychology. The best preparation at the undergraduate level is a psychology major with many supporting courses in biology, statistics, and research methods. Many schools around the country are also adding an introductory health psychology course to the curriculum, but similar material may be covered in courses with titles such as behavioral health care, behavioral medicine, health behavior change, and health promotion. Because the biopsychosocial model incorporates many different subject areas you can cultivate your interest in health psychology by working in a variety of related fields. Many social workers, occupational and physical therapists, nutrition and exercise physiologists, dieticians, and other health care workers also utilize the health psychological approach even if not the explicit label. Many county, state, and national organizations also hire students with backgrounds and interests in health psychology to work with related departments. Even within the field of psychology many social, personality, clinical, and counseling psychologists (some of the classic and traditional areas of psychology) may also take a strong health psychological approach in their work.

After an undergraduate degree, most health psychologists enroll in graduate school and work toward a master's (M.S.) or doctoral degree (Ph.D.). These degrees can take from 5 to 7 or more years and the content of the coursework will vary with the institution. Some graduate schools will focus more on the psychological aspects of the biopsychosocial model, including a greater number of advanced courses in psychology. Others will lean more heavily on the biological side of the model with more specialized courses in biology and medicine. If you use the most traditional way to look for graduate schools, the American Psychological Association's guide to graduate study, here is something to watch out for. There are a small (although growing) number of health psychology Ph.D. programs, but a larger number of clinical psychology programs that offer health psychology "tracks." There are also many schools that have a health psychology emphasis within their social psychology Ph.D. programs (e.g., UCLA). There are also schools with behavioral neuroscience or behavioral medicine programs whose curriculum is very close to that of health psychology programs. For one of the most up-to-date sources for programs with health psychology training, check the Society of Behavioral Medicine and health psychology education and training websites.

Applied health psychologists have a doctoral or master's degree and are licensed for the independent practice of psychology in areas such as clinical and counseling psychology, and board certification is available in health psychology through the American Board of Professional Psychology. Clinical and counseling doctoral students are required to complete a 1-year internship before obtaining their doctorates, and many of these programs offer some training in health psychology. After graduate school, a number of individuals choose to specialize in a particular area of the field and take on postdoctoral positions. Although these positions rarely pay much, they are excellent opportunities to work closely with experienced researchers in the field and learn much more about specific topics.

If this brief taste of what is available to you has whet your appetite for more information about being a health psychologist, the best place to look is Health Psychology's (APA Division 38) education and training website or a similar site hosted by the Society for Behavioral Medicine. You will find a listing of doctoral programs in health psychology, a guide to internships in health psychology, and a listing of postdoctoral programs in health psychology. This is an expanding, exciting field with a tremendous potential to change how long and how well we live. I hope you have enjoyed learning about it and join the ranks of health psychologists.

Chapter Summary

- Health psychology as a separate field has now been in existence for approximately 35 years, although its roots go back much further. It has many areas of specialization and organizations that cater to individuals from different fields.
- There is a great need for health psychology to focus more on cultural issues. There are significant cultural differences in health behaviors and health in general. Health psychologists have only recently begun to focus explicitly on differences in cultural groups. This focus calls for more training and cultural awareness. With the increasing diversity in North America, there is an urgent need for more cross-cultural health psychology research.
- Although it is clear that health issues vary as we age and that the causes of death vary for different age groups, health psychologists have yet to focus on developmental issues and the lifespan. Disparate literature studies reporting on developmental issues should be initiated for studies of health as we age.
- Additional work needs to be done on refining the biopsychosocial model. Still used more in the theoretical realm, the biopsychosocial model needs to be put into practice more often.
- The need for more cultural and developmental research in health psychology is going to require more multilevel and interdisciplinary collaborations. These collaborations will foster the design of more powerful interventions.
- Technology is changing rapidly. Research designs and interventions need to keep abreast of novel ways to collect data and monitor individuals. The greater use of portable computers, the Internet, and even multifunction cellular phones gives the health psychologist a wealth of new ways to reach people and change behavior.
- Interventions need to better account for the time course of diseases, different levels of analysis, cultural differences, and a focus on health threats across the lifespan.
- Training programs in health psychology need to be revised to keep up with the changing nature of the field and the increasing need for cultural competency.
- Health psychologists need to pay more attention to the use and utility of complementary and alternative medicines (CAMs). The uses of CAMs are growing, and they may prove to be effective aids to conventional treatments in addition to providing psychological buffers to illness.

Synthesize, Evaluate, Apply

- How would you summarize the state of the field of health psychology?
- How would you prioritize the different future directions described above?
- Generate your own description of health psychology, synthesizing what you have learned in this book.
- Are there other areas of culture, development, and health that have not been discussed in this book?

KEY TERMS, CONCEPTS, AND PEOPLE

behavioral telehealth, 417
biopsychocultural, 421
Current Procedural
   Terminology, 420

Division 38, 412
grouping variables, 414
multidimensional
   approaches, 416

National Electronic Clinical
   Trials and Research
   (NECTAR), 420
NIH Roadmap, 420

ESSENTIAL READINGS

Nicassio, P. M., Meyerowitz, B. E., & Kerns, R. D. (2004). The future of health psychology interventions. *Health Psychology, 23*(2), 132–137.

Smith, T. W., Kendall, P. C., & Keefe, F. J. (2002). Behavioral medicine and clinical health psychology: Introduction to the special issue, a view from the decade of behavior. *Journal of Consulting and Clinical Psychology, 70*(3), 459–462.

Suls, J., & Rothman, A. (2004). Evolution of the biopsychosocial model: Prospects and challenges for health psychology. *Health Psychology, 23*(2), 119–126.

Yali, A. M., & Revenson, T. A. (2004). How changes in population demographics will impact health psychology: Incorporating a broader notion of cultural competence into the field. *Health Psychology, 23*(2), 147–155.

WEB RESOURCES

Visit the companion website at **http://psychology.wadsworth.com/gurung1e/**, where you will find online resources for this book, including chapter-by-chapter quizzes, weblinks, and more! You can also visit Wadsworth Psychology Resource Center at **http://psychology.wadsworth.com** to access additional resources.

Health Psychology Education and Training
http://www.health-psych.org/edu.htm

References

Abel, E., & Chambers, K. B. (2004). Factors that influence vulnerability to STDs and HIV/AIDS among Hispanic women. *Health Care for Women International, 25,* 761–780.

Abraham, C., Sheeran, P., Spears, R., & Abrams, D. (1992). Health beliefs and promotion of HIV preventive intentions among teenagers: A Scottish perspective. *Health Psychology, 11,* 363–370.

Abraido-Lanza, A. F., Vasquez, E., & Echeverria, S. E. (2004). En las Manos de Dios [in God's Hands]: Religious and other forms of coping among Latinos with arthritis. *Journal of Consulting and Clinical Psychology, 72,* 91–102.

Abrams, D. B., Herzog, T. A., Emmons, K. M., & Linnan, L. (2000). Stages of change versus addiction: A replication and extension. *Nicotine and Tobacco Research, 2,* 223–229.

Ader, R., & Cohen, N. (1975). Behaviorally conditioned immunosuppression. *Psychosomatic Medicine, 37,* 333–340.

Ader, R., Felten, D. L., & Cohen, N. (1991). *Psychoneuroimmunology* (2nd ed.). San Diego, CA: Academic Press.

Adler, N. E., Boyce, T., Chesney, M. A., Cohen, S., Folkman, S., Kahn, R. L., et al. (1994). Socioeconomic status and health: The challenge of the gradient. *American Psychologist, 49,* 15–24.

Adler, N. E., & Ostrove, J. M. (1999). Socioeconomic status and health: What we know and what we don't. In N. E. Adler & M. Marmot (Eds.), *Socioeconomic status and health in industrial nations: Social, psychological, and biological pathways* (pp. 3–15). New York: New York Academy of Sciences.

Affleck, G., Tennen, H., & Apter, A. (2001). Optimism, pessimism, and daily life with chronic illness. In E. C. Chang (Ed.), *Optimism & pessimism: Implications for theory, research, and practice* (pp. 147–168). Washington, DC: American Psychological Association.

Affleck, G., Tennen, H., Urrows, S., & Higgins, P. (1992). Neuroticism and the pain/mood relation in rheumatoid arthritis: Insights from a prospective daily study. *Journal of Consulting and Clinical Psychology, 60,* 119–126.

Affleck, G., Tennen, H., Urrows, S., Higgins, P., Abeles, M., Hall, C., Karoly, P., & Newton, C. (1998). Fibromyalgia and women's pursuit of personal goals: A daily process analysis. *Health Psychology, 17,* 40–77.

Agarwal, D. P., & Seitz, H. K. (2001). *Alcohol in health and disease.* New York: Marcel Dekker.

Ai, A. L., Peterson, C., & Huang, B. (2003). The effect of religious-spiritual coping on positive attitudes of adult Muslim refugees from Kosovo and Bosnia. *International Journal for the Psychology of Religion, 13,* 29–47.

Aiken, L. G., West, S. G., Woodward, C. K., Reno, R. R., & Reynolds, K. D. (1994). Increasing screening mammography in asymptomatic women: Evaluation of a second-generation, theory-based program. *Health Psychology, 13,* 526–538.

Aiken, L. S., Gerend, M. A., & Jackson, K. M. (2001). Subjective risk and health protective behavior: Cancer screening and cancer prevention. In A. Baum, T. A. Revenson, & J. E. Singer (Eds.), *Handbook of health psychology* (pp. 727–746). Mahwah, NJ: Erlbaum.

Ainsworth, M. D. S. (1978). *Patterns of attachment: A psychological study of the strange situation.* Oxford, England: Erlbaum.

Ainsworth, M. S., Blehar, M. C., Water, E., & Wall, S. (1978). *Patterns of attachment: A psychological study of the strange situation.* Oxford, England: Erlbaum.

Aisenberg, E. (2001). The effects of exposure to community violence upon Latina mothers and preschool children. *Hispanic Journal of Behavioral Sciences, 23,* 378–398.

Ajzen, I. (1988). *Attitudes, personality, and behavior.* Homewood, IL: Dorsey Press.

Ajzen, I., & Madden, T. J. (1986). Prediction of goal-directed behavior: Attitudes, intentions, and perceived behavioral control. *Journal of Experimental Social Psychology, 22,* 453–474.

Akil, H., Mayer, D. J., & Liebeskind, J. C. (1976). Antagonism of stimulation-produced analgesia by naloxone, a narcotic antagonist. *Science, 191,* 961–962.

Albarracin, D., McNatt, P. S., Williams, W. R., Howworth, T., Zenilman, J., Ho, R. M., et al. (2000). Structure of outcome beliefs in condom use. *Health Psychology, 19,* 458–468.

Albert, C. M., Manson, J. E., Cook, N. R., Ajani, U. A., Gaziano, J. M., & Hennekens, C. E. (1999). Moderate alcohol consumption and the risk of sudden cardiac death among U. S. male physicians. *Circulation, 100,* 944–950.

Aldwin, C. M. (1994). *Stress, coping, and development: An integrative perspective.* New York: Guilford Press.

Aldwin, C. M., & Revenson, T. A. (1987). Does coping help? A re-examination of the relation between coping and mental health. *Journal of Personality and Social Psychology, 53,* 337–348.

Aldwin, C., Folkman, S., Schaefer C., Coyne, J. C., & Lazarus, R. S. (1980, August). *Ways of coping: A process measure.* Paper presented at the meeting of the American Psychological Association, Montreal.

Aldwin, C. M., Sutton, K. J., & Lachman, M. (1996). The development of coping resources in adulthood. *Journal of Personality, 64,* 837–871.

Alexander, E. (1950). *Psychosomatic medicine.* New York: Norton.

Allport, G. W. (1961). *Patterns and growth in personality.* New York: Holt.

Altabe, M. N. (2001). Issues in the assessment and treatment of body image disturbance in culturally diverse populations. In J. K. Thompson (Ed.), *Body image, eating disorders, and obesity: An integrative guide for assessment and treatment* (pp. 129–147). Washington, DC: American Psychological Association.

Alvord, L. A., & Van Pelt, E. C. (2000). *The scapel and the silver bear: The first Navajo woman surgeon combines western medicine and traditional healing.* New York: Bantam Books.

American Cancer Society. (2004). Estimated new cancer cases and deaths by sex for all sites, US, 2004. Retrieved from http://www.cancer.org/docroot/home/index.asp. December 2004.

American Cancer Society. (2005) Incidence and mortality rates by site, race, and ethnicity, US, 1997-2001. National Cancer Institute, Bethesda, Maryland.

American Diabetes Association. (2000). Type 2 diabetes in children and adolescents. *Pediatrics, 105,* 671–680.

American Heart Association. (2004). African Americans and cardiovascular disease statistics. Retrieved from http://www.americanheart.org/presenter.jhtml?identifier=1200000. December 2004.

American Psychiatric Association. (1994). *Diagnostic and statistical manual of mental disorders: DSM-IV* (4th ed.). Washington, DC: Author.

American Stroke Association. (2004). Reducing risk. Retrieved from http://www.strokeassociation.org/presenter.jhtml?identifier.jhtml?identifier=1200037. December 2004.

Amirkhan, J. H. (1990). A factor analytically derived measure of coping: The Coping Strategy Indicator. *Journal of Personality and Social Psychology, 59,* 1066–1074.

Anand, K. J. S., & Craig, K. D. (1996). Editorial: New perspectives on the definition of pain. *Pain, 67,* 3–6.

Anand, S., & Yusuf, S. (1998). Risk stratification for sympathetic atherosclerosis. In J. S. Ginsberg (Ed.), *Critical decisions in thrombosis and hemostasis* (pp. 179–189). Hamilton, Ontario, Canada: BC Decker.

Anda, R., Williamson, D., Jones, D., Macera, C., Eaker, E., Glassman, A., & Marks, J. (1993). Depressed affect, hopelessness, and the risk of ischemic heart disease in a cohort of U. S. adults. *Epidemiology, 4,* 285–294.

Andersen, R., Lewis, S. Z., Giachello, A. L., Aday, L. A., & Chiu, G. (1981). Access to medical care among the Hispanic population of the southwestern United States. *Journal of Health and Social Behavior, 22,* 78–89.

Anderson, B. L. (1992). Psychological interventions for cancer patients to enhance the quality of life. *Journal of Consulting and Clinical Psychology, 60,* 552–568.

Anderson, B. L. (2002). Behavioral outcomes following psychological interventions for cancer patients. *Journal of Consulting and Clinical Psychology, 70,* 590–610.

Anderson, B. L., Farrar, W. B., Golden-Kreutz, D., Kutz, L. A., MacCallum, R., Courtney, M. E., et al. (1998). Stress and immune responses following surgical treatment for regional breast cancer. *Journal of the National Cancer Institute, 90,* 30–36.

Anderson, B. L., Kiecolt-Glaser, J. K., & Glaser, R. (1994). A biobehavioral model of cancer stress and disease course. *American Psychologist, 49,* 389–404.

Anderson, B. L., & Tewfik, H. H. (1985). Psychological reactions to radiation therapy: Reconsideration of the adaptive aspects of anxiety. *Journal of Personality and Social Psychology, 48,* 1024–1032.

Anderson, J. M. (1993). Ethnocultural communities as partners in research. In R. Masie, L. L. Menseh, & K. A. McLeod (Eds.), *Health and cultures: Exploring the relationships* (Vol. 1, pp. 319–328). Oakville, Ontario, Canada: Mosaic Press.

Anderson, N. B. (1995). Behavioral and sociocultural perspectives in ethnicity and health: Introduction to the special issue. *Health Psychology, 14,* 589–591.

Anderson, N. H. (1990). *Contributions to information integration theory* (Vol. 1). Hillsdale, NJ: Erlbaum.

Anderson, R. T., Hogan, P., Appel, L., Rosen, R., & Shumaker, S. A. (1997). Baseline correlates with quality of life among men and women with medication-controlled hypertension. *Journal of the American Geriatrics Society, 45,* 1080–1085.

Angell, M. (1997). The Supreme Court and physician-assisted suicide: The ultimate right. *The New England Journal of Medicine, 336,* 50–53.

Antoni, M. H., Baggett, L., Ironson, G., LaPerriere, A., August, S., Klimas, N., et al. (1991). Cognitive-behavioral stress management intervention buffers distress responses and immunologic changes following notification of HIV-1 seropositivity. *Journal of Consulting and Clinical Psychology, 59,* 906–915.

Antoni, M., Cruess, D., Cruess, S., Lutgendorf, S., Kumar, M., Ironson, G., et al. (2001). Cognitive-behavioral stress management intervention effects on anxiety, 24-hr urinary norepinephrine output, and T-cytotoxic/suppressor cells over time among symptomatic HIV-infected gay men. *Journal of Consulting and Clinical Psychology, 68,* 31–35.

Antoni, M. H., Lehman, J. M., Kilbourn, K. M., Boyers, A. E., Culver, J. L., Alferi, S. M., et al. (2001). Cognitive-behavioral stress management intervention decreases the prevalence of depression and enhances benefit finding among women under treatment for early-stage breast cancer. *Health Psychology, 20,* 20–32.

Antonucci, T. C. (1991). Attachment, social support, and doping with negative life events in mature adulthood. In E. M. Cummings, A. L. Greene, et al. (Eds.), *Life-span developmental psychology: Perspectives on stress and coping* (pp. 261–276). Hillsdale, NJ: Erlbaum.

Antonucci, T. C., & Akiyama, H. (1987). An examination of sex differences in social support among older men and women. *Sex Roles, 17,* 737–749.

Antonucci, T. C., & Akiyama, H. (1995). Convoys of social relations: Family and friendships within a life span context. In R. Blieszner & V. H. Bedford (Eds.), *Handbook of aging and the family* (pp. 355–371). Westport, CT: Greenwood Press/Greenwood Publishing Group.

Apel, M., Klein, K., McDermott, R. J., & Westhoff, W. W. (1997). Restricting smoking at the University of Koln, Germany: A case study. *Journal of American College Health, 45,* 219–223.

Arias, D. C. (2004). Alternative medicines' popularity prompts concern. *Nation's Health, 34,* 6.

Armor, D. A., & Taylor, S. E. (1998). Situated optimism: Specific outcome expectancies and self regulation. In M. P. Zanna (Ed.), *Advances in experimental social psychology* (Vol. 30, pp. 309–379). New York: Academic Press.

Armor, D. A., & Taylor, S. E. (1998). When predictions fail: The dilemma of unrealistic optimism. In T. Gilovich, D. Griffin, & D. Kahneman (Eds.), *Heuristics and biases: The psychology of intuitive judgment* (pp. 334–347). New York: Cambridge University Press.

Armstrong, T. L., & Swartzman, L. C. (2001). Cross-cultural differences in illness models and expectations for the health care provider-client/patient interaction. In S. S. Kazarian & D. R. Evans (Eds.), *Handbook of cultural health psychology* (pp. 63–84). San Diego, CA: Academic Press.

Arnetz, B. B., Wasserman, J., Pertrii, B., Brenner, S. O., Levi, L., Eneroth, P., et al. (1987). Immune function in unemployed women. *Psychosomatic Medicine, 49,* 3–12.

Arntz, A., & de Jong, P. F. (1993). Anxiety, attention and pain. *Journal of Psychosomatic Research, 37,* 423–431.

Ashing-Giwa, K., & Ganz, P. A. (1997). Understanding the breast cancer experience of African-American women. *Journal of Psychosocial Oncology, 15,* 19–35.

Aspinwall, L. G., Kemeny, M. E., Taylor, S. E., Schneider, S. G., & Dudley, E. T. (1991). Psychosocial predictors of gay men's AIDS risk-reduction behavior. *Health Psychology, 10,* 432–444.

Aspinwall, L. G., & Taylor, S. E. (1992). Modeling cognitive adaptation: A longitudinal investigation of the impact of individual differences and coping on college adjustment and performance. *Journal of Personality and Social Psychology, 63,* 989–1003.

Aspinwall, L. G., & Taylor, S. E. (1997). A stitch in time: Self-regulation and proactive coping. *Psychological Bulletin, 121,* 417–436.

Astin, J. A., Marie, A., Pelletier, K. R., Hansen, E., Haskell, W. L. (1998). A Review of the Incorporation of Complementary and Alternative Medicine by Mainstream Physicians. *Archives of Internal Medicine, 158,* 2303–2310.

Auerbach, S. M. (1989). Stress management and coping research in the health care setting: An overview and methodological commentary. *Journal of Consulting and Clinical Psychology, 57,* 388–395.

Auerbach, S. M. (2000). Should patients have control over their own health care? Empirical evidence and research issues. *Annals of Behavioral Medicine, 22,* 246–259.

Ax, A. F. (1953). The physiological differentiation between fear and anger in humans. *Psychosomatic Medicine, 15,* 433–442.

Baba, V. V., Jamal, M., & Tourigny, L. (1998). Work and mental health: A decade in Canadian research. *Canadian Psychology, 39,* 94–107.

Babyak, M., Blumenthal, J. A., Herman, S., Khatri, P., Doraiswamy, M., Moore, K., et al. (2000). Exercise treatment for major depression: Maintenance of therapeutic benefit at 10 months. *Psychosomatic Medicine, 62,* 633–638.

Bachen, E. A., Marsland, A. L., Manuck, S. B., & Cohen, S. (1998). Immunomodulation: Psychological stress and immune competence. In T. F. Kresina (Ed.), *Handbook of immune modulating agents* (pp. 145–159). New York: Marcel Dekker.

Baer, J. S., Stacy, A., & Larimer, M. (1991). Biases in the perception of drinking norms among college students. *Journal of Studies on Alcohol, 52,* 580–586.

Baer, R. A. (2003). Mindfulness training as a clinical intervention: A conceptual and empirical review. *Clinical Psychology: Science and Practice, 10*, 125–143.

Bailey, F. J., & Dua, J. (1999). Individualism-collectivism, coping styles, and stress in international and Anglo-Australian students: A comparative study. *Australian Psychologist, 34*, 177–182.

Baker, B., Richter, A., & Anand, S. S. (2001). From the heartland: Culture, psychological factors, and coronary heart disease. In S. S. Kazarian & D. R. Evans (Eds.), *Handbook of cultural health psychology* (pp. 141–162). San Diego, CA: Academic Press.

Ball, D. M., & Murray, R. M. (1994). Genetics of alcohol misuse. *British Medical Bulletin, 50*, 18–35.

Ball, K., Berch, D. B., Helmers, K. F., Jobe, J. B., Leveck, M. D., Marsiske, M., et al. (2002). Effects of cognitive training interventions with older adults: A randomized controlled trial. *Journal of the American Medical Association, 288*, 2271–2281.

Ballantyne, C. M. (2004). Achieving greater reductions in cardiovascular risk: Lessons from statin therapy on risk measures and risk reduction. *American Heart Journal, 148*, S3–S8.

Ballard, T. J., Saltzman, L. E., Gazmararian, J. A., Spitz, A. M., Lazorick, S., & Marks, J. S. (1998). Violence during pregnancy: Measurement issues. *American Journal of Public Health, 88*, 274–276.

Ballard-Reisch, D. S. (1990). A model of participative decision making for physician/patient interaction. *Health Communication, 2*, 91–104.

Balls Organista, P., Organista, K., & Kurasaki, K. (2002). The relationship between acculturation and ethnic minority health. In K. M. Chun, P. Balls Organista, G. Marin, & S. Sue (Eds.), *Acculturation: Advances in theory, measurement, and applied research* (pp. 139–161). Washington, DC: American Psychological Association.

Band, P. R., Le, N. D., Fang, R., & Deschamps, M. (2002). Carcinogenic and endocrine disrupting effects of cigarette smoke and risk of breast cancer. *Lancet, 360*, 1044–1050.

Bandura, A. (1969). Social learning of moral judgments. *Journal of Personality & Social Psychology, 11*, 275–279.

Bandura, A. (1977). *Social learning theory.* Englewood Cliffs, NJ: Prentice Hall.

Barnes, P. M., Powell-Griner, E., McFann, K., & Nahin, R. L. (2004). Complementary and alternative medicine use among adults: United States, 2002. *Advance Data, 343*, 1–19.

Barrera, M., Wayland, L., D'Agostino, N. M., Gibson, J., Weksberg, R., & Malkin, D. (2003). Developmental differences in psychological adjustment and health-related quality of life in pediatric cancer patients. *Children's Health Care, 32*, 215–232.

Bastani, R., Marcus, A., & Hollatz-Brown, A. (1991). Screening mammography rates and barriers to use: A Los Angeles County survey. *Preventive Medicine, 20*, 350–363.

Barrett, B. (1995). Ethnomedical interactions: Health and identity on Nicaragua's Atlantic coast. *Social Science and Medicine, 40*, 1611–1621.

Barrett, B. (1998). When should there be liability for negligently causing psychiatric illness? *Work and Stress, 12*, 101–111.

Barrett, R. K. (1998). Sociocultural considerations for working Blacks experiencing loss and grief. In K. Doka (Ed.), *Living with grief: How we are—how we grieve* (pp. 83–96). Washington, DC: Taylor & Francis.

Barsky, A. J. (1988). *Worried sick: Our troubled quest for wellness.* New York: Little, Brown.

Barsky, A. J., Ahern, D. K., Bailey, E. D., Saintfort, F., Liu, E. B., & Peekna, H. M. (2001). Hypochondriacal patients' appraisal of health and physical risks. *American Journal of Psychiatry, 158*, 783–787.

Bartoshuk, L. M. (1988). Taste. In R. C. Atkinson, R. J. Herrnstein, G. Lindzey, & R. D. Luce (Eds.), *Stevens' handbook of experimental psychology: Perception and motivation* (Vol. 1). New York: John Wiley.

Bartoshuk, L. M., Rifkin, B., Marks, L. E., & Hooper, J. E. (1988). Bitterness of KCI and benzoate: Related to genetic status for sensitivity to PTC/PROP. *Chemical Senses, 13*, 517–528.

Bates, M. S., Edwards, W. T., & Anderson, K. O. (1993). Ethnocultural influences on variation in chronic pain perception. *Pain, 52*, 101–112.

Bates, M. S., Rankin-Hill, L., & Sanchez-Ayendez, M. (1997). The effects of the cultural context of health care on treatment of and response to chronic pain and illness. *Social Science & Medicine, 45*, 1433–1447.

Batty, D., & Thune, I. (2000). Does physical activity prevent cancer? Evidence suggests protection against colon cancer and probably breast cancer. *British Medical Journal, 321*, 1424–1425.

Baum, A., & Dougall, A. L. (2002). Terrorism and behavioral medicine. *Current Opinion in Psychiatry, 15*, 617–621.

Baum, A., O'Keefe, M. K., & Davidson, L. M. (1990). Acute stressors and chronic response: The case of traumatic stress. *Journal of Applied Social Psychology, 20*, 1643–1654.

Baumrind, D. (1991). Effective parenting during the early adolescent transition. In P. A. Cowan & M. Hetherington (Eds.), *Family transitions.* Hillsdale, NJ: Erlbaum.

Beauchamp, K., Baker, S., McDaniel, C., Moser, W., Zalman, D. C., Balinghoff, J., Cheung, A. T., & Stecker, M. (2001). Reliability of nurses' neurological assessments in the cardiothoracic surgical intensive care unit. *American Journal of Critical Care, 10*, 298–305.

Beck, A. T. (1976). *Cognitive therapy and the emotional disorders.* Oxford, England: International Universities Press.

Beck, A. T., Ward, C. H., Mendelson, M., Mock, J., & Erbaugh, J. (1961). An inventory for measuring depression. *Archives of General Psychology, 4*, 561–571.

Becker, M. H. (Ed.). (1974). The health belief model and personal health behavior. *Health Education Monographs, 2*, entire issue.

Beckman, H. B., & Frankel, R. M. (1984). The effect of physician behavior on the collection of data. *Annals of Internal Medicine, 101*, 692–696.

Beecher, H. K. (1955). The powerful placebo. *Journal of the American Medical Association, 159*, 1602–1606.

Belle, D. (1989). *Children's social networks and social supports.* Oxford, England: John Wiley.

Benotsch, E. G., Lutgendorf, S. K., Watson, D., Fick, L. J., & Lang, E. V. (2000). Rapid anxiety assessment in medical patients: Evidence for the validity of verbal anxiety ratings. *Annals of Behavioral Medicine, 22*, 199–203.

Ben-Zur, H. (2002). Coping, affect and aging: The roles of mastery and self-esteem. *Personality and Individual Differences, 32*, 357–372.

Berkanovic, E., & Telesky, C. (1985). Mexican-American, Black-American and White-American differences in reporting illnesses, disability and physician visits for illnesses. *Social Science and Medicine, 20*, 567–577.

Berkley, K. J. (1997). Sex differences in pain. *Behavioral and Brain Sciences, 20*, 371–380.

Berkman, L., & Syme, S. L. (1979). Social networks, host resistance, and mortality: A nine-year follow-up study of Alameda County residents. *American Journal of Epidemiology, 109*, 186–204.

Berkman, L. F. (1985). The relationship of social networks and social support to morbidity and mortality. In S. Cohen & S. L. Syme (Eds.), *Social support and health* (pp. 241–262). San Diego: Academic Press.

Berkman, L. F. (1995). The role of social relations in health promotion. *Psychosomatic Medicine, 57*, 245–254.

Berkman, L. F., & Syme, S. L. (1994). Social networks, host resistance, and mortality: A nine year follow-up study of Alameda County residents. In A. Steptoe & J. Wardle (Eds.), *Psychosocial processes and health: A reader* (pp. 43–67). New York: Cambridge University Press.

Berkman, L. F., Vaccarino, V., & Seeman, T. (1993). Gender differences in cardiovascular morbidity and mortality: The contribution of social networks and support. *Annals of Behavioral Medicine, 15,* 112–118.

Berlin, J. A., & Colditz, G. A. (1990). A meta-analysis of physical activity in the prevention of coronary heart disease. *American Journal of Epidemiology, 132,* 612–628.

Berman, B. A., & Gritz, E. R. (1991). Women and smoking: Current trends and issues for the 1990s. *Journal of Substance Abuse, 3,* 221–238.

Bernabei, R., Gambassi, G., Lapane, K., Landi, F., Gatsonis, C., Dunlop, R., (1998). Management of pain in elderly patients with cancer. Journal of the American Medical Association, 279, 1877–1882.

Bernstein, L., Henderson, B. E., Hanisch, R., Sullivan-Halley, J., & Ross, R. K. (1994). Physical exercise and reduced risk of breast cancer in young women. *Journal of the National Cancer Institute, 86,* 1403–1408.

Berrol, S. C. (1995). Growing up American: Immigrant children in America then and now. New York: Twayne.

Berry, J. W., Trimble, J. E., Olmedo, E. L. (1986). Assessment of acculturation. In W. J., Lonner & J. W. Berry (Eds.) *Field methods in cross-cultural research* (pp. 291–324). Thousand Oaks, CA: Sage.

Betencourt, H., & Fuentes, J. L. (2001). Culture and Latino issues in health psychology. In S. S. Kazarian & D. R. Evans (Eds.), *Handbook of cultural health psychology* (pp. 305–321). San Diego, CA: Academic Press.

Bexton, W. H., Heron, W., & Scott, T. H. (1954). Effects of decreased variation in the sensory environment. *Canadian Journal of Psychology, 8,* 70–76.

Bhui, K., & Fletcher, A. (2000). Common mood and anxiety states: Gender differences in the protective effect of physical activity. *Social Psychiatry and Psychiatric Epidemiology, 35,* 28–35.

Bijur, P. E., Kurzon, M., Overpeck, M. D., & Scheidt, P. C. (1992). Parental alcohol use, problem drinking, and children's injuries. *Journal of the American Medical Association, 267,* 3166–3171.

Billings, A. G., & Moos, R. H. (1984). Coping, stress, and social resources among adults with unipolar depression. *Journal of Personality and Social Psychology, 46,* 877–891.

Blair, S. N., Kohl, H. W., Gordon, N. F., & Paffenbarger, R. S. (1992). How much physical activity is good for health? *Annual Review of Public Health, 13,* 99–126.

Blaisdell, R. K. (1998). Culture and cancer in Kanaka Maoli (Native Hawaiians). *Asian American and Pacific Islander Journal of Health, 6,* 400.

Blanchard, C. G., Albrecht, T. L., Ruckdeschel, J. C., & Grant, C. H. (1995). The role of social support in adaptation to cancer and to survival. *Journal of Psychosocial Oncology, 13,* 75–95.

Blanchard, E. B., & Andrasik, F. (1985). Management of chronic headaches: A psychological approach. *Psychology practitioner guidebooks.* Elmsford, NY: Pergamon Press.

Blondel, B. (1998). Social and medical support during pregnancy: An overview of the randomized controlled trials. *Prenatal Neonatal Medicine, 3,* 141–144.

Blum, K., Noble, E., Sheridan, P. J., Montgomery, A., Ritchie, T., Jagadeeswaran, P., et al. (1990). Allelic association of human dopamine D₂ receptor gene in alcoholism. *Journal of the American Medical Association, 263,* 2055–2060.

Blumenthal, J. A., Babyak, M. A., Carney, R. M., Huber, M., Saab, P. G., Burg, M. M., et al. (2004). Exercise, depression, and mortality after myocardial infarction in the ENRICHD trial. *Medicine and Science in Sports and Exercise, 36,* 746–755.

Blumenthal, J. A., Babyak, M., Wei, J., O'Connor, C., Waugh, R., Eisenstein, E., et al. (2002a). Usefulness of psychosocial treatment of mental stress-induced myocardial ischemia in men. *American Journal of Cardiology, 89,* 164–168.

Blumenthal, J. A., Sherwood, A., Gullette, E. C. D., Georgiades, A., & Tweedy, D. (2002b). Biobehavioral approaches to the treatment of essential hypertension. *Journal of Consulting and Clinical Psychology, 70,* 569–589.

Blumer, D., & Heilbronn, M. (1984). Chronic pain as a variant of depressive disease: A rejoinder. *Journal of Nervous and Mental Disease, 172,* 405–407.

Bogg, T., & Roberts, B. W. (2004). Conscientiousness and health-related behaviors: A meta-analysis of the leading behavioral contributors to mortality. *Psychological Bulletin, 130,* 887–919.

Boland, R. (1997). HIV and depression. *American Journal of Psychiatry, 154,* 1632–1633.

Bolger, N. (1990). Coping as a personality process: A prospective study. *Journal of Personality and Social Psychology, 59,* 525–537.

Bolger, N., DeLongis, A., Kessler, R., & Wethington, E. (1989). The contagion of stress across multiple roles. *Journal of Marriage and Family, 51,* 175–183.

Bond, B., Hirota, L., Fortin, J., & Col, N. (2002). Women like me: Reflections on health and hormones from women treated for breast cancer. *Journal of Psychosocial Oncology, 20,* 39–56.

Bond, D. S., Lyle, R. M., Tappe, M. K., Seehafer, R. S., & D'Zurilla, T. J. (2002). Moderate aerobic exercise, T'ai Chi, and social problem-solving ability in relation to psychological stress. *International Journal of Stress Management, 9,* 329–343.

Borzekowski, D. L. G., Robinson, T. N., & Killen, J. D. (2000). Does the camera add 10 pounds? Media use, perceived importance of appearance, and weight concerns among teenage girls. *Journal of Adolescent Health, 26,* 36–41.

Bouchard, C. (1995). Genetics and the metabolic syndrome. *International Journal of Obesity, 19,* S52–S59.

Bouchard, C. (2001). Physical activity and health: Introduction to the dose-response symposium. *Medicine and Science in Sports and Exercise, 33,* S347–S350.

Bouchard, C., Tremblay, A., Despres, J. P., Nadeau, A., Lupien, P., Theriault, G., et al. (1990). The response to long-term overfeeding in identical twins. *New England Journal of Medicine, 322,* 1477–1482.

Bowlby, J. (1958). The nature of the child's tie to his mother. *International Journal of Psycho-analysis, 39,* 350–373.

Boykin-McElhaney, K., & Allen, J. P. (2001). Autonomy and social functioning: The moderating effect of risk. *Child Development, 72,* 220–235.

Bradford, D. (2005). African herbalism and spiritual divination. London: New Press.

Bradley, L. A., & Van der Heide, L. H. (1984). Pain-related correlates of MMPI profile subgroups among back pain patients. *Health Psychology, 3,* 157–174.

Bradley, R. H., & Corwyn, R. F. (2002). Socioeconomic status and child development. *Annual Review of Psychology, 53,* 371–399.

Braithewaite, R. L., Bianchi, C., & Taylor, S. E. (1994). Ethnographic approach to community organization and health empowerment. *Health Education Quarterly, 21,* 407–419.

Breslau, N., & Rasmussen, B. K. (2001). The impact of migraine: Epidemiology, risk factors, and co-morbidities. *Neurology. Special Headache-Related Disability in the Management of Migraine, 56,* S4–S12.

Breslow, R. A., Sorkin, J. D., Frey, C. M., & Kessler, L. G. (1997). Americans' knowledge of cancer risk and survival. *Preventive Medicine, 26,* 170–177.

Brett, J. F., Brief, A. P., Burke, M. J., George, J. M., Webster, J. (1990). Negative affectivity and the reporting of stressful life events. *Health Psychology, 9,* 57–68.

Brewer, W. (1974). There is no convincing evidence for operant or classical conditioning in adult humans. In W. Weimer & D. Palermo (Eds.), *Cognition and the symbolic processes* (pp. 115–138). Hillsdale, NJ: Erlbaum.

Brissette, I., Scheier, M. F., & Carver, C. S. (2002). The role of optimism in social network development, coping, and psychological adjustment during a life transition. *Journal of Personality and Social Psychology, 82,* 102–111.

Brisson, C., Laflamme, N., Moisan, J., Milot, A., Masse, B., & Vezina, M. (1999). Effects of family responsibilities and job strain on ambulatory blood pressure among white-collar woman. *Psychosomatic Medicine, 61,* 205–213.

Bronfrenbrenner, U. (1977). Toward an experimental ecology of human development. *American Psychologist, 32,* 513–531.

Bronzaft, A. L., & McCarthy, D. P. (1975). The effect of elevated train noise on reading ability. *Environment and Behavior, 7,* 517–527.

Brooks-Gunn, J., & Duncan, G. J. (1997). The effects of poverty on children. *Future of Children, 7,* 55–71.

Brown, D. R. (1992). Physical activity, aging, and psychological well-being: An overview of the research. *Canadian Journal of Sport Sciences, 17,* 185–193.

Brown, G. W., & Harris, T. (1978). Social origins of depression: A reply. *Psychological Medicine, 8,* 577–588.

Brown, J. D. (1991). Staying fit and staying well: Physical fitness as a moderator of life stress. *Journal of Personality and Social Psychology, 60,* 555–561.

Brown, K. W., & Moskowitz, D. S. (1997). Does unhappiness make you sick? The role of affect and neuroticism in the experience of common physical symptoms. *Journal of Personality and Social Psychology, 72,* 907–917.

Brownson, R. C., Chang, J. C., Davis, J. R., & Smith, C. A. (1991). Physical activity on the job and cancer in Missouri. *American Journal of Public Health, 81,* 639–643.

Brownson, R. C., Eyler, A. A., King, A. C., Brown, D. R., Shyu, Y., & Sallis, J. F. (2000). Patterns and correlates of physical activity among US women 40 years older. *American Journal of Public Health, 90,* 264–270.

Brumberg, J. J. (1997). *The body project: An intimate history of American girls.* New York: Vintage.

Burhansstipnov, L. (2000). Urban Native American health issues. *Cancer, 888,* 987–993.

Burleson, B. R., & Mortenson, S. R. (2003). Explaining cultural differences in evaluations of emotional support behaviors: Exploring the mediating influences of value systems and interaction goals. *Communication Research, 30,* 113–146.

Burns, V. E., Drayson, M., Ring, C., & Carroll, D. (2002). Perceived stress and psychological well-being are associated with antibody status after meningitis C conjugate vaccination. *Psychosomatic Medicine, 64,* 963–970.

Buske-Kirschbaum, A., Kirschbaum, C., Stierle, H., Lehnert, H., & Hellhammer, D. (1992). Conditioned increase of natural killer cell activity (NKCA) in humans. *Psychosomatic Medicine, 54,* 123–132.

Butow, P. N., Coates, A. S., & Dunn, S. M. (1999). Psychosocial predictors of survival in metastatic melanoma. *Journal of Clinical Oncology, 17,* 2256–2263.

Byers, T., & Doyle, C. (2004). Diet, physical activity, and cancer . . . what's the connection? Available at http://www.cancer.org/docroot/PED/content/PED_3_1x_Link_Between_Lifestyle_and_CancerMarch03.asp. Accessed May 15, 2005.

Byrd, T. L., Mullen, P. D., Selwyn, B. J., & Lorimor, R. (1996). Initiation of prenatal care by low-income Hispanic women in Houston. *Public Health Reports, 111,* 536–540.

Byrd-Bredbenner, C., Lagiou, P., & Trichopoulou, A. (2000). A comparison of household food availability in 11 countries. *Journal of Human Nutrition & Dietetics, 13,* 197–204.

Cooper, (1989). Incidence and perception of psychosocial stress: The relationship with breast cancer. *Psychological Medicine, 19,* 3290.

Caballero, A. R., Sunday, S. R., & Halmi, K. A. (2004). A comparison of cognitive and behavioral symptoms between Mexican and American eating disorder patients. *International Journal of Eating Disorders, 34,* 136–141.

Cahill, L., Prins, B., Weber, M., & McGaugh, J. L. (1994). Beta-adrenergic activation and memory for emotional events. *Nature, 371,* 702–704.

Calhoun, G., & Alforque, M. (1996). Prenatal substance afflicted children: An overview and review of the literature. *Education, 117,* 30–39.

Callister, L. C. (2003). Cultural influences on pain perceptions and behaviors. *Home Health Care Management and Practice, 15,* 207–211.

Calvo, M. G., Szabo, A., & Capafons, J. (1996). Anxiety and heart rate under psychological stress: The effects of exercise-training. *Anxiety, Stress and Coping: An International Journal, 9,* 321–337.

Campfield, L. A., Smith, F. J., & Burn, P. (1996). The OB protein (leptin) pathway—A link between adipose tissue mass and central neural networks. *Hormone and Metabolic Research, 28,* 619–632.

Cannon, W. B. (1914). The interrelations of emotions as suggested by recent physiological researches. *American Journal of Physiology, 25,* 256–282.

Cannon, W. B. (1929). *Bodily changes in pain, hunger, fear and rage.* Oxford, England: Appleton.

Cannon, W. B. (1932). *The wisdom of the body.* New York: Norton.

Cantor, M. H. (1979). Neighbors and friends: An overlooked resource in the informal support system. *Research on Aging, 1,* 434–463.

Cao, G., Booth, S. L., Sadowski, J. A., & Prior, R. (1998). Increases in human plasma antioxidant capacity after consumption of controlled diets high in fruits and vegetables. *American Journal of Clinical Nutrition, 68,* 1081–1087.

Caplan, G. (1964). *Principles of preventive psychiatry.* Oxford, England: Basic Books.

Cappell, H., & Greeley, J. (1987). Alcohol and tension reduction: An update on research and theory. In H. T. Blane & K. E. Leonard (Eds.), *Psychological theories of drinking and alcoholism* (pp. 15–50). New York: Guilford Press.

Carlson, L. E., Speca, M., Patel, K. D., & Goodey, E. Mindfulness-based stress reduction in relation to quality of life, mood, symptoms of stress, and immune parameters in breast and prostate cancer outpatients. *Psychosomatic Medicine, 65,* 571–581.

Carmichael Olson, H., Streissguth, A.P., Sampson, P.D., Barr, H.M., Bookstein, F.L., & Thiede, K. (1997). Association of prenatal alcohol exposure with behavioral and learning problems in early adolescence. *Journal of the American Academy of Child & Adolescent Psychiatry, 36*(9), 1187–1194.

Carstensen, L. L. (1987). Age-related changes in social activity. In L. L. Carstensen & B. A. Edelstein (Eds.), *Handbook of clinical gerontology* (Vol. 146, pp. 222–237). Elmsford, NY: Pergamon Press.

Carstensen, L. L., & Fisher, J. E. (1991). Treatment application for psychological and behavioral problems of the elderly in nursing homes. In P. A. Wisocki (Ed.), *Handbook of clinical behavior therapy with the elderly client. Applied clinical psychology* (pp. 337–362). New York: Plenum Press.

Carstensen, L. L., Isaacowitz, D. M., & Charles, S. T. (1999). Taking time seriously: A theory of socioemotional selectivity. *American Psychologist, 54,* 165–181.

Carter, C. S. (1998). Neuroendocrine perspectives on social attachment and love. *Psychoneuroendocrinology, 23,* 779–818.

Carvajal, S. C., Garner, R. L., & Evans, R. I. (1998). Dispositional optimism as a protective factor in resisting HIV exposure in sexually active inner-city minority adolescents. *Journal of Applied Social Psychology, 28,* 2196–2211.

Carver, C. S., & Scheier, M. F. (1994). Situational coping and coping dispositions in a stressful transaction. *Journal of Social and Personality Psychology, 56,* 267–283.

Carver, C. S., Pozo, C., Harris, S. D., Noriega, V., Scheier, M. F., Robinson, D. S., et al. (1993). How coping mediates the effect of optimism on distress: A study of women with early stage breast cancer. *Journal of Social and Personality Psychology, 65,* 375–390.

Carver, C. S., Pozo-Kaderman, C., Harris, S. D., Noriega, V., Scheier, M. F., Robinson, D. S., et al. (1994). Optimism versus pessimism predicts the quality of women's adjustments to early stage breast cancer. *Cancer, 73,* 1213–1220.

Carver, C. S., & Scheier, M. F. (1999). Stress, coping, and self-regulatory processes. In L. A. Pervin & O. P. John (Eds.), *Handbook of personality: Theory and research* (2nd ed.) (pp. 553–575). New York: Guilford Press.

Carver, C. S., Scheier, M. F., & Weintraub, J. K. (1989). Assessing coping strategies: A theoretically based approach. *Journal of Personality and Social Psychology, 56,* 267–283.

Case, R. B., Moss, A. J., Case, N., McDermott, M., & Eberly, S. (1992). Living alone after myocardial infarction: Impact on prognosis. *The Journal of the American Medical Association, 267,* 515–524.

Caspersen, C. J., Powell, K. E., & Christenson, G. M. (1985). Physical activity, exercise, and physical fitness: Definitions and distinctions for health related research. *Public Health Reports, 100,* 126–131.

Caspi, A., Begg, D., Dickson, N., Harrington, H., Langley, J., Moffitt, T. E., & Silva, P. A. (1997). Personality differences predict health-risk behaviors in young adulthood: Evidence from a longitudinal study. *Journal of Personality and Social Psychology, 73,* 1052–1063.

Cassel, J. (1976). The contribution of the social environment to host resistance. *American Journal of Epidemiology, 104,* 107–123.

Cassidy, J., & Shaver, P. R. (1999). *Handbook of attachment: Theory, research, and clinical applications.* New York: Guilford Press.

Catania, J. A., Binson, D., Dolcini, M. M., Moskowitz, J. T., & van der Straten, A. (2002). Frontiers in the behavioral epidemiology of HIV/STDs. In A. Baum, T. A. Revenson, & J. E. Singer (Eds.), *Handbook of health psychology* (pp. 777–800). Mahwah, NJ: Erlbaum.

Catania, J. A., Kegeles, S. M., & Coates, T. J. (1990a). Psychosocial predictors of people who fail to return for their HIV test results. *AIDS, 4,* 261–262.

Catania, J. A., Kegeles, S. M., & Coates, T. J. (1990b). Towards an understanding of risk behavior: An AIDS risk reduction model (ARRM). *Health Education Quarterly, 17,* 381–399.

Cattell, R. B. (1966). *The scientific analysis of personality.* Chicago: Aldine.

Cauce, A. M., Felner, R. D., & Primavera, J. (1982). Social support in high-risk adolescents: Structural components and adaptive impact. *American Journal of Community Psychology, 10,* 417–428.

Centers for Disease Control and Prevention. (2003). Deaths, final data for 2001, National vital statistics reports, 52. Retrieved from http://www.cdc.gov/nchs/data/nvsr52/nvsr52_03.pdf. December 2004.

Centers for Disease Control and Prevention. (2004). Deaths, final data for 2002, National vital statistics reports, 53. Retrieved from http://www.cdc.gov/nchs/fastats/infmort.htm. December 2004.

Champion, V., & Menon, U. (1997). Predicting mammography and breast self-examination in African American women. *Cancer Nursing, 20,* 315–322.

Champion, V. L. (1999). Revised susceptibility, benefits, and barriers scale for mammography screening. *Research in Nursing and Health, 22,* 341–348.

Champion, V. L., Ray, D. W., Heilman, D. K., & Springston, J. K. (2000). A tailored intervention for mammography among low-income African-American women. *Journal of Psychosocial Oncology, 18,* 1–13.

Chan, C.W. and Chang, J.K. (1976). The role of Chinese medicine in New York City's Chinatown. *American Journal of Chinese Medicine, 4*(1), 31–45.

Chandarana, P., & Pellizzari, J. R. (2001). Health psychology: South Asian perspectives. In S. S. Kazarian & D. R. Evans (Eds.), *Handbook of cultural health psychology* (pp. 411–444). San Diego, CA: Academic Press.

Chang, D. M., Chang, W. Y., Kuo, S. Y., & Chang, M. L. (1997). The effects of traditional antirheumatic herbal medicines on immune response cells. *Journal of Rheumatology, 24,* 436–441.

Chang, E. C. (1998). Dispositional optimism and primary and secondary appraisal of a stressor: Controlling for confounding influences and relations to coping and psychological and physical adjustment. *Journal of Personality and Social Psychology, 74,* 1109–1120.

Chassin, L., Rogosch, F., & Barrera, M. (1991). Substance use and symptomatology among adolescent children of alcoholics. *Journal of Abnormal Psychology, 100,* 449–463.

Chen, E. (2004). Why socioeconomic status affects the health of children. *Current Directions in Psychological Science, 13,* 112–115.

Chen, H., Haley, W. E., Robinson, B. E., & Schonwetter, R. S. (2003). Decisions for hospice care in patients with advanced cancer. *Journal of the American Geriatrics Society, 51,* 789–797.

Chesney, M., & Darbes, L. (1998). Social support and heart disease in women: Implications for intervention. In K. Orth-Gomer & M. Chesney (Eds.), *Women, stress, and heart disease* (pp. 165–182). Mahwah, NJ: Erlbaum.

Chesney, M. A., & Antoni, M. H. (2002). Innovative approaches to health psychology: Prevention and treatment lessons from AIDS. *Application and practice in health psychology.* Washington, DC: American Psychological Association.

Chesney, M. A., & Ozer, E. M. (1995). Women and health: In search of a paradigm. *Women's Health: Research on Gender, Behavior and Policy, 1,* 3–26.

Chilman, C. S. (1993). Hispanic families in the United States. In H. P. McAdoo (Ed.), *Family ethnicity: Strength in diversity* (pp. 141–163). Newbury Park, CA: Sage.

Christensen, A. J., Smith, T. W., Turner, C. W., Holman, J. M., & Gregory, M. C. (1990). Type of hemodialysis and preference for behavioral involvement: Interactive effects on adherence in end-stage renal disease. *Health Psychology, 9,* 225–236.

Christiansen, C. L., Wang, F., Barton, M. B., Kreuter, W., Elmore, J. G., Gelfand, A. E., & Fletcher, S. W. (2000). Predicting the cumulative risk of false-positive mammograms. *Journal of the National Cancer Institute, 92,* 1657–1666.

Chung, K. C., Hamill, J. B., Kim, H. M., Walter, M. R., & Wilkins, E. G. (1999). Predictors of patients satisfaction in an outpatient plastic surgery clinic. *Annals of Plastic Surgery, 42,* 56–60.

Chung, R. C., & Lin, K. (1994). Help-seeking behavior among Southeast Asian refugees. *Journal of Community Psychology, 22,* 109–120.

Ciechanowski, P. S., Walker, E. A., Katon, W. J., & Russo, J. E. (2002). Attachment theory: A model for health care utilization and somatization. *Psychosomatic Medicine, 64,* 660–667.

Clancy, S. M., & Dollinger, S. J. (1993). Photographic description of the self: Gender and age differences in social connectedness. *Sex Roles, 29,* 477–495.

Clark, D. O. (1995). Racial and educational differences in physical activity among older adults. *Gerontologist, 35,* 472–480.

Clark, M. (1959). *Health in the Mexican American culture.* Berkeley, CA: University of California Press.

Clark, P. I., Scarisbrick-Hauser, A., Gautam, S. P., & Wirk, S. J. (1999). Anti-tobacco socialization in homes of African-American and White parents, and smoking and nonsmoking parents. *Journal of Adolescent Health, 24,* 329–339.

Coates, T. J., McKusick, L., Kuno, R., & Stites, D. (1989). Stress management training reduces number of sexual partners but does not enhance immune function in men infected with HIV. *American Journal of Public Health, 79,* 885–887.

Cobb, S. (1976). Social support as a moderator of life stress. *Psychosomatic Medicine, 38,* 300–314.

Cockerham, W. C. (1997). Lifestyles, social class, demographic characteristics, and health behavior. In D. S. Gochman (Ed.), *Handbook of health behavior research. 1: Personal and social determinants* (pp. 253–265). New York: Plenum Press.

Coddington, R. D. (1972). The significance of life events as etiologic factors in the diseases of children. I. A survey of professional workers. *Journal of Psychosomatic Research, 16,* 7–18.

Cohen, S., Doyle, W. J., Skoner, D. P., Frank, E., Rabin, B. S., Gwaltney, J. M., Jr., et al. (1998). Types of stressors that increase susceptibility to the common cold in healthy adults. *Health Psychology, 17,* 214–223.

Cohen, S., Evans, G. W., Krantz, D. S., & Stokols, D. (1980). Physiological, motivational, and cognitive effects of aircraft noise on children: Moving from the laboratory to the field. *American Psychologist, 35,* 231–243.

Cohen, S., Glass, D. C., & Singer, J. E. (1973). Apartment noise, auditory discrimination, and reading ability in children. *Journal of Experimental Social Psychology, 9,* 407–422.

Cohen, S., & Herbert, T. B. (1996). Health psychology: Psychological factors and physical disease from the perspective of human psychoneuroimmunology. *Annual Review of Psychology, 47,* 113–142.

Cohen, S., Kamarck, T., & Mermelstein, R. (1983). A global measure of perceived stress. *Journal of Health and Social Behavior, 24,* 385–396.

Cohen, S., & Wills, T. A. (1985). Stress, social support, and the buffering hypothesis. *Psychological Bulletin, 98,* 310–357.

Cohen Silver, R., Holman, E. A., McIntosh, D. N., Poulin, M., & Gil-Rivas, V. (2002). Nationwide longitudinal study of psychological responses to September 11. *Journal of the American Medical Association, 288,* 1235–1244.

Colditz, G. A., & Frazier, A. L. (1995). Models of breast cancer show that risk is set by early events in life: Prevention efforts must shift focus. *Cancer Epidemiology, Biomarkers and Prevention, 4,* 567–571.

Cole, S. R., Bryant, C. A., McDermott, R. J., Sorrell, C., & Flynn, M. (1997). Beliefs and mammography screening. *American Journal of Preventive Medicine, 13,* 439–443.

Cole, S. W., & Kemeny, M. E. (1997). Psychobiology of HIV infection. *Critical Reviews in Neurobiology, 11,* 289–321.

Collins, F. S., & McKusick, V. A. (2001). Implications of the Human Genome Project for medical science. *Journal of the American Medical Association, 285,* 540–544.

Colon, M., & Lyke, J. (2003). Comparison of hospice use and demographics among European Americans, African Americans, and Latinos. *American Journal of Hospice and Palliative Care, 20,* 182–190.

Commerford, M. C., Gular, E., Orr, D. A., Reznikoff, M., & O'Dowd, M. A. (1994). Coping and psychological distress in women with HIV/AIDS. *Journal of Community Psychology, 22,* 224–230.

Compas, B. E., Connor-Smith, J. K., Saltzman, H., Thomsen, A. H., & Wadsworth, M. E. (2001). Coping with stress during childhood and adolescence: Problems, progress, and potential in theory and research. *Psychological Bulletin, 127,* 87–127.

Compton, M. M., & Cidlowski, J. A. (1986). Rapid in vivo effects of glucocorticoids on the integrity of rat lymphocyte genomic DNA. *Endocrinology, 118,* 38.

Contrada, R. J., Ashmore, R. D., Gary, M. L., Coups, E., Egeth, J. D., Sewell, A., et al. (2000). Ethnicity-related sources of stress and their effects on well-being. *Current Directions in Psychological Science, 9,* 136–139.

Contrada, R. J., & Guyll, M. (2001). On who gets sick and why: The role of personality, stress, and disease. In A. Baum, T. A. Revenson, & J. E. Singer (Eds.), *Handbook of health psychology* (pp. 59–81). Mahwah, NJ: Erlbaum.

Conway, T. L., Vickers, R. R., Weid, H. W., & Rahe, R. (1981). Occupational stress and variation in cigarette, coffee, and alcohol consumption. *Journal of Health and Social Behavior, 22,* 155–165.

Cook, J. J. (1998). Dad's double binds. Rethinking fathers' bereavement from a men's studies perspective. *Journal of Contemporary Ethnography, 17,* 285–308.

Cooper, C. L., Cooper, R. F., & Faragher, E. B. (1986). Incidence and perception of psychosocial stress: The relationship with breast cancer. *Psychological Medicine, 19,* 415–422.

Copeland, E. P., & Hess, R. S. (1995). Differences in young adolescents' coping strategies based on gender and ethnicity. *Journal of Early Adolescence, 15,* 203–219.

Cordova, M. J., Cunningham, L. L. C., Carlson, C. R., & Andrykowski, M. A. (2001). Posttraumatic growth following breast cancer: A controlled comparison study. *Health Psychology, 20,* 176–185.

Cormier, L. S., Cormier, W. H., & Weisser, R. J. (1984). *Interviewing and helping skills for health professionals.* Belmont, CA: Wadsworth.

Corrao, G., Bagnardi, V., Vittadini, G., & Favilli, S. (2000). Capture-recapture methods to size alcohol related problems in a population. *Journal of Epidemiology and Community Health, 54,* 603–610.

Corrao, G., Rubbiati, L., Bagnardi, V., Zambon, A., & Poikolainen, K. (2000). Alcohol and coronary heart disease: A meta-analysis. *Addiction, 95,* 1505–1524.

Cosway, R., Endler, N. S., Sadler, A. J., & Deary, I. J. (2000). The coping inventory for stressful situations: Factorial structure and associations with personality traits and psychological health. *Journal of Applied Biobehavioral Research, 5,* 121–143.

Cottington, E. M., Matthews, K. A., Talbott, E., & Kuller, L. H. (1986). Occupational stress, suppressed anger, and hypertension. *Psychosomatic Medicine, 48,* 249–260.

Covey, L. A., & Feltz, D. L. (1991). Physical activity and adolescent female psychological development. *Journal of Youth and Adolescence, 20,* 463–474.

Cowley, G. (1998). Can you eat to beat malignancy? A controversial diet book is just one sign of the revolutionary new thinking about food and health. *Newsweek, 132,* 60–67.

Cox, D. J., & Gonder-Frederick, L. (1992). Major developments in behavioral diabetes research. *Journal of Consulting and Clinical Psychology, 60,* 628–638.

Cox, T., & Ferguson, E. (1991). Individual differences, stress and coping. In C. L. Cooper & R. Payne (Eds.), *Personality and stress: Individual differences in the stress process. Wiley series on studies in occupational stress* (pp. 7–30). Oxford, England: John Wiley.

Coyne, J. C., & Gottlieb, B. H. (1996). The mismeasure of coping by checklist. *Journal of Personality, 64,* 959–991.

Coyne, J. C., & Racioppo, M. W. (2000). Never the twain shall meet? Closing the gap between coping research and clinical intervention research. *American Psychologist, 55,* 655–664.

Crabb, D. W. (1993). The liver. In M. Galanter (Ed.), *Recent developments in alcoholism: Vol. 11. Ten years of progress* (pp. 207–230). New York: Plenum Press.

Craig, K. D. (1998). The facial display of pain. In G. A. Finley & P. J. McGrath (Eds.), *Measurement of pain in infants and children* (pp. 103–122). Seattle, WA: IASP Press.

Cross, S. E., & Madson, L. (1997). Models of the self: Self-construals and gender. *Psychological Bulletin, 122,* 5–37.

Cruess, D. G., Antoni, M. H., Schneiderman, N., Ironson, G., McCabe, P., Fernandez, J. B., et al. (2000). Cognitive-behavioral stress management increases free testosterone and decreases psychological distress in HIV-seropositive men. *Health Psychology, 19,* 12–20.

Crystal, S., & Kersting, R. C. (1998). Stress, social support, and distress in a statewide population of persons with AIDS in New Jersey. *Social Work in Health Care, 28,* 41–60.

Culver, J. L., Arena, P. L., Wimberly, S. R., Antoni, M. H., & Carver, C. S. (2004). Coping among African-American, Hispanic, and non-Hispanic White women recently treated for early stage breast cancer. *Psychology and Health, 19,* 157–166.

Curbow, B., Somerfield, M. R., Baker, F., Wingard, J. R., & Legro, M. W. (1993). Personal changes, dispositional optimism, and psychological adjustment to bone marrow transplantation. *Journal of Behavioral Medicine, 16,* 423–443.

Curran, P. J., Stice, E., & Chassin, L. (1997). The relation between adolescent alcohol use and peer alcohol use: A longitudinal random coefficients model. *Journal of Consulting and Clinical Psychology, 65,* 130–140.

Cusumano, D. L., & Thompson, J. K. (2001). Media influence and body image in 8–11-year-old boys and girls: A preliminary report on Multidimensional Media Influence Scale. *International Journal of Eating Disorders, 29,* 37–44.

Cutrona, C. E. (1990). Stress and social support: In search of optimal matching. *Journal of Social and Clinical Psychology, 9,* 3–14.

Dafoe, W., & Huston, P. (1997). Current trends in cardiac rehabilitation. *Canadian Medical Association Journal, 156,* 527–533.

Dalton, M. A., Ahrens, M. B., Sargent, J. D., Mott, L. A., Beach, M. L., Tickle, J. J., et al. (2002). Relation between parental restrictions on movies and adolescent use of tobacco and alcohol. *Effective Clinical Practice, 5,* 1–10.

Dash, B., Junius, A. M. M., & Dash, V. B. (1997). *Handbook of Ayurveda.* New Delhi, India: Loftus Press.

David, J. P., & Suls, J. (1999). Coping efforts in daily life: Role of Big Five traits and problem appraisals. *Journal of Personality, 67,* 265–294.

David, P., & Johnson, M. A. (1998). The role or self in third-person effects about body image. *Journal of Communication, 48,* 37–58.

David, R. J., & Collins, J. W. (1997). Differing birth weight among infants of U. S.-born Blacks, African-born Blacks and U. S.-born Whites. *New England Journal of Medicine, 337,* 1209–1233.

Davidson, K., & Prkachin, K. (1997). Optimism and unrealistic optimism have an interacting impact on health-promoting behavior and knowledge changes. *Personality and Social Psychology Bulletin, 23,* 617–625.

Davidson, R. J., Kabat-Zinn, J., Schumacher, J., Rozenkranz, M., Muller, D., Santorelli, S. F., et al. (2003). Alterations in brain and immune function produced by mindfulness meditation. *Psychosomatic Medicine, 65,* 564–570.

Davis, C. G., Nolen-Hoeksema, S., & Larson, J. (1998). Making sense of loss and benefiting from the experience: Two construals of meaning. *Journal of Personality and Social Psychology, 75,* 561–574.

De Boer, J. B., Sprangers, M. A. B., Aaronson, N. K., Lange, J. M. A., & van Dam, F. S. (1996). A study of the reliability, validity and responsiveness of the HIV Overview of Problems Evaluation System (HOPES) in assessing the quality of life of patients with AIDS and symptomatic HIV infection. *Quality of Life Research, 5,* 339–347.

De Vellis, B. M. (1995). The psychological impact of arthritis: Prevalence of depression. *Arthritis Care and Research, 8,* 284–289.

De Vellis, B. M., Revenson, T. A., & Blalock, S. J. (1997). Rheumatic disease and women's health. In S. J. Gallant, G. P. Keita, & R. Royak-Shaler (Eds.), *Health care for women: Psychological, social, and behavioral influences* (pp. 333–347). Washington, DC: American Psychological Association.

Dean, B. B., Borenstein, J. E., Henning, J. M., Knight, K., & Merz, C. N. (2004). Can change in high-density lipoprotein cholesterol levels reduce cardiovascular risk? *American Heart Journal, 147,* 966–976.

Deapen, D., Lui, L., Perkins, C., Bernstein, L., & Ross, R. K. (2002). Rapidly rising breast cancer incidence rates among Asian-American women. *International Journal of Cancer, 99,* 747–750.

Deater-Deckard, K., Dodge, K. A., Bates, J. E., & Pettit, G. S. (1996). Physical discipline among African Americans and European American mothers: Links to children's externalizing behaviors. *Developmental Psychology, 32,* 1065–1072.

DeBernardo, R. L., Aldinger, C. E., Dawood, O. R., Hanson, R. E., Lee, S., & Rinaldi, S. R. (1999). An e-mail assessment of undergraduate's attitudes toward smoking. *Journal of American College Health, 48,* 61–66.

DeFrain, J., Millspaugh, E., & Xiaolin, X. (1996). The psychosocial effects of miscarriage: Implications for health professionals. *Families, Systems and Health, 14,* 331–347.

DeFronzo, R., Panzarella, C., & Butler, A. C. (2001). Attachment, support seeking, and adaptive inferential feedback: Implications for psychological health. *Cognitive and Behavioral Practive, 8,* 48–52.

Delahanty, D. L., & Baum, A. (2001). Stress and breast cancer. In A. Baum, T. A. Revenson, & J. E. Singer (Eds.), *Handbook of health psychology* (pp. 747–756). Mahwah, NJ: Erlbaum.

Demark-Wahnefried, W., Rimer, B. K., & Wimer, E. P. (1997). Weight gain in women diagnosed with breast cancer. *Journal of the American Dietetic Association, 97,* 519–529.

Dembrowski, T. M., MacDougall, J. M., Williams, R. B., Haney, T. L., & Blumenthal, J. A. (1985). Components of Type A, hostility, and anger in relationship to angiographic findings. *Psychosomatic Medicine, 47,* 219–233.

Dennerstein, L. (1996). Well-being, symptoms and the menopausal transition. *Maturitas, 23,* 147–157.

Depaola, S. J., Griffin, M., Young, J. R., & Neimeyer, R. A. (2003). Death anxiety and attitudes toward the elderly among adults: The role of gender and ethnicity. *Death Studies, 27,* 335–354.

Derogatis, L. R., Morrow, G. R., Fetting, J., Penman, D., Piasetsky, S., Schmale, A. M., et al. (1983). The prevalence of psychiatric disorders among cancer patients. *Journal of the American Medical Association, 249,* 953–957.

DeRosa, C. J., & Marks, G. (1998). Preventive counseling in HIV-positive men and self-disclosure of serostatus to sex partners: New opportunities for prevention. *Health Psychology, 17,* 224–331.

Derryberry, M. (1960). Health education: Its objectives and methods. *Health Education Monographs, 8,* 5–11.

Diamond, J. M. (1999). *Guns, germs, and steel: The fates of human societies.* New York: Norton.

Dibble, S. L., Vanoni, J. M., & Miaskowski, C. (1997). Woman's attitudes toward breast cancer screening procedures: Differences by ethnicity. *Women's Health Issues, 7,* 47–54.

Dickerson, S. S., & Kemeny, M. E. (2004). Acute stressors and cortisol responses: A theoretical integration and synthesis of laboratory research. *Psychological Bulletin, 130,* 355–391.

DiClemente, C. C., & Prochaska, J. O. (1982). Self-change and therapy change of smoking behavior: A comparison of processes of change in cessation and maintenance. *Addictive Behaviors, 7,* 133–142.

Dietz, W. H. (1998). Health consequences of obesity in youth: Childhood predictors of adult disease. *Pediatrics, 101,* 518–525.

Diez-Roux, A. V., Merkin, S. S., Arnett, D., Chambless, L., Massing, M., Nieto, F. J., et al. (2001). Neighborhood of residence and incidence of coronary heart disease. *New England Journal of Medicine, 345,* 99–107.

Dignan, M., Sharp, P., Blinson, K., Michielutte, R., Konen, J., Bell, R., et al. (1995). Development of a cervical cancer education program for Native American women in North Carolina. *Journal of Cancer Education, 9,* 235–242.

DiMatteo, M. R. (1991). *The psychology of health, illness, and medical care: An individual perspective.* Belmont, CA: Brooks/Cole Publishing.

DiMatteo, M. R. (2004a). Variations in patients' adherence to medical recommendations: A quantitative review of 50 years of research. *Medical Care, 32,* 200–209.

DiMatteo, M. R. (2004b). Social support and patient adherence to medical treatment: A meta-analysis. *Health Psychology, 23,* 207–218.

Ding, X., & Staudinger, J. L. (2005). Induction of drug metabolism by forskolin: The role of the pregnane X receptor and the protein kinase A signal transduction pathway. *The Journal of Pharmacology and Experimental Therapeutics, 312,* 849–856.

DiPietro, J. A., Costigan, K. A., Hilton, S. C., & Pressman, E. K. (1999). Effects of socioeconomic status and psychosocial stress on the development of the fetus. *Annals of the New York Academy of Sciences, 896,* 356–358.

DiPlacido, J., Zauber, A., & Redd, W. H. (1998). Psychosocial issues in cancer screening. In J. Holland, W. Breitbart, M. Massie, M. Lederberg, M. Loscalzo, R. McCorkle, et al. (Eds.), *Psychooncology* (pp. 161–176). New York: Oxford University Press.

Dise-Lewis, J. E. (1988). The Life Events and Coping Inventory: An assessment of stress in children. *Psychosomatic Medicine, 50,* 484–499.

Distefan, J. M., Gilpin, E. A., Sargent, J. D., & Pierce, J. P. (1999). Do movie stars encourage adolescents to start smoking? Evidence from California. *Preventive Medicine, 28,* 1–11.

Dohrenwend, B. S., & Dohrenwend, B. P. (1974). *Stressful life events: Their nature and effects*. Oxford, England: John Wiley.

Doll, R., Peto, R., Boreham, J., & Sutherland, I. (2004). Mortality in relation to smoking: 50 years' observations on male British doctors. *British Medical Journal, 328,* 1519.

Dougall, A. L., & Baum, A. (2002). Stress, health, and illness. In A. Baum, T. A. Revenson, & J. E. Singer (Eds.), *Handbook of health psychology* (pp. 321–338). Mahwah, NJ: Erlbaum.

Doumas, D. M., Margolin, G., & John, R. S. (2003). The relationship between daily marital interaction, work, and health-promoting behaviors in dual-earner couples: An extension of the work-family spillover model. *Journal of Family Issues, 24,* 3–20.

Duan, N., Fox, S. A., Derose, K. P., & Carson, S. (2000). Maintaining mammography adherence through telephone counseling in a church-based trial. *American Journal of Public Health, 90,* 1468–1471.

Dube, M. F., & Green, C. R. (1982). Methods of collection of smoke for analytical purposes. *Recent Advances in Tobacco Science, 8,* 42–102.

Duncan, C., Jones, K., & Moon, G. (1999). Smoking and deprivation: Are there neighbourhood effects? *Social Science and Medicine, 48,* 497–505.

Dunkel-Schetter, C., & Bennett, T. L. (1990). Differentiating the cognitive and behavioral aspects of social support. In B. R. Sarason & I. G. Sarason (Eds.), *Social support: An interactional view* (pp. 267–296). Oxford, England: John Wiley.

Dunkel-Schetter, C., Feinstein, L. G., Taylor, S. E., & Falke, R. L. (1992). Patterns of coping with cancer. *Health Psychology, 11,* 79–87.

Dunkel-Schetter, C., Gurung, R. A. R., Lobel, M., & Wadhwa, P. (2001). Psychosocial processes in pregnancy: Stress as a central organizing concept. In A. Baum, J. Singer, & T. Revenson (Eds.), *Handbook of health psychology* (pp. 495–518). New York: John Wiley.

Dunkel-Schetter, C., Sagrestano, L. M., Feldman, P., & Killingsworth, C. (1996). Social support and pregnancy: A comprehensive review focusing on ethnicity and culture. In G. R. Pierce, B. *and the family. Plenum series on stress and coping* (pp. 375–412). New York: Plenum.

Dunn, A. (1989). Psychoneuroimmunology for the psychoneuroendocrinologist: A review of animal studies of nervous system-immune system interactions. *Psychoneuroendocrinology, 14,* 251–272.

Dunn, A. L., Trivedi, M. H., & O'Neal, H. A. (2001). Physical activity dose-response effects on outcomes of depression and anxiety. *Medicine and Science in Sports and Exercise, 33,* S587–S597.

Dunston, G. M, Henry, L. W., Christian, J., Ofosu, M. D., & Callendar, C. O. (1989). HLA-DR3, DQ heterogeneity in American Blacks is associated with susceptibility and resistance to insulin dependent diabetes mellitus. *Transplantation Proceedings, 21,* 653–655.

Durkheim, E. (1951). *Suicide*. New York: Free Press.

Dusseldorp, E., van Elderen, T., Maes, S., Meulman, J., & Kraaij, V. (1999). A meta-analysis of psychoeducational programs for coronary heart disease patients. *Health Psychology, 18,* 506–519.

Dweck, C. S., & Sorich, L. (1999). Mastery-oriented thinking. In C. R. Snyder (Ed.), *Coping*. New York: Oxford University Press.

Eccleston, C. (1995). Chronic pain and distraction: An experimental investigation into the role of sustained and shifting attention in the processing of chronic persistent pain. *Behavior Research and Therapy, 33,* 391–405.

Eden, K. B., Orleans, C. T., Mulrow, C. D., Pender, N. J., & Teutsch, S. M. (2002). Advice from primary care providers about physical activity: A recommendation from the U. S. Preventive Services Task Force. *Annals of Internal Medicine, 137,* 40–41.

Edgar, L., Rosberger, Z., & Nowlis, D. (1992). Coping with cancer during the first year after diagnosis: Assessment and intervention. *Cancer, 69,* 817–828.

Edman, J. L., & Yates, A. (2004). Eating disorder symptoms among Pacific Island and Caucasian women: The impact of self dissatisfaction and anger discomfort. *Journal of Mental Health, 13,* 143–150.

Edut, O. (1998). *Adios, Barbie: Young women write about body image and identity*. New York: Seal Press.

Edwards, C. L., Fillingim, R. B., & Keefe, F. (2001). Race, ethnicity and pain. *Pain, 94,* 133–137.

Edwards, C. P. (1993). Behavioral sex differences in children of diverse cultures: The case of nurturance to infants. In M. E. Pereira & L. A. Fairbanks (Eds.), *Juvenile primates: Life history, development, and behavior* (pp. 327–338). New York: Oxford University Press.

Edwards, J. R., & Rothbard, N. P. (2000). Mechanisms linking work and family: Clarifying the relationship between work and family constructs. *Academy of Management Review, 25,* 179–199.

Eisler, I., Dare, C., Russell, G. F. M., Szmukler, G., le Grange. D., & Dodge, E. (1997). Family and individual therapy in anorexia nervosa: A 5-year follow up. *Archives of General Psychiatry, 54,* 1025–1030.

Elkin, I. (1994). The NIMH Treatment of Depression Collaborative Research Program: Where we began and where we are. In A. E. Bergin, & S. Garfield (Eds.), *Handbook of psychotherapy and behavior change* (4th ed., pp. 114–139). Oxford, England: John Wiley.

Ell, K., & Dunkel-Schetter, C. (1994). Social support and adjustment to myocardial infarction, angioplasty, and coronary artery bypass surgery. In S. A. Shumaker & S. M. Czajkowski (Eds.), *Social support and cardiovascular disease. Plenum series in behavioral psychophysiology and medicine* (pp. 301–332). New York: Plenum Press.

Ell, K., Nishomoto, R., Mediansky, L., Mantell, J., & Hamovitch, M. (1992). Social relations, social support and survival among patients with cancer. *Journal of Psychosomatic Research, 36,* 531–541.

Ellenberger, H. (1981). *The discovery of the unconscious*. New York: Basic Books.

Ellis, A. (1987). The impossibility of achieving consistently good mental health. *American Psychologist, 42,* 364–375.

Elmore, J. G., Moceri, V. M., Carter, D., & Larson, E. B. (1998). Breast carcinoma tumor characteristics in Black and White women. *Cancer, 83,* 2509–2515.

Engel, L. (1959). *New trends in the care and treatment of the mentally ill*. Oxford, England: National Association for Mental Health.

Epping-Jordan, J. E., Compas, B. E., & Howell, D. C. (1994). Predictors of cancer progression in young adult men and women: Avoidance, intrusive thoughts, and psychological symptoms. *Health Psychology, 13,* 539–547.

Escobar, A. (1999). Are all food pyramids created equal? *Family Economics and Nutrition Review, 12,* 75–78.

Escobar, J. I., Randolph, E. T., & Hill, M. (1986). Symptoms of schizophrenia in Hispanic and Anglo veterans. *Culture, Medicine and Psychiatry, 10,* 259–276.

Espino, D. V., & Maldonado, D. (1990). Hypertension and acculturation in elderly Mexican Americans: Results from 1982–84 Hispanic HANES. *Journal of Gerontology, 45,* M209–M213.

Everly, G. S., & Girdano, D. A. (1980). *The stress mess solution*. Bowie, MD: Robert J. Brady.

Evers, A. W. M., Kraaimaat, F. W., Geenen, R., & Bijlsma, J. W. J. (1997). Determinants of psychological distress and its course in the first year after diagnosis in rheumatoid arthritis patients. *Journal of Behavioral Medicine, 20,* 489–504.

Everson, S. A., Goldberg, D. E., Kaplan, G. A., & Cohen, R. D. (1996). Hopelessness and risk of mortality and incidence of myocardial infarction and cancer. *Psychosomatic Medicine, 58,* 113–121.

Exline, J. J., Yali, A. M., & Lobel, M. (1999). When God disappoints: Difficulty forgiving God and its role in negative emotion. *Journal of Health Psychology, 4,* 365–379.

Fadiman, A. (1997). *The spirit catches you and you fall down: A Hmong child, her American doctors, and the collusion of two cultures*. New York: Farrar, Straus and Giroux.

Fagot-Campagna, A., Pettitt, D. J., Engelgau, M. M., Burrows, N. R., Geiss, L. S., Valdez, R., et al. (2000). Type 2 diabetes among North American children and adolescents: An epidemiologic review and a public health perspective. *The Journal of Pediatrics, 136,* 664–672.

Fahey, J. L., & Flemming, D. S. (Eds.) (1997). *AIDS/HIV reference guide for medical professionals* (4th ed.). Baltimore: Williams & Wilkins.

Fahey, J. W., Zhang, Y., & Talalay, P. (1997). Broccoli sprouts: An exceptionally rich source of inducers of enzymes that protect against chemical carcinogens. *Proceeding of the National Academy of Sciences, USA, 94,* 10367–10372.

Farmer, M. E., Locke, B. Z., Moscicki, E. K., Dannenberg, A. L., Larson, D. B., & Radloff, L. S. (1988). Physical activity and depressive symptoms: The NHANES I epidemiologic follow-up study. *American Journal of Epidemiology, 128,* 1340–1351.

Farran, C. J., Paun, O., & Elliot, M. H. (2003). Spirituality in multicultural caregivers of persons with dementia. *Dementia: The International Journal of Social Research & Practice, 2,* 353–377.

Faucett, J., Gordon, N., & Levine, J. (1994). Differences in postoperative pain among four ethnic groups. *Journal of Pain and Symptom Management, 9,* 383–389.

Fawzy, F. I., Fawzy, N., Hyun, C. S., Guthrie, D., Fahey, J. L., & Morton, D. (1993). Malignant melanoma: Effects of an early structured psychiatric intervention, coping, and effective state on recurrence and survival six years later. *Archives of General Psychiatry, 50,* 681–689.

Feeney, J. A., & Ryan, S. M. (1994). Attachment style and affect regulation: Relationships with health behavior and family experiences of illness in a student sample. *Health Psychology, 13,* 334–345.

Feifel, H., & Strack, S. (1989). Coping with conflict situations: Middle-aged and elderly men. *Psychology & Aging, 4,* 26–33.

Feldman, P. J., Cohen S., Gwaltney, J. M., Jr., Doyle, W. J., & Skoner, D. P. (1999). The impact of personality on the reporting of unfounded symptoms and illness. *Journal of Personality and Social Psychology, 77,* 370–378.

Field, D. (1999). A cross-cultural perspective on continuity and change in social relations in old age: Introduction to a special issue. *International Journal of Aging and Human Development, 48,* 257–261.

Field, T. M. (1998). Massage therapy effects. *American Psychologist, 53,* 1270–1281.

Field, T. M. (2002). Infants' need for touch. *Human Development, 45,* 100–103.

Fields, H. F. (1987). *Pain.* New York: McGraw-Hill.

Fillingim, R. B. (2003). Sex-related influences on pain: A review of mechanisms and clinical implications. *Rehabilitation Psychology, 48,* 165–174.

Finckh, U. (2001). The dopamine D2 receptor gene and alcoholism: Association studies. In D. P. Agarwal & H. K. Seitz (Eds.), *Alcohol in health and disease* (pp. 151–176). New York: Marcel Dekker.

Fiori, M. C., Jorenby, D. E., Wetter, D. W., Kenford, S. L., Smith, S. S., & Baker, T. B. (1993). Prevalence of daily and experimental smoking among UW-Madison undergraduates, 1989–1993. *Wisconsin Medical Journal, 92,* 605–608.

Fischer, W. A., Fisher, J. D., & Rye, B. J. (1995). Understanding and promoting AIDS-preventive behavior: Insights from the theory of reasoned action. *Health Psychology, 14,* 255–264.

Fishbein, M., & Ajzen, I. (1975). *Belief, attitude, intention and behavior: An introduction to theory and research.* Boston: Addison-Wesley.

Fisher, J. D., Bell, P. A., & Baum, A. (1984). *Environmental psychology* (2nd ed.). New York: Holt, Rinehart & Winston.

Fiske, S. T. (2004). *Social beings: A core motives approach to social psychology.* New York: John Wiley.

Fitchett, G., Rybarczyk, B. D., DeMarco, G. A., & Nicholas, J. J. (1999). The role of religion in medical rehabilitation outcomes: A longitudinal study. *Rehabilitation Psychology, 44,* 333–353.

Flaherty, J., & Richman, J. A. (1989). Gender differences in the perception and utilization of social support: Theoretical perspectives and an empirical test. *Social Science & Medicine, 28,* 1221–1228.

Flannery, R. B., Sos, J., & McGovern, P. (1981). Ethnicity as a factor in the expression of pain. *Psychosomatics, 22,* 39–50.

Flegal, K. M., Carroll, M. D., Kuczmarski, R. J., & Johnson, C. L. (1998). Overweight and obesity in the United States: Prevalence and trends, 1960–1994. *International Journal of Obesity, 22,* 39–48.

Fleishman, J. A., & Fogel, B. (1994). Coping and depressive symptoms among young people with AIDS. *Health Psychology, 13,* 156–169.

Fleming, R., Baum, A., Gisriel, M. M., & Gatchel, R. J. (1982). Mediating influences of social support on stress at Three Mile Island. *Journal of Human Stress, 8,* 14–22.

Fletcher, G. F. (1996). The antiatherosclerotic effect of exercise and development of an exercise prescription. *Cardiology Clinics, 14,* 85–96.

Flor, H. (2001). Psycho physiological assessment of the patient with chronic pain. In D. C. Turk & R. Melzack (Eds.), *Handbook of pain assessment* (2nd ed., pp. 76–96). New York: Guilford Press.

Flor, H., Birbaumer, N., & Turk, D. C. (1990). The psychobiology of chronic pain. *Advances in Behavior Research & Therapy, 12,* 47–84.

Flor, H., Kerns, R. D., & Turk, D. C. (1987). The role of spouse reinforcement, perceived pain, and activity levels of chronic pain patients. *Journal of Psychosomatic Research, 31,* 251–259.

Foley, K. M. (1997). Competent care for the dying instead of physician-assisted suicide. *The New England Journal of Medicine, 54–58.*

Folkman, S., & Lazarus, R. S. (1988). *Ways of coping questionnaire.* Palo Alto, CA: Mind Garden.

Folkman, S., Lazarus, R. S., Gruen, R. J., & DeLongis, A. (1986). Appraisal, coping, health status, and psychological symptoms. *Journal of Personality and Social Psychology, 50,* 571–579.

Folkman, S., & Moskowitz, J. T. (2000). Positive affect and the other side of coping. *American Psychologist, 55,* 647–654.

Fontane, P. E. (1996). Exercise, fitness, feeling well: Aging well in contemporary society. II. Choices and processes. *American Behavioral Scientist, 39,* 288–305.

Ford, E. S. (1999). Body mass index and colon cancer in a national sample of adult US men. *American Journal of Epidemiology, 150,* 390–398.

Fordyce, W. E. (1988). Pain and suffering: A reappraisal. *American Psychologist, 43,* 276–282.

Fordyce, W. E. (1990). Environmental and interoceptive influences on chronic low back pain behavior: Response. *Pain, 43,* 133–134.

Forlenza, M. J., & Baum, A. (2000). Psychosocial influences on cancer progression: Alternative cellular and molecular mechanisms. *Current Opinion in Psychiatry, 13,* 639–645.

Fors, E. A., Sexton, H., & Gotestam, G. (2002). The effect of guided imagery and amitriptyline on daily fibromyalgia pain: A prospective, randomized, controlled trial. *Journal of Psychiatric Research, 36,* 179–187.

Fournier, M., de Ridder, D., & Bensing, J. (2002a). How optimism contributes to the adaptation of chronic illness: A prospective study into the enduring effects of optimism on adaptation moderated by the controllability of chronic illness. *Personality and Individual Differences, 33,* 1163–1183.

Fournier, M., de Ridder, D., & Bensing, J. (2002b). Optimism and adaptation to chronic disease: The role of optimism in relation to self-care options of Type I diabetes mellitus, rheumatoid arthritis and multiple sclerosis. *British Journal of Health Psychology, 7,* 409–432.

Fournier, M., de Ridder, D., & Bensing, J. (2003). Is optimism sensitive to the stressors of chronic disease? The impact of Type 1 diabetes mellitus and multiple sclerosis on optimistic beliefs. *Psychology and Health, 18,* 277–294.

Fox, B. H. (1998). A hypothesis about Spiegel et al.'s 1989 paper on psychosocial intervention and breast cancer survival. *Psychooncology, 7,* 361–370.

Francis, M. E., & Pennebaker, J. W. (1992). Putting stress into words: Writing about personal upheavals and health. *American Journal of Health Promotion, 6,* 280–287.

Frankel, R. M. (1995). Emotion and the physician-patient relationship. *Motivation and Emotion, 19,* 163–173.

Frankenhaeuser, M., Lundenberg, U., Fredrikson, M., Melin, B., Tuomisto, M., & Myrsten, A-L. (1989). Stress on and off the job as related to sex and occupational status in white-collar workers. *Journal of Organizational Behavior, 10,* 321–346.

Frankl, V. (1963). *Man's search for meaning.* Boston: Beacon.

Frasure-Smith, N., Lesperance, F., & Talajic, M. (1995). The impact of negative emotions on prognosis following myocardial infarction: Is it more than depression? *Health Psychology, 14,* 388–398.

Frasure-Smith, N., & Prince, R. H. (1987). The ischemic heart disease life stress monitoring program: Possible therapeutic mechanisms. *Psychology and Health, 1,* 273–285.

Freedman, J. L. (1975). *Crowding and behavior.* San Francisco: W. H. Freeman.

Freeman, M. A., Hennessy, E. V., & Marzullo, D. M. (2001). Defensive evaluation of antismoking messages among college-age smokers: The role of possible selves. *Health Psychology, 20,* 424-33.

Freeman, V. L., Meydani, M., Young, S., Pyle, J., Wan, Y., Arvizu-Durazo, R., et al. (2000). Prostatic levels of tocopherols, carotenoids, and retinol in relation to plasma levels and self-reported usual dietary intake. *American Journal of Epidemiology, 151,* 109–118.

Freud, S. (1940/1964). New introductory lectures on psychoanalysis. In J. Strachey (Ed.), *The standard edition of the complete psychological works of Sigmund Freud* (Vol. 22). London: Hogarth.

Friedman, G. D., Armstrong, M. A., Kipp, H., & Klatsky, A. L. (2003). Wine, liquor, beer, and mortality. *American Journal of Epidemiology. 158,* 585–595.

Friedman, H., Klein, T., & Specter, S. (1991). Immunosuppression by marijuana and components. In R. Ader & D. L. Felton (Eds.), *Psychoneuroimmunology* (pp. 931–953). San Diego, CA: Academic Press.

Friedman, H. S. (2000). Long-term relations of personality and health: Dynamisms, mechanisms, tropism. *Journal of Personality, 68,* 1089–2008.

Friedman, H. S., & Booth-Kewley, S. (1987). The "disease-prone personality." A meta-analytic view of the construct. *American Psychologist, 42,* 539–555.

Friedman, H. S., Hall, J. A., & Harris, M. J. (1995). Type A behavior, nonverbal expressive style, and health. *Journal of Personality and Social Psychology, 48,* 1299–1315.

Friedman, L. C., Webb, J. A., Weinberg, A. D., Lane, M., Cooper, H. P., & Woodruff, A. (1995). Breast cancer screening: Racial/ethnic differences in behaviors and beliefs. *Journal of Cancer Education, 10,* 213–216.

Friedman, M., Breall, W. S., Goodwin, M. L., Sparagon, B. J., Ghandour, G., & Fleischmann, N. (1996). Effect of Type A behavioral counseling on frequency of silent myocardial ischemia in coronary patients. *American Heart Journal, 132,* 933–940.

Friedman, M., & Rosenman, R. H. (1959). Association of specific overt behavior pattern with blood and cardiovascular findings: Blood cholesterol level, blood clotting time, incidence of arcus senilis, and clinical coronary artery disease. *Journal of the American Medical Association, 169,* 1286–1296.

Friedman, M., & Rosenman, R. H. (1974). *Type A behavior and your heart.* New York: Knopf.

Friedman, M., Thoresen, C. E., Gill, J. J., Ulmer, D., Powell, L. H., Price, V. A., et al. (1986). Alteration of Type A behavior and its effect on cardiac recurrences in post myocardial infarction patients: Summary results of the recurrent coronary prevention project. *American Heart Journal, 112,* 653–665.

Frone, M. R., Russell, M., & Cooper, M. L. (1995). Relationship of work and family stressors to psychological distress: The independent moderating influence of social support, mastery, active coping, and self-focused attention. In R. Crandall & P. L. Perrewé (Eds.), *Occupational stress: A handbook* (pp. 129–150). Philadelphia: Taylor & Francis.

Fudin, R., & Lembessis, E. (2004). The Mozart effect: Questions about the seminal findings of Rauscher, Shaw and colleagues. *Perceptual & Motor Skills, 98,* 389–406.

Fujimoto, W. Y. (1992). The growing prevalence of non-insulin-dependent diabetes in migrant Asian populations and its implications for Asia. *Diabetes Research and Clinical Practice, 15,* 167–183.

Fuller, T. D., Edwards, J. N., Sermsri, S., & Vorakitphokatron, S. (1993). Gender and health: Some Asian evidence. *Journal of Health and Social Behavior, 34,* 252–271.

Fulton, J. P., Rakowski, W., & Jones, A. C. (1995). Determinants of breast cancer screening among inner-city Hispanic women in comparison with other inner-city women. *Public Health Reports, 110,* 476–482.

Futterman, A. D., Kemeny, M. E., Shapiro, D., & Fahey, J. L. (1994). Immunological and physiological changes associated with induced positive and negative mood. *Psychosomatic Medicine, 56,* 499–511.

Gaines, S. O., Jr. (1997). Culture, ethnicity, and personal relationship processes. New York: Routledge.

Galanti, G. (2004). *Caring for patients from different cultures.* Philadelphia: University of Pennsylvania Press.

Gall, T. L., & Cornblat, M. W. (2002). Breast cancer survivors give voice: A qualitative analysis of spiritual factors in long-term adjustment. *Psycho-Oncology, 11,* 524–535.

Galligan, R. F., & Terry, D. J. (1993). Romantic ideals, fear of negative implications, and the practice of safe sex. *Journal of Applied Social Psychology, 23,* 1685–1711.

Gallo, J. J., Armenian, H. K., Ford, D. E., Eaton, W. W., & Khachaturian, A. S. (2000). Major depression and cancer: The 13-year follow-up of the Baltimore epidemiologic catchment area sample (United States). *Cancer Causes and Control, 11,* 751–758.

Gant, L. M., & Ostrow, D. G. (1995). Perceptions of social support and psychological adaptation to sexually acquired HIV among White and African American men. *Social Work, 40,* 215–224.

Ganzini, L., Harvath, T. A., Jackson, A., Goy, E. R., Miller, L. L., & Delorit, M. A. (2002). Experiences of Oregon nurses and social workers with hospice patients who requested assistance with suicide. *New England Journal of Medicine, 347,* 582–588.

Gao, F., Bailes, E., Robertson, D. L., Chen, Y., Rodenburg, C. M., Michael, S. F., et al. (1999). Origin of HIV-1 in the chimpanzee *Pan troglodytes. Nature, 397,* 436–441.

Garcia, H. B., & Lee, P. C. Y. (1989). Knowledge about cancer and use of health care services among Hispanic- and Asian-American older adults. *Journal of Psychosocial Oncology, 6,* 157–177.

Garcia, K., & Mann, T. (2003). From "I wish" to "I will": Social-cognitive predictors of behavioral intentions. *Journal of Health Psychology, 8,* 347–360.

Garnett, G. P., & Anderson, R. M. (1993). Contact tracing and the estimation of sexual mixing patterns: The epidemiology of gonococcal infections. *Sexually Transmitted Diseases, 20,* 181–190.

Garrison, V. (1977). Doctor, espirista, or psychiatrist: Health seeking behavior in a Puerto Rican neighborhood of New York City. *Medical Anthropologist, 1,* 165–191.

Garssen, B., & Goodkin, K. (1999). On the role of immunological factors as mediators between psychosocial factors and cancer progression. *Psychiatry Research, 85,* 51–61.

Gatchel, R. J. (2005). *Clinical essentials of pain management.* Washington, DC: American Psychological Association.

Gatchel, R. J., & Oordt, M. S. (2003a). *Clinical health psychology and primary care: Practical advice and clinical guidance for successful collaboration.* Washington, DC: American Psychological Association.

Gatchel, R. J., & Oordt, M. S. (2003b). Coping with chronic or terminal illness. In R. J. Gatchel & M. S. Oordt (Eds.), *Clinical health psychology and primary care: Practical advice and clinical guidance for successful collaboration* (pp. 213–233). Washington, DC: American Psychological Association.

Gazmararian, J. A., Adams, M. M., & Pamuk, E. R. (1996). Associations between measures of socioeconomic status and maternal health behavior. *American Journal of Preventive Medicine, 12,* 108–115.

Geertsen, R., Kane, R. L., Klauber, M. R., Rindflesh, M., & Gray, R. (1975). A re-examination of Suchman's views on social factors in health care utilization. *Journal of Health and Social Behavior, 16*, 226–37.

Gelernter, J., Goldman, D., & Risch, N. (1992). The A1 allele at the D2 dopamine receptor gene and alcoholism: A reappraisal. *Journal of the American Medical Association, 269*, 1673–1677.

George, L. K. (1989). Stress, social support, and depression over the life-course. In K. S. Markides & C. L. Cooper (Eds.), *Aging, stress and health* (pp. 241–267). Oxford, England: John Wiley.

Gerstein, D. R., & Green, L. W. (1993). *Preventing drug abuse: What do we know?* Washington, DC: National Academy Press.

Gesell, A. (1928). *Infancy and human growth.* Oxford, England: Macmillan.

Geyer, S. J. (1993). Urinalysis and urinary sediment in patients with renal disease. *Clinical Laboratory Medicine, 13*, 13–20.

Giblin, P. T., Poland, M. L., & Ager, J. W. (1990). Effects of social supports on attitudes, health behaviors and obtaining prenatal care. *Journal of Community Health, 15*, 357–368.

Gilanshah, F. (1993). Islamic customs regarding death. In D. P. Irish, K. F. Lundquist, & V. J. Nelsen (Eds.), *Ethnic variations in dying, death, and grief: Diversity in universality* (pp. 137–145). Philadelphia: Taylor and Francis.

Gilbert, S. C. (2003). Eating disorders in women of color. *Clinical Psychology: Science and Practice, 10*, 444–455.

Gilliland, F. D., Li, Y., Baumgartner, K. B., Crumley, D., & Samet, J. (2001). Physical activity and breast cancer risk in Hispanic and non-Hispanic White women. *American Journal of Epidemiology, 154*, 442–450.

Gilliland, S. S., Carter, J. S., Perez, G. E., Two Feathers, J., Kenui, C. K., & Mau, M. K. (1998). Recommendations for development and adaptation of culturally competent community health interventions in minority populations with Type 2 diabetes mellitus. *Diabetes Spectrum, 11*, 166–174.

Giolas, M. H., & Sanders, B. (1992). Pain and suffering as a function of dissociation level and instructional set. *Dissociation: Progress in the Dissociated Disorders, 5*, 205–209.

Glantz, S., Slade, J., Bero, L. A., Hanauer, P., & Barnes, D. E. (1998). *The Cigarette Papers.* Berkeley: University of California Press.

Glanz, K., Rimer, B. K., & Marcus-Lewis, F. M. (2002). Theory, research, and practice in health behavior and education. In K. Glanz, B. K. Rimer, & F. M. Lewis (Eds.), *Health behavior and health education: Theory, research, and practice* (pp. 22–43). San Francisco: Jossey-Bass.

Glass, D. C., & Singer, J. E. (1972). *Urban stress: Experiments on noise and social stressors.* New York: Academic Press.

Gleiberman, L., Harburg, E., Frone, M.R., Russell, M., & Cooper, M.L. (1995). Skin colour, measures of socioeconomic status, and blood pressure among blacks in Erie County, NY. *Annals of Human Biology, 22*, 69–73.

Gluck, M. E., & Geliebter, A. (2002). Racial/ethnic differences in body image and eating behaviors. *Eating Behaviors, 3*, 143–151.

Gogos, C. A., Ginopoulos, P., Salsa, B., Apostolidou, E., Zoumbos, N. C., & Kalfarentzos, F. (1998). Dietary omega-3 polyunsaturated fatty acids plus vitamin-E restore immunodeficiency and prolong survival for severely ill patients with generalized malignancy. *Cancer, 82*, 395–402.

Goldberg, M. G., DePue, J., Kazura, A., & Niaura, R. (1998). Models for provider-patient interaction: Applications to health behavior change. In S. A. Shumaker, E. B. Schron, J. K. Okene, & W. L. McBee (Eds.), *The handbook of health behavior change* (2nd ed., pp. 283–304). New York: Springer.

Goldenberg, I., Jonas, M., Tenenbaum, A., Boyko, V., Matetzky, S., Shotan, A., et al. (2003). Current smoking, smoking cessation, and the risk of sudden cardiac death in patients with coronary artery disease. *Archives of Internal Medicine, 163*, 2301–2306.

Goldman, L. K., & Glantz, S. A. (1998). Evaluation of antismoking advertising campaigns. *Journal of the American Medical Association, 279*, 772–777.

Goldman, M. S., DelBoca, F. K., & Darkes, J. (1999). Alcohol expectancy theory: The application of cognitive neuroscience. In K. E. Leonard & H. T. Blane (Eds.), *Psychological theories of drinking and alcoholism* (pp. 203–246). New York: Guilford Press.

Goldscheider, A. (1894). *Ueber den schmerz im physiologischer und klinischer hinsicht.* Berlin: Hirschwald.

Goldstein, A. O., Sobel, R. A., & Newman, G. R. (1999). Tobacco and alcohol use in G-rated children's animated films. *Journal of the American Medical Association, 281*, 1131–1137.

Goodkin, K., Feaster, D., Tuttle, R., Blaney, N., Kumar, M., Baum, M., et al. (1996). Bereavement is associated with time-dependent decrements in cellular immune function in asymptomatic HIV type 1-seropositive homosexual men. *Clinical and Diagnostic Laboratory Immunology, 3*, 109–113.

Goodman, E. (1999). The role of socioeconomic status gradients in explaining differences in US adolescents' health. *American Journal of Public Health, 89*, 1522–1528.

Goodwin, I. (2003). The relevance of attachment theory to the philosophy, organization, and practice of adult mental health care. *Clinical Psychology Review, 23*, 35–56.

Goodwin, R., & Giles, S. (2003). Social support provision and cultural values in Indonesia and Britain. *Journal of Cross-Cultural Psychology, 34*, 240–245.

Gordon, C. M., Carey, M. E., & Carey, K. B. (1997). Effects of a drinking event on behavioral skills and condom attitudes in men: Implications for HIV risk from a controlled experiment. *Health Psychology, 16*, 490–495.

Gordon, D. F., & Cerami, T. (2000). Cancers common in men. In R. M. Eisler & M. Hersen (Eds.), *Handbook of gender, culture, and health* (pp. 179–195). Mahwah, NJ: Erlbaum.

Gortmaker, S. L. (1985). Demography of chronic childhood diseases. In N. Hobbs & J. M. Perrin (Eds.), *Issues in the care of children with chronic illness: A sourcebook on problems, services, and policies* (pp. 135–154). San Francisco: Jossey-Bass.

Gotay, C. C., Muraoka, M. Y., & Holup, J. (2001). Cultural aspects of cancer prevention and control. In S. S. Kazarian & D. R. Evans (Eds.), *Handbook of cultural health psychology* (pp. 163–193). San Diego, CA: Academic Press.

Gottdiener, J. S., Krantz, D. S., Howell, R. H., Hecht, G. M., Klein, J., Falconer, J. J., & Rozanski, A. (1994). Induction of silent myocardial ischemia with mental stress testing: Relation to the triggers of ischemia during daily life activities and to ischemic functional severity. *Journal of the American College of Cardiology, 24*, 1645–1651.

Gottesman, D., & Lewis, M. (1982). Differences in crisis reactions among cancer and surgery patients. *Journal of Consulting and Clinical Psychology, 50*, 381–388.

Gottfredson, D. C., & Koper, C. S. (1996). Race and sex differences in the prediction of drug use. *Journal of Consulting and Clinical Psychology, 64*, 305–313.

Gottfried, A. W., Gottfried, A. E., Bathurst, K., Guerin, D. W., & Parramore, M. M. (2003). Socioeconomic status in children's development and family environment: Infancy through adolescence. In M. H. Bornstein & R. H. Bradley (Eds.), *Socioeconomic status, parenting and child development. Monographs in parenting series* (pp. 189–207). Mahwah, NJ: Erlbaum.

Grant, B. F., Hartford, T. C., Chou, P., Pickering, R., Dawson, D. A., Stinson, F. S., et al. (1991). Prevalence of DSM-III-R alcohol abuse and dependence, United States, 1988. *Alcohol, Health, and Research World, 15*, 91–96.

Grant, B. F., Hartford, T. C., Dawson, D. A., Chou, P., Dufor, M., & Pickering, R. (1994). Prevalence of DSM-IV alcohol abuse and dependence, United States, 1992. *Alcohol, Health, and Research World, 18*, 243–248.

Graugaard, P. K., & Finset, A. (2000). Trait anxiety and reactions to patient-centered and doctor-centered styles of communication: An experimental study. *Psychosomatic Medicine, 62*, 33–39.

Green, C. R., Baker, T. A., Sato, Y., Washington, T. L., & Smith, E. M. (2003). Race and chronic pain: A comparative study of young Black and White Americans presenting for management. *Journal of Pain, 4,* 176–183.

Green, L. W., Kreuter, M. W., Partridge, K. B., & Deeds, S. G. (1980). *Health education planning: A diagnostic approach.* Mountain View, CA: Mayfield.

Greenberg, J. A., & Pollack, B. (1981). Motivating students to not smoke. *Journal of Drug Education, 11,* 341–359.

Greenberg, M. A., & Stone, A. A. (1992). Emotional disclosure about trauma and its relation to health: Effects of previous disclosure and trauma severity. *Journal of Personality and Social Psychology, 63,* 75–84.

Greendale, G. A., Barrett-Conner, E., Edelstein, S., Ingles, S., & Halle, R. (1995). Lifetime leisure exercise and osteoporosis: The Rancho Bernardo study. *American Journal of Epidemiology, 141,* 951–959.

Greenwald, P., Clifford, C., Pilch, S., Heimendinger, J., & Kelloff, G. (1995). New directions in dietary studies in cancer: The National Cancer Institute. In J. B. Longnecker (Ed.), *Nutrition and biotechnology in heart disease and cancer* (pp. 229–239). New York: Plenum Press.

Greer, S., Morris, T., & Pettingale, K. W. (1979). Psychological responses to breast cancer: Effect on outcome. *Lancet,* 785–787.

Griffin, K., Rabkin, J. G., Remien, R. H., & Williams, J. B. (1998). Disease severity, physical limitations and depression in HIV-infected men. *Journal of Psychosomatic Research, 44,* 219–227.

Griffiths, W. (1972). Health education definitions, problems, and philosophies. *Health Education Monographs, 31,* 12–14.

Gronbaek, M., Deis, A., Sorensen, T. I. A., Becker, U., Schnohr, P., & Jensen, G. (1995). Mortality associated with moderate intake of wine, beer, or spirits. *British Medical Journal, 310,* 1165–1169.

Grossman, K., Grossman, K. E., Spangler, S., Suess, G., & Unzner, L. (1985). Maternal sensitivity and newborn orientation responses as related to quality of attachment in northern Germany. In I. Bretherton & E. Waters (Eds.), *Growing points of attachment theory. Monographs of the Society for Research for Child Development, 50*(1–2, Serial No. 209).

Grube, J. W., & Wallack, L. (1994). Television beer advertising and drinking knowledge, beliefs, and intentions among schoolchildren. *American Journal of Public Health, 84,* 254–259.

Grube, J. W., McGree, S. T., & Morgan, M. (1986). Beliefs related to cigarette smoking among Irish college students. *International Journal of the Addictions, 21,* 701–706.

Gruenewald, T. L., Taylor, S. E., Klein, L. C., & Seeman, T. E. (1999). Gender disparities in acute stress research [Abstract]. Proceedings of the Society of Behavioral Medicine's 20th Annual Meeting. *Annals of Behavioral Medicine, 21,* S141.

Grunberg, N. E., Brown, K. J., & Klein, L. C. (1997). Tobacco smoking. In A. Baum, S. Newman, J. Weinman, R. West, & C. McManus (Eds.), *Cambridge handbook of psychology, health, and medicine* (pp. 606–611). New York: Cambridge University Press.

Grunberg, N. E., Faraday, M. M., & Rahman, M. A. (2002). The psychobiology of nicotine self-administration. In A Baum, T. A. Revenson, & J. E. Singer (Eds.), *Handbook of health psychology* (pp. 249–262). Mahwah, NJ: Erlbaum.

Grunberg, N. E., & Klein, L. C. (1998). Biological obstacles to adoption and maintenance of health-promoting behaviors. In S. A. Shumaker, E. Schron, J. Ockene, & W. L. McBee (Eds.), *The handbook of health behavior changes* (2nd ed., pp. 269–282). New York: Springer.

Gump, B. B., & Matthews, K. A. (2000). Are vacations good for your health? The 9-year mortality experience after the multiple risk factor intervention trial. *Psychosomatic Medicine, 62,* 608–612.

Gupta, M. P., Gupta, M., Jakovcic, S., & Zak, R. (1996). Catecholamines and cardiac growth. *Molecular and Cellular Biochemistry, 163–164,* 203–213.

Gurung, R. A. R., Dunkel-Schetter, C., Collins, N., Rini, C., & Hobel, C. (2005). Psychosocial predictors of perceived prenatal stress. *Journal of Social and Clinical Psychology, 24,* 497–519.

Gurung, R. A. R., & Mehta, V. (2001). Relating ethnic identity, acculturation, and attitudes toward treating minority clients. *Cultural Diversity and Ethnic Minority Psychology, 7,* 139–151.

Gurung, R. A. R., Taylor, S. E., Kemeny, M., & Myers, H. (2004). "HIV is not my biggest problem": The impact of HIV and chronic burden on depression in women at risk for AIDS. *Journal of Social and Clinical Psychology, 23,* 490–511.

Gurung, R. A. R., Taylor, S. E., & Seeman, T. (2003). Accounting for changes in social support among married older adults: Insights from the MacArthur Studies of Successful Aging. *Psychology and Aging, 18,* 487–496.

Guthrie, N., & Carroll, K. K. (1999). Specific versus non-specific effects of dietary fat on carcinogenesis. *Progress in Lipid Research, 38,* 261–271.

Guthrie, R. (2003). *Even the rat was white.* New York: Harper and Row.

Guyton, A. C. (1977). *Basic human physiology: Normal function and mechanisms of disease.* Philadelphia: Saunders.

Haines, M. P. (1996). *A social norms approach to preventing binge drinking at colleges and universities.* Newton, MA: Higher Education Center for Alcohol and Drug Prevention.

Hak, A. E., Ma, J., Powell, C. B., Campos, H., Gaziano, J. M., Willet, W. C., & Stampfer, M. J. (2004). Prospective study of plasma carotenoids and tocopherols in relation to risk of ischemic stroke. *Stroke; a Journal of Cerebral Circulation, 35,* 1584–1588.

Hak, E., Wei, F., Nordin, J., Mullooly, J., Poblete, S., & Nichol, K. L. (2004). Development and validation of a clinical prediction rule for hospitalization due to pneumonia or influenza or death during influenza epidemics among community-dwelling elderly persons. *Journal of Infectious Diseases, 189,* 450–459.

Haley, W. E., Allen, R. S., Reynolds, S., Chen, H., Burton, A., & Gallagher-Thompson, D. (2002). Family issues in end-of-life decision making and end-of-life care. *American Behavioral Scientist, 46,* 284–298.

Haley, W. E., Turner, J. A., & Romano, J. M. (1985). Depression in chronic pain patients: Relation to pain, activity, and sex differences. *Pain, 23,* 337–343.

Hall, J. A., Epstein, A. M., DeCiantis, M. L., & McNeil, B. J. (1993). Physicians' liking for their patients: More evidence for the role of affect in medical care. *Health Psychology, 12,* 140–146.

Hanahan, D., & Weinberg, R. A. (2000). The hallmarks of cancer. *Cell, 100,* 57–70.

Hance, M., Carney, R. M., Freedland, K. E., & Skala, J. (1996). Depression in patients with coronary heart disease: A 12-month follow-up. *General Hospital Psychiatry, 18,* 61–65.

Hancock, L. (2000). *Tobacco use reduction guide for colleges and universities: Spring, 2000.* Richmond: Office of Health Promotion, Virginia Commonwealth University.

Hansen, W. B. (1993). School-based alcohol prevention programs. *Alcohol Health and Research World, 17,* 54–60.

Hanson, R. W., & Gerber, K. E. (1990). *Coping with chronic pain: A guide to patient self-management.* New York: Guilford Press.

Harburg, E., Gleiberman, L., Russell, M., & Cooper, M. L. (1991). Anger-coping styles and blood pressure in Black and White males: Buffalo, New York. *Psychosomatic Medicine, 53,* 153–164.

Harinath, K., Malhotra, A. S., Pal, K., Prasad, R., Kumar, R., Kain, T. C., et al. (2004). Effects of Hatha Yoga and Omkar meditation on cardiorespiratory performance, psychologic profile, and melatonin secretion. *Journal of Alternative and Complementary Medicine, 10,* 261–269.

Harmon, M. P., Castro, F. G., & Coe, K. (1996). Acculturation and cervical cancer: Knowledge, beliefs, and behaviors of Hispanic women. *Women and Health, 24,* 37–57.

Harrison, K. (2000). Television viewing, fat stereotyping, body shape standards, and eating disorder symptomatology in grade school children. *Communication Research, 27,* 617–640.

Harte, J. L., Eifert, G. H., & Smith, R. (1995). The effects of running and meditation on beta-endorphin, corticotrophin-releasing hormone and cortisol in plasma, and on mood. *Biological Psychology, 40,* 251–265.

Haug, M. R., & Ory, M. G. (1987). Issues in elderly patient/provider interactions. *Research on Aging, 9,* 3–44.

Hawkins, C., & Miaskowski, C. (1996). Testicular cancer: A review. *Oncology Nursing Forum, 23,* 1203–1213.

Hayden, M., Pignone, M., Phillips, C., & Mulrow, C. (2002). Aspirin for the primary prevention of cardiovascular events: A summary of the evidence for the U. S. Preventive Services Task Force. *Annals of Internal Medicine, 136,* 161–173.

Haynes, R. B., McKibbon, K. A., & Kanani, R. (1996). Systematic review of randomized controlled trials of the effects of patient adherence and outcomes of interventions to assist patients to follow prescriptions for medications. *The Cochrane Library, 2,* 1–26.

Hays, R. B., Turner, H., & Coates, T. J. (1992). Social support, AIDS-related symptoms, and depression among gay men. *Journal of Consulting and Clinical Psychology, 60,* 463–469.

Hazan, C., & Shaver, P. (1987). Romantic love conceptualized as an attachment process. *Journal of Personality and Social Psychology, 52,* 511–524.

Hazuda, H. P., Haffner, S. M., Stern, M. P., & Eifler, C. W. (1988). Effects of acculturation and socioeconomic status on obesity and diabetes in Mexican Americans. *American Journal of Epidemiology, 128,* 1289–1301.

He, J., Vupputuri, S., Allen, K., Prerost, M. R., Hughes, J., & Whelton, P. K. (1999). Passive smoking and the risk of coronary heart disease—A meta-analysis of epidemiologic studies. *New England Journal of Medicine, 340,* 920–926.

Healthy People 2010. Healthy people. Retrieved from http://www. healthypeople.gov/default.htm. May 2005.

Heaven, R., & Booth, T. (2003). Vodou Shaman: The Haitian Way of Healing and Power. New York: Destiny Press.

Hebert, J. R., Hurley, T. G., Olendzki, B. C., Teas, J., Ma, Y., & Hampl, J. S. (1998). Nutritional and socioeconomic factors in relation to prostate cancer mortality: A cross-national study. *Journal of the National Cancer Institute, 90,* 1637–1647.

Heckman, T. J., Kochman, A., Sikkema, K. J., Kalichman, S. C., Masten, J., & Goodkin, K. (2000). Late middle-aged and older men living with HIV/AIDS: Race differences in coping, social support, and psychological distress. *Journal of the National Medical Association, 92,* 436–444.

Heinberg, L. J., & Thompson, J. K. (1995). Body image and televised images of thinness and attractiveness: A controlled laboratory investigation. *Journal of Social and Clinical Psychology, 14,* 325–338.

Heitkamp, H. C., Schulz, H., Rocker, K., & Dickhuth, H. H. (1998). Endurance training in females: Changes in beta-endorphin and ACTH. *International Journal of Sports Medicine, 19,* 260–264.

Helgeson, V. S., & Cohen, S. (1996). Social support and adjustment to cancer: Reconciling descriptive, correlational, and intervention research. *Health Psychology, 15,* 135–148.

Helgeson, V. S., & Fritz, H. L. (2000). The implications of unmitigated agency and unmitigated communion for domains of problem behavior. *Journal of Personality, 68,* 1031–1057.

Helgeson, V. S., Cohen, S., Schultz, R., & Yasko, J. (1999). Education and peer discussion group interventions and adjustment to breast cancer. *Archives of General Psychiatry, 56,* 340–347.

Helgeson, V. S., Cohen, S., Schulz, R., & Yasko, J. (2000). Group support interventions for women with breast cancer: Who benefits from what? *Health Psychology, 19,* 107–114

Helgeson, V. S., Snyder, P., & Steltman, H. (2004). Psychological and physical adjustment to breast cancer over 4 years: Identifying distinct trajectories of change. *Health Psychology, 23,* 3–15.

Helmstetter, F. J., & Bellgowan, P. S. (1994). Effects of muscimol applied to the basolateral amygdala on acquisition and expression of contextual fear conditioning in rats. *Behavioral Neuroscience, 108,* 1005–1009.

Helmstetter, F. J., & Bellgowan, P. S. (1994). Hypoalgesia in response to sensitization during acute noise stress. *Behavioral Neuroscience, 108,* 177–185.

Helweg, W. A. Helweg, M. U. (1990) *An Immigrant success story: East Indians in America.* London: Hurst and Company.

Hemenover, S. H., & Dienstbier, R. A. (1996). Prediction of stress appraisals from mastery, extraversion, neuroticism, and general appraisal tendencies. *Motivation and Emotion, 20,* 299–317.

Henderson, B. N., & Baum, A. (2002). Neoplasms. In Boll, T. J., & Johnson, S. B. (Eds.), *Handbook of clinical health psychology* (Vol. 1, pp. 37–64). Washington, DC: American Psychological Association.

Henderson, G., & Springer-Littles, D. (1996). *A practitioner's guide to understanding indigenous and foreign cultures: An analysis of relationships between ethnicity, social class, and therapeutic intervention strategies.* Springfield, IL: Charles C Thomas.

Henderson-King, D., Henderson-King, E., & Hoffman, L. (2001). Media images and women's self evaluations: Social context and importance of attractiveness as moderators. *Personality and Social Psychology Bulletin, 27,* 1407–1416.

Herbert, T. B., & Cohen, S. (1993). Stress and immunity in humans: A meta-analytic review. *Psychosomatic Medicine, 55,* 364–379.

Herman-Stahl, M., & Petersen, A. C. (1996). The protective role of coping and social resources for depressive symptoms among young adolescents. *Journal of Youth and Adolescence, 25,* 733–753.

Herring, D., Britten, P., Davis, C., & Tuepker, K. (2000). Serving sizes in the food guide pyramid and on the nutrition facts label: What's different and why? *Nutrition Insights, 22.*

Hetherington, M. M., & Rolls, B. J. (1996). Sensory-specific satiety: Theoretical frameworks and central characteristics. In E. D. Capaldi (Ed.), *Why we eat what we eat: The psychology of eating* (pp. 267–290). Washington, DC: American Psychological Association.

Hiatt, R. A., Pasick, R. J., Perez-Stable, E. J., McPhee, S. J., Engelstad, L., Lee, M., et al. (1996). Pathways to early cancer detection in the multiethnic population of San Francisco Bay area. *Health Education Quarterly, 23,* S10–S27.

Hiatt, R. A., & Rimer, B. K. (1999). A new strategy for cancer control research. *Cancer Epidemiology, Biomarkers, and Prevention, 8,* 957–964.

Higginbotham, J. C., Trevino, F. M., & Ray, L. A. (1990). Utilization of curanderos by Mexican Americans: Prevalence and predictors. Findings from HHANES 1982–84. *American Journal of Public Health, 80,* 32–35.

Hightower, M. (1997). Effects of exercise participation on menstrual pain and symptoms. *Women Health 26,* 15227.

Hilgard, E. R. (1978). Covert pain in hypnotic analgesia: Its reality as tested by the real-simulator design. *Journal of Abnormal Psychology, 87,* 655–663.

Hill, A. (1993). The use of pain coping strategies by patients with phantom limb pain. *Pain, 55,* 347–353.

Hill, E. J., Hawkins, A. J., Ferris, M., & Weitzman, M. (2001). Finding an extra day a week: The positive influence of perceived job flexibility on work and family life balance. *Family Relations, 50,* 513–524.

Hill, P. C., & Pargament, K. I. (2003). Advances in the conceptualization and measurement of religion and spirituality: Implications for physical and mental health research. *American Psychologist, 58,* 64–74.

Hill, R. (1949). *Families under stress.* New York: Harper & Row.

Hilts, P. J. (1996). *Smoke Screen: The truth behind the tobacco industry cover-up.* Reading, MA: Addison-Wesley

Hines, A. M., & Caetano, R. (1998). Alcohol and AIDS-related sexual behavior among Hispanics: Acculturation and gender differences. *AIDS Education and Prevention, 10,* 533–547.

Hines, A. M., Snowden, L. R., & Graves, K. L. (1998). Acculturation, alcohol consumption and AIDS-related risky sexual behavior among African American women. *Women and Health, 27,* 17–35.

Hobfoll, S. E. (1989). Conservation of resources. *American Psychologist, 44,* 513–524.

Hochbaum, G. M. (1958). *Public participation in medical screening programs: A sociopsychological study* (PHS Publication No. 572). Washington, DC: Government Printing Office.

Hoffman-Goetz, L., Breen, N. L., & Meissner, H. (1998). The impact of social class on the use of cancer screening within three racial/ethnic groups in the United States. *Ethnicity and Disease, 8,* 43–51.

Holahan, C. J., Moos, R. H., Holahan, C. K., & Brennan, P. L. (1997). Psychosocial adjustment in patients reporting cardiac illness. *Psychology and Health, 12,* 345–359.

Holahan, C. J., Moos, R. H., & Schaefer, J. A. (1996). Coping, stress resistance, and growth: Conceptualizing adaptive functioning. In M. Zeidner & N. S. Endler (Eds.), *Handbook of coping: Theory, research, applications* (pp. 24–43). Oxford, England: John Wiley.

Holder-Perkins, V., & Wise, T. N. (2001). Somatization disorder. In K. A. Phillips (Ed.), *Somatoform and factitious disorders: Review of psychiatry* (Vol. 20, No. 3, pp. 1–26). Washington, DC: American Psychiatric Association.

Holland, J. C. (1989). Anxiety and cancer: The patient and the family. *Journal of Clinical Psychiatry, 50,* 20–25.

Holmes, T. H., & Rahe, R. H. (1967). The Social Readjustment Rating Scale. *Journal of Psychosomatic Research, 11,* 213–218.

Hooper, E. M., Comstock, L. M., Goodwin, J. M., & Goodwin, J. S. (1982). Patient characteristics that influence physician behavior. *Medical Care, 20,* 630–638.

Hoover, S. M. (2002). The culturalist turn in scholarship on media and religion. *Journal of Media and Religion, 1,* 25–36.

Horwitz, S. M., Morgenstern, H., DiPietro, L., & Morrison, C. L. (1998). Determinants of pediatric injuries. *American Journal of Diseases in Children, 142,* 605–611.

House, J. S., Umberson, D., & Landis, K. R. (1988). Structures and processes of social support. *Annual Review of Sociology, 14,* 293–318.

Hovelius, B. (1998). Kvinnors underordning inom halso-och sjukvarden. [Women hold a subordinate position in the medical and health care system] *Socialmedicinsk Tidskrift, 75,* 1–2, 4–7.

Howard, G., Wagenknecht, L. E., Burk, G. L., Diex-Roux, A., Evans, G. W., McGovern, P., et al. (1998). Cigarette smoking and progression of atherosclerosis: The Antherosclerosis Risk in Communities (ARIC) study. *Journal of the American Medical Society, 279,* 119–124.

Hu, F. B., Leitzmann, M. F., Stampfer, M. J., Colditx, G. A., Willett, W. C., Rimm, E. B., et al. (2001). Physical activity and television watching in relation to risk for Type 2 diabetes mellitus in men. *Archives of Internal Medicine, 161,* 1542–1549.

Huang, J. Z., & Joseph, J. G. (1999, May). *Does small area income inequality influence the hospitalization of children? A disease-specific analysis.* Paper presented at the meeting of the New York Academy of Sciences, Bethesda, MD.

Hubbell, F. A., Chavez, L. R., Mishra, S. I., & Valdez, R. B. (1996). Differing beliefs about breast cancer among Latinas and Anglo women. *Western Journal of Medicine, 164,* 405–409.

Huffman, J. W. (1981). Endometriosis in young teen-age girls. *Pediatric Annals, 10,* 44–49.

Hyun, O. L., Wanjeong, Y. A., Bok-Hee, Y., Miller, B. C., Schvaneveldt, J., & Lau, S. (2002). Social support for two generations of new mothers in selected populations in Korea, Hong Kong, and the United States. *Journal of Comparative Family Studies, 33,* 57–70.

Ickovics, J. R., Hamburger, M. E., Vlahov, D., Schoenbaum, E. E., Schuman, P., Boland, R. J., et al. (2001). Mortality, CD4 cell count decline, and depressive symptoms among HIV-seropositive women: Longitudinal analysis from the HIV Epidemiology Research Study. *Journal of the American Medical Association, 285,* 1466–1474.

Ickovics, J. R., Thayaparan, B., & Ethier, K. A. (2002). Women and AIDS: A contextual analysis. In A. Baum, T. A. Revenson, & J. E. Singer (Eds.), *Handbook of health psychology* (pp. 817–841). Mahwah, NJ: Erlbaum.

Irish, D. P., Lundquist, K. F., & Nelson, V. J. (Eds.). (1993). *Ethnic variations in dying, death, and grief: Diversity in universality.* Philadelphia: Taylor & Francis.

Ironson, G., Schneiderman, H., Kumar, M., & Antoni, M. H. (1994). Psychosocial stress, endocrine and immune response in HIV-1 disease. *Homeostasis in Health and Disease, 35,* 137–148.

Irwin, C. E., Cataldo, M. F., Matheny, A. P., & Peterson, L. (1992). Health consequences of behaviors: Injury as a model. *Pediatrics, 90,* 798–807.

Iverson, G. L, Stampfer, H. G., & Gaetz, M. (2002). Reliability of circadian heart pattern analysis in psychiatry. *Psychiatric Quarterly, 73,* 195–203.

Jackson, R. W., Treiber, F. A., Turner, J. R., Davis, H., & Strong, W. B. (1999). Effects of race, sex, and socioeconomic status upon cardiovascular stress responsively and recovery in youth. *International Journal of Psychophysiology, 31,* 111–119.

Jamner, L. D., Alberts, J., Leigh, H., & Klein, L. C. (1998). *Affiliative need and endogenous opioids.* Paper presented at the annual meetings of the Society of Behavioral Medicine, New Orleans, LA.

Janeway, C. A., & Travers, P. (1996). *Immuno biology: The immune system in health and disease.* New York: Garland Publishing.

Janz, N., Champion, V. L., & Strecher, V. J. (2002). The Health Belief Model. In K. Glanz, B. K. Rimer, & F. M. Lewis (Eds.), *Health behavior and health education: Theory, research, and practice* (pp. 45–66). San Francisco: Jossey-Bass.

Janz, N. K., & Becker, M. H. (1984). The Health Belief Model: A decade later. *Health Education Quarterly, 11,* 1–47.

Jeffery, R. W., French, S. A., Raether, C., & Baxter, J. E. (1994). An environment intervention to increase fruit and salad purchases in a cafeteria. *Preventive Medicine, 23,* 788–792.

Jemal, A., Clegg, L. X., Ward, E., Ries, L. A. G., Wu, X., Jamison, P. M., Wingo, P. A., Howe, H. L., Anderson, R. N., & Edwards, B. K. (2004). *Annual report to the nation on the status of cancer, 1975–2001, with a special feature regarding survival. Cancer, 101,* 3–27.

Jemal, A., Tiwari, R. C., Murray, T., Ghafoor, A., Samuels, A., Ward, E., et al. (2004). Cancer statistics, 2004. *CA—A Cancer Journal for Clinicians, 54,* 8–29.

Jemmott, J. B., Jemmott, L. S., & Fong, G. T. (1992). Reductions in HIV risk–associated sexual behaviors among Black male adolescents: Effects of an AIDS prevention intervention. *American Journal of Public Health, 82,* 372–377.

Jemmott, J. B., Jemmott, L. S., & Hacker, C. I. (1992). Predicting intentions to use condoms among African-American adolescents: The risk-associated behavior. *Ethnicity Discussions, 2,* 371–380.

Jennings, K. M. (1997). Getting a Pap smear: Focus group responses of African American and Latina women. *Oncology Nursing Forum, 24,* 827–835.

Jensen, M. P., & Karoly, P. (2001). Self-report scales and procedures for assessing pain in adults. In D. C. Turk & R. Melzack (Eds.), *Handbook of pain assessment* (2nd ed., pp. 15–34). New York: Guilford Press.

Jensen, M. P., Turner, J. A., & Romano, J. M. (1994). What is the maximum number of levels needed in pain intensity measurement? *Pain, 58,* 387–392.

Jensen, M. R. (1987). Psychobiological factors predicting the course of breast cancer. *Journal of Personality. Special Personality and Physical Health, 55,* 317–342.

Jerome, L. W., DeLeon, P. H., James, L. C., Folen, R., Earles, J., & Gedney, J. J. (2000). The coming of age of telecommunication in psychological research and practice. *American Psychologist, 55,* 407–421.

Jerram, K. L., & Coleman, P. G. (1999). The Big Five personality traits and reporting of health problems and health behaviour in old age. *British Journal of Health Psychology, 4,* 181–192.

Jessor, R., Turbin, M. S., & Costa, F. M. (1998). Protective factors in adolescent health behavior. *Journal of Personality and Social Psychology, 75,* 788–800.

Jillson-Boostrom, I. (1992). The impact of HIV on minority populations. In P. I. Ahmed & N. Ahmed (Eds.), *Living and dying with AIDS* (pp. 235–254). New York: Plenum.

John, O. P., & Srivastava, S. (1999). The Big Five Trait taxonomy: History, measurement, and theoretical perspectives. In L. A. Pervin & O. P. Oliver (Eds.), *Handbook of personality: Theory and research* (2nd ed., pp. 102–138). New York: Guilford Press.

Johnson, L. S. (1997). Developmental strategies for counseling the child whose parent or sibling has cancer. *Journal of Counseling and Development, 75,* 417–427.

Johnston, L. D., O'Malley, P. M., & Bachman, J. G. (2001). *Monitoring the future: National survey results on drug use, 1975–2000. Vol. II: College students and adults ages 19–40* (NIH Publication No. 01–4925). Bethesda, MD: National Institute on Drug Abuse.

Jones, E. E., Kannouse, D. E., Kelley, H. H., Nisbett, R. E., Valins, S., & Weiner, B. (Eds.) (1972). *Attribution: Perceiving the causes of behavior.* Morristown, NJ: General Learning Press.

Jones, F., & Fletcher, B. C. (1993). An empirical study of occupational stress transmission in working couples. *Human Relations, 46,* 881–903.

Julien, R. M. (2001). *A primer of drug action.* New York: Worth.

Just, J., Louie, L., Abrams, E., Nicholas, S. W., Wara, D., Stein, Z., et al. (1992). Genetic risk factors for perinatally acquired HIV-1 infection. *Pediatric and Perinatal Epidemiology, 6,* 215–224.

Kabat-Zinn, J. (2003). Mindfulness-based interventions in context: Past, present, and future. *Clinical Psychology: Science and Practice, 10,* 144–156.

Kahn, E. (1963). On crises. *Psychiatric Quarterly, 37,* 297–305.

Kahn, R. L., & Antonucci, T. C. (1984). *Social supports of the elderly: Family/friends/professionals.* Final Report to the National Institute on Aging (No. AG01632).

Kahn, R. L., Wolfe, D. M., Quinn, R. P., Snoek, J. D., & Rosenthal, R. A. (1964). *Organizational stress: Studies in role conflict and ambiguity.* Oxford, England: John Wiley.

Kalichman, S. C., Carey, M. P., Johnson, B. T. (1996). Prevention of sexually transmitted HIV infection: A meta-analytic review of the behavioral outcome literature. *Annals of Behavioral Medicine, 18,* 6–15.

Kalichman, S. C., Heckman, T., Kochman, A., Sikkema, K., & Bergholte, J. (2000). Depression and thoughts of suicide among middle-aged and older persons living with HIV-AIDS. *Psychiatric Services, 51,* 903–907.

Kalichman, S. C., & Ramachandran, B. (1999). Mental health implications of new HIV treatments. In D. G. Ostrow & S. C. Kalichman (Eds.), *AIDS prevention and mental health* (pp. 137–150). Dordrecht, the Netherlands: Springer.

Kalil, K. M., Gruber, J. E., Conley, J., & Sytniac, M. (1993). Social and family pressures on anxiety and stress during pregnancy. *Journal of Prenatal and Perinatal Psychology and Health, 8,* 113–118.

Kane, R. L., Klein, S. J., Bernstein, L., & Rothenberg, R. (1986). The role of hospice in reducing the impact of bereavement. *Journal of Chronic Diseases, 39,* 735–742.

Kanner, A. D., Coyne, J. C., Schaefer, C., & Lazarus, R. S. (1981). Comparison of two modes of stress measurement: Daily hassles and uplifts versus major life events. *Journal of Behavioral Medicine, 4,* 1–39.

Kaplan, G. A., & Keil, J. E. (1993). Socioeconomic factors and cardiovascular disease: A review of the literature. *Circulation, 88,* 1973–1998.

Kaplan, H. B. (Ed.) (1983). *Psychosocial stress: Trends in theory and research.* New York: Academic Press.

Kaplan, M., Marks, G., & Mertens, S. (1997). Distress and coping among women with HIV infection: Preliminary findings from a multiethnic sample. *American Journal of Orthopsychiatry, 6,* 47–53.

Kaplan, R. M., & Groessl, E. J. (2002). Applications of the cost-effectiveness methodologies in behavioral medicine. *Journal of Consulting and Clinical Psychology, 70,* 482–493.

Kaplan, R. M., & Simon, H. J. (1990). Compliance in medical care: Reconsideration of self-predictions. *Annals of Behavioral Medicine, 12,* 66–71.

Kaptchuk, T. J. (2000). *The web that has no weaver: Understanding Chinese medicine.* Chicago: Contemporary Books.

Karon, J. M., Rosenberg, P. S., McQuillan, G., Khare, M., Gwinn, M., & Petersen, L. R. (1996). Prevalence of HIV infection in the United States, 1984 to 1992. *Journal of the American Medical Association, 276,* 126–131.

Kashima, Y., Yamaguchi, S., Kim, U., Choi, S.-C., Gelfand, M. J., & Yuki, M. (1995). Culture, gender, and self: A perspective from individualism-collectivism research. *Journal of Personality and Social Psychology, 69,* 925–938.

Kastenbaum, R. (1999). Dying and bereavement. In J. C. Cavanaugh & S. K. Whitbourne (Eds.), *Gerontology: An interdisciplinary perspective* (pp. 155–185). New York: Oxford University Press.

Katz, B. P., Fortenberry, J. D., Zimet, G. D., Blythe, M. J., & Orr, D. P. (2000). Partner-specific relationship characteristics and condom use among adolescents with sexually transmitted infections. *Journal of Sex Research, 37,* 69–75

Katz, E. R., Kellerman, J., & Siegel, S. E. (1980). Behavioral distress in children with cancer undergoing medical procedures: Developmental considerations. *Journal Consulting and Clinical Psychology, 48,* 356–365.

Katzmarzyk, P. T. (2001). Obesity in Canadian children. *Canadian Medical Association Journal, 164,* 1563–1564.

Kawachi, I., Colditz, G. A., Speizer, F. E., Manson, J. E., Stampfer, M. J., Willett, W. C., et al. (1997). A prospective study of passive smoking and coronary heart disease. *Circulation, 95,* 2374–2379.

Kazarian, S. S., & Evans, D. R. (2001). *Handbook of cultural health psychology.* New York: Academic Press.

Keats, D. M. (2000). Cross-cultural studies in child development in Asian contexts. *Cross-Cultural Research: The Journal of Comparative Social Science, 34,* 339–350.

Keefe, F. J., Buffington, A. L. H., Studts, J. L., & Rumble, M. E. (2002). Behavioral medicine: 2002 and beyond. *Journal of Consulting and Clinical Psychology, 70,* 852–857.

Keefe, F. J., Smith, S. J., Buffington, A. L. H., Gibson, J., Studts, J. L., & Caldwell, D. S. (2002). Recent advances and future directions in the biopsychosocial assessment and treatment of arthritis. *Journal of Consulting and Clinical Psychology, 70,* 640–656.

Keefe, S. E., Padilla, A. M., & Carlos, M. L. (1979). The Mexican-American extended family as an emotional support system. *Human Organization, 38,* 144–152.

Keinan, G. (1997). Social support, stress, and personality: Do all women benefit from their husband's presence during childbirth? In G. R. Pierce, B. Lakey, I. G. Sarason, & B. R. Sarason (Eds.), *Sourcebook of social support and personality* (pp. 409–427). New York: Plenum Press.

Kelley, M. L., & Tseng, H. (1992). Cultural differences in child rearing: A comparison of immigrant Chinese and Caucasian American mothers. *Journal of Cross-Cultural Psychology, 23,* 444–455.

Kelly, C., Ricciardelli, L. A., & Clarke, J. D. (1999). Problem eating attitudes and behaviors in young children. *International Journal of Eating Disorders, 25,* 281–284.

Kelty, M. F., Hoffman, R. R., III, Ory, M. G., & Harden, J. T. (2000). Behavioral and sociocultural aspects of aging. In R. M. Eisler & M. Hersen (Eds.), *Handbook of gender, culture, and health* (pp. 139–160). Mahwah, NJ: Erlbaum.

Kemeny, M. E. (2003). An interdisciplinary research model to investigate psychosocial cofactors in disease: Application to HIV-1 pathogenesis. *Brain, Behavior, & Immunity, 17,* S62–S72.

Kemeny, M. E., Weiner, H., Duran, R., Taylor, S. E., Visscher, B., & Fahey, J. L. (1995). Immune system changes after the death of a partner in HIV-positive gay men. *Psychosomatic Medicine, 57,* 547–554.

Kendall, P. C. (1999). Clinical significance. *Journal of Consulting and Clinical Psychology, 67,* 283–284.

Kendrick, K. M., Da Costa, A. P., Broad, K. D., Ohkura, S., Guevara, R., Levy, F., & Keverne, E. B. (1997). Neural control of maternal behavior and olfactory recognition of offspring. *Brain Research Bulletin, 44,* 383–395.

Kennedy, S., Kiecolt-Glaser, J. K., & Glaser, R. (1988). Immunological consequences of acute and chronic stressors: Mediating role of interpersonal relationships. *The British Journal of Medical Psychology, 61,* 77–85.

Kerns, R. D., Turk, J. A., & Rudy, T. E. (1985). The West Haven-Yale Multidimensional Pain Inventory (WHYMPI). *Pain, 23,* 315 356.

Kerr, J. H., & Kuk, G. (2001). The effects of low and high intensity exercise on emotions, stress, and effort. *Psychology of Sport and Exercise, 2,* 173–186.

Kessler, R. C., Crum, R. M., Warner, L. A., Nelson, C. B., Schulenberg, J., & Antony, J. C. (1997). Lifetime co-occurrence of DSM-III-R alcohol abuse and dependence with other psychiatric disorders in the national comorbidity survey. *Archives of General Psychiatry, 54,* 313–321.

Kesteloot, H., Sasaki, S., Xie, J., & Joossens, J. V. (1994). Secular trends in cerebrovascular mortality. *Journal of Human Hypertension, 8,* 401–408.

Kiecolt-Glaser, J. K., Bane, C., Glaser, R., Malarkey, W. B. (2003). Love, marriage, and divorce: Newlyweds' stress hormones foreshadow relationship changes. *Journal of Consulting and Clinical Psychology, 71,* 176–188.

Kiecolt-Glaser, J. K., Garner, W., Speicher, C., Penn, G. M., Holliday, J., & Glaser, R. (1984). Psychosocial modifiers of immunocompetence in medical students. *Psychosomatic Medicine, 46,* 7–14.

Kiecolt-Glaser, J. K., & Glaser, R. (1991). Stress and immune function in humans. In R. Ader, D. L. Felten, & N. Cohen (Eds.), *Psychoneuroimmunology* (2nd ed., pp. 849–867). New York: Academic Press.

Kiecolt-Glaser, J. K., Glaser, R., Cacioppo, J. T., & Malarkey, W. B. (1998). Marital stress: Immunologic, neuroendocrine, and autonomic correlates. In S. M. McCann, J. M. Lipton, et al. (Eds.), *Annals of the New York Academy of Sciences* (Vol. 840, pp. 656–663). New York: New York Academy of Sciences.

Kiecolt-Glaser, J. K., Glaser, R., Dyer, C., Shuttleworth, E., Ogrocki, P., & Speicher, C. E. (1987). Chronic stress and immunity in family caregivers of Alzheimer's disease victims. *Psychosomatic Medicine, 49,* 523–535.

Kiecolt-Glaser, J. K., Page, G. G., Marucha, P. T., MacCallum, R. C., & Glaser, R. (1998). Psychological influences on surgical recovery: Perspectives from psychoneuroimmunology. *American Psychologist, 53,* 11209–11218.

Kilmer, R. P., Cowen, E. L., & Wyman, P. A. (2001). A micro-level analysis of developmental, parenting, and family milieu variables that differentiate stress-resilient and stress-affected children. *Journal of Community Psychology, 29,* 391–416.

Kilpatrick, D. C., Hague, R. A., Yap, P. L., & Mok, J. L. (1991). HLA antigen frequencies in children born to HIV-infected mothers. *Disease Markers, 9,* 21–26.

Kim, J., & Dellon, A. L. (2001). Pain at the site of tarsal tunnel incision due to neuroma of the posterior branch of the saphenous nerve. *Journal of the American Podiatric Medical Association, 91,* 109–113.

Kim, K., Yu, E. S., Chen, E. H., Kim, J., & Brintnall, R. A. (1998). Colorectal cancer screening: Knowledge and practices among Korean Americans. *Cancer Practice, 6,* 167–175.

Kirscht, J. P. (1971). Social and psychological problems of surveys on health and illness. *Social Science and Medicine, 5,* 519–526.

Klayman, D. L. (1985). Qinghaosu (Artemisinin): An antimalarial drug from China. *Science, 228,* 1049–1055.

Kleinman, A. (1980). *Patients and healers in context of cultures.* Berkeley: University of California Press.

Kleinman, A., Eisenberg, L., & Good, B. (1978). Culture, illness, and care: Clinical lessons from anthropological and cross-cultural research. *Annals of Internal Medicine, 88,* 251–258.

Klevens, R. M., Diaz, T., Fleming, P. L., Mays, M. A., & Frey, R. (1999). Trends in AIDS among Hispanics in the United States, 1991–1996. *American Journal of Public Health, 89,* 1104–1106.

Kline, A., & VanLandingham, M. (1994). HIV-infected women and sexual risk reduction: The relevance of existing models of change. *AIDS Education and Prevention, 6,* 390–402.

Kloner, R. A., Leor, J., Poole, W. K., & Perritt, R. (1997). Population-based analysis of the effect of the Northridge earthquake on cardiac death in Los Angeles, California. *Journal of the American College of Cardiology, 31,* 1174–1180.

Klonoff, E. A., & Landrine, H. (2001). Depressive symptoms and smoking among US Black adults: Absence of a relationship. *Journal of Health Psychology, 6,* 645–649

Knekt, P., Jarvinen, R., Seppanen, R., Hellovaara, M., Teppo, L., Pukkala, R., et al. (1997). Dietary flavonoids and the risk of lung cancer and other malignant neoplasms. *American Journal of Epidemiology, 146,* 223–230.

Knight, G. P., Bernal, M. E., Garza, C. A., Cota, M. K., & Ocampo, K. A. (1993). Family socialization and the ethnic identity of Mexican-American children. *Journal of Cross-Cultural Psychology, 24,* 99–114.

Knouse, S. B. (1991). Social support for Hispanics in the military. *International Journal of Intercultural Relations, 15,* 427–444.

Knox, P. (1998). *The business of healthcare.* Green Bay, WI: Bellin.

Kobasa, S. C., Maddi, S. R., & Kahn, S. (1982). Hardiness and health: A prospective study. *Journal of Personality and Social Psychology, 42,* 168–177.

Koenig, H. G., Pargament, K. I., & Nielsen, J. (1998). Religious coping and health status in medically ill hospitalized older adults. *Journal of Nervous and Mental Disease, 186,* 513–521.

Kohl, H. W., III. (2001). Physical activity and cardiovascular disease: Evidence for a dose response. *Medicine and Science in Sports and Exercise, 33,* S472–S483.

Kompier, M. A., & DiMartino, V. (1995). Review of bus drivers' occupational stress and stress prevention. *Stress Medicine, 11,* 253–262.

Koos, E. L. (1954). *The health of Regionville: What the people thought and did about it.* New York: Columbia University Press.

Korol, C. T., & Craig, K. D. (2001). Pain from the perspectives of health psychology and culture. In S. S. Kazarian & D. R. Evans (Eds.), *Handbook of cultural health psychology* (pp. 241–265). San Diego, CA: Academic Press.

Kout, P. (1992). Yoga and AIDS. *The Journal of the International Association of Yoga Therapists, 3.*

Kraemer, R. R., Dzewaltowski, D. A., Blair, M. S., Rinehardt, K. F., & Castracane, V. D. (1990). Mood alteration from treadmill running and its relationship to beta-endorphin, corticotropin, and growth hormone. *Journal of Sports Medicine and Physical Fitness, 30,* 241–246.

Krantz, D. S. (1995). Editorial: Health psychology: 1995–1999. *Health Psychology, 14,* 3.

Krantz, D. S., Helmers, K. F., Nebel, L. E., Gottdiener, J. S., & Rozanski, A. (1991). Mental stress and myocardial ischemia in patients with coronary disease: Current status and future direction. In A. P. Shapiro & A. Baum (Eds.), *Behavioral aspects of cardiovascular disease: Perspectives in behavioral medicine* (pp. 11–27). Mahwah: NJ: Erlbaum.

Krantz, D. S., & Lundgren, N. R. (1998).Cardiovascular disorders. In A. S. Bellack & M. Hersen (Eds.), *Comprehensive clinical psychology* (pp. 189–216). New York: Pergamon Press.

Krantz, D. S., & Manuck, S. B. (1984). Acute psychophysiologic reactivity and risk of cardiovascular disease: A review and methodologic critique. *Psychological Bulletin, 96,* 435–464.

Krause, N. (1998). Neighborhood deterioration, religious coping, and changes in health during late life. *Gerontologist, 38,* 653–664.

Kreimer, A. R., Alberg, A. J., Daniel, R., Gravitt, P. E., Viscidi, R., Garrett, E. S., et al. (2004). Oral human papillomavirus infection in adults is associated with sexual behavior and HIV serostatus. *Journal of Infectious Diseases, 189,* 686–699.

Kreuter, M., Strecher, V. J., & Glassman, B. (1999). One size does not fit all: The case for tailoring print materials. *Annals of Behavioral Medicine, 21,* 276–283.

Kreuzer, M., Krauss, M., Kreienbrock, L., Jockel, K. H., & Wichmann, H. E. (2000). Environmental tobacco smoke and lung cancer: A case-control study in Germany. *American Journal of Epidemiology, 151,* 241–250.

Kriska, A. (2000). Ethnic and cultural issues in assessing physical activity. *Research Quarterly for Exercise and Sport, 71,* 47–54.

Kristensen, M., Kucinskiene, Z., Bergdahl, B., Calkauskas, H., Urmonas, V., & Orth-Gomer, K. (1998). Increased psychosocial strain in Lithuanian versus Swedish men: The LiVicordia study. *Psychosomatic Medicine, 60,* 277–282.

Krohne, H. W. (1993). Vigilance and cognitive avoidance as concepts in coping research. In H. W. Krohne (Ed.), *Attention and avoidance: Strategies in coping with aversiveness* (pp. 19–50). Ashland, OH: Hogrefe & Huber Publishers.

Krystal, J. H., D'Souza, D. C., Petrakis, I. L., Belger, A., Berman, R. M., Charnery, D. S., et al. (1999). NMDA agonists and antagonists as probes of glutamatergic dysfunction and pharmacotherapies in neuropsychiatric disorders. *Harvard Review of Psychiatry, 7,* 125–144.

Kübler-Ross, E. (1970). The care of the dying: Whose job is it? *Psychiatry in Medicine, 1,* 103–107.

Kumanyika, S. K., Van Horn, L., Bowen, D., Perri, M. G., Rolls, B. J., Czajkowski, S. M., et al. (2000). Maintenance of dietary behavior change. *Health Psychology, 19,* 42–56.

Kusnecov, A. W. (2002). Behavioral conditioning of the immune system. In A. Baum, T. A. Revenson, & J. E. Singer (Eds.), *Handbook of health psychology* (pp. 105–116). Mahwah, NJ: Erlbaum.

La Perriere, A. R., Fletcher, M. A., Antoni, M. H., Ironson, G., Klimas, N., & Schneiderman, N. (1991). Aerobic exercise training in an AIDS risk group. *International Journal of Sports Medicine, 12,* S53–S57.

Lafferty, C. K., Heaney, C. A., & Chen, M. S., Jr. (1999). Assessing decisional balance for smoking cessation among Southeast Asian males in the US. *Health Education Research, 14,* 139–146.

Lamb, T. (2004). Yoga and asthma. Yoga Research and Education Center. Retrieved from www.yrec.org. May 2005.

Lampl, M., Frongillo, E. F., & Johnson, M. L. (1997). Stasis without saltation? *Annals of Human Biology 24,* 65–68.

Landrine, H., & Klonoff, E. A. (1992). Culture and health-related schemes: A review and proposal for interdisciplinary integration. *Health Psychology, 11,* 267–276.

Landrine, H., & Klonoff, E. A. (2001). Cultural diversity and health psychology. In A. Baum, T. A. Revenson, & J. E. Singer (Eds.), *Handbook of health psychology* (pp. 851–891). Mahwah, NJ: Erlbaum.

Landry, S. H., Denson, S. E., & Swank, P. R. (1997). Effects of medical risk and socioeconomic status on the rate of change in cognitive and social development for low birth weight children. *Journal of Clinical and Experimental Neuropsychology, 19,* 261–274.

Landsbergis, P. A., Schnall, P. L, Warren, K., & Pickering, T. G. (1994). Association between ambulatory blood pressure and alternative formulations of job strain. *Scandinavian Journal of Work, Environment and Health, 20,* 349–363.

Lang, F. R., & Carstensen, L. L. (1994). Close emotional relationships in late life: Further support for proactive aging in the social domain. *Psychology and Aging, 9,* 315–324.

Lang, F. R., Staudinger, U. M., & Carstensen, L. L. (1998). Perspectives on socioemotional selectivity in late life: How personality and social context do (and do not) make a difference. *Journals of Gerontology: Series B: Psychological Sciences and Social Sciences, 53B,* P21–P30.

Langer, E. J., & Rodin, J. (1976). The effects of choice and enhanced personal responsibility for the aged: A field experiment in an institutional setting. *Journal of Personality and Social Psychology, 34,* 191–198.

Lansford, J. E., Sherman, A. M., & Antonucci, T. C. (1998). Satisfaction with social networks: An examination of socioemotional selectivity theory across cohorts. *Psychology and Aging, 13,* 544–552.

Larson, R., & Asmussen, L. (1991). Anger, worry, and hurt in early adolescence: An enlarging world of negative emotions. In M. E. Colten & S. Gore (Eds.), *Adolescent stress: Causes and consequences—social institutions and social change* (pp. 21–41). Hawthorne, NY: Aldine de Gruyter.

Larsson, M. L., Frisk, L., Hallstrom, J., Kiviloog, J., & Lundback, B. (2001). Environmental tobacco smoke exposure during childhood is associated with increased prevalence of asthma in adults. *Chest, 120,* 711–718.

Laumann, E. O., Gagnon, J. H., Michael, R. T., & Michaels, S. (1994). *The social organization of sexuality: Sexual practices in the United States.* Chicago: University of Chicago Press.

Laursen, B. (1996). Closeness and conflict in adolescent peer relationships: Interdependence with friends and romantic partners. In W. M. Bukowski, A. F. Newcomb, et al. (Eds.), *The company they keep: Friendship in childhood and adolescence. Cambridge studies in social and emotional development* (pp. 186–210). New York: Cambridge University Press.

Lautenbacher, S., & Strian, F. (1991). Sex differences in pain and thermal sensitivity. *Perception and Psychophysics, 50,* 179–183.

Lawlis, G. F., Achterberg, J., Kenner, L., & Kopetz, K. (1984). Ethnic and sex differences in response to clinical and induced pain in chronic spinal pain patients. *Spine, 9,* 751–754.

Lazarus, R. S. (1966). *Psychological stress and the coping process.* New York: McGraw-Hill.

Lazarus, R. S. (1991). Progress on a cognitive-motivational-relational theory of emotion. *American Psychologist, 46,* 819–834.

Lazarus, R. S. (2000). Toward better research on stress and coping. *American Psychologist, 55,* 665–673.

Lazarus, R. S., & Folkman, S. (1984). *Stress, appraisal, and coping.* New York: Springer.

Lazarus, R. S., & Folkman, S. (1991). *Stress and coping.* New York: Columbia University Press.

Lazarus, R. S., & Launier, R. (1978). Stress-related transactions between person and environment. In L. A. Pervin & M. Lewis (Eds.), *Perspectives in interactional psychology* (pp. 287–322). New York: Plenum.

Leach, J. (1995). Psychological first-aid: A practical aide-memoire. *Aviation, Space, and Environmental Medicine, 66,* 668–674.

LeBlanc, A. J. (1993). Examining HIV-related knowledge among adults in the U. S. *Journal of Health and Social Behavior, 34,* 23–36.

Lee, I. M., Paffenbarger, R. S., & Hsieh, C. C. (1992). Physical activity and risk of prostatic cancer among college alumni. *American Journal of Epidemiology, 135,* 169–179.

Lee, I. M., & Skerrett, P. J. (2001). Physical activity and all-cause mortality: What is the dose-response relation? *Medicine and Science in Sports and Exercise, 33,* S459–S471.

Lee, M. C. (2000). Knowledge barriers, and motivators related to cervical cancer screening among Korean-American women: A focus group approach. *Cancer Nursing, 23,* 168–175.

Leigh, B. C., Schafer, J., & Temple, M. T. (1995). Alcohol use and contraception in first sexual experiences. *Journal of Behavioral Medicine, 18,* 81–95.

Leigh, B. C., & Stall, R. (1993). Substance use and risky sexual behavior for exposure to HIV: Issues in methodology, interpretation, and prevention. *American Psychologist, 48,* 1035–1045.

Lemos-Giraldez, S., & Fidalgo-Aliste, A. M. (1997). Personality dispositions and health-related habits and attitudes: A cross-sectional study. *European Journal of Personality, 11,* 197–209.

Leng, G. (1999). A year of acupuncture in palliative care. *Palliative Medicine, 13,* 163–164.

Lepore, S. J. (1997). Measurement of chronic stressors. In S. Cohen, R. C. Kessler, & L. U. Gordon (Eds.), *Measuring stress: A guide for health and social scientists* (pp. 102–120). London: Oxford University Press.

Lepore, S. J., & Evans, G. W. (1996). Coping with multiple stressors in the environment. In M. Zeidner & N. S. Endler (Eds.), *Handbook of coping: Theory, research, applications* (pp. 350–377). Oxford, England: John Wiley.

Lerman, C., Caporaso, N. E., Audrain, J., Main., D., Bowman, E. D., Lockshin, B., et al. (1999). Evidence suggesting the role of specific genetic factors in cigarette smoking. *Health Psychology, 18,* 14–20.

Leserman, J., Petitto, J. M., Golden, R. N., Gaynes, B. N., Gu, H., Perkins, D. O., et al. (2000). Impact of stressful life events, depression, social support, coping, and cortisol on progression of AIDS. *American Journal of Psychiatry, 157,* 1221–1228.

Lester, B. M., Boukydis, C. F., & Twomey, J. E. (2000). Maternal substance abuse and child outcome. In C. H. Zeahnah (Ed.), *Handbook of infant mental health* (2nd ed., pp. 161–175). New York: Guilford Press.

Leventhal, E. A., Hansell, S., Diefenbach, M., Leventhal, H., & Glass, D. C. (1996). Negative affect and self-report of physical symptoms: Two longitudinal studies of older adults. *Health Psychology, 15,* 193–199.

Leventhal, H., Diefenbach, M., & Leventhal, E. A. (1992). Illness cognition: Using common sense to understand treatment adherence and affect cognition interactions. *Cognitive Therapy and Research, 16,* 143–163.

Levitsky, L. L. (2000). Type 2 diabetes in children and adolescents. *Pediatrics, 105,* 671-680.

Levitsky, L. L. (2002). *Type 2 diabetes: The new epidemic of childhood.* Presented at the American Academy of Pediatrics Annual Meeting. Boston, MA.

Levitt, S., Kempen, P. M., Mor, V., Bernabei, R., Lapane, K. L., & Gambassi, G. (1999). Managing pain in elderly patients. *Journal of the American Medical Association, 281,* 605–606.

Levy, R. I. (1996). Essential contrasts: Differences in parental ideas about learners and teaching in Tahiti and Nepal. In S. Harkness & C. M. Super (Eds.), *Parents' cultural belief systems: Their origins, expressions, and consequences* (pp. 123–142). New York: Guilford Press.

Lichstein, K. L., Riedel, B. W., Wilson, N. M., Lester, K. W., & Aguillard, R. N. (2001). Relaxation and sleep compression for late-life insomnia. *Journal of Consulting and Clinical Psychology, 69,* 227–239.

Lichtenstein, E., & Lopez, K. (1999). Enhancing tobacco control policies in Northwest Indian tribes. In National Cancer Institute (Ed.), *Native outreach: A report to American Indian, Alaska Native, and Native Hawaiian communities* (pp. 57–65). Washington, DC: National Institutes of Health.

Lichtman, S. W., Pisarska, K., Berman, E. R., Pestone, M., et al. (1992). Discrepancy between self-reported and actual caloric intake and exercise in obese subjects. *New England Journal of Medicine, 327,* 1893–1898.

Liddell. A., & Locker, D. (1997). Gender and age differences in attitudes to dental pain and dental control. *Community Dental and Oral Epidemiology, 25,* 314–318.

Lieber, J. (1994). Conflict and its resolution in preschoolers with and without disabilities. *Early Education and Development, 5,* 5–17.

Liebeskind, J. C., Lewis, J. W., Shavit, Y., & Terman, G. W. (1983). Our natural capacities for pain suppression. *Advances in Pain Research and Therapy, 1,* 8–11.

Light, E., & Lebowitz, B. (1989). *Alzheimer's disease treatment and family stress: Directions for research.* Rockville, MD: National Institute of Mental Health.

Lin, T., & Lin, M. C. (1978). Service Delivery Issues in Asian-North American Communities. *American Journal of Psychiatry, 135,* 454–456.

Lindemann, E. (1944). Symptomatology and management of acute grief. *American Journal of Psychiatry, 101,* 141–148.

Linden, W., Lenz, J. W., & Stossel, C. (1996). Alexithymia, defensiveness and cardiovascular reactivity to stress. *Journal of Psychosomatic Research, 41,* 575–583.

Linden, W., Stossel, C., & Maurice, J. (1996). Psychosocial interventions for patients with coronary artery disease: A meta-analysis. *Archives of Internal Medicine, 156,* 745–752.

Lipton, J. A., & Marbach, J. J. (1984). Ethnicity and the pain experience. *Social Science & Medicine, 19,* 1279–1298.

Littrell, J. (1996). How psychological states affect the immune system: Implications for interventions in the context of HIV. *Health and Social Work, 21,* 287–295.

Litwak, E. (1985). *Helping the elderly: The complementary roles of informal networks and formal systems.* New York: Guilford Press.

Llabre, M. M., Klein, B. R., Saab, P. G., McCalla, J. B., & Schneiderman, N. (1998). Classification of individual differences in cardiovascualr responsivity: The contribution of reactor type controlling for race and gender. *International Journal of Behavioral Medicine, 5,* 213–229.

Lobell, M., Bay, R. C., Rhoads, K. V., & Keske, B. (1998). Barriers to cancer screening in Mexican-American women. *Mayo Clinic Proceedings, 73,* 301–308.

Lobell, M., Yali, A. M., Zhu, W., & DeVincent, C. (1998). Emotional reactions to the stress of high-risk pregnancy: The role of optimism and coping [Abstract]. *Annals of Behavioral Medicine, 20,* 29.

Locker, D., Shapiro, D., & Liddell, A. (1997). Overlap between dental anxiety and blood-injury fears: Psychological characteristics and response to dental treatment. *Behavior Research and Therapy, 35,* 585–590.

Longnecker, M. P., Gerhardsson de Verdier, M., Frumkin, H., & Carpenter, C. (1995). A case-control study of physical activity in relation to risk of cancer of the right colon and rectum in men. *International Journal of Epidemiology, 24,* 42–50.

Lorenz, K. (1935). The companion in the bird's world: The fellow-member of the species as releasing factor of social behavior. *Journal für Ornithologie. Beiblatt, 83,* 137–213.

Loue, S., Lane, S. D., Lloyd, L. S., & Loh, L. (1999). Integrating Buddhism and HIV prevention in U. S. Southeast Asian communities. *Journal of Health Care for the Poor and Underserved, 10,* 100–121.

Lubin, J. H., Richter, B. S., & Blot, W. J. (1984). Lung cancer risk with cigar and pipe use. *Journal of the National Cancer Institute, 73,* 377–381.

Luckow, A., Reifman, A., & McIntosh, D. N. (1998). *Gender differences in coping: A meta-analysis.* Poster session presented at the 106th Annual Convention of the American Psychological Association, San Francisco, CA.

Lutgendorf, S., Klimas, N. G., Antoni, M., Brickman, A., & Fletcher, M. A. (1995). Relationships of cognitive difficulties to immune measures, depression and illness burden in chronic fatigue syndrome. *Journal of Chronic Fatigue Syndrome, 1,* 23–41.

Lutz, D. J., & Sternberg, R. J. (1999). Cognitive development. In M. H. Bornstein & M. E. Lamb (Eds.), *Developmental psychology: An advanced textbook* (4th ed., pp. 275–311). Mahwah, NJ: Erlbaum.

Lynn, J. (2001). Serving patients who may die soon and their families: The role of hospice and other services. *Journal of the American Medical Association, 285,* 925–932.

MacDonald, R. A., Mitchell, L. A., Dillon, T., Serpell, M. G., Davies, J. B., & Ashley, E. A. (2003). An empirical investigations of the anxiolytic and pain reducing effects of music. *Psychology of Music, 31,* 187–203.

Macintyre, S. (1997). The Black report and beyond: What are the issues? *Social Science and Medicine, 44,* 723–45.

Maddi, S. R., & Kobasa, S. C. (1991). The development of hardiness. In A. Monat & R. S. Lazarus (Eds.), *Stress and coping: An anthology* (3rd ed., pp. 245–257). New York: Columbia University Press.

Madsen, W. (1955). Shamanism in Mexico. *Southwestern Journal of Anthropology, 3,* 48–57.

Maes, S., Leventhal, H., & de Ridder, D. T. D. (1996). Coping with chronic diseases. In M. Zeidner & N. S. Endler (Eds.). *Handbook of coping: Theory, research, applications* (pp. 221–251). Oxford, England: John Wiley.

Magill, L. (2001). The use of music therapy to address the suffering in advanced cancer pain. *Journal of Palliative Care, 17,* 167–172.

Mahler, H. I., & Kulik, J. A. (1991). Health care involvement preferences and social-emotional recovery of male coronary-artery-by-pass patients. *Health Psychology, 10,* 399–408.

Maisto, S. A., Carey, K. B., & Bradizza, C. M. (1999). Social learning theory. In K. E. Leonard & H. T. Blane (Eds.), *Psychological theories of drinking and alcoholism. The Guilford substance abuse series* (2nd ed., pp. 106–163). New York: Guilford Press.

Mann, T., Nolen-Hoeksema, S., Huang, K., Burgard, D., Wright, A., & Hanson, K. (1997). Are two interventions worse than none? Joint primary and secondary prevention of eating disorders in college females. *Health Psychology, 16*, 215–225.

Manson, J. E., Willett, W. C., Stampfer, M. J., Colditz, G. A., Hunter, D. J., Hankinson, S. E., et al. (1995). Body weight and mortality among women. *New England Journal of Medicine, 333*, 677–685.

Manson, S. M., Shore, J. H., Baron, A. E., Ackerson, L., & Neligh, G. (1992). Alcohol abuse and dependence among American Indians. In J. E. Helzer & G. J. Canino (Eds.), *Alcoholism in North America, Europe, and Asia* (pp. 113–130). London: Oxford University Press.

Manyam, B. V. (2004). Diabetes mellitus, ayurveda, and yoga. *Journal of Alternative and Complementary Medicine, 10*, 223–225.

Marcus, B. H. (1993). Binge eating in obesity. In C. G. Fairburn & G. T. Wilson (Eds.), *Binge eating: Nature, asssessment, and treatment* (pp. 77–96). New York: Guilford Press.

Marcus, B. H., Forsyth, L. H., Stone, E. K., Dubbert, P. M., McKenzie, T. L., Dunn, A. L., et al. (2000). Physical activity behavior change: Issues in adoption and maintenance. *Health Psychology. Special Maintenance of Behavior Change in Cardiorespiratory Risk Reduction, 19*, 32–41.

Marcus, D. A., Nash, J. M., & Turk, D. C. (1994). Diagnosing recurring headaches: HIS criteria and beyond. *Headache, 34*, 329–336.

Marin, G., Marin, B. V., Perez-Stable, E. J., Sabogal, F., & Otero-Sabogal, R. (1990). Changes in information as a function of a culturally appropriate smoking cessation community intervention for Hispanics. *American Journal of Community Psychology, 17*, 847–864.

Marinelli, R. D., & Plummer, O. K. (1999). Healthy aging: Beyond exercise. *Activities, Adaptation and Aging, 23*, 1–11.

Markey, C. N. (2004). Culture and the development of eating disorders: A tripartite model. *Eating Disorders: The Journal of Treatment & Prevention, 12*, 139–156.

Markey, C. N., Ericksen, A. J., Markey, P. M., & Tinsley, B. J. (2001). Personality and family determinants of preadolescents' participation in health-compromising and health-promoting behaviors. *Adolescent and Family Health, 2*, 83–90.

Marks, D. F. (1998). Addiction, smoking and health: Developing policy-based interventions. *Psychology, Health and Medicine, 3*, 97–111.

Marks, D. F. (1996). Health psychology in context. *Journal of Health Psychology, 1*, 7–21.

Markus, H. R., & Kitayama, S. (1991). Culture and the self: Implications for cognition, emotion, and motivation. *Psychological Review, 98*, 224–253.

Marlatt, G. A., & George, W. H. (1990). Relapse prevention and the maintenance of optimal health. In S. A. Shumaker, E. B. Schron, et al. (Eds.), *The handbook of health behavior change* (pp. 44–63). New York: Springer.

Marmot, M. (1994). Work and other factors influencing coronary health and sickness absence. *Work and Stress, 8*, 191–201.

Marmot, M., Smith, G. D., Stansfeld, S., Patel, C., North, F., Head, J., et al. (1991). Health inequalities among British civil servants: The Whitehall study. *Lancet, 337*, 1387–1393.

Marshall, G., Agarwal, S., Lloyd, C., Cohen, L., Henninger, E., & Morris, G. (1998). Cytokine dysregulation associated with exam stress in healthy medical students. *Brain Behavior and Immunology, 12*, 297–307.

Marsland, A. L., Bachen, E. A., Cohen, S., & Manuck, S. B. (2002). Stress, immunity, and susceptibility to infectious disease. In A. Baum, T. A. Revenson, & J. E. Singer (Eds.), *Handbook of health psychology* (pp. 683–695). Mahwah, NJ: Erlbaum.

Martel, F. L., Nevison, C. M., Rayment, F. D., Simpson, M. J. A., & Keverne, E. B. (1993). Opioid receptor blockade reduces maternal affect and social grooming in rhesus monkeys. *Psychoneuroimmunology, 18*, 307–321.

Martin, M. P., Dean, M., Smith, M. W., Winkler, C., Gerrard, B., Michael, N. L., et al. (1998). Genetic acceleration of AIDS progression by a promoter variant of CCR5. *Science, 282*, 1907–1911.

Martin, T. L., & Doka, K. J. (2000). *Men don't cry . . . women do: Transcending gender stereotypes of grief.* Oxford, England: John Wiley.

Martinez, R. G., Chavez, L. R., & Hubbell, F. A. (1997). Purity and passion: Risk and morality in Latina immigrants' and physicians' beliefs about cervical cancer. *Medical Anthropology, 17*, 337–362.

Mason, J. W. (1971). A re-evaluation of the concept of "non-specificity" in stress theory. *Journal of Psychiatric Research, 8*, 323–333.

Matarrazo, J., Weiss, S. M., Herd, J. A., Miller, N. E., & Weiss, S. M. (1984). *Behavioral health: A handbook of health enhancement and disease prevention.* New York: Wiley-Interscience.

Matarazzo, J. D. (1980). Behavioral health and behavioral medicine: Frontiers for a new health psychology. *American Psychologist, 35*, 807–817.

Maton, K. I. (1989). The stress-buffering role of spiritual support: Cross-sectional and prospective investigations. *Journal for the Scientific Study of Religion, 28*, 310–323.

Matsumoto, D. (2001). *The handbook of culture and psychology.* London: Oxford University Press.

Matthews, K. A. (1992). Myths and realities of the menopause. *Psychosomatic Medicine, 54*, 1–9.

Matthews, K. A., Shumaker, S. A., Bowen, D. J., Langer, R. D., Hunt, J. R., Kaplan, R. M., et al. (1997). Women's Health Initiative: Why now? What is it? What's new? *American Psychologist, 52*, 101–116.

Mattlin, J. A., Wethington, E., & Kessler, R. C. (1990). Situational determinants of coping and coping effectiveness. *Journal of Health and Social Behavior, 31*, 103–122.

Mau, M. K., Glanz, K., Severino, R., Grove, J. S., Johnson, B., Curb, J. D. (2001). Mediators of lifestyle behavior change in native Hawaiians: Initial findings from the Native Hawaiian Diabetes Intervention program. *Diabetes Care, 24*, 1770–1775.

Maunsell, E., Brisson, J., & Deschenes, L. (1995). Social support and survival among women with breast cancer. *Cancer, 76*, 631–637.

Maxwell, A. E., Bastani, R., & Warda, U. S. (1998). Mammography utilization and related attitudes among Korean-American women. *Women's Health, 27*, 89–107.

Maxwell, A. E., Bastani, R., & Warda, U. S. (1998). Mammography utilization and related attitudes among Filipino-American women. *Cancer Epidemiological Biomarkers and Prevention, 6*, 719–726.

Mayer, S. E., & Jencks, C. (1989). Growing up in poor neighborhoods: How much does it matter? *Science 243*, 1441–1445.

Mays, V. M., & Cochran, S. D. (1987). Acquired immunodeficiency syndrome and Black Americans: Special psychosocial issues. *Public Health Reports, 102*, 224–231.

Mays, V. M., So, B. T., Cochran, S. D., Detels, R., Benjamin, R., Allen, E., et al. (2002). HIV disease in ethnic minorities: Implications of racial/ethnic differences in disease susceptibility and drug dosage response for HIV infection and treatment. In A. Baum, T. A. Revenson, & J. E. Singer (Eds.), *Handbook of health psychology* (pp. 801–816). Mahwah, NJ: Erlbaum.

McCabe, M. P., & Ricciardelli, L. A. (2003). Sociocultural influences on body image and body changes among adolescent boys and girls. *Journal of Social Psychology, 193*, 5–26.

McCaul, K. D., Branstetter, A., Schroeder, D. M., & Glasgow, R. E. (1996). What is the relationship between breast cancer risk and mammography screening? A meta-analytic review. *Health Psychology, 15*, 423–429.

McCauley, J., Kern, D. E., Kolodner, K., Dill, L., & Schroeder, A. F. (1997). Clinical characteristics of women with a history of childhood abuse: Unhealed wounds. *Journal of the American Medical Association, 277,* 1362–1368.

McClintock, M. K. (1998). Whither menstrual synchrony? *Annual Review of Sex Research, 9,* 77–98.

McCormick, M. C. (1985). The contribution of low birth weight to infant mortality and childhood morbidity. *New England Journal of Medicine, 312,* 82–89.

McCormick, M. C., Brooks-Gunn, J., Shorter, T., Holmes, J. H., Wallace, C. Y., & Heagarty, M. C. (1990). Factors associated with smoking in low-income pregnant women: Relationship to birth weight, stressful life events, social support, health behaviors and mental distress. *Journal of Clinical Epidemiology, 43,* 441–448.

McCormick, R. A., Dowd, E. T., Quirk, S., & Zegarra, J. H. (1998). The relationship of NEO-PI performance to coping styles, patterns of use, and triggers for use among substance abusers. *Addictive Behaviors, 23,* 497–507.

McCrae, R. R. (1984). Situational determinants of coping responses: Loss, threat, and challenge. *Journal of Personality and Social Psychology, 46,* 919–928.

McCrae, R. R., & Costa, P. T. (1987). Validation of the five-factor model of personality across instruments and observers. *Journal of Personality and Social Psychology, 52,* 81–90.

McCubbin, H. I., & Patterson, J. M. (1983). The family stress process: The double ABCX model of adjustment and adaptation. *Marriage and Family Review, 6,* 7–37.

McDonald, L. M., & Korabik, K. (1991). Sources of stress and ways of coping among male and female managers. *Journal of Social Behavior and Personality. Special Handbook on Job Stress, 6,* 185–198.

McEwen, B. S. (1998). Protective and damaging effects of stress mediators. *New England Journal of Medicine, 338,* 171–179.

McEwen, B. S., Biron, C., Brunson, K., Bulloch, K., Chambers, W., Dhabhar, F., et al. (1997). The role of adrenocorticoids as modulators of immune function in health and disease: Neural, endocrine, and immune interactions. *Brain Research Reviews, 23,* 79.

McEwen, B. S., & Wingfield, J. C. (2003). The concept of allostasis in biology and biomedicine. *Hormones and Behavior, 43,* 2–15.

McFarland, B., Bigelow, D., Zani, B., Newsom, J., & Kaplan, M. (2002). Complementary and alternative medicine use in Canada and the United States. *American Journal of Public Health, 92,* 1616–1618.

McFarlane, J., Parker, B., & Soeken, K. (1996a). Abuse during pregnancy: Associations with maternal health and infant birth weight. *Nursing Research, 45,* 37–42.

McFarlane, J., Parker, B., & Soeken, K. (1996b). Physical abuse, smoking, and substance use during pregnancy: Prevalence, interrelationships, and effects on birth weight. *Journal of Obstetric, Gynecologic, and Neonatal Nursing, 25,* 313–320.

McGee, R., Williams, S., & Elwood, M. (1994). Depression and the development of cancer: A meta-analysis. *Social Science and Medicine, 38,* 187–192.

McGinnis, J. M., & Foege, W. H. (1993). Actual causes of death in the United States. *Journal of the American Medical Association, 270,* 2207–2213.

McGrath, J. E. (1970). *Social and psychological factors in stress.* Oxford, England: Holt, Rinehart, & Winston.

McGrath, P. A., & Gillespie, J. (2001). Pain assessment in children and adolescents. In D. C. Turk & R. Melzack (Eds.), *Handbook of pain assessment (2nd ed.)* (pp. 97–118). New York, NY: Guilford.

McGue, M. (1999). Behavioral genetic models of alcoholism and drinking. In K. E. Leonard & H. T. Blane (Eds.), *Psychological theories of drinking and alcoholism* (2nd ed., pp. 372–421). New York: Guilford Press.

McKenna, M. C., Zevon, M. A., Corn, B., & Rounds, J. (1999). Psychosocial factors and the development of breast cancer: A meta-analysis. *Health Psychology, 18,* 520–531.

McKusick, L., Horstman, W., & Coates, T. J. (1985). AIDS and sexual behavior reported by gay men in San Francisco. *American Journal of Public Health, 75,* 493–496.

McLoyd, V. C. (1990). The impact of economic hardship on Black families and children: Psychological distress, parenting, and socioeconomic development. *Child Development, 61,* 311–346.

McNally, R. J. (1997). Implicit and explicit memory for trauma-related information in PTSD. *Annals of the New York Academy of Sciences, 821,* 219–224.

McNicholl, J., & Smith, D. (1997). Host genes and HIV: The role of the chemokine receptor gene CCR5 and its allele (...32 CCR5). *Emerging Infectious Diseases, 3,* 261–272.

McPhee, S. J., Bird, J. A., Davis, T., Ha, N. T., Jenkins, C. N. H., & Le, B. (1997). Barriers to breast and cervical cancer screening among Vietnamese-American women. *American Journal of Preventive Medicine, 13,* 205–213.

McPhee, S. J., Bird, J. A., Ha, N. T., Jenkins, C. N. H., Fordham, D., & Le, B. (1996). Pathways to early cancer detection for Vietnamese women: Suc khoe la vang! (Health is gold!). *Health Education Quarterly, 23,* S60–S75.

McWilliams, L. A., Cox, B. J., & Enns, M. W. (2003). Use of the Coping Inventory for Stressful Situations in a clinically depressed sample: Factor structure, personality correlates, and prediction of distress. *Journal of Clinical Psychology, 59,* 423–437.

Meagher, M. W., Arnau, R. C., & Rhudy, J. L. (2001). Pain and emotion: Effects of affective picture modulation. *Psychosomatic Medicine, 63,* 79–90.

Meaney, M. J. (2001). Nature, nurture, and the disunity of knowledge. *Annals of the New York Academy of Sciences, 935,* 50–61.

Mechanic, D. (1995). Sociological dimensions of illness behavior. *Social Sciences and Medicine, 41,* 1207–1216.

Mehl-Medrona, L. (1998). *Coyote medicine: Lessons from Native American healing.* New York: Simon and Schuster.

Meichenbaum, D., & Cameron, R. (1983). Stress inoculation training: Toward a general paradigm for training coping skills. In D. Meichenbaum & M. E. Jaremko (Eds.), *Stress reduction and prevention* (pp. 115–154). New York: Plenum Press.

Meisel, S. R., Kutz, I., Dayan, K. I., Pauzer, H., Chetboun, I., Arbel, Y., et al. (1991). Effect of Iraqi missile war on incidence of acute myocardial infarction and sudden death in Israeli civilians. *Lancet, 338,* 660–661.

Mellman, T. A. (1997). Psychobiology of sleep disturbances in posttraumatic stress disorder. *Annals of the New York Academy of Sciences, 821,* 142–149.

Melzack, R. (1975). The McGill Pain Questionnaire: Major properties and scoring methods. *Pain, 1,* 277–299.

Melzack, R. (1999). Pain and stress: A new perspective. In R. J. Gatchel & D. C. Turk (Eds.), *Psychosocial factors in pain: Critical perspectives* (pp. 89–106). New York: Guilford Press.

Melzack, R., & Casey, K. L. (1968). Sensory, motivational, and central control determinants of pain: A new conceptual model. In D. Kenschalo (Ed.), *The skin senses* (pp. 423–443). Springfield, IL: Charles C Thomas.

Melzack, R., & Wall, P. D. (1965). Pain mechanisms: A new theory. *Science, 150,* 971–979.

Meredith, H. V. (1973). Somatological development. In B. B. Wolman (Ed.), *Handbook of general psychology.* Englewood Cliffs, NJ: Prentice Hall.

Merikangas, K. R. (1990). The genetic epidemiology of alcoholism. *Psychological Medicine, 20,* 11–22.

Metts, S., Manns, H., & Kuzic, L. (1996). Social support structures and predictors of depression in persons who are seropositive. *Journal of Health Psychology, (1),* 367–382.

Meyer, T. J., & Mark, M. M. (1995). Effects of psychosocial interventions with adult cancer patients: A meta-analysis of randomized experiments. *Health Psychology, 14,* 101–108.

Meyerowitz, B. E., Bull, A. A., & Perez, M. A. (2000). Cancers common in women. In R. M. Eisler & M. Herson (Eds.), *Handbook of gender, culture and health* (pp. 197–225). Mahwah, NJ: Erlbaum.

Meyerowitz, B. E., Richardson, J., Hudson, S., & Leedham, B. (1998). Ethnicity and cancer outcomes: Behavioral and psychosocial considerations. *Psychological Bulletin, 123,* 47–71.

Meyers, L. B., & Vetere, A. (2002). Adult romantic attachment styles and health-related measures. *Psychology, Health, and Medicine, 7,* 175–180.

Mezzetti, M., La Vecchia, C., Decarli, A., Boyle, P., Talamini, R., & Franceschi, S. (1998). Population attributable risk for breast cancer: Diet, nutrition, and physical exercise. *Journal of the National Cancer Institute, 90,* 389–394.

Miceli, P. J., & Mylod, D. E. (2003). Satisfaction of families using end-of-life care: Current successes and challenges in the hospice industry. *American Journal of Hospice & Palliative Care, 20,* 360–370.

Millard, R. W. (1993). Behavioral assessment of pain and behavioral pain management. In R. B. Patt (Ed.), *Cancer Pain* (pp. 85–97). Philadelphia: Lippincott.

Miller, A. M., & Champion, V. L. (1997). Attitudes about breast cancer and mammography: Racial, income, and educational differences. *Women's Health, 26,* 41–63.

Miller, G. M., & Cole, S. W. (1998). Social relationships and the progression of human immunodeficiency virus infection: A review of evidence and possible underlying mechanisms. *Annals of Behavioral Medicine, 20,* 181–189.

Miller, L. C., Bettencourt, B. A., DeBro, S. C., & Hoffman, V. (1993). Negotiating safer sex: Interpersonal dynamics. In J. B. Pryor & G. D. Reeder (Eds.), *The social psychology of HIV infection* (pp. 85–123). Hillsdale, NJ: Erlbaum.

Miller, M. C. (1992). Winnicott unbound: The fiction of Philip Roth and the sharing of potential space. *International Review of Psycho-Analysis, 19,* 445–456.

Miller, S. C., Mor, V., Wu, N., Gozalo, P., & Lapane, K. (2002). Does receipt of hospice care in nursing homes improve the management of pain at the end of life? *Journal of the American Geriatrics Society, 50,* 507–515.

Miller, S. M. (1987). Monitoring and blunting: Validation of a questionnaire to assess styles of information seeking under threat. *Journal of Personality and Social Psychology, 52,* 345–353.

Miller, S. M., & Diefenbach, M. A. (1998). The Cognitive-Social Health Information-Processing (C-SHIP) model: A theoretical framework for research in behavioral oncology. In D. S. Krantz & A. Baum (Eds.), *Technology and methods in behavioral medicine* (pp. 219–244). Mahwah, NJ: Erlbaum.

Miller, S. M., Shoda, Y., & Hurley, K. (1996). Applying cognitive-social theory to health-protective behavior: Breast self-examination in cancer screening. *Psychological Bulletin, 119,* 70–94.

Miller, W. R., & Thoresen, C. E. (2003). Spirituality, religion, and health: An emerging research field. *American Psychology, 58,* 24–35.

Mills, P. J., Berry, C. C., Dimsdale, J. E., & Nelesen, R. A. (1993). Temporal stability of task-induced cardiovascular, adrenergic, and psychological responses: The effects of race and hypertension. *Psychophysiology, 30,* 187–204.

Mischel, W. (1984). Convergences and challenges in the search for consistency. *American Psychologist, 39,* 351–364.

Mishra, S. I., Luce-Aoelua, P., & Hubbell, F. A. (1998). Identifying the cancer control needs of American Samoans. *Asian American and Pacific Islander Journal of Health, 6,* 277–285.

Mittleman, M. A., Maclure, M., Sherwood, J. B., Mulry, R. P., Tofler, G. H., Jacobs, S. C., et al. (1995). Triggering of acute myocardial infarction onset by episodes of anger. *Circulation, 92,* 1720–1725.

Mo, B. (1992). Modesty, sexuality, and breast health in Chinese-American women. *Western Journal of Medicine, 157*(3), 260–264.

Mokdad, A. H., Marks, J. S., Stroup, D. F., Gerberding, J. L. (2004). Actual causes of death in the United States, 2000. *Journal of American Medical Association. 291*(10): 1238–1245.

Montano, D., Kasprzyk, D., von Haeften, I., & Fishbein, M. (2001). Toward an understanding of condom use behaviours: A theoretical and methodological overview of Project SAFER. *Psychology, Health and Medicine, 6,* 139–150.

Monte, T. (1993). *World medicine: The east west guide to healing your body.* New York: Penguin Putnam.

Moore, J., Schuman, P., Schoenbaum, E., Boland, B., Solomon, L., and Smith, D. (1999). Severe adverse life events and depressive symptoms among women with, or at risk for, HIV infection in four cities in the United States of America. *AIDS, 13,* 2459–2468.

Moos, R. H., & Schaefer, J. A. (1993). Coping resources and processes: Current concepts and measures. In L. Goldberger & S. Breznitz (Eds.), *Handbook of stress: Theoretical and clinical aspects* (2nd ed., pp. 234–257). New York: Free Press.

Morgan, W. P. (1997). Methodological considerations. In W. P. Morgan (Ed.), *Physical activity and mental health* (pp. 3–32). Washington, DC: Taylor & Francis.

Morrill, A. C., Ickovics, J. R., Golubchikov, V., Beren, S. E., & Rodin, J. (1996). Safer sex: Predictors of behavioral maintenance and chance for heterosexual women. *Journal of Consulting and Clinical Psychology, 64,* 819–828.

Morris, J. N., Heady, J. A., Raffle, P. A. B., Roberts, C. G., & Parks, J. W. (1953). Coronary heart disease and physical activity of work. *Lancet, 2,* 1053–1057.

Morris, T., Greer, S., Pettingale, K. W., & Watson, M. (1981). Patterns of expression of anger and their psychological correlates in women with breast cancer. *Journal of Psychosomatic Research, 25,* 111–117.

Mortensen, E. L., Jensen, H. H., Sanders, S. A., & Reinisch, J. M. (2001). Better psychological functioning and higher social status may largely explain the apparent health benefits of wine: A study of wine and beer drinking in young Danish adults. *Archives of Internal Medicine, 161,* 1844–1849.

Moyad, M. A. (1999). Soy, disease prevention, and prostate cancer. *Seminars in Urologic Oncology, 17,* 97–102.

Mrazek, D. A., Klinnert, M., Mrazek, P. J., Brower, A., McCormick, D., Rubin, B. et al. (1999). Prediction of early-onset asthma in genetically at-risk children. *Pediatric Pulmonology, 27,* 85–94.

Muellersdorf, M., & Soederback, I. (2000). The actual state of the effects, treatments, and incidence of disabling pain in a gender perspective: A Swedish study. *Disabilities and Rehabilitation, 22,* 840–854.

Mulder, C., de Vroome, E., van Griensven, G., Antoni, M. H., & Sandfort, T. (1999). Distraction as a predictor of the virological course of HIV-1 infection over a 7-year period in gay men. *Health Psychology, 18,* 1072113.

Mullen, P. D., Hersey, J. C., & Iverson, D. C. (1987). Health behavior models compared. *Social Science and Medicine, 24,* 973–981.

Muller, J. E. (1999). Circadian variation and triggering of acute coronary events. *American Heart Journal, 137,* S1–S8.

Muller, J. E., Tofler, G. H., & Stone, P. H. (1989). Circadian variation and triggers of onset of acute cardiovascular disease. *Circulation, 79,* 733–743.

Murberg, T. A., Bru, E., & Stephens, P. (2002). Personality and coping among congestive heart failure patients. *Personality and Individual Differences, 32,* 775–784.

Murdoch, D., Pihl, R. O., & Ross, D. (1990). Alcohol and crimes of violence: Present issues. *The International Journal of the Addictions, 25,* 149–157.

Murphy, D., Mann, T., O'Keefe, Z., & Rotheram-Borus, M. J. (1998). Number of pregnancies, outcome expectancies, and social norms among HIV-infected young women. *Health Psychology, 17,* 470–475.

Murray, C. J., & Lopez, A. D. (1997). Mortality by cause for eight regions of the world: Global burden of disease study. *Lancet, 349,* 1269–1276.

Murray, E. J., & Segal, D. L. (1994). Emotional processing in vocal and written expression of feelings about traumatic experiences. *Journal of Traumatic Stress, 7,* 391–405.

Murray, V. (1992). Sexual career paths of Black adolescent females: A study of socioeconomic status and other life experiences. *Journal of Adolescent Research, 7,* 4–27.

Muscat, J. E., Richie, J. P., Thompson, S., & Wynder, E. L. (1996). Gender differences in smoking and risk for oral cancer. *Cancer Research, 56,* 5192–5197.

Mussolino, A. E., Looker, A. C., & Orwoll, E. S. (2001). Jogging and bone mineral density in men: Results from NHANES III. *American Journal of Public Health, 91,* 1056–1059.

Myers, H. F., & Rodriguez, N. (2002). Acculturation and physical health in racial and ethnic minorities. In K. M. Chun, P. B. Organista, & G. Marin (Eds.), *Acculturation: Advances in theory, measurement, and applied research.* Washington, DC: American Psychological Association.

Myers, L. B., & Midence, K. (Eds.). (1998). *The handbook of health behavior change* (2nd ed.). New York: Springer.

Myers, L. B., & Vetere, A. (2002). Adult romantic attachment styles and health-related measures. *Psychology, Health and Medicine, 7,* 175–180.

Nabi, R. L., & Horner, J. R. (2001). Victims with voices: How abused women conceptualize the problem of spousal abuse and implications for intervention and prevention. *Journal of Family Violence, 16,* 237–253.

Nashold, B., Somjen, G., & Friedman, H. (1972). Paresthesias and EEG potentials evoked by stimulation of the dorsal funiculi in man. *Experimental Neurology, 36,* 273–287.

Nathanson, C. A. (1977). Sex roles as variables in preventive health behavior. *Journal of Community Health, 3,* 142–55.

National Center for Health Statistics. (2004). *Vital and health statistics, 13,* 149. Hyattsville, MD: U. S. Public Health Service.

Nelson, D. E., Bland, S., Powell-Griner, E., Klein, R., Wells, H. E., Hogelin, G., & Marks, J. S. (2002). State trends in health risk factors and receipt of clinical preventive services among US adults during the 1990s. *Journal of the American Medical Association, 287,* 2659–2668.

Neumark-Sztainer, D., Wall, M. M., Story, M., & Perry, C. L. (2003). Correlates of unhealthy weight-control behaviors among adolescents: Implications for prevention programs. *Health Psychology, 22,* 88–98.

Newnham, J. (1998). Consequences of fetal growth restriction. *Current Opinion in Obstetrics and Gynecology, 10,* 145–149.

Ng-Mak, D. S. (1999). A further analysis of race differences in the National Longitudinal Mortality Study. *American Journal of Public Health, 89,* 1748–1752.

Niaura, R., & Abrams, D. B. (2002). Smoking cessation: Progress, priorities, and prospectus. *Journal of Consulting and Clinical Psychology, 70,* 494–509.

Nicassio, P. M., Meyerowitz, B. E., & Kerns, R. D. (2004). The future of health psychology interventions. *Health Psychology, 23,* 132–137.

Nicolosi, R. J., & Schaefer, E. J. (1992). Pathobiology of hypercholesterolemia and atherosclerosis: Genetic and environment determinants of elevated lipoprotein levels. In I. S. Ockene & J. K. Ockene (Eds.), *Prevention of coronary heart disease* (pp. 69–102). Boston: Little, Brown.

NIDA Research Report. (2000). Anabolic steroid abuse (DHHS Publication No. 00–3721). Washington, DC: Department of Health and Human Services.

Niedenthal, P. M., & Beike, D. R. (1997). Interrelated and isolated self-concepts. *Personality and Social Psychology Review, 1,* 106–128.

Niederhoffer, K. G., & Pennebaker, J. W. (2002). Sharing one's story: On the benefits of writing or talking about emotional experience. In C. R. Snyder & S. J. Lopez (Eds.), *Handbook of positive psychology* (pp. 573–583). London: Oxford University Press.

Niklason, L. E., & Langer, R. (2001). Prospects for organ and tissue replacement. *Journal of the American Medical Association, 285,* 573–576.

Nishiyama, K., & Johnson, J. V. (1997). Karoshi—Death from overwork: Occupational health consequences of Japanese production management. *International Journal of Health Services: Planning, Administration, Evaluation, 27,* 625–641.

Noppe, I. C. (2004). Gender and death: Parallel and intersecting pathways. In J. Berzoff & P R. Silverman (Eds.), *Living with dying: A handbook for end-of-life healthcare practitioners.* New York: Columbia University Press.

Norbeck, J. S., & Anderson, N. J. (1989). Psychosocial predictors of pregnancy outcomes in low-income Black, Hispanic, and White women. *Nursing Research, 38,* 204–209.

Norlander, T., Bood, S. A., & Archer, T. (2002). Performance during stress: Affective personality, age, and regularity of physical exercise. *Social Behavior and Personality, 30,* 495–508.

Norris, F., Byrne, C. M., & Diaz, E. (2002). The range, magnitude, and duration of effects of natural and human-caused disasters: A review of the empirical literature. A National Center for PTSD Fact Sheet. Retrieved from http://www.ncptsd.org/facts/disasters/fs_range.html. May 15, 2005.

Norris, F. H., Murphy, A. D., Kaniasty, K., Perilla, J. L., & Ortis, D. C. (2001). Postdisaster social support in the United States and Mexico: Conceptual and contextual considerations. *Hispanic Journal of Behavioral Sciences, 23,* 469–497.

Norrish, A. E., Jackson, R. T., Sharpe, S. J., & Skeaff, C. M. (2000). Prostate cancer and dietary carotenoids. *American Journal of Epidemiology, 151,* 119–23.

Nyamathi, A. M., Stein, J. A., & Brecht, M. L. (1995). Psychosocial predictors of AIDS risk behavior and drug use behavior in homeless and drug addicted women of color. *Health Psychology, 14,* 265–273.

Nyswander, D. B. (1966). Education for health: Some principles and their application. *Health Education Monographs, 14,* 65–70.

Obeidallah, D. A., Hauser, S. T., & Jacobson, A. M. (1999). The long branch of phase-environment fit: Concurrent and longitudinal implications of match and mismatch among diabetic and nondiabetic youth. *Journal of Adolescent Research, 14,* 95–121.

O'Conner, G. T., Buring, J. E., Yusuf, S., Goldhaber, S. Z., Olmstead, E. M., Paffebarger, R. S., et al. (1989). An overview of randomized trials of rehabilitation with exercise after myocardial infarction. *Circulation, 80,* 234–244.

Ockene, J., Kristeller, J. L., Goldberg. R., & Ockene, I. (1992). Smoking cessation and severity of disease: The coronary artery smoking intervention study. *Health Psychology, 11,* 119–126.

Ogden, J. (2003). Some problems with social cognition models: A pragmatic and conceptual analysis. *Health Psychology, 22,* 424–428.

Ogus, E. D., Greenglass, E. R., & Burke, R. J. (1990). Gender-role differences, work stress and depersonalization. *Journal of Social Behavior and Personality, 5,* 387–398.

Oken, B. S., Kishiyama, S., Zajdel, D., Bourdette, D., Carlsen, J., Haas, M., et al. (2004). Randomized controlled trial of yoga and exercise in multiple sclerosis. *Neurology, 62,* 2058–2064.

Olbrisch, M. E., Benedict, S. M., Ashe, K., & Levenson, J. L. (2002). Psychological assessment and care of organ transplant patients. *Journal of Consulting and Clinical Psychology, 70,* 771–783.

Olson, H. C., Streissguth, A. P., Sampson, P. D. Barr, H. M., Bookstein, F. L., & Thiede, K. (1997). Association of prenatal alcohol exposure with behavioral and learning problems in early adolescence. *Journal of the American Academy of Child and Adolescent Psychiatry, 36,* 1187–1194.

Olson, J. M., Roese, N. J., & Zanna, M. P. (1996). Expectancies. In E. T. Higgins & A. W. Kruglanski (Eds.), *Social psychology: Handbook of basic principles* (pp. 211–239). New York: Guilford Press.

Ondeck, D. M. (2003). Impact of culture on pain. *Home Health Care Management & Practice, 15,* 255–257.

Ong, L. M. L., DeHaes, J. C. J. M., Hoos, A. M., & Lammes, F. B. (1995). Doctor-patient communication: A review of the literature. *Social Science and Medicine, 40,* 903–918.

Oomen, J. S., Owen, L. J., & Suggs, L. S. (1999). Culture counts: Why current treatment models fail Hispanic women with Type 2 diabetes. *The Diabetes Educator, 25,* 220–225.

Ornish, D., Brown, S. E., Scherwitz, L. W., Billings, J. H., Armstrong, W. T., Ports, T. A., McLanahan, S. M., Kirkeeide, R. L., Brand, R. J., & Gould, K. L. (1990). Can lifestyle changes reverse coronary heart disease? The lifestyle heart trial. *Lancet, 336,* 129–133.

Ornish, D., Scherwitz, L. W., Billings, J. H., Gould, K. L., Merritt, T. A., Sparler, S., et al. (1998). Intensive lifestyle changes for reversal of coronary heart disease. *Journal of the American Medical Association, 280,* 2001–2007.

Orth-Gomer, K., Chesney, M., & Wenger, N. K. (1998). *Women, stress, and heart disease.* Mahwah, NJ: Erlbaum.

Orth-Gomer, K., & Johnson, J. V. (1987). Social network interaction and mortality: A six year follow-up study of a random sample of the Swedish population. *Journal of Chronic Diseases, 40,* 949–957.

Orth-Gomer, K., Rosengren, A., & Wilhelmsen, L. (1993). Lack of social support and incidence of coronary heart disease in middle-aged Swedish men. *Psychosomatic Medicine, 55,* 37–43.

Orth-Gomer, K., Wamala, S. P., Horsten, M., Schenck-Gustafsson, K., Schneiderman, N., & Mittleman, M. A. (2000). Marital stress worsens prognosis in women with coronary heart disease: The Stockholm female coronary risk study. *Journal of the American Medical Association, 284,* 3008–3014.

Osborne, L., & Mason, J. (1993). HLA A/B haplotype frequencies among U. S. Hispanic and African American populations. *Human Genetics, 91,* 326–332.

Padian, N. S., Shiboski, S., Glass, S., & Vittinghoff, E. (1997). Heterosexual transmission of HIV in northern California: Results from a 10 year study. *American Journal of Epidemiology, 146,* 350–357.

Padilla, A. M., & Ruiz, R. A. (1973). *Latino mental health: A review of literature.* Washington, DC: U. S. Government Printing Office.

Paffenbarger, R. S., Hyde, R. T., Wing, A. L., & Hsieh, C. (1986). Physical activity, all-cause mortality, and longevity of college alumni. *New England Journal of Medicine, 314,* 605–613.

Paffenbarger, R. S., Lee, I., & Leung, R. (1994). Physical activity and personal characterisitcs associated with depression and suicide in American college men. *Acta Psychiatrica Scandinavica, 89,* 16–22.

Pakenham, K. I., Dadds, M. R., & Terry, D. J. (1994). Relationship between adjustment to HIV and both social support and coping. *Journal of Consulting & Clinical Psychology, 62,* 1194–1203.

Pargament, K. I. (1997). *The psychology of religion and coping: Theory, research, practice.* New York: Guilford Press.

Pargament, K. I. (2002). The bitter and the sweet: An evaluation of the costs and benefits of religiousness. *Psychological Inquiry, 13,* 168–181.

Pargament, K. I., Koenig, H. G., & Perez, L. M. (2000). The many methods of religious coping: Development and initial validation of the RCOPE. *Journal of Clinical Psychology, 56,* 519–543.

Pargament, K. I., Smith, B. W., Koenig, H. G., & Perez, L. (1998). Patterns of positive and negative religious coping with major life stressors. *Journal for the Scientific Study of Religion, 37,* 710–724.

Parhan, T. A. & Helms, J. E. (1985). Attitudes of racial identity and self-esteem: An exploratory investigation. *Journal of College Student Personnel, 26,* 143–151.

Park, C. L., Cohen, L. H., & Murch, R. L. (1996). Assessment and prediction of stress-related growth. *Journal of Personality, 64,* 71–105.

Park, C. L., & Folkman, S. (1997). The role of meaning in the context of stress and coping. *General Review of Psychology, 2,* 115–144.

Parker, B., McFarlane, J., & Soeken, K. (1994). Abuse during pregnancy: Effects on maternal complications and birth weight in adult and teenage women. *Obstetrics and Gynecology, 84,* 323–328.

Parker, S., Tong, T., Bolden, S., & Wingo, P. (1997). Cancer statistics, 1997. *CA—A Cancer Journal for Clinicians, 47,* 5–27.

Parkes, C. M., Stevenson-Hinde, J., & Marris, P. (1991). *Attachment across the life cycle.* New York: Tavistock/Routledge.

Parry, J., & Ryan, A. (1995). *A cross cultural look at death, dying and religion.* Stamford, CT: Wadsworth.

Parsons, O. A. (1994). Determinants of cognitive deficits in alcoholics: The search continues. *Clinical Neuropsychologist, 8,* 39–58.

Pate, R. H. (1995). Certification of specialities: Not if, but how. *Journal of Counseling & Development, 74,* 181–184.

Patterson, C. J., Fulcher, M., & Wainright, J. (2002). Children of lesbian and gay parents: Research, law, and policy. In B. L. Bottoms, M. Kovera Bull, et al. (Eds.), *Children, social science and the law* (pp. 176–199). New York: Cambridge University Press.

Patterson, D. R., Adcock, R. J., & Bombardier, C. H. (1997). Factors predicting hypnotic analgesia in clinical burn pain. *International Journal of Clinical and Experimental Hypnosis, 45,* 377–395.

Patterson, J. (2002). Integrating family resilience and family stress theory. *Journal of Marriage and Family, 64,* 349–360.

Patterson, J. M. (2002). Understanding family, resilience. *Journal of Clinical Psychology, 58,* 233–247.

Patterson, J. M., & Garwick, A. W. (1994). Levels of meaning in family stress theory. *Family Process, 33,* 287–304.

Patterson, J. M., & McCubbin, H. I. (1987). Adolescent coping style and behaviors: Conceptualization and measurement. *Journal of Adolescence, 10,* 163–186.

Pattison, E. M. (1977). Ten years of change in alcoholism treatment and delivery systems. *American Journal of Psychiatry, 134,* 261–266.

Paus, T. (1999). Imaging the brain before, during, and after transcranial magnetic stimulation. *Neuropsychologia, 37,* 219–224.

Pearlin, L. I., & Schooler, C. (1978). The structure of coping. *Journal of Health and Social Behavior, 19,* 2–21.

Pearlin, L. I., & Skaff, M. M. (1995). Stressors and adaptation in late life. In M. Gatz (Ed.), *Emerging issues in mental health and aging* (pp. 97–123). Washington, DC: American Psychological Association.

Penley, J. A., & Tomaka, J. (2002). Associations among the Big Five, emotional responses and coping with acute stress. *Personality and Individual Differences, 32,* 1215–1128.

Penn, N. E., Kramer, J., Skinner, J. F., Velasquez, R. J., Yee, B. W. K., Arellano, L. M., et al. (2000). Health practices and health-care systems among cultural groups. In R. M. Eisler & M. Hersen (Eds.), *Handbook of gender, culture, and health* (pp. 105–138). Mahwah, NJ: Erlbaum.

Pennebaker, J. W., & Beall, S. K. (1986). Confronting a traumatic event: Toward an understanding of inhibition and disease. *Journal of Abnormal Psychology, 95,* 274–281.

Pennebaker, J. W., & Graybeal, A. (2001). Patterns of natural language use: Disclosure, personality, and social integration. *Current Directions in Psychological Science, 10,* 90–93.

Penninx, B. W. J. H., Guralnik, J. M., Pahor, M., Ferrucci, L., Cerhan, J. R., Wallace, R. B., et al. (1998). Chronically depressed mood and cancer risk in older persons. *Journal of the National Cancer Institute, 90,* 1888–1896.

Pereira, M. A., Kriska, A. M., Collins, V. R., Dowse, G. K., Tuomilehto, J., Alberti, K. G. (1998). Occupational status and cardiovascular disease risk factors in the rapidly developing, high-risk population of Mauritius. *American Journal of Epidemiology, 148,* 148–159.

Perez-Stable, E. J., Sabogal F., Otero-Sabogal R., Hiatt R. A., & McPhee S. J. (1992). Misconceptions about cancer among Latinos and Anglos. *Journal of the American Medical Association, 268,* 3219–3223.

Perkins, H. W. (Ed.). (2003). *The social norms approach to preventing school and college age substance abuse: A handbook for educators, counselors, and clinicians.* San Francisco: Jossey-Bass.

Perkins, H. W., Meilman, P., Leichliter, J., Cashin, J., & Presley, C. (1999). Misperceptions of the norms for the frequency of alcohol and other drug use on college campuses. *Journal of American College Health, 47,* 253–258.

Perkins, P., Cooksley, C. D., & Cox, P. D. (1996). Breast cancer: Is ethnicity an independent prognostic factor for survival? *Cancer, 78,* 1241–1247.

Perry-Jenkins, M., Repetti, R. L., & Crouter, A. C. (2002). Work and family in the 1990s. *Journal of Marriage and the Family, 62,* 981–998.

Persky, V., Kempthorne-Rawson, J., & Shekelle, R. (1987). Personality and risk of cancer: 20-year follow-up of the Western Electric study. *Psychosomatic Medicine, 49,* 435–449.

Petridou, E., Zavitsanos, X., Dessypris, N., Frangakis, C., Mandyla, M., Doziadis, S., & Trichopoulous, D. (1997). Adolescents in high-risk trajectory: Clustering of risky behavior and the origins of socioeconomic health differentials. *Preventive Medicine: An International Journal Devoted to Practice & Theory, 26,* 215–219.

Pettingale, K. W. (1985). Towards a psychobiological model of cancer: Biological considerations. *Social Science and Medicine, 20,* 779–787.

Petrie, K. J., Booth, R., Pennebaker, J. W., Davidson, K. P., & Thomas, M. (1995). Disclosure of trauma and immune response to Hepatitis B vaccination program. *Journal of Consulting and Clinical Psychology, 63,* 787–792.

Pfefferbaum, B., Adams, J., & Aceves, J. (1990). The influence of culture on pain in Anglo and Hispanic children with cancer. *Journal of the American Academy of Child and Adolescent Psychiatry, 29,* 642–647.

Pham, C. T., & McPhee, S. J. (1992). Knowledge, attitudes, and practices of breast and cervical cancer screening among Vietnamese women. *Journal of Cancer Education, 7,* 305–310.

Phillips, D. (1996). Medical professional dominance and client dissatisfactions: A study of doctor-patient interaction and reported dissatisfaction with medical care among female patients at four hospitals in Trinidad and Tobago. *Social Science and Medicine, 42,* 1419–1425.

Phillips, W. T., Kiernan, M., & King, A. C. (2002). The effects of physical activity on physical and psychological health. In A. Baum, T. A. Revenson, & J. E. Singer (Eds.), *Handbook of health psychology* (pp. 627–659). Mahwah, NJ: Erlbaum.

Phinney, J., & Rosenthal, D. (1992). Ethnic identity formation in adolescence: Process, context, and solution. In G. Adams, T. Gulotta, & R. Montemayor (Eds.), *Identity formation during adolescence* (pp. 145–172). Newbury Park, CA: Sage.

Phinney, J. S. (1996). When we talk about American ethnic groups, what do we mean? *American Psychologist, 51,* 918–927.

Pickin, C., & St. Leger, S. (1993). *Assessing health need using the life cycle framework.* Buckingham, England: Open University Press.

Pierce, G. R., Lakey, B., Sarason, I. G., & Sarason, B. R. (1997). Sourcebook of social support and personality. In G. R. Pierce, B. Lakey, I. G. Sarason, & B. R. Sarason (Eds.), *The Plenum series in social/clinical psychology.* New York: Plenum Press.

Pilowsky, I., & Spence, N. D. (1975). Patterns of illness behavior in patients with intractable pain. *Journal of Psychosomatic Research, 19,* 279–287.

Pines, A. M., Ben-Ari, A., Utaso, A., & Larson, D. (2002). A cross-cultural investigation of social support and burnout. *European Psychologist, 7,* 256–264.

Pi-Sunyer, X. (1998). A clinical view of the obesity problem. *Science, 299,* 859–861.

Polich, J., Pollock, V. E., & Bloom, F. E. (1994). Meta-analysis of P300 amplitude from males at risk for alcoholism. *Psychological Bulletin, 115,* 55–73.

Pollock, S. E. (1986). Human responses to chronic illness: Physiologic and psychosocial adaptation. *Nursing Research, 35,* 90–95.

Pomerleau, O. F., & Kardia, S. L. R. (1999). Introduction to the featured section: Genetic research on smoking. *Health Psychology, 18,* 3–6.

Popkin, B. M., & Udry, J. R. (1998). Adolescent obesity increases significantly in second- and third-generation U. S. immigrants: The National Longitudinal Study of Adolescent Health. *Journal of Nutrition, 128,* 701–706.

Porter, J. R., & Washington, R. E. (1993). Minority identity and self-esteem. *Annual Review of Sociology, 19,* 139–161.

Porter, R. (2002). *Blood and guts: A short history of medicine.* New Delhi, India: Penguin.

Potter, J. D., & Steinmetz, K. (1996). Vegetables, fruit, and phytoestrogens as preventative agents. *IARC Science Publications, 139,* 61–90.

Powell, L. H., Shahabi, L., & Thoresen, C. E. (2003). Religion and spirituality: Linkages to physical health. *American Psychologist, 58,* 36–52.

Probst, J. C., Greenhouse, D. L., & Selassie, A. W. (1997). Patient and physician satisfaction with an outpatient care visit. *Journal of Family Practice, 45,* 418–425.

Prochaska, J. O., & DiClemente, C. C. (1983). Stages and processes of self-change in smoking: Towards an integrative model of change. *Journal of Consulting and Clinical Psychology, 51,* 390–395.

Prochaska, J. O., Redding, C. A., & Evers, K. E. (2002). The transtheoretical model and stages of change. In K. Glanz, B. K. Rimer, & F. M. Lewis (Eds.), *Health behavior and health education: Theory, research, and practice* (pp. 99–120). San Francisco: Jossey-Bass.

Pryzdoga, J., & Chrisler, J. C. (2000). Definitions of gender and sex: The subtleties of meaning. *Sex Roles, 43,* 553–569.

Ptacek, J. T., Smith, R. E., & Zanas, J. (1992). Gender, appraisal, and coping: A longitudinal analysis. *Journal of Personality, 60,* 747–771.

Raglin, J. S. (1997). Anxiolytic effects of physical activity. In W. P. Morgan (Ed.), *Physical activity and mental health. Series in health psychology and behavioral medicine* (pp. 107–126). Philadelphia: Taylor & Francis.

Rahe, R. H. (1972). Subjects' recent life changes and their near future illness reports. *Annals of Clinical Research, 4,* 250–265.

Rainville, P., Carrier, B., Hofbauer, R. K., Bushnell, M. C., & Duncan, G. H. (1999). Dissociation of sensory and affective dimensions in pain using hypnotic modulation. *Pain, 82,* 159–171.

Ramakrishna, J., & Weiss, M. G. (1992, September). Health, illness, and immigration: East Indians in the United States. *The Western Journal of Medicine, 157*(3), 265–271.

Rand, C. S., & Weeks, K. (1998). Measuring adherence with medication regimens in clinical care and research. In S. A. Shumaker, E. B. Schron, et al. (Eds.), *The handbook of health behavior change* (2nd ed., pp. 114–132). New York: Springer.

Rapoff, M. A. (1999). *Adherence to pediatric medical regimens.* New York: Kluwer Academic/Plenum Publishers.

Rauscher, F. H., Shaw, G. L., & Ky, K. N. (1995). Listening to Mozart enhances spatial-temporal reasoning: Towards a neurophysiological basis. *Neuroscience Letters, 185,* 44–47.

Ravussin, E., & Rising, R. (1992). Daily energy expenditure in humans: Measurements in a respiratory chamber and by doubly labeled water. In J. M. Kinney & H. N. Tucker (Eds.), *Energy metabolism: Tissue determinants and cellular corollaries* (pp. 81–96). New York: Raven Press.

Ravussin, E., Valencia, M. E., Esparza, J., Bennett, P. H., & Schulz, L. O. (1994). Effects of a traditional lifestyle on obesity in Pima Indians. *Diabetes Care, 17,* 1067–1074.

Rawl, S. M., Champion, V. L., Menon, U., & Foster, J. L. (2000). The impact of age and race on mammography practices. *Health Care for Women International, 21,* 583–597.

Ray, C., Jefferies, S., & Weir, W. R. (1995). Life-events and the course of chronic fatigue syndrome. *British Journal of Medical Psychology, 68,* 323–331.

Ready, T. (1988). Too few minorities in AIDS tests, critics say, scientists "ignoring" Blacks, Hispanics, women. *Washington Watch, 1.*

Reaven, P. D., Barrett-Conner, E., & Edelstein, S. (1991). Relation between leisure-time physical activity and blood pressure in older women. *Circulation, 83,* 559–565.

Redd, W. H., & Jacobsen, P. (2001). Behavioral intervention in comprehensive cancer care. In A. Baum, T. A. Revenson, & J. E. Singer (Eds.), *Handbook of health psychology* (pp. 757–776). Mahwah, NJ: Erlbaum.

Reed, G. M., Kemeny, M. E., Taylor, S. E., & Visscher, B. R. (1999). Negative HIV-specific expectations and AIDS-related bereavement as predictors of symptom onset in asymptomatic HIV-positive gay men. *Health Psychology, 18,* 354–363.

Reed, G. M., Kemeny, M. E., Taylor, S. E., Wang, H. Y., & Visscher, B. R. (1994). Realistic acceptance as a predictor of decreased survival time in gay men with AIDS. *Health Psychology, 13,* 299–307.

Reid, D. P. (1989). *The Tao of health, sex, and longevity: A modern practical guide to the ancient way.* New York: Simon & Schuster.

Reis, A. L. (1993). Adherence in the patient with pulmonary disease. In J. E. Hodgkin, G. L. Conners, & C. W. Bell (Eds.), *Pulmonary rehabilitation* (2nd ed., pp. 86–101). Philadelphia: Lippincott.

Renaud, S. C., Gueguen, R., Siest, G., & Salamon, R. (1999). Wine, beer, and mortality in middle-aged men from eastern France. *Archives of Internal Medicine, 159,* 1865–1870.

Repetti, R. L. (1998). The promise of a multiple roles paradigm for women's health research. *Women's Health: Research on Gender, Behavior, and Policy, 4,* 273–80.

Repetti, R. L., Taylor, S. E., & Seeman, T. E. (2002). Risky families: Family social environment and the mental and physical health of offspring. *Psychological Bulletin, 128,* 330–366.

Repetti, R. L., & Wood, J. (1997). Effects of daily stress at work on mothers' interactions with preschoolers. *Journal of Family Psychology, 11,* 90–108.

Reynolds, D. V. (1969). Surgery in the rat during electrical analgesia induced by focal brain stimulation. *Science, 164,* 444–445.

Reynolds, P., & Kaplan, G. A. (1990). Social connections and risk for cancer: Prospective evidence from the Alameda County Study. *Behavioral Medicine, 16,* 101–110.

Ricciardelli, L. A., & McCabe, M. P. (2001). Dietary restraint and negative effect as mediators of body dissatisfaction and bulimic behavior in adolescent girls and boys. *Behavior Research and Therapy, 39,* 1317–1329.

Richards, J. M., Pennebaker, J. W., & Beall, W. E. (1995). *The effects of criminal offense and disclosure in prison inmates.* Paper presented at the Midwest Psychological Association, Chicago.

Richardson, P. J., Wodak, A. D., Atkinson, L., Saunders, J. B., & Jewitt, D. E. (1986). Relationship between alcohol intake, myocardial enzyme activity, and myocardial function in dilated cardiomyopathy: Evidence for the concept of alcohol induced heart muscle disease. *British Heart Journal, 56,* 165–170.

Richmond, M. (2004). *Practice organization action alert.* APAPO Government Relations Office.

Ries, L. A. G. (1996). Cancer rates. In A. Harras, B. K. Edwards, W. J. Blot, & L. A. G. Ries (Eds.), *Cancer rates and risks* (pp. 9–54). NIH Publication No. 96–961). Bethesda, MD: National Cancer Institute.

Rigotti, N. A., Lee, J. E., & Wechsler, H. (2000). US college students' use of tobacco products: Results of a national survey. *Journal of the American Medical Association, 264,* 699–705.

Riley, J. L., Wade, J. B., Myers, C. D., Sheffield, D., Papas, R. K., & Price, D. D. (2002). Racial/ethnic differences in the experience of chronic pain. *Pain, 100,* 291–298.

Rime, B. (1995). Mental rumination, social sharing, and the recovery from emotional exposure. In J. W. Pennebaker (Ed.), *Emotion, disclosure, & health* (pp. 271–291). Washington, DC: American Psychological Association.

Rimer, B. K. (1994). Mammography use in the US: Trends and the impact of interventions. *Annals of Behavioral Medicine, 16,* 317–326.

Rimer, B. K. (2002). Perspectives on intrapersonal theories of health behavior. In K. Glanz, B. K. Rimer, & F. M. Lewis (Eds.), *Health behavior and health education: Theory, research, and practice* (pp. 144–164). San Francisco: Jossey-Bass.

Rimm, E. B., & Ellison, R. C. (1995). Alcohol in the Mediterranean diet. *American Journal of Clinical Nutrition, 61,* 1378S–1382S.

Risberg, G. (1994). Sexual violence as a health problem: Caregivers' reluctance to ask questions makes rehabilitation of women more difficult. *Lakartidningen, 91,* 4770–4771.

Robert, S. A. (1999). Socioeconomic risk factors for breast cancer: Distinguishing individual- and community-level effects. *Epidemiology, 15,* 4422450

Robins, L. N., Locke, B. Z., & Regier, D. A. (1991). An overview of psychiatric disorders in America. In L. N. Robins & D. A. Regier (Eds.), *Psychiatric disorders in America: The epidemiologic Catchment Areas Study* (pp. 328–366). New York: Free Press.

Robinson, T. N., Patrick, K., Eng, T. R., & Gustafson, D. (1998). An evidence-based approach to interactive health communication: A challenge to medicine in the information age. *Journal of Psychosomatic Research, 47,* 439–447.

Rogers, E. M. (1983). *Diffusion of innovations.* New York: Free Press.

Rogers, S. J., Parcel, T. L., & Menaghan, E. G. (1991). The effects of maternal working conditions and mastery on child behavior problems: Studying the intergenerational transmission of social control. *Journal of Health and Social Behavior, 32,* 145–164.

Roizen, J. (1997). Epidemiological issues in alcohol-related violence. In M. Galanter (Ed.), *Recent developments in alcoholism* (pp. 7–40). New York: Plenum.

Roland, A. (1991). *In search of self in India and Japan: Toward a cross-cultural psychology.* Princeton, NJ: Princeton University Press.

Rollman, G. B. (2003). Sex makes a difference: Experimental and clinical pain responses. *Clinical Journal of Pain, 19,* 204–207.

Rolls, B. J., & Shide, D. J. (1992). Moth naturalistic and laboratory-based studies contribute to the understanding of human eating behavior. *Appetite, 19,* 76–77.

Rook, K. S., & Schuster, T. L. (1996). Compensatory processes in the social networks of older adults. In G. R. Pierce, B. R. Sarason, et al. (Eds.), *Handbook of social support and the family. Plenum series on stress and coping* (pp. 219–248). New York: Plenum Press.

Rosario, M., Nahler, K., Hunter, J., & Gwadz, M. (1999). Understanding the unprotected sexual behaviors of gay, lesbian, and bisexual youths: An empirical test of the cognitive-environmental model. *Health Psychology, 18,* 272–80.

Rosenbaum, E., Gautier, H., Fobair, P., Neri, E., Festa, B., Hawn, M., et al. (2004). Cancer supportive care, improving the quality of life for cancer patients: A program evaluation report. *Supportive Care in Cancer, 12,* 293–301.

Rosenberg, M. (1965). Society and the adolescent self image. Princeton, NJ: Princeton University Press.

Rosenberg, P. S., & Biggar, R. J. (1998). Trends in HIV incidence among young adults in the United States. *Journal of the American Medical Association, 279,* 1894–1899.

Rosenblatt, P. C. (1993). Cross-cultural variation in the experience, expression, and understanding of grief. In D. P. Irish, K. F. Lundquist, & V. J. Nelsen (Eds.), *Ethnic variations in death, dying, and grief.* Washington, DC: Taylor & Francis.

Rosenhan, D. L., & Seligman, M. E. P. (1989). *Abnormal psychology* (2nd ed.). New York: Norton.

Rosenman, R. H., & Friedman, M. (1974). Neurogenic factors in pathogenesis of coronary heart disease. *The Medical Clinics of North America, 58,* 269–279.

Rosenstock, I. M. (1960). What research in motivation suggests for public health. *American Journal of Public Health, 50,* 295–301.

Rosenstock, I. M. (1974). Historical origins of the health belief model. In M. H. Becker (Ed.), *The health belief model and personal health behavior* (pp. 1–8). Thorofare, NJ: Slack.

Rosenstock, I. M., Strecher, V. J., and Becker, M. H. (1988). The health belief model and HIV risk behavior change. In J. Peterson & R. DiClemente (Eds.), *Preventing AIDS: Theory and practice of behavior interventions* (pp. 5–24). New York: Plenum Press.

Ross, C. E., & Mirowsky, J. (1979). A comparison of life-event-weighting schemes: Change, undesirability, and effect-proportional indices. *Journal of Health and Social Behavior, 20,* 166–177.

Rossouw, J. E., Anderson, G. L., Prentice, R. L., LaCroix, A. Z., Kooperberg, C., Stefanick, M. L., et al. (2002). Risks and benefits of estrogen plus progestin in healthy postmenopausal women: Principal results from the Women's Health Initiative randomized controlled trial. *Journal of the American Medical Association, 288,* 321–333.

Roter, D. L., & Hall, J. A. (1992). *Doctors talking with patients/patients talking with doctors: Improving communication in medical visits.* Westport, CT: Auburn House/Greenwood Publishing Group.

Roter, D. L., Stewart, M., Putnam, S. M., Lipkin, M., Jr., Stiles, W., & Inui, T. S. (1997). Communication patterns of primary care physicians. *Journal of the American Medical Association, 277,* 350–356.

Rotheram-Borus, M. J., & Duan, N. (2003). Next generation of preventive interventions. *Journal of the American Academy of Child and Adolescent Psychiatry, 42,* 518–526.

Rotheram-Borus, M. J., Song, J., Gwadz, M., Lee, M., Van Rossem, R., & Koopman, C. (2003). Reductions in HIV risk among runaway youth. *Preventative Science, 4,* 173–187.

Roy, M. P., Steptoe, A., & Kirschbaum, C. (1998). Life events and social support as moderators of individual differences in cardiovascular and cortisol reactivity. *Journal of Personality and Social Psychology, 75,* 1273–1281.

Royce, R. A., Sena, A., Cates, W., Jr., & Cohen, M. S. (1997). Sexual transmission of HIV. *New England Journal of Medicine, 336,* 1072–1078.

Rozanski, A., Bairey, C. N., Krantz, D. S., Friedman, J., Resser, K. J., Morell, M., et al (1994). Mental stress and the induction of silent myocardial ischemia in patients with coronary artery disease. In A. Steptoe & J. Wardle (Eds.), *Psychosocial processes and health: A reader* (pp. 147–165). New York: Cambridge University Press.

Rozanski, A., Blumenthal, J. A., & Kaplan, J. (1999). Impact of psychological factors on the pathogenesis of cardiovascular disease and implications for therapy. *Circulation, 99,* 2192–2217.

Rozin, P. (1990). Development in the food domain. *Developmental Psychology, 26,* 555–563.

Rudolph, K. D., & Hammen, C. (1999). Age and gender as determinants of stress exposure, generation, and reactions in youngsters: A transactional perspective. *Child Development, 70,* 660–677.

Rundall, T. G., & Wheeler, J. R. (1979). The effect of income on use of preventive care: An evaluation of alternative explanations. *Journal of Health and Social Behavior, 20,* 397–406.

Russel, M., Cooper, M. L., Frone, M. R., & Welte, J. W. (1991). Alcohol drinking patterns and blood pressure. *American Journal of Public Health, 81,* 452–457.

Russell, M. (1990). The influence of sociodemorgraphic characteristics on familial alcohol problems: data from a community sample. *Alcohol Clinical Experimental Research, 14,* 221–226.

Ryan, G. W. (1998). What do sequential behavioral patterns suggest about the medical decision-making process? Modelling home case management of acute illnesses in a rural Cameroonian village. *Social Science and Medicine, 46,* 209–225.

Ryff, C. D., & Singer, B. (2003a). Thriving in the face of challenge: The integrative science of human resilience. In F. Kessel, P. L. Rosenfield, & N. Anderson (Eds.), *Expanding the boundaries of health and social science: Case studies in interdisciplinary innovation* (pp. 181–205). London: Oxford University Press.

Ryff, C. D., & Singer, B. (2003b). Flourishing under fire: Resilience as a prototype of challenged thriving. In C. L. M. Keyes & J. Haidt (Eds.), *Flourishing: Positive psychology and the life well-lived* (pp. 15–36). Washington, DC: American Psychological Association.

Ryndes, T., Connor, S., Cody, C., Merriman, M., Bruno, S., Fine, P., et al. (2001). Report on the alpha and beta pilots of end result outcome measures constructed by the outcomes forum, a joint effort of the National Hospice and Palliative Care Organization and the National Hospice Work Group. Available at www.nhpco.org.

Saab, P. G., McCalla, J. R., Coons, H. L., Christensen, A. J., Kaplan, R., Johnson, S. B., et al. (2004). Technological and medical advances: Implications for health psychology. *Health Psychology, 23,* 142–146.

Sable, M. R., Stockbauer, J. W., Schramm, W. F., & Land, G. H. (1990). Differentiating the barriers to adequate prenatal care in Missouri, 1987–88. *Public Health Report, 105,* 9–555.

Sagrestano, L. M., Feldman, P., Rini, K. C., Woo, G., & Dunkel-Schetter, C. (1999). Ethnicity and social support during pregnancy. *American Journal of Community Psychology, 27,* 869–898.

Salmon, P. (2001). Effects of physical exercise on anxiety, depression, and sensitivity to stress: A unifying theory. *Clinical Psychology Review, 21,* 33–61.

Salovey, P., Rothman, A. J., & Rodin, J. (1998). Health behavior. In D. T. Gilbert, S. T. Fiske, et al. (Eds.), *The handbook of social psychology* (Vol. 2, 4th ed., pp. 633–683). New York: McGraw-Hill.

Sandborn, K. M. (2000). Predicting depressive symptoms after miscarriage: A path analysis based on the Lazarus paradigm. *Journal of Women's Health and Gender-Based Medicine, 9,* 191–207.

Sanders, S. H., Brena, S. F., Spier, C. J., Beltrutti, D., McConnell, H., & Quintero, O. (1992). Chronic low back pain patients around the world: cross-cultural similarities and differences. *The Clinical Journal of Pain, 8,* 317–23.

Sandlund, E. S., & Norlander, T. (2000). The effects of Tai Chi Chuan relaxation and exercise on stress responses and well-being: An overview of research. *International Journal of Stress Management, 7,* 139–149.

Saper, R. B., Eisenberg, D. M., Davis, R. B., Culpepper, L., & Phillips, R. S. (2004). Prevalence and patterns of adult yoga use in the United States: Results of a National Survey. *Alternative Therapies and Health Medicine, 10,* 44–49.

Sapolsky, R. M. (1991). Poverty remains. *The Sciences* (September-October), 8.

Sapolsky, R. M. (1998). *Why zebras don't get ulcers: An updated guide to stress, stress-related disease and coping.* New York: Freeman.

Sapolsky, R. M. (2002). *A primate's memoir.* New York: Touchstone Books.

Sarafino, E. P. (2001). *Behavior modification: Principles of behavior change* (2nd ed.). Mountain View, CA: Mayfield.

Saran, P. (1985). Asian Indian Experience in the United States. Cambridge, MA.: Schenkman.

Sarason, B. R., Sarason, I. G., & Gurung, R. A. R. (2001). Close personal relationships and health outcomes: A key to the role of social support. In B. R. Sarason & S. Duck (Eds.), *Personal relationships: Implications for clinical and community psychology* (pp. 15–41). Chichester, England: Wiley.

Sarason, I. G., Johnson, J. H., & Siegel, J. M. (1978). Assessing the impact of life changes: Development of the life experiences survey. *Journal of Consulting and Clinical Psychology, 46,* 932–946.

Sargent, J. D., Dalton, M. A., Beach M. L., Mott, L. A., Tickle, J. J., Ahrens, M. B., et al. (2002). Viewing tobacco use in movies: Does it shape attitudes that mediate adolescent smoking? *American Journal of Preventive Medicine, 22,* 137–145.

Sargent, J. D., Dalton, M. A., Heatherton, T., & Beach, M. (2003). Modifying exposure to smoking depicted in movies: A novel approach to preventing adolescent smoking. *Archives of Pediatrics and Adolescent Medicine, 157,* 643–648.

Schaal, B., Tremblay, R. E., Soussignan, R., & Susman, E. J. (1996). Male testosterone linked to high social dominance but low physical aggression in early adolescence. *Journal of the American Academy of Child and Adolescent Psychiatry, 35,* 1322–1330.

Schachter, S. (1959). *The psychology of affiliation: Experimental studies of the sources of gregariousness.* Oxford, England: Stanford University Press.

Schachter, S. (1980). Nonpsychological explanations of behavior. In L. Festinger (Ed.), *Retrospective on social psychology* (pp. 131–157). New York: Oxford University Press.

Schachter, S., & Singer, J. E. (1962). Cognitive, social, and physiological determinants of emotional state. *Psychological Review, 69,* 379–399.

Schaefer, C. A., & Gorsuch, R. L. (1991). Psychological adjustment and religiousness: The multivariate belief-motivation theory of religiousness. *Journal for the Scientific Study of Religion, 30,* 448–461.

Schaie, K. W. (1993). The Seattle Longitudinal Study: A thirty-five-year inquiry of adult intellectual development. *Zeitschrift für Gerontologie, 26,* 129–137.

Schedlowski, M., Jacobs, R., Stratman, G., Richter, S., Hadicke, A., Tewes, U., et al. (1993). Changes of natural killer cells during acute psychological stress. *Journal of Clinical Immunology, 13,* 119–126.

Scheier, M. F., & Bridges, M. W. (1995). Person variables and health: Personality predispositions and acute psychological states as shared determinants for disease. *Psychosomatic Medicine, 57,* 255–268.

Scheier, M. F., Matthews, K. A., Owens, J. F., Magovern, G. J., et al. (1989). Dispositional optimism and recovery from coronary artery bypass surgery: The beneficial effects on physical and psychological well-being. *Journal of Personality and Social Psychology, 57,* 1024–1040.

Scheier, M. F., Matthews, K. A., Owens, J. F., Magovern, G. J., Lefebvre, R. C., Abbott, R. A., et al. (2003). Dispositional optimism and recovery from coronary artery bypass surgery: The beneficial effects of physical and psychological well-being. In P. Salovey & A. J. Rothman (Eds.), *Social psychology of health: Key readings in social psychology* (pp. 342–361). New York: Psychology Press.

Scheier, M. F., Weintraub, J. K., & Carver, C. S. (1986). Coping with stress: Divergent strategies of optimists and pessimists. *Journal of Personality and Social Psychology, 51,* 1257–1264.

Scherck, K. A. (1997). Recognizing a heart attack: The process of determining illness. *American Journal of Critical Care, 6,* 267–273.

Scherwitz, L., Graham, L. E., & Ornish, D. (1985). Self-involvement and the risk factors for coronary heart disease. *Advances, 2,* 6–18.

Schnall, P. L., Landsbergis, P. A., & Baker, D. (1994). Job strain and cardiovascular disease. *Annual Review of Public Health, 15,* 381–411.

Schreurs, K. M., & de Ridder, D. T. D. (1997). Integration of coping and social support perspectives: Implications for the study of adaptation to chronic diseases. *Clinical Psychology Review, 17,* 89–112.

Schroeder, D. H., & Costa, P. T. (1984). Influence of life event stress on physical illness: Substantive effects or methodological flaws? *Journal of Personality and Social Psychology, 46,* 853–863.

Schucklit, M. A. (1994). Low level of response to alcohol as a predictor of future alcoholism. *American Journal of Psychiatry, 151,* 184–189.

Schutte, J. W., Valerio, J. K., & Carrillo, V. (1996). Optimism and socioeconomic status: A cross-cultural study. *Social Behavior and Personality, 24,* 9–18.

Schwarzer, R. (1992). *Self-efficacy: Thought control of action.* Washington, DC: Hemisphere.

Schwarzer, R., Dunkel-Schetter, C., & Kemeny, M. (1994). The multidimensional nature of received social support in gay men at risk of HIV infection and AIDS. *American Journal of Community Psychology, 22,* 319–339.

Schwarzer, R., & Schwarzer, C. (1996). A critical survey of coping instruments. In M. Zeidnes & N. S. Endler (Eds.), *Handbook of coping: Theory, research, applications* (pp. 107–132). Oxford, England: John Wiley & Sons.

Seeman, T. E., Singer, B. H., Horwitz, R. I., & McEwen, B. S. (1997). Price of adaptation: allostatic load and its health consequences—MacArthur studies of successful aging. *Archives of Internal Medicine, 157,* 2259–2268.

Seeman, T. E., & Syme, S. L. (1987). Social networks and coronary artery disease: A comparison of the structure and function of social relations as predictors of disease. *Psychosomatic Medicine, 49,* 341–354.

Segerstrom, S. C., & Miller, G. E. (2004). Psychological stress and the human immune system: A meta-analytic study of thirty years of inquiry. *Psychological Bulletin, 130,* 601–630.

Segerstrom, S. C., Taylor, S. E., Kemeny, M. E., & Fahey, J. L. (1998). Optimism is associated with mood, coping and immune change in response to stress. *Journal of Personality and Social Psychology, 74,* 1646–1655.

Seligman, M. E. P., & Csikszentmihalyi, M. (2000). Positive psychology: An introduction. *American Psychologist, 55,* 5–14.

Sellick, S. M., & Zaza, C. (1998). Critical review of 5 nonpharmacologic strategies for managing cancer pain. *Cancer Prevention and Control, 2,* 7–14.

Selye, H. (1956). *The stress of life.* New York: McGraw-Hill.

Shavitt, S., Sanbonmatsu, D. M., Smittipatana, S., & Posavac, S. S. (1999). Broadening the conditions for illusory correlation formation: Implications for judging minority groups. *Basic and Applied Social Psychology, 21,* 263–279.

Shearer, H. M., & Evans, D. R. (2001). Adherence to health care. In S. S. Kazarian & D. R. Evans (Eds.), *Handbook of cultural health psychology* (pp. 113–138). San Diego, CA: Academic Press.

Sheikh, A. A. (Ed.). (2003). *Healing images: The role of imagination in health.* Amityville, NY: Baywood Publishing.

Shekelle, R. V., Hulley, S. B., Neaton, J. D., Billings, J. H., Borhani, N. O., Gerace, T. A., et al. (1985). The MRFIT behavior pattern study II: Type A behavior and incidence of coronary heart disease. *The American Journal of Epidemiology, 122,* 559–570.

Sher, K. J. (1991). *Children of alcoholics: A critical appraisal of theory and research.* Chicago: University of Chicago Press.

Sher, K. J., & Trull, T. J. (1994). Personality and disinhibitory psychopathology: Alcoholism and antisocial personality disorder. *Journal of Abnormal Psychology, 103,* 92–102.

Shilts, R. (2000). *And the band played on: Politics, people, and the AIDS epidemic.* New York: Stonewall Inn.

Shneidman, E. S. (1980). A possible classification of suicidal acts based on Murray's need system. *Suicide and Life-Threatening Behavior, 10,* 175–181.

Shopland, D. R. (1996). US cigar consumption. *Journal of the National Cancer Institute, 89,* 999.

Shopland, D. R., Eyre, H. J., & Pechacek, T. F. (1991). Smoking-attributable cancer mortality in 1991: Is lung cancer now the leading cause of death among smokers in the United States? *Journal of the National Cancer Institute, 83,* 1142–1148.

Shorris, E. (1992). *Latinos: A biography of the people.* New York: Norton.

Shumaker, S., & Czajkowski, S. M. (Eds.). (1994). *Social support and cardiovascular disease. Plenum series in behavioral psychophysiology and medicine.* New York: Plenum Press.

Shumaker, S. A., & Hill, D. R. (1991). Gender differences in social support and physical health. *Health Psychology. Special Gender and Health, 10,* 102–111.

Siegel, K., Karus, D., Raveis, V. H., & Hagan, D. (1998). Psychological adjustment of women with HIV/AIDS: Racial and ethnic comparisons. *Journal of Community Psychology, 26,* 439–455.

Siegler, I. C., Bastian, L. A., Steffens, D. C., Bosworth, H. B., & Costa, P. T. (2002). Behavioral medicine and aging. *Journal of Consulting and Clinical Psychology, 70,* 843–851.

Sikkema, K. J., Hansen, N. B., Kochman, A., Tate, D. C., & Difranciesco, W. (2004). Outcomes from a randomized controlled trial of a group intervention for HIV positive men and women coping with AIDS-related loss and bereavement. *Death Studies, 28,* 187–209.

Sikkema, K. J., Wagner, L. I., & Bogart, L. M. (2000). Gender and cultural factors in prevention of HIV infection among women. In R. M. Eisler & M. Hersen (Eds.), *Handbook of gender, culture, and health* (pp. 299–319). Mahwah, NJ: Erlbaum.

Simonds, J. F. (1976). Psychiatric status of diabetic youth in good and poor control. *International Journal of Psychiatry in Medicine, 7,* 133–151.

Sims, E. R. (1987). Relaxation therapy as a technique for helping patients cope with the experience of cancer: A selected review of the literature. *Journal of Advanced Nursing, 12,* 583–591.

Singh, R. B., Dubnov, G., Niaz, M. A., Ghosh, S., Singh. R., Rastogi, S., et al. (2002). Effect of an Indo-Mediterranean diet on progression of coronary artery disease in high risk patients (Indo-Mediterranean Diet Heart Study): A randomized single-blind trial. *Lancet, 360,* 1455–1462.

Skaff, M. M., Pearlin, L. I., & Mullan, J. T. (1996). Transition in the caregiving career: Effects on sense of mastery. *Psychology and Aging, 11,* 247–257.

Skevington, S. M. (1995). *Psychology of pain.* Oxford, England: John Wiley.

Skinner, B. F. (1938). *The behavior of organisms.* Englewood Cliffs, NJ: Appleton-Century-Crofts.

Skinner, E. A., Edge, K., Altman, J., & Sherwood, H. (2003). Searching for the structure of coping: A review and critique of category systems for classifying ways of coping. *Psychological Bulletin, 129,* 216–269.

Slater, M. A., Hall, H. F., Atkinson, J. H., & Garfin, S. R. (1991). Pain and impairment beliefs in chronic low back pain: Validation of the Pain and Impairment Relationship Scale (PAIRS). *Pain, 44,* 51–56.

Slavin, L. A., Rainer, K. L., McCreary, M. L., & Gowda, K. K. (1991). Toward a multicultural model of the stress process. *Journal of Counseling & Development: Special Multiculturalism as a Fourth Force in Counseling, 70,* 156–163.

Sloman, R., Brown, P., Aldana, E., & Chee, E. (1994). The use of relaxation for the promotion of comfort and pain relief in persons with advanced cancer. *Contemporary Nursing, 3,* 333–339.

Smedley, B. D., & Syme, S. L. (Eds.). (2000). *Promoting health: Intervention strategies from social and behavioral research.* Washington, DC: National Academy Press.

Smilkstein, G., Helsper-Lucas, A., Ashworth, C., Montano, D., & Pagel, M. (1984). Prediction of pregnancy complications: An application of the biopsychosocial model. *Social Science and Medicine, 18,* 315–321.

Smith, B. W., Pargament, K. I., Brant, C., & Oliver, J. M. (2000). Noah revisited: Religious coping by church members and the impact of the 1993 Midwest flood. *Journal of Community Psychology, 28,* 169–186.

Smith, C. A., Wallston, K. A., & Dwyer, K. A. (1995). On babies and bathwater: Disease impact and negative affectivity in the self-reports of persons with rheumatoid arthritis. *Health Psychology, 14,* 64–73.

Smith, G. T., Goldman, M. S., Greenbaum, P. E., & Christiansen, B. A. (1995). Expectancy for social facilitation from drinking: The divergent paths of high-expectancy and low-expectancy adolescents. *Journal of Abnormal Psychology, 104,* 32–40.

Smith, M. S., & Wallston, K. A. (1992). How to measure the value of health. *Health Education Research, 7,* 129–135.

Smith, T. W., & Ruiz, J. M. (2002). Psychosocial influences on the development and course of coronary heart disease: Current status and implications for research and practice. *Journal of Consulting & Clinical Psychology, 70,* 548–568.

Smith, T. W., Kendall, P. C., & Keefe, F. J. (2002). Behavioral medicine and clinical health psychology: Introduction to the special issue, a view from the decade of behavior. *Journal of Consulting and Clinical Psychology, 70,* 459–462.

Smith, T. W., Orleans, C. T., & Jenkins, C. D. (2004). Prevention and health promotion: Decades of progress, new challenges, and an emerging agenda. *Health Psychology, 23,* 126–131.

Smith, T. W., & Suls, J. (2004). Introduction to the special section on the future of health psychology. *Health Psychology, 23,* 115–118.

Smyth, J. M., & Pennebaker, J. W. (2001). What are the health effects of disclosure? In A. Baum, T. A. Revenson, & J. E. Singer (Eds.), *Handbook of health psychology* (pp. 339–348). Mahwah, NJ: Erlbaum.

Snell, J. E. (1967). Hypnosis in the treatment of the "hexed" patient. *American Journal of Psychiatry, 124,* 311–316.

Snell, J. L., & Buck, E. L. (1996). Increasing cancer screening: A meta-analysis. *Preventive Medicine, 25,* 702–707.

Snow, M. G., Prochaska, J. O., & Rossi, J. S. (1992). Stages of change for smoking cessation among former problem drinkers: A cross-sectional analysis. *Journal of Substance Abuse, 4,* 107–116.

Solomon, G. F., Segerstrom, S. C., Grohr, P., Kemeny, M., & Fahey, J. (1997). Shaking up immunity: Psychological and immunologic changes after a natural disaster. *Psychosomatic Medicine, 59,* 114–127.

Somerfield, M. R., & McCrae, R. R. (2000). Stress and coping research: Methodological challenges, theoretical advances, and clinical applications. *American Psychologist, 55,* 620–625.

Sonstoem, R. J. (1997). Physical activity and self-esteem. In W. P. Morgan (Ed.), *Physical activity and mental health* (pp. 127–143). Washington, DC: Taylor & Francis.

Soudijn, K. A., Hutschemaekers, G. J. M., & Van de Vijver, F. J. R. (1990). Culture conceptualizations. In F. J. R. Van de Vijver and G. J. M. Hutschemaeker (Eds.), *The investigation of culture: Current issues in cultural psychology* (pp. 19–39). Tilburg: Tilburg University Press.

Spiegel, D. (1996). Cancer and depression. *British Journal of Psychiatry, 168,* 109–116.

Spiegel, D., Bloom, J. R., Kraemer, H. C., & Gottheil, E. (1989, October 14). Effects of psychosocial treatment on survival of patients with metastatic breast cancer. *Lancet,* 888–891.

Sprangers, M. A. (1996). Response-shift bias: a challenge to the assessment of patients' quality of life in cancer clinical trials. *Cancer Treatment Review, 22,* 55–62.

Stack, C. B., & Burton, L. M. (1993). Kinscripts. *Journal of Comparative Family Studies, 24,* 157–170.

Stack, S. (2003). Media coverage as a risk factor in suicide. *Journal of Epidemiology and Community Health, 57,* 238–240.

Stampfer, M. J., Hu, F. B., Manson, J. E., Rimm, E. B., & Willett, W. C. (2000). Primary prevention of coronary heart disease in women through diet and lifestyle. *New England Journal of Medicine, 343,* 16–22.

Stanfeld, S. A., Rael, E. G., Head, J., Shipley, M., & Marmot, M. (1997). Social support and psychiatric sickness absence: A prospective study of British civil servants. *Psychological Medicine, 27,* 35–48.

Stanton, A. L., Collins, C. A., & Sworowski, L. (2001). Adjustment to chronic illness: Theory and research. In A. Baum, T. A. Revenson, and J. E. Singer (Eds.), *Handbook of health psychology* (pp. 387–404). Mahwah, NJ: Erlbaum.

Stanton, A. L., & Snider, P. R. (1993). Coping with a breast cancer diagnosis: A prospective study. *Health Psychology, 12,* 16–23.

Statsiewicz, P. R., & Lisman, S. A. (1989). Effects of infant cries on alcohol consumption in college males at risk for child abuse. *Child Abuse and Neglect, 13,* 463–470.

Stein, J. A., Fox, S. A., & Murata, P. J. (1991). The influence of ethnicity, socioeconomic status, and psychological barriers on use of mammography. *Journal of Health and Social Behavior, 32,* 101–113.

Steinberg, W., & Tenner, S. (1994). Acute pancreatitis. *New England Journal of Medicine, 330,* 1198–1210.

Steinmaus, C., Nunez, S., & Smith, A. H. (2000). Diet and bladder cancer: A meta-analysis of six dietary variables. *American Journal of Epidemiology, 151,* 693–702.

Stern, D. (1995). *The Motherhood Constellation: a unified view of parent-infant psychotherapy.* New York: Basic Books.

Stice, E., Shaw, H., & Nemeroff, C. (1998). Dual pathway model of bulimia nervosa: Longitudinal support for dietary restraint and affect-regulation mechanisms *Journal of Social and Clinical Psychology, 17,* 129–149.

Stone, A. A., Bovbjerg, D. H., Neale, J. M., Napoli, A., Valdimarsdottir, H., Cox, D., et al. (1992). Development of common cold symptoms following experimental rhinovirus infection is related to prior stressful life events. *Behavioral Medicine, 18,* 115–120.

Strawbridge, W. J., Shema, S. J., Cohen, R. D., Roberts, R. E., & Kaplan, G. A. (1998). Religiosity buffers effects of some stressors on depression but exacerbates others. *Journals of Gerontology: Series B: Psychological Sciences and Social Sciences, 53B*, S118–S126.

Streissguth, A. P., Sampson, P. D., Olson, H. C., Bookstein, F. L., Barr, H. M., Scott, M., et al. (1994). Maternal drinking during pregnancy: Attention and short-term memory in 14-year old offspring—A longitudinal prospective study. *Alcohol: Clinical and Experimental Research, 19*, 202–218.

Strodl, E., Kenardy, J., & Aroney, C. (2003). Perceived stress as a predictor of the self-reported new diagnosis of symptomatic CHD in older women. *International Journal of Behavioral Medicine, 10*, 205–220.

Stroebe, M. S., Hansson, R. O., Stroebe, W., & Schut, H. (Eds.). (2001). *Handbook of bereavement research: Consequences, coping, and care.* Washington, DC: American Psychological Association.

Stroebe, M. S., & Stroebe, W. (1983). Who suffers more? Sex differences in health risks of the widowed. *Psychological Bulletin, 93*, 279–301.

Stroebe, M., Stroebe, W., & Schut, H. (2001). Gender differences in adjustment to bereavement: An empirical and theoretical review. *Review of General Psychology, 5*, 62–83.

Strong, J. P., Malcom, G. T., McMahan, C. A., Tracy, R. E., Newman, W. P., Herderick, J. F., et al. (1999). Prevalence and extent of atherosclerosis in adolescents and young adults: Implications for prevention from the pathobiological determinants of atherosclerosis in youth study. *Journal of the American Medical Association, 281*, 727–735.

Suarez, L., Rouche, R. A., Nichols, D., & Simpson, D. M. (1997). Knowledge, behavior, and fears concerning breast and cervical cancer among older low-income Mexican-American women. *American Journal of Preventative Medicine, 13*, 137–142.

Suchday, S., Tucker, D. L., & Krantz, D. S. (2002). Diseases of the circulatory system. In T. J. Boll, S. B. Johnson, et al., *Handbook of clinical health psychology: Vol. 1. Medical disorders and behavioral applications* (pp. 203–238). Washington, DC: American Psychological Association.

Suchman, E. A. (1965). Social patterns of illness and medical care. *Journal of Health and Human Behavior, 6*, 2–16.

Sue, D. (2000). Health risk factors in diverse cultural groups. In R. M. Eisler and M. Hersen (Eds.), *Handbook of gender, culture, and health* (pp. 85–104). Mahwah, NJ: Erlbaum.

Sue, S., Nakamura, C. Y., Chung, R., & Yee-Bradbury, C. (1994). Mental health research on Asian Americans. *Journal of Community Psychology, 22*, 181–187.

Suleiman, A. B. (2001). The untapped potential of telehealth. *International Journal of Medical Informatics, 61*, 103–112.

Suls, J., & Rothman, A. (2004). Evolution of the biopsychosocial model: Prospects and challenges for health psychology. *Health Psychology, 23*, 119–125.

Sundquist, K., Lindstrom, M., Malmstrom, M., Johansson, S. E., & Sundquist, J. (2004). Social participation and coronary heart disease: A follow-up study of 6900 women and men in Sweden. *Social Science and Medicine, 58*, 615–622.

Sung, J. F., Blumenthal, D. S., Coates, R. J., & Alema-Mensah, E. (1997). Knowledge, beliefs, attitudes, and cancer screening among inner-city African-American women. *Journal of the National Medical Association, 89*, 405–411.

Sussman S., Dent C. W., Severson H. H., Burton D., & Flay B. R. (1998). Self-initiated quitting among adolescent smokers. *Preventative Medicine, 27*, A19–A28.

Sutton, S., Bickler G., Sancho-Aldridge J., & Saidi G. (1994). Prospective study of predictors of attendance for breast screening in inner London. *Journal of Epidemiology and Community Health, 48*, 65–73.

Svoboda, R. E. (1992). *Ayurveda: Life, health, and longevity.* New Delhi, India: Penguin.

Swanson, K. M. (2000). Predicting depressive symptoms after miscarriage: A path analysis based on the Lazarus paradigm. *Journal of Women's Health and Gender-Based Medicine, 9*, 191–206.

Syrjala, K. L., Donaldson, G. W., Davis, M. W., Kippes, M. E., & Carr, J. E. (1995). Relaxation and imagery and cognitive-behavioral training reduce pain during cancer treatment: A controlled clinical trial. *Pain, 63*, 189–198.

Szasz, T. S., & Hollender, M. H. (1956). A contribution to the philosophy of medicine: The basic models of the doctor-patient relationship. *Archives of Internal Medicine, 97*, 585–592.

Takahashi, K. (1986). Examining the strange-situation procedure with Japanese mothers and 12-month-old infants. *Developmental Psychology, 22*, 265–270.

Tanasescu, M., Cho, E., Manson, J. E., & Hu, F. B. (2004). Dietary fat and cholesterol and the risk of cardiovascular disease among women with Type 2 diabetes. *The American Journal of Clinical Nutrition, 79*, 999–1005.

Tang, T. S., Solomon, L. J., McCracken, L. M. (2000). Cultural barriers to mammography, clinical breast exam, and breast self-exam among Chinese women 60 and older. *Preventive Medicine, 31*, 575–583.

Taylor, A. H., Doust, J., & Webborn, N. (1998). Randomised controlled trial to examine the effects of a GP exercise referral programme in Hailsham, East Sussex, on modifiable coronary heart disease risk factors. *Journal of Epidemiology and Community Health, 52*, 595–601.

Taylor, R. S., Brown, A., Ebrahim, S., Jolliffe, J., Noorani, H., Rees, K., Skidmore, B., et al. (2004). Exercise-based rehabilitation for patients with coronary heart disease: Systematic review and meta-analysis of randomized controlled trials. *American Journal of Medicine, 116*, 682–692.

Taylor, S. E. (1983). Adjustment to threatening events: A theory of cognitive adaptation. *American Psychologist, 38*, 1161–1173.

Taylor, S. E., Kemeny, M. E., Apsinwall, L. G., Schneider, S. G., Rodriguez, R., & Herbert, M. (1992). Optimism, coping, psychological distress, and high-risk sexual behavior among men at risk for acquired immunodeficiency syndrome (AIDS). *Journal of Personality and Social Psychology, 63*, 460–473.

Taylor, S. E., Kemeny, M. E., Reed, G. M., Bower, J. E., & Gruenewald, T. L. (2000). Psychological resources, positive illusions, and health. *American Psychologist, 55*, 99–109.

Taylor, S. E., Klein, L. C., Lewis, B. P., Gruenewald, T. L., Gurung, R. A. R., & Updegraff, J. A. (2000). Biobehavioral responses to stress in females: Tend-and-befriend, not fight-or-flight. *Psychological Review, 107*, 411–429.

Taylor, S. E., Lerner, J. S., Sage, R. M., Lehman, B. J., & Seeman, T. E. (2004). Early environment, emotions, responses to stress, and health. *Journal of Personality, 72*, 1365–1393.

Taylor, S. E., Lewis, B. P., Gruenewald, T. L., Gurung, R. A. R., Updegraff, J. A., & Klein, L. C. (2002). Sex differences in biobehavioral responses to threat: Reply to Geary and Flinn. *Psychological Review, 109*, 751–753.

Taylor, S. E., Lichtman, R. R., & Wood, J. V. (1984). Attributions, beliefs about control, and adjustment to breast cancer. *Journal of Personality and Social Psychology, 46*, 489–502.

Taylor, S. E., Repetti, R. L., & Seeman, T. (1997). Health psychology: What is an unhealthy environment and how does it get under the skin? *Annual Review of Psychology, 48*, 411–447.

Taylor, S. E., Sherman, D. K., Kim, H. S., Jarcho, J., Takagi, K., & Dunagan, M. S. (2004). Culture and social support: Who seeks it and why? *Journal of Personality and Social Psychology, 87*, 354–362.

Temoshok, L. (1987). Personality, coping style, emotion and cancer: Toward an integrative model. *Cancer Surveys, 6*, 837–857.

Tennen, H., Affleck, G., Armeli, S., & Carney, M. A. (2000). A daily process approach to coping: Linking theory, research, and practice. *American Psychologist, 55*, 626–636.

Thadhani, R., Camargo, C. A., Stampfer, M. J., Curhan, G. C., Willett, W. C., & Rimm, E. B. (2002). Prospective study of moderate alcohol consumption and risk of hypertension in young women. *Archives of Internal Medicine, 162*, 569–576.

Theakston, J. A., Stewart, S. H., Dawson, M. Y., Knowlden-Loewen, S. A. B., & Lehman, D. R. (2004). Big Five personality domains predict drinking motives. *Personality & Individual Differences, 37,* 971–984

Theorell, T., Blomkvist, V., Jonsson, H., Schulman, S., Berntorp, E., & Stigenendal, L. (1995). Social support and the development of immune function in HIV infection. *Psychosomatic Medicine, 57,* 32–36.

Theorell, T., & Harenstam, A. (2000). Influence of gender on cardiovascular disease. In R. M. Eisler & M. Herson (Eds.), *Handbook of gender, culture, and health* (pp. 161–177). Mahwah, NJ: Erlbaum.

Thoits, P. A. (1983). Multiple identities and psychological well-being: A reformulation and the test of the social isolation hypothesis. *American Sociological Review 48,* 174–187.

Thomas, R. M. (1999). *Human development theories: Windows on culture.* Thousand Oaks, CA: Sage.

Thorburn, S., Harvey, S. M., & Ryan, E. A. (2005). HIV prevention heuristics and condom use among African-Americans at risk for HIV. *AIDS Care, 17,* 335–344.

Throne, L. C., Bartholomew, J. B., Craig, J., & Farrar, R. P. (2000). Stress reactivity in fire fighters: An exercise intervention. *International Journal of Stress Management, 7,* 235–246.

Thune, I., & Furberg, A. S. (2001). Physical activity and cancer risk: Dose-response and cancer, all sites and site-specific. *Medicine and Science in Sports and Exercise, 33,* S530–S550.

Tobin, A. J., & Dusheck, J. (2001). *Asking about life.* Pacific Grove, CA: Brooks/Cole.

Tomich, P. L., & Helgeson, V. S. (2004). Is finding something good in the bad always good? Benefit finding among women with breast cancer. *Health Psychology, 23,* 16–23.

Tope, D. A., Ahles, T. A., & Silberfarb, P. M. (1993). Psycho-oncology: Psychological well-being as one component of quality of life. *Psychotherapy and Psychosomatics, 60,* 129–147.

Torrey, E. F. (1969). The case for the indigenous therapist. *Archives of General Psychiatry, 20,* 365–373.

Tovian, S. M. (2004). Health services and health care economics: The health psychology marketplace. *Health Psychology, 23,* 119–125.

Tracey, D. J., Walker, J. S., & Carmody, J. J. (2000). Chronic pain: Neural basis and interactions with stress. In D. T. Kenny & J. G. Carison (Eds.), *Stress and health: Research and clinical applications* (pp. 105–125). Amsterdam, Netherlands: Harwood Academic Publishers.

Triandis, H. C. (1996). The psychological measurement of cultural syndromes. *American Psychologist, 51,* 407–415.

Trichopoulou, A., & Lagiou, P. (1997). Healthy traditional Mediterranean diet: An expression of culture, history, and lifestyle. *Nutrition Reviews, 55,* 383–390.

Triest-Robertson, S., Gurung, R. A. R., Brosig, C., Whitfield, N., & Pfutzenreuter, M. (2001, March). *Assessing satisfaction with hospital pain management.* Paper presented at the meeting of the Society for Behavioral Medicine, Seattle, WA.

Troiano, R. P., Flegal, K. M., Kuczmarski, R. J., Campbell, S. M., & Johnson, C. L. (1995). Overweight prevalence and trends for children and adolescents. The National Health and Nutrition Examination Surveys, 1963 to 1991. *Archives of Pediatrics and Adolescent Medicine, 149,* 1085–1091.

Trompenaars, F. (1997). *Riding the waves of culture: Understanding cultural diversity in business.* London: Nicholas Brealey.

Trotter, R. T., & Chavira, J. A. (1997). *Curanderismo: Mexican American folk healing.* Athens, GA: University of Georgia Press.

Trudeau, L., Lillehoj, C., Spoth, R., & Redmond, C. (2003). The role of assertiveness and decision making in early adolescent substance initiation: Mediating processes. *Journal of Research on Adolescence, 13,* 304–328.

Tucker, J. S., Orlando, M., & Ellickson, P. L. (2003). Patterns and correlates of binge drinking trajectories from early adolescence to young adulthood. *Health Psychology, 22,* 79–87.

Turbin, M. S., Jessor, R., & Costa, F. M. (2000). Adolescent cigarette smoking: Health-related behavior of normative transgression? *Prevention Science, 1,* 115–124.

Turk, D. C. (2001a). Combining somatic and psychosocial treatment for chronic pain patients: Perhaps 1 + 1 does = 3. *Clinical Journal of Pain, 17,* 281–283.

Turk, D. C. (2001b). Treatment of chronic pain: Clinical outcomes, cost-effectiveness, and cost benefits. *Drug Benefit Trends, 13,* 36–38.

Turk, D. C. (2002a). A diathesis-stress model of chronic pain and disability following traumatic injury. *Pain Research & Management, 7,* 9–20.

Turk, D. C. (2002b). Clinical effectiveness and cost-effectiveness of treatments for patients with chronic pain. *Clinical Journal of Pain, 18,* 355–365.

Turk, D. C. (2002c). Cognitive-behavioral techniques and cost-effectiveness of treatments for patients with chronic pain. *Catalog of Selected Documents in Psychology, 10,* 17.

Turk, D. C. (2002d). Suffering and dysfunction in fibromyalgia syndrome. *Journal of Musculoskeletal Pains, 10,* 85–96.

Turk, D. C., Meichenbaum, D., & Genest, M. (1983). *Pain and behavioral medicine: A cognitive-behavioral perspective.* New York: Guilford.

Turk, D. C., & Melzack, R. (Eds.). (2001). *Handbook of pain assessment* (2nd ed., pp. 97–118). New York: Guilford Press.

Turk, D. C., & Nash, J. M. (1996). Psychological issues, in chronic pain. In R. K. Portenoy, K. Foley, & R. Kanner (Eds.), *Contemporary Neurology* (pp. 245–260). Philadelphia: Davis.

Turk, D. C., & Okifuji, A. (2002). Psychological factors in chronic pain: Evolution and revolution. *Journal of Consulting and Clinical Psychology, 70,* 678–690.

Turk, D. C., & Rudy, T. E. (1986). MAP-ping out the terrain. *Journal of Pain and Symptom Management, 1,* 235–237.

Turk, D. C., & Salovey, P. (1984). Chronic pain as a variant of depressive disease: A critical reappraisal. *Journal of Nervous and Mental Disease, 172,* 398–404.

Turner, D. C. (1996). The role of culture in chronic illness. *American Behavioral Scientist, 39,* 717–728.

Turner, D. C., Cobb, J. M., & Steptoe, A. (1996). Psychosocial stress and susceptibility to upper respiratory tract illness in an adult population sample. *Psychosomatic Medicine, 58,* 404–412.

Turner, R. J., & Avison, W. R. (1992). Innovations in the measurement of life stress: Crisis theory and the significance of event resolution. *Journal of Health and Social Behavior, 33,* 36–50.

Tuzcu, E. M., Kapadia, S. R., Tutar, E., Ziada, K. M., Hobbs, R. E., McCarthy, P. M., et al. (2001). High prevalence of coronary atherosclerosis in asymptomatic teenagers and young adults: Evidence from intravascular ultrasound. *Circulation, 103,* 2705–2710.

Uchino, B. N., Cacioppo, J. T., & Kiecolt-Glaser, J. K. (1996). The relationship between social support and physiological processes: A review with emphasis on underlying mechanisms and implications for health. *Psychological Bulletin, 119,* 488–531.

Udwadia, F. E. (2000). *Man and medicine: A history.* New Delhi, India: Oxford University Press.

Ulbrich, P. M., & Bradsher, J. E. (1993). Perceived support, help seeking, and adaptation to stress among older Black and White women living alone. *Journal of Aging and Health, 5,* 365–386.

Ullrich, P. A. & Lutgendorf, S. L. (2002). Journaling about stressful events: Effects of cognitive processing and emotional expression. *Annals of Behavioral Medicine, 24,* 244–250.

Ulrich, R. S. (1984). View through a window may influence recovery from surgery. *Science, 224,* 420–421.

Unger, J. B., McAvay, G., Bruce, M. L., Berkman, L., & Seeman, T. (1999). Variation in the impact of social network characteristics on physical functioning in elderly persons: MacArthur Studies of Successful Aging. *Journals of Gerontology: Series B: Psychological Sciences & Social Sciences, 54B,* S245–S251.

U. S. Department of Health and Human Services. (2000). Best practices for comprehensive tobacco control programs. Retrieved from http://www.hsca.com/mcmbersonly/USDHHSlink.htm. June 2004.

U. S. Department of Health and Human Services. (2003). Racial and ethnic disparities in infant mortality rates: 60 Largest U.S. Cities, 1995–1998. Morbidity and Mortality Weekly Report, 51. Retrieved from http://www.hsca.com/membersonly/USDHHSlink. htm. December 2004.

U. S. Department of Labor. (2003). Occupational stress: Counts and rates. Compensation and Working Conditions. Retrieved from http://www.bls.gov/. January 2005.

Uvnas-Moberg, K. (1996). Neuroendocrinology of the mother–child interaction. Trends in Endocrinology and Metabolism, 7, 126–131.

van der Velde, F. W., & van der Pligt, J. (1991). AIDS-related health behavior: Coping, protection motivation, and previous behavior. Journal of Behavioral Medecine, 14, 429–451.

Van Itallie, T. B. (1985). Health implications of overweight and obesity in the United States. Annals of Internal Medicine, 103, 983–989.

van Servellen, G., Sarna, L., Nyamathi, A., Padilla, G. V., Brecht, M. L., & Jablonski, K. J. (1998). Emotional distress in women with symptomatic HIV disease. Issues in Mental Health Nursing, 19, 173–188.

Van't Spijker, A., Trijsburg, R. W., & Duivenvoorden, H. J. (1997). Psychological sequelae of cancer diagnosis: A meta-analytical review of 58 studies after 1980. Psychosomatic Medicine, 59, 280–293.

Van Zanden, J. W. V. (2002). Human development. New York: McGraw-Hill.

Vega, W. A., Kolody, B., Aguilar-Gaxiola, S., Alderete, E., Catalano, R., & Caraveo-Anduaga, J. (1998). Lifetime prevalence of DSM-III-R psychiatric disorders among urban and rural Mexican Americans in California. Archives of General Psychiatry, 55, 771–782.

Verbrugge, L. M. (1985). Triggers of symptoms and health care. Social Science and Medicine, 20, 855–876.

Veroff, J., Kulka, R., & Douvan, E. (1981). Mental health in America: Patterns of help-seeking from 1957 to 1976. New York: Basic Books.

Vessey, M., Painter, R., & Yeates, D. (2003). Mortality in relation to oral contraceptive use and cigarette smoking. Lancet, 362, 185–191.

Vickers, A., Ohlsson, A., Lacy, J. B., & Horsley, A. (2002). Massage for promoting growth and development of preterm and/or low birth-weight infants. Cochrane Database System Review, 2, CD000390.

Victor, M. (1993). Persistent altered mentation due to ethanol. Neurology Clinic, 11, 639–661.

Viney, L. L., Walker, B. M., Robertson, T., Lilley, B., & Evan, C. (1994). Dying in palliative care units and in hospital: A comparison of the quality of life of terminal cancer patients. Journal of Consulting and Clinical Psychology, 62, 157–166.

Vinson, M. A. (1989). Acute transient memory loss. American Family Physician, 39, 249–254.

Volicer, B. J., Isenberg, M. A., & Burns, M. W. (1977). Medical-surgical differences in hospital stress factors. Journal of Human Stress, 3, 3–13.

von Knorring, L., Oreland, L., & von Knorring, A. (1987). Personality traits and platelet MAO activity in alcohol and drug abusing teenage boys. Acta Psychiatica Scandinavica, 75, 307–314.

Voydanoff, P. (2002). Linkages between the work-family interface and work, family, and individual outcomes: An integrative model. Journal of Family Issues, 23, 138–164.

Waddell, G., Main, C. J., Morris, E. W., DiPaola, M., & Gray, I. C. (1984). Chronic low-back pain, distress and illness behavior. Spine, 9, 209–213.

Wadhwa, P. D., Dunkel-Schetter, C., Chicz-DeMet, A., Porto, M., & Sandman, C. A. (1996). Prenatal psychosocial factors and the neuroendocrine axis in human pregnancy. Psychosomatic Medicine, 58, 432–446.

Wadhwa, P. D., Sandman, C. A., Porto, M., Dunkel-Schetter, C., & Garite, T. J. (1993). The association between prenatal stress and infant birth weight and gestational age at birth: A prospective investigation. American Journal of Obstetrics and Gynecology, 69, 858–865.

Waitzkin, H. (1985). Information giving in medical care. Journal of Health and Social Behavior, 26, 81–101.

Wakefield, M., Flay, B., Nichter, M., & Giovino, G. (2003). Role of the media in influencing trajectories of youth smoking. Addiction, 98, 79–103.

Waldron, I. (1991). Effects of labor force participation on sex differences in mortality and morbidity. In M. Frankenhaeuser, U. Lundberg, & M. Chesney (Eds.), Women, work, and health: Stress and opportunities (pp. 17–38). New York: Plenum Press.

Waldron, I. (1995). Contributions of changing gender differentials in behaviour to changing gender differences in mortality. In D. Sabo and D. Gordon (Eds.), Men's health and illness: Gender, power and the body. London: Sage.

Walker, J. S., & Carmody, J. J. (1998). Experimental pain in healthy human subjects: Gender differences in nociception and in response to ibuprofen. Anesthesia and Analgesia, 86, 1257–1262.

Wallace, L. M., Priestman, S. G., Dunn, J. A., & Priestman, T. J. (1993). The quality of life of early breast cancer patients treated by two different radiotherapy regimens. Clinical Oncology, 5, 228–233.

Wallin, P., & Clark, A. L. (1964). Religiosity, sexual gratification, and marital satisfaction in the middle years of marriage. Social Forces, 42, 303–309.

Wallston, K. A. (1992). Hocus-pocus, the focus isn't strictly on locus: Rotter's social learning theory modified for health. Cognitive Therapy and Research. Special Cognitive Perspectives in Health Psychology, 16, 183–199.

Wamala, S. P., Mittleman, M. A., Horsten, M., Schenck-Gustafsson, K., & Orth-Gomer, K. (2000). Job stress and the occupational gradient in coronary heart disease risk in women. The Stockholm Female Coronary Risk Study. Social Science and Medicine, 51, 481–489.

Wan, T. H., & Soifer, S. J. (1974). Determinants of physician utilization: A causal analysis. Journal of Health and Social Behavior, 15, 100–108.

Wankel, L. M., & Berger, B. G. (1990). The psychological and social benefits of sport and physical activity. Journal of Leisure Research, 22, 167–182.

Wannamethee, S. G., & Shaper, A. G. (1992). Blood lipids: The relationship with alcohol intake, smoking, and body weight. Journal of Epidemiology and Community Health, 46, 197–202.

Wannamethee, S. G., & Shaper, A. G. (1999). Type of alcoholic drink and risk of major coronary heart disease events and all-cause mortality. American Journal of Public Health, 89, 685–690.

Wannamethee, S. G., Shaper, A. G., & Alberti, G. M. M. (2000). Physical activity protects against diabetes and heart disease. Geriatics, 35, 78.

Ward, M. M., Mefford, I. N., Parker, S. D., Chesney, M. A., Taylor, C. B., Keegan, D. L., et al. (1983). Epinephrine and norepinephrine responses in continuously collected human plasma to a series of stressors. Psychosomatic Medicine, 45, 471–86.

Wardle, J., & Pope, R. (1992). The psychological costs of screening for cancer. Journal of Psychosomatic Research, 36, 609–624.

Ware, J. E., Jr., Snow, K. K., Kosinski, M., & Gandek, B. (1993). SF-36 health survey. Manual and interpretation guide. Boston: The Health Institute, New England Medical Center.

Wasylkiw, L., & Fekken, G. C. (2002). Personality and self-reported health: Matching predictors and criteria. Personality and Individual Differences, 33, 607–620.

Waters, E., Merrick, S., Treboux, D., Crowell, J., & Albersheim, L. (2000). Attachment security in infancy and early adulthood: A twenty-year longitudinal study. Child Development, 71, 684–689.

Watson, D., & Hubbard, B. (1996). Adaptational style and dispositional structure: Coping in the context of the five-factor model. *Journal of Personality, 64,* 737–774.

Waxler-Morrison, N., Hislop, T. G., Mears, B., & Kan, L. (1991). Effects of social relationships on survival for women with breast cancer: A prospective study. *Social Science & Medicine, 33,* 177–183.

Way, E. L., & Chen, C. F. (1999). Modern clinical applications related to Chinese traditional theories of drug interactions. *Perspectives in Biology and Medicine, 42,* 512–525.

Wechsler, H., Kelley, K., Seibring, M., Kuo, M., & Rigotti, N. A. (2001). College smoking policies and smoking cessation programs: Results of a survey of college helath center directors. *Journal of American College Health, 49,* 205–212.

Wechler, H., Moeykens, B., Davenport, A., Castillo, S., & Hansen, J. (2000). The adverse impact of heavy episodic drinkers on other college students. *Journal of Studies on Alcohol, 56,* 628–634.

Weihs, K., & Reiss, D. (1996). Family reorganization in response to cancer: A developmental perspective. In L. Baider, C. L. Cooper, et al. (Eds.), *Cancer and the family* (pp. 3–29). Oxford: John Wiley.

Weinberger, M., Hiner, S. L., & Tierney, W. M. (1987). In support of hassles as a measure of stress in predicting health outcomes. *Journal of Behavioral Medicine, 10,* 19–31.

Weinhardt, L. S., Carey, M. P., Johnson, B. T., & Bickman, N. L. (1999). Effects of HIV counseling and testing on sexual risk behavior: A meta-analytic review of published research, 1985–1987. *American Journal of Public Health, 89,* 1397–1405.

Weinraub, M., Horvath, D. L., & Gringles, M. B. (2002). Single parenthood. In M. H. Bornstein (Ed.), *Handbook of parenting: Vol. 3: Being and becoming a parent* (2nd ed., pp. 109–140). Mahwah, NJ: Erlbaum.

Weinrich, S., Ellison, G., Weinrich, M., Ross, K. S., & Reis-Starr, C. (2001). Low sun exposure and elevated serum prostate specific antigen in African American and Caucasian men. *American Journal of Health Studies, 17,* 148–156.

Weinstein, N. D., & Sandman, P. M. (1992). A model of the precaution adoption process: Evidence from home radon testing. *Health Psychology, 11,* 170–180.

Weisman, A. D., & Worden, J. W. (1972). Risk-rescue rating in suicide assessment. *Archives of General Psychiatry, 26,* 553–560.

Welin, L., Larsson, B., Svardsudd, K., Tibblin, B., & Tibblin, G. (1992). Social network and activities in relation to mortality from cardiovascular diseases, cancer and other causes: A 12 year follow up of the study of men born in 1913 and 1923. *Journal of Epidemiology and Community Health, 46,* 127–132.

Welsh, S., Davis, C., & Shaw, A. (1993). *USDA's Food Guide: Background and Development* (Miscellaneous Publication No. 1514). Washington, DC: U. S. Government Printing Office.

West, S. G., & Aiken, L. S. (1997). Towards understanding individual effects in multiple component prevention programs: Design and analysis strategies. In K. Bryant, M. Windle, & S. West (Eds.), *The science of Prevention: Methodological advances from alcohol and substance abuse research* (pp. 167–209). Washington, D. C.: American Psychological Association.

Westbrook, M. T., & Viney, L. L. (1983). Age and sex differences in patients' reactions to illness. *Journal of Health and Social Behavior, 24,* 313–324.

Westman, M. (2001). Stress and strain crossover. *Human Relations, 54,* 717–752.

Westman, M., & Etizon, D. (1995). Crossover of stress, strain, and resources from one spouse to another. *Journal of Organizational Behavior, 16,* 169–181.

Westman, M., & Vinokur, A. D. (1998). Unraveling the relationship of distress levels within couples: Common stressors, empathic reactions, or crossover via social interaction? *Human Relations, 51,* 137–156.

Wethington, E. (2000). Expecting stress: Americans and the "midlife crisis." *Motivation and Emotion: Special Integrating Quantitative and Qualitative Approaches, 24,* 85–103.

Wethington, E., McLeod, J. D., & Kessler, R. C. (1987). *The importance of life events for explaining sex differences in psychological distress.* In R. C. Barnett, L. Biener, & G. K. Baruch (Eds.), *Gender and stress* (pp. 144–156). New York: Free Press.

Wetzler, H. P., Lum, D. L., & Bush, D. M. (2000). Using the SF-36 survey in primary care. In M. E. Maruish (Ed.), *Handbook of psychological assessment in primary care settings* (pp. 583–621). Mahwah, NJ: Erlbaum.

Whelton, S. P., He, J., Whelton, P. K., & Muntner, P. A. (2004). Meta-analysis of observational studies on fish intake and coronary heart disease. *The American Journal of Cardiology, 93,* 1119–1123.

White, A. R., & Ernst, E. (1999). A systematic review of randomized controlled trials of acupuncture for neck pain. *Rheumatology, 38,* 143–147.

Whiteside, T. L., & Herberman, R. B. (1994). Role of human natural killer cells in health and disease. *Clinical and Diagnostic Laboratory Immunology, 1,* 125–133.

Whitfield, K. E., Weidner, G., Clark, R., & Anderson, N. B. (2002). Sociodemographic diversity and behavioral medicine. *Journal of Consulting and Clinical Psychology, 70,* 463–481.

Whiting, B., & Whiting, J. (1975). *Children of six cultures.* Cambridge, MA: Harvard University Press.

Whitten, P., Kingsley, C., Cook, D., Swirczynski, D., & Doolittle, G. (2001). School-based telehealth: An empirical analysis of teacher, nurse, and administrator perceptions. *Journal of School Health, 71,* 173–180.

Wiggins, J. S., & Trapnell, P. D. (1997). Personality structure: The return of the Big Five. In R. Hogan, J. A. Johnson, et al. (Eds.), *Handbook of personality psychology* (pp. 737–765). San Diego, CA: Academic Press.

Wilcox, S., & King, A. (1999). Health behaviors and aging. In W. R. Hazzard, J. P. Blass, W. H. Ettinger, J. B. Halter, & J. G. Ouslander (Eds.), *Principles of geriatric medicine and gerontology* (pp. 287–302). New York: McGraw-Hill.

Willett, J. B., & Singer, J. D. (1995). It's déjà vu all over again: Using multiple-spell discrete-time survival analysis. *Journal of Educational and Behavioral Statistics, 20,* 41–67.

Willett, W. C., & Trichopoulos, D. (1996). Nutrition and cancer: A summary of the evidence. *Cancer Causes and Control, 7,* 178–180.

Williams, D. R. (1995). The concept of race in health services research: 1966–1990. *Hospital Services Research, 30,* 261–274.

Williams, D. R., & Collins, C. (1995). U. S. socioeconomic and racial differences in health: Patterns and explanations. *Annual Review of Sociology, 21,* 349–377.

Williams, G. D., Stinson, F. S., Sanchez, L. L., & Dufour, M. C. (1998, December). *Apparent per capita alcohol consumption: National, state, and regional trends, 1977–1996* (NIAAA Surveillance Report No. 47). Washington, DC: U. S. Government Printing Office.

Williams, P. G., Holmbeck, G. N., & Greenley, R. N. (2002). Adolescent health psychology. *Journal of Consulting and Clinical Psychology, 70,* 828–842.

Williams, R. B. (1987). Refining the Type A hypothesis: Emergence of the hostility complex. *The American Journal of Cardiology, 60,* 27J–32J.

Willich, S. N. (1995). Circadian influences and possible triggers of sudden cardiac death. *Sport Science Review, 4,* 31–45.

Wills, T. A., & Cleary, S. D. (1999). Peer and adolescent substance use among 6th–9th graders: Latent growth analysis of influence versus selection mechanisms. *Health Psychology, 18,* 453–463.

Wing, R. R., & Polley, B. A. (2002). Obesity. In A. Baum, T. A. Revenson, & J. E. Singer (Eds.), *Handbook of health psychology* (pp. 263–279). Mahwah, NJ: Erlbaum.

Winnicott, D. W. (1965). *The maturational processes and the facilitating environment: Studies in the theory of emotional development.* Oxford, England: International Universities Press.

Winslow, R. W., Franzini, L. R., & Hwang, J. (1992). Perceived peer norms, casual sex, and AIDS risk prevention. *Journal of Applied Social Psychology, 22,* 1809–1827.

Wismer, B. A., Moskowitz, J. M., Chen, A. M., Kang, S. H., Novotny, T. E., Min, K., et al. (1998). Mammography and clinical breast examination among Korean American women in two California counties. *Preventive Medicine, 27*, 144–151.

Wolfe, J., & Proctor, S. P. (1996). The Persian Gulf War: New findings on traumatic exposure and stress. *PTSD Research Quarterly, 7*, 1–8.

Wood, J. V., Taylor, S. E., & Lichtman, R. R. (1985). Social comparison in adjustment to breast cancer. *Journal of Personality and Social Psychology, 49*, 1169–1183.

Wood, M. D., Vinson, D. C., & Sher, K. J. (2002). Alcohol use and misuse. In A. Baum, T. A. Revenson, & J. E. Singer (Eds.), *Handbook of health psychology* (pp. 280–318). Mahwah, NJ: Erlbaum.

Woodward, M., Oliphant, J., Lowe, G., & Tunstall-Pedoe, H. (2003). Contribution of contemporaneous risk factors to social inequality in coronary heart disease and all causes mortality. *Preventative Medicine, 36*, 561–568.

Wortley, P. M., & Fleming, P. L. (1997). AIDS in women in the United States. *Journal of the American Medical Association, 278*, 911–916.

Wright, C. C., Barlow, J. H., Turner, A. P., & Bancroft, G. V. (2003). Self-management training for people with chronic disease: An exploratory study. *British Journal of Health Psychology, 8*, 456–476.

Wyatt, G. E. (1994). The sociocultural relevance of sex research: Challenges for the 1990s and beyond. *American Psychologist, 49*, 748–754.

Wyatt, G. E., Myers, H. F., Williams, J. K., Kitchen, C. R., Loeb, T., Carmona, J. V., et al. (2002). Does history of trauma contribute to HIV risk for women of color? Implications for prevention and policy. *American Journal of Public Health, 92*, 660–666.

Wyllie, A. H. (1980). Glucocorticoid-induced thymocyte apoptosis is associated with endogenous endonuclease activation. *Nature, 284*, 555–556.

Wynder, E. L., Cohen, L. A., Muscat, J. E., Winters, B., Dwyer, J. T., & Blackburn, G. (1997). Breast cancer: Weighing the evidence for a promoting role of dietary fat. *Journal of the National Cancer Institute, 89*, 766–775.

Wyper, M. A. (1990). Breast self-examination and the Health Belief Model: Variations on a theme. *Research in Nursing and Health, 13*, 421–428.

Yali, A. M., & Revenson, T. A. (2004). How changes in population demographics will impact health psychology: Incorporating a broader notion of cultural competence into the field. *Health Psychology, 23*, 147–155.

Yeager, K. K., Anda, R. F., Macera, C. A., Donehoo, R. S., & Eaker, E. D. (1995). Sedentary lifestyle and state variation in coronary heart disease. *Public Health Reports, 110*, 100–102.

Yi, H., Stinson, F. S., Williams, G. D., & Bertolucci, D. (1998, December). *Trends in alcohol-related fatal traffic crashes, United States: 1975–1996* (Surveillance Report No. 46, National Institute on Alcohol Abuse and Alcoholism). Washington, DC: U. S. Department of Health and Human Services.

Yi, J. K. (1994). Breast cancer screening practices by Vietnamese women. *Journal of Women's Health, 3*, 205–213.

Yi, K. (1998). Diet, lifestyle, and colorectal cancer: Is hyperinsulinemia the missing link? *Nutritional Review, 56*, 275–279.

Ying, Y. W. (1995). Cultural orientation and psychological well-being in Chinese Americans. *American Journal of Community Psychology, 23*, 893–911.

Young, A. J., Lowe, G. M. (2001). Antioxidant and prooxidant properties of carotenoids. *Archives of Biochemistry and Biophysiology, 385*, 20–27.

Zakowski, S. G., Ramati, A., Morton, C., Johnson, P., & Flanigan, R. (2004). Written emotional disclosure buffers the effects of social constraints on distress among cancer patients. *Health Psychology, 23*, 555–563.

Zaza, C., Sellick, S. M., Willian, A., Reyno, L., & Browman, G. P. (1999). Health care professionals' familiarity with non-pharmacological strategies for managing cancer pain. *Psycho-Oncology, 8*, 99–111.

Zeidner, M., & Hammer, A. L. (1992). Coping with missile attack: Resources, strategies, and outcomes. *Journal of Personality, 60*, 709–746.

Zhang, H., Liang, M. J., & Ye, H. L. (1995). Clinical study on the effects of Bu Yang Huan Wu decoction on coronary heart disease. *Chinese Journal of Integrated Traditional and Western Medicine, 15*, 213–215.

Zhou, Z. H., Hu, Y. H., & Pi, D. H. (1991). Clinical and experimental observations of treatment of peptic ulcer with Wie Yan An (easing peptic ulcer) capsule. *Journal of Traditional Chinese Medicine, 2*, 34–39.

Zimmer, M. H., & Zimmer, M. (1998). Socioeconomic determinants of smoking behavior during pregnancy. *Social Science Journal, 35*, 133–142.

Zimmerman, J. (1979). Case study in self-determinism: A model for client-assisted self help. *Psychological Record, 29*, 201–217.

Zola, I. K. (1964). Illness behavior of the working class: Implications and reccomendations. In A. Shostak & W. Gomberg (Eds.), *Blue collar world: Study of the American worker* (pp. 350–362). Englewood Cliffs, NJ: Prentice-Hall.

Zuckerman, M. (1990). Some dubious premises in research and theory on racial differences. *American Psychologist, 45*, 1297–1303.

Zuniga, M. E. (1992). Families with Latino roots. In E. W. Lynch & M. J. Hanson (Eds.), *Developing cross-cultural competence: A guide for working with young children and their families* (pp. 151–179). Baltimore: Paul H. Brookes.

Name Index

Subject Index